Voting for Reform

Voting for Reform

Democracy, Political Liberalization, and Economic Adjustment

edited by
Stephan Haggard and Steven B. Webb

PUBLISHED FOR THE WORLD BANK
OXFORD UNIVERSITY PRESS

Oxford University Press

OXFORD   NEW YORK   TORONTO
DELHI   BOMBAY   CALCUTTA   MADRAS   KARACHI
KUALA LUMPUR   SINGAPORE   HONG KONG   TOKYO
NAIROBI   DAR ES SALAAM   CAPE TOWN
MELBOURNE   AUCKLAND
and associated companies in
BERLIN   IBADAN

Published by Oxford University Press, Inc.
200 Madison Avenue, New York, N.Y. 10016

Oxford is a registered trademark of Oxford University Press.

First printing June 1994

Library of Congress Cataloging-in-Publication Data

Voting for reform : democracy, political liberalization, and economic
   adjustment / edited by Stephan Haggard and Steven B. Webb.
   p. cm.
   Includes bibliographical references and index.
   ISBN 0–19–520987–7
   1. Economic policy–Case studies. 2. Structural adjustment
(Economic policy)—Case studies. 3. Democracy—Case studies.
I. Haggard, Stephan. II. Webb, Steven Benjamin, 1947–   .
III. International Bank for Reconstruction and Development.
HD82.V63   1994
338.9—dc20   94–5012
                                                          CIP

Contents

v

Foreword

EVEN THOUGH THE EMERGING CONSENSUS on development policy is far from unanimous or infallible, policymakers and advisers know much more about how to design a technically sound adjustment program than they do about how to get adequate political support to sustain such a program. The link of policy reform to politics is especially critical where the political system is undergoing fundamental transformation at the same time. The most dramatic evidence for this comes from Eastern and Central Europe and the successor states to the Soviet Union, where democracy and policy reform are both new. The connection between the two is also crucial in the countries of Africa, Asia, Latin America, and the Middle East, where structural adjustment and political liberalization are new or incomplete.

To examine the political context and implications of reform in developing countries, the World Bank initiated a research project on the political economy of structural adjustment in the context of democratization and political liberalization. This volume presents some of the studies from the project. They contribute to an ongoing inquiry by the development policy community—economists, political scientists, and policymakers—on how the democratic process and economic reform can be brought together.

The book highlights four key political challenges to economic reform.

These challenges are in many cases common to countries at various stages of economic development. Countries can and should learn from each others' experience. The point is reinforced by illustrating the four challenges with examples from the United States.

The first challenge arises from the fact that democratic governments, rather than concentrating on areas where resources are most needed, generally tend to homogenize the benefits of spending, thereby spreading the benefits very thinly. The United States exhibits multiple symptoms of this problem; a particularly good illustration is found in our regional development efforts. The U.S. government now classifies as "depressed" and eligible for special assistance geographical areas home to 93 percent of our population. At least a small component of the B-1 bomber is produced in each of the fifty states and in 410 out of 435 congressional districts. Our social welfare programs are notoriously untargeted, with far more benefits from social security and medicare going to the upper third of the population in terms of income than to the lower third.

The second challenge is exemplified by the problem of dairy farmers or New York City teachers. Relatively small but highly concentrated interest groups exert disproportionate influence on policy outcomes because of their willingness to stake all their chips on the resolution of a single issue. The vast majority of voters would prefer that milk prices and New York teachers' salaries come down to market-clearing levels. Few in that vast majority, however, are prepared to vote only on that issue, while a much larger fraction of the small minority are prepared to vote and are prepared to work for candidates only on that basis. Thus, the perverse outcome can arise that the will of the minority prevails, even under democratic conditions. The systematic difficulty is the overresponsiveness of democratic politicians to the demands of narrow but well-organized interest groups.

The third challenge, bias toward the status quo, is exemplified by the sugar growers' problem. When a group like sugar growers in the United States gets a special favor, that special favor then becomes capitalized into the price of their land and other asset inputs. After it is capitalized in the price of a sugar farm, and particularly when the current owner actually paid that price, it appears unfair to take the benefit away. Democratic governments, and to some extent nondemocratic governments as well, are reluctant to take steps that will tangibly and measurably make somebody worse off in relation to the current status, whether or not that status is justified.

Another striking example came in the course of the U.S. tax reform debate in 1986. One of the liveliest issues was whether business lunches, including those with three martini drinks, would continue to enjoy tax-deductible status. The proposition was highly controversial, but nobody who ate, or drank, a three-martini lunch had any role in the debate. The constituency for preserving deductibility was made up of all the restaurants that had come into being on the basis of the assumption that those rules would continue. It is not that the constituency had earned excess profits or had gotten rich especially; they had only been earning a fair return on their investment. But removing the provision would cause a capital loss. As a consequence, the rule was only barely altered. The obvious lesson is to avoid creating rents that will then be difficult to take away when they no longer make sense several years later. The tougher question is how to implement desirable change after the distortion is part of the status quo. Relevant to this point, Dani Rodrik's essay in this volume offers the thesis that the ratio of the net social efficiency gain to the magnitude of the reallocations is crucial in determining which reforms happen and which do not.

The fourth challenge is the propensity for democracies to be shortsighted, leading to the deficit problem in the American context and many others. The political science literature has shown that governments divided between parties are more prone to shortsightedness than those that are not divided. And it is not difficult to see why. The essential economics of worker ownership consists of the observation that if an enterprise (including a whole economy) is run for the benefit of today's workers, who no longer will be owners and cannot sell their shares when they leave, the enterprise will not have an adequate incentive to pay attention to the future. The same is true of a government. Voters rarely judge the government on the basis of the economy's outcome several years down the road. With a divided government, as has often been the case in the United States, the problem is compounded because the credit or blame for any outcome, current or future, is shared in voters' minds by Republicans and Democrats. This further weakens the incentive to accept paying a political price in the short run to generate society's economic gain in the long run.

These four challenges, which obviously play out in different ways in different parts of the world, capture a large part of the difficulty in achieving economic reform in new democracies as well. It is no accident that democracies do well when they have to fight external wars, which have the marvelous function of aligning everybody's primary objectives. Without a common and clear threat, however, these mechanisms explain the frequent failures of policy reform. Churchill probably got it right: "No one pretends that democracy is perfect or all-wise. Indeed, it has been said that democracy is the worst form of government except all those other forms that have been tried from time to time."

The research on political economy does not need to describe in more detail how the mechanisms of these challenges operate, though that is interesting. Rather, the task is to find politically acceptable ways of designing institutions to minimize these problems. If communism is the surest way to destroy an economy and bombing is the second surest way, rampant populism is probably a very close third. What we need are ways to preserve the benefits of democracy without letting popular forces destroy the economy that supports them. The essays here make an important start in answering these questions.

Lawrence H. Summers
U.S. Undersecretary of the Treasury
for International Affairs

Preface

THE WORLD BANK BEGAN IN THE 1980s to evaluate in a systematic way its experiences with structural adjustment. Three reports on adjustment lending and their predecessors all identified the government's ownership of the program as a critical prerequisite for successful adjustment lending, but the origins of such ownership remained largely a mystery.

Policymakers and advisers in the World Bank and elsewhere thus saw a need to understand how the political aspects of the design and implementation of adjustment programs affect their success. Although the Bank abstains from interference in the internal politics of its members, deciding on economic adjustment is a political process, and the outcome of adjustment has political consequences. Thus from the need to understand the political context and effects of Bank lending arose an array of questions: In which political and economic situations are adjustment programs most likely to get the political support essential for their success? Given the political and economic context, what kinds of modifications in program design help improve the quality of programs actually implemented? How can international financial institutions contribute to the political sustainability of reforms?

Theory alone could not answer such questions. Broader cross-sectional, time-series samples could be used to test some narrowly focused questions, as we have done elsewhere with patterns of inflation and fiscal deficits that accompany political transitions. But only case studies could provide adequate institutional detail.

Several projects had already compiled impressive collections of case studies, and to get beyond them we decided first to focus on the conjuncture of democracy and adjustment, and second to emphasize the testing of a common set of hypotheses. We also decided to concentrate on reforms in the areas of fiscal, monetary, exchange rate, and trade policy. Other policy reforms were equally important in many cases, but only these seemed to have enough universal importance to support cross-country comparisons. While the small sample size of a case study approach would preclude standard statistical tests of the hypotheses, the case studies would permit us to investigate in more detail how and why a particular case fit with our hypotheses.

In choosing the countries, we wanted examples that combined at least some success in structural adjustment and in political liberalization, if not democratization. The number of such countries was limited in 1990 when we designed the project, particularly since we also wanted examples that covered diverse economic adjustment challenges. Within two years, there were many more countries we could have chosen from, because of the political changes in Central Europe and the former Soviet Union and in Africa and Latin America. We have taken heart that the topic of our study has become more and more relevant and that the new examples tended to fit the patterns and predictions of our study. The eight countries studied here demonstrate the diversity of challenges to economic reform and of political situations even within the set that combined political liberalization with economic reform. Nevertheless, the project does not claim to cover all important issues. For instance, events of recent years highlight two issues that clearly warrant further study. One is the challenge of political liberalization contemporaneously with the total reconstruction of an economy, as in Eastern Europe and Central Asia now. Second is the challenge of dealing with ethnic and racial divisions. But these must wait for another day.

To address the range of questions that we had in mind, the research team for each country needed to combine expertise in economics and political science, as well as knowledge of the institutions of the country. We were very fortunate in finding such persons who were willing join the project (see the brief biographies of the contributors toward the end of the book). We also included experts in the theoretical aspects of political economy to strengthen the framework of the project. The lively and constructive interaction among members of the whole team made a critical contribution to the success of the project.

In developing the project, we received helpful suggestions from many people, including Thomas Callaghy, Alex Cukierman, Jessica Einhorn, Barbara Geddes, John Holsen, Nora Lustig, Sylvia Maxfield, Joan Nelson, Barbara Nunnberg, and Michael Stevens. We owe a particular debt to Robert Kaufman; through his close collaboration, his ideas worked their way into this project at numerous points. We also express especial gratitude to Vittorio Corbo and Johannes Linn for their enthusiastic support of the project, through many constructive conversations in developing its design and steadfast help in guiding it through the bureaucracy of the World Bank. This was not an easy project for an institution like the Bank to undertake, and we wish to thank the country operations departments for agreeing to let us work on their countries.

Outlines and issues papers for each of the studies were discussed at an extended team meeting in Washington in May 1991, before we went out to do the field research. Economists from the relevant country operations departments joined in that meeting and gave us much helpful guidance for refining our research plans. In May 1992 at a public conference in Washington, the papers of the project were presented and discussed. Formal discussants there included Vittorio Corbo, Donald Emerson, Miguel Fernández-Ordóñez, Bulent Gultekin, James Hansen, Ishrat Husain, Johannes Linn, Katherine Marshall, William McCleary, Lyn Squire, Arturo Valenzuela, Stan Wellisz, Jennifer Widner, and Prosper Youm. Lawrence H. Summers made the opening presentation, and Richard Feinberg, Moises Niam, and Mancur Olson led a panel discussion at the end of the conference. They and the many other participants of the conference pushed forward our ideas and helped with the final preparation of the chapters of this volume. Four anonymous referees provided many helpful comments on this volume. Elizabeth Forsyth provided excellent help in copyediting the volume.

Financial support for the project came from the Policy Research Department of the World Bank and the International Center for Economic Growth. They also supported the project with their intellectual guidance and institutional endorsement. Alfred Imhoff, Carol Rosen, and Michael Treadway in the Office of the Publisher guided the preparation and production of the volume. This has been a team effort in many dimensions, in which we have been lucky to have the chance to participate.

Stephan Haggard   *Steven B. Webb*
San Diego, California   *Washington, D.C.*

Introduction

STEPHAN HAGGARD AND STEVEN B. WEBB

THE WIDESPREAD MOVEMENT TOWARD POLITICAL LIBERALIZATION and democratization is one of the most dramatic historical developments of the last two decades (Diamond, Linz, and Lipset 1990; Huntington 1991; O'Donnell, Schmitter, and Whitehead 1986). This wave of political change began in Southern Europe in the mid-1970s when dictatorships in Greece, Portugal, and Spain relinquished power. In 1983 in Turkey, a three-year military intervention came to a close. By the mid-1980s, all of the South American militaries except those in Chile and Paraguay had retreated to the barracks, and by 1990 they too had followed suit. In the 1980s, transitions began in a number of Asian countries, including the Republic of Korea, Pakistan, the Philippines, Taiwan (China), and Thailand. At the end of the decade, communist governments in Eastern Europe and the Soviet Union collapsed. In the early 1990s, economic crisis, the end of the cold war, and increasing pressure from external aid and lending agencies began to weaken authoritarian governments in Africa as well.

This period of political change has coincided with the most severe economic crisis affecting the developing world since the Great Depres-

For comments on drafts of this introduction, the authors wish to thank Rick Doner, Barbara Geddes, Carol Graham, Simon Johnson, Robert Kaufman, Dani Rodrik, Nicholas van de Walle, and three anonymous reviewers.

sion. Governments there, particularly in Latin America and Africa, have come under strong internal and external pressure to undertake politically risky stabilization and structural adjustment measures. The challenge of reform is even more daunting in the former socialist economies, which must construct virtually the entire institutional apparatus of a market economy and a democratic government.

In the postwar period, the developing countries have had difficulty combining stable democracy with well-functioning market economies; some analysts have wondered whether the two are compatible in poor countries (O'Donnell 1973; Dornbusch and Edwards 1991). We would expect new democratic governments to face particular challenges in managing economic policy, including strong distributional claims from previously excluded groups and highly uncertain institutional settings. We know from the historical experience of the advanced industrial states that democracy and market-oriented policies can be made compatible over the long run. What are the chances that the developing countries can emulate this experience?

To address this question, this volume analyzes how political liberalization and democratization influence the efforts of governments to initiate and sustain economic reforms. This chapter draws heavily on eight country studies that form the core of the volume. It also takes into account recent theoretical developments in the political economy of adjustment (see chapters 2 and 3), cross-national quantitative studies conducted in conjunction with this project (Cukierman, Webb, and Neyapti 1992; Haggard, Kaufman, and Webb 1992), and a growing, but still small, literature on the political economy of democratic transitions and policymaking in new democracies (Bates and Krueger 1993; Bresser Pereira, Maraval, and Przeworski 1993; Haggard and Kaufman 1992; Williamson 1993).

The case studies in this volume capture a wide range of differences with respect to region, level of development, and extent of political and economic reform. All eight countries have undergone some degree of political liberalization, although not all can be considered democratic. The countries analyzed in the second part—Spain, Turkey, Poland, and Chile—have had relatively well-defined democratic transitions, although outgoing military elites have continued to exercise some influence over post-transition politics in Turkey and Chile. In none of these four cases, however, have there been signs of political reversal; democracy appears to be consolidated. The case studies in part 3, by contrast, have experienced ambiguous political transitions. Political liberalization has occurred gradually within a dominant party context in Senegal and Mexico and been reversed or delayed in Thailand and Nigeria. The prospects for democratization in these four cases remain uncertain. All eight countries have attempted, albeit with varying degrees of success, to implement adjustment programs. All except Spain have done so with support from the international financial institutions.

The studies use political economy to explain policy choice, including both the timing and content of policies when they are initiated and the success of the government in implementing and sustaining reforms over time. Most economists are primarily concerned with the effects of policy on economic outcomes; the choice of policy itself is treated either as exogenous or as a response to economic parameters and concerns with efficiency. By contrast, we view policy not so much as a function of its intended economic effects but as the outcome of interactions among politicians, bureaucrats, and interest groups operating within a set of institutional constraints.

The country studies focus on two clusters of policies: adjustments of monetary and fiscal policy and reforms of the trade and exchange rate regime. There are legitimate disagreements on what constitutes appropriate policy in both areas, including in the countries under study, and it is not our purpose to argue for a particular macroeconomic or trade policy stance. Nonetheless, our premise is that fiscal and monetary policies are central to short-term stabilization efforts, regardless of whether incomes policies and other heterodox measures are also employed. Similarly, reforms of the trade and exchange rate regime play a role in expanding exports and equilibrating the balance of payments, even when they are accompanied by other industrial policy measures. These two areas do not exhaust the range of reform issues facing developing, and particularly former socialist, countries. Nonetheless, they do represent the broader array of stabilization and structural adjustment measures facing new democracies over the past two decades and thus provide a useful entry for comparative analysis.

The studies each analyze one or more reform episodes, which are outlined in table 1-1. The reforms were usually spurred by the economic programs of new governments. Several studies compare reform efforts by successive administrations; thus the number of cases studied actually exceeds the number of countries. As table 1-1 shows, the reforms were usually supported by various forms of structural adjustment lending from the World Bank and International Monetary Fund.[1]

The findings of these studies are summarized in four sections. The first examines the effects of political liberalization and the transition to democracy itself, with an emphasis on different sequences of economic and political reform. In countries where military governments have undertaken economic reform prior to initiating the transition to democracy, and those reforms have yielded tangible benefits, policy gains will, in all likelihood, not be reversed by the transition. Many new democratic governments do not enjoy the luxury of a strong economic inheritance, however, and in a number of new democracies, incoming governments have made matters worse. Nonetheless, the "democracy first" sequence has produced successful reform efforts when new governments have acted swiftly at the outset of their term to exploit political advantages associated with the transition.

Table 1-1. Reform Episodes Analyzed in the Country Studies, 1980s

Country; type of adjustment lending during the standby period	Comments
Chile, 1988–92 EFF (1985–89) SAL II (1986–87) SAL III (1987–89) Standby (1989–90)	Focus on the period from the 1988 plebiscite through the transition to the democratic Aylwin government (1990–present)
Mexico, 1987–88 Standby (1986–88) Trade policy SECAL (1986–90) Second trade policy SECAL (1988) Agricultural SECAL (1988–90)	Focus on the Economic Solidarity Pact from its inception in December 1987 through the end of the de la Madrid administration (December 1988)
Nigeria, 1979–92 Fertilizer SECAL (1983–86) Trade SECAL (1986–89) Standby (1987–88) Second trade SECAL (1988–90) Standby (1989–90) Educational SECAL (1990–94) Standby (1991–92)	Compares policies of the Shagari (1979–83) and Buhari (1983–85) governments with the adjustment efforts of the Babangida government (1985–92), with emphasis on the structural adjustment program of 1986
Poland, 1989–91 Financial SECAL (1992–95) Restructuring and privatization SECAL (1991–98) Standby (1990–91) SAL I (1991–94)	Focus on the transition period and governments of Mazowiecki (1989–90) and Bielecki (1991), with emphasis on the Balcerowicz program of 1990
Senegal, 1980–91 EFF (1980–83) SAL I (1981–83) Standby (1981–82) Standby (1982–83) Standby (1985–86) SAL II (1986–87) SAF (1986–88) Standby (1986–87) Standby (1987–88) Enhanced SAF (1988–91)	Examines the adjustment programs of the Diouf governments (1981–83, 1983–88, 1988–91) and particularly the economic adjustment plan of 1984
Spain, 1975–86	Compares the transition period (1975–77) and programs of the Center Democratic Union (1977–82) and the Spanish Socialist Workers Party (1982–86) governments
Thailand, 1980–88 SAL I (1982–83) Standby (1982–83) SAL II (1983–84) Standby (1985–87)	Focuses on reforms of the fourth (1983–86) and fifth (1986–88) Prem governments

Country, type of adjustment lending during the standby period	Comments

Turkey, 1980–91
  Standby (1979–80)
  SAL I (1980–81)
  Standby (1980–83)
  SAL II (1981–82)
  SAL III (1982–83)
  Standby (1983–84)
  SAL IV (1983–85)
  Standby (1984–85)
  SAL V (1984–86)
  Agricultural SECAL (1985–89)
  Financial SECAL (1986–90)
  Energy SECAL (1987–90)
  Second financial SECAL
    (1988–90)
	Examines the first program under the democratic Demirel government (1980), the period of military rule (1980–83), and two Özal governments (1983–87; 1987–91)

Note: Standby refers to an IMF Standby Arrangement; SAL, a World Bank structural adjustment loan; EFF, an IMF Extended Fund Facility agreement; SAF, an IMF structural adjustment facility; SECAL, a World Bank sector adjustment loan.
Source: World Bank 1992.

The second section focuses on the institutions of new democracies by examining how differences in the party and electoral system and in bureaucratic organization affect the choice of policy. These institutions are not easily changed, but other features of government structure are to a greater extent. We suggest how the decisionmaking apparatus within the government can increase or decrease the efficiency of economic policy, a finding with direct implications for institutional reform.

The third section examines interest groups and the coalition-building process on the premise that no reform program can be fully consolidated unless it has an adequate basis of political support. If interest groups determine policy, and interests in the period before reform tend to favor the status quo, how is reform ever possible? The answer to this paradox is that interests are not fixed but rather change in response to features of the program itself. This section examines the political role of labor and business in the adjustment process, paying particular attention to how the speed and sequence of reform and the strategic use of compensation affect the level of political support.

The fourth section examines the international influences on the policy process. There is no evidence from the countries studied that external actors tipped the political scales in favor of reform when the domestic institutional and coalitional environment was unfavorable; there is evidence that lending in such settings postponed adjustment. Providing support to committed governments did, however, increase the domestic political credibility of the reformers, both by improving overall performance and by increasing their freedom of maneuver.

Democratization and Economic Reform

New democracies differ in the sequence of economic and political reform (Haggard and Kaufman 1992, 1993). In some cases, including Chile, Thailand, and Turkey, military elites undertook major stabilization and structural adjustment initiatives *prior* to political liberalization; Korea and Taiwan (China) also fit this pattern. By the time of the transition, these efforts had yielded positive results and the military could thus liberalize or withdraw from power under relatively auspicious economic circumstances.

Not only were the economic problems facing these countries less severe by the time democracy was introduced or restored, but the success of past policy had created a base of political support for the underlying economic model. In Turkey, Turgut Özal won the transitional presidential election of 1983 partly because he was the only civilian candidate allowed to stand. However, he was also identified with the economic reforms he had initiated under democratic auspices and sustained for the most part during the three years of military rule preceding the election. In Chile, a coalition of opposition parties led by the Christian Democratic Party won the presidency. Recognizing the importance of establishing its credibility with the military, the middle classes, and the right, the Christian Democratic Party took a position on economic issues that was even more cautious and less populist than the pro-Pinochet candidate, Hernán Büchi. Yet this stance was not simply strategic; it also reflected a broader consensus among the political elite of the prodemocracy coalition on the merits of a broadly market-oriented economic strategy. Both countries faced the problem of how to balance the incorporation of new groups with the implementation of economic reforms, but they did so in the context of relatively strong growth that eased otherwise difficult tradeoffs.

In other cases, by contrast, the sequence of political and economic liberalization was reversed. Outgoing authoritarian governments had failed to adjust, and new democratic governments inherited severe economic crises. Among the cases presented here, Poland fits this pattern most clearly. It is arguably characteristic of Senegal as well and also typifies the transitions of several Latin American countries not studied in this volume, such as Argentina and Bolivia. Crises had advantages as well as disadvantages for new democratic governments. Past policy had generally been discredited, and support, including support from the private sector, for the outgoing authoritarian regime had collapsed. The incoming government thus enjoyed a widespread, if diffuse, mandate to change policy. Yet the adjustment problems themselves were extremely severe, and the public would at some point hold the new government accountable for poor performance, even if its source could justifiably be attributed to the outgoing government.

Comparative analysis suggests that new democratic leaders facing crises achieved stabilization and structural adjustment objectives most successfully when they moved swiftly to capitalize on the political gains associated with the transition to democracy. Of the countries in this study, Poland provides the most dramatic example of this process. Johnson and Kowalska (chapter 6) show how opposition to stabilization and market-oriented reform was swept away in the broad support granted to Poland's new Solidarity government. Even the communists, who still held a significant share of legislative seats following the transition, were unwilling to oppose the Balcerowicz program.

Initial support for difficult programs was also secured by explicitly trading political gains for economic sacrifices. Spain provides the archetype of this strategy, although the economic setting was more auspicious. Bermeo and García-Durán (chapter 4) detail how labor and the left abandoned a confrontational posture and accepted wage restraint in order to smooth and secure the transition. Arriagada Herrera and Graham (chapter 7) show how the Chilean opposition's moderate stance on economic issues formed part of a larger political settlement. The opposition leadership showed restraint on economic questions in order to assure the military and the right, thus advancing the cause of democratic consolidation. In Senegal, Abdou Diouf sought to secure support for economic reform and deflect attention from the economic crisis through further political liberalization.

In other countries, however, the government did not or could not exploit this positive tradeoff effectively. In Argentina, Bolivia, and Brazil, as well as a number of the republics that emerged from the collapse of the Soviet Union, new democratic leaders failed to initiate decisive action at the beginning of their terms. Policy and performance deteriorated, and the honeymoon effect associated with the transition dissipated. Leaders in all three Latin American countries—Raúl Alfonsín, Hernán Siles, and José Sarney—spent the remainder of their terms attempting unsuccessfully to recoup lost credibility, cycling through a series of failed or partial stabilization efforts.

Herbst and Olukoshi (chapter 11) show a third pattern in Nigeria. The government of Ibrahim Babangida attempted to implement concurrently economic reforms and a gradual process of political liberalization from above. This combined effort at political and economic reform, also visible in some of the former Soviet republics, appears to create particular difficulties: rather than reinforcing the government's reform effort, the controlled nature of the political liberalization provided a focal point for opposition challenges. In Nigeria, opposition forces took advantage of

the political opening to mobilize against Babangida's structural adjustment program and, by proxy, against the government itself. Increased
political pressures forced the government to choose between the objectives of political and economic liberalization. Babangida opted for political control, overriding opponents of the structural adjustment program
on a number of issues. Yet the effort to stage-manage the political transition ultimately led to sacrifices in the program as elections approached.

In sum, new democratic governments typically enjoy a period in which
the costs of adjustment can be traded against political gains. This political space for initiating reforms is particularly critical for governments
that come to power during crises. When the transition occurs under good
economic conditions, new democratic governments have the luxury of
making adjustments in an incremental fashion. In periods of crisis, however, delay leads to further economic deterioration, which dissipates the
support for reform and may even erode support for democracy itself
(Haggard and Kaufman 1993, chap. 9).

The success of this strategy for initiating reform is by no means assured. New reform initiatives must be followed by sustained follow-up
and implementation. This process of consolidating reform depends on
the program's economic success, yet it also depends on the routine legislative, electoral, and interest group constraints that characterize any
democracy.

Institutions and Economic Policy

The most common approach to policymaking in democracies—both
among academics and nonspecialists—is to focus on the role of interest
groups. The model is a simple one. Policy reform has distributive consequences for different groups, which organize to protect their incomes and
rents. Politicians respond to constituent pressures because they seek to
remain in office, and they exchange policy distortions for political support. The fate of any reform effort thus hinges on the political balance of
power between the winners and losers in the reform effort.

Distributive conflicts over adjustment policy are explored in more detail in the next section of this introduction and in the discussion of trade
policy in the essay by Rodrik (chapter 3 of this volume). This section
focuses on two features of the institutional setting: the party and electoral system and the decisionmaking structures within the executive itself. As Geddes (1992, p. 1) argues, "Institutional characteristics either
mute or magnify the effects of interest group pressures on government
decisionmakers."

The Party System

The nature of the party system strongly influences how support and
opposition are organized, and thus the prospects for reform. Although

the executive enjoys some leeway in initiating reform efforts, particularly at the outset of a new government, sustaining reform in a democracy requires an adequate base of legislative support. Even in the presence of such support, opposition politicians have an incentive to campaign against the costs associated with reform; without such support, executives are isolated, vulnerable to attack, and more likely either to reverse course or to lose office to antireform candidates. Although numerous characteristics of the party and electoral system might plausibly influence reform efforts, this book focuses on the extent of polarization and fragmentation.[2] The formal models outlined by Alesina in chapter 2 suggest that polarized party systems, in which wide ideological differences separate the main political contenders, encourage bidding wars between competing political forces and produce destabilizing swings in policy. The populist policy cycles in Latin America illustrate this pattern among developing countries (Dornbusch and Edwards 1991). There is some debate over the effects of fragmentation, or the tendency toward the proliferation of political parties.[3] Nonetheless, fragmentation makes coalition rule more likely, increases the difficulty of reaching compromises, and contributes to the instability of governments—all factors that can effect government policy (Roubini and Sachs 1989).

Mexico constitutes an important limiting case in this analysis of the role of the party system. Although Mexico has undergone some political liberalization since the mid-1970s, the system is still dominated by a powerful single party, the Institutional Revolutionary Party (PRI), which can control, co-opt, and reconcile contending social interests. This structure did not, however, prevent Mexico from getting into serious economic trouble in the early 1980s; indeed, internal divisions within the party over the course of economic policy contributed to the government's delay in undertaking corrective measures. Kaufman, Bazdresch, and Herredia (chapter 9) show, however, that once the leadership of the party changed, the PRI's long-standing corporatist links with labor and the private sector did allow the president to secure agreement to, and compliance with, the heterodox stabilization program contained in the Economic Solidarity Pact of 1989.

The very dominance of the PRI in the Mexican political system raises questions about Mexico's relevance—or desirability—as a model for other countries. In two countries examined here, outgoing authoritarian leaders altered constitutions in order to limit previous tendencies to polarization and fragmentation. These cases—Turkey and Chile—permit comparisons between the performance of different party systems within the same country.

In Turkey, the political and economic difficulties of the late-1970s can be attributed in no small measure to an increasingly polarized political system. The 1983 election was limited to three parties hand-picked by the military, and the new constitution drafted by the military contained rules, including electoral thresholds for gaining parliamentary representation, that served to eliminate smaller parties from participation altogether. These prohibitions and rules initially helped the conservative Motherland Party gain large legislative majorities that facilitated its adjustment initiatives but ultimately gave rise to a political backlash that eased the barriers to political entry. As Öniş and Webb (chapter 5) show, this new political opening corresponded to increased difficulties in managing both fiscal and trade policy.

In Chile, Augusto Pinochet went further, setting up a number of what Arriagada Herrera and Graham (chapter 7) call "authoritarian enclaves" in the new democratic order. Not only were electoral rules written to strengthen the legislative representation of the right, but Pinochet directly appointed a number of senators in order to guarantee a conservative majority.

Poland also provides an example of the outgoing regime bequeathing itself nondemocratic enclaves of authority in the new constitution, with the key difference being that the outgoing party by and large opposed reform. By reserving a number of seats in the Parliament (Sejm) for the communists, Solidarity and its coalition partners that formed the first democratic government were barred from having a legislative majority. Yet the Solidarity leadership exploited its popularity by launching a reform program at a time when it constituted a broad umbrella movement. Johnson and Kowalska (chapter 6) argue that, while the program was sustained, its political difficulties can be traced to the emergence of a highly fragmented party system beginning in the summer of 1990. New groupings in the legislature voiced legitimate concerns about the program, but the proliferation of small, weak parties made governance substantially more complicated.

The Spanish case also demonstrates the advantages of a strong majority government. The first post-transition government of the Center Democratic Union faced legislative difficulties with its program due to its minority status in the legislature. Complex intracoalitional politics within the party also contributed to ministerial turnover. The party's socialist successor, the Spanish Socialist Workers Party, by contrast, did not have to rely on coalition partners at all, enjoyed an absolute majority in the legislature, and faced little coherent opposition. This dominance allowed it to push through a more comprehensive program than that of its predecessor, even though its ideological orientation was center-left, while that of the Center Democratic Union was center-right.

Gauging the actual extent of polarization and fragmentation within the party system can be difficult if one looks simply at the number of parties or their ideological stance. The party system in Thailand is highly fragmented, but the country has had relatively consistent economic policy and undertook important reforms during a period of political liberalization. As Doner and Laothamatas argue in chapter 10, the extent of polarization is low and the apparently fragmented system "can be understood as a single dominant coalition composed of three major parties." Moreover, the parties are weak relative to the prime minister and technocrats, who continue to wield extensive power over the country's economic agenda. As in Mexico, these arrangements call into question the extent to which Thailand could be considered genuinely democratic, even before the military coup of 1991.

By contrast, Senegal appears to be a less fragmented political system. Diouf enjoyed an overwhelming legislative majority after the 1983 elections, placing him in a strong position to initiate a new reform thrust. But Ka and van de Walle show in chapter 8 that the ruling party was little more than a collection of diverse political factions and networks of clients, many of which had interests directly opposed to adjustment. Rather than reconciling these diverse interests, the ruling party provided a vehicle through which they could block reform.

Nigeria represents the most interesting experiment in shaping the party system. The Babangida government sought to avoid ethnic polarization and to circumvent traditional party politicians by dictating that only two parties would contest the transitional elections initially scheduled for 1992, one "a little to the left," the other "a little to the right." The government mandated, however, that the platforms of both parties explicitly had to support the structural adjustment program. Despite this effort at electoral engineering, as of this writing, Babangida had not honored the election results by letting the winner take power.

Electoral Cycles

Closely related to the question of party structure is the effect that the timing of elections has on the timing of reform. Early models of the political-business cycle argued that parties in power manipulated macroeconomic policy to maximize their electoral chances, stimulating the economy as elections approached and stabilizing it immediately afterward (for reviews see Alesina 1988; Nordhaus 1990; and chapter 2 of this volume). Empirical evidence supporting the model is weak for the advanced industrial states (Alesina 1988; Alt 1985; Alt and Chrystal 1983, chap. 5), and the theory is questionable: in Brian Barry's well-known criticism, models of the political-business cycle assume "a collection of rogues competing for the favors of a larger collection of dupes" (Barry 1985, p. 300). Under assumptions of rational expectations, the electorate would discount anticipated government actions, reducing their effects and thus the incentive to manipulate policy for political ends.

In response to these problems, the theoretical literature on political-business cycles has taken two alternative tacks. Alesina (1988) has developed a rational partisan model in which differences in government behavior are attributable to differences in the underlying coalitional base of parties. In these models, party behavior depends on ideological orientation. Partisan models also generally support the arguments presented in the previous section concerning party polarization and emphasize that sharply polarized party systems will be characterized by particularly virulent electoral cycles. This is the case not only because of differences in party platforms but also because of the high degree of uncertainty surrounding the electoral contest itself.

Rogoff and Sibert (1988) and Rogoff (1990), by contrast, have developed a rational opportunistic model in which informational asymmetries between the government and citizens generate a political-business cycle. Many institutional factors that offset such asymmetries in the industrial countries are absent in the developing world, including an informed public, independent media coverage of economic policy, and forms of consultation that expand the information available to groups about government policies and their likely effects. Lower levels of income, extensive poverty, and the absence of welfare systems to cushion the costs of economic crisis might also shorten the time horizons of voters. Under such conditions, electoral support might plausibly be linked to government delivery of short-term material benefits.

The one published cross-national study of the electoral cycle in developing countries—Ames's analysis of Latin American expenditure data for 1947–82—found significant effects of the electoral cycle (Ames 1987, pp. 23–33). Comparative case study research by Joan Nelson (1990) and her colleagues also found some evidence of policy cycles tied to elections. One pooled time-series analysis (Haggard, Kaufman, and Webb 1992) with a broad sample of countries that controlled for political variables such as type of regime and transition found no significant difference in the level of fiscal deficits or inflation in the years before, during, or after the election. The study did find, however, that when a country *already* had high inflation, the government was less likely to initiate a stabilization program in the year before or during an election.

This finding is generally confirmed by the case studies, particularly when the transition is followed by a series of nonconcurrent elections (usually for different levels of government). Economic policy in Poland was temporarily disrupted by the complex political battles surrounding the presidential election in the summer of 1990 and by the parliamentary elections of late 1991. Turkey (1987 and 1991) and Nigeria (1990–91) show evidence of election-related expansions, and the momentum of the Senegalese program began to slow prior to the 1988 election, although numerous other factors ultimately contributed to its demise.

Conversely, new programs were typically initiated following elections, often associated with the transition itself: Turkey (1980 and 1983), Senegal (1984), Poland (1990), and Spain (1976, 1982) provide examples. Dramatic adjustment programs in Brazil under Fernando Collor de Mello (1990), Argentina under Carlos Menem (1991), and Bolivia under Víctor Paz Estenssoro (1985) confirm the independent effects of electoral cycles as opposed to changes in regime. In each case, reforms were launched by the second post-transition government, which came to office by exploiting the failures of the first.

There is one clear exception to this rule among the cases presented in this volume. In Mexico, the government launched the Economic Solidarity Pact just prior to a presidential election. Yet this exception proves the rule: the PRI's dominance of the political system meant precisely that elections did not pose any fundamental uncertainties. The top figure in the outgoing de la Madrid government associated with the economic program—Carlos Salinas de Gortari—was the incoming president.

Several other well-known election-eve stabilizations have occurred outside our sample. Particularly in countries where inflation was extremely high and becoming a political liability, stabilizing promptly seemed to promise political as well as economic gains. In Argentina, the Austral Plan came just a few months before key congressional elections and the Primavera Plan in 1988 was a gambit to win the presidential election in 1989. Brazil's 1986 Cruzado Plan was also initiated just before congressional elections. These programs succeeded in bringing down inflation temporarily with minimal economic dislocation, yet they foundered on the inability of the government to undertake more difficult supporting measures, particularly with reference to fiscal policy. As a result, the programs unraveled, and the ruling party in both countries was punished electorally for that failure.

Reform of Bureaucracies

Frequently, the most vociferous opposition to a change in policy comes not from interest groups, legislators, or voters, but from ministers and bureaucrats within the government or even from the executive himself. One of the most consistent findings of the research presented in this volume is the crucial role played by bureaucratic organizations in both initiating and consolidating reform efforts. In every successful reform effort, politicians delegated decisionmaking authority to units within the government that were insulated from routine bureaucratic processes, from legislative and interest group pressures, and even from executive pressure (Geddes 1992). In some cases, bureaucratic agencies associated with old policies were eliminated outright.

Of course, insulating key parts of the bureaucracy from political pressure only assists the cause of reform if the bureaucrats are technically capable of designing and carrying out the measures. In general, middle-income countries in the sample had relatively strong bureaucratic traditions to begin with, and strengthening the quality of governance further was an element of new adjustment efforts. In Nigeria, Poland, and Senegal, however, shortcomings of the bureaucracy arguably contributed to difficulties in the program's implementation. For low-income countries in particular, increasing the decisionmaking and administrative capacity of the government constitutes a crucial precondition for initiating coherent programs, although it does not provide a panacea where the broader political milieu is unfavorable.

That political setting varied across our cases. In Chile, the military undertook bureaucratic reform with the explicit intention of tying the hands of its democratic successor. Yet in other cases, new democratic governments initiated institutional reforms in order to advance their programmatic objectives in the face of bureaucratic opposition, usually by establishing bureaus with close or exclusive ties to the chief executive, which held decisionmaking powers previously spread among several ministries.

Thailand and Mexico, countries in which the process of democratization was the least advanced, again constitute limiting cases, with a particularly high level of bureaucratic insulation. In Thailand, control over macroeconomic policy had long been dominated by a highly insulated technocratic team, including a particularly strong central bank and a budgetary process that limits legislative involvement. Trade policy was also relatively insulated in the Ministry of Finance, although the revenue motive did not always guarantee that bureaucratic interests favored liberalization, and interest groups gained greater access to trade policymaking as politics were liberalized. The reforms of the early 1980s were overseen by a Council of Economic Ministers, headed by the prime minister. Doner and Laothamatas (chapter 10) argue that the council "was in effect a supercabinet, authorized to make decisions that were binding on the entire cabinet." The prime minister's personal advisers, career bureaucrats, and nonparty politicians dominated party politicians, who were in any case relatively weak. When the balance of power between bureaucrats and politicians tilted toward the latter after 1988, policymaking became less coherent.

The Mexican case is more complex, because the bureaucracy in the past was divided between orthodox groups that emphasized market-oriented approaches to macroeconomic management and developmentalist factions that urged a more activist role for the state. The crisis of the mid-1980s propelled market-oriented officials in the budget and financial ministries to prominence; not coincidentally, this group was led by Carlos Salinas de Gortari, who later became president.

Chile and Turkey display important contrasts in the origins and purposes of the insulating institutions for economic policy, although both countries reintroduced democracy in a controlled way. In Chile, outgoing military officials built institutional arrangements to favor more insulated decisionmaking by ideological allies. Although most of the arrangements were in the area of political-military affairs, at least two were in the economic arena: a new law governing the central bank and a requirement that any change of tariffs be approved by both houses of the legislature, including the Senate, where special rules guaranteed control by the military-right parties. Although the opposition initially protested the central bank law as another authoritarian imposition, its own political interest in a moderate policy stance allowed a negotiated compromise to be reached on the composition of the board of the new bank. The result substantially strengthened the institution's autonomy and enhanced the prospects for macroeconomic stability.

In Turkey, the new democratic regime was more committed to organizational reform than its military predecessor. Rather than try to reform the old bureaucrats, Özal created a new agency and transferred key powers to it. He created an undersecretariat for treasury and foreign trade under a new minister of state for economic affairs, who reported directly to him. This institutional reform streamlined policymaking but also gave the prime minister greater control over patronage. As political pressures on the government mounted, the insulation of this office from the political fray necessarily waned. The changes were initially motivated by an effort to improve coordination and to reduce the power of etatist segments of the bureaucracy, and this objective was achieved in the early period, when a variety of reforms were initiated.

Senegal and Spain show similar patterns. On winning an electoral mandate, Diouf strengthened his direct hold on the Senegalese administration by eliminating the post of prime minister, promoting technocrats throughout the bureaucracy, and creating special coordinating committees to promote interministerial communication and more effective decisionmaking. These bodies were dominated by technocrats and were designed precisely to divert power from the established agencies, which tended to act like private interest groups engaged in lobbying. In Spain, economic policymaking under the Spanish Socialist Workers Party was concentrated in the hands of the well-known economist Miguel Boyer, who drew three previously separate economics ministries together under his own command and became known as the *superministro*.

Nigeria presents a contrasting case. Initially, Babangida established a presidential advisory committee to oversee the structural adjustment program. The committee was independent of ministerial control; headed by a prominent economist, it became central to the formulation of stabilizing budgets as well as the larger reform effort. In 1987, in response to growing opposition to the effects of the program, the president revised the composition of the committee to include noneconomists, who played an important role in pushing the government to adopt a reflationary budget in 1988.

Insulating reformers within the bureaucracy is important for initiating adjustment, but success in sustaining and consolidating reform requires building bases of support. In the absence of such bases of support, insulated technocratic agencies become politically isolated and programs become vulnerable to reversal. It is to the strategy of building support among the beneficiaries of the reform process that we now turn.

Building Coalitions for Reform

Outside the legislative arena and the government itself, political opposition to and support for reform come from interest group leaders and other political entrepreneurs who react to the program's anticipated effects on their constituents. Interest groups are important not only because of their lobbying activity and role in mobilizing electoral support but also because of their capability for spearheading collective action outside routine political channels: labor and investment strikes, capital flight, demonstrations, riots, and even insurrection.

In formulating and launching a program, politicians can counter opposition with the technical expertise of their staff, their power over the agenda, broad political mandates, and exploitation of political and institutional circumstances. Over the longer run, however, the implementation of adjustment measures must be seen as a process of coalition-building (Waterbury 1989).

The configuration of interest group support is likely to change as an economy undergoes stabilization and structural adjustment. Indeed, if the interest group configuration does not change, it is unclear how the status quo could ever be transcended. The resolution to this paradox is that the political success of a program depends not only on its distributive consequences but also on the organization of groups and their relationship to the political system. Even if the aggregate benefits are widespread, politicians may not be able to capture these gains politically if institutional arrangements weaken or dissipate support from beneficiaries and strengthen antireform forces (Geddes 1992). A critical aspect of the political management of policy reform therefore involves encouraging the reorganization of interests: expanding the representation and weight of interest groups that benefit from the reforms and either marginalizing or compensating the losers.

Interest Groups and the Government

The interest groups relevant to a particular adjustment effort vary depending on the policy area. In some cases, such as trade policy, narrowly focused organizations, such as sectoral lobbies, can play a crucial role. In general, business associations and urban labor in both the public and private sectors have proven to be the most important organized interests in middle-income countries. Agricultural interests also come into play in several of our case studies, particularly Poland and Senegal.

LABOR. Organized labor almost always loses in the initial phase of a traditional adjustment program. Tight fiscal and monetary policies reduce aggregate demand and employment and hit directly at public sector employment and wages. The political models of inflation and stabilization reviewed by Alesina in chapter 2 often explicitly or implicitly have a labor-business conflict at their core. Trade policy also affects the interests of workers, although theoretically, the relevant cleavages should not divide labor from capital but should depend on the sectoral location of labor. As Rodrik argues in chapter 3, trade liberalization pressures the import-substituting sector, and real devaluation hits the producers of nontraded goods. In both cases, organized labor is expected to resist reform efforts.

Thus, getting labor to agree to temporary setbacks is crucial. Labor is typically subject to a variety of controls under authoritarian regimes, and this has been one reason for their relative success in implementing stabilization efforts. In some cases, such as Korea and Turkey, controls on labor extended into the democratic period. Genuine democratization is, however, likely to allow more extensive and active labor union organization and militancy. This happened in Spain under the Center Democratic Union, in Turkey after 1987, in Senegal, and of course in Poland, where labor led the fight against the communist government.

Whether labor resisted and blocked reform depended in part on its degree of organization and sectoral location. Devaluation and trade liberalization were more contentious and subject to reversal where labor found other allies opposed to adjustment, like the rural religious and business leaders in Senegal, or where labor was concentrated in strategic sectors, such as coal mining in Poland. A high concentration of workers in state-owned enterprises complicates stabilization plans because efforts to control wages or lay off workers are immediately politicized; this was a problem in Nigeria, Poland, and Turkey.

In some cases with strategically placed unions (Mexico) or resurgent unions following democratization (Spain), stabilization and adjustment succeeded anyway. This suggests that the most critical factors are how unions relate to the government and political parties and how they are represented in the political system as a whole. Previous studies, particularly of Europe, have found that corporatist arrangements (Katzenstein 1985), close ties with governing social-democratic parties (Cameron 1984; Hicks 1988; Lange and Garrett 1985), or ties with broad cross-class parties (Haggard and Kaufman 1992) can integrate labor into the political system in ways that provide the basis for compromise, social pacts, and enhanced policy credibility.

The cases of successful adjustment generally fit one of these patterns. Mexico again constitutes a limiting case, because corporatist organization was used for the purposes of control: the government was able to secure labor concessions in support of the Economic Solidarity Pact. Yet this outcome is not limited to more restrictive governments; democracies can achieve similar results. Center-left governments in Spain and in Poland secured the acquiescence of labor, at least in the short run; so, too, did the Concertación in Chile, a coalition led by the Christian Democrats but with socialist participation. By contrast, where labor had weak links with the government, but strong ties with class-based leftist or populist parties or movements, as in Nigeria, Spain under the Center Democratic Union, and Turkey before September 1980 and after 1987, reform proved more difficult.

One reason for this apparently anomalous result—social-democratic governments extracting concessions from labor—may be that such governments are particularly concerned with establishing their credibility with the private sector. Leadership of the Spanish Socialist Workers Party in Spain and of the Concertación in Chile had this concern. A second reason is that center-left governments more often enjoy credibility with labor and are thus in a better position to protect labor's long-term interests in return for short-term restraint. Right-of-center governments, in contrast, are less likely to offer long-term improvements for labor and more likely to resort to short-run concessions in the face of labor pressure, such as wage increases that outstrip productivity or expanded public employment, even if these undermine the program. This pattern was particularly clear in Turkey and in Spain under the Center Democratic Union.

BUSINESS. Although organized labor almost always fares poorly in the initial phases of stabilization and adjustment programs, the interests of business are usually more mixed. Some measures, such as wage restraint, regulatory reform, and privatization, can garner support among all segments of business while others, such as trade liberalization, face resistance from adversely affected sectors. In Thailand and Turkey, this ambivalence extended to the level of the individual firm or group, since diversified financial-industrial groups were involved in importing, import-substituting, and export activities simultaneously.

This policy ambivalence presents the government with a wider array of options for dealing with the business sector. Policy reforms can be packaged or linked to compensate firms for unpopular measures. Contrary to conventional political economy expectations, relatively low levels of business resistance to trade reform were found in the countries studied here, in part because policies were packaged effectively. In both Turkey and Thailand, import-dependent businesses were compensated for a costly devaluation by means of the gradual pace of import liberalization and an expansion of export subsidies. In addition, the devaluation itself protected the import-competing sector, as explained in Rodrik's essay (chapter 3). In Nigeria, where the system of import-licensing benefited relatively few firms, the government packaged a large devaluation with the elimination of the system of licenses, which expanded legal entry into the import business.

Trade policy reform in Senegal also included accompanying measures, including wage restraint, intended to lower costs since devaluing the nominal exchange rate was precluded by membership in the Franc Zone.

But the size of the cut in nominal wages required to achieve a real devaluation and the strength of unions representing public sector employees made it impossible to achieve the program's objectives for wage policy. Other industrial policy measures designed to assist business proved to be either inadequate to the task or poorly implemented, and the battered private manufacturing sector succeeded in partially reversing the liberalization measures.

In Mexico, Spain, Poland, Thailand, and Turkey, the packaging extended beyond the bounds of trade policy. Rodrik explains how periods of depreciation and macroeconomic crisis may be good times to launch trade reforms, contrary to usual thinking, precisely because the politically disruptive redistributive effects of trade policy are either small compared with macroeconomic developments or partly offset by movements in the exchange rate. In Mexico, a protected business sector put up surprisingly little resistance to a program that linked much-wanted stabilization with sweeping trade liberalization. In Spain, the manifest benefits of entering the European Community and a concerted effort to increase the flexibility of labor markets offset the dislocation associated with trade liberalization.

The strategy of providing offsetting gains does not necessarily guarantee that trade policy reform will be institutionalized; political leaders must also change patterns of organization to maximize support and minimize the access of rent-seeking antireform groups. Mexico and Senegal provide a sharp contrast in this regard. In Mexico, the government not only did away with the licensing system but also substantially reduced the discretionary power of the agency (Secofi) that had been an important source of access for firms seeking special exemptions from trade policy decisions. At the same time, new consultative mechanisms favored representation by large financial-industrial groups that were in a reasonably good position to survive—and even benefit from—liberalization; the Prem government devised similar consultative mechanisms in Thailand.

In Senegal, by contrast, the government failed to reach out to those elements in the private sector that benefited from reform, mostly a weakly organized group of small-scale traders. The government was unwilling and unable to break long-standing networks of patronage, and technocrats retained a disdain for the private sector, considering it parasitic and corrupt. Thus, the antireform element within the state was much more familiar to the private sector, through rent-seeking and clientelist networks, than were the free-marketeer reformers.

Governments seeking to liberalize trade clearly gain by building ties to private sector organizations with export interests and by weakening institutions that provide access for firms in the import-substituting sector. Building consultative ties to broad-based industry groups should therefore have advantages over consultative mechanisms that empower narrow sectoral organizations. Encompassing peak organizations played a role in blunting business opposition to reform in both Thailand and Mexico. In Mexico, the complex heterodox adjustment program would have failed without extensive private sector participation and consultation.

In Turkey, by contrast, failure to institutionalize procedures for maintaining a dialogue with relevant peak associations allowed representation to remain in personalistic and particularistic channels, which whittled away some elements of the trade reform. In Poland and Senegal, little effort was made to build bases of support in the private sector, which contributed to the fragility of the reform in those two countries.

Program Design

Political institutions linking the government with key interest groups clearly affect the likely success of a program, but the design of the program itself also affects the response of interest groups. Although policymakers and economists have devoted substantial attention to the problem of designing programs to elicit the desired *economic* response, programs will only be sustained if they elicit a favorable *political* response as well. This depends, in turn, on how different groups experience gains and losses as a result of stabilization and structural adjustment measures. Three dimensions of program design are relevant here: the speed of implementation, the sequencing and packaging of different types of policy reforms, and the use of compensation mechanisms.

SPEED OF IMPLEMENTATION. To some extent, economic conditions dictate the speed with which policymakers can act. Hyperinflation or the depletion of foreign exchange reserves demands swift action. When reform is organization-intensive, and requires the creation of new procedures and agencies or fundamental reorganization of existing institutions, moving fast may be technically impossible. Typically, however, the government does have some control over the pace of reform. If so, the crucial policy question is which economically feasible reform path is *politically* optimal.

For exchange rate corrections, stabilization, and most domestic price reforms, the economically optimum pace of reform is generally considered to be rapid. Delay in these areas not only has high economic costs but, as a growing literature has emphasized, casts doubt on the credibility of the reform effort itself. There is somewhat more debate on the optimal pace of trade reform, with some arguing for rapid liberalization and others presenting the case for gradualism (see chapter 3). Privatization and financial sector reform, by contrast, typically have slower economically optimal speeds because complementary institutional changes are needed to make these policy adjustments effective.

In the debate about politics and the speed of adjustment, the dominant line of argument is that rapid reform makes political as well as economic sense. The closer the program is to the economically optimal pace, the sooner and stronger will be the growth response. Delay and partial reform, by contrast, can have perverse economic consequences and, as a result, even increase opposition to reform. Political economy models by Murphy, Shleifer, and Vishny (1992) and van Wijnbergen (1992) produce such results.

Advocates of rapid reform argue that the problem of short-term political reactions to the program is often overstated. First, rapid reforms do not necessarily have high political costs; rapid stabilization of hyperinflation, for example, usually garners broad support for the government. Second, most governments have some leeway to ride out the opposition. Political honeymoons gave the government leeway for rapid reform in Turkey in 1983–84, Senegal in 1984, Nigeria in 1985–86, Poland in 1990, and Spain in both 1977 and 1983, although it is clear in retrospect that the Turkish, Senegalese, Nigerian, and Polish governments did not use their honeymoons fully. Finally, pushing reform rapidly might actually *weaken* interest groups tied to the status quo or at least exploit the delay in the mobilization of antireform forces (Douglas 1990). Turkey's reforms in 1983 and Poland's in 1990 took effect before interest groups could mobilize their opposition. The slow pace of reform in Senegal, by contrast, gave opposing interests ample time to organize.

Moreover, governments are not necessarily punished for pushing reforms through the system. Among our case studies, political leaders gained from undertaking adjustment programs in Mexico, Spain, and Turkey. Conversely, governments in Nigeria, Poland, and Senegal lost political support not simply because the costs of the program were too high, but because delays and inconsistency in its implementation added to and prolonged the costs of adjustment.

A final argument for moving rapidly, and one that has gained particular attention among economists, centers on the government's credibility (Alesina and Tabellini 1988; Calvo 1989; Froot 1988; Przeworski 1991, pp. 168–71; van Wijnbergen 1985). Rodrik (1989), for example, develops a model in which economic agents are uncertain whether the government is serious about reform or not. It shows that a truly reform-minded government can signal its commitment by undertaking reforms of a magnitude or at a pace that uncommitted governments would be unwilling to attempt.

Such a radical strategy carries risks, however. If the government retreats by slowing or reversing policy reforms, it can lose credibility, and the program may fail as a result. In the next period, the government must take even bolder action in order to signal its commitment. Yet such actions are less credible due to the legacy of past failures, whereas a more gradual approach might have built up a legacy of success.

There are costs of moving too rapidly, costs that may lead the electorate to reverse the program before it has had time to bear fruit; Dewatripont and Roland (1992a, 1992b) developed a formal model that yields this result. Under these conditions, it is preferable to demonstrate the positive results of initial reforms, thereby expanding the coalition of support and whittling away at the opposition, before proceeding further.

What evidence do the cases shed on the debate about the pace of stabilization? The initial macroeconomic imbalances in Chile and Thailand, and therefore the costs associated with adjustment, were comparatively slight. Both governments enjoyed the benefits of relatively robust growth, and the new Chilean government also had the advantage of a honeymoon period for reversing Pinochet's election-year expansion.

Mexico, Turkey, and Poland provide more meaningful comparisons for developing countries experiencing severe crises. Rapid adjustment was feasible and credible in Mexico because of unusually strong institutional structures. Turkey's large devaluation in 1980 and trade liberalization in 1983–84 brought rapid trade and output growth and contributed to political support for reform. Although costs associated with the adjustment program perhaps contributed to the increasing polarization of the political system before the coup in 1980, these political developments probably would have occurred even if the government had not acted swiftly. Poland's shock program had political benefits as well as costs. Debate continues on the extent of the output lost in 1990–91, but the rapid adjustment of prices followed by stabilization reduced scarcities and enhanced the availability of consumer goods, a major gain offsetting the other dislocations of the program.

Although rapid paths of reform sometimes encounter problems, none failed in the countries studied here. By contrast, gradual approaches to tackling macroeconomic imbalances usually failed. Gradualism (if it can even be considered a strategy) faltered in Turkey in the late 1980s and in Nigeria and Senegal. It succeeded in Spain only because large inflows of foreign investment and a strong initial fiscal position provided the government leeway; these conditions do not exist in most countries needing to stabilize.

With respect to trade liberalization, however, a more clear-cut case can perhaps be made for gradualism. Mexico was able to initiate and sustain a rapid trade reform, partly because it could control or influence interests that were negatively affected but also because it packaged the trade reform with a successful program of macroeconomic stabilization. Such attempts did not prove sustainable in Nigeria, Poland, and Senegal, however, where macroeconomic failures also led to reversals in trade policy. Gradualism helped with the Turkish trade reforms in the mid-1980s, the Spanish trade reforms, and the reforms of trade and industrial strategy undertaken by the Thai government in the 1980s. Gradualism provided the opportunity for firms to adjust to the new environment and in effect constituted a form of compensation.

SEQUENCING AND PACKAGING. Many of the observations on the speed of implementation also apply to the question of sequencing and of whether reforms should be undertaken in stages or all at once. A large literature has addressed the question of the optimal sequencing of trade, financial, and macroeconomic policy reforms from an economic perspective. The lesson drawn from the Southern Cone experiences of the 1970s is that it was important to stabilize the economy before liberalizing trade and the capital account. Recently, however, there has been greater recognition that combining trade and macroeconomic reforms can increase the credibility of the overall reform effort. Where excessive or inefficient government involvement in production is a problem, privatization at an early stage in the adjustment process expands the weight of groups interested in sustaining or pressing on with the program.

In chapter 3, Rodrik develops the idea that the political attractiveness of reforms depends on the ratio of the gain in income to the amount of redistribution. Trade reforms generally have a low ratio of efficiency gain to redistribution; Harberger triangles are small relative to the rectangles. Macroeconomic policy reforms, by contrast, have a high ratio of gains to redistribution. This is an argument for packaging reforms and helps explain the large number of successful trade liberalizations undertaken by developing countries in the 1980s, including Mexico, Spain, and Turkey and the initial success in Poland. The experiences of Nigeria, Poland, and Senegal show that if the macroeconomic reform falters, trade reforms are also likely to suffer. In Turkey, protectionist interests also experienced some partial reversals, but these deviations were relatively modest. The cases generally support the proposition that bundling reforms has a political economy rationale.

COMPENSATION. The theme of compensation already arose in the discussion of the government's relationship with labor and business, but the topic deserves more extended analysis. Various arguments have been forwarded for including compensation schemes in policy reform programs (see Graham 1993). If a reform will raise aggregate output, an appropriate scheme for compensating losers can make the reform Pareto-improving: every individual will be either better off or no worse off than before. Not only is this morally appealing, but it makes political sense. If individuals are certain that the risk of reform is reduced in this way, they will probably support the reform effort. Indeed, to make the reform politically feasible under a democratic setting, it should only be necessary to devise a compensation scheme under which at least a majority would be better or no worse off.

Policy analysts and applied economists have treated compensation with greater skepticism. First, the ability of governments to use compensatory schemes is severely limited by financial and managerial resources (see Dewatripont and Roland 1992a, 1992b). Second, the groups most able to secure compensation are not necessarily the most severely affected by either the crisis or the efforts to adjust to it (Nelson 1992); "compensation" may mean simply paying off the politically powerful. Contrary to the sentiments expressed in the United Nations Children's Fund (UNICEF) study on *Adjustment with a Human Face* (Cornia, Jolly, and Stewart 1987), it is not evident that cushioning the effects of adjustment on the poor is *politically* important, although economic and moral grounds may exist for doing so.[4] Finally, a major objective of adjustment programs is to reduce and reorient the government's use of subsidies and other interventions that contribute to inefficiency, rent seeking, and corruption. Compensation schemes, unless very well designed and implemented, can run counter to these objectives.

The case studies suggest that compensation is crucial to securing support for stabilization and adjustment programs. In the more successful cases—Chile, Mexico, Spain, and Thailand—compensation came in the form of complementary measures that provided effective compensation while enhancing welfare and economic opportunity over the longer term and minimizing rent-seeking opportunities. The successful schemes typically did not include *direct* compensation for losing groups.

The Concertación in Chile and the Spanish Socialist Workers Party in Spain came to power with the expectation that they would protect the interests of labor and the poor, but they realized that doing this through wage increases and direct subsidies would derail needed fiscal adjustments. Instead, they took measures to improve the distribution of health and education services, expand the social safety net for the poor, and liberalize social legislation. Direct compensation schemes succeeded economically in Chile in the early 1980s because they were well targeted, but they certainly did not win support for the Pinochet government or for the adjustment program, according to opinion polls cited in chapter 7. These measures worked for the Concertación because of political agreements that surrounded the transition. Labor and the rural poor were core constituencies for the Concertación parties, and they knew that their interests would be addressed in the long term. The government of the Spanish Socialist Workers Party in Spain was similarly able to use limited welfare measures to win political support. International agreements to enhance opportunities for Mexicans and Chileans to export to the United States and for Spaniards, Poles, and Turks to export to Europe acted as compensation to firms accustomed to selling in a protected domestic market. So did export incentives in Thailand and Turkey, which sped not only the growth of exports but also the expansion of the proadjustment export interests.

More direct compensation has occurred in the countries studied here, but their influence on the political economy of adjustment is unclear. In Turkey, workers in the formal sector and in agriculture were the group most hurt by the adjustment in the early and mid-1980s. As the expansion of democracy in the late 1980s brought them back into the political process, the government tried to compensate for previous losses and win support by giving generous wage increases and raising farm price supports. Wage increases in the private sector were justified by growth in productivity and came about through market forces, especially after the rights of unions to organize and strike were reinstated. The increase in public sector wages and support prices, however, contributed substantially to the deterioration of fiscal policy. In any case, labor and agriculture voted mostly for the opposition parties in 1991, bringing them to power, although not with a mandate for reversing the adjustment program.

In Senegal, various compensation schemes helped moderate opposition to the government, but as in Turkey, they did not garner political support for the program; moreover, the implementation of some programs resembled the traditional patronage that the Socialist Party had always pursued and contributed to fiscal slippage (see also Graham 1991). In Poland, the government partially compensated agriculture through tax breaks and special export subsidies, but this support did not stem the increasingly vocal criticism of the government and the program, even from the Solidarity farm organizations.

The case studies presented in this volume point to the conclusion that compensation measures are useful components of adjustment programs. It is important, however, to distinguish between compensation in the form of complementary policies that offset the costs associated with reform, and have other benefits, and compensation in the form of direct subsidies and transfers. The latter did have some positive effect in the area of trade policy by expanding export-oriented groups but later constituted a problem when efforts were made to reduce the subsidies.

International Influences on the Adjustment Process

Although politics and policy vary widely across countries, even when they face similar international constraints, international influences cannot be ignored. Not only do world markets for goods and capital influence economic performance, but international agencies and foreign governments can influence policy outcomes as well. A full examination of these issues is beyond the scope of this project (see Kahler 1992), but three influences deserve some discussion: the conditionality bargain, the existence of export opportunities, and external ideas and advice about policy. The cases suggest that conditional external support is unlikely to tip the domestic political balance in favor of reform when opposition is strong, but that its presence (or absence) can bolster (or weaken) the standing of reformers within the government. Over the longer run, material assistance may be less important than training and socialization, which can change the political actors and alter the domestic debate surrounding the adjustment process.

Conditionality

All the countries in the sample, with the exception of Spain, received loans from the International Monetary Fund and the World Bank for at least part of the time they were undergoing structural adjustment. Do the international organizations have policy leverage as a result? Or should one conclude, as Kahler (1992) does, that governments committed to policy reform will probably undertake them in any case and that those opposed will resist?

The attempt by external actors to exercise policy influence has been the subject of a growing literature (Berg and Batchelder 1985; Dell 1981; Fishlow 1990; Haggard 1986; Kahler 1990, 1992; Killick 1984; Mosley 1987; Mosley, Harrigan, and Toye 1991; Polak 1991; Remmer 1986; Williamson 1983). Mosley, Harrigan, and Toye (1991, chap. 3), for example, argue that conditionality can be modeled as a bargaining game consisting of three steps: a negotiating process that sets the conditions, an implementation process in which the government decides how far to honor the promises made in the first step, and a response by the external aid and lending agencies to the government's actions. As Putnam (1988) argues, such bargaining games always consist of two levels: the implementation of the agreement struck internationally is contingent on a variety of political factors that the government does not necessarily control. Governments may therefore defect from an agreement involuntarily because of opposition from important constituents.

How does the provision of conditional resources affect the political economy of reform? On the one hand, providing extra resources can help increase its political sustainability by allowing the country greater consumption than otherwise would have been possible. External assistance also allows the country to sustain a higher level of investment, which in turn should lead to greater economic benefits in later years. At a more political level, external assistance can be linked to the compensatory measures outlined above, either directly or indirectly. On the other hand, the lack of external support, or even external demands for resource transfers such as debt repayment or reparations, can weaken the political position of reform advocates. This applies not only during the current crisis, but in important historical cases such as German reparations in the interwar period (Berg and Sachs 1989; Maxfield 1990; Webb 1988, 1989).

In none of the case studies did a low level of external support for a program totally undermine the position of reformers, although this may reflect the particular sample. It is clear that external support had positive political effects in Poland and in Turkey in the early 1980s. The political ascent of the reformers within these two governments was partly tied to their ability to secure external financing, and external support made it easier for them to deal with the subsequent opposition. In both cases, domestic political and economic crises already inclined the leadership in the direction of reform, and therefore the influence of external resources is difficult to judge.

Turkey and Thailand show how external aid influenced the stance of the military. In both cases, the military did not traditionally favor devaluation and did not see any benefits in stimulating a more outward-oriented economy. They were, however, receptive to arguments that promised to restore external financing and went along with devaluations in order to secure loans. Whether external assistance can have such an influence on larger, more diffuse interest groups is uncertain.

For policy purposes, the opposite finding seems more significant. When resources are made available to governments disposed *against* reform, such as Mexico in the late 1970s, Turkey in the late 1980s (on fiscal reform), and Senegal during parts of the 1980s, the financing allowed governments to postpone, rather than pursue, adjustment. This pattern is consistent with the findings of the World Bank's third report on adjustment lending. While countries that received intensive adjustment lending had significantly higher growth rates than those that did not, total official capital flows contributed to higher growth only in low-income countries, not in middle-income ones (World Bank 1992).

International Trade Agreements

Although the discussion of external influences on economic policy in developing countries typically focuses on international financial institutions, the studies presented here show that the prospect of trade concessions from important partners can greatly increase the attractiveness of a reform program. Spain's membership in the European Community was widely desired and recognized as one of the benefits not only of trade reform, but also of democratization. For Turkey and Poland, the prospect of joining the European Community is far less certain, but even the distant hope of membership has probably contributed to the reform momentum for trade policy. Mexico's free trade agreement with the United States and Canada was reached after the country had already substantially liberalized trade, but the recognition that a return to macroeconomic instability would endanger the agreement helped sustain support for the Economic Solidarity Pact. These cases reinforce the obvious point that the advanced industrial states must provide a favorable climate if outward-oriented policies are to have their full effect.

Ideas

This discussion has focused on the material benefits provided by external actors. International networks and socialization also influence policy choices by transmitting policy-relevant knowledge and attitudes (Kahler 1990, 1992). These channels of influence include not only foreign advisers, but also the training of technocrats at foreign universities, government-sponsored exchange programs, and work experience in multinational corporations.

The case studies demonstrate clearly that these channels of influence had a powerful effect on the nature of the policy debate within governments. In Chile, Mexico, Spain, and Turkey, members of the economic team had either studied at American universities or worked at the World Bank or the International Monetary Fund. Turgut Özal, the prime minister of Turkey, worked at the World Bank in the 1970s and gathered many of his ideas on trade liberalization and adjustment at that time. In Chile, the influence of "the Chicago boys" on policy is well known, but internationally sponsored think tanks there also played an important role in keeping economists from all parts of the political spectrum in touch with the international evolution of ideas on economic policy.

In all the countries studied, foreign advisers from multilateral institutions, universities, and think tanks actively provided policy advice; in Poland and other East European and Central Asian countries, the influx of foreign advisers has been particularly large (although their influence may not be as great as the advisers advertise). External policy advice generally improved the technical quality of policymaking, but the fact that the influences were external created some political problems. Reform proposals were more attractive when they could be shown to be homegrown. Opposition to external policy ideas was particularly strong in countries with long histories of political interference by great powers, as in Mexico and Turkey, or outright imperialism, as in African countries.

Nigeria and Turkey demonstrate these points. In Nigeria, Babangida opened to public discussion the question of whether the country should adopt an International Monetary Fund program; the proposal was rejected in a wide-ranging national debate in which nationalism and the violation of sovereignty by international organizations were the central theme of the opposition. The Babangida government immediately adopted a similar program without international support. Although the International Monetary Fund's detractors complained bitterly that they had been duped, nationalist resistance to the reform was blunted to some extent. When the Turkish government faced severe macroeconomic and balance of payments problems at the beginning of 1980, it decided to develop its own program, with only informal input from the International Monetary Fund. The government believed that the program would be more politically acceptable if officials went to the World Bank and the International Monetary Fund for approval and financial support after it had been initiated.

The conclusion seems clear: although external advisers have an important role to play, the training of indigenous economists and technicians is more likely to have a longer-term influence on the domestic policy debate.

Implications for International Financial Institutions

The goal of policy-oriented economic research is clear: to identify policies that are optimal according to some criterion—whether it is efficiency, stability, equality, or long-term growth—and to urge their adoption by the relevant political authorities. The purpose of political analysis is somewhat less obvious, particularly for the community of external aid agencies and international financial institutions. Moreover, important arguments can be made that political calculations should *not* enter into their operations. First, the clients of international financial institutions are member governments, and any dealings with a country are through its government or with government approval. Introducing noneconomic calculations runs the risk of politicizing already delicate operations and weakening both the design of programs and the commitment of governments.

Despite these legitimate concerns, external aid and lending agencies, and particularly the international financial institutions, should be concerned with the political economy of reform for at least four reasons. First, both prudential considerations and their mandate to promote economic development demand that they evaluate the prospects that a given reform program will be sustained. Political considerations are relevant in making that evaluation. There is no sense lending to a government that lacks the political interest or capacity to pursue a program to its conclusion. Lending in such circumstances may even establish perverse incentives, allowing governments to postpone reform and continue with misguided policies.

Second, a reform program undertaken under difficult political circumstances, such as those in new democracies, must be designed with particular attention to improving its political viability. Political considerations will not necessarily dilute a program's economic integrity; rather, appropriate strategy and tactics play a crucial role in constructing the coalitions of support that will sustain programs over the longer run.

Third, bilateral aid and lending agencies and international financial institutions can play a constructive role in the design and reform of institutions. It is clearly beyond the mandate of the international institutions to press for a change in a country's party system. It is appropriate, however, to urge a government to establish a political dialogue with affected groups or to argue for a more independent central bank. The renewed concern with "governance" among the international financial institutions is based on a stronger premise: the quality and credibility of decisionmaking policy can be improved by increasing the flow of information between government and the private sector, increasing accountability, and making government action more transparent and more democratic. Institutional reform is already a component of program design in many areas, from the budget process and central banking to state-owned enterprises and the administrative structure surrounding particular projects. Perhaps the greatest contribution of political analysis is to suggest how institutions can be designed to increase the political incentives for growth-enhancing policies.

A final consideration returns to the central purpose of this project: the relationship between democratization and economic reform. Throughout, this chapter has asked what effects political arrangements have on economic adjustment efforts while recognizing the intrinsic value of promoting stable democratic rule. It also asked how the sometimes conflicting objectives of pluralist politics and growth-promoting economic policies could be made complementary.

No country has undertaken major structural adjustments without political difficulty. No magic formula will dispense with the political opposition to reform. Thus it is important to remain modest not only about what is known but also about what outsiders can do. Nonetheless, there are some lessons for reconciling democratic rule with market-oriented reform.

The process of democratization poses difficulties for the management of economic policy because of the reemergence of social demands on the government; this dilemma is particularly acute during periods of economic crisis. Yet governments that aggressively launched adjustment programs following the transition could exploit a tradeoff between political gains and temporary economic losses. Governments that delayed, by contrast, had difficulty re-establishing their credibility. Similar findings hold for the electoral cycle. The implications for the timing of external support are straightforward: external aid agencies and international financial institutions must stand ready to support aggressive and wide-ranging reforms immediately following changes of government. They must also recognize that there are times when little will be accomplished.

It is important to distinguish between the *initiation* and *consolidation* of reform. Even when economic and political conditions favor an aggressive adjustment strategy, such a strategy will fail unless attention is given to sustaining support; this is particularly true in new democracies. The urgency that surrounds crisis situations and the desire to reverse inherited legacies make radical action appear attractive, but unless they build political support, such programs can leave a destructive legacy not only of economic failure but of political polarization as well.

Some of the findings concerning political institutions, such as those concerning the polarization and fragmentation of the party system, do not generate clear policy recommendations for outside actors, although they certainly have implications for the design of new democracies. Institutional weaknesses in one area can be offset in part by innovations in others, however. A particularly strong finding is that successful policy reform efforts were preceded by reforms within the bureaucracy itself, reforms that pried policymaking away from existing channels and centralized decisionmaking processes across relevant agencies. These changes elevated the policy role of technical staff with fresh ideas as a counterweight to bureaucratic and interest group opposition. The institutional changes and delegation of authority were characteristic not only of the less democratic cases, such as Mexico and Thailand, but also of Spain and Poland.

Institutional changes can help both launch and consolidate reforms by, for example, changing the trade policy machinery or strengthening the central bank or budgetary process. Regardless of the institutional structure, governments will still confront opposition. In most of the adjustment programs that succeeded, governments explicitly used compensatory mechanisms to blunt such opposition. Generally, successful compensation took the form of complementary measures, such as political concessions or reforms in government spending priorities, rather than that of subsidies or wage increases. When direct compensation was tried, as in Spain in the early 1980s or Senegal and Turkey in the late 1980s, it undermined the program, because it had direct fiscal effects and weakened the argument that fiscal, wage, or exchange rate adjustments were necessary.

The question of compensation is closely related to how reforms are packaged. The studies suggest that packaging reforms tends to increase their political viability, both because a wider array of groups see some direct benefit and because measures that impose costs on some group can be matched with others that promise gains. This type of explicit packaging of reforms was characteristic of successful programs in Mexico, Poland, Spain, Thailand, and Turkey.

Institutional reform, compensation, and skillful packaging are important stratagems for political leaders to consider. But the essence of democracy is that the allocation of the costs and benefits of reform is the subject of bargaining among competing groups. Sometimes such bargaining is inefficient and fails to produce economically optimal outcomes, which makes it tempting to limit or defer the democratic control of policymaking. The history of the 1970s and 1980s shows, however, that authoritarian rule does not necessarily produce positive results and that, in any case, governments cannot suppress or marginalize indefinitely the interests of major groups.

A counterintuitive finding of this project is that organizational ties with negatively affected groups can, if managed correctly, increase the credibility of the government. Not only do such arrangements provide assurances that the program will benefit groups such as labor in the medium term, but they also provide a forum in which trust can be built and tradeoffs negotiated. Such institutional arrangements are not always available, though, and opposition groups may be too fragmented and divided to permit such a corporatist solution. In the absence of such organizational options, other institutional mechanisms must be used to build bases of support.

In democracies, the main channel for accomplishing this objective is the party and electoral system. The findings in this regard are not as pessimistic as simple rent-seeking models would lead one to believe. Any change in the status quo generates opposition, but political leaders in the countries studied were punished as often for failing to undertake needed reforms as for moving too quickly. Given the negative image that adjustment programs have in many developing countries, this is not a trivial finding.

In any case, establishing the credibility of reform and institutionalizing its gains under democratic rule ultimately require building support for the program through the party system and with the electorate at large. Thus the title of this book: structural adjustment is not complete until the public has voted for reform.

Notes

1. These include structural adjustment loans and sector adjustment loans from the World Bank and regular standby arrangements, extended fund facility agreements, and structural adjustment facility loans from the International Monetary Fund. Sector adjustment loans are omitted from table 1-1.

2. To date, surprisingly few studies have examined this crucial topic. See Roubini and Sachs 1989; Haggard and Kaufman 1993, chaps. 5 and 9.

3. Defendants of proportional representation, which generally encourages a larger number of political parties than plurality systems, argue that such systems are more democratic in the sense of being more representative.

4. Graham 1993 argues, however, that even if compensating the poor is not politically significant for specific adjustment measures, doing so can help create new progovernment bases of support that are valuable to political leaders.

References

Alesina, Alberto. 1988. "Macroeconomics and Politics." NBER Macroeconomics Annual, pp. 13–52. Cambridge, Mass.: National Bureau of Economic Research.

Alesina, Alberto, and Guido Tabellini. 1988. "Credibility and Politics." European Economic Review 32, pp. 542–50.

Alt, James A. 1985. "Political Parties, World Demand, and Unemployment." American Political Science Review 79:4, pp. 1016–40.

Alt, James A., and K. Alec Chrystal. 1983. Political Economics. Berkeley: University of California Press.

Ames, Barry. 1987. Political Survival: Politicians and Public Policy in Latin America. Berkeley: University of California Press.

Barry, Brian. 1985. "Does Democracy Cause Inflation? Political Ideas of Some

Economists." In Leon N. Lindberg and Charles Maier, eds., *The Politics of Inflation and Economic Stagnation*. Washington, D.C.: Brookings Institution.

Bates, Robert, and Anne Krueger, eds. 1993. *Political and Economic Interactions in Economic Policy Reform*. Cambridge, Eng.: Blackwell.

Berg, Andrew, and Jeffery Sachs. 1989. "The Debt Crisis: Structural Explanations of Country Performance." NBER Working Paper 2607. National Bureau of Economic Research, Cambridge, Mass.

Berg, Elliot, and Alan Batchelder. 1985. "Structural Adjustment Lending: A Critical Review." *World Bank CPD* 8521. Washington, D.C.

Bresser Pereira, Luiz Carlos, Jose Maria Maraval, and Adam Przeworski. 1993. *Economic Reforms in New Democracies: A Social-Democratic Approach*. New York, N.Y.: Cambridge University Press.

Calvo, Guillermo A. 1989. "Incredible Reforms." In Guillermo Calvo and others, eds., *Debt, Stabilization, and Development: Essays in Memory of Carlos Díaz-Alejandro*. London: Blackwell.

Cameron, David R. 1984. "Social Democracy, Corporatism, Labour Quiescence, and the Representation of Economic Interests in Advanced Capitalist Society." In John H. Goldthorpe, ed., *Order and Conflict in Contemporary Capitalism*. Oxford, Eng.: Clarendon Press.

Cornia, Giovanni, Richard Jolly, and Frances Stewart. 1987. *Adjustment with a Human Face: Protecting the Vulnerable and Promoting Growth*. Oxford, Eng.: Clarendon Press.

Cukierman, Alex, Steven B. Webb, and B. Neyapti. 1992. "Measuring Central Bank Independence and Its Effect on Policy Outcomes." *World Bank Economic Review* 6, no. 3, pp. 353–98.

Dell, Sidney. 1981. *On Being Grandmotherly: The Evolution of IMF Conditionality*. No. 144/Princeton Studies in International Finance. Princeton, N.J.: Princeton University, Department of Economics, International Finance Section.

Dewatripont, M., and G. Roland. 1992a. "Economic Reform and Dynamic Political Constraints." *Review of Economic Studies* 59, pp. 703–30.

———. 1992b. "The Virtues of Gradualism and Legitimacy in the Transition to a Market Economy." *Economic Journal* 102 (March), pp. 291–300.

Diamond, Larry, Juan R. Linz, and Seymour Martin Lipset, eds. 1990. *Politics in Developing Countries: Comparing Experiences with Democracy*. Boulder, Colo.: Lynne Rienner Publishers.

Dornbusch, Rudiger, and Sebastian Edwards, eds. 1991. *The Macroeconomics of Populism in Latin America*. Chicago, Ill.: University of Chicago Press.

Douglas, Roger. 1990. "The Politics of Successful Structural Reform." *Wall Street Journal,* January 26–27, p. 6.

Fishlow, Albert. 1990. "Conditionality and Willingness to Pay: Some Parallels from the 1890s." In Barry Eichengreen and Peter Lindert, eds., *The International Debt Crisis in Historical Perspective*. Cambridge, Mass.: M.I.T. Press.

Froot, Kenneth. 1988. "Credibility, Real Interest Rates, and the Optimal Speed of Trade Liberalization." *Journal of International Economics* 25, pp. 71–93.

Geddes, Barbara. 1992. "The Effect of Political Institutions on the Feasibility of

Structural Adjustment." Background paper prepared for the World Bank project on the political economy of structural adjustment in new democracies, World Bank, Washington, D.C.

Graham, Carol. 1991. "Emergency Social Programs in Senegal." Brookings Institution, Washington, D.C. Processed.

_____. 1993. "Market Transitions and the Poor: Comparative Studies in Sustaining Reform." Brookings Institution, Washington, D.C. Processed.

Haggard, Stephan. 1986. "The Politics of Adjustment: Lessons from the IMF's Extended Fund Facility." In Miles Kahler, eds., *The Politics of International Debt,* pp. 157–86. Ithaca, N.Y.: Cornell University Press.

Haggard, Stephan, and Robert Kaufman, eds. 1992. *The Politics of Economic Adjustment: International Constraints, Distributive Conflicts, and the State.* Princeton, N.J.: Princeton University Press.

_____. 1993. "The Political Economy of Democratic Transitions." University of California, San Diego. Processed.

Haggard, Stephan, Robert Kaufman, and Steven B. Webb. 1992. "Democracy, Dictatorship, and Inflation in Middle-Income Countries." Harvard University, Rutgers University, and World Bank, Washington, D.C. Processed.

Hicks, Alexander. 1988. "Social Democratic Corporatism and Economic Growth." *Journal of Politics* 50, pp. 677–704.

Huntington, Samuel. 1991. *The Third Wave: Democratization in the Late Twentieth Century.* Norman: University of Oklahoma Press.

Kahler, Miles. 1990. "International Political Economy." *Foreign Affairs* 69 (fall), pp. 139–51.

_____. 1992. "External Influence, Conditionality, and the Politics of Adjustment." In Stephan Haggard and Robert Kaufman, eds., *The Politics of Economic Adjustment: International Constraints, Distributive Conflicts, and the State.* Princeton, N.J.: Princeton University Press.

Katzenstein, Peter. 1985. *Small States in World Markets: Industrial Policy in Europe.* Ithaca, N.Y.: Cornell University Press.

Killick, Tony, and others. 1984. *The Quest for Economic Stabilization.* London: Heinemann.

Lange, Peter, and Geoffrey Garrett. 1985. "The Politics of Growth: Strategic Interaction and Economic Performance in the Advanced Industrial Democracies, 1974–1980." *Journal of Politics* 49, pp. 792–827.

Maxfield, Sylvia. 1990. *Governing Capital: International Finance and Mexican Politics.* Ithaca, N.Y.: Cornell University Press.

Mosley, Paul. 1987. *Conditionality as Bargaining Process: Structural Adjustment Lending, 1980–86.* Princeton Studies in International Finance. Princeton, N.J.: Princeton University, International Finance Section.

Mosley, Paul, Jane Harrigan, and John Toye, eds. 1991. *Aid and Power: The World Bank and Policy-Based Lending,* 2 vols. London: Routledge.

Murphy, Kevin M., Andrei Shleifer, and Robert W. Vishny. 1992. "The Transition to a Market Economy: Pitfalls of Partial Reform." *Quarterly Journal of Economics* (August), pp. 889–906.

Nelson, Joan. 1990. "Conclusion." In Joan Nelson, ed., *Economic Crisis and Policy Choice: The Politics of Adjustment in the Third World.* Princeton, N.J.: Princeton University Press.

———. 1992. "Poverty, Equity, and the Politics of Adjustment." In Stephan Haggard and Robert Kaufman, eds., *The Politics of Economic Adjustment: International Constraints, Distributive Conflicts, and the State.* Princeton, N.J.: Princeton University Press.

Nordhaus, William D. 1990. "Alternative Approaches to the Political-Business Cycle." *Brookings Papers on Economic Activity* 2, pp. 1–68.

O'Donnell, Guillermo. 1973. *Modernization and Bureaucratic Authoritarianism: Studies in South American Politics.* Politics of Modernization Series 9. Berkeley: University of California, Institute of International Studies.

O'Donnell, Guillermo, Philippe C. Schmitter, and Laurence Whitehead, eds. 1986. *Transitions from Authoritarian Rule: Prospects for Democracy.* Baltimore, Md.: Johns Hopkins University Press.

Polak, Jacques. 1991. *The Changing Nature of IMF Conditionality.* Princeton Studies in International Finance. Princeton, N.J.: Princeton University, International Finance Section.

Przeworski, Adam. 1991. *Democracy and the Market: Political and Economic Reforms in Eastern Europe and Latin America.* New York: Cambridge University Press.

Putnam, Robert. 1988. "Diplomacy and Domestic Politics: The Logic of Two-Level Games." *International Organization* 42:3, pp. 427–60.

Remmer, Karen. 1986. "The Politics of Economic Stabilization: IMF Standby Programs in Latin America, 1954–1984." *Comparative Politics* 19 (October), pp. 1–25.

Rodrik, Dani. 1989. "Promises, Promises: Credible Policy Reform via Signalling." *Economic Journal: The Journal of Royal Economic Society [UK]* 99 (September), pp. 756–72.

Rogoff, Kenneth. 1990. "Equilibrium Political Budget Cycles." *American Economic Review* 80:1 (March), pp. 21–36.

Rogoff, Kenneth, and Anne Sibert. 1988. "Elections and Macroeconomic Policy Cycles." *Review of Economic Studies* 55:1 (January), pp. 1–16.

Roubini, Nouriel, and Jeffrey Sachs. 1989. "Political and Economic Determinants of Budget Deficits in the Industrial Democracies." *European Economic Review* 33 (May), pp. 903–33.

van Wijnbergen, Sweder. 1985. "Trade Reform, Aggregate Investment, and Capital Flight: On Credibility and the Value of Information." *Economics Letters* 19, pp. 369–72.

———. 1992. "Intertemporal Speculation, Shortages, and the Political Economy of Price Reform." *Economic Journal* 102 (November), pp. 1395–1406.

Waterbury, John. 1989. "The Political Management of Economic Management and Reform." In Joan Nelson, ed., *Fragile Coalitions: The Politics of Economic Adjustment,* pp. 39–56. New Brunswick, N.J.: Transaction Books.

Webb, Steven B. 1988. "Latin American Debt Today and German Reparations after World War I: A Comparison." *Weltwirtschaftliches Archiv [Review of World Economics]* 124:4, pp. 745–74.

_____. 1989. *Hyperinflation and Stabilization in Weimar Germany.* New York: Oxford University Press.

Williamson, John. 1983. *IMF Conditionality.* Washington, D.C.: Institute for International Economics.

_____, ed. 1993. *The Political Economy of Policy Reform.* Washington, D.C.: Institute for International Economics.

World Bank. 1992. "Adjustment Lending and the Mobilization of Private and Public Resources for Growth." Policy and Research Series 22. Washington, D.C.

2

Political Models
of Macroeconomic Policy
and Fiscal Reforms

ALBERTO ALESINA

ECONOMISTS TYPICALLY STUDY POLICYMAKING USING MODELS in which a benevolent social planner optimally chooses economic policy instruments in order to maximize the welfare of a representative individual, given certain resource constraints. From a *normative* point of view, these models are an extremely important tool of analysis. From a *positive* point of view, they cannot explain the occurrence of frequent and large departures from first-best policies. In addition, models with a social planner cannot explain why different countries at different points in time exhibit extremely different economic performances even though they face similar economic problems and have comparable resources.

A political-economic approach takes into account the institutional constraints and rigidities in which policymaking occurs by emphasizing the role of distributive conflicts, ideological and opportunistic incentives of the politicians, and other factors. Once these political variables are appropriately brought into the analysis, economic policy decisions that, at first view, appear wildly incoherent and suboptimal, can be interpreted as the rational outcome of a political-economic equilibrium. Such an approach not only is valuable from a positive perspective but also is

The author is grateful to several members of the World Bank Political Economy of Structural Adjustment Project, especially Stephan Haggard and Steven Webb, for their useful comments. He retains full responsibility for the content of this chapter.

rich in normative implications. In fact, it provides insights into how to design institutions that facilitate the achievement of efficient economic outcomes. Given the current transition to democracy occurring in Eastern Europe, such problems of institutional design are truly at the heart of the current policy debate.

This chapter highlights how recent developments in political economics contribute to the understanding of macroeconomic policy and, more specifically, of the timing, design, and likelihood of success of stabilizations achieved through monetary and fiscal reforms.

In addressing these important issues, two basic and very general forces will always be crucial factors: (1) the policymakers' incentive to retain power and (2) society's polarization and degree of social conflict. These two elements of the analysis play a crucial role in both democratic and dictatorial systems, although they may manifest themselves differently, in different institutional contexts.[1]

This chapter is organized as follows. First, the role of rationality in political-economic models and related methodological issues are discussed. Second, the timing of macroeconomic policy in general, and of fiscal reforms in particular, is addressed in relation to the timing of elections. This section focuses on how ideological and opportunistic considerations influence the choice of when to implement certain policies. It also reviews the literature on opportunistic and partisan political cycles and emphasizes what this literature offers to countries engaging simultaneously in policy reforms and democratization. Third, the related issue is examined of why stabilizations are delayed. The emphasis here is on why suboptimal economic outcomes such as hyperinflation and out-of-control budget deficits are not corrected for extended periods of time, even when something will obviously have to be done sooner or later. This section also emphasizes which political-institutional features are most likely to produce the timely adoption of successful stabilization programs.

Why Use Rational Models?

Political-economic models are often invoked to explain observations that seem to conflict with standard economic rationality. Thus, one is immediately tempted to abandon altogether the notion of rational behavior—defined as the maximization of individual utility under constraints—which also implies that all the available information is used to form expectations. Much too often, political-economic models hold the view that societies can be characterized as a bunch of crooks (the politicians) who manipulate a bunch of naive children (the citizens). It is often too easy to explain apparent departures from efficient collective behavior as the result of naïveté behavior, lack of understanding of basic economic relationships, shortsightedness, forgetfulness, or incoherence.

Interpretive schemes and models in which behavior and expectations that are not rational play a crucial role should be used only as a last resort, after first considering other explanations.

Two compelling arguments justify this view. The first is that economic rationality (the maximization of individual utility under constraints) underlies our basic economic models. Why should analysts be so ready to assume that economically rational investors, consumers, and workers suddenly become dumb voters and naive citizens?

The second argument is that one of the most important contributions that the political-economic approach can make is to explain the large differences observed in the economic performance of countries with similar economic problems, resources, and level of development. If the observed outcomes are explained as a lack of rationality, then one has to believe that what differentiates various countries in the world is the degree of rationality of their citizens, consumers, voters, and leaders. This view is far from appealing.

The most common objections to the assumption of rationality in political-economic models can be summarized as follows:

First, voters have no incentive to gather information, and empirical evidence shows that they know very little about politics. Rationality simply requires that an agent uses efficiently all the information he has; rationality has nothing to do with the amount of information available. The vast literature on decision theory under uncertainty and game theory with imperfect information shows how the behavior of poorly informed, rational agents can be very different from that of naive agents (see Tirole 1989). Second, in many political models, very little is required of voters; in several spatial models of elections, for instance, voters are only required to know which party is on the left of the other.

Second, even economists are studying models with limited or near rationality. In fact, several economists have studied models that emphasize how small departures from rational behavior can lead to significant economic effects (see Akerlof and Yellen 1985a, 1985b for applications of near-rational models to product and labor markets). This idea is quite interesting, although the kind of irrationality often invoked in political-economic models is not small; on the contrary, it is very large and on a completely different order of magnitude than that of near-rational models in economics. For example, in traditional models of fiscal illusion, voters are not supposed to understand that more public goods imply higher taxes sooner or later (see, for instance, Brennan and Buchanan 1980). In the traditional models of the political-business cycle pioneered by Nordhaus (1975), voters are not supposed to learn from the past that incumbents manipulate the economy before each election. These are definitively not examples of near rationality.

Third, not only are individuals self-motivated, they also have ideologies and may care about their fellow citizens, or at least some of them.

This is not inconsistent with rationality. In fact, this chapter discusses models in which partisan politicians act as if they followed an ideology, in addition to being self-interested. A rational approach only requires political and economic behavior to be consistent with given preferences, constraints, and information. Furthermore, an ideology can be interpreted as a systematic statement of preferences concerning political outcomes that are related to the resources and constraints of different actors.

Fourth, individuals cannot be expected to make all the necessary and complicated calculations needed to act rationally. Consumers are not required to take partial derivatives in order to compute marginal rates of substitutions when they shop in supermarkets. Nevertheless, economists believe in basic consumer theory and in the idea that demand curves are downward sloping. The same arguments apply to politics.

Fifth, leaders are not capable of acting rationally, because they and their advisers do not have enough technical preparation to adopt the correct policy decisions. In most cases, the crucial ingredients of policy reforms are simple. The real difficulties are political: for instance, how to share the burden of adjustment, how to implement the program without creating social unrest, and so on. Political issues are much more difficult than the technical issues of how to design the perfect program, from the point of view of economic theory. This is not meant to deny that good technical advice to leaders is not important; nevertheless, political conflicts and constraints are often much more difficult to overcome than technical difficulties. Otherwise, one would be led to the conclusion that, for instance, the far below-average economic performance of Latin America is due to the below-average competence of its economic advisers, a distasteful hypothesis. This does not mean, however, that government competence is irrelevant. More-competent governments are more likely than less-competent governments to minimize the costs of adjustments.

Political Cycles and Economic Cycles

Based largely on sections 1 and 2 of Alesina and Roubini (1990), this section reviews the theory and empirical evidence of political cycles in economic policymaking. Most of this literature has been developed with reference to advanced democracies, but some provides insights for analyzing systems that are not democratic or are in transition to democracy.

Different models of political cycles emphasize either the opportunistic or the partisan incentives of policymakers. In opportunistic models, policymakers maximize only their probability of being reelected or, more generally, their probability of surviving in office. In partisan models, different political parties represent the interests of different constituencies and, when in office, follow policies that are favorable to their supporting groups. Traditionally, left-wing parties are more concerned with the problems of unemployment, while right-wing parties are relatively more willing to bear the costs of unemployment to reduce inflation.

This literature has developed in two clearly distinct phases. The first one, in the mid-1970s, is due to the work of Nordhaus (1975) and Lindbeck (1976) on opportunistic cycles and by Hibbs (1977) on partisan cycles. These papers share a prerational expectations model of the economy and are based on the existence of an exploitable Phillips curve, relating inflation and unemployment.

The second phase took off in the mid-1980s as a branch of the game-theoretic approach to the positive theory of macroeconomic policy pioneered by Barro and Gordon (1983) and Kydland and Prescott (1977). Cukierman and Meltzer (1986), Persson and Tabellini (1990), Rogoff (1990), and Rogoff and Sibert (1988) developed rational opportunistic models; Alesina (1987) developed a rational partisan model. These models depart from their predecessors in two important dimensions. First, the assumption of economic agents' rationality makes real economic activity less directly and predictably influenced by economic policy in general and by monetary policy in particular. Second, voters' rationality implies that they cannot be systematically fooled in equilibrium; that is, a repeated, openly opportunistic behavior would be punished by the voters.

The Political-Business Cycle

The assumptions underlying Nordhaus's political-business cycle can be characterized as follows:

(2-1) The economy is described by a stable Phillips curve in which growth (and unemployment) depends on unexpected inflation.

(2-2) Inflation expectations are adaptive; that is, current expected inflation depends only on past inflation.

Combining these assumptions leads to the result that an increase in inflation *always* leads to a reduction in unemployment (and an increase in growth). Since expectations are adaptive, they catch up with a lag to actual inflation.

(2-3) Policymakers control the level of aggregate demand by means of monetary and fiscal instruments.

(2-4) Politicians are opportunistic: they only care about holding office, and they do not have partisan objectives.

(2-5) Voters are mainly retrospective: they judge the incumbent's performance by economic performance during the term of office and heavily discount past observations. Also, voters cannot distinguish between good economic conditions caused by luck and those caused by skillful policies.

Under these assumptions, Nordhaus derives the following testable implications: (a) every government follows the same policy, (b) toward the end of his term in office, the incumbent stimulates the economy to take advantage of the short-run more favorable Phillips curve, (c) the rate of inflation increases around election time as a result of the pre-electoral economic expansion; after the election, inflation is reduced with contractionary policies.[2] Thus one should observe high growth and low unemployment before each election and a recession after each election.

Models of Rational Political-Business Cycles

Cukierman and Meltzer (1986), Persson and Tabellini (1990), Rogoff (1990), and Rogoff and Sibert (1988) have developed the model of the political-business cycle in a rational direction. In a nutshell, this line of work removes the second assumption and substitutes it with the following:

(2-2′) Economic agents have rational expectations concerning all the relevant economic variables.

(2-2″) Voters cannot perfectly assess the level of competence of the incumbent; that is, they can only imperfectly distinguish the effects of unlucky shocks to the economy from the effect of the government's lack of competence in handling the economy.

Assumption 2-5, which implies naive retrospective voting behavior, is substituted by the following:

(2-5′) Each voter chooses the candidate who is expected to deliver the highest utility for himself, given his rational expectations of postelectoral economic outcomes. In particular, the voters try, as best as they can given their information, to disentangle the effects on the economy of exogenous shocks from the effects of economic policy.

The competence of policymakers is defined as their ability to reduce waste in the budget process, to promote growth without inflation, or to react quickly to unexpected shocks. An important component of competence is the degree to which government officials are corrupted.

The basic assumption of this model is that policymakers are more informed than citizens about their own competence. By taking advantage of this informational asymmetry, and by trying to appear as competent as possible, politicians behave in a way leading to a Nordhaus-type political-business cycle. However, given voters' rationality and awareness of politicians' incentives, politicians are limited in their opportunistic behavior. If politicians appear to be too openly opportunistic, they might be punished by voters. Thus, electoral cycles in these rational models are more short-lived, smaller in magnitude, and less regular than they are in Nordhaus's model.

For example, Rogoff (1990) and Rogoff and Sibert (1988) consider a budgetary problem and the empirical implications of opportunistic cycles for monetary and fiscal variables rather than for unemployment and output. Specifically, these papers suggest that, before elections, monetary and fiscal policies should be relatively loose. Fiscal stabilizations with tax increases would tend to be postponed until after the election, while spending programs and transfer payments would be anticipated before the election. However, these short-run budget manipulations may not affect either the growth in gross national product or unemployment.

The Partisan Theory

A strong version of the partisan theory (Hibbs 1977, 1987), based on a nonrational expectation mechanism, adopts assumptions 2-1, 2-2, and 2-3. Assumptions 2-4 and 2-5 are substituted by:

(2-4′) Politicians are partisan, in the sense that different parties maximize different objective functions. Left-wing parties attribute a higher cost to unemployment, relative to inflation, than right-wing parties do.

(2-5″) Each voter is aware of partisan differences and votes for the party that offers the policy closest to the preferred outcome.

The assumption of partisanship is justified by the distributional consequences of unemployment. Hibbs shows that, in the United States, in periods of high unemployment, low growth, and low inflation, the relative share of income of the upper middle class increases and vice versa. Obviously, since both inflation and unemployment are bad, both political parties proclaim that, if elected, they will fight both of them. The partisan model does not require the right-wing party, for example, to *prefer* high unemployment to low unemployment. It simply requires the right to be willing to bear more costs—unemployment—to reduce inflation. Hibbs (1987) discusses at length how, in the United States, the official electoral platforms of the two major parties place different emphasis on the costs of unemployment and inflation.

This model implies that different parties choose different points on the Phillips curve: output growth and inflation should be permanently higher and unemployment permanently lower with left-wing than with right-wing governments. More generally, fiscal policy will have a partisan bias (for instance, capital taxation will be used more extensively by the left).

Rational Partisan Theory

Alesina (1987, 1988) develops a rational partisan theory by adopting assumptions 2-1, 2-2′ , 2-3, 2-4′ , and 2-5″. This model generates a political cycle if nominal wage contracts are signed at discrete intervals (which do not coincide with the political terms of office) and if electoral outcomes are uncertain. Given the sluggishness with which wages are adjusted, changes in the inflation rate associated with changes in government temporarily deviate real economic activity from its natural level.

More specifically, the following testable implications can be derived from the model: (a) at the beginning of a right-wing (left-wing) government, output growth is below (above) its natural level and unemployment is above (below) it; (b) after expectations, prices, and wages adjust, output and unemployment return to their natural level, and after this period of adjustment, which should last no more than a couple of years, the level of economic activity should be independent of the party in office; and (c) the rate of inflation should remain higher throughout the term of a left-wing government; that is, the time-consistent (but suboptimal) inflation rate remains higher for left-wing parties even after the level of economic activity returns to its natural level because of a credibility problem. The public knows that the left has a strong incentive to follow expansionary policies to reduce unemployment. Thus, expected inflation is high when the left is in office. In particular, because of rational expectations, after the initial adjustment to the new regime, expected inflation is high enough so that the government does not have an incentive to inflate more. Actual inflation is equal to expected inflation, and unemployment is at its natural level. Persson and Tabellini (1990) present a recent survey of these credibility models.

In summary, this rational model differs from the traditional partisan one because it emphasizes how differences in growth and unemployment associated with changes in government are only temporary. For example, a left-wing or a populist government, strongly committed to reducing unemployment by means of expansionary aggregate demand policies, is bound to succeed only in the short run. After a brief period in which unemployment may actually fall, such a government will find itself trapped in a high-inflation equilibrium with no benefit on the unemployment side. According to Hibbs's model, a left-wing government could permanently lower the rate of unemployment by permanently increasing the rate of inflation.

Empirical Evidence for OECD Democracies

Three recent papers by Alesina (1988), Alesina, Cohen, and Roubini (1992), and Alesina and Roubini (1990) have provided several tests of political cycle models on a sample of all the democracies in the Organization for Economic Cooperation and Development (OECD) for the period 1960–87. Their conclusions can be summarized in two general points: (1) the new rational approaches to modeling opportunistic and partisan cycles are much more successful empirically than their predecessors; and (2) partisan effects are rather strong on economic outcomes, such as growth, unemployment, and inflation,[3] while opportunistic effects are small in magnitude and appear only on policy instruments, particularly budget deficits.[4]

The traditional political-business cycle model by Nordhaus is generally rejected quite strongly and unambiguously for growth and unemployment. On the contrary, some evidence of opportunistic budgetary and monetary electoral cycles is found. These findings are consistent with the rational view, which emphasizes the limited latitude available to policymakers seeking systematically to fool voters by appropriately timed recessions and expansions.

The data also seem to be explained better by a rational version of the partisan theory than by the traditional Hibbs specification of this theory. In fact, differences in growth rates and unemployment have a partisan connotation but are observable only in the short run, for about eighteen to twenty-four months after a change of government. In this period, the difference in growth and unemployment between left-wing and right-wing governments is quite substantial, although it completely disappears after about two years. Furthermore, Alesina and Roubini (1990) find that the partisan theory of macroeconomic policy fits better and is more appropriate for countries that have either a two-party system or, at least, two clearly identifiable right and left coalitions, with clearly marked shifts from one to the other. For instance, countries that provide a better fit for the theory include Australia, France, Germany, New Zealand, the United Kingdom, and the United States. On the contrary, this approach does not successfully describe countries with large middle-of-the-road coalition governments, such as Belgium or Italy.

Political Cycles in Nondemocracies and the Problem of Transition to Democracy

Empirical research on political cycles in non-OECD democracies is much more limited, and, therefore, any new results in this area would be valuable. It is important to distinguish between dictatorships and periods of transition to democracy.

Dictatorships are a heterogeneous group, beginning with the distinction between strong and weak dictators. The survival of strong dictators is not seriously threatened, given a certain domestic and international political and military balance. Strong dictators are themselves heterogeneous. Some have promoted economic growth and macroeconomic stability in their countries. Others have wrecked their countries' economy. Given such differences, any attempt to show that dictatorships as a group exhibit a superior (or inferior) economic performance than democracies as a group would be inconclusive. More generally, the vast literature on democracy and growth has not reached conclusive evidence regarding their relationship (see Roubini 1990 for a recent survey of this literature).

Weak dictators are in danger of being overthrown. In fact, if social discontent increases, the dictator's probability of survival decreases (see Grossman 1991 for an interesting formalization of the probability of successful insurrections against dictators). When a dictator is in such danger, his incentives may not differ too much from those of an incumbent president or prime minister in a democracy before an uncertain election. Thus, one may look for opportunistic policies and loose fiscal policies when weak dictators are in danger of being overthrown. Ames (1987) studies the opportunistic behavior of Latin American rulers, with particular reference to budget cycles and fiscal and military policies. This author shows that Latin American dictators have followed fiscal policies that, in some respects, are a magnified example of the kind of opportunistic policies described above. Ames documents how rulers in danger of being overthrown used public expenditure to please key constituencies and, in particular, the military.

In fact, immediately before dictators are overthrown, they employ the worst opportunistic and self-interested policies, for two reasons. First, collapsing dictators are struggling for survival and are willing to do anything, since they feel that they have no future. Any consideration of good economic management is secondary to the goal of remaining politically (and physically) alive. Second, if a dictator becomes convinced that his time horizon in office is very short, he may simply decide to steal from the country's wealth for his personal gain and that of his close supporters.

As a result, collapsing dictators are likely to bequeath to their successors economies with serious macroeconomic imbalances, and new democracies thus inherit difficult economic problems. In addition, new democratic governments may feel particularly strong partisan pressures to do something for social groups that have recently obtained a voice in the political arena. Furthermore, new democracies are particularly subject to the risk of being overthrown and even more so when the groups and constituencies supporting the old regime have a voice and a political or military presence. As a result, new democracies face a difficult problem of survival and may find it particularly difficult to follow tough policies implying short-run economic costs: new democracies may have to be opportunistic to survive. Unfortunately, as argued above, new democracies may come to office exactly at a time when tough policies are called for and cannot be postponed.

Haggard and others (1990) analyze both opportunistic and partisan cycles in a sample of middle-income countries with particular emphasis on periods of transition to democracy. Haggard and Kaufman (1989) convincingly argue that transitional democracies face more difficult pressures and show worse economic outcomes than either established democracies or dictatorships. Some recent results on economic growth are consistent with this observation. Alesina and others (1991) show that, on average, the growth performance of dictatorships and democracies is indistinguishable. Also, they find that a high probability that the government will collapse reduces growth. These observations are consistent with the view that highly unstable periods of transition are worse for the economy than periods of stability.

Finally, the partisan theory implies a positive relationship between the degree of political and social polarization and the variability of macroeconomic policies, which, in turn, affects the variability and level of economic outcomes. In fact, as emphasized above, the partisan theory is based on the view that because different parties have different distributional preferences, they also have different preferences for macroeconomic policies (Hibbs 1987). The more different these distributional preferences are, the more volatile is macroeconomic policy. From this perspective, populist cycles in Latin America magnify partisan cycles in OECD democracies. Populist policies are, in fact, defined as the use of aggregate policies (monetary and fiscal) to redistribute income and wealth (Dornbusch and Edwards 1992). Populist governments are often followed by right-wing regimes that attempt to reverse these redistributions.

These macroeconomic policy cycles often introduce a large variance and unpredictability to expectations of future policies. Such uncertainty is likely to be associated with poor economic performance by making long-run planning more difficult. Recent results by Alesina and others (1991) and Özler and Rodrik (1991) suggest that the degree of political uncertainty and instability is linked with the level of investments and growth in large samples of countries, including Latin America.

Delays in Policy Reforms

One of the most puzzling observations in political economics is that several countries follow policies, for extended periods of time, that are recognized as not being feasible in the long run: in particular, rapidly accumulating public debts with skyrocketing ratios of debt to gross national product and hyperinflation. These observations are particularly puzzling when, as is quite common, the longer a country waits, the more costly the stabilization program is when finally adopted. Similar arguments apply to the apparently inexplicable delays in reforming trade policies to eliminate socially inefficient forms of protection. In its most general terms, the puzzle is the following: why are certain reforms delayed that are efficient in the sense that they increase aggregate welfare?

Clearly, no single model can explain every delay in reforming policy. Different explanations may play a role in different cases, although certain arguments appear, in general, to be more convincing than others. The following paragraphs review the least compelling explanations.

The first one is that countries that delay reforms do not understand that such reforms are unavoidable. This is not convincing since in most cases the macroeconomic imbalances are so macroscopic that the need for a monetary and fiscal stabilization is undeniable. Reasonable persons can, in some cases, disagree about the speed, urgency, and design of a stabilization program for technical reasons. Most often, however, these technical discussions reflect underlying distributional conflicts.

A second explanation is that governments wait to stabilize until exogenous shocks make the stabilization program less costly. Thus, there is an option value in waiting, as suggested by Orphanides (1990). Such an approach does not explain why, as is often the case, countries do not stabilize as soon as favorable shocks occur and why many stabilizations take place without any prior realization of particularly favorable economic shocks.

A third argument is that since stabilizations are costly in the short run, they are postponed until things get really bad. This is irrational, since the longer a country waits, the more costly the stabilization becomes. According to this model, different countries' experiences would be explained by different degrees of rationality, an argument that is hardly convincing.

Explanations based on collective rationality or an understanding of basic economic relationships are more sound. The remainder of this section highlights a few, organized by four types of models:

(1) War of attrition models based on an uncertain distribution of the costs of delaying the stabilizations
(2) Models focusing on the conflicting interests of specific social groups, such as labor and capital
(3) Models emphasizing the uncertain outcome of the stabilization
(4) Models emphasizing the role of certain institutional arrangements, such as the degree of independence of the central bank.

Stabilization as a War of Attrition

Alesina and Drazen (1991) argue that, often, the process leading to a monetary and fiscal stabilization can be described as a war of attrition between socioeconomic groups with conflicting distributional interests. The basic idea follows. Consider an economy where, for whatever reason, a budget deficit appears. A stabilization is defined as an increase in regular income taxes that eliminates the deficit. For simplicity and without loss of generality, government spending is assumed to be constant.

Before a stabilization occurs, government spending and the interest on the external debt are paid by the government, in part by borrowing abroad and in part by means of a highly distortionary tax. For concreteness, the tax before stabilization is thought of as an inflation tax, and it is assumed to be more distortionary than regular income taxes. In such a situation, a social planner managing an economy populated by identical individuals would *not* delay the stabilization program. In fact, delays are socially costly for two reasons: first, until the stabilization occurs, distortionary means of taxation are used; second, the longer one waits, the more the debt accumulates, and the higher the interest the government pays.

Even though a social planner would stabilize immediately, the political conflict between heterogeneous groups over how the burden of the stabilization will be allocated leads to rational delays. Suppose that the burden of the stabilization is not divided equally among groups. In particular, assume that there are two competing groups and that the loser will pay more than half of the stabilization costs (that is, income taxes). Suppose, further, that the two groups are not identical: in particular, they differ in the utility loss suffered in the period before stabilization. For instance, the high-cost group is the one whose costs of living in an unstable economy are particularly high. An important element necessary to obtain delayed stabilization is that each group's costs of delaying the stabilization are privileged information. Each group knows only its own costs and has a probability distribution over the opponent's costs.

The stabilization occurs when one of the two groups concedes, that is, accepts being the loser and agrees to pay a high fraction of the taxes needed to eliminate the deficit. Stabilization does not occur immediately because each group has a rational incentive to wait, hoping that the opponent will concede first. In equilibrium, the group with the highest costs of waiting will concede, but it is the passage of time that will reveal which is the high-cost group. The concession time is determined by the condition that the marginal costs of not conceding—the costs of remaining in the unstable economy for another instant—are equal to the marginal gains from remaining, which are given by the probability that the opponent will concede in the next instant, multiplied by the gains of being the winner (paying less than half the costs of stabilization). The asymmetry of information is important in generating the delay. If it is known from the start which group has the highest costs of waiting, then the loser is known from the start. Thus, the loser concedes immediately in order to avoid the costs of delays.

This war of attrition can be generalized to the case of n groups, with $n > 2$. This extension is immediate if the game ends when one of the groups concedes. The extension is more complicated and technically more demanding if, after the first group concedes and pays a high fraction of the costs, a new war of attrition begins between the remaining groups $(n - 1)$, over how the remainder of the stabilization costs will be allocated.

Alesina and Drazen (1991) derive several results concerning the expected time of stabilization, which make this war of attrition model useful for empirical analysis.

(1) *Political cohesion:* The more unequal the distribution of the costs of stabilization, other things being equal, the longer the stabilization is delayed.

If these costs are shared equally, stabilization occurs immediately, since there is no gain from being the winner. The more unequal the distribution of costs is, the higher the gain from being the winner and the higher the incentive to wait the opponent out. This suggests that stabilization will be delayed more in countries with less cohesion and with more political polarization and instability, in which it is more difficult to reach an equitable social contract with a fair allocation of costs.

(2) *Costs of delaying:* an increase in the costs of postponing the stabilization reduces the delay.

This somewhat obvious result becomes rather interesting if one thinks of these costs not only as the economic costs of inflation but also as political costs. For instance, the costs of political action that each group must pay in order to avoid being imposed upon increase that group's share of the costs of the stabilization. These costs of political action may be loss of wages and leisure time incurred by striking urban workers, the risks incurred by armed insurrectionists, the monetary costs incurred by the capitalists financing their representatives in the legislature, and so forth. Political institutions that make it easier for even small interest groups to block the legislative process by veto power are conducive to delayed stabilization. For instance, strictly proportional electoral systems are more likely to generate coalition governments in which legislative action requires the consensus of a large number of parties, each of which can veto an action. Thus even a small interest group can veto a stabilization program and procrastinate the war of attrition.

(3) *Income distribution:* The degree of income inequality has ambiguous effects on the amount of delay.

If political and economic resources are very unequally distributed, so that it is immediately obvious which group is stronger and has more resources to wait longer, the war of attrition ends immediately, since the identity of the winner is certain. However, if resources are dispersed across groups, maintaining the asymmetric distribution of information about relative costs, then delays increase.

Alesina and Drazen (1991, pp. 1172–74) argue that this war of attrition model is consistent with three elements that are often (but not always) observed in stabilization processes:

(1) There is an agreement over the need of a fiscal change but a political stalemate over how the burden of higher taxes or expenditure cuts should be allocated. In the political debate over the stabilization, this distributional question is central.

(2) When stabilization occurs it coincides with a *political* consolidation. Often, one side becomes politically dominant. The burden of stabilization is sometimes quite unequal, with the politically weaker group bearing a larger burden. Often this means the lower classes, with successful stabilizations being regressive.

(3) Successful stabilizations are usually preceded by several failed attempts; often a previous program appears quite similar to the successful one.

Further progress in an empirical direction can be made by defining more clearly what exactly is meant by a concession. In theory, a concession means simply that one of the groups accepts the role of loser. In practice, a concession may take different forms. One is a clear electoral victory for one side. This may make the legislative action easier for the winning side and raise to an unsustainable level the political costs to the opponent of vetoing stabilization plans. A second is the acceptance by one side of granting extraordinary powers to the government to avoid legislative deadlocks. A third is the recall of strikes, riots, and other political actions taken by the workers' movement if they are perceived to be too costly and unsustainable. A fourth is the achievement of a compromise accepted by all parts governing how the burden of stabilization will be allocated. Alesina (1988), Alesina and Drazen (1991), Casella and Eichengreen (1991), and De Long and Eichengreen (1991) discuss various case studies of successful and failed stabilizations from the point of view offered by the war of attrition model and discuss various forms of concession.

Drazen and Grilli (1990) extend the war of attrition model by emphasizing the possible benefits of economic crises. They show that if an exogenous shock aggravates the economic conditions, the war of attrition may be resolved because the costs of not stabilizing are even higher. In some cases, such crises increase aggregate welfare: in fact, the costs of the adverse shock are more than compensated by the benefits of the anticipated stabilization.

Finally, the war of attrition idea is applicable not only to delays in fiscal stabilizations but also to many other delays in the adoption of efficient reforms, such as the removal of price controls or trade restrictions. For a war of attrition to occur, the proposed reform should have substantial distributional effects and some uncertainty must exist about the relative strength of the various groups.

Class Conflicts

Different classes may have different perspectives about the urgency of a stabilization, and some may actually gain from delaying the stabilization. In other words, an unstable economy benefits some groups. For instance, in one model stabilization may be delayed if the asset holders perceive that they can escape taxation by exporting their assets abroad. He considers an economy with three broadly defined classes: capital owners, middle-class or skilled workers, and unskilled workers. Suppose that, because of a fiscal imbalance, aggregate demand is high and inflation is increasing; a social planner, once again, would choose to stabilize immediately. However, a political equilibrium may lead to postponements for the following reason. Suppose that in the period of high aggregate demand and high inflation, profits are increasing and wages of unskilled workers are indexed and approximately constant in real terms. Profits are increasing with aggregate demand, as are returns to capital.

Capitalists would like to postpone the stabilization, if they think that they gain first, because of the increasing returns, and that they can then move their profits abroad to escape the tax increase needed to stabilize. Unskilled workers are too poor to be taxed after stabilization. Thus, the cost of stabilization falls mostly, or exclusively, on the middle class. While the middle class would prefer to stabilize immediately to minimize overall costs, capitalists and unskilled workers may prefer to postpone the stabilization. If capitalists and unskilled workers together have enough political influence, the stabilization is delayed.

This model captures two important insights, which are much more general than the specific example: first, not everybody loses during the period preceding stabilization; second, the very rich and the very poor may be on the same side against the middle class. In fact, in several well-known cases of hyperinflation, the middle class has suffered the most.

Alesina and Tabellini (1989) present a view somewhat related to that of the above model. Even though they do not focus explicitly on stabilization, they show that the possibility of exporting capital leads to socially inefficient policies. Governments close to the interests of capitalists tend to borrow abroad and redistribute resources to capitalists, who then escape taxation by exporting capital, forcing the rest of the economy to pay the interest on the government's foreign borrowing.

In summary, these types of models suggest that in some cases certain coalitions actually benefit from a macroeconomic imbalance and manage to postpone the adjustment for their own advantage.

Uncertain Outcomes of the Stabilization

Fernández and Rodrik (1991) consider the case of a policy reform that improves the welfare of the majority of the population. For concreteness, removal of a tariff is the reform under consideration. All producers in the export sectors are better off with the reform; a fraction of producers in the import-competing sector have to move to the export sector and are better off after the reform and their move. Suppose that these two groups are a majority of the population. However, because of uncertainty about which agents in the import-competing industry will benefit from the reform, a majority of the population may vote against it. For certain parameter values, even though, after the fact, a majority of the population is better off with the reform, all things being equal, the majority is *not* in favor of it. This result holds even in the case of risk neutrality, but it is reinforced when agents are risk averse.

This model emphasizes that uncertainty concerning the identity of the losers from a proposed reform may create a bias toward maintaining an inefficient status quo. Even though Fernández and Rodrik (1991) consider a trade reform, clearly their approach is much more general and applicable to fiscal reforms as well.

Milesi-Ferretti (1991) suggests another reason, based on uncertain outcomes, why monetary and fiscal stabilizations may be postponed. He considers a model in which the costs of stopping inflation are uncertain and depend upon how competent the government is in managing the reform; that is, there are competent governments, which manage to stabilize with small economic costs, and incompetent ones, which are capable of stabilizing but do so at higher costs.

If a stabilization is started and the government is discovered to be incompetent, the public may choose to elect the opposition, which is expected to be more competent. If, instead, the government does not begin a program, nothing is learned about the government's competence. In this case, if the public favors the opposition, the latter would have to solve the same problem faced by today's government. Thus, if it is in the interest of the current government to do nothing for fear of failure because of incompetence, the public may have no incentive to vote for the opposition because the latter would do the same, when in office. What is crucial, here, is that the *government itself does not know its own level of competence*, otherwise the choice of doing something or doing nothing would reveal some of the government's private information concerning its own competence.

This model is particularly appropriate for cases in which a policy reform is relatively new and has never been attempted before, making it difficult to predict the costs and the government's competence on such grounds. The case of policy reforms in Eastern Europe comes immediately to mind. More generally, the case of new democratic governments facing economic crises may be a good example for this model. A new democratic leadership may be reasonably unknown to the public, since the new leadership has never been in office before. At the same time, the new democratic opposition is also new to the political arena. Thus, there might be very little available information on both the new democratic government and the new opposition.

Institutions

Different institutional arrangements may be more or less conducive to macroeconomic management and to a swift reaction to economic crises needing stabilization. The discussion of wars of attrition suggested that multiparty systems with coalition governments may find it difficult to achieve quick agreement on how to stabilize. This is because each member of a coalition government may have the power to veto and block any program that is disliked by a certain (even small) constituency. Coalition governments are more often observed in parliamentary democracies with proportional representation. Therefore, the institution of proportionality may not be conducive to swift fiscal reforms when they are needed. Empirical results by Roubini and Sachs (1989a, 1989b) and Grilli, Masciandaro, and Tabellini (1991) on OECD democracies are consistent with these observations. They show that prolonged periods of fiscal imbalance leading to the accumulation of relatively high ratios of debt to gross national product have been common in parliamentary democracies with large coalition governments. On the other hand, single-party governments have reacted more quickly to prevent persistent deficits.

These arguments are not directly applicable to dictatorships. However, they are somewhat related to the previous discussion of strong versus weak dictators. A weak dictator may be the analog of a weak coalition government in a democracy. A weak dictator may have to please several constituencies with conflicting interests in order to survive and would find it difficult to resolve a fiscal crisis promptly.

A second institutional feature that may affect fiscal management and the implementation of fiscal reforms is the possibility of conflicts within a state or a bureaucracy over the allocation of spending and taxation. Fiscal federalism (that is, geographic decentralization of fiscal decisions) may make it difficult to act quickly when quick action is needed. First, if local authorities can, up to a point, transfer locally generated deficits to the federal system, they may choose to do so in time of need; that is, one may observe a prisoner's dilemma situation, in which different states or regions fail to cooperate. Second, there might be, once again, a veto power with which various states or regions block stabilization plans decided at the federal level.

A similar argument may apply to conflicts within a bureaucracy. Obviously, the relevance of these conflicts would depend on the degree to which the bureaucracy is independent of elected officers.

Third, an institutional feature that could be very important in the context of a discussion of monetary and fiscal stability is the degree to which the central bank is politically independent. A central bank independent of the treasury and firmly committed to monetary control reduces the degree of monetization of budget deficits. This has two effects: it keeps inflation under control, and it forces the government to find other sources of financing, ultimately forcing the government to raise taxes or cut spending (see Alesina and Grilli 1992; Lohmann 1992; and Rogoff 1985 for theoretical discussions of the benefits of central bank independence).

Several authors have noted how, within industrial economies, countries with low inflation have independent central banks. Furthermore, such low inflation has not been accompanied by high unemployment, high real interest rates, or other undesirable, real consequences. Thus, central bank independence seems to have helped monetary stability with very small "real" costs. These observations emerge from work by Alesina (1988), Alesina and Grilli (1992), Alesina and Summers (1993), Bade and Parkin (1982), and Grilli, Masciandaro, and Tabellini (1991). Clearly, the difficult part of this empirical analysis is how to classify the degree of independence of different central banks. Although this body of research has reached a reasonable consensus on a reliable classification of the degree of central bank independence for advanced industrial economies, much work remains to be done for all the other countries. Cukierman, Webb, and Neyapti (1992) address this very important question.

Although a central bank with an established reputation of independence may improve policymaking, the process of establishing such a reputation may lead to periods of policy instability. In fact, suppose that the treasury runs budget deficits and does not raise taxes in an attempt to induce the central bank to monetize. The bank refuses to do so, precisely to establish a reputation of independence and induce the treasury to raise taxes and cut spending. This situation may lead to a sort of war of attrition between the treasury and the central bank. Both institutions pursue their uncoordinated policies in order to force the opponent to concede, as in models by Loewy (1988), Sargent and Wallace (1981), and Tabellini (1986). Before one of the two players gives in, taxes are not raised and the deficit is not monetized; such a combination leads to a rapidly growing ratio of debt to gross national product. On the one hand, institutional arrangements guaranteeing the independence of the central bank should ensure that such an institutional war of attrition does not occur because the treasury knows that the central bank will not concede. On the other hand, a war of attrition will not occur when the central bank has no independence at all, and the treasury can obtain as much monetization as it desires.

Inflation, Taxation, and Political Stability: Empirical Evidence

There are three ways of testing political-economic models of inflation, deficits, stabilization, or lack thereof: case studies, a comparative method in which several cases are examined jointly, and econometric studies of several countries. The first two approaches have been adopted mostly (but not exclusively) by political scientists. The third has been used mostly (but not exclusively) by economists. A survey of the empirical literature is, obviously, well beyond the scope of this chapter. The following paragraphs highlight some recent cross-sectional econometric analysis with large samples of countries.

Haggard and others (1990) examine the statistical relationships between the type of political regime and the ideological nature of different government and economic outcomes, such as inflation, budget deficits, and the adoption of stabilization programs. They find that periods of transition from authoritarian regimes to democracy are often associated with economic instability. New democracies have a particularly difficult time implementing stabilization programs. This finding is quite consistent with a war of attrition model. After the collapse of an authoritarian and repressive regime, conflicting distributional claims of various socioeconomic groups are likely to emerge. Legislative deadlock and inaction are typical of such situations.

Cukierman, Edwards, and Tabellini (1992) and Edwards and Tabellini (1991) show that, after controlling for various economic determinants of inflation, a strong association is evident between government instability and use of seigniorage as a source of tax revenues. Thus, weak governments are less capable of using noninflationary taxes to cover government spending.

Roubini and Sachs (1989a, 1989b) and Grilli, Masciandaro, and Tabellini (1991) find that, within OECD democracies, the high-debt countries are almost exclusively parliamentary democracies with a highly proportional electoral system; conversely, almost all the countries with such electoral systems have high public debt. This evidence is broadly consistent with the war of attrition model: in strictly proportional parliamentary systems, wars of attrition are more likely to occur because each member of the coalition holds veto power. Similar evidence for developing countries is found by Özler and Tabellini (1991), who show that external debt in a large panel of developing countries for the period 1973–82 is positively related to a reasonable indicator of political instability.

An important problem in this literature on government instability as an explanatory variable for inflation and fiscal imbalance is that of joint endogeneity. It is certainly true that government instability may cause inflation. However, high inflation and, more generally, economic instability may lead to government collapse. In the context of a study of the correlation between economic growth and coups d'état, Londregan and Poole (1990) have shown how to deal econometrically with this problem of joint endogeneity. Alesina and others (1991) have used this method to study the joint determination of economic growth and government changes in both democracies and nondemocracies. They find that both directions of causality are present: a high probability of a government collapse reduces growth; conversely, low growth increases the likelihood of a change in government.

A similar analysis that accounts for issues related to joint endogeneity would be desirable for the study of inflation and fiscal imbalances as well.

Conclusions

This chapter has reviewed recent formal developments in political economics that study the relationship between the timing of macroeconomic policy and political institutions. Two important issues have been the focus of this review: political-business cycles and monetary and fiscal stabilization policies.

Rather than review the results described in the previous pages, this section highlights several issues open for further research.

- Although a reasonably sound and extensive body of theoretical and empirical research exists on political-business cycles in advanced industrial democracies, much less has been done for developing countries. This research should tackle difficult issues, such as how to test for such cycles in nondemocracies.
- The periods of transition from dictatorships to democracies are extremely interesting situations for studying political-economic interactions. Researchers should devote careful and specific attention to such periods.
- Authoritarian regimes appear to be a heterogeneous group. Some have promoted growth and economic stability and have done better than the average democracy. Others have destroyed their economies. A further understanding of what explains these large differences is likely to have very high intellectual returns.
- The normative aspects of political economy should also be very high on the research agenda. Should a new democracy be advised to adopt majoritarian systems, set up independent central banks, include balanced-budget clauses in the constitution, limit the number of times incumbents can run for office, delegate fiscal authority to local authorities to have a bicameral system, and elect the president directly? These are only a few of the many questions facing new democracies.

Notes

1. This chapter is not meant to be an exhaustive survey of the literature. For recent surveys of the literature on political-business cycles, see Alesina 1988 and Nordhaus 1989. For a survey of the literature on the political economy of development in developing countries, see Roubini 1990. For a survey of the theoretical contributions in the new political macroeconomics, with emphasis on fiscal policy, see Persson and Tabellini 1990 and Alesina and Tabellini 1990. For a survey of the traditional literature on public choice, see Mueller 1989.

2. Whether inflation starts to increase before or only after the election depends on the exact specification of the model. See Lindbeck 1976 for a discussion of this point.

3. The United States offers quite a good case for this theory. For a general theoretical and empirical model of macroeconomic outcomes and elections in the United States, see Alesina, Londregan, and Rosenthal 1990.

4. Alvarez, Garret, and Lange 1991 have investigated the role of labor organizations in a partisan model of macroeconomic policy.

References

Akerlof, G., and J. Yellen. 1985a. "Can Small Deviations from Rationality Make Significant Differences to Economic Equilibria?" *American Economic Review* 75, pp. 708–21.

———. 1985b. "A Near-Rational Model of Business Cycles with Wage and Price Inertia." *Quarterly Journal of Economics* 100, pp. 823–38.

Alesina, Alberto. 1987. "Macroeconomic Policy in a Two-Party System as a Repeated Game." *Quarterly Journal of Economics* 101, pp. 651–78.

_____. 1988. "Macroeconomics and Politics." NBER *Macroeconomics Annual,* pp. 13–52. Cambridge, Mass.: National Bureau of Economic Research.

Alesina, Alberto, Gerald Cohen, and Nouriel Roubini. 1992. "Macroeconomic Policy and Elections in OECD Economies." *Economics and Politics* 4, pp. 1–30.

Alesina, Alberto, and Allan Drazen. 1991. "Why Are Stabilizations Delayed?" *American Economic Review* 81, pp. 1170–89.

Alesina, Alberto, and Vittorio Grilli. 1992. "The European Central Bank: Reshaping Monetary Politics in Europe." In M. Canzoneri, Vittorio Grilli, and P. Mosson, eds., *The Creation of a Central Bank.* Cambridge, Mass.: Cambridge University Press.

Alesina, Alberto, J. Londregan, and H. Rosenthal. 1990. "A Political-Economy Model of the United States." NBER Working Paper. National Bureau of Economic Research, Cambridge, Mass. Processed.

Alesina, Alberto, S. Özler, Nouriel Roubini, and P. Swagel. 1991. "Political Instability and Economic Growth." Unpublished ms. Processed.

Alesina, Alberto, and Nouriel Roubini. 1990. "Political Cycles in OECD Economies." NBER Working Paper 3478. National Bureau of Economic Research, Cambridge, Mass.

Alesina, Alberto, and L. Summers. 1993. "Central Bank Independence and Economic Performance: Some Comparative Evidence." *Journal of Money, Credit, and Banking* (May), pp. 151–62.

Alesina, Alberto, and Guido Tabellini. 1989. "External Debt, Capital Flight, and Political Risk." *Journal of International Economics* 27 (November), pp. 199–220.

_____. 1990. "A Positive Theory of Fiscal Deficit and Government Debt." *Review of Economic Studies* 57 (July), pp. 403–14.

Alvarez, M., J. Garret, and P. Lange. 1991. "Government Partisanship, Labor Organizations, and Macroeconomic Performance." *American Political Science Review* 85, pp. 539–56.

Ames, Barry. 1987. *Political Survival: Politicians and Public Policy in Latin America.* Berkeley: University of California Press.

Bade, Robert, and Michael Parkin. 1982. "Central Bank Laws and Inflation." Unpublished ms. Processed.

Barro, R., and D. Gordon. 1983. "Rules, Discretion, and Reputation in a Model of Monetary Policy." *Journal of Monetary Economics* 12 (July), pp. 101–22.

Brennan, R., and J. Buchanan. 1980. *The Power to Tax.* London: Cambridge University Press.

Casella, A., and B. Eichengreen. 1991. "Halting Inflation in Italy and France after World War II." Unpublished ms. Processed.

Cukierman, Alex, Sebastian Edwards, and Guido Tabellini. 1992. "Seigniorage and Political Instability." *American Economic Review* 82, pp. 537–55.

Cukierman, Alex, and Allan Meltzer. 1986. "A Positive Theory of Discretionary Policy, the Cost of a Democratic Government, and the Benefit of a Constitution." *Economic Inquiry* 24, pp. 367–88.

Cukierman, Alex, Steven B. Webb, and B. Neyapti. 1992. "Measuring Central Bank Independence and Its Effect on Policy Outcomes." *World Bank Economic Review*, 6, no. 3, pp. 353–98.

De Long, B., and B. Eichengreen. 1991. "The Marshall Plan: History's Most Successful Structural Adjustment Program." Unpublished ms. Processed.

Dornbusch, Rudiger, and Sebastian Edwards, eds. 1992. *Macroeconomic Policy and Income Distribution in Latin America*. Chicago: University of Chicago Press and National Bureau of Economic Research, Harvard University.

Drazen, Allan, and Vittorio Grilli. 1990. "The Benefits of Crises for Economic Reform." NBER Working Paper 3527. National Bureau of Economic Research, Cambridge, Mass.

Edwards, Sebastian, and Guido Tabellini. 1991. "Explaining Fiscal Deficits and Inflation in Developing Countries." NBER Working Paper 3493. National Bureau of Economic Research, Cambridge, Mass.

Fernández, Raquel, and Dani Rodrik. 1991. "Resistance to Reform: Status Quo Bias in the Presence of Individual-Specific Uncertainty." *American Economic Review* 81 (December), pp. 1146–56.

Grilli, Vittorio, D. Masciandaro, and Guido Tabellini. 1991. "Political and Monetary Institutions and Public Finance Policies in the Industrial Democracies." *Economic Policy* 13, pp. 41–89.

Grossman, H. 1991. "A General Equilibrium Theory of Insurrections." *American Economic Review* 81, pp. 912–22.

Haggard, Stephan, and Robert Kaufman. 1989. "Economic Adjustment in New Democracies." In Joan Nelson, ed., *Fragile Coalitions: The Politics of Economic Adjustment*. New Brunswick, N.J.: Transaction Books.

Haggard, Stephan, Robert Kaufman, K. Shariff, and Steven Webb. 1990. "Politics, Inflation, and Stabilization in Middle-Income Countries." Unpublished ms. Processed.

Hibbs, D. 1977. "Political Parties and Macroeconomic Policy." *The American Political Science Review* 7 (December), pp. 1467–87.

———. 1987. *The American Political Economy*. Cambridge, Mass.: Harvard University Press.

Kydland, F., and E. Prescott. 1977. "Rules Rather than Discretion: The Inconsistency of Optimal Plans." *Journal of Political Economy* 85, pp. 473–90.

Lindbeck, A. 1976. "Stabilization Policies in Open Economies with Endogenous Politicians." *American Economic Review Papers and Proceedings* 66, pp. 1–19.

Loewy, M. 1988. "Reaganomics and Reputation Revisited." *Economic Inquiry* 26 (April), pp. 253–64.

Lohmann, S. 1992. "Optimal Commitment in Monetary Policy: Credibility vs. Flexibility." *American Economic Review* 82, pp. 273–87.

Londregan, J., and K. Poole. 1990. "Poverty, the Coup Trap, and the Seizure of Executive Power." *World Politics* 42 (January), pp. 151–83.

Milesi-Ferretti, Gian Maria. 1991. "Dynamic Models of Strategic Policy Making." Ph.D. diss., Harvard University, Cambridge, Mass.

Mueller, D. 1989. *Public Choice II*. London: Cambridge University Press.

Nordhaus, William D. 1975. "The Political Business Cycle." *Review of Economic Studies* 42 (April), pp. 169–90.

_____. 1989. "Alternative Models to Political Business Cycles." Brookings Papers on Economic Activity 2. Brookings Institution, Washington, D.C.

Ophranides, A. 1990. "The Timing of Stabilizations." Unpublished ms. Processed.

Özler, S., and Dani Rodrik. 1991. "Political Instability and Investment in LDCs." *Journal of Development Economics* 42, pp. 412–37.

Özler, S., and Guido Tabellini. 1991. "External Debt and Political Instability." NBER Working Paper. National Bureau of Economic Research, Cambridge, Mass.

Persson, Torsten, and Guido Tabellini. 1990. *Macroeconomic Policy, Credibility, and Politics.* London: Harwood Academic Publishers.

Rogoff, Kenneth. 1985. "The Optimal Degree of Commitment to an Intermediate Monetary Target." *Quarterly Journal of Economics* 100 (November), pp. 1169–90.

_____. 1990. "Political Budget Cycles." *American Economic Review* (March), pp. 1–16.

Rogoff, Kenneth, and Anne Sibert. 1988. "Equilibrium Political Business Cycles." *Review of Economic Studies* 55 (January), pp. 1–16.

Roubini, Nouriel. 1990. "The Interaction between Macroeconomic Performance and Political Structures and Institutions: The Political Economy of Growth and Development." Unpublished ms., Yale University, New Haven, Conn., February.

Roubini, Nouriel, and Jeffrey Sachs. 1989a. "Government Spending and Budget Deficits in the Industrialized Countries." *Economic Policy* 8 (spring), pp. 99–132.

_____. 1989b. "Political and Economic Determinants of Budget Deficits in the Industrial Democracies." *European Economic Review* 33 (May), pp. 903–33.

Sargent, T., and N. Wallace. 1981. "Some Unpleasant Monetarist Arithmetic." *Federal Reserve Bank of Minneapolis Quarterly Review* (January), pp. 1–17.

Tabellini, Guido. 1986. "Money, Debt, and Deficits in a Dynamic Game." *Journal of Economic Dynamics and Control* 6 (December), pp. 77–102.

Tabellini, Guido, and Alberto Alesina. 1990. "Voting on the Budget Deficit." *American Economic Review* (March), pp. 17–32.

Tirole, J. 1989. *The Theory of Industrial Organization.* Cambridge, Mass.: M.I.T. Press.

3

The Rush to Free Trade in
the Developing World:
Why So Late? Why Now? Will It Last?

Dani Rodrik

A WORK ON THE POLITICAL ECONOMY OF TRADE LIBERALIZATION in developing countries must address at least two puzzles. First, why has trade liberalization in these countries traditionally been so contentious? There is probably no area in economics where professional opinion is so united: the vast majority of economists see free trade, warts and all, as superior to protection. The attraction of free trade resides at one level in the theoretical elegance of the principle of comparative advantage—which, as Paul Samuelson once put it, is the only proposition in economics that is at once true and nontrivial.[1]

Even when the theory is complicated by second-best considerations under which trade restrictions can enhance efficiency, most economists remain in favor of free trade on practical grounds. Yet import-substitution policies relying on trade restrictions have been the orthodoxy among policymakers in developing countries for much of the postwar period. Until recently, policymakers usually resisted advice from academics and lending agencies to open up their economies to international competition (on the general subject of the political economy of

The author is grateful to Stephan Haggard, Jim Leitzel, David Ellwood, Steven Webb, and seminar participants at Harvard University, Federal Reserve Bank of San Francisco, the World Bank, and University of California, Berkeley, for their comments. He also wishes to thank the Hoover Institution, where he was a National Fellow while writing this chapter.

Table 3-1. Recent Trade Policy Reforms in Selected Developing Countries

Country	Reform
Argentina	Tariffs were reduced starting in October 1988; import licensing was abolished except for twenty-two items (vehicles and parts); in 1991, a three-level tariff structure was introduced (0, 11, and 22 percent)
Bolivia	Trade regime was overhauled in 1985, and quantitative restrictions were eliminated; as of April 1990, two basic tariff rates exist: 5 percent for capital goods and 10 percent for others
Brazil	Major trade reform was announced in March 1990 as part of the Collor stabilization package; almost all quantitative restrictions were to be phased out and replaced by tariffs; the average tariff was reduced to 25 percent in 1990 (from 37 percent); an average tariff rate of 14 percent was sought by 1994
Chile	Substantial reform occurred after 1973, with the elimination of quantitative restrictions and a uniform tariff rate of 10 percent (except for motor vehicles) achieved by 1979; the uniform tariff was raised to 35 percent briefly during the macroeconomic crisis of the early 1980s but was subsequently reduced to 15 percent
Ghana	Import licensing was substantially liberalized, and a uniform tariff was introduced for most imports
Indonesia	Trade has been continually reformed since 1986; by the end of 1988, only 20 percent of imports (by value) were subject to licensing
Jamaica	Quantitative restrictions were eliminated, and tariffs were lowered to 20 to 30 percent for most items
Mexico	Quantitative restrictions were substantially liberalized beginning in mid-1985; few import licensing requirements remain; tariffs were reduced to an average 11 percent by 1988; the maximum rate is 20 percent; Mexico acceded to GATT in 1986

policymaking in developing countries, see Bates 1988; Haggard and Webb 1993; Meier 1991; Rodrik 1992c; for earlier cases of liberalization, see Papageorgiou, Choksi, and Michaely 1990).

The second puzzle has to do with recent trends in developing countries. Since the early 1980s, developing countries have flocked to free trade as if it were the Holy Grail of economic development. Bolivia, Ghana, Mexico, Morocco, Turkey, and, more recently, scores of other countries in Africa, Asia, and Latin America have made considerable progress in dismantling their protectionist trade regimes, doing away with import licenses and quantitative restrictions. Argentina and Brazil have begun the same process in the past couple of years. Even India appears to have embarked on the road to trade liberalization after decades of heavy-handed dirigisme. Table 3-1 provides capsule summaries of some of the more significant reforms. Together with the historic transformation and opening of the Eastern European economies, these developments represent a genuine revolution in policymaking. The puzzle is why is it occurring now and why in so many countries all at once?

Country	Reform
Morocco	Protection was significantly reduced after 1983 through the elimination of some quantitative restrictions and the reduction of tariff rates; the maximum tariff was reduced from 400 to 45 percent
Nigeria	Trade liberalization was initiated in 1986; the import licensing system was reformed and substantial cuts undertaken in tariffs
Pakistan	In July 1988, a reform program was initiated to shift from nontariff measures to tariffs; import licensing was eliminated for a wide range of products; the maximum tariff was reduced to 125 percent (from 225)
Peru	The newly elected Fujimori government embarked on a stabilization package in August 1990, including substantial trade reform; all quantitative restrictions were eliminated, and the tariff system was simplified to include three rates (15, 25, and 50 percent) only; in March 1991, the top rate was reduced to 20 percent
Senegal	Most quantitative restrictions were removed during 1986–88; tariffs were selectively reduced
Tunisia	Licensing was removed from more than half of import items by mid-1990; the maximum tariff was reduced to 43 percent (from 220)
Turkey	The general trend has been toward liberalization since 1980, including substantial liberalization of quantitative restrictions and licensing procedures
Venezuela	Comprehensive import liberalization was introduced in 1989; most import prohibitions were abolished, and tariffs were reduced to a maximum rate of 50 percent (from 80 percent); Venezuela acceded to GATT in 1990

Source: United Nations Conference on Trade and Development 1991; Whalley 1989; Williamson 1990; World Bank 1989; and national sources.

The key to these two puzzles might appear at first to be one and the same. The reasons for the recent conversion to outward orientation must be sought, at least initially, in the dissolution of the forces and motives that led policymakers to resist reforms in the past. However, this line of reasoning does not take us too far. The reasons for the free trade bandwagon are more or less unique and derive from the intense, prolonged macroeconomic crisis that surrounded developing countries during the 1980s. This crisis overshadowed the distributional considerations that had blocked trade reform until the 1980s. A combination of special circumstances made governments eventually choose openness over further restrictions, the latter being the historical outcome during crises brought on by unfavorable external circumstances.

The reasons that developing countries initially adopted import-substitution policies and widespread trade restrictions are well known. Early on, nationalist policymakers, as well as many development economists, perceived such restrictions as laying the basis for industrialization and development. A temporary period of protection was required, it was felt, for infant industries to grow and become competitive. Over time, the problems with the infant-industry argument became increasingly evident. The negative examples were the countless cases of infant industries that refused to mature in old age and spawned inefficiencies throughout the economy. The positive examples were the East Asian tigers (Hong Kong, Republic of Korea, Singapore, and Taiwan [China]), where the early administration of outward-oriented policies was yielding spectacular results by the 1970s. Yet despite the accumulating evidence, trade reform remained sporadic and was often reversed.

To understand why requires understanding what trade policy does and how it affects different groups in society. A large part of this chapter is devoted to presenting a framework in which such an analysis can be carried out, including discussion of the channels through which commercial and exchange rate policies work and their respective distributional impacts. The main theme in this part of the chapter is that the central political difficulty in undertaking trade reform is the exceedingly high ratio of redistribution to aggregate gain that trade reform typically generates. The political cost-benefit ratio of trade reform, which will be defined more precisely, is generally very high. This is the source of the contentiousness of trade policy in normal times.

The second part of the chapter turns to the reforms of the 1980s, arguing that it is the pervasive crisis during those years that enabled these reforms. Desperate policymakers packaged reforms in the fiscal, monetary, and exchange rate areas—which were intimately linked to the crisis—with reforms in commercial policies—which were by and large only incidental. The depth of the crisis reduced distributional considerations to second-order importance and eliminated previous resistance. This raises the question of the sustainability of the reforms. If and when normal times and politics as usual return, will these reforms be undercut by the re-emergence of the previous distributional coalitions? The last section of the chapter suggests some reasons to hope that they will not. The status-quo bias that helped entrench the previous policy regime is now likely to work in reverse. Provided macroeconomic stabilization proves successful and inflation and external balances are brought under control, backtracking from the reforms will not be easy.

Trade Reform, Distribution, and Economic Efficiency

We start by reviewing the standard partial-equilibrium analysis of trade liberalization. The general-equilibrium analysis—to which we must necessarily resort when reform involves more than a few items—is more complicated, but the wrinkles involved need not concern us for the moment. The next section extends the analysis in the general-equilibrium direction.

Figure 3-1 shows the domestic demand and supply (S) schedules for an import-competing commodity, say, steel. Let the import restriction take the form of a quota, with only a specified amount of imported steel allowed in the country. To simplify further, we assume that the home economy is small in the world market for steel (that is, the world price for steel is a given) and that domestically produced and imported steel are perfect substitutes for each other. The exchange rate is fixed at unity. The (fixed) world price is indicated in the diagram by p^*. Adding up horizontally the domestic supply with the import quota yields the supply curve faced by domestic consumers (S_q) inclusive of imports. The intersection of domestic demand with S_q (point C) gives the domestic price of steel in equilibrium, p_d. The gap between p_d and p^* is the protection provided to the domestic industry by the quota. It also represents the unit rent created by the quota. These rents accrue typically to holders of import licenses who get them through, depending on the context, political connections, bribery, or sheer luck.[2]

Now consider the consequences of eliminating the import quota. If domestic consumers can import as much steel as they want at price p^*, the new, free trade equilibrium is found at the intersection of the domestic demand schedule with the perfectly flat schedule for world supply (point D). The domestic price falls from p_d to p^*. Consequently, imports and domestic consumption increase, while domestic production decreases and quota rents vanish. The reform enhances the efficiency of resource allocation: previously, resources worth p_d were tied up in the domestic steel industry; releasing these resources and increasing imports at price p^*, achieves a net gain.

Figure 3-1. Trade Reform and Income Distribution

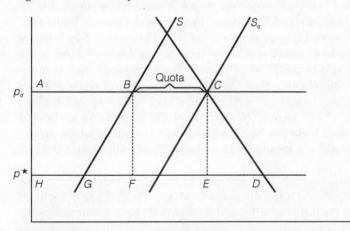

Note: The distributional effect of removing the quota on imports is −ABGH for import-competing producers, −BCEF for import license holders, and +ACDH for the rest of the economy; the net gain is BFG + CDE.

A detailed welfare analysis of the reform can be carried out to see who loses, who gains, and by how much. There are three groups of interest here: users of steel,[3] domestic producers of steel, and license holders. The lower panel of figure 3-1 shows the consequences for each of these groups. The gain to users of steel (or the economy in general) is captured by the area under the demand curve, $ACDH$. The loss to steel producers is the area under the domestic supply curve, $ABGH$. License holders, in turn, lose the quota rents amounting to the area $BCEF$. This leaves a net efficiency gain to the economy from removing the quota that amounts to the sum of two triangles, BFG and CDE.

At this point in the analysis the economics professor usually stops and rests his case, feeling smug after this unassailable demonstration of the superiority of free trade. Most students are probably left a bit uneasy the first time they are subjected to this logic. What is striking about the analysis is perhaps less the end product—the two triangles of efficiency gains—than the massive transfers of income from one group to another— the rectangles that appear or vanish—that are necessary to get there. License holders and steel producers lose out on chunks of income, while consumers (who may include downstream producers using steel as an input) gain by a magnitude that barely exceeds these losses. This leaves a net efficiency gain that amounts to two paltry triangles. In other words, the ratio of net gain to redistribution involved is quite small.

Economists have long been aware of the links between trade policy and income distribution. Some of the most fundamental theorems of trade theory concern precisely the distributional consequences of free trade (for example, the Stolper-Samuelson theorem; Stolper and Samuelson 1941). Development economists have spent much effort trying to ascertain whether these consequences are normatively desirable or not— that is, whether free trade improves equity. A good recent analysis is the study by Bourguignon and Morrisson (1989), which contains both cross-country regression analyses and case studies. Their main conclusion is that protection has a negative effect on income distribution.[4] More to the point, they find that the effect of trade policies on distribution is quantitatively very significant, even though their measure of trade policy is crude and subject to error. Everything else held constant, they find the income share of the richest 20 percent of the population to be 4–5 percentage points higher in highly protectionist countries, where protectionist is defined by a mean effective rate of protection greater than 30 percent.

This suggests, then, that the prospect of too much redistribution may be the central political difficulty in trade reform. From the perspective of policymakers, the pure reshuffling of income must be counted as a political cost. In politics, rents and revenues that accrue on a regular basis create entitlements. Whether viewed as desirable or not, taking income away from one group is rarely easy for a politician to accomplish. And although most policy reforms undercut such entitlements, trade reform does so with a vengeance. Of course, the efficiency benefit of the reform is itself a source of political gain: it amounts to an increase in the size of the national pie, representing improvement in the well-being of at least some groups in society at no cost to others.

Such considerations can be formalized by devising an index of the political cost-benefit ratio (PCBR) of policy reform, defined as follows:

$$(3\text{-}1) \qquad \text{PCBR} = \frac{1}{2}\left[\frac{(\Sigma_j|\Delta\text{income}_j| - \text{net gain})}{\text{net gain}}\right]$$

where net gain stands for the efficiency gain of the reform, j indexes groups (or individuals) in society, and Δ income$_j$ is the change in the income of group j. Note that net gain can also be expressed as $\Sigma_j(\Delta$ income$_j)$. The numerator is the sum of the absolute values of the income effects of the policy on different groups (net of the efficiency gain) and, therefore, is a measure of the total redistribution resulting from the policy. This is divided by two to get rid of the double-counting. In this way, the numerator becomes equivalent to the sum of losses suffered by the groups adversely affected by the reform. Hence, the numerator captures the political cost of the reform, while the denominator captures its benefit. The index is meant to quantify the notion that, for any amount of increase in the size of the national pie, as the amount of reshuffling of income required to achieve that increase grows, so does the cost of the change to policymakers. More specifically, the PCBR index answers the following question: how many dollars of income are shuffled from one group to another for every dollar of net efficiency gain?

Although the index is meant to be nothing more than a heuristic device, it can be given a solid theoretical foundation. Suppose, for example, that the policymaker wants to maximize a conventional social welfare function, subject to the constraint that no group of individuals is made worse off by the reform compared with the status quo. The policymaker has at his disposal only distortionary subsidies and taxes to undertake the requisite compensation. Then the cost-benefit calculus undertaken by the policymaker will bear a certain similarity to the index discussed above. In fact, the PCBR index can be viewed as representing a special case of the problem just stated. The appendix to this chapter provides a formal statement of this and more details.

This index has values that range between zero and infinity. When a policy is purely redistributive and achieves no net gain, the value of the index goes to infinity. When a policy increases some groups' incomes without taking income away from any other group (that is, when it is Pareto efficient), the index takes a value of zero. The latter case corresponds to the economist's proverbial "manna from heaven": it would be politically very desirable if it could be made a reality.

The preceding discussion already provided a hint that trade reform performs poorly when judged by this index. To see how poorly, we relate expression 3-1 to parameters of relevance to trade reform, distinguishing, once again, among consumers, import-competing producers, and rentiers. Let m denote import volume, q import-competing production, c total consumption of the importable, p the domestic price of the importable, p^* the world price, and t the (ad valorem) tariff-equivalent of the trade restriction initially. To a first-order approximation,[5] the income effects of trade reform can be summarized as follows:

$$
\begin{aligned}
\text{Consumers} &= -c\Delta p \\
\text{Producers} &= q\Delta p \\
\text{Rentiers} &= m\Delta p + tp^*\Delta m \\
\text{Net gain} &= tp^*\Delta m.
\end{aligned}
$$

(Note the identity $m = c - q$.) Therefore, the index can be written as follows:

$$
(3\text{-}2) \qquad \text{PCBR} = \frac{-c\Delta p}{tp^*\Delta m} = \frac{1}{\mu\epsilon t}
$$

where μ is the share of imports (at border prices) in domestic consumption and ϵ is the absolute value of the import demand elasticity. The expression on the right-hand side relates the PCBR index to recognizable parameters. The index is increasing in t, μ, and ϵ.

Table 3-2 shows the range of values that the PCBR index can take under plausible combinations of these parameters. The import demand elasticity is fixed at 2 (which is relatively generous), and the other two parameters vary. In most reasonable circumstances, the PCBR lies above 5. In words, an index of 5 indicates that for each dollar of net income generated, five dollars of income are being reshuffled among different groups in the economy. This puts the analysis much closer to the pure redistribution case than to the Pareto-efficient case. Put bluntly, trade reform is politically inefficient.[6]

In fact, things are typically worse. By its very nature, trade liberalization creates a lot of winners whose identities cannot be discerned beforehand. That is because not all of the general-equilibrium ramifications of reform can be sorted out with perfect foresight. After reform, some entrepreneurs in import-substituting sectors will transform themselves into successful exporters; some new, unanticipated export opportunities will be created. Only after reform takes root does the full configuration of gainers and losers become evident. This kind of uncertainty leads to a systematic bias against policy reform: reforms that would receive adequate political support after the fact may fail to receive support beforehand when some of the gainers (or losers) from reform cannot yet be identified (Fernández and Rodrik 1991). Hence, the uncertainty surrounding the distributional effects compounds the immediate difficulties raised by the distributional consequences themselves.

*Table 3-2. Plausible Values of the PCBR Index
under Trade Reform*

		(t)	
μ	*0.20*	*0.50*	*0.70*
0.10	25.00	10.00	7.15
0.20	12.50	5.00	3.58
0.40	6.25	2.50	1.79

Note: $\epsilon = 2$.

These arguments raise the question of why, if trade reform is politically so costly, it is ever undertaken. The maintained assumption behind the PCBR index is that altering the distribution of income is politically costly. This need not always apply. In particular, policymakers may want to reshape distribution—or be indifferent to it—following a transformation in political regime or a change in the underlying configuration of power. Indeed, historically sharp changes in trade policy have almost always been preceded (or accompanied) by changes in the political regime. This was true of the first significant move to free trade in modern history—the repeal of the Corn Laws in England in 1846—a move that reflected the growing political power of urban interests over landed interests. It was also true of the most significant case of reform in the developing world until the 1980s: the reforms that took place after Pinochet's coup in Chile in 1973. More evidence on this will be discussed later in this chapter. Not all political transformations result in trade reform, but sharp changes in trade policy are typically the result of such transformations.

What about the gradual, steady liberalization in the industrial world under the aegis of the General Agreement on Tariffs and Trade (GATT) during the postwar period? It is harder to credit changes in political regime for this process. The political acceptability of these reforms derived instead from the joint influence of two factors: (a) the gradualist nature of the reforms and (b) a favorable external environment in the form of unprecedented economic growth. The latter served to mask the distributive consequences of liberalization and allowed everyone to share in the benefits of recovery and, later on, increased prosperity. The gradual nature of the liberalization, meanwhile, ensured that these distributive effects would remain second order relative to the consequences of overall economic growth. The lesson is a simple, but valuable, one: the congruence of gradualism with increasing, all-around prosperity provides the most comfortable environment for trade reform.[7]

A Closer Look at the Distributive Consequences of Trade Reform

Since trade reform and distribution are so closely related, it is helpful to have a framework for analysis in which the links are laid out. As the

Table 3-3. Matrix for Trade Policy Analysis

Commodity group	Domestic price	Relation to world price	Typical goods or services	Income group most directly affected
Importable	p_m	$ep_m^*(1 + t_m)$	Intermediate goods, capital goods, consumer durables	Import-substitution industrialists, holders of import licenses, organized labor
Exportable	p_x	$ep_x^*/(1 + t_x)$	Cash crops, light manufactures	Agricultural producers, export-oriented entrepreneurs
Nontradable	p_n	n.a.	Construction, labor services	Informal sector, unorganized labor

n.a. Not applicable.

Note: e, exchange rate (home currency per foreign currency); t_m, tariff equivalent of all import restrictions (including license premiums); t_x, tax equivalent of all export restrictions; prices with asterisks denote world prices (in foreign currency).

reforms in question occur across the board, the framework should accommodate economy-wide (that is, general-equilibrium) repercussions. This section provides a sketch of such a framework.

Three sets of commodities and services must be distinguished: (a) importables, (b) exportables, and (c) nontradables. Each of these groups is associated with an "average" domestic price, denoted by p_m, p_x, and p_n, respectively. This classification is meant to be exhaustive; that is, all commodities and services produced in the economy should fit in one of these categories.[8] Table 3-3 shows the typical commodities classified under these headings; intermediate goods (such as chemicals) and capital goods, for example, are typically importables.

The table also shows how the domestic price of each aggregate relates to its world price. The domestic price (in pesos) of importables equals their world price (in dollars) multiplied by the exchange rate (defined as pesos per dollar) times 1 plus t_m, the tariff equivalent of all import restrictions. Not only duties and other taxes but also the ad valorem price equivalent of quota restrictions and other nontariff measures are included under t_m. In fact, t_m itself is usually not directly observable when trade restrictions, as so often, are primarily of a nontariff nature. It can be recovered, however, by comparing the price of domestic products with the price of close substitutes on world markets. The domestic price of exportables (for example, coffee or clothing) is related to the world price in a similar manner, where the export tax, t_x, captures the ad valorem price equivalent of all export restrictions. Note that an import tariff increases the domestic price of importables—the price paid by consumers and received by producers—while an export tax reduces the domestic price of the exportables.

Finally, note that prices of nontradables do not bear any systematic relationship (at least in the context of trade policy) to prices of similar goods on world markets. Since haircuts and cement are normally non-tradable (the first because of restrictions on labor mobility, the second because of transport costs), no arbitrage relationship exists that would pin down domestic prices in relation to foreign prices.[9] Hence, p_n is determined exclusively by domestic demand and supply. The most important category of nontradables is labor services. The wage rate is consequently the most important nontradable price. When import-competing goods are protected by quantitative restrictions, they too become nontradables at the margin.

Table 3-3 also shows the identities of the income groups whose fortunes are most closely tied to each of these prices. Hence, the incomes of import-substituting industrialists, of import-license holders, and often of organized labor are determined in the first instance by p_m, the importable price. The price of exportables, p_x, serves the same purpose for agricultural producers and export-oriented entrepreneurs. The nontradable price, p_n, determines income in the informal sector and unorganized labor.

Now, the well-being of each of these groups is determined not only by the price they receive for their production; other prices matter too, since these affect the costs of inputs and consumption. Real incomes are determined, therefore, by relative prices and not the absolute level of any single price. To draw the links between trade policy and distribution, it is important to know how specific relative prices are affected by trade policy.

But which relative prices? Since three prices exist in the economy, there are only two relative prices that are of independent interest, but there are many different ways of expressing them. For reasons that will be clear shortly, it is convenient to focus on (a) the relative price of importables to exportables and (b) the relative price of tradables to nontradables. These two relative prices are key to the resource allocation effects of trade policy, and any political-economy analysis must begin with them.

Using the definitions in table 3-3, the first of these can be expressed as follows:

$$(3-3) \qquad \frac{p_m}{p_x} = \left(\frac{p_m^*}{p_x^*}\right)(1 + t_m)(1 + t_x).$$

The second relative price is obtained by lumping importables and exportables into a basket called tradables. Formally, the price of tradables, p_t, is a weighted average of p_m and p_x:

$$(3-4) \qquad p_t = [ep_m^*(1 + t_m)]^\alpha \left[\frac{ep_x^*}{(1 + t_x)}\right]^{1-\alpha}$$

$$= e[p_m^*(1 + t_m)]^\alpha \left[\frac{p_x^*}{(1 + t_x)}\right]^{1-\alpha}$$

where α is the weight on importables. The second relative price is then given by the ratio of the price of tradables to nontradables:

$$(3\text{-}5) \qquad \frac{p_t}{p_n} = \left\{ \frac{e[p_m^*(1 + t_m)]^\alpha \left[\dfrac{p_x^*}{(1 + t_x)}\right]^{1-\alpha}}{p_n} \right\}$$

This ratio is also called the real exchange rate.

From an economic standpoint, the distinction between these two is useful because each has a distinct effect on resource allocation. On the one hand, changes in p_m/p_x are associated inversely with changes in an economy's openness: the higher this relative price is, the smaller the share of imports *and* exports is in national income (all else remaining equal) and the higher the level of import-substituting production. On the other hand, changes in p_t/p_n are typically associated with changes in the trade (or current account) balance: the higher this relative price is, the more positive the trade balance (again, all else remaining equal) is. These resource-allocation effects also define the criteria by which the success of commercial policy and of exchange rate policy should be measured: successful trade liberalization will increase the ratio of imports to gross national product (GNP) and of exports to GNP on a sustained basis; successful devaluation will reduce the trade deficit (or increase the surplus) without affecting domestic levels of inflation and unemployment. Finally, the two relative prices have distinct distributional consequences. The first relative price captures distributional conflict within tradables' sectors, whereas the second focuses on distribution across the tradables-nontradables cleavage.

Armed with these two relative prices, it is now possible to analyze the consequences of trade policy for the real incomes of different groups in society. For each policy in question, the analysis examines how these relative prices are affected and reads the implications for different groups with the help of the classification in table 3-3.

Commercial Policy

The term "commercial policy" captures the set of policies that have direct implications for the domestic prices of importables and exportables and thus affect the relative price p_m/p_x. As shown in equation 3-3, these are import and export taxes of various sorts, including quantitative restrictions, licensing, advance deposits on imports, prohibitions, and (often) commodity marketing boards. Note that the relative price of importables and exportables does not depend on the exchange rate, as e enters both the numerator and the denominator and cancels out; that is, exchange rate policy is distributionally neutral between import-competing and export-oriented interests. There are two notable exceptions, however. First, when some import-competing sectors are protected by quotas, rendering them nontradable at the margin, a real depreciation of the currency will hurt these sectors and benefit exporters (as well as remaining import-competing activities). Second, a devaluation under foreign currency rationing will act just like import liberalization. The latter case is discussed below.

Note the symmetry in the way that import and export taxes enter equation 3-3: import tariffs and export taxes have identical effects.[10] A 10 percent export tax has the same effect on p_m/p_x—and hence on the openness of the economy and on distribution within tradables—as a 10 percent import tariff and vice versa.[11] This demonstrates that import protection imposes a penalty on exporters that is identical to a direct export tax. Conversely, an export tax benefits import-competing interests. The logic works for subsidies also, as long as one keeps in mind that a subsidy is a negative tax. Hence, an export subsidy takes away some import protection and hurts import-competing interests as much as a direct reduction in protection.

Finally, commercial policy per se has no direct distributive consequence for groups that derive their income from nontradables, such as unorganized labor (or the informal sector). Equation 3-5 shows that a reduction in the import tariff would tend to increase the real incomes of labor (as p_t/p_n is reduced) but only as long as the nominal exchange rate (e) remains unchanged. If the import liberalization is packaged with a devaluation (see below), the effect on labor is ambiguous.

The situation may be quite different for organized labor in import-competing industries, where high profits may be shared with labor unions and be reflected in wage premia relative to the rest of the economy. The relaxation of import controls will bite into these labor "rents" and hurt these groups directly.

Exchange Rate Policy

Exchange rate policy affects a different relative price, that between all tradables and nontradables. This can be seen in expression 3-5, in which e enters the numerator. This is an important distinction between commercial policy and exchange rate policy and is often missed in general discussions of trade policy. At the risk of being repetitive, the distinction is summarized in table 3-4. A devaluation increases the domestic price of tradables and, all else remaining equal, raises p_t/p_n. Unlike commercial liberalization, a devaluation is likely to squeeze unorganized labor and reduce real wages in terms of tradables (provided wages are determined predominantly by conditions in the nontradable sector). The reduction in real wages is the flip side of the increase in competitiveness brought about by devaluation. Also, a devaluation affects all tradable sectors symmetrically: both import-competing and export-oriented interests benefit from it, while commercial liberalization pits these two sectors against each other.

With respect to real wages, one point bears stressing. It is useful to

Table 3-4. Commercial Policy and Exchange Rate Policy

Policy	Relative price affected	Resource-allocation effect	Distributive effect
Commercial	p_m/p_x	Openness	Import-competing versus export-oriented interests
Exchange rate	p_t/p_n	Trade balance	All tradables versus nontradables; real wages

distinguish between two concepts of the real wage: the product real wage and the consumption real wage. The product real wage is the nominal wage divided by the price of tradables, and it determines the competitiveness of domestic tradables. The consumption real wage is the nominal wage divided by an aggregate price index that includes the price of nontradables; it measures the purchasing power of wages and is the more appropriate index of workers' well-being. If nontradables are sufficiently important in workers' consumption basket and wages rise sufficiently more than the price of nontradables, consumption real wages could increase as a consequence of devaluation, while the product real wage falls.

Moreover, unlike commercial policy, which can be made effective by fiat, the economic success of exchange rate policy depends on the response of p_n (or wages). Equation 3-5 shows that the value of the real exchange rate p_t/p_n depends both on e and on p_n. For an increase in the nominal exchange rate to bring about an increase in the real exchange rate (that is, to achieve a real depreciation), p_n must not rise proportionately. As mentioned, p_n is determined by domestic supply and demand conditions. Making exchange rate policy effective, therefore, requires restrictive demand management policies that do not allow p_n (or wages) to rise along with e. This is the source of the oft-repeated admonishment to developing countries that exchange rate devaluation (expenditure switching) should be coupled with restrictive monetary and fiscal policies (expenditure reduction) to have an effect on the external balance. Economic effectiveness calls for income redistribution.

Devaluation When Foreign Exchange Is Rationed

A sharp distinction has been drawn here between the impacts of commercial and exchange rate policy on distribution and the allocation of resources. In some circumstances, however, the distinction disappears, and a devaluation becomes identical to commercial liberalization. This occurs when foreign exchange is rationed by the government and a black market exists for foreign exchange.

In the presence of a black market, there are at least two exchange rates: an official exchange rate, call it $\bar{e}$, at which only a limited number of transactions are carried out due to rationing by the central bank, and the black market rate, e_b, which represents the marginal cost of foreign exchange and to which importers must resort in order to satisfy their needs in excess of the official allocation (naturally, $e_b > \bar{e}$). This is shown in figure 3-2. Exporters must turn in their foreign exchange receipts at the lower price $\bar{e}$. Hence, domestic prices of importables and exportables are now given by $p_m = e_b p_m^*(1 + t_m)$ and $p_x = \bar{e} p_x^* / (1 + t_x)$. The relative price of importables to exportables becomes

$$(3\text{-}3') \qquad \frac{p_m}{p_x} = \left(\frac{e_b}{\bar{e}}\right)\left(\frac{p_m^*}{p_x^*}\right)(1 + t_m)(1 + t_x)$$

where the exchange rates have not canceled out (compare equation 3-3). The gap between $\bar{e}$ and e_b represents rents that accrue to groups with access to dollars at the official rate (since these dollars are worth the black market price). Therefore, the rationing of foreign currency creates a situation that is entirely analogous to the imposition of a trade restriction. This can be seen from equation 3-3': an increase in the exchange rate premium (that is, a larger gap between e_b and $\bar{e}$) works just like an increase in t_m or t_x.

Now consider a devaluation of the official rate (an increase in $\bar{e}$), which prompts an increase in the supply of foreign exchange as exporters respond by increasing their activity. As shown in figure 3-2, that leads, in turn, to a decrease in the black market exchange rate. The net effect is a fall in $e_b/\bar{e}$, which amounts to a fall in the price of importables relative to the price of exportables (see equation 3-3'). Now the devaluation works

Figure 3-2. Foreign Currency Rationing and Multiple Exchange Rates

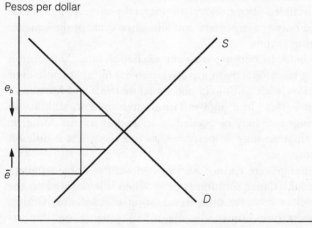

Pesos per dollar

Quantity of foreign currency

just like commercial liberalization and will have all the same consequences for resource allocation and distribution. In particular, the rents accruing to groups with access to official dollars will diminish. This is the case of a trade-liberalizing devaluation. By increasing the availability of foreign exchange, previously rationed, the devaluation allows more exports and more imports. Import-competing groups that would normally benefit from a devaluation are now hurt.

Compensated and Uncompensated Trade Liberalization

Consider a reduction in import barriers. In the medium to long run, there is no reason why the liberalization should have an adverse effect on the trade balance; even in the absence of adjustments in the exchange rate, endogenous changes in the price of nontradables will generally be enough to return the economy to external balance. In the shorter run, the situation may be a bit more complicated if p_n is not sufficiently flexible or, what amounts to the same thing in most contexts, if the operation of labor markets is plagued by rigidities. To make the point as starkly as possible, let us assume that p_n is fixed and does not adjust once import barriers are lifted.

Equation 3-5, on close inspection, shows that a reduction in t_m reduces the numerator of p_t/p_n and hence appreciates the real exchange rate. This makes domestic production less competitive and can be expected to deteriorate the external balance. Intuitively, cheaper imports replace domestic output. An endogenous reduction in p_n would insulate the external balance from the effect of the liberalization. In its absence, the government can achieve the same insulation by undertaking a devaluation. An increase in e raises the numerator in p_t/p_n and prevents the appreciation of the real exchange rate and the loss of competitiveness. With a compensating devaluation of this sort, the effects of liberalization are limited to those discussed above under commercial policy. The devaluation gives an added boost to exporters and alleviates some of the squeeze on import-competing groups.

The alternative is to do nothing with the exchange rate. This option was selected during the 1980s by many governments fighting triple-digit (and higher) inflation (such as Bolivia and Israel in 1985 and Mexico in 1988). The reason is that, in a high-inflation environment, stability in the nominal exchange rate may be needed as an anchor for the domestic price level. A devaluation may be perceived as too risky, lest it unleash inflationary expectations.

Clearly, the exchange rate cannot be targeted on the domestic price level and the external balance simultaneously. When it is targeted on the domestic price level, a compensating devaluation is ruled out. Consequently, the liberalization imposes a magnified squeeze on import-competing interests to the benefit of nontradable sectors. The ensuing deterioration in the current account balance can continue as long as there are capital inflows willing to sustain it. Living beyond one's means in this fashion can even create a sense of euphoria, but politically this can be dangerous. Powerful import-substituting interests are more likely to oppose vigorously an uncompensated liberalization than a compensated one. In Chile, for example, the early stages of liberalization during 1975–78 took place in the context of a depreciating real exchange rate. Industrialists complained in earnest only after 1979, when the real exchange rate started to appreciate. Similarly, in Mexico liberalization during 1985–87 did not have detrimental effects on industry thanks to a depreciating exchange rate; starting in 1988, when the peso was stabilized and the trade reform speeded up, liberalization began to bite considerably more.

Distributive Consequences for the State

The discussion so far has left out a very important claimant on national income, the state (or the bureaucracy). The willingness of policymakers to undertake trade reform is often shaped as much by the perceived impact on the fiscal resources of the state or on the wealth of well-placed bureaucrats as by the pressure from below. The analysis of distribution closes by discussing briefly the main channels through which trade policy transfers resources to and from the state.

First and most directly, import and export taxes are a source of revenue for the public treasury. Trade taxes (including the profits of marketing boards) play a particularly important role in the poorest countries, where such revenues can make up between one-quarter and half of central government income. Under most circumstances, trade liberalization may be expected to reduce these revenues. But there are a couple of important exceptions to this rule. First, the initial stages of trade liberalization usually eliminate quantitative restrictions, often replacing them by tariffs. Such an imposition of tariffs should channel resources that previously ended up as quota rents toward public coffers. Second, when trade restrictions get too high and overvaluation of the exchange rate becomes extreme, trade taxes are typically dissipated in smuggling and other illicit activities. Correcting such problems can sharply increase government revenue despite the overall liberalization. A significant example of this took place in Ghana after 1983.

Exchange rate policy also has important implications for government finance, but the effects tend to be more subtle. Since exchange rate policy aims at changing the price of tradables relative to nontradables, the income effect on the public sector can be found by answering the following question: are nontraded goods and services a net source of income for the government or not? When they are, as when payroll taxes constitute an important component of government revenue and much of public spending goes to purchase tradables (military hardware, for example), a devaluation will leave the state sector poorer. When they are not, as is the case in oil-producing economies, the public sector benefits from a devaluation. Turkey and Venezuela are good examples of these cases, respectively. Sometimes the question is put differently: is the government a net seller or buyer of dollars in relation to the private sector? Useful as a first approximation, this question betrays a partial-equilibrium logic where a general-equilibrium one is needed.

As discussed above, much of trade policy is concerned with the creation and elimination of rents (Krueger 1974). These rents are often captured by individual bureaucrats. A government official who is entrusted with the disposition of scarce import licenses or foreign currency is endowed with a very valuable resource. Whether he cashes in on this resource by accepting bribes or simply basks in the self-importance created by his job, asking him to give up this resource willingly may be asking too much. This explains why restrictive trade regimes and foreign exchange crises often create within the government a powerful lobby in favor of their continuation and why successful implementation of reforms may require the replacement of middle echelons within the economic bureaucracy. Indonesia, which substituted a Swiss inspection firm for its customs bureaucracy, is a good case in point.

Why Has There Been So Much Trade Liberalization Lately?

It is time to address the second puzzle stated at the outset of this chapter: if trade reform is politically so difficult to undertake, why are so many countries doing it now? The mystery is heightened because the current wave of trade reform is taking place in an environment not conducive to its success: high inflation blunts the impact of relative-price changes achieved by trade reform, and recession makes the required reallocation of resources more costly.

Focusing on the distributional consequences of trade policy provides one potential key to the puzzle. Perhaps the powerful interests that benefited from protection and had successfully blocked reform were weakened by the debt crisis of the 1980s, which would explain the general move toward liberal policies. But the argument would require a demonstration that import-competing interests, the ones most severely hurt by reform, were weakened disproportionately. Such an argument would be difficult to construct. Of course, the debt crisis highlighted the urgency of earning foreign exchange and thus may have increased the political strength of exporters. By the same token, the need to conserve foreign exchange must have played into the hands of import-substituting groups. The crisis of 1982 and the ensuing macroeconomic mess were costly all around. It is not at all evident that import-competing groups bore the brunt of the effects or that they systematically lost out on the political front.

On the international scene, there were two clear winners: the World Bank and the International Monetary Fund (IMF). The crisis forced developing countries to line up at the gates of these Bretton Woods institutions, pleading for the imprimatur that would unlock debt rescheduling arrangements and new capital flows. The renewed importance of these institutions gave unprecedented salience to their orthodox arguments on economic management, that is, the need for trade liberalization, realistic exchange rates, and conservative monetary and fiscal policies. The bargaining was especially one-sided in Africa, where governments were poorly endowed with the technical expertise to evaluate and reshape standard prescriptions and lacked powerful patrons among rich countries, which would help moderate World Bank and IMF demands (for a recent study of the World Bank's relations with governments, see Mosley, Harrigan, and Toye 1991).

That the World Bank and the IMF became uncommonly powerful in their dealings with the governments of developing countries during the 1980s is indisputable. Yet it would be a mistake to picture the process of policy reform as one in which orthodox economic policies were externally imposed on unwilling policymakers. In some African cases, this characterization may have come close to being true—witness, for example, the cycle of reform and reversal in Zambia. But more often than not, reform has had a significant homegrown component, exceeding on occasion the World Bank's or the IMF's expectations and stipulations. The Mexican liberalization since 1987, for example, has been more ambitious and has proceeded faster than some World Bank officials thought was prudent at the time. The recent Argentine, Brazilian, and Indian conversions cannot be credited to the Bretton Woods institutions either; these large countries have a long history of avoiding and evading World Bank conditionality on liberalization. External actors have played at best a modest role in initiating recent reforms.

The bulk of the credit must go instead to the dire economic circumstances in which most developing countries found themselves as a consequence of the prolonged macroeconomic crisis of the 1980s. The experience of high inflation and negative growth year after year eventually prepared the ground for embracing an entirely new set of policies. The continued deterioration in economic conditions shaped a general consensus that something had to be done. Put differently, the perceived overall gain from restoring the economy's health became, after a point, so large that it swamped distributional considerations.[12]

This point can be demonstrated using the PCBR index developed previously, which shows that the political cost-benefit ratio of trade reform declines dramatically when it is introduced in the context of stabilization policy. Consider a trade reform that is part of an overall economic stabilization package. The stabilization aims to reduce inflation and revive the economy by eliminating the foreign exchange stranglehold. The question of why trade reform is included in the package alongside the standard fiscal and monetary measures will be addressed later; suffice it to say that in practice trade reform arrived as part of an overall macroeconomic package of this sort. Now, stabilization differs from trade liberalization in one key respect: unlike trade liberalization, it holds the promise of generating benefits that will be shared by all. Few coherent interest groups can be identified as net gainers from triple-digit inflation and economic collapse, and hence most interest groups stand to benefit from an end to both.[13] Moreover, the deeper the crisis, the larger the overall net benefits from recovery.

The PCBR index for this reform can be calculated by tracking the effects of both the liberalization and the stabilization. The across-the-board benefit of stabilization is denoted by γ, the percentage increase in net income that accrues to all groups in the economy as a result of stabilization. γ is a proxy for the depth of the crisis (as well as for the likely success of the stabilization). Further, let θ denote the share of consumption of importables in GNP and ω the percent reduction in the price of importables relative to exportables as a consequence of the reform. The PCBR index for the stabilization-cum-liberalization package can now be expressed as:

$$(3-6) \qquad \text{PCBR} = \frac{1}{\mu \epsilon t + (\gamma / \omega \theta)}.$$

It is now a matter of simple algebra to demonstrate that when the all-around benefit of stabilization (γ) is large, it swamps the redistributive aspect of the trade reform. Table 3-5 shows how the PCBR index falls sharply with γ. When $\gamma = 0$, the PCBR index takes its usual high value—5.0 under the present parameter combinations. In the presence of a stabilization program that promises to make all groups better off by 10 percent $(\gamma = 0.1)$, the index plummets to 0.69. With $\gamma = 0.25$, the index declines further to 0.30. Since relatively small increases in the growth rate of an economy can cause large jumps in the level of the present discounted value of income, an expectation that a successful stabilization will increase well-being 10 to 25 percent is not far off the mark.[14] Hence trade reform can suddenly start to look politically attractive if (a) it is perceived as an integral part of a stabilization package, and (b) the macroeconomy stands engulfed in a deep crisis.

Table 3-5. The PCBR Index with Stabilization-cum-Trade Reform

γ	PCBR
0.00	5.00
0.10	0.69
0.25	0.30
0.50	0.16
1.00	0.08

Note: $t = 0.5$; $\mu = 0.2$; $\epsilon = 2.0$; $\theta = 0.4$; $\omega = 0.2$.

Table 3-6. The Correlates of Trade Reform for Countries with Strong and Fast Reform Episodes

Country and year	Change in political regime	Perception of complete economic collapse
Argentina, 1976	x	x
Chile, 1956		x
1974	x	x
Greece, 1953		
Indonesia, 1966	x	x
Israel, 1952		x
Peru, 1979		
Philippines, 1960	x	
Singapore, 1968	x	
Spain, 1977	x	
Sri Lanka, 1977	x	
Turkey, 1980		x
Yugoslavia, 1965		

Source: Papageorgiou, Choksi, and Michaely 1990.

The argument that economic crisis can promote reform is consistent with the evidence (scanty as it is) from earlier decades also. A recent World Bank research project analyzes liberalization episodes in nineteen developing countries during the period after World War II and before the debt crisis (Papageorgiou, Choksi, and Michaely 1990). Table 3-6, taken from this research, lists thirteen cases classified as episodes of "strong" and "fast" trade reform. The vast majority of these reforms—ten out of thirteen—took place in the context of either a change in political regime or a generalized perception of complete economic collapse, or both. The close association between economic collapse and reform was even more evident in the 1980s, when each occurred again and again: no significant case of trade reform in a developing country in the 1980s took place outside the context of a serious economic crisis.

Two questions remain to be answered. First, why did the changes in trade policy take the form of liberalization rather than of closing up? After all, the logic of the argument is symmetric with respect to trade policy reforms in either direction. Second, why were trade reforms packaged with stabilization, if the relationship between trade policy and the debt crisis is incidental? (For an argument that the relationship is indeed incidental, see Rodrik 1992b.) That is, why did policymakers perceive a need for commercial policy reforms on top of monetary, fiscal, and exchange rate reforms?

The answer to the first question is that the countries concerned for the most part initially did choose to protect rather than to liberalize. This reaction constituted the traditional response to foreign exchange crises: when dollars become scarce, policymakers in developing countries impose rationing and tighten quantitative restrictions. This is what happened in the early stages of the debt crisis. Turkey, which entered its debt crisis early in 1977, mucked around with halfway measures for two-and-a-half years until it decided to liberalize in 1980. Mexico started to liberalize in earnest in late 1987 (but some of the measures were announced in 1985—still three years after the debt crisis hit). Peru was an extreme case of turning inward under García and until the Fujimori government took over. Argentina and Brazil took the better part of the decade before they decided to liberalize. Hence, liberalization was selected only after the alternative had been tried repeatedly and discredited. The crisis called for something new; import controls were not it.

The second issue—the packaging of stabilization with liberalization— is more mystifying. One factor was that the crisis had discredited the entire pattern of previous economic policymaking, including the commercial policy regime. To have credibility, policymakers had to make a clean break with the past, and this included doing away with the import-substitution regime. It may be too much to assume that the policymakers themselves were fully aware of the distinctions and of the full set of causal relations among the trade regime, the macroeconomic stance, and the economic crisis. Also, the World Bank must be given credit for having invented and successfully marketed the concept of "structural adjustment," a concept that packaged together microeconomic and macroeconomic reforms. Structural adjustment was sold as the process that countries needed to undergo in order to save their economies from the crisis. For governments that bought into the package, the distinction between sound macroeconomic policies that maintain external balance and stable prices, on the one hand, and policies that determine openness, on the other, was obfuscated.

Sustaining the Reforms

The argument made in the previous section is perhaps not very encouraging for the sustainability of trade liberalization into the 1990s. If the argument is correct, the reforms were enabled not by the dissolution of powerful import-competing coalitions, but by a deep economic crisis— necessarily of a temporary nature—that relegated distributional issues to second place behind the need to stabilize the macroeconomy. Once the crisis is over and politics as usual returns, will these coalitions not reassert themselves and demand a return to import protection? Possibly so. But there are reasons to think that it will not be easy for policymakers to turn their backs on the reforms.

The experience of Chile provides an instructive example. During the 1970s, a radical trade reform was imposed on Chilean business by a repressive dictatorial regime impervious to interest-group pressure. By the early 1980s, import-substitution policies had been replaced by a simple uniform tariff of 10 percent (motor vehicles being the sole exception). With the return of democracy at the end of the decade, a reasonable guess might have been that protectionist business interests would rise to the occasion and push for a return to some of the old policies under which they had prospered. Yet nothing of the sort happened. In fact, during the presidential election campaign in the fall of 1989, the trade regime never became an issue. All major groups, it would seem, were ready to live with free trade.

One reason that the open trade regime has not been challenged in Chile is the comparative success of its economy. While many of its neighbors were reeling under triple-digit inflation and negative growth, Chile managed to keep its inflation rate at or below 20 percent and grew at highly respectable rates. Why mess with success?

One lesson from the Chilean experience, then, is that when policies are demonstrated to work, they will gain legitimacy. When the economy starts to recover and inflation is firmly under control, some of the success—rightly or wrongly—will be attributed to the open trade policies. Indeed, probably the most important determinant of the sustainability of the liberalization will be the success of macroeconomic stabilization. In countries where inflation and external imbalances are brought under control, the reform package, including its commercial component, will have legitimacy and will be resistant to political attack. Bolivia provides an additional example: the memory of the successful 1985 stabilization after hyperinflation has created a political consensus on the desirability of liberal trade policies. Where stabilization fails, on the other hand, trade reform too will be prone to reversal.

A second lesson from the example of countries like Chile and Bolivia is that all policies create constituencies for their continuation. Outward-oriented policies generate new profit opportunities for entrepreneurs, some of whom may have been engaged only in import-substituting activities prior to reform. As new, previously unpredictable export activities appear, a new class of export-oriented businessmen is created. These entrepreneurs now have a stake in the new policy regime and will fight any attempt to reverse it. The distributional complications discussed in the first half of the chapter now operate in reverse: going back to protection will be difficult precisely because so much (re)redistribution will be involved.

Such status quo bias will help enlightened policymakers stick with open trade policies. But the policymakers themselves have also taken measures to avoid reversal. Governments in many countries have been imaginative in devising strategies for institutionalizing the reforms. Mexico, for example, first bound its tariff rates under the GATT and then began negotiations with the United States to enter a free trade agreement. By making reversal extremely costly, these actions have helped solidify the reforms. The appropriate strategies naturally depend on the context, but some helpful ones include adopting a uniform tariff to make individual tariff rates less susceptible to special-interest pleading from business;

reorganizing the economic bureaucracy to reduce the power of officials who benefited directly from the previous licensing and rationing system;[15] and quickly establishing a credible export subsidy program to ensure that there is an interest group with a stake in outward orientation. These and other strategies are discussed at greater length elsewhere (see Panagariya and Rodrik 1991; Rodrik 1989a, 1989b, 1992a).

Creative policymakers will no doubt come up with more of these strategies. But institutional innovation notwithstanding, a point already made bears repeating: nothing will help sustain open trade policies more than a stable macroeconomic environment. The success of recent reforms, therefore, will ultimately depend less on their own direct effects than on the success of macroeconomic policy.

Appendix 3-1: The Political Cost-Benefit Ratio

A conventional utilitarian social welfare function is defined as follows:

$$V(\sigma_1, \ldots, \sigma_k; t) \equiv \Sigma_i U_i(\sigma_1, \ldots, \sigma_k; t)$$

where σi stands for various subsidies (and taxes) available to the policymaker for undertaking compensation, t is the generic trade policy instrument, and $U_i(\cdot)$ stands for group (or individual) i's utility function. Note that utility functions are reduced forms defined directly over the policy instruments. Since σ_i will generally be distortionary, $U_i(\cdot)$ and $V(\cdot)$ have the standard interpretation as in the literature on public finance.

The policymaker selects the tax or subsidy scheme to ensure that no group is made worse off subsequent to a trade reform than in the status quo. Denoting the status quo level of utility of group i by $\bar{U}_i$, this problem can be written as follows:

$$(3A-1) \quad \underset{\{\sigma_i\}}{\text{Max}} \ V(\sigma_1, \ldots, \sigma_k; t) \ s.t. \ U_1(\sigma_1, \ldots, \sigma_k; t) \geq \bar{U}_1$$

$$U_n(\sigma_1, \ldots, \sigma_k; t) \geq \bar{U}_n.$$

The associated Lagrangean expression is given by:

$$\mathscr{L} = V(\sigma_1, \ldots, \sigma_k; t) + \Sigma_i \mu_i [U_i(\sigma_1, \ldots, \sigma_k; t) - \bar{U}i]$$

where μ_i are the Lagrange multipliers ($\mu_i \geq 0$). $V(\cdot)$ is assumed to be sufficiently well-behaved so that the second-order conditions for this problem are satisfied. Let $\{\sigma_i^*(t)\}$ represent the solution to this problem. We can then derive the maximum-value function $V^*(t)$:

$$V^*(t) = V[\sigma_1^*(t), \ldots, \sigma_k^*(t); t].$$

To the policymaker who must compensate the losers by using distortionary taxes and subsidies, the net benefit of trade reform is now given by $dV^*(t)/dt$. By the envelope theorem,

$$\frac{dV^*(t)}{dt} = \frac{\partial \mathscr{L}}{\partial t}$$

$$= \left[\frac{\partial V(\cdot)}{\partial t}\right] + \Sigma_i \mu_i \left[\frac{\partial U_i(\cdot)}{\partial t}\right].$$

Note that the constraints in equation 3A-1 will bind in the post-reform equilibrium only for groups that are made worse off; it will not bind for the winners. Hence, μ_i is equal to zero for beneficiary groups and greater than zero for losing groups. Consequently, $dV^*(t)/dt$ can be written as

(3A-2) $$\frac{dV^*(t)}{dt} = \left[\frac{\partial V(\cdot)}{\partial t}\right] + \underset{\{\text{losers}\}}{\Sigma} \mu_i \left[\frac{\partial U_i(\cdot)}{\partial t}\right].$$

The first term here is simply the efficiency gain of the reform, and for a reduction in t, it will normally be positive. The second term represents the cost of compensating the losers: it is the weighted sum of utility losses suffered by groups adversely affected by the reform, with the weights being the Lagrange multipliers. Note that these multipliers summarize the (marginal) resource cost of compensation. For an efficiency-enhancing reform, the sign on the second term is always opposite to that on the first.

The PCBR discussed in the text can now be seen to represent a special case of the calculus expressed in equation 3A-2, with gains and losses measured in income rather than utility. The denominator of the PCBR is the first term of equation 3A-2. The numerator, which equals the sum of losses, is the second term, with all μ_i that are positive set equal to unity.

Dixit and Norman (1986) have shown that under certain conditions (some curvature in the production-possibility frontier and the existence of a commodity for which all consumers are net buyers or sellers), a full set of commodity and factor taxes can ensure the Pareto-superiority of free trade over autarky (even in the absence of lump-sum taxes). In terms of the framework here, the Dixit-Norman result would imply that expression 3A-2 is unambiguously negative and, therefore, that the PCBR is always less than unity. However, this need not be the case when the tax or subsidy scheme has administrative costs, when less than a full set of tax or subsidy instruments exists, or when there is a government revenue requirement.

Notes

1. Samuelson was challenged by a mathematician who disdained economics to come up with such a proposition; he confessed to being at a loss until he came up with the principle of comparative advantage. That it is true, Samuelson pointed out, need not be explained at great length to a mathematician. That it is nontrivial, he said, was evidenced by the long history of errors committed by individuals who had not understood it.

2. In rare cases, the government auctions import licenses to the highest bidders. In this instance, quota rents accrue to the government in the form of revenue from the auction.

3. Since steel is an intermediate product, these consumers are typically producers as well. The demand curve for steel reflects the derived demand for the commodity, taking into account all the links among industries up the processing chain, including consumers of final products that use steel (such as cars).

4. However, there is an alternative way of interpreting this evidence. Recent studies have shown that growth-damaging policies are more likely to be undertaken in countries where the distribution of income is skewed, at least where democratic regimes are concerned (see Alesina and Rodrik 1991, 1992; Persson and Tabellini 1991). Hence causality may well go in the other direction, such as from inegalitarian distribution to high levels of trade protection.

5. The approximation is based on calculus; that is, it ignores some interaction terms. It will be more accurate the smaller the trade reform.

6. To the extent that rent-seeking behavior dissipates some of the rents of trade protection, the efficiency gains of reform may be larger than those measured here. However, the rent-seeking literature generally exaggerates these gains. If individuals can waste resources competing for the rents generated by, say, quotas, they can also waste resources lobbying the government for the reimposition of quotas that have been taken away. Altering the incentives for rent-seeking behavior goes beyond simple changes in the level of trade protection.

7. Of course, the two may be related. Growth may be fostered by the ongoing liberalization, but given the lags and uncertainty involved, the relationship is unlikely to be exploitable for political purposes.

8. Some commodities can be simultaneously imported and exported, raising a difficulty as to whether they should be classified as importable or exportable. With sufficient disaggregation, this will rarely be a serious problem in the context of developing countries.

9. There are always exceptions: Venezuela exports cement to Florida as it is cheaper to transport cement via the ocean than to bring it overland by train or truck. In fact, in late 1991, cement producers in Florida were trying to bring antidumping action against Venezuelan exporters.

10. This result, known as the Lerner symmetry theorem, is surprisingly general. All that it requires is that the trade balance be insulated from the effect of the tariff or tax, as would occur when p_n is perfectly flexible or e is adjusted to maintain the trade balance unchanged. Often, however, and especially in the short run, macroeconomic equilibrium may fail to occur, and the symmetry may break down. The claims made in this paragraph lose their force when this is the case (see the discussion below on compensated and uncompensated trade liberalizations).

11. Sometimes this equivalence is stated in a different way: a 10 percent increase in tariffs is identical to a 10 percent increase in the export tax. As a moment's reflection will show, this does not follow from equation 3-3, unless t_m and t_x are initially zero.

12. Witness, for example, the following description of the Ghanaian experience: "Rent seekers who can control import licenses are usually a potent source of opposition to devaluation, but the crisis had become so bad in Ghana that the group benefiting from administrative allocation of foreign exchange was extremely limited. Indeed, by the early 1980s, the economy had deteriorated to such an extent that even senior government officials, who normally benefit from access to imported goods even in times of shortage, reported that they were going hungry and were concerned that they could not find food for their families" (Herbst 1991). For a formal model on the benefits of crisis for economic reform, which closely parallels the argument here, see also Drazen and Grilli (1990).

13. This does not mean that stabilization does not generate distributional conflict; Alesina and Drazen (1991) present a model based on such conflict. But in this model (and in reality), the conflict over stabilization is based not on who gains and who loses from stabilization, but on who gains more and who gains less. Therefore, the distributional conflict is on a lower order of magnitude than in the case of trade liberalization.

14. Let the stabilization increase the growth rate of the economy by only one percentage point, from 0 to 1 percent. Assume that individuals have a time discount rate of 8 percent. Then, this relatively small increase in the growth rate translates into a 14.3 percent increase in the level of individuals' wealth (present discounted value of income).

15. Onis (forthcoming) provides a good discussion of some of these institutional innovations in post-1983 Turkey: "The post-1983 governments aimed explicitly at weakening the role of the traditional bureaucratic elites . . . Installing a managerial bureaucracy in the form of a select group of U.S. educated technocrats, recruited from outside the ranks of traditional bureaucracy, hence largely independent from both societal and intrabureaucratic pressures, has been perceived as a necessary condition for the consistent implementation of the economic program."

References

Alesina, Alberto, and Allan Drazen. 1991. "Why Are Stabilizations Delayed?" *American Economic Review* 81, pp. 1170–88.

Alesina, Alberto, and Dani Rodrik. 1991. "Distributive Politics and Economic Growth." NBER Working Paper 3668. Harvard University, National Bureau of Economic Research, Cambridge, Mass.

_____. 1992. "Distribution, Political Conflict, and Economic Growth: A Simple Theory and Some Empirical Evidence." In Alex Cukierman and others, eds., *The Political Economy of Business Cycles and Growth*. Cambridge, Mass.: M.I.T. Press.

Bates, Robert H., ed. 1988. *Toward a Political Economy of Development: A Rational Choice Perspective*. Berkeley: University of California Press.

Bourguignon, François, and Christian Morrisson. 1989. *External Trade and Income Distribution*. Paris: Development Center of the Organization for Economic Cooperation and Development.

Dixit, Avinash, and Victor Norman. 1986. "Gains from Trade without Lump-Sum Compensation." *Journal of International Economics* 21, pp. 111–22.

Drazen, Allan, and Vittorio Grilli. 1990. "The Benefits of Crises for Economic Reforms." NBER Working Paper 3527. National Bureau of Economic Research, Cambridge, Mass.

Fernández, Raquel, and Dani Rodrik. 1991. "Resistance to Reform: Status Quo Bias in the Presence of Individual-Specific Uncertainty." *American Economic Review* 81 (December), pp. 1146–55.

Haggard, Stephan, and Steven Webb. 1993. "What Do We Know about the Political Economy of Economic Policy Reform?" *World Bank Research Observer* 8:2 (July), pp. 143–68.

Herbst, Jeffrey. 1991. "Exchange Rate Reform in Ghana: Strategy and Tactics." Robert S. McNamara Program Tenth Anniversary Publication. Economic Development Institute, World Bank, Washington, D.C.

Krueger, Anne. 1974. "The Political-Economy of the Rent-Seeking Society." *American Economic Review* 64:3, pp. 291–303.

Meier, Gerald M., ed. 1991. *Politics and Policy Making in Developing Countries*. San Francisco: ICS Press.

Mosley, Paul, Jane Harrigan, and John Toye, eds. 1991. *Aid and Power: The World Bank and Policy-Based Lending*, 2 vols. London: Routledge.

Önis, Ziya. Forthcoming. "Redemocratization and Economic Liberalization in Turkey: The Limits of State Autonomy." *Studies in Comparative International Development*.

Panagariya, Arvind, and Dani Rodrik. 1991. "Political Economy Arguments for a Uniform Tariff." NBER Working Paper 3661. National Bureau of Economic Research, Cambridge, Mass.

Papageorgiou, Demetris, Armeane Choksi, and Michael Michaely. 1990. *Liberalizing Foreign Trade: Lessons of Experience in the Developing World*. Cambridge, Mass.: Basil Blackwell.

Persson, Torsten, and Guido Tabellini. 1991. "Is Inequality Harmful to Growth?" NBER Working Paper. National Bureau of Economic Research, Cambridge, Mass.

Rodrik, Dani. 1989a. "Credibility of Trade Reform: A Policy Maker's Guide." *World Economy* 12:1 (March), pp. 1–16.

———. 1989b. "Promises, Promises: Credible Policy Reform via Signalling." *Economic Journal* 99 (September), pp. 756–72.

———. 1992a. "Conceptual Issues in the Design of Trade Policy for Industrialization." *World Development* 20 (March), pp. 309–20.

———. 1992b. "The Limits of Trade Policy Reform in LDCs." *Journal of Economic Perspectives* 6 (winter), pp. 87–105.

———. 1992c. "Political Economy and Development Policy." *European Economic Review* 36 (January), pp. 329–36.

Stolper, Wolfgang, and Paul Samuelson. 1941. "Protection and Real Wages." *Review of Economic Studies* 9, pp. 58–73.

United Nations Conference on Trade and Development. 1991. *Trade and Development Report*. Geneva, Switzerland.

Whalley, John. 1989. "Recent Trade Liberalization in the Developing World: What Is Behind It, and Where Is It Headed?" NBER Working Paper 3057. National Bureau of Economic Research, Cambridge, Mass.

Williamson, John. 1990. *The Progress of Policy Reform in Latin America*. Policy Analyses in International Economics 28. Washington, D.C.: Institute for International Economics.

World Bank. 1989. *Strengthening Trade Policy Reform*, vol. 2. Washington, D.C.

Spain: Dual Transition Implemented
by Two Parties

NANCY BERMEO WITH JOSÉ GARCÍA-DURÁN

SCHOLARS AND POLICYMAKERS OFTEN CITE POST-FRANCO SPAIN AS A MODEL of successful structural adjustment. Although the success of Spain's program was marred by the worst unemployment in Western Europe, its achievements in other realms were extraordinary. That these achievements took place in a nation struggling to establish a democracy makes the Spanish case especially interesting as a model for other states undergoing similar economic and political transitions today. Structural adjustment in Spain was gradual, spanning at least three decades. It took place under dictatorship and democracy and under socialist and centrist governments. This variation makes the Spanish case especially useful for examining the political variables affecting program success.

In keeping with the gradual nature of Spain's structural adjustment, this chapter covers events taking place in three contiguous historical periods. The first part focuses on the first years of Spain's transition to democracy, and the second focuses on the economic policies of the first freely elected post-Franco government (that of the Center Democratic Union, or UCD), which ruled Spain from July 1977 until December 1982. The final part concentrates on the structural adjustment program carried

The authors thank the World Bank for funding and Lisa Arone and Omar Encarnación for valuable research assistance.

89

out by the Socialist Workers' Party of Spain (PSOE) in its first term in office, from 1982 to 1986.

Although many secondary sources portray the UCD program as a failure and the PSOE program as a success, this chapter shows that the parties actually implemented two phases of same program. It examines the political factors behind both the achievements and the limitations of each government's adjustment initiatives and explains why, despite similar goals, economic liberalization took one form under the centrist UCD and another under the center-left PSOE.

Three major features distinguish the governments of the two parties. First, the UCD was elected at the beginning of the transition to democracy, while the PSOE came to power after the transition period had ended. The ongoing process of democratization was a mixed blessing for the UCD. On the one hand, the pressures and concessions intrinsic to democratization delayed certain aspects of the economic reform program. On the other hand, the UCD's ability to trade in political as well as material goods enabled it to purchase enough restraint to push key reforms forward. The democratization process helped the UCD's reform program because it gave the reformers more to trade and more credibility, but it also limited the arenas in which the reforms could take place. No policies that might threaten the stability of the newly emerging democracy could be implemented. The political risks of economic reform had decreased by the time the PSOE came to power, which enabled it to build on the progress made by the UCD and to deepen the structural adjustment process.

A second feature distinguishing the two periods is that the UCD ruled as a minority government, commanding only 47 percent of parliamentary seats, compared with the PSOE's impressive 58 percent. The UCD's electoral and organizational weaknesses hampered not only the approval of supporting legislation but also the bureaucratic solidarity that implementation required. Constant ministerial infighting and turnover gave the UCD an image of indecisiveness, which led the public both to underestimate the party's achievements and to punish the party at the polls. Both the passage and the implementation of structural adjustment legislation are greatly dependent on party strength and solidarity.

The third factor distinguishing these cases is that the parties had different relationships with organized labor. The UCD was a new, center-right party with no institutional ties to Spanish trade unions. The PSOE, on the other hand, was a center-left party that had existed for generations and had strong ties to what became the largest federation of trade unions in the nation. These differences produced an ironic outcome when the parties tried to move forward with structural adjustment. The PSOE was able to move more decisively and extract more concessions from labor precisely because it had more credibility with trade unions. The UCD had to compromise the pace and scope of its economic reforms because it was neither trusted enough to extract as many concessions from labor nor secure enough to impose more forceful solutions.

Spain's Transition to Democracy

Spain's transition to democracy was orchestrated from above by civilian elites within the dictatorial regime. After Francisco Franco died in November 1975, his designated successor, Juan Carlos, became king and chief executive. Franco stated that with Juan Carlos on the throne, the future of the regime was *bien atado*, or well secured; but, like a package that was tied too tightly, the old regime soon changed shape and burst apart.

King Juan Carlos was committed to constitutional monarchy rather than dictatorship and soon took steps to dismantle the old order. On July 3, 1976, he named Adolfo Suárez to be president of the government and thereby initiated a political process that changed Spanish history forever. Suárez was not an obvious choice to lead the democratic transition. He had spent his entire professional life within the ranks of Franco's bureaucracy and eventually became the head of Franco's political organization, the National Movement. Although Suárez represented a new generation that had not fought in the civil war, he was not trusted by the opposition. Indeed, many prodemocracy leaders characterized his appointment as "a formidable mistake" (Carr and Fusi 1981, p. 217).

Despite an inauspicious start, Suárez moved rapidly to reform the political system. By the end of March 1977—only eight months after gaining office—Suárez had already laid most of the foundation for a liberal democracy: recognizing the right to strike, legalizing all political parties, proclaiming a major political amnesty, gaining legislative approval of a new electoral law, and legalizing free trade union federations. In April 1977, he disbanded the National Movement and legalized the Spanish Communist Party. The first free elections since the civil war were held on June 15, 1977. Suárez himself emerged triumphant with 34 percent of the vote and leadership of the newly created UCD.

Suárez was elected during an economic crisis. As the 1977 balloting took place, gross fixed capital formation was declining for the second year in a row (OECD 1977, p. 6). Inflation was rising to 20 percent despite declining inflation in the countries of the Organization for Economic Cooperation and Development (OECD) and despite weak domestic demand. Unemployment was rising sharply as well, reaching levels that had not been seen in decades (OECD 1977, p. 11).[1] The current account of the balance of payments was deteriorating rapidly with a deficit that jumped from 3.5 to 5.1 percent of the gross domestic product (GDP) in a single year, and most of the gap was being financed through commercial borrowing, raising external indebtedness to $11 billion (OECD 1977, p. 15).[2] A 1977 OECD report on Spain found it necessary "to stress the importance of the disequilibria that characterized the Spanish economy" (OECD 1977, p. 32). Yet, the UCD's attempts to right these disequilibria were constrained by both the nature of Spain's evolving political institutions and pressures from civil society.

Economic Policymaking under the UCD

The UCD's economic program was designed by the well-known economist Enrique Fuentes Quintana, who had been a junior member of the team that launched the nation's first stabilization program in 1959. The 1959 program had been greatly influenced by advisers from international lending agencies (Muns 1986, pp. 31–37), as was the UCD's program. The 1962 World Bank report on Spain had become a national best-seller shortly after its release and was the bible for Spain's economic reformers throughout the 1960s. Its arguments for liberalizing and restructuring the Spanish economy were already widely accepted among Spanish economists by the time the UCD came to power. The growing consensus on a neoliberal solution to the nation's economic problems was reinforced by advisers from the International Monetary Fund (IMF) and OECD, who offered both private and public endorsements of structural adjustment at key moments before and after negotiation of the Moncloa Pacts (*El País*, November 9 and 16, 1977). Looking at the pacts with "confidence and enthusiasm" (*El País*, December 21, 1977), IMF officials loaned Spain $290.3 million in early 1978 to support its stabilization efforts (*Wall Street Journal*, February 8, 1978). The IMF report on the period from 1977 to 1979 agreed with the "fundamental lines" of the government's economic policies (*El País*, March 7, 1980, p. 45), but the UCD never sought another IMF loan, seeking instead to lessen the terms of IMF conditionality because the political price for meeting further loan requirements might otherwise be too high (*El País*, October 2, 1980, p. 47).

The party produced a vast array of economic legislation during the sixty-six months it controlled the national government. Its most important structural adjustment initiatives involved external liberalization, fiscal reform, a moderate increase in the flexibility of the labor market, and a reduction in the rate of growth of nominal wages.

The main element of the external liberalization was a 1978 decree allowing foreign banks to operate in Spain. In only four years, the number of foreign banks jumped from four to thirty-four, and their assets rose from 2 to 9 percent of the national total. Finance capital did not oppose the change because legislation limited the new institutions' capacity to expand and forced them to seek credit from Spanish banks. The new banks became good clients of the Spanish interbank market and an effective stimulus for reforming the banking system.

Although the UCD initiated negotiations for membership in the European Community a few months after assuming office, the admission process proved slower than expected due to resistance from the community itself. Trade liberalization was thus limited to minor changes in the tariff regime (de la Dehesa, Ruiz, and Torres 1990, pp. 180–81).

The UCD's fiscal reforms established a new tax on wealth and increased taxes on luxury goods and incomes above a certain level. Property taxes became the responsibility of local governments, and, for the first time in history, the filing of income tax forms became standard practice for all Spaniards. These reforms were not undertaken to compensate for deficit spending (for there was none at the time). They were taken instead as part of a cross-class commitment to building a modern welfare state (Pérez-Díaz 1987a, p. 229).

To reform the labor market, the UCD legalized temporary contracts and reduced the number of steps necessary to dismiss individual workers (Toharia 1988, p. 137). Franco had left Spain with a heavily regulated labor market, which discouraged temporary and part-time employment and allowed employees to be fired only with substantial compensation and state review (Pérez-Díaz 1987a, p. 237). Legislation for increased flexibility in the labor market was seen by business leaders and UCD economists as key to recovering profits and investments. The problem of overstaffing and the need for part-time and temporary workers seemed especially grave as the nation faced membership in the European Community. If rigidities continued, the government feared that local capital would be less competitive and foreign capital would go elsewhere.

The UCD's incomes policy was an important part of the government's anti-inflationary drive, but it was also sought as a sign that trade unions supported the government's more general effort to modernize the economy within a democratic context. UCD officials wisely recognized that controlling wages required a consensual approach and thus brought representatives of the relevant class associations together to try to forge a common position in the late summer of 1977. These attempts failed because class associations were themselves in a process of transition. The owners' association (the Spanish Confederation of Business Organizations, or CEOE), which was still forming, was struggling with problems of unity. Labor was represented by officials of at least four political leanings: communist, socialist, regionalist, and ultra-left. With so many participants struggling to build or solidify support in their own organizations, no one was willing to risk the controversy that compromise would inevitably involve.

After class associations failed to reach an accord, Suárez invited party leaders to forge an agreement instead. They did so in October 1977 in what are now called the Moncloa Pacts. A party-based pact was easier to forge because the ultra-left had no parliamentary representation and was, therefore, excluded from the bargaining process altogether. Most important, party leaders were more moderate and compromising than interest group leaders, just as the social science literature would predict (Huntington 1968, pp. 397–421).

The pacts were best known for their provisions regarding wage restraint, but their scope was, in fact, very broad. The accords incorporated the government's monetary, fiscal, and budgetary policies and promised to define a "new framework for labor relations" that would provide "maximum flexibility" for contracting employment (Fuentes Quintana 1988, p. 41). They included other provisions relevant to structural reform (Confederación Sindical de Comisiones Obreras 1989, p. 42):

- Limitation of state consumption expenditures
- Institution of a more progressive tax system
- Gradual decrease in the rate of increase in the money supply
- Further liberalization of the financial system
- Increase in tax revenue after further tax reform
- Closer monitoring of expenditures in health and social security, public works, and education
- Rationalization of public enterprises through parliamentary control, decentralization, and increased participation of workers and consumers.

Promises to reform public enterprise and restructure industry were added, too (Fuentes Quintana 1988, pp. 40–41).

The UCD's promises of structural reform were only partially fulfilled. In the area of labor flexibility, a 1981 law set limits on the number of workers who could be hired on a temporary basis (Toharia 1988, p. 138). Individual dismissals still had to go through a government agency, and collective dismissals still had to be approved by the Ministry of Labor, even if a preliminary agreement had been reached between workers and management (Toharia 1988, p. 137).

The progress made on industrial restructuring and public sector reform was similarly mixed. During its last eighteen months in office, the UCD managed to pass two industrial reconversion laws (one in June 1981 and another in June 1982), but "insufficiencies in their means and scope" as well as "serious deficiencies in their implementation" limited their impact (Aceña and Comín 1992, pp. 464–65).

Although the UCD's economic policies fell short of its own goals, the overview of results presented in table 4-1 illustrates significant achievements. The overall rate of inflation was reduced from almost 25 percent in 1977 to 14 percent in 1982, the rate of wage inflation was reduced from 30 to 15 percent, and the share of imports plus exports to GDP increased from 30 to 38 percent, marking an opening of the economy. The fiscal reform resulted in an increase in government revenue of a full 5 percent of GDP. Thus, despite the second oil shock, the UCD succeeded in controlling inflation of prices and wages and in modernizing the tax system. The UCD government succeeded partially in restoring growth in GDP, liberalizing trade, and controlling the growth of the money supply (despite some expansion due to the 1982 election). UCD policy was less

Table 4-1. *Economic Indicators in Spain under the UCD, 1977–82*
(percent unless otherwise noted)

Indicator	1977	1978	1979	1980	1981	1982
Inflation rate (consumer price index)	24.5	19.7	15.6	15.6	14.5	14.3
Unemployment rate	5.2	7.0	8.7	11.5	14.3	16.2
Growth in:						
GDP	3.3	1.8	0.2	1.5	0.2	1.2
Money	19.4	19.2	19.6	17.4	16.2	18.3
Nominal hourly wage	30.2	26.2	23.3	18.7	19.0	15.4
Ratio to GDP of:						
Government interest payments	0.0	0.0	0.0	0.7	0.7	0.9
Government borrowing requirement	0.0	0.0	0.0	−2.6	−3.9	−5.6
Government revenue	26.8	27.4	28.8	30.2	31.7	31.9
Exports	14.4	15.2	15.0	15.8	18.1	18.7
Imports	16.5	14.4	14.7	18.1	20.1	20.5
Long-term foreign capital	2.4	1.2	1.6	2.0	2.2	1.0
External debt	−10.7	−8.8	−7.9	−8.9	−10.3	−13.0
Exports plus imports	30.3	28.9	29.0	33.2	37.4	38.4
Current account ratio	−1.6	1.0	0.5	−2.4	−2.6	−2.3
Government borrowing as a share of all bank credit	8.3	9.6	10.8	12.0	14.7	16.9
Balance of payments (billions of pesetas)	−200.1	−264.3	−465.4	−635.1	−873.9	−1,093.3
Nominal exchange rate index	97	103	93	100	116	129
Real exchange rate index	116	111	95	100	112	118

Source: IMF, various years; unpublished data from the Bank of Spain and the WEFA Group, Philadelphia, Pa.

successful in several other areas. The government's expenditures and deficit rose sharply as a percentage of GDP. The government was unable to eliminate most labor market rigidities and made little or no progress on privatization or in restructuring industry. Moreover, stabilization was achieved only at the cost of a significant increase in unemployment from 6 to almost 18 percent. What political factors account for this mixed pattern of policy implementation?

The Constraints on UCD Reforms

The mixed pattern of policy implementation is partially explained by the timing of the UCD's economic reforms. The honeymoon period that might have supported a more sweeping structural adjustment program was delayed because the basic institutions of Spanish democracy were still being formed when the UCD came to power. Structural adjustment programs are often facilitated by a honeymoon effect in the immediate aftermath of democratization, particularly if both business and labor desire an end to dictatorship. The UCD did not enjoy such a honeymoon because the party came to power when the process of democratization was still under way, and when there was still some uncertainty about whether business and labor would give democracy priority over other goals. The nation's new constitution was not even debated in Parliament until nearly a year after the UCD's election. The text was not approved until October 31, 1978, and the national referendum endorsing the constitution was not held until December 6, 1978. All of the government's structural adjustment initiatives were announced before these critical events took place. The design and implementation of the party's economic policies were greatly affected by the desire to forge a democratic constitution and to preserve a nascent democracy in the face of high levels of mobilization and sporadic but serious acts of terrorism. Adolfo Suárez spoke openly of the political constraints on economic policymaking, admitting (in a speech on the Moncloa Pacts in Parliament) that the "coincidence" of the economic crisis and the political transition "limited the room for maneuver" (Suárez 1977, p. 147).

The political values of peak association leaders—especially those of labor—were not well understood as the transition to democracy began, and the UCD leadership was not at all certain that a honeymoon would be granted. Since labor unions had taken the grave risk of engaging in dramatic mobilizations during the dictatorship, the prospects that they would continue to do so in the less restrictive conditions of democracy seemed high indeed. The impression that factions within Spain's labor movement might prove intransigent was reinforced by the UCD's failed attempt to engineer a pact between peak associations in the late summer of 1977.

A larger discussion of relations between the UCD and labor will be presented shortly. The theoretical point to be made here is that in 1977 and 1978, there was some uncertainty about how highly labor would value the purely political rewards associated with democracy. Concrete material rewards might prove more alluring, and mobilization for these rewards might destabilize democracy itself.

The most dynamic sectors of Spanish capital had come to favor democracy years before the collapse of Franco's dictatorship (Carr and Fusi 1981, pp. 77–78; Rojo 1969, p. 178), and entrepreneurs who were oriented toward the European Community (and therefore, democratization) were elected to head the national owners association. These facts enhanced the likelihood that the business community would grant a policy honeymoon to the UCD, but uncertainty remained about the resilience and scope of democratic norms among right-wing forces in general. Would the democratic elements of the business community prevail if mass mobilization and strikes created increased political disorder? No one had enough information to be certain, and rumors of possible right-wing coups abounded (Carr and Fusi 1981, p. 221).

The timing of the UCD's rise to power meant that the party's structural adjustment program would inevitably be compromised. UCD leaders had drawn lessons from the tragic consequences of the nonconsultative policymaking in the second republic (interview with former PSOE minister, Madrid, January 29, 1992; see also Fuentes Quintana 1990). Even more important, party leaders recognized that the economic changes they sought could not be brought about by government actions alone. The preservation of order was key to maintaining democracy and recouping investment, and this meant (among other things) a decrease in the strike rate and in labor mobilization in general. A decrease in inflation was seen as essential too because extremist forces on both ends of the political spectrum might feed on the panic associated with spiraling prices.

In the context of a nascent democracy, neither the rapidly rising strike rate nor the inflationary rise in real wages could be controlled by government decree. Bargaining was essential, particularly because controlling strikes and controlling inflation were potentially antithetical. If the inflationary wage spiral was not suppressed with the consent of labor, the strike rate might continue to rise. The tradeoffs required for bargaining to succeed help explain the modesty of the party's structural adjustment initiatives. The party was unable to enjoy a honeymoon and was obliged to bargain, rather than simply legislate, because its leadership could not risk toppling a democracy still under construction.

The timing of the economic reform program was not the only factor shaping its implementation and scope. Constraints imposed by Spain's state institutions and organized interests were also important. The constitution ratified during the UCD's second year in office enshrined a parliamentary monarchy. The finished document listed some 169 articles and established the king as head of state and commander in chief. He was given the power to appoint the prime minister (who was effectively the head of government) but only after consulting with the party leaders of the Cortes (or Parliament) and only if the Cortes gave a vote of confidence to the candidate chosen.

The king had been such a pivotal figure in the democratization process that the socialists and communists were in a difficult position on the issue of republicanism as the constitution was being designed. Historically, both parties had been opposed to any form of monarchy, but both knew that intransigence on the issue of republicanism might endanger the movement toward democracy itself (Gunther and Higley 1992, p. 45). In the end, both parties limited their opposition to speeches supporting republicanism, and the articles related to the monarch and his powers passed with little opposition (Bonime-Blanc 1987, p. 70; Gunther 1987, p. 44).

In reaction to the centralization of authority under the Franco dictator-

Table 4-2. Results of National Elections in Spain, 1977–86

	1977				1979				1982				1986			
	Votes		Seats		Votes		Seats		Votes		Seats		Votes		Seats	
Party	Number	Percent	Number	Percent	Number	Percent	Number	Percent	Number	Percent	Number	Percent	Number	Percent	Number	Percent
Center-left Socialist Party of Spanish Workers	5,371	28.9	118	33.7	5,477	30.5	121	34.5	10,127	48.4	202	57.7	8,887	44.0	184	52.6
Right-wing Popular Party	1,448	8.0	16	4.6	1,094	6.1	9	2.6	5,479	26.6	106	30.3	5,245	26.0	105	30.0
Centrist Center Democratic Union	6,310	34.0	165	47.1	6,291	35.1	168	48.0	1,495	6.3	12	3.4	0	0.0	0	0.0
Democratic and Social Center	0	0.0	0	0.0	0	0.0	0	0.0	604	2.9	2	0.6	1,863	9.2	19	4.0
Left-wing Spanish Communist Party	1,710	9.2	20	5.7	1,940	10.8	23	6.6	865	4.1	4	1.1	0	0.0	0	0.0
United Left	0	0.0	0	0.0	0	0.0	0	0.0	0	0.0	0	0.0	930	4.6	7	2.0
Popular Socialist Party	817	4.4	6	1.7	0	0.0	0	0.0	0	0.0	0	0.0	0	0.0	0	0.0
Regional	1,232	6.6	25	7.1	1,697	9.3	25	7.1	1,617	9.3	24	6.9	2,033	9.9	35	10.0

Note: Number of votes is in the thousands.

Source: Gunther, Sani, and Shabad 1988, p. 402.

ship, Spain's constitution-makers eschewed presidentialism and designed a system in which the executive depended on a Congress to pass legislation. Two chambers of the Cortes were established. The secondary chamber was the Senate, which had the power to delay but not veto legislation. The most important chamber was the Congress, which was elected by universal suffrage on the basis of proportional representation. The balance of power between Congress and the executive was one of "contained competition" (Bonime-Blanc 1987, p. 80).

The UCD's position within the institutions of the evolving Spanish state was far from ideal, and this factor constrained party policy as much as any other. Weakness in the national legislature was the party's principal problem. Spain's electoral system was based on proportional representation with a 3 percent threshold below which no party could obtain a seat. Seats were allocated by the D'Hondt method, which led, in the Spanish case, "to the overrepresentation of the two largest parties and the underrepresentation of smaller parties."[3] Right-wing and moderate parties were also favored because the less populated, rural and conservative districts of Spain received a disproportionate share of assembly seats (Gunther, Sani, and Shabad 1988, p. 45). Even with these advantages, the UCD lacked a sufficient number of seats to guarantee passage of any of its legislation without compromise. As table 4-2 illustrates, the party never gained a legislative majority in the national assembly.

A strong executive might have overcome the barriers inherent in the legislature, but in Spain's prime ministerial system, the chief executive needed the approval of Parliament. Without controlling the majority of seats in Parliament, both Suárez and his UCD successor, Leopoldo Calvo Sotelo, were constantly forced to bargain with opposition parties.[4] A compromised adjustment program was the inevitable result.

The UCD's economic policymakers freely admit that their government's weak position in the legislature affected economic policy (García-Diez 1991, p. 34). Fiscal policy was especially susceptible to parliamentary pressures. As a key actor in the earlier reforms asserted, "The elections of 1979 left the state's flank open to pressures for public spending" (Fuentes Quintana and Requeijo 1984, p. 28). The negative implications of increased spending might have been mitigated by increased revenue from fiscal reform, but fiscal reform was also constrained by the UCD's weakness in Parliament. Bemoaning the problems of minority government, Fuentes Quintana recalls that debates on tax reforms were so prolonged that key bills were still on the floor when the legislature disbanded for new elections in 1979 (Fuentes Quintana and Requeijo 1984, p. 28). The UCD's initial fiscal reforms were successful but could not be advanced further. Its failure to reduce deficit spending and, thus, to correct a serious problem in its adjustment program were very much affected by the party's weak position in Parliament.

Parliament was not the only state institution that affected the UCD's structural adjustment policies. The state bureaucracy also accounted for slippage in the party's original program. The UCD's problems with the bureaucracy were linked to problems within the party itself. The UCD was a coalition of fourteen small parties centered around a diverse range of notables. At least five factions within the party derived from groups that had at one time sought to be independent entities. Its factional nature meant that the party was plagued with ministerial crises throughout its years in power. The state bureaucracy was one of the few resources that Suárez could use to hold his coalition together, and he made a regular practice of placating various party factions with bureaucratic appointments. This led to large cabinets ranging from nineteen to twenty-three members and to a "fragmentation of governmental policy activity because each ministry followed only the programmatic lines of its individual head" (Huneeus 1985, p. 203).

Ministerial heads changed rapidly throughout the UCD's years in power, and this made a coherent structural adjustment program extremely difficult. The first Suárez cabinet underwent its first change only two months after being formed, and individual ministers changed two more times. The second and third Suárez cabinets were also reshuffled three times, with the second and third shakeups affecting eleven and fourteen ministers, respectively (Bar, Blondel, and Muller-Rommel 1988, p. 105). Calvo Sotelo's government underwent four revisions in twenty-two months. In five years of UCD government, there were four different labor ministers alone.[5] The different and often incongruent policy leanings of the government's many ministers and ministries were regularly reported in the press (*El País*, June 6, 1981), and the public viewed the party's policy as not being cohesive.

The problem of party divisions was exacerbated when Adolfo Suárez resigned as prime minister in January 1981. An unsuccessful military coup ensued when his successor—Calvo Sotelo—was unable to secure the endorsement of Parliament. The coup was a turning point in the consolidation of Spain's democracy, but it had only a temporary effect on party unity. Calvo Sotelo was given an overwhelming parliamentary endorsement after the coup was scotched, but the battles within the party that had hampered economic policymaking in the past soon worsened.

In August 1982, Adolfo Suárez himself left the UCD, and in November of that year, the influential social democrat Fráncisco Fernández-Ordóñez resigned from the party and took eleven other deputies and five senators with him. Faced with an almost total paralysis of policymaking and severe erosion of support, Calvo Sotelo called early elections for October 1982. The UCD suffered a devastating electoral defeat and relinquished the task of structural adjustment to the Socialist Party. Spain's bureaucratic structures were not inevitably a barrier to structural adjustment, but the lack of cohesion of the party itself prevented the UCD from using state institutions to its advantage.

The Role of Labor

The fact that the UCD was a center-right party with no institutional ties to labor greatly inhibited its structural adjustment plans. UCD leaders recognized that "support within the trade union movement was an important base for the implementation of economic policy" (Huneeus 1985, pp. 220–21). Yet, attempts to create a centrist federation failed. Because the nation's largest union federations were linked with the largest left-wing opposition parties, the UCD was put on the policy defensive.

Spain's labor movement had long been opposed to a "transition from above" and had, until the end of 1976 at least, publicly favored a *ruptura,* a transition from below. Suárez had to lobby hard and long to convince the trade unions that his desire to dismantle the old regime was genuine, and although labor's abandonment of the ruptura posture reflected its "recognition of Suárez's desire to negotiate a full democratization" (Fishman 1990, p. 140), the leader of the UCD was still struggling with his image as electoral democracy began. This explains why, throughout his early months in office, Suárez shunned meetings with the official leadership of the CEOE, while meeting on a regular basis with official representatives of labor (interview with CEOE leaders, Madrid, January 31, 1992).

The party sought to respond to labor because Spain's trade unions were one of the strongest groups in civil society. They were not highly organized compared with certain European counterparts, but they were better organized (at that time) than the Spanish employers' associations, and this mattered greatly.

Fuentes Quintana was surely referring to the disruptive capabilities of labor when he argued that the "social ramifications" of the economic crisis made plans based only on economic criteria "impossible or ineffectual" (Fuentes Quintana 1990, p. 39). According to Víctor Pérez-Díaz, the weakness of the new regime and its leadership encouraged the political class "to give in to the demands of those social groups which had more electoral clout, which had greater access to public opinion, and whose capacity for causing public disturbances was greater. Initially, this meant that unions took precedence over employers associations" (Pérez-Díaz 1987a, p. 229).

There can be no doubt that Spain's trade unions (and its working class in general) facilitated the construction of democracy (Fishman 1990, p. 140; also see Zufiaur 1985, p. 202), but labor also made good use of its capacity to cause disturbances as the new democracy began. Spain had higher levels of worker conflict than any other nation in Europe (Zufiaur 1985, p. 203). Thousands of workers were affiliating with the newly legalized trade unions, and twice as many were aligning themselves with the communist Workers Commissions as with the socialist General Union of Workers (CCOO and UGT; Pérez-Díaz 1981, 1987b, p. 234). Support for the right within the trade union movement was minuscule. The num-

ber of workers on strike increased by at least half a million during the
UCD's first year in office, and this was seen to threaten not simply the UCD
as a government but democracy itself (Maravall 1984, p. 27).

Given the political landscape at the time, it is not surprising that the
UCD made many concessions to labor. Many of these were embodied in
the Moncloa Pacts. Although the pacts contained the bases of structural
adjustment policies, they also contained measures to compensate labor
for bearing the burdens that adjustment would inevitably produce:

- An increase in state spending on job creation and unemployment
  insurance
- A 30 percent increase in state investment for employment maintenance
- A disproportionate increase in the size of pension payments for
  those receiving the least
- The progressive extension of unemployment insurance to all the
  unemployed
- Price controls
- Government subsidies for the development of trade unionism.

The UCD's structural adjustment program was clearly based on a series of
publicly acknowledged tradeoffs in which the representatives of labor
promised to moderate their wage demands and strike activity in exchange for a series of concessions. Not surprisingly, Felipe González,
future president under the PSOE, described the pacts as a program "in
which everyone gave something up, and everyone got something in return" (González in a speech before the Cortes, quoted in Aguero 1978, p.
256). Ramón Tamames, then a member of the Spanish Communist Party,
asserted that the pacts "repaid workers for their sacrifices on wage issues," with fiscal reform, increased public spending, and other changes
(Tamames 1986, p. 230).

To say that the UCD made concessions to labor is not to argue that the
party was wholly or consistently responsive to the petitions of the Spanish working class nor that workers were ever won over by the UCD's
concessions. In 1979, the UCD was unable to orchestrate an extension of
the wage policies of the Moncloa agreements, in part because labor
leaders were convinced that the UCD had not complied with many of the
promises it had offered the year before (Palacio Morena 1988, p. 573).
The party took unilateral action instead and fixed wage increases at 13
percent through a decree passed on December 26.

The promulgation of this decree shows that the UCD was capable of
insulating itself from labor demands. But the actions of trade unions in
the aftermath of the decree show that (in 1979 at least) Spain's working
class still commanded some threatening political resources. Well more
than 5.5 million workers went out on strike in 1979, an all-time high for
the transition period. The mobilization was clearly the result of a broad
effort to challenge the government's wage guidelines (Fishman 1990, p.
217), and, as table 4-3 illustrates, the challenge was extensive.

Table 4-3. Characteristics of Strikes Held in Spain, 1970–87

Year	Strikes	Workers affected	Hours of work lost
1970	817	366,146	6,750,900
1971	601	266,453	8,186,500
1972	688	304,725	7,469,400
1973	811	441,042	11,120,200
1974	1,193	625,971	11,180,900
1975	855	556,371	10,355,120
1976	1,568	3,638,952	110,016,240
1977	974	2,317,026	92,522,050
1978	1,356	3,633,004	128,738,478
1979	1,789	5,752,304	171,067,049
1980	1,669	2,461,061	108,625,662
1981	2,582	3,358,214	74,559,793
1982	2,582	1,634,062	57,834,829
1983	2,714	2,997,468	78,372,920
1984	3,091	5,495,477	122,072,450
1985	2,029	4,538,788	64,180,987
1986	2,239	1,793,187	50,795,973
1987	3,194	3,222,700	81,968,568

Source: Unpublished data from the Spanish Confederation of Business Organizations.

The last year in which the party tried to control wages outside a consultative framework was 1979. The December decree was followed by a series of accords that continued trading wage (and strike) controls for other nonwage benefits. As the chronology of the accords and summary of their main wage and nonwage provisions presented in table 4-4 suggest, the interactions between labor and the UCD were extremely complex. Much policy activity took place outside these accords, and the scope of this chapter permits only an overview of what occurred in either setting. The UCD was certainly not consistently responsive to labor demands, but with approximately 35 percent of the work force unionized and the capacity to bring more than 5.5 million workers out on strike, Spain's labor movement was not easily ignored.

Labor was not the only nongovernmental protagonist in the pacts, of course. Entrepreneurial associations were important as well. As the next section indicates, however, the UCD leadership never succeeded in winning support from organized business. Entrepreneurs felt that the party took business support for granted or assumed it was not required.

The Role of Business

The most visible representatives of the capitalist elite were highly critical of the UCD throughout its tenure in office. This was ironic because a substantial majority of Spain's businesspeople placed themselves in the center of the ideological spectrum, where the UCD itself was fixed (de la Sierra, Caballero, and Pérez Escanilla 1981, pp. 54–56). The nature of

Table 4-4. Characteristics of Social Accords Negotiated in Spain,
1977–86

Pact	Duration	Focus	Signatories	Wage band (percent)
Negotiated during the UCD governments				
Moncloa Pacts	1978	Political and economic reforms	Parliamentary parties	20–22
Interconfederal Framework	1980–81	Labor relations	CEOE, General Union of Workers	13–16
National Employment Agreement	1982	Employment creation	Government, CEOE, General Union of Workers, Workers Commissions	9–11
Negotiated during the first PSOE government				
Interconfederal Accord	1983	Labor relations	CEOE, General Union of Workers, Workers Commissions	9.5–12.5
Economic and Social Agreement	1985–86	Economic reforms	Government, CEOE, General Union of Workers	5.5–7.5

Source: El País, 1978–86; Confederación Sindical de Comisiones Obreras 1989.

the party's relationship with labor explains part of this irony, but the UCD's relationship with business requires a more elaborate discussion.

Spain's most important entrepreneurial association is the CEOE, the Spanish Confederation of Business Organizations, which was founded on June 29, 1977, as an amalgam of three other entrepreneurial groups: the Independent Business Association, the Spanish Business Confederation, and the General Business Confederation (Folgado Blanco 1989). These groups (like the parties that made up the UCD) were diverse in their histories, but they eventually found a compromise candidate—Carlos Ferrer—to be president of the organization. Ferrer, who had headed the Fomento de Trabajo in Barcelona, quickly became an opinion leader within the association as a whole (Díaz-Varela and Guindal 1990, p. 60). Within a few years of its founding, the CEOE attracted a broad range of the nation's businesses, totaling 80 percent of all industrial employment (Roca 1987, p. 250). Its political character was not well understood when the UCD came to power. No one knew if the organization could deliver votes or not.

Ferrer was a centrist within the entrepreneurial elite. This seemed to bode well for the organization's future relations with the centrist ruling party, but important policy differences plagued the potential alliance from the start. Many of the policy differences emerged because the UCD had strong social democratic elements in its program in its early years. The party statutes asserted that "economic policy should correct the market and guarantee a public sector that serves to provide a much more equal division of income, wealth, and social power" (UCD 1979, p. 157).

This image of an interventionist, redistributive state stood alongside calls for economic liberalization. The UCD's vice president for economic affairs explained that the first democratic government sought an economic policy that was "both more liberal *and* more social democratic." A sincere desire to reduce the role of an interventionist state stood side by side with a commitment to create a modern European-style welfare state (García-Diez 1991, p. 36). Given the political pressures emanating from trade unions, it is not surprising that the desire to create a welfare state was more easily realized. As a result, the CEOE criticized the UCD's policies under Adolfo Suárez as "excessively interventionist" (Huneeus 1985, p. 368).

Complaints about interventionism might have been fewer if the business community had felt that it had more say in the form that interventionism might take, but business organizations protested that their voices were ignored in the policymaking process. Carlos Ferrer was convinced that "the UCD did not take the CEOE into consideration" until it was absolutely forced to (Díaz-Varela and Guindal 1990, p. 159), and a future president of Madrid's Circle of Entrepreneurs believed that the UCD governments had a "certain aversion to businessmen" as a whole (Ysasi-Ysasmendi 1984, p. 19). Social scientists concluded that the UCD governments pushed their policies forward, "paying little attention to the criticisms of the employers' class" (Pérez-Díaz 1987b, p. 135; Huneeus 1985, p. 229), and García-Diez himself pointed out that "during the period of 1977–1982, the government's relations with trade union federations were, in general, *better* than those with organized business" (García-Diez 1991, p. 38, emphasis added).

There were several moments in which relations between the UCD and the CEOE showed signs of improvement. Business expectations rose, for example, in February of 1978 when CEOE leader Augustín Rodríguez Sahagún was named industry minister and Fernando Abril Martorell took over as vice president for economic affairs. Expectations also rose in 1981 when Leopoldo Calvo Sotelo replaced Adolfo Suárez as prime minister. Calvo Sotelo had been prominent in the business community for many years, and the CEOE believed that Abril gave them better access to Suárez and the policymaking process in general (Díaz-Varela and Guindal 1990, p. 161; Huneeus 1985, p. 368).

Despite these and other changes in personnel, the UCD's economic policies rarely escaped the censure of the nation's business elite. Even the

1979 wage decree met with serious criticism. The largest business association in Catalonia argued that the wage guidelines would drive many firms into bankruptcy (*El País,* December 30, 1978). The organization of small and medium firms (CEPYME) condemned the move altogether, and the CEOE argued that the law was based on false figures and "preelectoral vices" (*El País,* December 29, 1978). The decree had set wage increases at 3 percentage points above what the CEOE had sought in bilateral negotiations.

The UCD governments are thought to have grown more conservative over time, but the party's public relationship with the business community changed very little. The last pact of the UCD governments (the National Employment Agreement) was still criticized by employers' groups even though the CEOE was one of its signatories. Although a communist federation leader praised the pact for incorporating "practically all the points that the CCOO and UGT wanted included" (*El País,* June 6, 1981), CEOE leader Arturo Gil insisted that "this is not the accord we wanted . . . the shadow of the elections has compromised the policies" (Gil 1982, pp. 355–56).

The policy differences distancing the business community from the UCD went well beyond debates about wage increases. In the area of trade, the CEOE criticized the UCD for seeking to enter the European Community "at any price" (Calvo Sotelo 1990, p. 166). In the area of labor policy, it insisted that the workers' statutes of 1980 did not "meet the demands of the business class [because] they conserved rigidities relating to individual contracts and collective dismissals" (Iglesias 1990, p. 151). In the area of fiscal policy, it criticized the UCD for elevating tax pressures without considering the policy's long-term effects. The UCD's property and inheritance taxes were "shackles on private initiative" and would discourage saving. The tax reforms as a whole were a strong disincentive to entrepreneurial activity. It is not surprising that Calvo Sotelo described business attitudes toward the UCD as "hostile" (Calvo Sotelo 1990, pp. 167–68).

The uneasy relationship between the business community and the UCD had mixed effects on the party's adjustment program. Better relations might have meant more rapid elimination of rigidities in the labor market, but they might also have meant greater relaxation of the tight credit policies that were pivotal to controlling inflation. Better relations would probably have had little effect on welfare spending because Spain's business community largely supported the welfare state.

In the long term, however, the troubled relationship undercut the recuperation of private investment, one of the primary goals of the adjustment program. The UCD was able to bring down inflation and increase the share of profits in value added, but private investment did not respond (Toharia 1988, p. 128). As UCD leader García-Diez himself recognized, entrepreneurs "felt insecure" and even "betrayed" by the policies of the UCD (García-Diez 1991, p. 38). Despite its progress in meeting several of the business community's most important demands, the party never created the investment climate that domestic capitalists sought.

Although organized business did not play a major role in shaping UCD policy, it did contribute to the frailty of the party's hold on power. Carlos Ferrer abandoned what the press called "his habitually tough criticisms of the UCD" shortly before the 1982 national elections (*Cambio 16,* March 15, 1982), but the attitude of the CEOE was thought to be "one of the fundamental factors" leading to the party's electoral crisis and defeat (Roca 1987, p. 251).

Economic Policymaking under the PSOE: Deepening the Structural Adjustment Process

The socialist electoral victory in October 1982 was a political watershed marking the largest electoral plurality in Spanish history and the first time that any socialist party would rule the nation outside a coalition. The 1982 elections also marked the consolidation of Spain's new democracy for they showed that yesterday's losers could be today's winners, even if the party in question was socialist.

The PSOE Reforms

The PSOE had used the period between the 1981 coup and the 1982 elections to strengthen its electoral appeal. Its Twenty-ninth Congress of October 1981 furnished an ideal setting in which to display the unity and decisiveness that the UCD lacked. The Spaniards who turned away from the UCD and voted socialist in 1982 did so not because their ideology had shifted to the left, but because they had been alienated by the infighting and indecision of the UCD (Gunther, Sani, and Shabad 1988, p. 403).

The PSOE presented a more centrist electoral program than in previous years. Although it clearly had Keynesian overtones and marked itself as leftist on foreign policy issues, its economic program did not promote anticapitalist themes. The program promised to create 800,000 new jobs in four years but did not specify the precise role that the state would play in the creation of these jobs or in the economy more generally. The program emphasized modernization and efficiency in preparation for entering the European Community and in this sense differed little from the program of the UCD.

The campaign platform was built around the vague but appealing promise of *cambio,* or "change," but the exact nature of the change in the area of economic policy was not clarified until after the election was won. After entering office, the socialists announced that liberalization of the economy would be accelerated, that they could not create 800,000 new jobs, and that their priorities would be to close the inflation differential with the European Community and to complete the general reforms set out by Fuentes Quintana in 1977. The platform had promised vague general reforms for the sake of modernization, but the postelection programs clearly indicated that these reforms would liberalize the economy.

The design of the PSOE program was largely a reaction to problems that the UCD had either exacerbated or been unable to solve. The inflation differential with Europe stood at 4.6 percent. The real exchange rate was at its 1977 level, and the current account was in deficit for its third consecutive year. There was an urgent need to create a more efficient apparatus for collecting taxes to fund both the payment of interest on debt and the compensation of the many newly unemployed. Liberalization of financial markets had not succeeded in creating a market for the short-term public debt needed for open market operations. The market for government paper was restricted to financial institutions, excluding the general public.

The possibilities of stimulating more private investment (and thus, employment) were limited by at least three factors: rigidities in the labor market remained almost unchanged, employers feared uniformity of wages, and most important, firms were still trying to reduce indebtedness, the costs of which were constantly increasing. To add to these difficulties, negotiations with the European Economic Community had proceeded slowly, so markets and competition remained uncertain.

The socialists' attempts to improve this situation coincided closely with the policies recommended by the IMF team that had visited Spain in December of 1981. The team had praised many of the UCD's achievements but recommended a stepped up liberalization of the economy, including devaluation, financial liberalization, budget cuts, export promotion, industrial reconversion, and social security reform (*El País,* December 27, 1981, p. 37). Felipe González cleverly rationalized the coincidence between the PSOE's plans and the IMF's proposals as an attempt to do what was necessary immediately and independently in order to avoid an imposed program later. Austerity became more palatable when symbolically linked to national sovereignty.

The government's most important monetary reforms included an initial 8 percent devaluation of the peseta, with a 22 percent devaluation for the whole year. Reserve requirements of the banks were increased 1 percentage point, and the rate of increase in the quantity of money was reduced 3 percentage points.

The socialists' most important fiscal reform was the attempt to cut state spending through an austerity budget announced in April 1983. As table 4-5 indicates, few budget categories escaped cutbacks in their share of total spending. Government spending increased in all four years of the PSOE's first administration, but this was due to nondiscretionary budget lines, such as interest on the public debt.

The PSOE tried to control regional spending by curtailing some of the independent fiscal power of regional governments, but this was declared

Table 4-5. Budget Expenditures in Spain, 1982 and 1983

	1982		1983	
Allocation	Percentage of central government expenditure	Percentage of GDP	Percentage of central government expenditure	Percentage of GDP
Public debt	1.96	0.36	7.54	1.44
President's office	1.48	0.27	1.43	0.27
Foreign affairs	0.53	0.10	0.45	0.09
Justice	1.43	0.26	1.52	0.29
Education and science	11.49	2.13	9.91	1.89
Labor	24.42	4.52	2.25	0.43
Industry and energy	5.22	0.97	3.78	0.72
Agriculture	3.81	0.70	3.78	0.72
Defense	10.17	1.88	10.74	2.05
Interior	4.85	0.90	4.46	0.85
Public works	5.45	1.01	4.15	0.79
Economy	0.35	0.06	0.08	0.01
Transportation and communications	6.65	1.23	7.33	1.40
Health and social security[a]	1.29	0.24	0.88	0.17
Culture	0.83	0.15	0.74	0.14
Treasury	1.22	0.23	1.58	0.30
Regions	6.49	1.20	10.11	1.93
Interregional compensation funds	3.70	0.68	3.98	0.76
Industrial reconversion	0.46	0.09	17.35	3.31
Other	8.2	1.51	7.94	1.50

Note: Total expenditures were ptas3,621,023.5 million in 1982 and ptas4,244,936.8 million in 1983; GDP was ptas19,567.3 billion in 1982 and ptas22,234.7 billion in 1983.

a. In the initial 1983 budget, social security, unemployment, and other compensatory programs were given a separate budget line valued at ptas749,579.0 million. This budget line disappears in the actual government expenditures tables but suggests that the socialists were willing to increase spending for social security.

Source: Unpublished figures from the Bank of Spain; IMF, various years.

unconstitutional. Other more successful initiatives to control state spending included limitations on salaries in the public sector, an income tax hike of 20 percent (announced in September 1983), and improvement in the system for collecting taxes. Social security costs were to be controlled by a massive plan to reform pensions. The PSOE's pension reform legislation (passed in 1985) involved substantial cuts in benefits and saved approximately $600 million.

The PSOE's trade liberalization policy focused on Spain's entry into the European Economic Community, which was set in June 1984. The changes involved in the Treaty of Adhesion included a 10 percent annual reduction of tariffs and abolition of the border adjustment tax (López-Claros 1988, pp. 27–28).

The revision of the foreign investment regulations in 1985 further liberalized the capital flow between Spain, the European Community, and the rest of the world, which resulted in a 43 percent increase in direct foreign investment in the following year. By 1992, under the Treaty of Accession, Spanish tariffs on industrial exports from European Community countries were to be completely phased out, and tariffs on imports from countries outside the European Community were likewise to be reduced to levels consistent with those of the European Community Common External Tariff. All nontariff trade barriers with the European Community were to be eliminated by 1990.

The PSOE was like the UCD in that both parties were interested in using incomes policy as a means of controlling inflation and promoting investment. The socialists continued to promote wage pacts, but agreements reached between 1983 and 1986 demanded more from the work force than the pacts negotiated previously. Real wage increases came to an end, and the share of wages in gross national product dropped. In February 1983, the Interconfederal Framework Agreement set a wage band of 9.5 to 12.5 percent, with a consumer price index forecast at 11.5 to 12.5 percent. In 1984, there was no accord at all, but the Economic and Social Agreement signed in October of that year set wage increases between 5.5 and 7.5 percent, with rates of inflation predicted to be 7 percent (Domínguez 1990, p. 93; Share 1989, p. 75).

The PSOE made rapid, though controversial, changes in the flexibility of the Spanish labor market. Until the PSOE's first administration, part-time employment in Spain was ten times less frequent than the European Community average, and temporary contracts were rare (López-Claros 1988, p. 26). In 1984, the socialists passed major laws to facilitate hiring workers on a temporary or part-time basis. These special employment contracts were rationalized with the argument that these jobs—whatever their shortcomings—were better than no jobs at all. The percentage of new hires in the category of special employment rose from 28 percent in 1982 to almost 40 percent in 1985.[6]

In addition to promoting alternatives to the permanent full-time labor contract, the PSOE also attempted to lower barriers to dismissing workers. In a highly ambiguous article of the Economic and Social Agreement, the party committed itself to following the labor dismissal policy advocated by the European Community. For the Workers Commissions and the CEOE, this meant a policy of *despido libre,* or free dismissal. The General Union of Workers and the PSOE denied this, but inclusion of the article left the door open to taking rapid steps toward passing free dismissal in the future.

The most difficult part of the PSOE's adjustment program was the implementation of industrial restructuring. This meant the firing of

83,000 Spanish workers—more than one-quarter of the laborers in the targeted steel, shipbuilding, and textile industries. The layoffs were to take place both in private and public firms, but the PSOE was the principal target for blame because it provided the enabling legislation (Wozniak 1991, pp. 12–15).

As a corollary to its restructuring policy, the PSOE promoted the privatization of state industries and the streamlining of the National Institute of Industry (INI), the huge state holding company started by Franco. Losses of the INI were reduced for the first time since 1975, dropping 10 percent between 1983 and 1984 (*El País,* January 20, 1985). Between 1984 and 1986, the PSOE sold off or dissolved more than thirty enterprises including the SEAT car company and the national truck company (see *Cambio 16,* November 3, 1986; Bermeo 1990, p. 3).

The socialists' policies helped prepare the nation for the vast changes associated with entering the European Community and for the economic expansion that took place from 1986 to 1990 (see table 4-6 for an overview of the macroeconomic trends during the PSOE's first term in government).

Table 4-6. Economic Indicators in Spain during the Adjustment Period, 1982–86
(percent unless noted)

Indicator	1982	1983	1984	1985	1986
Inflation rate (consumer price index)	14.3	12.2	11.3	8.7	8.7
Balance of payments (billions of pesetas)	−1,093.3	−1,408.3	−2,113.2	−1,062.6	−1,463.4
Growth in					
GDP	1.2	1.8	1.8	2.3	3.3
Money	18.3	16.4	14.5	14.2	12.3
Nominal hourly wage	15.4	15.2	12.4	9.8	10.5
Ratio to GDP of					
Government revenue	31.9	34.0	33.8	35.0	36.4
Government borrowing requirement	−5.6	−4.8	−5.5	−7.0	−5.7
Government interest payments	0.9	1.3	2.0	3.2	4.1
Exports	18.7	21.2	23.6	23.3	20.0
Imports	20.5	21.8	21.3	21.1	17.8
Long-term foreign capital	1.0	2.0	2.0	−1.5	−1.4
External debt	−13.0	−14.7	−14.8	−11.7	−8.4
Government borrowing as a share of all bank credits	16.9	19.9	18.4	21.1	22.6
Nominal exchange rate index	129	160	170	177	163
Real exchange rate index	118	137	137	137	119

Source: IMF, various years; unpublished data from the Bank of Spain and the WEFA Group, Philadelphia, Pa.

Inflation was reduced 6 percentage points, and the rate of increase in the quantity of money and of hourly wages dropped as well. Government revenue as a percentage of GDP rose 5 points, and the primary deficit was substantially reduced. The current account changed from negative to positive, allowing repayment of part of the foreign debt. Real wages did not decrease but their growth was substantially moderated, and the financial situation of individual firms improved markedly. The low degree of indebtedness and increased savings by firms provided the basis for a substantial increase in private investment in the next five years. New financial markets were created, and entrance into the European Community decreased many market uncertainties. Luck was with the socialists: investment was recuperating throughout the world by 1984.

Despite these many achievements, the socialists failed to accomplish some of their goals. Unemployment increased 6 percentage points, in part because the restructuring drive was successful. The public deficit continued to increase as a share of GDP, in part because of the rising cost of unemployment benefits and in part because of the growth of interest payments. The increase in public deficits led to financial crowding out, which in turn hampered the creation of new jobs in the private sector.

The Constraints on PSOE Reforms

Why was the socialist government able to tackle more reforms than its predecessor? Important changes in Spanish civil society had taken place between 1977 and 1982, and the international economic environment had improved in significant ways. Most important, perhaps, the Socialist Party as an organization was dramatically different from the UCD. It both enjoyed and created a more autonomous position within the institutions of the Spanish state.

THE ROLE OF LABOR. The role of organized labor is especially interesting for one might guess that the long-standing association between the Socialist Party and the Spanish working class would produce policies subject to even more constraints than those of the UCD. This was not the case. It was the Socialist Party, not the UCD, that implemented those aspects of the structural adjustment program that were the least popular with labor. The restructuring of industry, pension reform, and the loosening of the labor market took place largely after the socialist's electoral victory.

Two factors explain this policy outcome. On the one hand, the socialists' links to labor increased the credibility of both their arguments about the need for structural adjustment in general and their promises regarding compensation. On the other hand, changes in the strength and image of the trade union movement enabled the party to insulate itself from labor when compensatory programs were deemed undesirable. An analysis of the party's programs for industrial reconversion and pension reform illustrates these points.

Industrial reconversion posed a serious challenge to the Socialist Party's image with the working class. The localized resistance to restructuring—including strikes, sequestrations, and even a kidnapping—"caused constant embarrassment for the PSOE" (Share 1989, p. 75). Resistance reflected a clear drop in PSOE popularity in Asturias, Barcelona, Galicia, Madrid, and the Basque Country but did not cause a significant reversal of the party's adjustment policies. The PSOE's response to labor pressure was not to reverse policy but to construct elaborate compensation schemes instead.

Rather than offering its potential opposition an expanded welfare state across the board, the PSOE offered specific compensation to the groups most likely to be adversely affected by the reforms. The party spent ptas820 billion—or 2.5 percent of GDP—on 791 firms by 1986 (*Cambio 16,* July 11, 1983, p. 80). Workers who lost jobs because of reconversion were, under certain conditions, given three years of unemployment subsidy (Economist Intelligence Unit 1992, p. 8). Workers who lost their jobs after the age of fifty-five were given benefits indefinitely (López-Claros 1988, p. 18). The regions in which the restructuring took place were named zones of reindustrialization, and their new and old enterprises were given tax deductions, investment subsidies, and other assistance to expand employment. Nationally, job training and educational programs were expanded to target first-time job seekers—the largest single social group within the unemployed (interview with José María Maravall, former education minister, Madrid, January 1992). Table 4-7 indicates the growth of compensatory programs under the PSOE.

Although party leaders were convinced that stronger compensation programs decreased resistance to the structural adjustment program, there were limits to what the government could spend. The PSOE was, like its predecessor, willing to trade state resources for labor's toleration, but since deepening the structural adjustment program required greater

Table 4-7. Growth of Compensatory Programs under the PSOE in Spain, 1983–89

Year	Percentage of unemployed receiving benefits	Unemployment benefits (pesetas)	Benefits for other programs (pesetas)	Percentage change
1983	—	564,349.3	658,470.7	n.a.
1984	36.9	621,480.3	729,275.8	10.8
1985	41.0	830,446.7	911,014.4	24.9
1986	41.5	951,960.9	1,043,749.5	14.6
1987	42.8	1,026,308.0	1,150,971.3	10.3
1988	44.5	1,146,842.4	1,273,698.8	10.7
1989	52.0	1,314,843.0	1,458,396.5	14.5

— Not available.
n.a. Not applicable.
Source: Instituto Nacional de Empleo, presented in Espina 1990, pp. 456, 470–71.

Table 4-8. Distribution of Delegates Elected in Trade Union Elections in Spain, by Federation, 1978–86

Federation	1978		1979		1982		1986	
	Number	Percent	Number	Percent	Number	Percent	Number	Percent
General Union of Workers (socialist federation)	41,897	21.7	48,194	29.3	51,672	36.7	66,411	40.9
Workers Commissions (communist federation)	66,540	34.5	50,817	30.9	47,016	33.4	56,065	34.5
Union of Workers' Trade Unions	7,474	3.9	14,296	8.7	6,527	4.6	6,152	3.8
Nationalist	1,931[a]	1.0	5,696[b]	3.5	6,293[b]	4.5	7,506[c]	4.6
Not affiliated	75,270	38.9	45,614	27.6	29,262	20.8	26,164	16.1

a. Solidarity of Basque Workers only.
b. Solidarity of Basque Workers and National Trade Union Confederation of Galacian Workers.
c. Includes all subnational federations.
Source: Comisión Ejecutiva Confederal 1987, p. 28.

sacrifice, the costs of mitigating conflict rose, increasing deficit spending. Structural adjustment was thus advanced in the areas of industrial restructuring and privatization, but the compensatory schemes that made restructuring tolerable undercut attempts to control government spending.

The PSOE's pension reform law attempted to set those limits as a decisive blow in the battle against the deficit (Boyer Salvador 1985, p. 436). The party moved ahead with a bold reform program that

- Increased the number of years needed to work to qualify for a pension
- Reduced payments through a change in the formula for calculating payments
- Cut the rate of growth of disability pensions 6 percentage points.

This aspect of the government's program had no compensatory components and, as a result, met with more resistance than any other economic policy passed by the first PSOE government (Domínguez 1990, p. 97). The General Union of Workers mounted major demonstrations against the reform and was joined by the Workers Commissions. Unlike the resistance to restructuring, this resistance was not localized. It even led Nicolás Redondo, leader of the General Union of Workers, to give up his PSOE seat in Parliament. Yet, the party did not capitulate, and the pension reform became law. Here, and in the promotion of part-time labor, the party showed a surprising capacity to insulate itself from the pressures of the organized working class.

This capacity derived in part from the changes that Spain's trade union movement had undergone since the early years of the UCD government. Three major changes had decreased labor's ability to constrain policy: a more moderate union federation had gained ascendancy in the labor movement as a whole, levels of unionization had dropped off dramatically, and rising levels of unemployment had decreased the likelihood of successful strikes.

Whereas the UCD faced a trade union movement in which the communist Workers Commissions had the ascendancy, the PSOE faced a movement dominated by its own affiliate: the more moderate General Union of Workers. Table 4-8 illustrates the gradual rise of the federation within Spain's labor movement as a whole.

By the time the PSOE came to power, the General Union of Workers had pulled ahead of the Workers Commissions and controlled almost 37 percent of all delegates. The vote of affiliated and nonaffiliated workers—with an 80 percent turnout—made the victory especially meaningful (Domínguez 1990, p. 88).

The ascendancy of the General Union of Workers within the labor movement was accompanied by a dramatic drop in union affiliation more generally. By 1982, authoritative sources suggested that only 20 percent of the labor force was affiliated with a union, and "most sources inside the labor movement spoke unofficially of a figure of 13 percent or even lower" (Fishman 1990, p. 187). The trade union movement, which had been characterized as "the engine of change and political reform" during the early years of the transition, would be described instead as "notoriously weak" and even "the weakest of any Western democracy" (Iglesias 1990, p. 146; Share 1989, p. 131; Fishman 1990, p. 4).

Working-class support for the General Union of Workers, and the decrease in trade union affiliation more generally, reflected a basically moderate working-class culture, which the heady days of the mid-1970s had obscured. As Víctor Pérez-Díaz (1987b, p. 136) discovered, "The radicalism that many (including a good part of the political class) attributed to the working class in the early years of the transition turned out to be a mirage." Class consciousness was weaker than had been assumed, and the once-feared labor movement turned out to be moderate and self-restrained in many ways (Fishman 1990, p. 2; Share 1989, p. 110). Determining whether the drop in affiliation was the result of a change in opinion or merely the correction of an image that had been distorted at the outset requires more investigation, but it is likely that some, if not much, of working-class moderation came from rapidly rising levels of unemployment. By 1983, more than 2 million Spaniards had joined the ranks of the officially unemployed, and, as table 4-9 indicates, the increase in unemployment did not abate until 1988, two years after the Socialist Party's first term in office.

A wide range of analysts recognized that the fear of unemployment hampered labor's ability to mobilize strike actions (Fishman 1990, pp. 201–03; Iglesias 1990, p. 154). Labor conflicts were limited, by and large, to the public sector and to plants experiencing layoffs or pay suspensions (García de Blas 1985, p. 331). Conflicts were common as restructuring proceeded, but resistance was generally localized (Wozniak 1991, pp. 2–3).

As a result of all these changes, trade unions seemed less threatening— on the national level—than at any other period in the transition. This gave the PSOE a level of maneuverability the UCD lacked.

THE ROLE OF BUSINESS. What role did organized business play in PSOE policymaking? Was the party's insulation from labor the result of a policy alliance with capital instead? Spain's business community had certainly become more confident and better organized by the time the socialists gained power. The organizational weakness that had characterized Spain's business elite in the early years of the transition had dissipated by 1982 (Maravall 1984, p. 26). By the early 1980s, the CEOE was well funded, extensive, and cohesive (Martínez 1984). The defensiveness that had characterized the employers' public positions in earlier years seemed to have diminished as well. Carlos Ferrer asserted publicly that the so-

Table 4-9. Registered Unemployment in Spain, 1978–88

Year	Thousands of persons
1978	818.5
1979	1,037.2
1980	1,277.3
1981	1,566.2
1982	1,872.6
1983	2,207.3
1984	2,475.4
1985	2,642.0
1986	2,758.6
1987	2,924.2
1988	2,858.3
1989	2,550.3

Source: Ministerio de Asuntos Sociales 1990.

cialists needed the business community like people "needed bread" (*Cambio 16,* April 10, 1982, p. 63), and the president of the Circle of Entrepreneurs in Madrid believed that the business class was more outspoken than ever before (Ysasi-Ysasmendi 1984, p. 20). Opinion polls suggested that the Spanish public increasingly saw entrepreneurs as key to providing employment and, thus, to ending Spain's economic crisis (Marzal 1985, p. 82).

There can be little doubt that Felipe González made a special effort to open channels of communication with leaders of the business community (interviews with business leaders, Madrid, January 1992). Just a few weeks after the socialists came to power, Carlos Ferrer announced that there was "better communication with this government than with its predecessors" (Díaz-Varela and Guindal 1990, p. 89). Both Miguel Boyer and González were popular with business leaders (Martínez 1984, p. 88; Pérez-Díaz 1987a, p. 164), and although the CEOE certainly criticized the PSOE on many occasions, the acerbity that characterized its criticisms of the UCD was absent (Pérez-Díaz 1985, p. 16).

The PSOE improved business-government relations, but it would be a mistake to conclude that organized capital had a determinate role in shaping socialist policies. Under the leadership of Miguel Boyer, the PSOE economic team had a clear vision of what it sought to do and moved ahead according to its own plan. Often, though not always, the party's goals corresponded with those of organized capital, but the PSOE's goals emerged more from the convictions of Spanish economists than from the pressure of any class associations. The PSOE showed itself capable of acting against the wishes of organized capital, just as it showed itself capable of acting against the interests of labor. The party was dependent on capital for modernizing the Spanish economy, but when the expressed interests of domestic business contradicted the party's policy blueprint, the PSOE behaved with autonomy. The goal of the PSOE—to attract foreign investment—helps explain this.

The party's credit policies were a source of some controversy and illustrate the sort of autonomy the PSOE exercised (Círculo de Empresarios 1984, p. 306). Bankers complained that they "tightened their belts more under six months of socialist government than during the Franquista and the UCD years combined," and since many believed that finance capital was the most powerful group within the CEOE, this resistance was particularly significant (*Actualidad Económica,* September 8, 1981, p. 14; see also Lancaster 1985; Martínez 1984). Although the party's "nonaccommodating stance" helped decelerate inflation, it contradicted a policy demand that the CEOE had been making since 1978: that high interest rates should not be used as a means to control inflation (López-Claros 1988, p. 6). The government's decision to give public monies to trade unions and its willingness to take employers to court for violating the union-inspired forty-hour workweek are two more examples of government capacity to contradict the expressed desires of organized capital (Iglesias 1990, p. 158).

Pérez-Díaz (1984) has properly characterized the relationship between the PSOE and capital as one of "reciprocal-instrumentalism." Although, overall, PSOE policies were more in line with the demands of capital than with those of labor, business leaders recognized that their constraints on party policymaking were limited. Spain's entrepreneurs felt distanced from both right-wing and left-wing parties (Pérez-Díaz 1987b, p. 141) and lamented that the socialists "listened to the business community only when its opinions matched the policies which the government itself wanted to carry out" (Ysasi-Ysasmendi 1984, p. 20).

An overview of economic policymaking during the first PSOE administration reveals a party capable of acting with some autonomy from each of the nation's class associations. The party succeeded in deepening the structural adjustment program not because any domestic organization pressured it to do so, but because party economists were convinced that they had no alternative. The government decreed that restructuring would take place "whether or not business or labor agreed" (Roca 1987, p. 262). The sources of the PSOE's autonomy derived from the nature of the party itself and from its advantageous position within the institutions of the Spanish state.

The PSOE and the Institutions of the Spanish State

The factor that seems most closely related to the successful deepening of the structural adjustment program is party strength. Party strength has two dimensions: an external one related to electoral popularity and an internal one related to organizational cohesion. The PSOE was strong on both dimensions, which enabled it to take risks that the UCD could not.

The PSOE commanded 57 percent of the seats in the lower house, and this made its legislative tasks much easier. Whereas Suárez and Calvo Sotelo had to cope with opposition both outside and inside their party, González headed an organization with an undisputed leader and a solid public image. Rule changes at the 1979 party congress had greatly reduced the role of minorities in the party (Daley and Wozniak 1992, p. 28), and the organization was controlled by parliamentarians who had defeated critical factions before assuming office. By the time the socialists won the national elections, "the stage was set," as Gillespie (1989, p. 420) puts it, "for a period of party subordination to . . . government."

The parliamentary party was not completely subordinated (as the resignation of Redondo illustrates), and the government's inability to control deficit spending was related in part to its need to placate the left wing of the party with compensatory programs. On the vast majority of policy issues, however, party discipline was maintained. Outsiders, as well as socialist cabinet members, unanimously emphasize the connection between party strength and the successful implementation of structural adjustment (Fernández Ordóñez, Angel, and Servén 1992; Segura 1990, p. 63; Toharia 1988, p. 129; interviews with PSOE cabinet members, Madrid, January 1992).

Another quality that assisted the PSOE in implementing structural adjustment was the weakness of its electoral opposition. The impact of the PSOE's strength might have been diminished if the party had faced another strong organization in the electoral arena, but this was not the case. Whereas the UCD government was justifiably concerned about votes lost to its left and its right, the socialists faced a very different party panorama. The Spanish Communist Party was in a state of crisis and had captured only four legislative seats. The party to the socialist's immediate right—the UCD—had captured only twelve seats, suffering what one analyst called the most disastrous electoral decline "of any ruling party in European history" (Share 1989, p. 101).

The deepening of the structural reform program involved serious electoral risks, but party leaders recognized that their competition was weak and that the risks of lost votes were therefore not overwhelming. The party lost 3 million votes between the elections of 1982 and 1986 but still maintained an absolute majority in the legislature for its second term. An electorally weak and politically divided party (such as the UCD) could never have withstood the loss of votes that a deepened structural adjustment program inevitably involved.

The party's position in the state bureaucracy was a second major factor accounting for its capacity to implement successful structural reforms. The bureaucratic conflicts and changes that gave the UCD reforms an image of fragmentation were almost absent under the PSOE. The first González cabinet was revised only once in four years, and the second (starting in July 1986) underwent no changes at all (Bar, Blondel, and Muller-Rommel 1988, p. 105). Felipe González took no votes in cabinet meetings and made the final cabinet decisions himself (González 1985; Bar, Blondel, and Muller-Rommel 1988, p. 117).

Economic policymaking was concentrated in the hands of Miguel Boyer, who drew three previously separate economics ministries together under his own command and became known as the *superministro*. His personal qualities enabled him to function as a sort of capstone, holding the key components of the political-economic class together (Morán 1990, p. 353). He had been in the party since the early 1960s and had been a friend to González since the latter arrived in Madrid, long before democratization. He was a well-known and well-respected economist who not only influenced the economic thinking of the president himself but had the contacts and experience in private and public industry critical to reconstructing business confidence. His additional work experience in the Bank of Spain had enabled him to gain a good knowledge of the nation's economic bureaucracy. Equally important, he was an influential professor of macroeconomics at the University of Madrid. His early morning classes—taught before he began work at his other posts—were an important training ground for the younger economists who would participate in and reinforce Spain's economic liberalization.[7]

As Boyer maintained control of the top levels of the economic bureaucracy, the party made important changes in other areas. Policy implementation was further facilitated by the insertion of political appointees in intermediate posts in the administrative service, and some thirty administrators (including three men who had been ministers under Franco) were fired from state enterprises (*Cambio 16*, January 17, 1983). The Ministry of Industry, which was pivotal to restructuring industry, was put in the hands of Carlos Solchaga, another proponent of liberalization.

These changes gave the PSOE's economic policy an air of coherence that the UCD's policies never had. Boyer admitted to making a special effort to create a policymaking bureaucracy that "would make incoherence and discrepancies extremely difficult" (Boyer Salvador 1983, p. 39), and business magazines reported that "the only ideas which reign in [the Presidential Palace] are those of economic rationality" (*Dinero*, September 10, 1984, p. 13).

The PSOE's cohesive economic bureaucracy insulated it from trade unionists, if not from business elites. Unionists from the General Union of Workers feared that the economics bureaucracy was instigating entrepreneurs to be even less concessionary than they would normally be, and the press reported that unionists had come to fear secret agreements between PSOE technocrats and the CEOE (Domínguez 1990, p. 92; *El País*, December 1, 1984, p. 43). Direct contact between González and the secretary general of the union was rare (*El País*, January 8, 1984). Not surprisingly, when unions protested pension reforms and helped precipitate Boyer's resignation in 1985, the deepening of structural adjustment continued under the leadership of Boyer's replacement, Carlos Solchaga.

Conclusions

The constraints emanating from domestic institutions reveal much about why and when the implementation of different aspects of Spain's structural adjustment programs proved successful. Yet, why was a structural adjustment program adopted in the first place? The question is most interesting in regard to the PSOE because a party with a large working-class constituency would be expected not to adopt such a position. What made the PSOE willing to take the risks of implementing a more complete structural adjustment program?

The answer to this question has a great deal to do with Spain's long-standing and widely felt desire to gain entrance into the European Community. The consensus on joining the community had been reasonably high at the mass level since at least 1968 (anonymous 1985, p. 293; interviews with PSOE officials, Madrid, January 1992). By 1977, there was a very broad consensus on this goal and on the goal of becoming like other European democracies in a more general sense as well.

The desire of Spaniards of all classes to enter the European Community and compete effectively with other European economies facilitated the sacrifices necessary for structural adjustment. State policymakers almost always rationalized their actions to control inflation, restructure industry, increase the flexibility of labor markets, or tighten fiscal policy with European comparisons.

Their arguments proved convincing because Spanish civil society was also thinking in terms of Europe. The militants in Spanish trade unions had important fraternal links with unions in the states of the European Community, and millions of working-class Spaniards had first-hand knowledge of Europe through immigration. The leadership of the CEOE was solidly behind the idea of Europeanization, too (Pascual 1984, pp. 17–92; Pérez-Díaz 1987b, p. 157; Carlos Ferrer in *El País,* March 9, 1981). Most important perhaps, the European model was well known and well regarded among the Spanish voting public. Decades of tourism, television, and travel had given them a positive (if somewhat distorted) image of their ultimate economic goal.

Spain's economists reinforced the idea that there was "no other choice" by offering no serious policy alternatives (interviews with economists, Madrid and Barcelona, July 1991 and January 1992). There was, of course, debate within the PSOE about the merits of structural adjustment, but almost all trained economists agreed on the need for structural reform. The merits of economic liberalization had been extolled in Spain's macroeconomics classes since at least the time of the first stabilization program in 1959. One of the legacies of that program's success was a fairly homogeneous community of macroeconomic teachings. This homogeneity helps explain why the blueprints for economic policy varied so little from one ruling party to another. Most macroeconomists in most parties had heard the same lectures, read the same books, and adopted the same basic principles.[8] These lessons were reinforced again and again by foreign economists in international lending agencies. The outcome of the PSOE's initiatives seemed less uncertain as a result.

The outcome of the PSOE's initiatives also seemed less risky because Spaniards were familiar with the meaning of structural adjustment by 1982. Prior to the socialists' adoption of a reform program, Spain had undertaken successful structural adjustment in 1959 and then again, to some extent, under the UCD. Most important, structural adjustment was always presented as part of Spain's preparation for the European Community. The agreement to enter the European Community not only made the PSOE's structural adjustment program more palatable, it also stimulated a faster and stronger growth response from business.

A comparison of political constraints on the domestic front explains both the differences and the similarities between the UCD and PSOE initiatives. The UCD made progress in controlling inflation and (before the second oil shock) in improving the balance of trade. The PSOE program continued these corrections and went even further into industrial and pension restructuring, privatization, and labor flexibility. Investment finally began to rise in 1985, just as the socialist's first term in office was coming to an end. The jobs created through new investment were far from sufficient to end double-digit unemployment, and high unemployment and deficit spending remained intractable problems for both the UCD and the PSOE.

Three major factors explain the pattern of policy implementation just described. The strength of the ruling party is the most obvious. Economic reform programs are much more likely to be delayed and compromised if the ruling party lacks a legislative majority. Without internal solidarity and centralized leadership, the party cannot attain the ministerial coordination that a full-fledged adjustment program requires.

The relations between the ruling party and labor seem to be an important explanation for successful structural adjustment as well. Parties with organizational and personal links to the actors most likely to object to the reforms occupy the best position to strike the bargains that a deepened reform process requires.

A third explanation for successful structural reform concerns timing and political distance from the uncertainties of the transition to democracy itself. The UCD did not enjoy a policy honeymoon because it was burdened with engineering the transition to democracy and with constructing a new party. Structural adjustment threatened both these goals for the UCD. The risks of structural adjustment had, however, diminished a great deal by the time the PSOE came to power. The economic risks of deepening the adjustment program seemed lower for at least three reasons. Economists seemed to have reached a consensus on what needed to be done. The proximity of "Europe 1992" made the changes seem unavoidable. And, finally, the risks of more gradual initiatives had been amply demonstrated by the problems of the previous administration.

By 1982, the ruling party's political risks had altered along with the international economy. King Juan Carlos had shown himself to be not only a powerful symbol of national unity but also a staunch defender of democracy. The implications of policy-related strikes and demonstrations were less grave because Spain's democracy was basically consolidated. The costs of lost votes were diminished because the parties to the PSOE's left and right posed no credible electoral threat. Most important, the Spanish public (including the working class) had shown itself to be moderate in ideology and willing to make short-term sacrifices for the long-term benefits of membership in the European Community.

This brings the discussion to the major international factor explaining the differences in the UCD and PSOE policies. Membership in the European Community provided an appealing political rationale for structural adjustment. Once the terms were secured, membership provided new incentives for growth and better access to foreign borrowing. Since the terms of membership were not finalized until the PSOE came to power, the beneficial effects of membership on structural adjustment were delayed.

What was the role of democratic institutions in general in the process? Democratic institutions raised the costs of structural adjustment, in a sense, because electoral considerations forced both the UCD and the PSOE to use state resources to compensate potential voters for short-term material losses. This is one of the reasons why neither party was able to eliminate deficit spending. Overall, though, democratic institutions helped the process of structural adjustment in Spain. Despite difficulties, the creation of democratic institutions assisted Spain's adjustment process because it gave greater credibility to the reformers and the reforms. This comparison of structural adjustment under centrist and socialist parties in Spain shows that the adjustment process actually became easier as political democracy was consolidated.

Notes

1. The actual level at the time was only 5.1 percent—a figure leaders in the developing world would probably envy—but in the context of Spain, this seemed both high and ominous.

2. All dollar amounts are U.S. dollars. A billion is 1,000 million.

3. The D'Hondt method, also known as the "highest average" method, determines seat allocation by dividing the total number of votes received by a party by the number of seats already designated to the party plus one. In the first round of counting, when no seats have been assigned, the first seat is awarded to the party with the most votes (the denominator equals 1, since 0 + 1 = 1). To allocate the second seat, the denominator remains 1 for all parties save the largest party, which because it already has a seat now has a denominator of 2. Distribution continues until all seats are distributed. This system tends to favor the most popular parties and to penalize "small parties in the extreme" unless party strength is distributed across many parties or there are many seats to be determined for each district (thus requiring many rounds of allocation, which benefits the smaller parties). The overwhelming predominance of the UCD and PSOE (alternately the first and second party in forty-six of the fifty districts) and the small number of seats in each district (only six provinces have ten or more seats) guaranteed the overrepresentation of the two largest parties. See Gunther, Sani, and Shabad 1988, pp. 47–50.

4. Calvo Sotelo was the UCD leader who became Spain's prime minister in January 1981 after Suárez resigned.

5. The UCD's labor ministers were Manuel Jiménez de Parga, Rafael Calvo Ortega, Salvador Sánchez Terán, and Félix Pérez Miyares.

6. In 1978, only 11 percent of all hires were of this type (see Fina, Meixide, and Toharia 1989, p. 123). The Workers Commissions claimed that the PSOE had created a "paradise for temporary work" and that by 1986 only 9 percent of all new contracts were permanent (see Gutiérrez 1990, p. 114). By 1990, the percentage of salaried workers with temporary contracts again fell to 30 percent. This caused an increase in the need for unemployment benefits (see Segura and others 1991, p. 71).

7. Just a few days after his election, González dined privately with CEOE leaders Carlos Ferrer, José María Cuevas, and Carlos Pérez de Bricio to discuss PSOE economic policy and to announce that Miguel Boyer would be economics, finance, and commerce minister. Boyer, who was well known and well respected in the business community, attended the dinner along with Alfonso Guerra (see Díaz-Varela and Guindal 1990, p. 219).

8. The Centro de Investigaciones Sociológicas conducted research in 1968 suggesting that 74 percent of the adult population supported entry.

References

Aceña, Pablo Martín, and Francisco Comín. 1992. INI 50 años de industrialización en España. Madrid: Espasa Calpe.

Actualidad Económica. 1981. September 8.

Aguero, Felipe. 1978. Felipe González: Socialismo es libertad. Barcelona: Galba.

Anonymous. 1985. "La opinión pública española ante la CEE, 1968–1985." Revista Española de Investigaciones Sociológicas 29 (January-March), pp. 289–396.

Bar, Antonio, Jean Blondel, and Ferdinand Muller-Rommel. 1988. Cabinets in Western Europe. London: St. Martin's Press.

Bermeo, Nancy. 1990. "The Politics of Public Enterprise in Portugal, Spain, and Greece." In Ezra Suleiman and John Waterbury, eds., The Political Economy of Public Sector Reform and Privatization. Boulder, Colo.: Westview Press.

Bonime-Blanc, Andrea. 1987. Spain's Transition to Democracy: The Politics of Constitution-Making. Boulder, Colo.: Westview Press.

Boyer Salvador, Miguel. 1983. "Interview." Cambio 16, March 1.

———. 1985. "El déficit público: Algunas conclusiones." Papeles de la Economía Española 23, pp. 431–35.

Calvo Sotelo, Leopoldo. 1990. Memoria viva de la transición. Barcelona: Plaza and Janes/Cambio 16.

Cambio 16. Various years, 1982–86.

Carr, Raymond, and Juan Pablo Fusi. 1981. Spain: Dictatorship to Democracy. London: George Allen and Unwin.

Círculo de Empresarios. 1984. "La reconversión industrial: Un posible análisis." Papeles de la Economía Española 21, pp. 291–309.

Comisión Ejecutiva Confederal. 1987. Resultados: Elecciones sindicales '86. Madrid, June.

Confederación Sindical de Comisiones Obreras. 1989. De los pactos de la moncloa al AES. Madrid: Secretaría de Formación y Cultura.

Daley, Anthony, and Lynne Wozniak. 1992. "Anomie or Enemmi: Labor and the

Left in France and Spain in the 1980s." Paper presented at the eighth international conference of Europeanists, Chicago, Ill., March 27–29.

de la Dehesa, Guillermo, José Juan Ruiz, and Angel Torres. 1990. "Liberalizing Foreign Trade: The Experience of Spain." In Demetris Papageorgou, Michael Michaely, and Armeane M. Choksi, eds., *Liberalizing Foreign Trade*. New York: Basil Blackwell.

de la Sierra, Fermín, Juan José Caballero, and J. Pedro Pérez Escanilla. 1981. *Los directores de grandes empresas españolas ante el cambio social*. Madrid: Centro de Investigaciones Sociológicas.

Díaz-Varela, Mar, and Mariano Guindal. 1990. *A la sombra del poder*. Barcelona: Tibidabo.

Dinero. 1984. September 10.

Domínguez, Justo. 1990. "Diez años de relaciones industriales en España." In Angel Zaragoza, ed., *Pactos sociales, sindicatos y patronal en España*. Madrid: Siglo Veintiuno.

Economist Intelligence Unit. 1992. *Country Report Spain*, no. 4. London.

Espina, Alvaro. 1990. *Empleo, democracia, y relaciones industriales en España*. Madrid: Ministerio de Trabajo y Seguridad Social.

Fernández Ordóñez, Miguel Angel, and Luís Servén. 1992. "Economic Reform in Southern Europe: The Spanish Experience." Paper presented at the conference on economic reform: recent experiences in market and socialist economies, El Escorial, Madrid, July 6–8.

Fina, Luís, Alberto Meixide, and Luís Toharia. 1989. "Reregulating the Labor Market amid an Economic and Political Crisis." In Samuel Rosenberg, ed., *The State and the Labor Market*. New York: Plenum Press.

Fishman, Robert. 1990. *Working Class Organization and the Return to Democracy in Spain*. Ithaca, N.Y.: Cornell University Press.

Folgado Blanco, José. 1989. *Concertación social y política presupuestaria*. Madrid: Universidad Autónoma de Madrid.

Fuentes Quintana, Enríque. 1988. "Tres decenios de la economía española en perspectiva." In José Luís García Delgado, ed., *España*, vol. 2, *Economía*. Madrid: Espasa Calpe.

———. 1990. "De los pactos de la moncloa a la constitución (julio 1977–diciembre 1978)." In José Luís García Delgado, ed., *Economía española de la transición y la democracia*. Madrid: Centro de Investigaciones Sociológicas.

Fuentes Quintana, Enríque, and Jaime Requeijo. 1984. "La larga marcha hacia una política económica inevitable." *Papeles de la Economía Española* 21.

García de Blas, Antonio. 1985. "La negociación colectiva en España: Situación y perspectivas." *Papeles de la Economía Española* 22, pp. 329–42.

García-Diez, Juan Antonio. 1991. "La economía de la transición española." *Claves* (December), pp. 32–39.

Gil, Arturo. 1982. "Opiniones sobre el ANE." *Papeles de la Economía Española* 8, pp. 355–60.

Gillespie, Richard. 1989. *The Spanish Socialist Party*. New York, N.Y.: Oxford University Press.

González, Felipe. 1985. "Interview." *El País*, November 17.

Guerra, Antonio. 1978. *Felipe González: Socialismo es libertad*. Barcelona: Galba.

Gunther, Richard. 1987. "Democratization and Party Building: The Role of Party Elites in the Spanish Transition." In Robert P. Clark and Michael H. Haltzel, eds., *Spain in the 1980s*, pp. 35–66. Cambridge, Mass.: Ballinger Publishing Co.

Gunther, Richard, and John Higley, eds. 1992. *Elites and Democratic Consolidation*. Cambridge, Eng.: Cambridge University Press.

Gunther, Richard, Giacomo Sani, and Goldie Shabad. 1988. *Spain after Franco: The Making of a Competitive Party System*. Berkeley: University of California Press.

Gutiérrez, Antonio. 1990. "Concertación social y coyuntura política en España." In Angel Zaragoza, ed., *Pactos sociales, sindicatos y patronal en España*. Madrid: Siglo Veintiuno.

Huneeus, Carlos. 1985. *La Unión de Centro Democrático y la transición a la democracia en España*. Madrid: Centro de Investigaciones Sociológicas.

Huntington, Samuel P. 1968. *Political Order in Changing Societies*. New Haven, Conn.: Yale University Press.

Iglesias, Rodrigo. 1990. "La concertación social desde la perspectiva de las organizaciones empresariales." In Angel Zaragoza, ed., *Pactos sociales, sindicatos y patronal en España*. Madrid: Siglo Veintiuno.

IMF (International Monetary Fund). Various years. *International Financial Statistics Yearbook*. Washington, D.C.

Lancaster, Thomas D. 1985. "Spanish Public Policy and Financial Power." In Thomas Lancaster and Gary Prevost, eds., *Politics and Change in Spain*. New York, N.Y.: Praeger.

López-Claros, Augusto. 1988. *The Search for Efficiency in the Adjustment Process: Spain in the 1980s*. Washington, D.C.: International Monetary Fund.

Maravall, José María. 1984. *La política de la transición*. Madrid: Taurus.

Martínez, Robert Esteban. 1984. "Business Elites in Democratic Spain." Ph.D. diss., Yale University, Department of Politics, New Haven, Conn.

Marzal, Antonio. 1985. "Actitudes empresariales y actitudes de los empresarios." *Papeles de la Economía Española* 22, pp. 62–83.

Ministerio de Asuntos Sociales. 1990. *Boletín estadístico de datos básicos, trimestre 4*. Madrid.

Morán, Fernando. 1990. *España en su sitio*. Barcelona: Plaza and Janes/*Cambio 16*.

Muns, Joaquín. 1986. *Historia de las relaciones entre España y el Fondo Monetario Internacional, 1958–1982*. Madrid: Alianza Editorial/Banco de España.

OECD (Organization for Economic Cooperation and Development). 1977. *Country Report: Spain*. Paris.

El País. Various years, 1977–86.

Palacio Morena, Juan Ignacio. 1988. "Relaciones laborales y tendencias organizativas de los trabajadores y de los empresarios." In José Luís García Delgado, ed., *España Economía*, vol. 2, pp. 561–94. Madrid: Espasa-Calpe.

Pascual, Julio. 1984. *En defensa de la empresa: Alegato en crónica, 1976–1984.* Madrid: Unión Editorial, S.A.

Pérez-Díaz, Víctor. 1981. "Los obreros españolas ante la empresa en 1980." *Papeles de la Economía Española* 7, pp. 282–309.

_____. 1984. "Gobernabilidad y mesogobiernos: Autonomías regionales y neo-corporatismo en España." *Papeles de la Economía Española* 21, pp. 40–76.

_____. 1985. "Los empresarios y la clase política." *Papeles de la Economía Española* 22, pp. 2–37.

_____. 1987a. "Neo-Corporatist Experiments in a New and Precariously Stable State." In Ilja Scholten, ed., *Political Stability and Neo-Corporatism.* London: Sage Publications.

_____. 1987b. *El retorno de la sociedad civil.* Madrid: Instituto de Estudios Económicos.

Roca, Jordi. 1987. "Corporatism in Post-Franco Spain." In Ilja Scholten, ed., *Political Stability and Neo-Corporatism.* London: Sage Publications.

Rojo, Luís Angel. 1969. "Panorama económico." Reprinted in Jacinto Hombravella, ed., *Trece economistas españoles.* Barcelona: Okos-tau, 1975.

Segura, Julio. 1990. "Del primer gobierno a la integración en la CEE: 1983–1985." In José Luís García Delgado, ed., *Economía española de la transición y la democracia.* Madrid: Centro de Investigaciones Sociológicas.

Segura, Julio, F. Durán, Luís Toharia, and S. Bentolila. 1991. "Análisis de la contratacíon temporal en España." Madrid: Ministerio de Trabajo y Seguridad Social.

Share, Donald. 1989. *Dilemmas of Social Democracy: The Spanish Socialist Workers' Party in the 1980s.* New York, N.Y.: Greenwood Press.

Suárez, Adolfo. 1977. "Mensaje sobre la situación económica." *Un Nuevo Horizonte para España,* November 2.

Tamames, Ramón. 1986. *The Spanish Economy.* London: C. Hurst.

Toharia, Luís. 1988. "Partial Fordism: Spain between Political Transition and Economic Crisis." In Robert Boyer, ed., *The Search for Labor Market Flexibility.* New York: Clarendon/Oxford University Press.

UCD (Center Democratic Union). 1979. *La solución a un reto: Tesis para una sociedad democrática occidental.* Madrid: Unión Editorial, S.A.

Wall Street Journal. 1978. February 8.

Wozniak, Lynn. 1991. "Industrial Modernization and Working Class Protest in Socialist Spain." Working Paper 165. University of Notre Dame, Department of Government and International Studies, Notre Dame, Ind.

Ysasi-Ysasmendi, José Joaquín. 1984. "Queremos ser un lobby." *Actualidad Económica,* April 5.

Zufiaur, José María. 1985. "El sindicalismo español en la transicíon y la crisis." *Papeles de la Economía Española* 22, pp. 202–34.

5

Turkey: Democratization and Adjustment from Above

ZIYA ÖNIŞ AND STEVEN B. WEBB

TURKEY IN THE 1980S UNDERTOOK BOTH MAJOR STRUCTURAL REFORMS of its economy and the restoration of democracy. In many respects it succeeded on both fronts, but it completed only part of the agenda for democratization and had some conspicuous failures of economic policy. These were closely linked with the way in which the program became subservient to short-term political concerns. The Turkish experience illustrates how a small group of technocrats outside the traditional bureaucracy, organized under a strong leader, can play a key role in initiating and implementing structural adjustment policies. Turkey's transition to democracy was controlled from above, as the military and the succeeding government gradually broadened the scope for popular participation in politics. This helped to contain distributional pressures and to

The authors benefited from many comments on drafts of this chapter, especially those of Ismail Arslan, Nurcan Akturk, Bülent Gültekin, Deniz Gökçe, Stephan Haggard, Attila Karaosmanoğlu, Sven Kjellstrom, Anne Krueger, William McCleary, Dani Rodrik, İlkay Sunar, Paulo Viera da Cunha, and participants at the May 1992 conference on Voting for Reform: The Political Economy of Structural Adjustment in New Democracies. Any errors that remain are the responsibility of the authors. Bilin Neyapti provided excellent research assistance. Interviews with the following persons were also insightful: Sabri Akdemir, Nurcan Akturk, Jeffrey Bàlkind, Yavuz Canevi, Ömer Dinçkök, Yavuz Ege, Gazi Erçel, Deniz Kirazci, Ercan Kumçu, Mieko Nishimizu, Enver Taçoğlu, Okan Üçer, and various business leaders.

maintain the principal reform measures in the initial years of political liberalization.

Political liberalization from above kept power concentrated in the executive, however, and became a disadvantage during the later stages of the adjustment process, when Turkey faced the challenge of simultaneously sustaining the momentum of reform and extending the scope of democracy. Thus, paradoxically, a concentrated and insulated policymaking process, which helped to initiate and implement reform during the early stages, progressively became a liability for sustaining the program. The top-down political liberalization perpetuated the paternalistic tradition of Turkish government and its lack of strong consultative links with peak associations of interest groups. This undermined the consolidation of both reform and democracy. Because peak associations were weak, the party system bore undue pressure to mobilize political support for the government's economic program.

Political developments affected the prospects for economic reform in diverse ways that are well illustrated by the evolution of trade and macroeconomic policies. Trade reforms succeeded in making the Turkish economy more efficient and much more outward oriented, and the economic success of the reforms engendered political support for them. Output grew steadily, and exports grew spectacularly during the 1980s (see table 5-1). The government and ruling party usually reaped only part of these political benefits, however, and efforts to use trade policy to get explicit voter support led to partial reversals of the program.

In contrast to trade, fiscal policy witnessed frequent, serious reversals. The resulting high inflation, high real interest rates, unstable real exchange rate, and uncertainty about future fiscal policy made economic recovery slower and less stable than it could have been. The ruling party of 1983–91 paid the political price for these failures, although it also reaped some short-term political benefits from the spending and credit policies that underlay the macroeconomic problems.

This chapter starts with a historical overview of the political and economic transformation in Turkey, followed by a section describing the institutions involved formally and informally in making economic policy. These include the constitution, bureaucracy, political parties, and interest groups. The third section looks at how these institutions and the dynamics of the democratization process affected the evolution of trade and macroeconomic policy. The final section draws lessons from the Turkish experience for the political management of policy reform.

Historical Overview

The political developments in Turkey in the 1980s can be usefully broken into four periods: the political crisis up to the time of the military intervention, the military interregnum, the initiation of democracy, and the consolidation of democracy.

Table 5-1. Economic Indicators in Turkey, 1975–90
(percent unless noted)

Turkey	1975	1976	1977	1978	1979	1980	1981	1982	1983	1984	1985	1986	1987	1988	1989	1990
Growth in																
GDP	8.9	8.4	7.5	-2.9	2.1	-0.8	4.4	5.0	3.7	5.7	5.1	8.3	7.4	3.6	1.0	—
Real exports	2.0	21.0	-18.0	14.0	-9.0	4.0	85.0	40.0	14.0	20.0	12.0	-1.0	27.0	20.0	5.0	10.0
Money	—	23.4	33.8	36.5	61.7	74.4	88.2	51.1	29.7	58.7	55.3	43.8	45.6	55.0	72.0	51.4
Inflation (current price index)	—	17.0	27.0	45.0	59.0	110.0	37.0	31.0	31.0	48.0	45.0	35.0	39.0	75.0	70.0	64.0
Ratio to GDP of																
Current account deficit	-4.6	-4.9	-6.6	-2.4	-2.0	-6.0	-3.4	-1.8	-3.8	-2.8	-1.9	-2.5	-1.2	2.3	1.2	-2.4
Exports of goods and services	6.5	7.0	4.9	5.7	4.9	6.6	10.4	14.9	15.7	19.6	20.9	17.6	20.8	24.6	22.5	15.6
Public sector borrowing requirement	—	—	—	—	—	—	-1.1	5.3	1.7	9.7	6.4	4.8	8.0	6.1	7.2	9.5
Ratio to exports of																
Foreign debt service	11.0	11.0	16.0	16.0	21.0	28.0	29.0	29.0	29.0	23.0	32.0	32.0	33.0	35.0	34.0	37.0
Foreign debt[a]	136.0	127.0	192.0	219.0	318.0	403.0	255.0	205.0	200.0	170.0	177.0	239.0	223.0	193.0	193.0	219.0

Real, dollar-weighted exchange rate index	195	194	206	204	231	243	178	143	144	119	100	114	128	137	111	145
Real wages in manufacturing																
Consumer price index deflated	107	112	133	138	142	119	125	118	118	104	100	96	102	97	94	—
Wholesale price index deflated	101	109	126	124	115	107	121	118	118	103	100	100	111	111	110	—
Unemployment rate	—	—	—	—	7.8	9.7	11.6	11.6	11.7	11.8	11.7	10.5	9.5	8.0	8.1	7.7

— Not available.

Note: For indexes, 1985 = 100.

a. Public and publicly guaranteed debt.

Source: IMF data; World Bank staff estimates; United Nations Industrial Development Organization (UNIDO); State Planning Organization; State Institute of Statistics 1991.

Political Crisis

The first period stretches back into the 1970s, when the economic and political systems were experiencing increasing difficulties. The import-substitution strategy of the 1960s and 1970s generated an economy highly dependent on imports and foreign borrowing but with limited capacity to export. The government borrowed imprudently to mitigate the growth-retarding impact of the first oil shock but could not borrow its way out of the second shock in 1979. Foreign lenders had cut off credit to Turkey after a debt crisis in 1977, and by 1979 other foreign exchange inflows were declining, as workers abroad reduced their remittances and exports declined because of exchange rate overvaluation and shortages of imported inputs. The oil shock of 1979, then, resulted in a severe balance of payments crisis that forced the country to curtail imports and produced shortages of essentials.

Political instability increased along with economic instability during the late 1970s. Political violence, already serious, worsened in the course of 1979. A series of coalition governments failed to stabilize the economy, much less to adopt the reforms required to avert a crisis. Turkey had a program with the International Monetary Fund (IMF) in 1978, which was canceled because lack of fundamental reforms made the program go off track. Another IMF program, negotiated in the summer of 1979 by the center-left government of social democrat Bulent Ecevit, was well on its way to a similar fate by the end of the year (Okyar 1983). At the beginning of 1980, Turkey was unable to import the essentials for surviving the winter: oil, coal, and coffee. Many homes and government buildings went without heat in that exceptionally cold winter.

In November 1979, a center-right coalition headed by Suleyman Demirel took over and brought in a new economic team, led by Turgut Özal. To end the crisis, the government introduced a major package of adjustment measures in January 1980. Initially, it mainly addressed the debt crisis and balance of payments problem, but it started the process of reorienting all policy toward a market-based economy. Strikes and political violence continued through the summer, aggravated in part by the economic dislocation originating from the adjustment.

Military Interregnum

The military took over in September 1980, dissolving Parliament, outlawing political parties and radical unions, arresting political leaders—executing some—and suspending many political and human rights. The military kept Özal as head of the economic team. Structural adjustment continued under military leadership, although the Turkish military did not traditionally favor open trade and market-oriented economic policies. The military was divided over Özal's plans to reduce the role of the state in running the economy, but it could not argue with his success in stimulating exports and securing foreign financing.

In June 1982, the Banker's Crisis, in which Turkey's largest money broker and securities house collapsed, led to Özal's resignation and replacement by Adnan Başer Kafaoğlu, a military man with a more traditional etatist orientation. The military had only a vague vision of a mixed economy; it only knew that it did not want communism and did not want any scandal or financial crisis. In the remaining year of military government, policy deteriorated as budget deficits deepened and the exchange rate was increasingly overvalued. This episode illustrates that the military was not the primary force behind the policy reform movement and that it followed policies that would sustain its popularity in the short run.

The military anticipated that it would have five or six years to restore political and macroeconomic stability, but it had even less. In the tradition of previous military interventions, all sides accepted that military rule would be temporary. Once the political violence was stopped, public opinion from all but the extreme right called for a return to democracy. The Europeans and Americans also wanted a return to democracy, and former U.S. Secretary of State Alexander Haig pressed the issue during his visit to Turkey in September of 1983.

Initiating Democracy

In November 1982, a new constitution was adopted by referendum, and a year later the military permitted elections. Strict limits were placed on party participation, and only three parties were allowed to contest the election. The newly formed Motherland Party (ANAP), led by Özal, won the election, defeating the parties endorsed by the military, and took power. The rest of the 1980s witnessed a series of elections that broadened the scope of democratic control and participation. Although economic reform and political liberalization on one front or another continued through the 1980s, there were also important delays and reversals of reform, especially in deficit reduction, bank restructuring, and privatization of state enterprises.

Turkey constitutes a unique case of structural adjustment because of the continuity of its leadership. Turgut Özal reemerged as prime minister following the general elections of November 1983, and the ruling party was centered around the core team that had designed and initiated the structural adjustment program of 1980. A key part of ANAP's political appeal was the success of its economic program. Although the party made appeals in other dimensions as well—distance from the military, more distance from the left, some association with Islamic fundamentalism, and some appeals to Turkish nationalism—it repeatedly campaigned in a referendum on its economic program.

The new government used the political honeymoon, following the resumption of elected government, to pass quickly a second wave of economic reforms focusing on the import regime and the capital account. Soon after, in 1984, came a series of measures to liberalize the foreign investment regime. ANAP's popularity was bolstered by high rates of economic growth in the mid-1980s, which contrasted with the dismal performance of the economy at the peak of the crisis. ANAP could portray itself as the party of the new era, while projecting the reemerging opposition parties as institutions of an old order that had ended in abject failure. In the local elections of 1984, six parties competed, and ANAP received a strong plurality: 40 percent of the vote. The Social Democracy Party followed with only 23 percent.

In 1985, when it was time to name a new chief of staff of the military, the old chief nominated his successor, as was the custom. Özal rejected the nominee, however, and chose someone else. This was significant in two ways. First, it demonstrated an unprecedented degree of civilian control over the military and signaled a much reduced possibility of another military takeover. Second, whereas the original nominee, like his predecessor, was from the branch of the military that favored etatist economic policy, Özal chose a general who accepted the need for an open, market-oriented economy.

Completing Democratization

Although the return to democracy started with the general elections of November 1983, freely competitive politics in Turkey resumed only in 1987. Leading politicians of the pre-1980 period—notably, Demirel and Ecevit—were permitted to contest the general elections of November 1987 after a ten-year ban on their participation in politics, originally imposed by the military, was lifted early by a referendum in September 1987. After that point, Özal increasingly diverted his attention from economic policy toward purely political issues.

The general election in November 1987 proved to be a turning point in the fortunes of both the ANAP government and the structural adjustment process. In spite of a decisive victory, the further opening up of the political system presented ANAP with a novel set of challenges that were largely absent in the preceding era: the public reappearance of key political figures of the pre-1980 order and the reemergence of distributional pressures, particularly involving wages and agricultural subsidies. The problem of macroeconomic instability continued and became more severe.

The popularity of ANAP declined dramatically in the eighteen months following its victory in the general election of 1987. The municipal elections of March 1989 proved to be a turning point, with ANAP emerging as the third party, with a mere 22 percent of the vote. The party never fully recovered. In 1989, Özal was elected to the presidency (by the ANAP-dominated Parliament) and, in accordance with the constitution, resigned from the party. He still tried to run the party and the government unofficially, through his successor Yildirim Akbulut, but his move upward left a leadership vacuum in the ANAP government and allowed infighting between key policymakers. Ozal's election to the presidency undermined the legitimacy of the government; opposition leaders, whose parties had strong support in the most recent elections and polls, claimed that he did not have a mandate to assume the presidency since ANAP had received only 22 percent of the vote in the municipal elections. The problems with internal coordination and domestic legitimacy weakened implementation of the structural adjustment program.

Fiscal instability and chronically high inflation contributed to the loss of popularity of ANAP in the late 1980s. Despite some improvement in its electoral performance compared with 1989, it lost the general election of October 1991. This election returned coalition politics to Turkey and initiated a new era, following eight years of uninterrupted ANAP rule and eleven years during which Özal dominated economic policy. Agriculture and labor were the principal losers in the structural adjustment process, and these two groups determined the outcome of the 1991 election. They were the principal bases of support for the two parties that became the ruling coalition partners after the general election in November 1991: the True Path Party (DYP) and the Social Democratic Populist Party (SHP).

Institutional Structure and Change

Before turning to a detailed chronology of the trade and macro-economic policies in the periods outlined above, this section examines the formal and informal institutions of decisionmaking, which have received relatively little attention in previous studies of Turkish political economy (Arícanlí and Rodrik 1990; Celasun and Rodrik 1989; Keyder 1987; Krueger and Turan 1993; Öniş and Riedel 1993; Waterbury 1992). Although the structural adjustment process in Turkey in the 1980s was closely associated with the personality of Özal, the political and bureaucratic institutions were also important. He often took the initiative in restructuring institutions, and the nature of these changes affected the course of structural adjustment.

Formal and Informal Constitution of Decisionmaking

The transition to democracy involved changes in the constitution, but the meaning of the document depended on the political culture inherited from the past and on how it was interpreted in practice. The following section lays out the features of the political culture and constitution that were most relevant to economic policy.

POLITICAL CULTURE. A strong patrimonial state tradition, which dates back to the Ottoman period, remains a key element of Turkey's political culture (Heper 1985; Mardin 1973). Central to this tradition is the idea of the "father state," an institution that guarantees the livelihood of broad strata of the population. For lower-income groups, a major form of provision involves employment opportunities within the large public sector. For business groups, entrepreneurs, or producers, state provision takes the form of a wide variety of subsidies. For example, the founder and head of Turkey's largest industrial group, Vehbi Koç, credited the success of his firm and others like it, not to the energy and skill of the entrepreneurs, but rather to the support of the state (Koç 1992).

A counterpart to the patrimonial state tradition in Turkey is the weakness of autonomous interest associations and of their links to the state. Politicians and bureaucrats will not enter into institutionalized contact with interest organizations concerning the formation and implementation of policy. The weakness of links with formal interest associations encourages the development of extensive patron-client networks and, under the constraints of parliamentary democracy, leads to attempts to build up popular support through the dispersion of patronage on a large scale.

This tradition affected the structural adjustment process in two ways. First, a highly centralized and insulated state apparatus helped to initiate stabilization and structural adjustment and to maintain the momentum of the process during its early stages. The absence of strong formal links with interest associations or organized groups in civil society proved to be a disadvantage, however, during the later stages of structural adjustment. At that time, the problem became one of consolidating, institutionalizing, and maintaining the momentum of the economic reform process.

The consolidation of democracy itself was also emerging as an overriding objective. Consequently, the strength of the state in being able to dispense patronage did not carry over to—and indeed weakened—its ability to create a growth-oriented market environment. It lacked the political strength to discipline firms and resist rent-seeking pressure. Although the paternalistic political culture continued in Turkey, civil society strengthened somewhat after 1983, and developments such as reduced tolerance for corruption signaled the rise of an alternate, more modern political culture.

ELECTORAL AND CONSTITUTIONAL CHANGES. Constitutional changes in the 1980s restored democracy only in stages and assured that some elements from each previous stage would remain for a time. Compared with the typical European parliamentary system, the Turkish constitution of 1982 granted the president and prime minister more power than other parts of government. At first, General Erven, who had led the military takeover, remained president after 1983, and then in 1989 Parliament elected Özal, head of the ruling party, to be president. Also, the participation of parties and of former politicians was severely circumscribed in 1983, and only beginning in 1987 could a broad spectrum of parties and politicians participate fully in elections and Parliament. Parties based on economic groups, regions, and ethnicity were expressly forbidden.

The electoral system, first used in 1983 and modified just before the elections of 1987, was consciously designed to eliminate minor parties, especially regional ones, and to avoid the instability associated with coalition governments in the late 1970s. The military directly tackled the problem of an excessive number of parties by only allowing three parties (ANAP, the Populist Party, and the National Democracy Party) to contest the 1983 elections. In the 1987 and 1991 general elections, the multiple-member-constituency electoral system with high thresholds was the key indirect instrument that effectively excluded minor parties from representation. A party had to pass both a national threshold of 10 percent and a local threshold that depended on the nature of the electoral district. If a party failed to satisfy the national requirement, it could not return deputies anywhere, regardless of its performance in a particular electoral district. Minor parties were particularly disadvantaged in small electoral districts.[1]

In 1987, the four minor parties received 20 percent of the vote and thus elected no deputies (see table 5-2). Yet, their presence had a significant impact because it shifted the balance away from the two major opposition parties and to the governing party. The electoral system enabled ANAP to receive two-thirds of the seats in Parliament with only 36 percent of the total vote. The weak popular mandate reduced its ability to confront public opinion, but it was still in a better position than if it had headed a minority government.

RULE BY DECREE AND THE ROLE OF PARLIAMENT. The military interlude and the constitution of 1982, which set the terms for returning to democracy, concentrated power at the center. The pattern of a strong executive and a weak Parliament continued after democracy was reestablished in 1983. A central feature of the ANAP governments was a concentrated decisionmaking structure, with the responsibility for key economic decisions being confined to the prime minister, an inner or core cabinet, and a small group of top-level bureaucrats. The dominance of the executive over the Parliament and even over the peripheral cabinet was reflected in the emergence of government decrees as the major instrument for introducing policy changes during the period. These decrees offered flexibility and could introduce decisions rapidly without unnecessary delays or inertia. Yet, the propensity to rely on government decrees rather than on legislation often led to arbitrary decisionmaking. Government decrees frequently changed policy and caused uncertainty on the part of economic agents, leading to shorter investment horizons and reducing the credibility of the adjustment measures.

Table 5-2. Results of Major National and Municipal Elections in Turkey, 1983–91
(percentage of total)

Party	General elections, November 1983		Municipal elections, March 1984 vote	General elections, November 1987		Municipal elections, March 1989 vote	General elections, October 1991	
	Vote	Seats		Vote	Seats		Vote	Seats
Motherland Party (ANAP)	45.0	53.0	40.0	36.0	66.0	22.0	24.0	26.0
Populist Party	31.0	29.0	8.0	n.a.	n.a.	n.a.	n.a.	n.a.
Social Democratic Party	n.a.	n.a.	23.0	n.a.	n.a.	n.a.	n.a.	n.a.
Social Democratic Populist Party (SHP)	n.a.	n.a.	n.a.	25.0	22.0	29.0	21.0	20.0
True Path Party (DYP)	n.a.	n.a.	13.0	19.0	12.0	25.0	27.0	40.0
Democratic Left Party (DSP)	n.a.	n.a.	n.a.	9.0	n.a.	9.0	11.0	2.0
Nationalist Work Party	n.a.	n.a.	n.a.	3.0	n.a.	4.0	n.a.	n.a.
National Democracy Party	23.0	18.0	7.0	n.a.	n.a.	n.a.	n.a.	n.a.
Welfare Party	n.a.	n.a.	4.0	7.0	n.a.	10.0	17.0[a]	14.0[a]
Reformist Democracy Party	n.a.	n.a.	n.a.	0.8	n.a.	0.9	n.a.	n.a.
Socialist Party	n.a.	n.a.	n.a.	n.a.	n.a.	n.a.	0.4	n.a.
Independents	1.0	n.a.	2.0	0.5	n.a.	0.6	0.1	n.a.

n.a. Not applicable; did not participate.
Note: Numbers may not total 100 because of rounding or lack of voter preference.
a. Includes Nationalist Work Party, which joined the Welfare Party in a coalition.

Political Parties

The military outlawed all political parties when it took over in 1980. When democracy returned in 1983, all parties had to have new names, and they could not have explicit links to economic interest groups or regions. To some extent, old wine ended up in bottles very similar to the old ones, except for the labels. A few major realignments occurred, however, and the economic platforms were all substantially different. The structural adjustment experience fundamentally changed the issues of debate on economic policy.

THE RULING PARTY. The base of support for ANAP was predominantly urban and from groups other than unionized workers, as the distribution of votes by provinces during the general elections of 1991 reveals. ANAP's best performance was registered in Istanbul, where the party won thirty-three out of fifty seats (with DYP and SHP gaining a mere five seats each). In Izmir and Ankara, ANAP also did well but by smaller margins. Among the major urban centers, Adana was the only one where ANAP lost, which is not surprising given its agricultural hinterland. The pro-urban character of ANAP is also confirmed by its good record in the comparatively prosperous provinces of the Aegean region in the west.

ANAP started as a coalition, with a liberal wing and a conservative wing (Ergüder 1991b). Religion was important for securing the loyalty of the conservative faction and for holding the basic coalition together. Özal himself was closely associated with the Islamic fundamentalist party (the National Salvation Party) for which he ran for Parliament and lost in 1977, and his older brother was a well-known religious leader. Thus, ANAP had widespread appeal in the 1980s because it represented a mixture of neoliberal and Islamic ideologies, without choosing between them. ANAP's electoral base changed after major losses in the municipal elections of March 1989. Compared with the 1987 election, the losses were particularly pronounced in urban centers (Çakmak 1990). During the 1980s, ANAP confronted SHP in urban centers and DYP in rural areas. In the elections of 1991, ANAP lost some of its support to the Welfare Party, which had a strong Islamic orientation, and consolidated its position particularly in the districts of the Inner Anatolia region. After shedding its religious or conservative components under new leadership in the beginning of the 1990s, ANAP emerged in the election of 1991 with a more homogeneous outlook as an urban-centered and secular party, committed to the neoliberal model. It became an attractive choice for the relatively prosperous strata and the managerial and business elites. The result was a party with a much diminished electoral base.

What explains ANAP's electoral success in the 1980s, particularly considering the intense distributional problems generated by the structural adjustment program? At least well into 1990, the electoral fortunes of

ANAP were closely tied to the popularity and performance of its leader. Özal played a major role in the success of ANAP between 1983 and 1987. He portrayed himself as a leader with influence abroad and as the architect of the new program for economic recovery. Equally striking was his ability to portray the crisis of the late 1970s, the most acute crisis in recent Turkish history, as the failure of the opposition. He projected ANAP as a new party with a novel economic program for the 1980s and other parties as a continuation of the pre-1980 politics whose policies had already been tried and ended in abject failure. Özal bolstered his position as leader of the party by keeping tight party discipline, choosing candidates, and dispensing with those who deviated from the party line.

It might appear paradoxical to view ANAP as a party of the new era, since it was one of the three parties allowed to contest the general elections of November 1983. ANAP was not, however, the party that the top military leadership wished to see in government after the 1983 elections. The military implicitly backed the National Democracy Party headed by an ex-general, Turgut Sunalp. Part of ANAP's unexpected success in 1983 derived from being the party that dissociated itself most from the military. It also helped that Özal had been out of office since the Banker's Crisis of June 1982.

As was traditional, particularly for parties on the right, ANAP used patron-client networks to maintain support. The electorate expected disproportionate benefits to come from close association with the top party leadership. For example, ANAP did well around Malatya, Özal's hometown, and in provinces on the east coast of the Black Sea region, home of Mesut Yilmaz, the party leader in 1990–91. Employment opportunities in the public enterprise sector and bureaucracy were the traditional avenues for patronage, and that is a major reason why Turkey's public sector remained largely intact throughout the 1980s. Credit from public banks and frequent rescue operations for troubled private firms also distributed patronage. The public sector continued to dominate the financial system, and, in fact, the share of total bank credit held by public banks expanded during the 1980s. Lucrative public sector contracts and preferential access to the output of public enterprises, which was being sold at prices that lagged behind inflation, constituted other avenues through which firms favored by the government could benefit in return for political support.

Two new means of disposing patronage emerged during the 1980s: extrabudgetary funds and local budgets. Through extrabudgetary funds, discussed in detail later, ANAP governments directed public expenditures to specific groups or regions with the explicit objective of attracting electoral support. Local governments distributed patronage not only through their spending but also through their authority, which ANAP transferred to them, to issue construction licenses.

ANAP's success also derived from the relative weakness of the opposition. Opposition parties in Turkey enjoyed much less access to state resources than the governing party. By controlling the large public sector, ANAP used patronage to augment its electoral base. The weakness of the opposition parties during most of the 1980s, however, was not due primarily to their weak financial base but rather to their inability to formulate a coherent and convincing alternative to the government's economic program.

Finally, part of ANAP's success derived from the electoral laws described above. This was particularly true in the 1987 elections, in which the party increased its share of seats in the Parliament while receiving a declining share of the national vote.

OPPOSITION PARTIES. After the transition to democracy started in 1983, two major opposition parties arose: the Social Democratic Populist Party (SHP) and the True Path Party (DYP), which descended directly from the two principal political parties of the pre-1980 era. The SHP may be regarded as the reincarnation of the Republican People's Party, which dated back to the very beginning of the republic in 1923. The Republican People's Party was the dominant institution in the single-party era until multiparty democracy began in 1950. Subsequently, in the late 1960s, it became the center-left Social Democratic Party. After the 1984 municipal election, the Populist Party merged with the Social Democratic Party, which participated only in the 1984 municipal election, to become the Social Democratic Populist Party and the principal center-left party in the 1980s. Compared with the Populist Party, the SHP was a more typical social democratic party in its prolabor stance and electoral base.

Starting with the municipal election of 1984, the number of parties in an election was no longer limited, and several new parties emerged. Ecevit (initially acting through his wife) started another socialist party, the Party of the Democratic Left (DSP), as a vehicle for his return to political life, because he did not regard the SHP as a true social democratic party. The Prosperity Party also formed as a reincarnation of the National Salvation Party, representing Islamic fundamentalism. The Communist Party and the parties based on ethnicity (mainly Kurdish) were still banned, however, as were former politicians until 1987.

After 1983, the SHP drew its support primarily from urban wage earners and lower- and middle-level public sector employees. Although it was the main political outlet for wage earners and lower-income groups, its links with the union movement remained weak. This was mostly due to constitutional restrictions on the interaction between political parties and interest group associations. It was also partly due to the failure of party leadership to develop links with unionized wage earners, particularly when the regime loosened up at the end of the 1980s. They took for granted the votes of industrial union members. The party remained the principal opposition party until the elections of November 1991. For most of the decade, redistribution in favor of lower-income groups constituted the focal point of the party's economic program. Important elements of the party's etatist heritage remained intact throughout the 1980s.

In the municipal elections of March 1989, the social democrats increased their share of votes nationally and won most of the key municipalities. Ironically, ANAP's partial recovery during the general elections of 1991 was predominantly an urban phenomenon and occurred at the expense of the social democrats. This may be explained by factors independent of the process of structural adjustment. Social democrats remained deeply divided into two parties (the SHP and DSP) and into factions within the SHP. In addition to internal conflicts, the weakness of the left was accentuated by its almost exclusive focus on redistribution with no serious discussion of how a major redistribution program would be compatible with acceptable rates of saving, investment, and economic growth. Consequently, social democrats could not come up with an economic program that would allow them to win an outright majority. The international climate, in which market-oriented reforms represented an almost universal phenomenon, also weakened the appeal of the left.

Undoubtedly, a major contributor to the sharp decline in the SHP's popularity was the poor performance of its municipal governments during the 1989–91 period, partly because of management problems and partly because of the broader economic context, including the tendency of the ANAP government to offer less funding to cities run by the SHP. Also, the DYP offered a populist but less ideological alternative, which gained it votes in a number of traditional strongholds of the SHP.

The DYP was the clear successor to the Justice Party, the principal center-right party of the pre-1980 era (Acar 1991). Demirel led the Justice Party with a charismatic style up to September 1980 and resumed leadership of the DYP after the referendum in 1987. The DYP drew its support primarily from rural areas and small business. Rural support proved to be a considerable asset, since more than 40 percent of the population in Turkey still lives in rural areas and is employed in agriculture. The vote of the agricultural regions was decisive for the DYP's emergence as the leading party in 1991. Both the SHP and DYP differed from ANAP in their explicit concern with income distribution and the position of lower-income groups.

Although the major parties converged on most key aspects of the structural adjustment program by the early 1990s, important differences between ANAP and the other parties remained. There was a consensus on the irreversibility of trade and capital account liberalization as well as on the importance of the key institutions of the neoliberal model, such as the capital market and the foreign exchange market. There was not, however, a similar consensus concerning reform of the public sector; both the

SHP and DYP were less disposed to privatization than ANAP, which certainly did not move quickly on the issue either.

Interest Groups

Compared with corporatism in Western Europe, the peak interest associations of business and labor contributed little to the formation or implementation of policy in the 1980s, in spite of the privileged position of private business. The insulation of the executive policymaking elite from societal and interest group pressures proved to be a decisive advantage for initiating and implementing the early phases of the structural adjustment program. Yet, as the restoration of democracy brought new distributional claims into the picture in the second half of the 1980s, the pattern of insulated decisionmaking increasingly became a disadvantage for sustaining macroeconomic discipline and the overall momentum of the program.

BUSINESS ASSOCIATIONS. The interaction between government and business occurred mainly at a personal level, involving direct contacts between key entrepreneurs, on the one hand, and the prime minister plus a small core of ministers and top-level bureaucrats, on the other (Buğra 1991; Heper 1991). Business and government had more contact with one another in the late 1980s, as senior officials and sometimes Özal himself attended the Taksim Round Table discussions, and they went together on missions abroad to promote Turkish exports. Indeed, the chance to meet with Özal sometimes became more important than the promotion of exports. Also, by the late 1980s, the young business leaders of TÜSİAD (the Turkish Industrialists' and Businessmen's Association) were meeting regularly with senior bureaucrats at the treasury and the central bank to discuss a variety of broad policy issues. The contacts did not go farther to become part of the official decision process, however. This occurred partly because the constitution of 1982 restricted the activities of interest groups, but also because Turkey had a paternalistic state tradition, with a strong center confronting a weakly organized periphery and civil society (Heper 1985; Mardin 1973; Özbudun 1991). In the early 1990s, business leaders still complained that the government would announce important policy measures without prior consultation and certainly without bargaining and reaching an agreement with the representatives of organized interest groups.

Turkish business associations have weak organizations, reflecting the fragmented nature of the business community itself. The two main organizations, TOBB (the National Union of Chambers of Commerce and Commodity Exchanges) and TÜSİAD, reflect the divisions and conflicts within the business community. TOBB, with a total of 687,000 members drawn from all parts of the country, regards itself as the sole legitimate representative of business interests and opinion. It bases its claim on the size and nature of its membership, which is compulsory for all firms, including industry. By weight of their numbers, small Anatolian businesses dominate the organization. By contrast, TÜSİAD comprises only the elite of the business community, namely the large-scale conglomerates, located almost exclusively in the Istanbul area.

Neither institution adequately represents the varied interests of the business community. For TOBB, the problems are, first, that it is too all encompassing to have a well-defined interest and, second, that the government finances and dominates its leadership. In practice, the government uses TOBB as an instrument to divide and rule business and as a source of public business support for government policies. TÜSİAD, in contrast, is a voluntary association and thus required by law to act in the general public interest. It lacks the unifying purpose of a true interest group organization and does not lobby for its members' interests. Given the one-member, one-vote system in TOBB elections, members of the TÜSİAD, who economically dominate their industries, are unable to exercise corresponding influence in TOBB. Furthermore, the majority of TOBB membership closely monitors TOBB's relations with TÜSİAD, which seriously constrains the development of a closer relationship between the two organizations (Arat 1991; Özbudun 1991). The conflict between TOBB and TÜSİAD illustrates the fragmented nature of business representation in Turkey. Yet, the line of cleavage does not simply divide small from large business. Important conflicts of interest have arisen within the community of large-scale conglomerates, which TÜSİAD represents, particularly between outward-oriented firms and those with a predominantly inward orientation.[2]

Large family-controlled conglomerates play a leading role in manufacturing in Turkey, producing both exports and import-competing goods and owning banks. Often their shift from import-competing goods to exports involves mainly a transition to higher-quality lines of production. Most of the manufacturing production before 1980 went to the heavily protected domestic market. By the late 1970s, however, many firms saw that the import-substituting model had become unsustainable, and they began to support more export-oriented policies.

Both businessmen and bureaucrats in the 1980s were fully aware of the fragmented nature of the business community and its principal interest organizations (interviews with business leaders). Consequently, top bureaucrats did not regard these associations as a united front representing their members' interests and did not enter into institutionalized dialogue with them. This process, in turn, encouraged individual contacts among businessmen, bureaucrats, and politicians. For the economy as a whole, the cost was unsystematic and unpredictable policy that encouraged rent seeking. At any point in time, however, key members of each group gained from the system of individual contacts: businessmen got favors, bureaucrats got options for moving into top private sector jobs, and politicians got political support and also freedom from having to deal with a unified and powerful business lobby.

At the microlevel, the special sectoral committees could have become a key forum for institutionalizing discussion of government-business relations, but they did not. Before 1980, these committees, with representatives of state agencies, the business community, and academia, were an important source of discussion and information for the State Planning Organization's five-year plans. These microlevel committees continued to exist in the 1980s—120 provided input to the sixth five-year development plan, which extended into the 1990s—but their importance declined as the five-year plans themselves were marginalized. The committee reports are useful in identifying the development trends and prospects in relevant sectors or subsectors, but they contain few major policy recommendations because their scope remained microsectoral. The major firms with political clout did not bother with the committees, because they had direct access to the politicians who made the final decisions.

LABOR. In the late 1970s Turkey had two main labor organizations: the Confederation of Labor Unions in Turkey (Türk-İs), the larger of the two, and the Confederation of Revolutionary Labor Unions (DISK), the more leftist and confrontational. DISK had been achieving large wage gains and organizing mass demonstrations in the big cities, thereby gaining size and influence. The military regime, as soon as it took over, banned strikes and suspended collective bargaining over wages. It outlawed DISK and jailed its leaders. Türk-İs remained in existence, but with much reduced opportunities for representing the interests of labor. Labor unions, like other interest groups, were not allowed to have any direct connection with political parties. Unlike persons in business, workers had virtually no personal connection with the political elite.

The military government created new labor institutions to replace those it destroyed or weakened. It set up a council of arbitration to settle wage disputes, which repeatedly gave nominal wage increases below the previous and projected rates of inflation. Wages were typically set with two-year contracts. The first-year increase usually provided only a partial catch-up, and the second-year increase was predetermined and based on a forecast of inflation that was usually lower than what actually occurred (Vieira da Cunha, Webb, and Isaac 1990). The government wanted cheap labor but not unemployment, which would have increased political unrest. To make the harsh wage regime politically sustainable, even in the short term, it was combined with an agreement by all major private and public sector employers not to lay off workers. This may have acted to some extent as a disincentive for firms to hire new workers; and unemployment did remain a problem through much of the 1980s. In effect, the government protected some elements of wage labor, namely those who would have been laid off, at the expense of those who would have kept their jobs even with high real wages.

The ANAP government in the mid-1980s did little to relax the inhibitions on union power. The persecution of labor leaders virtually stopped, but it had in any case become unnecessary for curtailing union power, at least in the short run. All strikes were outlawed until 1987, and they are still banned in the financial and public sectors. Binding arbitration was required until 1987, and real wages stayed low.

None of the three parties permitted in the 1983 election represented labor interests in the formal sense of consulting with labor unions in developing their economic programs, but the Populist Party made electoral appeals to the economic interests of wage labor. The Social Democratic Populist Party, which became the principal center-left party in the 1980s, was a more typical social democratic party in its prolabor stance and electoral base.

Three characteristics of labor unions in Turkey precluded labor in the 1980s, or before, from becoming an active party to a tripartite corporatist agreement with the state and private business. First, labor unions in Turkey lacked the technical base, the social status, the vision of longer-term interest, and the self-confidence required to participate effectively in economic decisionmaking at the national level. Second, collective bargaining in Turkey was organized at the level of industrial sectors; consequently, sectoral unions were key actors involved in the wage bargaining process. Although Türk-İs played a coordinating role, its ability as a peak association to control and discipline individual sectoral labor unions was limited. Hence, even if Türk-İs were to become a member of a corporatist arrangement for economic policymaking, coordination of the economy would not necessarily improve, since Türk-İs would have little power to make its constituent unions conform to the council's decisions. Finally, the negative experience of labor in the 1980s was and remains an obstacle to incorporating labor into a corporatist framework. The direct exclusion of labor during the early years of the decade undermined trust in the value of cooperating with the government and created the perception that corporatist institutions were a means of imposing labor discipline without requiring parallel sacrifices from other social groups.

The various phases of industrial labor relations in Turkey in the 1980s support the hypothesis that either totally excluding labor from the policy process or, at the other extreme, including labor through corporatist agreements facilitates structural adjustment. But intermediate arrangements lead to problems. Prior to the military takeover in September 1980, labor unions were strong in their ability to bargain with employers, including the government, but they were excluded from the policymaking process after the right-center Justice Party replaced the Social Democrats in November 1979. The Turkish government completely excluded labor in the early 1980s. The resultant decline of real wages greatly helped the authorities to engineer real devaluations of the exchange rate, which stimulated Turkey's exports. After 1987 the rights of unions were restored, but not in the context of an inclusive corporatist arrangement, and this contributed to macroeconomic instability.

AGRICULTURE. Most agricultural producers lost during the structural adjustment process of the 1980s. Although the devaluation helped stimulate exports of fruit and a few other products, most products were not exported, and many faced some competition from imports, including wheat. The agricultural sector received significant subsidies through high support prices and fertilizer subsidies, and the adjustment reduced them both. The decline in subsidies affected both the level of support prices and the number of commodities covered (Olgun 1991). The share of national income going to agriculture declined from 26 percent in 1978–79 to 21 percent in 1984–85 and to 18 percent in 1989–90, while the share of the labor force in agriculture only declined from 58 percent in 1980 to 46 percent in 1990 (Ozmucur 1991; State Institute of Statistics 1991).

The principal organization representing agricultural interests was the Turkish Union of Chambers of Agriculture. The agricultural community loudly criticized what it considered to be the obvious pro-urban bias of the ANAP governments. In spite of this vocal criticism, agricultural interests for most of the 1980s could not shift policy in their favor, although they did keep the support price system for a few key products like wheat. A turning point arrived, however, with the municipal elections of March 1989, in which the True Path Party, a party with strong rural support, emerged ahead of ANAP. Then the government began to pay more attention to rural interests. Thus it was through the party system and electoral competition, rather than through direct representation by the relevant interest association, that the agricultural sector exerted an influence over national politics (Ergüder 1991a).

Bureaucracy and the Cabinet

Besides the office of the prime minister itself, three institutions in the central government were crucial for the structural transformation of Turkish economic policy in the 1980s: the State Planning Organization, the Undersecretariat for Treasury and Foreign Trade (the treasury), and the Central Bank of the Republic of Turkey (the central bank). Other ministries and the Parliament played mostly passive roles. Since the election of 1983, and particularly since the installation of Özal's choice for chief of staff in 1985, the military stayed out of politics and played no role in economic policymaking.

RESTRUCTURING THE BUREAUCRACY. Prior to 1980, the principal agencies for economic policy were the Ministry of Finance and Customs, the Ministry of Commerce, and the State Planning Organization. All three were involved with trade policy and the allocation of foreign exchange. The State Planning Organization was the premier economic agency in the 1960s and 1970s. It produced the five-year plans and enforced their implementation. The state-owned enterprises had to meet the plan's targets, and numerous incentives existed to pressure private firms to meet them, especially the State Planning Organization's control of import and investment licenses. The organization's staff believed in the efficacy of state-led development and, accordingly, staked their careers on this presumption. The State Planning Organization and the Ministry of Finance handled fiscal policy and, through the subordinated central bank, monetary policy as well. All three agencies were staffed and directed predominantly by persons who believed that state-directed development was the most appropriate approach for Turkey.

Coordination problems between the economic ministries date back at least until the 1970s, when Turkey had a series of coalition governments. At that time, each party in the coalition got certain ministries, in which it built patronage empires and carried out portions of its electoral program. To maintain some coherence for the government as a whole, coordination committees of the relevant ministers functioned in various policy areas, including economics. The military and the Özal governments continued this tradition.

The Özal governments undertook two major reorganizations of the economic bureaucracy, in 1983 and 1991, and several minor ones. The reorganizations had three objectives:

- To deal with the problem of coordination
- To reward political friends and punish enemies
- To take power away from the parts of the bureaucracy opposed to Özal's economic program.

These objectives were not mutually exclusive, but they did conflict at times.

In the early 1980s, the third objective—taking power from the old, etatist bureaucrats—was predominant. The key move, which Özal took in 1983 as soon as he returned to power, was to create the Undersecretariat for Treasury and Foreign Trade and to put it under a new Ministry of State for Economic Affairs. This minister was also (although not permanently) made deputy prime minister, as Özal had been in 1980–83. Thus, rather than try to reform the old bureaucrats, he created a new agency and transferred key powers to it. Until 1989, Özal headed the economic team, which consisted of the inner cabinet of four or five politicians and three technocrats: the undersecretary for treasury and foreign trade, the head of the central bank, and (in a weaker role) the head of the State Planning Organization. The old agencies were left intact but relegated to less crucial functions, such as revenue collection (Ministry of Finance) and forecasting (State Planning Organization).

Sometimes key economic policymakers were appointed to head the agencies (Yusuf Özal at the State Planning Organization and Ekrem Pakdemirli at the Ministry of Finance, both in 1987), but they did not represent the views of their agencies. They held the positions in order to be part of the economic team and, in effect if not by design, to stop any etatist initiatives from being launched by traditional elements in their agencies.

In the middle and late 1980s, the objective of having facilities for distributing favor became more important because the ANAP government, initially elected in the context of a restricted democracy, faced electoral challenges to its rule as the scope for democracy expanded. The electoral payoff of this strategy for ANAP was less than anticipated, however, because the internationally oriented businesspersons, chief beneficiaries of the structural adjustment program and thus the most natural constituency for ANAP, were not inclined to make favor-seeking in Ankara the focal point of their entrepreneurial efforts. They were more frustrated than appeased by the prospect of their profits depending on shifting decrees. They preferred a predictable and stable regulatory environment to getting favors today that could be taken away tomorrow. In the late 1980s, coordination also became more problematic as Özal turned his attention more to politics, particularly after the 1989 municipal elections, which ANAP lost, and moved up to the presidency. In a reorganization in June 1991, virtually all economic policymaking was put under one minister of state for economy, who was also named deputy prime minister. Trade, fiscal, and monetary policy were put under him, along with the State Planning Organization, the central bank, and the major state banks. This move was certainly not inevitable, indeed it was hardly anticipated, but it did aim to address a widely recognized problem in getting the different branches of the economic bureaucracy to cooperate.

Professionalization versus Politicization

To smooth the implementation of the structural adjustment program, the ANAP governments sought to restructure the bureaucracy and to institute a top-down management structure (Heper 1990). The most visible manifestation of this trend was the appointment to top positions within the economic bureaucracy of a select group of young U.S.-educated technocrats with a strong commitment to the neoliberal model. These men, popularly known as the Princes, were dependent on and loyal to Özal and became key figures in the implementation of the economic program during the latter half of the 1980s.[3] The top-down restructuring created several nodes of competent technocrats who could carry out a reform program when the political leaders wanted it. As one would expect, the old-line bureaucrats resented having their traditional policies rejected and their career plans thwarted.

Alongside the positive trend in the direction of restructuring the bureaucracy and augmenting its technical capacity, a negative countertrend of de-professionalization sometimes occurred at top levels of the bureaucracy during the 1980s. The erosion occurred as the domain of political appointments expanded into the middle levels (that of general manager). Promotions from within the agencies became less common. The central bank avoided this, and so too did the treasury to some extent. The growing prevalence of political appointments severely reduced the autonomy and collective identity of the bureaucracy (Heper 1989). Two institutions illustrate the extremes of professionalization and politicization: the central bank and the extrabudgetary funds, respectively.

THE CENTRAL BANK. The central bank, which dates back to 1930, underwent changes in the 1980s that facilitated the structural adjustment program. Since the mid-1980s, the central bank has been the principal point of entry into the government for economists favoring neoliberal policies and a base for disseminating their ideas. By the end of the 1980s, the central bank had the institutional capacity, although not always the mandate, to take independent action that could influence policy outcomes.

Prior to 1983, it had no autonomy from the Ministry of Finance. With the reorganization in 1983, it was moved out of the Ministry of Finance and put under the Ministry of State for Economy, to which the new treasury undersecretariat also reported. Yavuz Canevi was named governor, moving up from being director of the foreign exchange desk. Educated in the Faculty of Political Science at the University of Ankara, like most bureaucrats of the time, Canevi had moved over from the old Ministry of Finance in the late 1970s. He was accompanied by several other bureaucrats, such as Zekeriya Yildirim, whose key distinction was that they also had some foreign graduate training and command of a foreign language. Canevi became undersecretary of treasury and foreign trade, after Pakdemirli, and Yildirim became acting governor of the central bank after Canevi's departure. Eventually, they moved to the private sector, but only after starting a tradition of intellectual leadership and internationalist orientation.

In 1986, the degree of international intellectual influence at the central bank increased further with the arrival of Rüşdü Saracoğlu—initially as director of research—his two successors in that position (Bülent Gültekin and Hasan Ersel), and another senior official (Ercan Kumçu). All had graduate training in economics or finance from U.S. or British universities and brought with them a number of young economists with similar backgrounds. Rather than emphasize legal procedures and lines of authority, like their predecessors who only had training as financial auditors from the political science faculty, these new economists emphasized using a statistical basis for policy decisions and evaluating them in terms of functional outcomes. Saracoğlu, governor of the central bank from

1987 to 1993, and other economists of this new breed now occupy all positions of importance in the bank. Gültekin, on leave from the Wharton Business School, left the bank to head the Public Participation Fund (an agency for the privatization of state-owned enterprises) and, after returning to Wharton, served as a political adviser to ANAP. In 1993 he replaced Saracoğlu as governor. No other economists have spread from the central bank to other agencies within the bureaucracy, although the relatively high caliber of their analysis and its resonance with work done at the Organization for Economic Cooperation and Development (OECD), IMF, and World Bank have given the central bank a strong voice in discussions of macroeconomic policy.

Although the central bank has remained within the economics ministry, it gained some independence there, at the price of becoming more dependent on the prime minister. The central bank law of 1970 stipulated that the governor would be elected by the shareholders (the treasury owns 70 percent) for a term of three years and could be dismissed by them, which effectively requires a vote of the whole cabinet. When Saracoğlu was appointed governor in 1987, the term was lengthened to five years, strengthening his position in the bureaucracy and especially the treasury. Saracoğlu's power grew because he retained the confidence of Özal and his designated successors in the prime minister's office and thus outlasted his counterparts at the treasury.[4] Although Saracoğlu and top officials at the central bank retained their positions after the change of government in 1991, at least for a time—in contrast to the complete turnover at the top in treasury, finance, and elsewhere—the way in which the central bank had to increase its monetary financing for the government in 1992 indicates the limits of its autonomy.

EXTRABUDGETARY FUNDS, THE SORCERER'S APPRENTICE. From the point of view of sustaining structural adjustment, the proliferation of extrabudgetary funds was the biggest organizational mistake of the 1980s. Prior to 1980, there were thirty-three funds, all small and some dating back to the 1940s, but twenty-four were added in 1980–83 and forty-eight more in 1984–90. The largest funds as of 1991 were the Public Participation Fund, the Mass Housing Fund, the Support Price Stabilization Fund, and the Defense Industries Support Fund. Smaller funds included the Justice Administration Improvement Fund, Mosque Construction Assistance Fund, Cement Fund, Fund for Measurement and Tuning Services, Universities Research Development Fund, and Tobacco Fund (Undersecretariat for Treasury and Foreign Trade 1992, p. 53). These funds were initially created as agencies to fund priority economic activities, in spite of the temporary borrowing constraints on the central government, and as a way to make imported consumer goods, like cigarettes and alcoholic beverages, socially and politically acceptable by taxing them for popular purposes. In 1984, the new government announced that a surcharge was to be levied on luxury goods, with the revenues earmarked for the Mass Housing and Public Participation Fund, which provided low-income housing, particularly in urban areas.

The funds were assigned to different ministries, usually according to their area of concern. Soon each ministry wanted to have one or more funds, for they were convenient ways to avoid the scrutiny of the budget process. A parliamentary law was necessary to set up a fund and to define the goods on which it could set levies, but after that, the amount of the levy and the expenditure of the fund could be set by decree. The variable levies were set by the appropriate deputy undersecretary for treasury and foreign trade, in consultation with the relevant fund. The check on the creation of new funds usually came from the revenue side; interest groups and legislators resisted additional taxes, but this did not stop their proliferation, especially where trade taxes had protectionist effects (Oyan, Aydín, and Konukman 1991). The revenue of the funds grew from 1.3 percent of gross national product (GNP) in 1981 to more than 11 percent in 1990—more than half of all public sector revenue (Oyan and Aydín 1991, pp. 121, 125).

The levies created economic distortions in several dimensions. They distorted both production and consumption decisions, except in the now small minority of cases when they were imposed on goods with negative externalities in consumption, like cigarettes. Mostly they resembled tariffs on narrowly defined categories of goods. From a macroeconomic perspective, the funds changed aggregate spending and taxation with usually no reference to what the overall stance of fiscal policy should be. The funds occasionally made transfers to the general budget, as occurred in 1987. When a fund ran a deficit, however, it borrowed as necessary. Although the loans to the funds carried a government guarantee, they were not coordinated in the government's debt management strategy. Borrowing covered an average of 25 percent of total expenses for funds in 1988–91 (Undersecretariat for Treasury and Foreign Trade 1992, p. 57). In 1989–91, borrowing by the funds shifted strongly to foreign sources.

The funds created rent-seeking opportunities that distorted the political process. First, they removed economic decisionmaking from the normal bureaucratic routines and from the possibility of democratic oversight. Second, the expenditures of the funds were often used to reward municipalities that voted for ANAP. The import levies were also an important means to offer selective protection against import competition for industries the government wanted to reward. The levy system reduced the transparency of the import protection regime. The actual level of protection for any branch of industry was much more difficult to ascertain than that from tariffs. The locus of rent seeking also shifted to an administrative arena, where specialized knowledge both of administrative procedures and of the particular markets provided advantages.

Political control over the funds became less centralized over time. At first, Özal controlled the funds closely, as he did other aspects of economic policy. As the number of funds grew, however, he could no longer monitor them. After he ascended to the presidency in 1989, control of most activities of the funds devolved to the ministries. Until the end of the ANAP period, the only remaining coherence was that all the ministers were from the same party. In 1992, the new government moved to centralize control of the funds under the treasury.

International Economic Community

International organizations—the OECD, the European Community, the World Bank, and the IMF—played a big role in Turkey's adjustment program but did not dictate most of its content. In the late 1970s, when Turkey's commercial debt crisis became acute, the OECD consortium, motivated partly by the fall of the shah of Iran and the Soviet invasion of Afghanistan, orchestrated the rescheduling of Turkey's commercial and bilateral debt. The possibility of membership in the European Community also motivated Turkey's reforms.

The IMF and the World Bank influenced both the evolution of economic philosophy in Turkey and the short-term choice of policy. Özal worked at the World Bank in the 1970s, where he was impressed with the arguments in favor of more open trade regimes. Saracoğlu worked at the IMF prior to coming to the central bank, and staff of the World Bank and IMF developed close working relationships with many staff in the central bank, State Planning Organization, and treasury.

The World Bank and IMF were, of course, key players in the development of policy packages in the early 1980s. There was a big need for balance of payments support, and the backing of external official financing and technical advice helped tip the balance within the Demirel government and under the military. The government needed, however, to be seen publicly as taking the initiative. The January 1980 measures, for example, were launched in advance of formal agreements; the first structural adjustment loan was not signed until April and the new IMF standby loan was not signed until June, although informal talks had begun in December 1979. "The World Bank was in a far better position to operate in secret than the Fund [IMF]. As an instrument, the SALS [structural adjustment loans], and particularly the specific conditions attached to them, were virtually unknown to the public, and this enabled the Turkish government gradually to present the measures agreed with the [World] Bank as its own policy. With hindsight, now that it has actually materialized as a medium-term strategy, the adjustment program also appears more consistent than could have been foreseen in early 1980, when the aim, as in previous years, was to resolve the acute crisis and the debate centered on the Fund's restrictive conditions" (Wolff 1987, p. 117). Both the World Bank and the IMF continued to engage in an active dialogue over policy throughout the 1980s. Turkey received five structural adjustment loans in 1980–84 and then gained approval of four sector adjustment loans in 1984–88, making it by far the largest recipient of balance of payments support in that period. Turkey had standby arrangements with the IMF in 1980, 1983, and 1984. The influence of both institutions declined in the late 1980s, especially since the Turkish economy ran balance of payments surpluses in 1988–89 and restored its access to international capital markets.

Policy Outcomes

The actors and institutions described above implemented three phases of trade and macroeconomic reforms. Turkey was largely successful in sustaining the trade and exchange rate reforms because they brought about large and beneficial structural change in the economy and created constituencies to support them. In the macroeconomic policy area, Turkey had occasional success in slowing inflation, reducing the budget deficit, and stabilizing the exchange rate, but the propensity of the political party system to rely on patronage made these achievements temporary. Macroeconomic imbalances repeatedly undermined the adjustment process and diluted its benefits. Nevertheless, the adjustment succeeded in shifting the whole context for macroeconomic policy by creating more open financial and trade policy regimes. By the end of the 1980s, market forces had developed to act as constraints on the public sector: the state both had to pay the real interest rate and had to endure the inflation that were the consequences of its macroeconomic shortcomings. By 1990, state enterprises operated with more competition from the domestic and foreign private sector.

First Reform Wave, Trade Issues, 1980–82

The first wave of reforms started with the January 24 measures in 1980 and continued until Özal's ouster in the summer of 1982. From then until the end of the military government in November 1983, there were some minor reversals of reform, although most of the reforms were sustained and provided a foundation from which further reforms could proceed.

In the January 24 measures, the exchange rate and export subsidies were the most critical trade reform initiatives; the government's objective was to increase the profitability of the tradable goods sector quickly, relying on existing capacity. Some import liberalization also occurred, but as Celasun and Rodrik (1989, p. 720) conclude, the adjustments in trade policy prior to 1984 were modest, and "it is perhaps more appropriate to regard the improvement in the macroeconomic context as the enabling cause of trade liberalization, as opposed to the other way around."

The first phase of trade reform emphasized export promotion and other measures to eliminate the foreign exchange constraints that had crippled the Turkish economy by the winter of 1979–80. Turkish growth since 1960 had been based on inward-oriented expansion: exports were less than 5 percent of gross domestic product (GDP). With little foreign exchange coming in, the government controlled its allocation closely and imposed harsh penalties on persons caught holding it without authorization. Extensive regulations for licensing trade and allocating foreign exchange fostered the expansion of rent-seeking activities (Krueger 1974a, 1974b; Krueger and Aktan 1992).

In response to the oil shocks of the early 1970s, Turkey had borrowed heavily from abroad, running its external debt up to almost four times its exports, although only about 20 percent of GDP. When the 1979 oil shock hit, credit lines had already dried up, and the government did not have the foreign exchange to meet its debt payments. Import restraints tightened further. The experience of a winter in Ankara without heat or coffee and with the spread of political violence made Turks willing to take the economic and political risks posed by measures to open the economy.

Trade policy and exchange rate reforms were central to the stabilization and adjustment program introduced on January 24, 1980, shortly after Demirel's government took office. The most important reform was the 33 percent devaluation of the Turkish lira and elimination of almost all multiple exchange rate practices. Over the course of the year, a number of small devaluations followed until May 1981, when adjustment began on a daily basis. The reforms also liberalized access to foreign exchange, particularly for exporters and banks involved in the export business. These included all the groups or conglomerates that dominate Turkish manufacturing, trade, and banking. For them, the remaining constraints on holding foreign exchange were not binding, since their import-export businesses and foreign offices gave ample opportunities for legally holding marks and dollars.

The devaluations had more than a passing effect in clearing the foreign exchange market, because other measures contributed to bringing inflation below the rate of depreciation, thus effecting a real devaluation. The two main policies were to reduce both the fiscal deficit and real wages. Real wages declined sharply with the rapid inflation in early 1980, and labor policy under the military kept them from recovering (table 5-1 shows the pattern of real wages and the real exchange rate, calculated in terms of the wholesale price index purchasing power). After the military government disbanded some unions and forbade strikes, binding arbitration suppressed real wages. The agreement not to lay off workers dis-

Table 5-3. Export Incentives in Turkey, 1980–89
(percent)

Incentive	1980	1981	1982	1983	1984	1985	1986	1987	1988	1989
Total export subsidy rate	22	21	22	24	14	19	25	23	15	8
Export tax rate	1	4	10	12	11	7	6	5	4	2
Duty-free imports	6	5	4	6	3	10	14	12	4	n.a.
Preferential export credits or foreign exchange allocation	16	13	7	7	n.a.	n.a.	n.a.	n.a.	n.a.	n.a.
Cash grants and corporate tax rebates	n.a.	n.a.	n.a.	n.a.	n.a.	3	6	7	6	6

n.a. Not applicable.
Source: Bateman and Arslan 1989.

guised unemployment as underemployment and spread its cost over most of the work force. As the economy recovered, underemployment declined, as did unemployment. Unwinding the policies that suppressed both real wages and unemployment became a problem mainly at the end of the decade.

Export promotion measures included a variety of incentives, several of which constituted direct subsidies. Export credits were the most important in 1980–81, running as high as 40 percent for industrial exports (see table 5-3). Tax rebates were initially designed to compensate exporters for indirect taxes and to substitute a value added tax rebate, which is allowed under the General Agreement on Tariffs and Trade (GATT). The term "rebate" is really a misnomer, however. First, the subsidy rate was not related to the total amount of taxes paid by the exporter and could exceed it. Second, the rebate scheme was introduced *before* the value added tax; when the actual value added tax rebate was added, the prior rebate scheme remained as a pure subsidy. Over the long term, these subsidies were undesirable distortions. In the short run, however, they may have accelerated the expansion of trading and manufacturing firms in the export sector. These firms became a vested interest, supporting the internationalist stance of the Özal government.

The export subsidy rates for the manufacturing sector from 1980 through 1983 averaged 22 percent (see table 5-3; Milanovic 1986). In the first two years of the program, this subsidy was largely in the form of export credits and varied widely; some sectors, such as metal products, received subsidies higher than 100 percent. Milanovic's calculations show that the highest subsidy rates appeared to go to sectors in which import-substitution had been of long-standing, including ferrous and nonferrous metals, electrical and nonelectrical machinery, and transport equipment. These sectors were mostly dominated by public sector enterprises. Private firms tended to be more involved in export-oriented subsectors, because they could produce the higher-quality products demanded in the export markets.

Not all exports were effectively subsidized. Agriculture, traditionally a stronghold for the Justice Party, lost subsidies. The January 1980 measures established a Price Support and Stability Fund at the central bank. This fund, one of the first new extrabudgetary funds, was financed by a levy equal to the difference between export receipts and domestic support prices for agricultural products. In effect, a tax on agricultural exports would be used to subsidize basic agricultural inputs purchased by farmers but also to finance export-oriented investments and to protect exporters somewhat from risk.

Some liberalization of imports occurred in the early 1980s. Since 1958, when Turkey initiated its annual import programs, all imports were divided between a liberalized and a quota list (see table 5-4). The liberalized list contained goods considered essential for meeting the ob-

Table 5-4. *Advance Deposits on Imports in Turkey, Various Years,*
1980–83
(percentages)

Type of list	Before January 24, 1980	After January 24, 1980	January 1981 to December 1983
Liberalized list I			
Importers	40	30	20
Industrialists	25	15	10
Liberalized list II			
Importers	40	20	20
Industrialists	25	10	10
Quota list			
Importers	10	20	n.a.
Industrialists	2.5	10	n.a.
Public sector imports	n.a.	0	n.a.
Additional deposit requirements			
Acceptance credits	n.a.	1	n.a.
Imports against documents and suppliers credits	50	20	n.a.

n.a. Not applicable.
Source: OECD 1981, p. 48.

jectives of the economic plan; the quota list contained less-essential goods and competing imports. The quota list was reduced slightly in 1980 and eliminated in 1981. Most of the items on the quota list were placed on the liberalized list of goods, and the government retained a positive list system of prohibited goods and a licensing system. Advance deposit requirements were also lowered, although a distinction was still drawn between importers, who were required to pay more substantial deposits, and industrialists, who were required to pay less (see table 5-5). Perhaps the most dramatic liberalization pertained to exporters. Import taxes on raw materials and intermediary goods destined to be incorporated in Turkish exports were reduced to zero, providing the exporter had the foreign exchange to finance the transaction.

Macroeconomic Issues

Only a few of the January 24, 1980, measures directly addressed the deficit and inflation, because the shortage of foreign exchange was the most immediate problem and no one realized how comprehensive a solution would be necessary. Some key measures had the immediate effect of increasing inflation: devaluing the currency, abolishing the Price Control Committee, and requiring state-owned enterprises to balance their budgets and allowing them to do so by raising prices. As devaluation and elimination of price controls reduced production bottlenecks in the

Table 5-5. Average Tariff Rates in Turkey, 1987–89
(unweighted averages)

Sector	1987	1988	November 1989
All categories	30	24	11
Agriculture	22	18	11
Mining (and petroleum)	17	18	6
Manufacturing	31	25	11
Consumer goods	45	35	17
Intermediate goods	21	17	6
Capital goods	32	30	10

Source: Bateman and Arslan 1989, tables 2, 4.

medium-term, supply and output expanded, reducing the pressure of inflation. The price increases to balance the budgets of state-owned enterprises were necessary to reduce unsustainable deficits and long-term inflation. The increases were equivalent to excise taxes and were indispensable to the stabilization effort. In order to ensure that the price increases, as well as the devaluation, were not totally passed along into inflation, money and credit expansion had to be slowed. Monetary policy tightened under the guidance of the newly created Money and Credit Committee but not enough to prevent an unprecedented, for Turkey, increase in average prices. Interest rates were liberalized in July 1980 so that the effects of tight money would pass through to the rest of the economy, although collusion among banks delayed this effect until the following winter (Saracoğlu 1987).

Even though the January measures improved the trajectory of the Turkish economy, average prices increased; most wages and prices in the nontraded sector did not keep up with overall inflation and thus fell in real terms. Although many of the resulting changes in relative prices were necessary, they caused intense frustration among some groups and fueled the continuing political violence.

With the military takeover, Özal received a mandate to proceed directly with whatever fiscal adjustment he thought necessary. He boasted in the press that he was acting only on economic considerations and that he was ignoring all political considerations (Ulagay 1987), suggesting that the military government freed him from the short-run political considerations that were later to play such havoc with fiscal policy.

Inflation remained high through 1980, roughly 110 percent over the course of the year, but dropped quickly in 1981 to around 37 percent a year, where it remained through 1983 (see table 5-1). Most of the increase in the average level of prices in 1980 was a one-time adjustment to recognize previously suppressed inflation, but this made it no less painful to most Turks, especially those who had been enjoying rents in the form of excess real wages and privileged access to scarce foreign exchange.

Some of these groups were active in the protests that marked the summer of 1980.

Why did inflation persist at more than 30 percent annually after mid-1981? With two-year, overlapping wage contracts, a key element in achieving the real devaluation was the persistence of inflation in the face of lower nominal wage increases in the second contract year. These increases were based on lower inflation projections (Vieira da Cunha, Webb, and Isaac 1990). Also, the military government did not want to press fiscal austerity and tight money to the point where its supporters would suffer. This comes out most clearly in the Bankers' Crisis in the summer of 1982, when the military insisted on relaxing the stabilization measures to prevent politically damaging bankruptcies, a reminder that military governments are not immune to interest group pressures.

The military expected to stay in control longer than three years, either directly or through a hand-picked successor, and therefore thought that the gradual disinflation policy they had been following would have time to complete its course. Leading up to the election in 1983, they did not realize how important the issue remained for people, and ANAP campaigned on a platform making inflation the principal target for policy reform.

Politics

Ideas for the 1980 reform package developed in several places. Some economists in the bureaucracy and academia were already advocating devaluation and trade liberalization in the late 1970s. The industrial groups in TÜSİAD formed the core of interests that would ultimately benefit from an open economy, and in 1978 they published an article in which Turgut Özal argued for most of the policies ultimately included in the package.[5] The World Bank, the International Finance Corporation, and the IMF were also advocating such policies, both on the basis of their own analysis and as a conduit for Turkish business opinion (interview with Gazi Erçel). Özal worked at the World Bank in the early 1970s, and the experience strongly influenced his views on economic policy (Özal 1991). It seems entirely plausible that Özal himself was the only node at which all these influences—academic, business, and international financial institutions—converged.

Demirel and Özal briefed the top military leaders, and presumably officials of the World Bank and IMF as well, to assure their support but did not tell all of the ministers what would be in the package. Even the finance minister was not informed, although many of his staff had worked on bits and pieces of the program. The top technocrats often took pride in the extent to which they had pulled off a surprise move, and for measures like the exchange rate devaluation, such secrecy was crucial (Krueger and Turan 1993; interviews with Yavuz Canevi and Gazi Erçel).

In this first phase, the reform package benefited many groups, in contrast to the inflation and foreign exchange shortage, so that many of the usual disputes over distribution were put aside. This made the political choices easier. Export promotion, through exchange rate undervaluation as well as direct subsidy, quickly increased the aggregate supply of foreign exchange. The increase took place directly through higher export earnings and also through greater availability of external finance in response to the growth of exports.[6] Since imports were vital inputs to virtually all sectors—import-competing and nontraded as well as for export—virtually everyone in Turkey benefited from relaxation of the severe import constraints that had been imposed in the crisis of the late 1970s. The international community of Turkey's financiers was also pleased. The emphasis on promoting exports and restoring financing flows in the first phase stimulated some recovery of employment. Given the continuing weight of import-substituting industries in the economy, and presumably their political clout as well, no effort was made to confront these producers directly through extensive liberalization, despite the additional protection they received from the devaluation itself. Firms with substantial import-competing lines, such as Koç, whose products include cars and home appliances, still lobbied for protection in those particular sectors, but they also favored the framework of a more open economy with a competitive real exchange rate. The main interests that lost were agriculture and labor.[7]

How important were political events for trade and exchange rate policy? Obviously, the change of government from Ecevit to Demirel in November 1979 was crucial. Ecevit in that period would never have brought a market-oriented, TÜSİAD-supported technocrat like Özal to head the economic team. The biggest question concerns the relation of policy reform to the military coup. The behind-the-scenes pressure exerted by the military in January 1980 to convince the government to address the political and social disorder was also a factor, although civilians had to sell the military on the need for radical adjustment measures. The political turmoil did not prevent the initiation of adjustment, but it probably would have derailed the program if the military had not intervened. The military did not take over in order to promote (or prevent) the economic policies of the Demirel-Özal government, but rather to quell political unrest, which most of the population agreed had become intolerable. The political violence predated the January 1980 adjustment measures, and its continuation was only partially in reaction to them.

The January 1980 measures angered the unions, both because they reduced real wages and because unions were excluded from the design process. Strikes and other forms of labor unrest, often violent, became increasingly common during the summer of 1980. Although some of this would have occurred in any case, as a symptom of long-term political factors, the short-run impact of the January measures contributed to making the disruptions severe enough to motivate the military to inter-

vene. Turkey's experience with the initial phase of the adjustment program in 1980 certainly supports the hypothesis that political management of adjustment becomes difficult, if not impossible, when a strong
labor movement is not incorporated into the policy process.

During its tenure in power, the military supported adjustment pas-
sively during the years when Özal remained in charge of economic policy,
but not after it put in its own man. By cracking down on unions and
imposing tighter social discipline generally, the military helped create the
political environment in which stabilization and adjustment began to
take effect. After Özal's departure from the government in 1982, along
with the core of his economic team, the military government reversed the
real depreciation that had been launched with maximum devaluation in
1980; some real appreciation took place in 1982. The military, with a
relatively etatist wing still dominant, did not push ahead with deficit
reduction because of the events of 1980; it did not take over for the
purpose of imposing a strict adjustment program.

The centralized, top-down institutions of policymaking under Özal
and the military were well suited to policymaking in the first phase of
adjustment, when moving fast was important for resolving the crisis and
capitalizing on the fresh memory of crisis to push through bold
initiatives.

Sustaining and Extending Reform with Democratization in the Mid-1980s

A second phase of reform began after the election of November 1983,
and most of the positive lessons for politically managing structural adjustment in a new democracy emerged from Turkey's experience in the
mid-1980s. Özal's government was committed to a more market-
oriented approach. This included deemphasizing subsidies, actively managing the exchange rate, and liberalizing imports, including the removal
of quantitative restrictions and a reform of tariffs. Some changes, such as
the shift to a negative list system, were sudden, but others, including the
lowering of tariffs, were introduced gradually and selectively. The scope
of liberalization was also partly offset by taxes and surcharges that,
although apparently initiated for revenue reasons, had clear protective
effects. Nonetheless, both the level and dispersion of nominal and effective rates of protection were reduced.

The military government had already restarted the devaluation policy
before the election, and Özal continued it through the first half of 1984.
During the second half of 1984 and the first half of 1985, the real
exchange rate was once again allowed to appreciate. The reasons for this
are unclear but probably reflect some lag in the adjustment of the rate to
domestic inflation, which was higher than anticipated. In order to continue the export drive, the government resumed aggressive devaluation in
1986 (see table 5-1).

The continued moderation or suppression of wage demands was a critical factor in keeping domestic inflation below the rate of exchange depreciation in the mid-1980s. From 1982 to 1988, industrial wages rose less than domestic inflation and exchange depreciation in every year but 1987, leading to declining real wages. The policy and political reasons for this outcome are obvious. Strikes remained illegal in the private sector until 1987, and for public sector unions they were still illegal in 1991. Wage labor was definitely a minority of the economically active population, however, and ANAP had some success in appealing even to labor on more diffuse economic issues, such as general prosperity (lower unemployment), and on religious or nationalist grounds.

The system of import lists was revised in December 1983. Although many restrictions remained, this revision entailed a substantial liberalization. Under the old system, everything not on the lists of quantitative restrictions was prohibited; the new system had three lists and all other imports were *permitted* without a limit on quantity. Intermediate inputs and investment goods were easier to import, although licenses were still required. Some consumer goods were still prohibited, but many were unlisted or readily importable with the payment of a special levy on luxuries. The State Planning Organization handled the licensing but no longer used its discretion to reward or punish firms according to whether they were meeting targets (Baysan and Blitzer 1991). After 1983, the number of categories of goods requiring import licenses declined in every year, except 1985, from 821 in 1983 to 33 in 1889.

Tariff rates were adjusted in December 1983 and again in January 1984. Some rates went down and others went up, but the overall effect was strongly liberalizing, especially in January. Explicitly to cushion the impact of liberalizing the licensing system, tariff protection was reduced less in sectors that lost the most licensing protection. Most consumer imports were completely liberalized from quantitative restrictions, but their tariffs were increased, particularly through dollar-denominated levies imposed by extrabudgetary funds. Tariffs were reduced substantially for most capital goods, but most remained on one list or another, usually the second. For intermediate goods, protection from both licensing and tariffs was reduced.

The institutions for distributing incentive certificates consciously emulated the Japanese and Korean models of creating general trading companies. Trading companies with exports in 1983 of $30 million, of which at least 75 percent had to consist of industrial and mining products, were issued certificates automatically.[8] The annual export requirement was to be raised each year by 10 percent. The policy contributed further to the concentration of Turkish business and also to the creation of a self-conscious interest group favoring an outward orientation but not necessarily free trade (Öniş 1992).

Foreign exchange regulations were also liberalized in December 1983 and January 1984. Banks were allowed to deal freely in foreign exchange at a market rate, as long as it was within 6 percent of the (frequently adjusted) official rate. Turkish citizens were allowed to hold foreign exchange and to open domestic bank accounts denominated in foreign exchange; but they could not yet freely convert lira to foreign exchange. Except for allowing foreign exchange deposits, these regulatory changes only made official and more irrevocable the situation that had been de facto since 1980. Nevertheless, the changes were important because before 1980 the power of the government—specifically the Ministry of Finance—to allocate scarce foreign exchange had been an important channel for rent seeking and for enforcement of the central planning targets. Thus, official liberalization of the foreign exchange regime complemented the relaxation of the licensing system and demonstrated the government's commitment to moving toward a more market-directed economy.

Özal had promised in the 1983 campaign to bring inflation under 10 percent within a year, but his government never achieved this objective. In 1984, the new government concentrated on its other electoral pledge: to end the economic hardships associated with stabilization. Özal decided to try supply-side tax cuts, combined with expanded public investment, export subsidies, and accelerated depreciation of the lira, in order to stimulate economic growth. The policies did not have the hoped-for effect of stimulating private investment, which remained well below the levels of the 1970s, but the package did stimulate aggregate demand and thus output growth. Because the expansion resulted more from a shift of the demand curve than from a shift of the supply curve, inflation increased again, from 31 percent in 1982–83 to 48 percent in 1984.

The rising inflation surprised and alarmed Özal and the OECD, IMF, and World Bank as well. These supporting external agencies worked closely with the treasury, the central bank, and the State Planning Organization to develop a stabilization program. Again, the ability of the upper bureaucracy to act decisively when it had Özal's support was crucial. Reducing export subsidies and introducing a value added tax also contributed to the stabilization, as well as to the fundamentals of Turkey's structural adjustment.

For political and institutional reasons, these measures did not realize their full fiscal potential. When export growth flagged in 1985–86, the government again raised export subsidies. To enforce collection of the value added tax, it set up an elaborate rebate scheme. Besides drastically reducing the effective rate of the value added tax, the scheme became a large entitlement program whose removal or serious reduction would arouse political protest. Also, the government did not follow through on complementary fiscal measures, such as permanently reducing subsidies to state-owned enterprises and raising corporate income taxes.[9]

The policy reforms of 1983–84 were planned in advance of the election by Özal and his top advisers, and, at least in broad outline, trade liberalization formed part of ANAP's electoral platform (Keesings Contemporary Archives 1984, p. 32926). The ability of the government to modify quickly the trade incentive in January was an important result of the bureaucratic reforms in December, namely creation of the Undersecretariat for Treasury and Foreign Trade. Several studies by the World Bank in the mid-1980s helped prepare the trade measures, but this was a case not of imposing reforms through conditionality, but more of offering technical assistance in an endeavor fully supported by the government.

To win political support for his program, Özal exploited the absence of an alternative economic program. He pointed to the improved performance of the economy and to Turkey's renewed ability to attract external resources on a large scale, which contributed to the rapid recovery of the economy in the early 1980s (Celasun 1990; Celasun and Rodrik 1989). ANAP's popularity in the mid-1980s also derived from measures that may be termed popular capitalism. Achieving positive real rates of interest on bank deposits was instrumental in generating a new group of middle-income rentiers who directly benefited from the program and added to ANAP's base of support. Similarly, the early features of the privatization program contributed to ANAP's success in the mid-1980s. The sale of revenue-share certificates was a popular mechanism for extending property ownership to middle- and lower-income groups. The extensive housing program and the development of infrastructure extended basic amenities to many parts of the country.

Although trade reform was surely a less important factor in appealing to voters, it was not implemented in the face of substantial opposition. This was because much of the import-competing manufacturing was done by large conglomerates, and what they lost from import liberalization was more than made up for by improved business opportunities in the financial and export sectors. An opportunity was lost, however, to bring a broad spectrum of industrialists and other exporters into the decisionmaking process. Individual businessmen continued to petition for specific favors but were only consulted informally on major changes; organized interest groups were not consulted at all.

Policy Oscillations after 1987

Although the elections of 1987 largely completed the process of reestablishing electoral democracy in Turkey, major aspects of economic reform remained unfinished, especially liberalizing imports and reducing fiscal deficits and inflation. Some of this agenda was completed by 1991 but much was not, and policy reversals were common. Often the difficulties in sustaining reform derived from the attempts of ANAP to hold onto power as the scope of the democratic system expanded.

Trade Policy

Although there were no clear breaks in trade policy in the late 1980s, the pattern of "two steps forward, one step backward" was common.[10] In 1986–88, liberalizing trends coexisted with the growth of backdoor barriers in the form of surcharges and taxes, but then in 1989–90 the movement toward freer trade resumed its course. That movement was not complete or uniform, however, for two reasons. First, the responsibility for trade policy was somewhat fragmented, and the centralized bureaucratic process that characterized the decisions of the mid-1980s eroded. Second, a wider range of firms was brought in to discuss the measures beforehand. By the end of the decade, despite tremendous export performance and an improvement over the system of the 1970s, Turkey retained many features of an import-substituting system, with nominal protection in some sectors offset by subsidies to exporters.

The high volume of trade by the late 1980s suggests that distortions had decreased markedly. The actual pattern of trade corresponded roughly with what one would surmise was Turkey's comparative advantage, so the static welfare loss from the trade restraints was probably low. The majority of the welfare loss was probably dynamic, arising because uncertainty discouraged investment and therefore reduced growth of productivity. Protection varied considerably because of extra-budgetary fund levies, although their absolute level was not high, often dropping to zero. This variation seems to have become more discretionary and created many opportunities for rent seeking. The multiplicity of tariffs, levies, quantitative restrictions, and incentives makes it hard to know at any point in time how the relative prices of inputs and outputs for a sector compared with those in the world market.[11] The lack of transparency and frequent changes were confusing not only to bureaucrats and academics but also to firms. They were not sure how trade regulations affected the relative profitability of two activities, but they were relatively sure that those regulations would change in a year or two.

The geometry of Turkey's trade reforms, shown in figure 5-1, sheds light on the political economy. The trade liberalization of the early 1980s had two politically favorable features. First, the degree of distortion was very large initially, so the triangles of efficiency gain were a larger fraction of the transfers. As Rodrik shows elegantly in chapter 3 of this volume, this increases the likelihood of reform. Also, Turkey was a classic case of the trade reform being packaged with a stabilization and external financing package that provided large and quick gains, overshadowing the distributional issues in the early 1980s. In the mid-1980s, the triangles of efficiency gains were smaller, and policymakers had to rely on rising income through steady economic growth to distract people from the distributional issues. By the late 1980s, the tremendous expansion of trade made the rectangles of redistribution very long and thus large even for small changes in the tariff rate. Large reductions in tariffs

Figure 5-1. Social Costs of Trade Barriers in Turkey

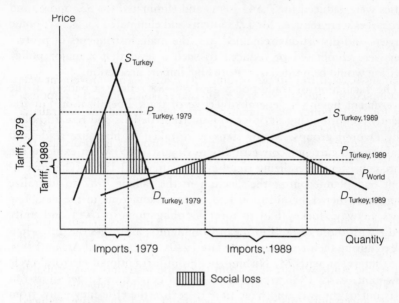

Source: Önis and Webb 1992.

were no longer possible, and large increases were out of the question. Even small changes became big favors because the volume was so high. Protection became politicized again, in the context of a basically open trade regime.

In 1986–88, import policy vacillated. For instance, the number of items subject to restrictive licensing was reduced in May 1986, but the advance deposits for imports were increased, after being virtually eliminated in 1984–85. The import surcharge earmarked for the Price Stability and Support Fund was increased in 1986 and again in 1987. In 1988 the number of items requiring import licenses, which had crept up to 111, was reduced to 33, and customs tariffs were lowered for 234 items, including basic industrial inputs. This brought all tariff rates under 50 percent, although this was partially offset by applying surcharges to more goods and raising the stamp duty on imports. By 1988 total import taxes were only 13 percent of the total value of imports and 37 percent of the value of dutiable imports (Bateman and Arslan 1989, table 9). Most goods entered the country duty free.

In 1989 and 1990, the direction of change became clearer, moving toward major liberalization of import licensing and tariffs, the main instruments of protectionism in the past. In August and September 1989, tariffs (and surcharges) were lowered on more than 300 items, mostly consumer goods. (During 1989, the import regime was modified at least seven times.) In January 1990 the list of items subject to import licensing was abolished, all import deposit guarantees were eliminated, customs duties were reduced for 7,545 items and eliminated for 333 more, and surcharges were reduced for 1,255 items and eliminated for 2,357. Some barriers and distortions remained, but the main instruments of protection were eliminated or reduced to such a level that a major policy decision would be needed to restore high import protection.

The vacillation of trade policy in 1986–88 reflects a pattern of the government having a general objective of trade liberalization but frequently compromising in order to limit trade deficits and reward politically favored groups. Major steps were taken to liberalize trade and establish full currency convertibility in August 1989. What explains the more consistent liberalizing trend evident after mid-1989? The government had planned after the election in the fall of 1987 to liberalize imports further. Liberalization had to come sometime in the next few years anyway. Turkey had to meet its obligations to GATT and unify tariffs with those of the European Community, a process the Turks had halted during their troubles of the late 1970s (Bateman and Arslan 1989, p. 5; interview with M. Nishimizu). From a traditional electoral-cycle viewpoint, early 1988 would have been a good time to get short-run costs out of the way and have time to realize the efficiency gains from liberalization before the next election. At that time, however, the government faced a recession resulting from its anti-inflation stabilization efforts and decided to defer import liberalization. Also, there were still immediate concerns about external credit and foreign exchange constraints. By late 1988, the situation had changed: the economy was booming, led by export growth that was strong enough to generate a current account surplus. In December 1988 the Turks confirmed in a speech to the European Community Ad-hoc Committee that they would fulfill all remaining obligations to reduce tariffs on an accelerated schedule by 1995 (Bateman and Arslan 1989, p. 5).

Short-run political concerns also added to the pressure for liberalization: high inflation had persisted for more than a year, and polls conducted just after the municipal elections in March 1989 singled out inflation as the most important cause for ANAP's unexpected setback. To stem the ebb of his popularity, Özal felt that he had to do more to combat inflation. He had, since the 1970s, argued that liberalizing imports would combat inflationary pressure from domestic monopolies. It would lower the price of imports, with a direct impact on price indexes and therefore on wage demands, and would reduce aggregate demand for domestic products as purchases switched to imported goods.[12]

There have been two wild cards in the array of protectionist instruments in Turkey: levies by the extrabudgetary funds and exemptions from customs duties for incentive programs. The protective effect of the import levies imposed by the extrabudgetary funds increased in the late 1980s. In 1987, these levies contributed approximately 6 percentage points to an overall rate of nominal protection of almost 26 percent.

More interesting from a political economy perspective, however, is the sectoral incidence of the levies and the way in which they contributed to a highly uneven tariff structure. In general, consumer goods and agricultural products managed to secure the highest level of protection from the levies, with relatively less for capital goods and virtually none for intermediate goods. Some traditional consumer goods industries, including beverages and cigarettes, and the transport sector have been able to secure very high levels of protection, such as 83 percent for automobiles (Bateman and Arslan 1989).

Exemptions from import duties were widely granted in the 1980s as a way to encourage certain economic activities, particularly investment and export production. In 1988 more than two-thirds of imports were exempt from all import taxes, not just customs duties. A little more than half of imports were duty free because they were for investment or export production (Bateman and Arslan 1989). Exemptions were sometimes granted as purely political favors. In some notable cases, an importer had a large shipment waiting in port, and a short-term exemption would be granted for that particular category. Obviously, the importer in question would gain a tremendous advantage over his competitors, at the expense of the public treasury and of stable incentives for domestic producers. Other widely known abuses, like export subsidies granted for fictitious exports by politically favored firms, became an embarrassment to the government and contributed to ANAP's setbacks in the municipal elections of March 1989.

Contemporaneous with the growth of backdoor import protection in the late 1980s was a return to more aggressive export support measures, such as duty-free imports, tax rebates, and subsidized credit (table 5-3 shows the changing structure of export incentives).

Macroeconomic Slippage

The macroeconomic situation in Turkey in the late 1980s deteriorated seriously, and two of the major causes were political: electoral cycles and the increased union power of a work force eager to restore real wages, especially in the public sector. In the 1987 electoral campaign, Özal promised to reduce inflation but did not state any specific target, as he had in 1983. Those targets had been badly missed, so Özal softened his promises and started talking of inflation as a price of high growth (Ulagay 1990).

Turkey's macroeconomic problems and attempted solutions in the late 1980s were related to the elections, but no clear pattern is discernible. This illustrates two important points:

- The government always wanted lower inflation but would sometimes tolerate higher inflation, especially if it would come after an election.
- The macroeconomy was not predictable enough for the government

to plan cycles of inflation or deflation in a way that would improve consistently its electoral performance.

Before the election, the government increased deficits to finance more public works projects and subsidies and to cover losses incurred by state-owned enterprises whose prices were being temporarily depressed. After the election, public prices would have to be increased to cover costs, and this would give a big boost to the inflation rate, especially since the public sector products were often inputs. The general election in 1987 exemplified this most clearly (Kjellstrom 1990). Central bank credit to the government grew 40 percent in 1986, 60 percent in 1987, and 40 percent in 1988 (central bank and World Bank staff estimates).

In the aftermath of the March 1989 elections, the ANAP government made a concerted effort to compete with DYP in order to enlarge its rural electoral base. A direct manifestation of these efforts involved a striking increase in agricultural subsidies via the traditional instrument—the support pricing scheme—which, in turn, contributed to the growing fiscal instability in the late 1980s and the early 1990s.

Exchange rate policy became more complex in the late 1980s. The government still wanted the exchange rate to help stimulate exports and control inflation, although it could not do both at once. The government relinquished its direct control of the exchange rate, which it left more as a market response to other policies, especially monetary and fiscal.

From 1986 to mid-1988, the government wanted strong exports to complete the restoration of its external creditworthiness and hence resumed its aggressive devaluation policy, linking the adjustment to recent inflation. Money growth stayed high to sustain the undervaluation and to provide monetary financing of deficits. Both fiscal and real exchange rate factors thus contributed to the problem of inflation (Vieira da Cunha, Webb, and Isaac 1990). Saracoğlu and others at the central bank realized that reducing inflation would be impossible with a devaluation policy aimed at reducing the real exchange rate. The well-publicized lessons of the Southern Cone experience showed that using the nominal exchange rate as an anti-inflationary instrument was risky and ultimately ineffective, especially when the fiscal deficit was not yet under control. A prerequisite for an anti-inflation policy at the central bank, in the presence of high budget deficits, was letting the exchange rate float.

By late 1988, Turkey was running a current account surplus, and in October 1988 the government decided to let the rate float. When a run on the lira ensued, the central bank responded not by backtracking on the floating rate but rather by sharply tightening credit in the recently developed interbank overnight money market. The central bank subsequently loosened credit when the crisis passed, keeping the real exchange rate at about its pre-October level.[13] In contrast to the bad impression created by the failed stabilization attempt in early 1988, the central bank seized the high ground, demonstrating that tight credit and high interest

rates were an effective and sometimes necessary means to fight speculation against the national currency and prevent rapid depreciation that
could lead to runaway inflation. The floating exchange rate was obviously managed, through the market, to prevent short-term gyrations, but
henceforth the central bank would be able to let economic fundamentals
take their course.

After 1988, Turkey's exchange rate policy was motivated mainly by
macroeconomic considerations, and the effects on trade were incidental
and largely undesired. Although the real exchange rate continued to have
important effects on trade, the nominal exchange rate policy was no
longer driven primarily by trade considerations. In 1989–91, rising fiscal
deficits combined with tight monetary policy to produce rising real interest rates, capital inflow, and real appreciation, as the nominal depreciation slowed relative to the rate of inflation. The fiscal deficits rose for the
usual political reasons: the government thought it could win votes by
increasing spending and could avoid losing votes by holding down taxes.
It lacked the institutional links that would let it appeal to many groups
on any basis other than special favors of spending or tax breaks. The
government fought inflation only with tight monetary policy, realizing
that this also had the effect of making the real exchange rate overvalued,
especially in 1990 (Krueger and Turan 1993).

The government's influence over the real exchange rate also declined in
the late 1980s as the relaxation of legal constraints on the labor movement led to increasing strike activity and more generous wage settle-
ments. Nevertheless, the share of labor costs in value added was still
lower in Turkey in 1990–91 than in the rest of Southern Europe and than
in Turkey itself in the 1970s (OECD 1990/91, p. 99; Özmucur 1991).
Wages had not yet had a major effect on the real exchange rate, but the
direction of pressure was definitely upward.

The pattern of labor union activity in the late 1980s and early 1990s in
some ways resembled the pattern of the late 1970s. Unions conceived
their role as that of a self-interested pluralistic pressure group, pushing
for the highest wage increases possible. They did not develop a longer-
term vision in which sustainable real wage increases would be limited to
increases in productivity. A comparison of the two key wage rounds in
1989 and 1991 reveals the evolution of union attitudes. The wage round
of 1989 was mainly defensive, a long-overdue attempt to recover what
workers had lost in real terms during the decade. The wage round of
1991 was offensive, however, and aimed to secure the maximum real
wage increase. This is understandable, given that labor's trust was destroyed by a long period of exclusion and by the refusal of business and
other key groups to make reciprocal concessions, such as accepting adequate taxation.

Real wages rebounded strongly starting in 1989, and this accompanied
a real revaluation in purchasing terms (see table 5-1). The major private
sector firms could afford to give substantial wage increases, especially in

the export sectors, because they had enjoyed high profits in the 1980s and had been able to make productivity-enhancing investments. In the public sector, however, wage increases proved much more burdensome. Most state-owned firms had not increased their productivity in the 1980s as fast as the private sector had, so the wage increases often exceeded their profit margins, necessitating central government subsidies, price increases, and reduced sales.

Fiscal and Monetary Policy

Going into the 1987 election, the government stimulated a boom with fiscal expansion while repressing inflation by restraining devaluation and public sector prices, making them fall behind in real terms. Immediately after the election, it raised public sector prices to stem the losses incurred by public enterprises and resumed devaluations at a pace that kept the real exchange rate competitive. The government realized that the measures would cause average prices to rise but expected, or at least hoped, that this would produce a one-time blip in the inflation rate and not persist. The rise of electricity prices and other inputs to industry pushed inflation up from less than 40 to almost 80 percent, and it did not come down quickly. Voters who had elected ANAP for its record of economic management felt betrayed and turned against the party in the municipal elections of March 1989.

In 1988 the government tried and failed to have stabilization led by fiscal retrenchment. The stabilization program of February 1988, designed to restabilize the economy, caused a sharp fall in the growth rate, but without reducing inflation. Inflation rates of 60 to 70 percent were increasingly the norm in the latter half of the decade, rising from an initial base of 25 to 30 percent in 1983. This contrasted sharply with a key promise of the ANAP government in 1983 to reduce inflation to 10 percent within a single year (Ulagay 1987). As the decade progressed, this promise became less and less credible, and the government lost its resolve. It began to rationalize that inflation was the price of rapid development, replacing earlier declarations that controlling inflation was the government's central priority.

Technocrats in the central bank, treasury, and State Planning Organization understood well the policy changes necessary to reduce inflation—namely to reduce fiscal deficits in a sustainable way—so that the central bank could slow the growth of domestic credit without starving the private sector. The policy dialogue with the IMF and the World Bank in 1987–90 explored the deficit-inflation issue with the Turkish government, and at the staff level these groups reached fundamental agreement. The politicians, at least some of whom also understood the economics involved, decided against tighter fiscal policy in the end, although several reforms may have helped lay the basis for disinflation later.[14]

Following the example of the Bundesbank and central banks in other industrial countries, the treasury and central bank agreed that there should be an annual monetary program. The events of 1989–91, and even 1992, illustrate the difficulty and ultimately the impossibility of establishing an independent central bank unless the government is committed to low fiscal deficits. The staff of the treasury and the central bank developed a monetary program in 1989, although without public announcement. It failed because of excess credit demands from the government. The next year, with more foresight, the central bank and treasury waited until the latter could make a commitment—sign a protocol—not to borrow more than a certain amount from the central bank. Only then did the central bank announce a monetary program, to which it kept. The protocol did not stop the treasury from increasing its borrowing, which was financed that year by borrowing in the domestic capital market, where inflows of foreign capital were strong.

Events in the first half of 1991 illustrate the importance of establishing the precedent and expectation of the monetary program. At the beginning of 1991, the minister of state for economy did not have the treasury issue a commitment on the deficit and financing. The central bank responded by declining to issue a monetary plan. The treasury further insisted that the central bank double its rate of financing to the government in order to hold down the cost of borrowing. The central bank recognized that it could not sustain both interest rate and exchange rate targets and, rather than use up its foreign exchange reserves to hold temporarily to the two targets, it let the Turkish lira fall rapidly under market pressure. The treasury then retreated. It was by then too late in the year for a formal protocol and monetary program, but the treasury did agree to a fixed nominal limit on its monthly borrowing from the central bank, which would progressively decline in real terms. The central bank accepted the increase in money base at the beginning of the year but after March kept reserve money growing at a rate slightly below the growth rate for 1990, which was within the range of the monetary program for 1991.

More disagreement surfaced within the bureaucracy as the central bank became more autonomous during the latter half of the 1980s. The February 1988 stabilization program, following the small crisis associated with the pre-election boom of 1987, was prepared essentially by the central bank with no input from the State Planning Organization (although the report itself that formed the basis of the February measures was publicized as the joint product of the three key agencies: the central bank, the State Planning Organization, and the treasury). The first conflict revolved around the exchange rate policy, with the State Planning Organization on one side and the central bank and the treasury on the other. The State Planning Organization opposed the real appreciation of the exchange rate in 1989 and 1990 because of its negative impact on the tradable sector and the long-run competitiveness of the economy. The perspective was supported by econometric evidence, which identified the real exchange rate as the key determinant of export performance in the Turkish case (Arslan and van Wijnbergen 1990; Barlow and Şenşes 1992; for an alternate view see Celasun and Rodrik 1989). The second disagreement was between the central bank and the treasury, which disagreed about the timing of capital account liberalization and of the transition to convertibility. The central bank opposed the August 1989 measures liberalizing the capital account, arguing that such measures were premature, considering the degree of macroeconomic instability. Finally, the central bank's monetary program became a subject of disagreement. Following the introduction of its monetary program in 1990, the central bank was criticized by the other two key agencies, which argued that a monetary program would not be effective unless it was coordinated with other macroeconomic policies, particularly control over the budget deficit.

The problems of coordinating the key bureaucratic agencies were aggravated further by the political vacuum following Özal's election to the presidency in November 1989. Işin Çelebi, minister of state, took a basically pro–State Planning Organization stance, on the exchange rate issue in particular, while Güneş Taner, the other minister responsible for the economy, agreed with the central bank and the treasury, particularly on the exchange rate issue. Disagreement over the exchange rate policy reflected the State Planning Organization's greater emphasis on growth and long-run competitiveness plus the central bank's and the treasury's corresponding concern with stabilization and inflation. The central bank increased its influence at the expense of the State Planning Organization, the premier institution for the pre-1980 era. This pattern was clearly validated by the attempt to restructure the economic bureaucracy a few months prior to the general elections of 1991. A primary objective was to take implementation functions away from the State Planning Organization and give it a more advisory role.

Political Management

Following the second ANAP victory in the November 1987 elections, Özal's direct involvement with economic management diminished, leading after that to fragmentation and lack of coordination in economic decisionmaking. That year was also a turning point because wage pressures reemerged, repayment of the foreign debt (both the interest and the principal) became an increased burden on the budget and macroeconomic balances, and the increasing fiscal deficits heightened the conflict between growth and competitiveness, on the one hand, and short-run stabilization, on the other.

The ANAP party failed to establish a strong base of support from the groups benefiting from structural adjustment. The failure to reap political support from the beneficiaries of stabilization reflected mainly the government's failure to sustain stabilization. When political support wavered, the government did not hark back to the success of the 1980 stabilization and call for a return to sound fiscal policy; rather, it usually tried populist measures that were fiscally damaging, such as restraining public sector price increases, increasing public sector wages, and spending more on popular local projects. Trade liberalization, by contrast, did expand the group of winners from structural adjustment. But because the policies often changed unpredictably and without consultation with the groups most directly affected—the top-down management style—the creation of a large group of gainers did not translate into corresponding political support for the ANAP government. ANAP could run as the party of successful structural adjustment in 1983 and 1987, but this reputation had faded by 1991.

Lessons from Turkey

The wide variation in economic and political outcomes in Turkey since the beginning of the 1980s offers the opportunity to draw important lessons on what to do and what not to do in politically managing structural adjustment. This chapter concludes first by summarizing the balance of achievements and then indicating the lessons that seem to transcend the Turkish circumstances.

Balance of Achievements

The Turkish adjustment accomplished a major structural reorientation of the economy. The share of output for export rose from 5 percent in 1979 to 23 percent in 1989, and real output roughly doubled. The financial markets not only were open internationally, in stark contrast to the situation before 1980, but also developed depth and sophistication. Even in areas where the program must be judged a failure as of the end of 1991—reducing fiscal deficits, inflation, income inequality, and the size of the inefficient public enterprise sector—the transformations of trade and finance fundamentally altered the context of the problems, changing their effects on the private sector and changing the options for the government to deal with them.

Although the first phase of economic adjustment was sustained, but not initiated, in an authoritarian context, the Turks restored democracy when the reform was incomplete. ANAP won office on the platform of economic success and eventually lost in part because of economic failure. The electoral defeat of ANAP in 1991 did not mean, however, the demise of the coalitions supporting structural adjustment or liberalization. The long period of ANAP rule helped consolidate reforms to such a degree that all the principal parties agreed on a broadly similar economic program. The ideological differences between the left and the right—state directed versus market oriented—substantially diminished. Despite the persistence of significant distributional conflicts, broad agreement on the desirability of market-oriented reforms constituted an important source of optimism for the future of structural adjustment in an era of coalition politics. Without sharp ideological conflicts, coalition politics in the 1990s seem unlikely to duplicate the highly unstable pattern of the late 1970s.

Although the reforms of the early 1980s greatly reduced the importance of rent seeking, particularly with regard to foreign trade, patronage politics by ANAP became more widespread again in the latter half of the decade as some features of the import-substitution regime continued. Hence, the initial strength that ANAP derived from control of state resources became a disadvantage as the dispensing of favors led to growing resentment and reaction on the part of the wider populace. Also, over-invoicing exports—or creating fictitious exports to take advantage of favorable export subsidies—and the subsequent failure of the government to discipline or penalize adequately the companies involved created political discontent. Fictitious exports also jeopardized the popularity of exporters, as a group, and the attempts since 1980 to build a coalition supporting exports.

Although the private sector became much more vibrant and competitive in world markets, a large public sector remained basically intact at the end of the ANAP era and created rent-seeking opportunities. Many people became disaffected by ANAP's arbitrary distribution of rents from the central government. Traditional sources of patronage politics included state economic enterprises, public banks, and public sector contracts. The extrabudgetary funds created new avenues for distributing rents. Fiscal decentralization during the period, involving the proliferation of extrabudgetary funds and the granting of increased spending authority to municipalities, also tended to amplify fiscal disequilibrium.

Top-down Political Liberalization

The hierarchical structure of ANAP, under a strong and dominant leader, helped the party in the early and mid-1980s but was increasingly a disadvantage during the latter half of the decade. Özal's style of leadership and his unwillingness to delegate power prevented a smooth transition of leadership within the party. Part of ANAP's defeat in the 1991 elections occurred because some of its constituency transferred to the smaller Islamic fundamentalist party, which increased its share of the vote strikingly compared with the 1987 elections.

Furthermore, the political vacuum left by Özal's ascendance to the presidency created divisions within the party and the government itself. These divisions were partly responsible for the problems with macroeconomic coordination. The divisions within the party led eventually to the withdrawal of important parts of the conservative-religious faction. Under the leadership of Mesut Yilmaz, a representative of the liberal

wing, ANAP recovered some of its old cohesion and vitality but not sufficiently to prevent defeat in the election of 1991.

Empowered Technocrats

From a comparative perspective, the Turkish experience up to late
1987 shows the effectiveness of having a key individual lead a select
group of technocrats in securing the degree of consistency and bureaucratic cohesion needed to initiate structural adjustment. Yet, once the leader
departs, coordination becomes a problem in the absence of an autonomous and internally coherent bureaucracy.

In retrospect, the failures of macroeconomic policy in the late 1980s
can be traced to three forces. First, a broad consultative process was not
institutionalized to cultivate popular support for macroeconomic stability. Second, the top bureaucrats lacked autonomy from the politicians
and, hence, were unable to counteract the pressures to expand the fiscal
deficit. Third, problems of coordination and conflict plagued the bureaucracy itself, and these were accentuated further by the appointment in
1989 of two separate ministers (Güneş Taner and Işin Çelebi), both of
whom tried to assume responsibility for running the economy.

The highly centralized and insulated policy apparatus that Özal created in the early 1980s helped initiate and sustain reform through its
early stages. Yet, insulation and lack of institutionalized links with interest groups increasingly became a disadvantage for coordinating policy
and managing distributional conflicts under conditions of fully competitive politics.

Dealing with Interest Groups

Political management of the reform process requires coalition-building
to deal with interest groups. This means developing each part of the
reform package so that it contributes to the overall objectives of the
program and at the same time satisfies the relevant groups enough for
them to go along with the overall program, even if some parts are not to
their liking. Turkey had mixed success in this regard.

The support of large-scale business was the domestic counterpart of
extensive external assistance, and both factors contributed to the success
of structural adjustment efforts. Conglomerates occupy a pivotal position in the Turkish economy. By 1980, the major conglomerates represented by TÜSİAD had recognized that the import-substitution model,
which involved sales to a heavily protected home market, was no longer
feasible, and they smoothed the path for trade liberalization. They had
been the bastions of import substitution during the 1960s and 1970s but
emerged as the principal exporters in the 1980s. The dominant role of
export-import companies, most of which were subsidiaries of major conglomerates, in the export surge of the 1980s clearly supports this
proposition.

The absence of serious distributional pressures on policymakers for a considerable period (due to the authoritarian regime during the 1980–83 phase and limited political liberalization during the 1983–87 era) also proved to be a key factor contributing to a process of smooth adjustment from a position of acute crisis. Real wage flexibility, due to the political exclusion of labor up to 1987, contributed to the short-run economic success of structural adjustment, although with obvious costs for the objective of democracy and income equality. The pattern of labor relations after 1987, which fits neither the "exclusion" nor the "corporatist intermediation" categories, clearly has been a source of instability. TÜSİAD recently sponsored a study recommending the creation of an economic and social council, which would bring together, in a formal and legally recognized setting, representatives of business (TOBB, TÜSİAD, Turk-Trade, and TISK, the employers' association), labor (Türk-İş and DISK, recently legalized), agriculture (TÖZB), and the government. The council would work to create a consensus on the framework for economic policy and on the specific measures to effect it. It would provide feedback and guidance during the implementation process (Öniş and Sunar 1992).

Packaging and Tradeoffs between Macroeconomic and Trade Reforms

The Turkish case illustrates both the benefits of packaging trade and macroeconomic reforms, in order to make both more politically acceptable, and the dangers of letting trade and financial sector reforms attract financing that permits the country to avoid fiscal structural adjustment.

The crisis of 1979–80 created for most Turks a mental association between the scarcity of imported goods and the problems of the old economic policy regime. Consequently, through the 1980s, trade reforms were widely recognized as being in the interest of the average man rather than as concessions to foreign or internationalist interests. Export subsidies in the form of low-interest credit and tax rebates played an important role because they encouraged exports and helped Turkey build a coalition in support of exports. Thus an unorthodox instrument helped the government buy support for the more conventional instruments such as exchange rate devaluation and import liberalization.

Packaging fiscal reforms to help stabilize the economy with trade and exchange rate reforms to alleviate the balance of payments crisis in the early 1980s made both kinds of reform more attractive politically. Another pattern in the late 1980s, however, made additional and more radical trade and exchange rate reforms *instead of* enacting the necessary macroeconomic measures, especially reducing the fiscal deficit. This exacerbated economic problems over the longer term, although it did help the government get continued financing over the short term and alleviated other symptoms of macroeconomic problems.

Speed of Reform

A large portion of the reforms were initiated in two windows of political opportunity when the government had a mandate for dramatic action: in the balance of payments crisis of 1980 and in the honeymoon of 1983–84 that followed democratization. Making reforms rapidly was important at these junctures. Later in the 1980s, as the democratic process became more routine, reforms succeeded when they were carefully prepared in consultation with the groups affected. Crash programs and gradualism were thus appropriate for different circumstances.

External Influences

The substantial external assistance that Turkey received in the early 1980s contributed to a large supply response and, hence, to a speedy recovery, which reduced the costs of stabilization and structural adjustment. The scale and speed of the recovery helped policymakers justify the program to broad segments of the population, override opposition, and consolidate a coalition in favor of reform. Given the acute import-starvation of the Turkish economy at the peak of the crisis, rapid recovery would not have been feasible in the absence of external assistance on a substantial scale. Slow recovery would have jeopardized the future of the program.

In the late 1980s, however, Turkey's success in getting external financing from commercial as well as official sources and the success of the government in getting domestic financing unfortunately allowed the government to pursue expansionary fiscal policies for short-term political motives. This caused serious problems with inflation and eventually with other types of macroeconomic instability.

Membership in GATT helped promote trade liberalization, as did prospects of joining the European Community. The rules of GATT helped, for example, eliminate export rebates in 1988. The government strongly favored admission to the European Community, but most top officials recognized that the prospects for admission were remote. They timed the application in 1987 to be part of the campaign to get domestic political approval for that round of trade liberalization.

Challenges for the 1990s

The twin challenges that Turkey faced as it entered the 1990s were to consolidate and broaden democracy and to renew the efforts at economic reform. Consolidating democracy would involve expanding human rights and the avenues for political discussion of economic interests. The experience of the 1980s had modernized the economy and removed many of the ideological impediments to policy formation, which had paralyzed it in the 1970s. The political culture remained paternalistic, however, so that the democratic incentives to seek popular support were channeled into patronage and the direct provision of benefits. This made good macroeconomic policy almost impossible. To meet the challenge of economic reform as well would require political and institutional innovations that resolve distributional conflicts—over issues like wages, taxation, and agricultural support prices—and avoid populist solutions.

Appendix 5-1: The Budget Process

The problems in coordinating agencies responsible for economic policy in Turkey are well illustrated by the routine established after 1983 for making the annual government budget. In the first phase, the Budget Department in the Ministry of Finance gathers current expenditure request forms from various parts of the central government and collates them. The State Planning Organization puts together the investment budget. This is a political process, with requests coming from various ministries and members of Parliament, who are the conduits for any interest group pressure. (Only ANAP deputies participated in the process during their tenure in power; opposition parties were totally shut out of the process.) The State Planning Organization receives the requests and collates and reconciles them with the five-year plan. The draft budgets for the state-owned enterprises are done in the treasury, with input from the State Planning Organization on the investment program. In the second phase, the State Planning Organization, the treasury, and the Budget Department of the Ministry of Finance bring together their parts of the draft budget and reconcile them with the macroeconomic program for the coming year. The treasury prepares this program on the basis of the macroeconomic forecasting done in the State Planning Organization. The output from the three agencies, known as the technical budget, is passed to the High Planning Council. Here the prime minister and other top politicians make final adjustments and then submit the budget to Parliament for approval. Further changes in Parliament are usually minor—mainly adjusting salary levels and making a few changes in public investment.

Implementing the budget is the task of the treasury. Some divergence between the planned budget and the outcome is inevitable since the budget is formulated in nominal terms when inflation makes it impossible for the government to forecast accurately the path of prices over the year. If the government wants to convince Parliament of the need for fiscal tightening, it understates revenues. If the Budget Commission, an interagency organization, decides on spending cuts (usually across the board), it passes these on to the Ministry of Finance to enact. (With regard to extrabudgetary funds, the treasury usually tries to understate revenues and claw back revenue from them.) Unanticipated inflation or political pressures may lead the government to implement an extra-contractual adjustment of public sector wages.

Notes

1. Local thresholds are determined by dividing the total number of votes in the constituency by the total number of seats allocated to the constituency. The local threshold therefore varies, from a minimum of 20 percent in the largest forty-eight constituencies with six seats each (also in districts with five seats) to a maximum of 50 percent in constituencies with only two seats each. Furthermore, in forty-six constituencies only one member is elected on the basis of a simple majority, which also hinders the participation of small parties.

2. This conflict has manifested itself particularly in the textile sector. Exporters of clothing want cheap imports of raw materials (fabric, yarn, and fiber) contrary to the interests of local producers.

3. Some of the Princes and their followers started out with a degree from the Faculty of Political Science in Ankara—the equivalent of the French École Nationale—but then went on for a graduate degree in the United States or Europe. Some even worked for a time in the private sector before entering the government, and some began their studies at Boğaziçi or Middle East Technical University in engineering or economics.

4. Bienen and van de Walle (1991) show the generality of the pattern whereby people who remain in office longer gain in power.

5. Krueger and Turan (1993) advise caution in attributing the adoption of the program to pressure from TÜSİAD. The article by Özal in 1977 is well within the tradition of having the president of TÜSİAD, then Feyyaz Berker of the Tekfen Group, sponsor a position piece without being able to mobilize the organization to lobby for it directly with the government.

6. Diwan (1990) explains how export promotion measures, which would create distortions and inefficiencies in other contexts, can increase welfare when they are integral to a strategy for debt rescheduling.

7. Boratav 1990; Özmucur 1991. Many small businesses lost from the stabilization package because of the costs of high interest, but small business activities were so varied that a comprehensive assessment is not possible. Many small firms profited, for example, from export-oriented expansion.

8. All dollar amounts are U.S. dollars.

9. Unlike the typical case of persistent moderate inflation (Dornbusch and Fischer 1991), monetary financing of government deficits played an important role in Turkey up through 1988 (van Wijnbergen, Anand, and Rocha 1988). Expansion of central bank credit to the private sector was not a serious contributor to inflation.

10. This expression in Turkish alludes to a famous and generally successful battle tactic of the Ottoman army, ritualized by the Janissary bands. To achieve victory against the opponents of reform, as against the enemies of the olden empire, the tactic requires discipline to ensure that the forward steps greatly outnumber the backward.

11. Quantitative studies of effective protection, such as that by Olgun, Togan, and Akder (1989, cited in OECD 1990/91, pp. 86–89), are based on legal tariff rates, and they do not systematically take into account the effects of quantitative restrictions and export incentives.

12. To some extent, these effects would be mitigated because import liberalization would cause the real exchange rate to depreciate by increasing the demand for foreign exchange. Depreciation would push import prices back up and increase the demand for exports, but this would take longer than the anti-inflationary effects.

13. There was great concern about distress in the banking system at this time, making the central bank reluctant to boost real interest rates permanently. Also, continued tight money would cause the real exchange rate to appreciate, and the central bank presumably did not want the floating rate regime immediately associated with overvaluation. Stopping inflation almost always leads to some overvaluation, whether or not the exchange rate is used as an instrument of control (Dornbusch 1980), but the central bank in 1988 was not in a position to lead a full-fledged disinflation program.

14. The Ministry of Finance, under Pakdemirli, did, in 1989, develop a comprehensive tax reform that would have raised more revenue and improved efficiency by, for instance, establishing a corporate income tax. The proposal was rejected, however, after big business protested.

References

Acar, Feride. 1991. "The True Path Party, 1983–1989." In Metin Heper and Jacob M. Landau, eds., *Political Parties and Democracy in Turkey.* London: I. B. Tauris Co.

Arat, Yeşim. 1991. "Politics and Big Business: Janus-Faced Link to the State." In Metin Heper, ed., *Strong State and Economic Interest Groups: The Post-1980 Turkish Experience,* pp. 135–48. Berlin: Walter de Gruyter.

Arícanlí, Tosun A., and Dani Rodrik, eds. 1990. *The Political Economy of Turkey: Debt, Adjustment, and Sustainability.* London: Macmillan.

Arslan, İsmail, and Sweder van Wijnbergen. 1990. "Turkey: Export Miracle or Accounting Trick?" Policy, Research, and External Affairs Working Paper Series 220. World Bank, Washington, D.C.

Barlow, Robin, and Fikret Senşes. 1992. "The Turkish Export Boom: Just Reward or Just Lucky?" Middle East Technical University, Ankara, March. Processed.

Bateman, Deborah, and İsmail Arslan. 1989. "A Note on Turkey's Trade Regime." Processed.

Baysan, Tercan, and Charles Blitzer. 1989. "Turkey." In A. M. Choksi, M. Michaely, and D. Papageorgiou, eds., *Liberalizing Foreign Trade,* vol. 6, Oxford: Basil Blackwell.

Bienen, Henry, and Nicholas van de Walle. 1991. *Of Time and Power: Leadership Duration in the Modern World.* Stanford, Calif.: Stanford University Press.

Boratav, Korkut. 1990. "Inter-Class and Intra-Class Relations of Distribution under Structural Adjustment: Turkey during the 1980s." In Tosun Arícanlí and Dani Rodrik, eds., *The Political Economy of Turkey: Debt, Adjustment, and Sustainability.* London: Macmillan.

Buğra, Ayşe. 1991. "Political Sources of Uncertainty in Business Life." In Metin Heper, ed., *Strong State and Economic Interest Groups: The Post-1980 Turkish Experience,* pp. 151–62. Berlin: Walter de Gruyter.

Çakmak, Cem. 1990. "1987 genel seçimleri ve 1989 yerel seçimleri: Bir karşilaştirma." METU *Studies in Development* 17:1–2, pp. 1–23.

Celasun, Merih. 1990. "Fiscal Aspects of Adjustment in the 1980s." In Tosun Arícanlí and Dani Rodrik, eds., *The Political Economy of Turkey: Debt, Adjustment, and Sustainability.* London: Macmillan.

Celasun, Merih, and Dani Rodrik. 1989. "Debt, Adjustment, and Growth: Turkey." In Jeffrey D. Sachs and Susan Collins, eds., *Developing Country Debt and Economic Performance,* vol. 3, pp. 720. Chicago, Ill.: University of Chicago Press.

Diwan, Ishac. 1990. "Linking Trade and External Debt Strategies." *Journal of International Economics* 29, pp. 293–310.

Dornbusch, Rudiger. 1980. *Open Economy Macroeconomics.* New York, N.Y.: Basic Books.

Dornbusch, Rudiger, and Stanley Fischer. 1991. "Moderate Inflation." NBER Working Paper 3896. National Bureau of Economic Research, Cambridge, Mass.

Ergüder, Üstün. 1991a. "Agriculture: The Forgotten Sector." In Metin Heper, ed., *Strong State and Economic Interest Groups: The Post-1980 Turkish Experience,* pp. 71–78. Berlin: Walter de Gruyter.

_____. 1991b. "The Motherland Party, 1983–1989." In Metin Heper and Jacob M. Landau, eds., *Political Parties and Democracy in Turkey,* pp. 152–69. London: I. B. Tauris Co.

Heper, Metin. 1985. *The State Tradition in Turkey.* Walkington, Eng.: Eathen Press.

_____. 1989. "The Motherland Party Governments and Bureaucracy in Turkey, 1983–1989." *Governance* 2, pp. 457–68.

_____. 1990. "The State and De-Bureaucratization: The Turkish Case." *International Social Science Journal* 126, pp. 605–15.

_____, ed. 1991. *Strong State and Economic Interest Groups: The Post-1980 Turkish Experience.* Berlin: Walter de Gruyter.

Keesings Contemporary Archives. *Record of World Events.* 1984. pp. 32926.

Keyder, Çağlar. 1987. *State and Class in Turkey: A Study in Capitalist Development.* London: Verso.

Kjellstrom, Sven. 1990. "Turkish Political Economy." World Bank, Country Economics Department, Washington, D.C. Processed.

Koç, Vehbi. 1992. Speech made at the Third Izmir Congress on the Turkish economy.

Krueger, Anne O. 1974a. *Foreign Trade Regimes and Economic Development: Turkey.* New York: Columbia University Press for National Bureau of Economic Research.

_____. 1974b. "The Political Economy of the Rent-Seeking Society." *American Economic Review* 64:3, pp. 291–303.

Krueger, Anne O., and Okay H. Aktan. 1992. *Swimming against the Tide: Turkish Trade Reform in the 1980s.* San Francisco: International Center for Economic Growth, ics Press.

Krueger, Anne O., and Ilter Turan. 1993. "The Politics and Economics of Turkish Policy Reforms in the 1980s." In Robert Bates and Anne O. Krueger, eds., *Political and Economic Interactions in Economic Policy Reform.* London: Basil Blackwell.

Mardin, Şerif. 1973. "Center-Periphery Relations: A Key to Turkish Politics?" *Deadalus* 102, pp. 169–90.

Milanovic, Branko. 1986. *Export Incentives and Turkish Manufacturing Exports, 1980–84.* World Bank Staff Working Paper 786. Washington, D.C.: World Bank.

OECD (Organization for Economic Cooperation and Development). 1981. *OECD Economic Survey: Turkey,* March. Paris.

_____. 1990/91. *Economic Survey: Turkey, March 1991.* Paris.

Okyar, Osman. 1983. "Turkey and the IMF: A Review of Relations, 1978–82." In John Williamson, ed., *IMF Conditionality.* Washington, D.C.: Institute for International Economics.

Olgun, Hasan. 1991. "Turkey." In Anne O. Krueger, Maurice Schiff, and Alberto Valdes, eds., *The Political Economy of Agricultural Pricing Policy,* vol. 3,

Africa and the Mediterranean. Baltimore, Md.: Johns Hopkins University Press.

Olgun, Hasan, Sübidey Togan, and Halis Akder. 1989. *Recent Developments in Turkey's External Economic Relations*. Ankara: Turktrade Publications.

Öniş, Ziya. 1992. "Organization of Export-Oriented Industrialization: The Turkish Foreign Trade Companies in Comparative Perspective." In T. Nas and M. Odekon, eds., *The Politics and Economics of Turkish Liberalization*. London: Associated Universities Press.

Öniş, Ziya, and James Riedel. 1993. *Economic Crises and Long-Term Growth in Turkey*. Washington, D.C.: World Bank.

Öniş, Ziya, and İlkay Sunar. 1992. *Sanayilesmede yönetime ve toplumsal uzlasma*. Istanbul: TÜSİAD YAYÍNÍ.

Öniş, Ziya, and Steven B. Webb, 1992. "Political Economy of Policy Reform in Turkey," World Bank, Country Economics Department, Washington, D.C.

Oyan, Oğuz, and Ali Ríza Aydín. 1991. *Türkiye'de Maliye ve Fon Politikalarí: Alternatif Yönelisler*. Ankara: Adím Yavíncílík.

Oyan, Oğuz, Ali Ríza Aydín, and Aziz Konukman. 1991. *Türkiye'de Fon Sisteminin Kamu Kesimi İçindeki Yeri ve Ekonomik Etkileri*. Ankara: TOBB YAYÍNÍ.

Özal, Turgut. 1991. Speech, November.

Özbudun, Ergun. 1991. "The Post-1980 Legal Framework for Interest Group Associations." In Metin Heper, ed., *Strong State and Economic Interest Groups: The Post-1980 Turkish Experience*, pp. 41–53. Berlin: Walter de Gruyter.

Özmucur, Süleyman. 1991. "Gelirin fonksiyonel dağílímí, 1948–1991." Boğaziçi University Research Paper ISS/EC 91-06. Boğaziçi University, Istanbul.

Saracoğlu, Rüşdü. 1987. "Economic Stabilization and Structural Adjustment: The Case of Turkey." In Vittorio Corbo, Morris Goldstein, and Mohsin Khan, eds., *Growth-Oriented Adjustment Programs*. Washington, D.C.: IMF and World Bank.

State Institute of Statistics. 1991. *Statistical Indicators for 1923–1990*. Ankara.

Ulagay, Osman. 1987. *Özal ekonomisinde paramiz pul olurken kim kazandi, kim kaybetti*. Ankara: Bilgi Yayinevi.

————. 1990. *Enflasyuno asmak icin*. Istanbul: AFA Yaginlari.

Undersecretariat for Treasury and Foreign Trade. 1992. *Treasury Monthly Indicators*. Ankara: UTFT, January.

van Wijnbergen, Sweder, Ritu Anand, and Roberto Rocha. 1988. "Inflation, External Debt, and Financial Sector Reform in Turkey: A Quantitative Approach to Consistent Fiscal Policy." World Bank, Washington, D.C. Processed.

Vieira da Cunha, Paulo, Steven Webb, and A. Isaac. 1990. "The Dynamics of Inflation in Turkey in the 1980s." World Bank, Washington, D.C. Processed.

Waterbury, John. 1992. "Export-Led Growth and the Center-Right Coalition in Turkey." *Comparative Politics* 24:2 (January), pp. 127–45.

Wolff, Peter. 1987. *Stabilization Policy and Structural Adjustment in Turkey, 1980–1985: The Role of IMF and World Bank in an Extremely Supported Adjustment Process*. Berlin: German Development Institute.

Poland: The Political Economy
of Shock Therapy

SIMON JOHNSON AND MARZENA KOWALSKA

AT THE BEGINNING OF 1990, AFTER INHERITING A DISASTROUS macro-economic situation, the first noncommunist Polish government in forty years implemented a radical program of reform that brought inflation under control, eliminated shortages, produced a current account surplus, and made the currency convertible. This program was sustained by a strong political coalition with widespread social support, as well as by considerable assistance from western governments, which provided not only financial aid and a debt reduction agreement but also important intellectual and technical support for the program.

Despite its undeniable successes, the program ran into serious political difficulties. The results of the first year were in many ways impressive, but economic performance in the second year deteriorated markedly. Facing a new set of economic difficulties, the second noncommunist government no longer had the political room to maneuver enjoyed by its predecessor. Problems with state enterprises and the budget mounted until they constituted a new crisis. By the end of 1991, this crisis had combined with the results of the first free parliamentary elections to

For their comments on drafts of this chapter, the authors thank Stephan Haggard, Michael Lav, Branko Milanovic, Steven Webb, Stanislaw Wellisz, and participants in the May 1991 and May 1992 World Bank conferences on the political economy of structural adjustment in new democracies.

produce the resignation of Jan Krzysztof Bielecki's government and of the program's architect, Leszek Balcerowicz.

Some elements of the program remain intact, and it is very unlikely that Poland could ever go back to its previous economic system. Nevertheless, despite its remarkable initial success, the Polish stabilization program ran into serious difficulties. What happened in Poland? There are three main puzzles about the political economy of adjustment in Poland. First, how did Solidarity—a social movement with strong trade union roots—come to support a government with such a radical promarket reform program? Second, given the costs imposed by this program, why did it face hardly any effective opposition during its first year (1990)? Third, given the initial economic and political success of the program, what caused the serious political problems encountered in its second year (1991)?

This chapter shows that Solidarity, as a movement, did not have clear plans about the economic policies it would implement if it came to power in 1989. Solidarity did surprisingly well in the June 1989 election, and this success immediately altered thinking about what was feasible in Poland. While the economic situation deteriorated rapidly, only two groups of Polish economists presented coherent policy proposals. The authors of the seemingly less radical proposal were brought into a government supported both by public opinion and by a remarkable political coalition. The shock nature of the economic program took advantage of these initial conditions and rapidly created irreversible macroeconomic and institutional changes.

The program initially met with surprisingly little organized opposition even though it imposed significant costs on many people. In part this was because the effects of the program tended to divide rather than unify social groups. Most groups, with the significant exception of farmers, had trouble organizing against it because they were disoriented and confused about how best to respond and did not have effective political representation of their group interests. Of course, these groups were represented by Solidarity, but this encompassing organization had broad anticommunist goals and strongly supported the program. At least through the summer of 1990, no new political groupings could harness society's disorientation and disaffection. Seen in retrospect, the election of Lech Walesa to the presidency in December 1990 actually strengthened the program by establishing a political figure able to transcend particular interests.

The program's problems emerged more clearly when the existing political blocs—both Solidarity and the former communists—began to divide and compete. In part because of the new electoral rules and in part because of acute social divisions, these new groups were extremely fragmented. Political groups in the Parliament moved rapidly from strongly supporting the program to positioning themselves against it in order to win votes in the parliamentary election of 1991. Beginning in mid-1990, the program encountered new economic problems—particularly due to the severe recession in industry and the perceived crisis in agriculture— that called for important policy adjustments. The new political situation made those adjustments very difficult to pursue.

Political changes in 1989 provided the initial impulse for economic reform, and the political agreements of that year provided a strong basis for the program. But political institutions hardly changed in the following year, despite the new economic system, and political arrangements based on the roundtable agreements of 1989 now became the program's most serious obstacle. Furthermore, the same social fragmentation that helped minimize opposition to the program in its first year now fed directly into the fragmentation of party politics and the corresponding paralysis of policy.

This chapter explains how the Balcerowicz Plan was created, considers why it did not face strong opposition even when its costs had become clear, examines how the political situation changed with the growth of new political groups willing to articulate social grievances, and considers the results of the reform process to the end of 1991. It concludes with an overall assessment of the plan. To help clarify the complex details of Polish politics, a glossary of party names is presented in appendix 6-1.

Breakdown of the Old System, 1988–89

The beginning of serious economic reform in Poland can be traced to 1980–81 when, under pressure from the newly legalized Solidarity movement, the government initiated new legislation. Implementation of these measures was interrupted by the military coup of December 1981, but the military-backed government itself soon tried to institute gradual economic reform in an attempt to make state firms more efficient and buy social peace. However, successive communist governments in the 1980s proved unwilling to follow through on their threats to bankrupt recalcitrant firms, and their reforms affected the behavior of firms only minimally. This first stage of economic reform ended with recentralization, a familiar pattern of communist reform in which bureaucrats fight to regain lost privileges.

According to official statistics, the Polish economic situation in the second half of the 1980s was not too bad, with real gross domestic product (GDP) and industrial production rising and inflation in 1986 and 1987 remaining around 20 percent a year. The reality was much less favorable, with shortages of many goods, poor-quality production, and low growth in productivity. The most pressing problem was that Poland could not service its foreign debt. A current account deficit persisted for transactions in convertible currencies at the end of the 1980s, and the slight trade surplus in transferable rubles could not be used to service debt denominated in hard currencies.

A so-called second stage of reform was designed in 1987 and implemented in 1988. Although these reforms had only weak popular support, the communists felt they had no alternative.[1] The domestic economic situation was bad and showed no signs of improving; Poland faced international pressure from creditor western countries and possibly from the Soviet Union. The reforms emphasized microeconomics, which meant altering the incentive structure to push firms toward market transactions. In particular, price controls were reduced in scope, the direct supervision of wages by ministries was abandoned, and managers were left to handle all negotiations with workers. This was intended to depoliticize wage bargaining, but nothing was done to strengthen the incentives for state managers to resist wage demands. The reform thus strengthened the power of workers over managers. Legally and in practice, the question of who owned the firms became very confused.

The second stage of reform started with a large relative price correction in February 1988; the result was a sharp increase in food prices, implying a 20 to 30 percent fall in real wages. The quick response was a spontaneous wave of strikes not organized by the Solidarity leadership, and managers of state firms showed little inclination to resist wage claims. Measured real wages increased sharply in February and March and again after mid-year as the financial controls on state enterprises broke down. The most important result was the rapid increase in prices, followed by further increases in the inflation rate later in the year.

A new communist prime minister, Mieczyslaw Rakowski, was installed in September in a last attempt to save the party's monopoly on political power. This new government sought to reform policies governing private enterprise, foreign investment, and the banking system, but these changes came too late to avert the acceleration of inflation and the breakdown of tax collections during 1989. Economic problems forced the government to negotiate again with representatives of the opposition, and although these negotiations ultimately created a new government, the route from the roundtable to the Balcerowicz Plan was quite complicated.

The Roundtable Agreements

The roundtable discussions of early 1989—they began in February and ended in April—resulted in a decisive reorganization of Poland's political institutions. The final agreements were designed to eliminate the communists' monopoly on power only gradually; once in place, the new institutions proved extremely difficult to change.

The political part of the agreements contained four general principles. First, citizens were given the freedom to create political, social, and professional organizations. All parts of Solidarity were legalized, allow-ing independent organizations of workers, farmers, and students to resume their activities, thus creating political pluralism. Second, opposi-tion groups were given real opportunities to have access to all forms of media, thus creating freedom of expression. Third, new electoral rules were adopted with the intention of making Parliament more representa-tive, and the courts were declared independent. Fourth, the principle of strong municipal self-government was adopted. These principles were intended to guide political developments in Poland over at least the next two to three years.

During the roundtable discussions, clear differences arose concerning the sequence of reforms. The government and Communist Party thought it was preferable to introduce rapid changes in the legislature and execu-tive, a process they hoped to control from the top down. In contrast, representatives of Solidarity thought the introduction of democracy should come from the bottom up through changes in the legal system, the mass media, and municipal self-government. Solidarity preferred to move more gradually on institutional change, forcing the Communist Party to give up its powers step by step.

What did the new political institutions look like? First, the roundtable re-created the post of president, which had been eliminated in 1952. The president's role was to be that of a stabilizer, and participants at the roundtable assumed that General Wojciech Jaruzelski would initially play this role. With this in mind, the presidential term of office was set at six years. The president had limited emergency powers but could dissolve Parliament if the Sejm (the lower house) failed to appoint a government or failed to pass the social and economic plan, the descendant of the five-year plan. The president could also veto any legislation passed by Parlia-ment, which could then override the veto.

The most important and complex changes concerned Parliament. Drawing on Poland's historical tradition, the roundtable negotiators re-created a second chamber of Parliament (the Senate), which would serve as a check on the powers of the Sejm. The Senate could discuss and propose amendments to legislation, including the budget, that had passed the Sejm. The Sejm would need a two-thirds' majority to reject the Senate's amendments.

Transitional provisions maintained the communists' power in the Par-liament. The Sejm and Senate were to be elected in 1989 for four years. In the Sejm, 65 percent of the deputies were to be from the Polish United Workers Party (the Communist Party) and its five small allied parties. Candidates from Solidarity and other independent groups who did not belong to these five parties were allowed to compete in free elections against procommunist forces for the remaining 35 percent of the seats. The allocation of seats to appointed and freely elected deputies, both within and across constituencies, was to be decided by the Council of

State, but it was agreed that in every constituency at least one seat would be reserved for an independent candidate. Election to the Senate, by contrast, was to be completely free, without any restrictions on the number of seats that could be won by the opposition. For both the Sejm and the Senate, a candidate could be elected on the first round only if he or she received more than 50 percent of the valid votes cast. If no one obtained such an absolute majority, a runoff election would decide between the top two candidates.

These details proved important in the following months and years, although often in unforeseen ways. Allowing Solidarity access to political power initially provided a strong push to serious economic reform in 1989 and 1990, while granting former communists control of the Sejm later became a significant brake on reform.

Economics of the Roundtable Agreements

In contrast to the deep political changes agreed at the roundtable, the economic agreements were much more cautious and partial. Solidarity's representatives were deeply divided. Some were skeptical about jumping to a market economy and preferred to advance the cause of self-management in state enterprises. Others held strong, promarket liberal views. The resulting agreements sought to improve existing economic policies while protecting the living standards of workers.

The agreements stipulated that the real value of subsidies to food products should be maintained during 1989 and then fall gradually beginning in 1990. At the same time, monopolistic organizations were to be dismantled and agricultural prices freely determined by demand and supply. Minimum purchase prices were to be guaranteed for agricultural goods, and some price controls were to remain on productive inputs to agriculture. In sum, these policies were designed to be gradual.

An important agreement on indexation was also passed: wages were supposed to rise by 80 percent of the increase in consumer prices. This part of the agreement was opposed by the procommunist All-Poland Alliance of Trade Unions, which demanded 100 percent indexation. Wages in the budget sphere, which includes education, health services, and general administration of the state, were to rise in line with increases in industrial wages. Pensions were to be indexed, with the indexation payments made directly from the government's budget.

This agreement had two important consequences. First, the fuse was lit on a hyperinflationary time bomb. Freeing the prices of agricultural output pushed inflation still higher, while the introduction of explicit wage indexation both accelerated inflation and made disinflation much more difficult. Defusing this bomb was the first priority of the Balcerowicz Plan, and commitments to indexation continued to be a problem for the budget throughout 1990 and 1991. Second, the roundtable hardly dealt with the privatization of state property and instead stressed self-management, which effectively strengthened workers' councils.

Interregnum, Summer 1989

In retrospect, the period following the roundtable was a transition from communism to democracy, from a controlled to a market-based economy. At the time, however, the situation was far from clear and remained extremely fluid from June to September. Events and decisions made in this period had important consequences that were not always predictable.

The Elections of 1989

Two electoral rounds took place in June. The full election results, shown in table 6-1, represented an unexpected triumph for Solidarity, which won all but one of the seats in the Senate as well as all of the seats in the Sejm it was allowed to contest—despite having to run against many candidates who were formally independent but received support from the communists. In addition, some deputies who won seats reserved for the communist coalition had tacit Solidarity support.

Almost all the (communist) candidates on the national list were defeated on the first round. This embarrassment resulted in the rapid elimination of the national list and the election of a further 10 percent of representatives from constituencies, with two (procommunist) candidates elected for each additional seat. A final sign of the widespread support for Solidarity was the low turnout in the second round, when almost no Solidarity-backed candidates were running.

The new balance of political power in Parliament was signaled by the election of General Jaruzelski to the presidency in July. Although no other candidates ran, General Jaruzelski added to the drama by waiting to announce his candidacy until the day before the election. He was

Table 6-1. Representation of Parliamentary Clubs in Poland's Sejm and Senate as of July 31, 1989

	Sejm		Senate	
Club and affiliation	Number of Seats	Percentage of total	Number of seats	Percentage of total
Solidarity				
Citizens' Parliamentary Club	161	35.0	99	99.0
Communist coalition				
Polish United Workers Party	173	37.6	0	0.0
United Peasant Party	76	16.5	0	0.0
Democratic Party	27	5.9	0	0.0
Union PAX	10	2.2	0	0.0
Christian Social Union	8	1.7	0	0.0
Polish Social Catholic Union	5	1.1	0	0.0
Independent	0	0.0	1	1.0
Total	460	100.0	100	100.0

Source: Sejm 1991.

elected by the most narrow margin possible—only one vote more than he needed—and only with the tacit support of some members of the Citizens' Parliamentary Club, which was backed by Solidarity.[2]

There was general astonishment that, given the closeness of the contest, some members of Solidarity abstained and implicitly supported the general, who was associated with the imposition of martial law. Even more surprising was that one deputy from the Communist Party and several from the Democratic and the United Peasant parties did not support the general. The communist monolith was beginning to crack, but so was the Citizens' Parliamentary Club.

Members of Solidarity who supported Jaruzelski said that an implicit agreement had been reached at the time of the roundtable and that preventing his election would risk internal anarchy and damage Poland's international position, a reference to the threat of intervention by the Soviet Union. The opponents replied that supporting Jaruzelski legitimized the communist system and betrayed the trust of voters (Domaranczyk 1990).

Formation of the Solidarity Government

The June election was a clear vote against the communists. Solidarity lacked a detailed program, however, and the very important question remained of the extent to which Solidarity should involve itself in government. On August 3, in this tense situation, Jaruzelski nominated General Czeslaw Kiszczak to be prime minister. Kiszczak had previously been minister of internal affairs and was one of the architects of martial law; the immediate response was a wave of politically motivated protest strikes. In the Sejm, Kiszczak's nomination was supported by 237 deputies and opposed by 173, including not only all members of Solidarity's Citizens' Parliamentary Club but also five deputies from the Communist Party, twenty-one from the United Peasant Party, and three from the Democratic Party. This vote clearly showed the growing lack of unity within the 65 percent of deputies supposedly controlled by the communists.

The Citizens' Parliamentary Club had been considering taking a more active role in government ever since the June elections. Even before the president was chosen, the slogan "Your President, Our Prime Minister" had been presented to the public in Gazeta Wyborcza (July 3, 1989) by one of the most influential opposition politicians: Adam Michnik.

The idea of a Solidarity government was, however, received with considerable although not universal skepticism.[3] Ironically, some of the strongest objections were raised by Tadeusz Mazowiecki, who soon became prime minister of the coalition government.[4] The main argument against Solidarity forming a government was that it lacked a comprehensive economic program. Solidarity had, after all, been an illegal opposition movement until recently and had not had an opportunity to prepare such a program. Moreover, its members lacked administrative experience and would have to contend with a bureaucracy, media, and military completely dominated by members of the communist *nomenklatura* and closely linked with other communist countries. Solidarity representatives in the government would only legitimize unpopular policy decisions, a fear exacerbated when the Rakowski government liberalized food prices on August 1. Instead of producing a serious program of reforms, it was feared, a Solidarity-supported government would help the Communist Party regain social support and legitimize existing state institutions.

The decisive move came when Lech Walesa, on August 7, declared himself opposed to General Kiszczak becoming prime minister and proposed a coalition government with ministers from Solidarity, the Democratic Party, and the United Peasant Party. On August 19, two days after Kiszczak gave up trying to form a new government, General Jaruzelski appointed Tadeusz Mazowiecki as prime minister. Mazowiecki and his government were overwhelmingly confirmed by the Sejm. Solidarity had swept its opponents from the political battlefield, and, despite being only a minority in the Sejm, controlled the legislative initiative. The critical question remained, however, of whether the new government could find an economic strategy that was politically viable.

Origins of the Economic Program

After resolving the presidential crisis and forming a new government, the next step was to introduce a program of radical economic reform. Observers of Poland have seen a major puzzle in this program: why did a political movement with strong trade union roots choose a program that delivered lower real wages, higher unemployment, and less production? This question is particularly intriguing because Solidarity's economic goals at the time of the roundtable were less ambitious.

As the macroeconomic situation worsened rapidly during the summer of 1989, only two alternative programs were debated and seriously considered by the Citizens' Parliamentary Club. Both were prepared by groups associated with leading promarket economists: Janusz Beksiak and Leszek Balcerowicz. For most of the summer, Beksiak's group was the most influential. Created at the beginning of July on the initiative of Jacek Kuron, it had close ties to the Citizens' Parliamentary Club. Leading roles were played by three well-known liberal professors: Janusz Beksiak (a member of roundtable talks who had opposed the final economic agreements), Stefan Kurowski, and Jan Winiecki.

Although some important differences existed between the proposals of the Beksiak group and those of the Balcerowicz group, both programs had a great deal in common (Beksiak and others 1989). Both diverged significantly from the economic sections of the roundtable agreements by proposing more radical ultimate goals and immediate policy measures. Both clearly rejected the option of improving socialism (that is, merely changing the operating conditions for state-owned enterprises, strengthening the welfare state, and emphasizing self-management).[5] Both also agreed that it was necessary to implement the market mechanism rapidly, to liberalize prices immediately, and to make the currency convertible.

The Beksiak group emphasized the need for quick institutional changes, such as privatization and reform of the banking and financial system, which they thought should be implemented at the same time as a tight macroeconomic policy. The Balcerowicz group argued that the first priority was macroeconomic stabilization, which should precede major institutional changes.

The Beksiak group opposed controlling wage increases through a special excess wage tax (the so-called *popiwek*) and supported controlling consumption rather than incomes, whereas the Balcerowicz group saw the popiwek as a practical and effective measure. The Beksiak group also thought that the exchange rate should be fixed against the dollar for only a very short period, until the end of hyperinflation, and then be freely determined by supply and demand. Similarly, they suggested more flexible rules and a bigger role for the market in determining interest rates. On both these points, the Balcerowicz group preferred to retain some government controls.

Despite these differences, both groups were seeking to introduce a market economy as fast as possible. They, and other commentators, justified this strategy with four arguments. First, society had grown tired during the 1980s of the slow-paced communist reforms, which had high social costs and few noticeable benefits. Second, the victory of Solidarity in the June election raised hopes that radical changes were possible. Third, the new acceleration of inflation increased the appeal of radical economic policies. Fourth, Poles held a deep-rooted idea that the market would produce higher welfare and that the communists refused to introduce the market because they feared it would reduce their power, which was based, in part, on controlling goods in short supply.

An influential role during this period was played by Jeffrey Sachs of Harvard University and his colleague David Lipton. Sachs and Lipton had, for several months, been involved in intense discussions with senior political leaders and economic advisers of Solidarity concerning the economic and political aspects of the reform program. They played a significant role in developing reform ideas during 1989 and were instrumental in ensuring that these ideas were practicable and workable. In July, at the request of key Solidarity leaders, they prepared and circulated the first comprehensive stabilization-cum-market reform program to be considered by the new Solidarity Parliamentary Club.

In that memorandum, Sachs and Lipton (1989) proposed "a single, stable exchange rate for the zloty, which will guarantee that all prices of internationally traded goods (both imports and exports) will be determined by the prices in the world market."[6] The immediate convertibility of the zloty (combined with the immediate elimination of price controls and subsidies) became a cornerstone of their advice. It was radically different from the advice of the World Bank and almost all other economists, who envisioned a multiyear period in which to achieve convertibility of the zloty (more than five years in the case of a World Bank mission).

As accomplished U.S. economists, Sachs and Lipton could offer the opinion of independent objective analysts, and in the summer of 1989, many of their arguments were more important politically, particularly within the Solidarity Parliamentary Club, than those of Beksiak and Balcerowicz. Sachs also had experience with successful overnight convertibility and debt reduction in the Bolivian stabilization program. Sachs and Lipton focused political attention on the need to prevent the further acceleration of inflation and to stabilize the economy fully. They also offered technical analyses on monetary policy and international finance, worked closely with the so-called Brussels Group in preparing Solidarity's original request for $10 billion of aid, and also pressed for reducing the Polish debt from the beginning.[7] These were important conceptual breakthroughs. In addition, their participation strengthened the international credibility of the reform program.

It is perhaps not surprising that some of the principal Polish participants downplay the U.S. advisers' role. Dabrowski (1991) states that the economic program presented to the International Monetary Fund (IMF) in September 1989 was primarily prepared by the Balcerowicz group itself, although Sachs and Lipton advised them on the draft. Clearly, the principal Polish advisers had independently arrived at the need for a radical reform program, and they prepared the key decisions necessary for its implementation. Nevertheless, Sachs and Lipton were extremely influential not only at the inception of the program but also during negotiations with the IMF and the G-7 governments and until at least the end of 1991.

The question remains of why Balcerowicz and not Beksiak was asked to become finance minister. The answer seems to lie with the preferences of the new prime minister, Tadeusz Mazowiecki. Mazowiecki was skeptical of the radical program of Beksiak, whom he remembered as a liberal participant in the roundtable and as a critic of the final agreements (Kuron 1991).[8] The Balcerowicz program seemed more controlled and perhaps more careful. Despite Jacek Kuron's proposal in 1989 that the Beksiak and Balcerowicz groups unify their efforts and join the government (Kuron 1991), Mazowiecki chose only Balcerowicz.

By September, the remarkable political and social situation gave Balcerowicz a free hand to design and implement his program. This was just as well: the final action of the communist government was to free food prices in August without making any other significant economic and institutional changes. Wage indexation meant that higher food prices immediately increased nominal wages and general price indexes. The result was a considerable acceleration of inflation, which caused a fall in real tax revenues—because taxes were not indexed and there were lags in collection—and a serious budget crisis. Poland appeared to be on the edge of runaway hyperinflation, and urgent action was needed.

Design of the Balcerowicz Plan, Fall 1989

Very quickly, Balcerowicz established the outline of an economic reform program, which was circulated in the West during September 1989 in the form of a memorandum.[9] This memorandum stated that "the government of Poland intends to transform the Polish economy into a market economy, with an ownership structure changing in the direction of that found in the advanced industrial economies" (Ministry of Finance 1989, p. 1). The macroeconomic language of this memorandum was orthodox: "We see monetary and price stabilization as an immediate task and a precondition for structural adjustment" (p. 2). It also included several radical proposals, such as removing most price controls, beginning rapid privatization, and bankrupting some state firms. A timetable was outlined, and it proved to be very close to what actually happened, particularly with January–March 1990 described as the "critical phase of the anti-inflationary drive" (appendix to the memorandum, p. 2). This was a clear and unambiguous statement of intentions, and it proved to be an effective means to rally international support.

The Polish government also expected to receive a standby loan from the IMF of $700 million (90 percent of Poland's quota) in December and a World Bank structural adjustment loan of $500 million during January–March 1990. In addition, the memorandum requested a $1 billion stabilization loan from industrial countries and appealed "for relief from debt service payments during the next thirty-six months, to be followed by significant and permanent debt reduction in the future."

Prior to negotiations with the IMF and the World Bank, the new government took several measures in late September and early October. It sought directly to limit wage inflation by modifying the excess wage tax—which had been used extensively under the communists—to make it more onerous and by suspending the payment of bonuses from fourth-quarter profits.

Cuts were made in budgetary subsidies and other current expenditures, as well as in budgetary investment spending. Tax payments were accelerated, and higher penalties were introduced for late payments. According to official estimates, these measures reduced the budget deficit by 2 to 3 percent of GDP.

Some administered prices were increased (energy prices were raised sharply in October), more price controls were removed, the quantitative ceilings on bank credit were tightened (in real terms), and the official exchange rate was devalued repeatedly to improve competitiveness and reduce the parallel market premium.

These partial measures did not have immediate positive effects, however. Output continued to decline and investment to fall, the balance of trade worsened, and inflation fell but remained high.

Negotiations with the IMF were held in Warsaw during the months of October, November, and December. At the same time, Poland was negotiating with the World Bank for a structural adjustment loan of $300 million, with the goal of disbursing half during 1990, as well as for two project loans with expected disbursements of $150 million in 1990. Although the IMF approved a standby loan of SDR 570 million (about $725 million) in early February, it helped arrange a bridge loan from the Bank for International Settlements in late December. Poland also arranged a special stabilization loan from some industrial countries of $1 billion, all of which was held in New York to help guarantee the convertibility of the zloty.

Although negotiations with the IMF were clearly crucial in designing the policy, the Polish government did not wait for formal approval of a standby loan. How did this program attain sufficient political support to be passed, particularly in a Sejm where procommunist forces were still very strong?

The essence of the Balcerowicz Plan was publicly unveiled on November 7, twenty-five days after the new government was created. This plan, which included thirteen laws and seven resolutions of the Sejm, was approved by the Council of Ministers on December 13 and presented to the Sejm on December 17. In the Sejm, the six most important points of debate were the speed of transformation to the market, the size of unemployment, the scale and form of economic intervention by the state, the correct policy toward state enterprises, the speed and scale of privatization, and the desirability of ownership by the workers.

The most active deputies in this debate were from the former Communist Party, the Democratic Party, and the Citizens' Parliamentary Club. They were concerned about the lack of state intervention in the market and what this implied for the costs borne by workers, particularly in state-owned enterprises. Many of these deputies feared the costs would be too high and questioned whether society would tolerate them. Some predicted that the high costs of economic reforms and resulting social dissatisfaction would cause a crisis for the political move toward democracy.

Despite these fears, the government's package of laws was passed without significant problems. The very acceptance of this legislation was a remarkable success, because this was still a "contract Sejm" in which Solidarity had only 35 percent of the seats. Three main reasons account for this political success.

First, the Communist Party adopted the slogan "Your Government,

Our Program," suggesting that the new program had been prepared by the Rakowski government and thus rationalizing its support. Second, the 65 percent of deputies in the Sejm who owed their position to being nominated by the communist coalition probably voted in favor of the Balcerowicz Plan in an attempt to legitimize themselves. Society clearly expected and wanted radical reforms, so any attempt to block the legislation would have been regarded as antidemocratic and been unpopular. Third, the majority of the Citizens' Parliamentary Club supported the program because it was the policy of a government created by Solidarity.

Some deputies of the Citizens' Parliamentary Club preferred a gradual introduction of markets over several years and more government measures to reduce the social costs of the transition. Although they did not vote against the program or leave the parliamentary club, these twenty-one deputies formed their own informal group—the Group for the Protection of Workers' Interests—consisting of about 10 percent of Solidarity's parliamentarians. Its most important member was Ryszard Bugaj, chair of the Sejm Commission on Economic Policy, Budget, and Finance. Bugaj later became the leader of a new organization, Solidarity of Workers.

Despite these early divisions among Solidarity's parliamentary representatives, the end of 1989 brought a clear political triumph for the Mazowiecki government. A radical reform program passed through the Parliament without serious problems and received overwhelming social support. The political conditions for designing a radical program of reform could not have been more favorable.

With such strong political support, the reform package implemented on January 1, 1990, was exactly what the government wanted.[10] The program had five main elements that, taken together, deserved the popular description of shock therapy.

First, the exchange rate for payments on the current account was unified at Zl 9,500 per $1. The new exchange rate was calculated using the effective rate for exporters in the fourth quarter of 1989, adjusted for the removal of export subsidies and tax breaks and for estimated inflation in January, with what was perceived to be a small margin. According to the IMF, this implied a real effective zloty depreciation of 40 percent in January on the basis of retail prices. The intention was to stabilize the nominal exchange rate for current account transactions for three months and then adjust it to maintain a competitive real exchange rate in terms of labor costs. The parallel (so-called *kantor*) market for households was retained, and the government made no commitment to intervene in that market. Instead, it promised to raise interest rates if the kantor rate rose more than 10 percent above the official rate.

Second, a very restrictive incomes policy was established for the first four months of 1990. Tax penalties of 200 to 500 percent were levied on increases in wage bills that exceeded 30 percent of the actual increase in consumer prices in January and 20 percent in February through April. Inflation was expected to decline by the end of April, so the tax-free increase in the wage bill was allowed to be 60 percent for May and June. This indexation coefficient for the second half of the year was to be discussed with the IMF in May. The excess wage tax was expected to differ from the versions used by the communist regimes because there were to be no exemptions.

At the same time, many prices were liberalized. Although discussed, a price freeze was rejected because major changes in relative prices and a brief corrective inflation were needed. The government hoped real wages in the state sector would fall one-third to compensate firms for the end of the massive interest rate subsidies, which constituted an estimated 25 percent of total labor costs.

Third, the goal of fiscal policy was to achieve a state budget deficit of less than 1 percent of GDP with a small surplus on extrabudgetary funds. This represented a significant adjustment, because the budget deficit had been more than 8 percent of GDP in 1989. In the budgetary plan, subsidies were to be cut by 8 percent of GDP, with the subsidy on coal being the only significant one remaining. Higher outlays totaling about 6 percent of GDP were also planned, however, primarily to create new social safety nets for the future unemployed. Income tax relief was also planned and would contribute an extra 4 percent of GDP.

Fourth, on January 1, the refinance rate of the National Bank of Poland was raised to 36 percent a month (up from 7 percent a month in December), which was higher than the inflation expected for January and February. The explicit goal was to adjust nominal interest rates as necessary during 1990 in order to maintain positive real interest rates. Preferential interest rates for various investments were abolished. Interest rate subsidies for housing and agriculture were retained, but their level was reduced and their cost was placed clearly on the budget.

Fifth, trade was substantially liberalized. Almost all foreign trade monopolies were liquidated. Quotas for most goods were replaced with a uniform tariff. As a result, Poland established an extremely liberal trade regime, although this was soon modified considerably.

The program had been assembled quickly, but thorough preparations were in place by January 1, 1990. Solidarity's political coalition remained strongly supportive of the program on almost all issues, with the significant exception of the government's privatization proposals. Opinion polls showed a high degree of approval for Balcerowicz and his new "professional" approach to economic policy. There was overwhelming foreign support for the program, and part of Balcerowicz's political appeal in 1989 was his favorable standing with international creditors and multilateral financial institutions. The program's credibility was boosted by the creation of a $1 billion stabilization fund in December 1989 from the loans and grants of seventeen western countries. Poland also received access to loans from both the IMF and World Bank (Poland received about $800 million in foreign credits in 1991, up from $428 million in 1990 and $226 million in 1989). Furthermore, at the beginning of 1990, Poland was able to suspend payments on commercial bank debt without disrupting any of these external financial arrangements.

Implementation and Initial Results, 1990

The most important performance indicators at the beginning of the program were the criteria set by the IMF. Although these criteria were initially perceived as being quite tough, the program performed better on a whole range of measures than required in 1990, particularly during the first half of the year (see table 6-2). Real wages fell much more sharply than required, and the government budget moved rapidly into surplus. The fall in net domestic assets was much larger than required, and net foreign reserves of the banking system actually increased. With the exception of net foreign reserves, this outstanding success did not continue during the second half of 1990; still, for the year as a whole, Poland more than satisfied the first five criteria set by the IMF.[11]

The first quarter of 1990 showed a remarkable change in economic conditions. The budget moved quickly into surplus. Real credit from the banking system fell sharply. The exchange rate remained stable, the zloty was fully convertible for current account transactions, foreign exchange reserves actually increased (exports rose rapidly), and the hard currency trade surplus for the first quarter was $778 million. Inflation declined quickly, even though 90 percent of all prices were liberalized.

In addition, the Paris Club of western government creditors agreed to a new rescheduling agreement in February. This agreement rescheduled all of the interest and principal that fell due between January 1990 and March 1991, plus all arrears from the end of 1989, with fourteen years' maturity and eight years' grace. The president of the World Bank visited Poland in February, and lending of around $2.5 billion was promised over three years. This lending was to be accelerated so that $531 million would be disbursed in the 1990 financial year and $925 million during the 1991 financial year.

Despite these external successes, there were growing worries about the domestic effects of reform. Using aggregate statistics, it is hard to judge whether the economic stabilization program improved or worsened the living conditions of the average Pole. Measured real incomes fell considerably, as did measured real wages and consumption. However, disaggregated indicators show a more ambiguous result: the average monthly salary in 1990 allowed a consumer to purchase more of some goods and less of others than in 1986 and 1987. A serious problem with these

Table 6-2. IMF Criteria and Poland's Performance in 1990

Criteria	First six months		Entire year	
	Agreement	*Results*	*Agreement*	*Results*
IMF *basic criteria*				
Percentage change in real wages in five main sectors (compared with 1989)	−18.0	−38.0	−31.0	−32.0
Credit for government sector (percent of GDP)	0.7	−8.0	0.0	−1.4
Deficit of government sector (percent of GDP)	1.6	−10.0	−0.1	−3.0
Percentage change in real net domestic assets	−28.0	−58.0	−24.0	−51.0
Change in net foreign reserves of the banking system (millions of dollars)	−165.0	3,100.0	245.0	2,650.0
Reduction in short-term foreign debt (millions of dollars)	400.0	183.0	700.0	0.0
Additional criteria				
Change in GDP	—	−15.0	−5.0	−12.0
Change in the real money supply	−25.0	−41.0	−4.0	−42.0
Change in real credit for the nongovernment sector	0.0	−18.0	20.0	0.0
Inflation	75.0	172.0	94.0	250.0

— Not specified.
Source: Gomulka 1991.

numbers is that pervasive shortages existed throughout the 1980s, and especially in 1988 and 1989. As a result, although a good was listed at a particular price in 1988 or 1989, it could not necessarily be bought at that price. In contrast, since the beginning of 1990, there have been no shortages in Poland. The rapid change from excess demand to equilibrium in the market for consumer goods makes it very difficult to calculate whether average consumption per capita fell or rose (Lipton and Sachs 1990 discuss these problems of measurement at length). Clearly, however, the real purchasing power of incomes and consumption cannot have fallen as much as official statistics suggest.

The major economic problem was the sharp fall in industrial output of the state sector. Official statistics showed a fall in excess of 20 percent for the first quarter, much larger than had been forecast. Unemployment also rose sharply, although there was strong evidence that a large fraction of the registered unemployed had not previously been employed. At the same time, hardly any bankruptcies occurred, contrary to initial expectations. These developments spurred sharp debate within the government about whether the macroeconomic policy was too tight.

Two key disappointments were that measured GDP fell as much as 12 percent and inflation continued to be higher than targeted. This was the first hint that the Polish economy would not respond to shock therapy as expected. To understand what happened and how economic performance determined subsequent social and political developments requires examining economic developments in rather more detail.

Prices and Wages

The recurring problem of the Balcerowicz Plan was inflation. Defeating inflation while eliminating shortages was the first priority of the stabilization program, and the initial results were impressive. Yet inflation refused to die completely, and its continuation was used by political opponents of the program to argue that the policies had not worked.

Prices rose steeply in January 1990, primarily as a result of increases in key prices controlled by the government that ranged from 100 percent for gasoline to 250 percent for natural gas, 300 percent for electricity, and 400 percent for black coal. Steep increases in energy prices were accompanied by a reduction in subsidies on food and industrial products (subsidies were retained on milk, the lowest quality of cheese, and mining). Most remaining price controls were removed, with the result that prices were freed for 90 percent of all goods, up from 50 percent at the end of 1989. Interest rates also rose sharply, which probably helped push prices up by increasing the costs of operating housing cooperatives and thus rents (see table 6-3 for monthly inflation throughout the reform period). Of particular importance is the politically sensitive "headline" inflation rate, which is calculated by comparing average prices in a month with average prices in the preceding month. Inflation in January 1990 was almost 80 percent, considerably higher than had been forecast.[12]

This error was embarrassing for the government, although hardly surprising given how hard it is to predict the effect of such large increases in the price of energy. Because it still had strong political support, the government did not face a crisis and was able to cite surprisingly low inflation in March. As expected, the initial surge of prices was followed by a rapid deceleration of inflation.

In the first three months of 1990, the wholesale trade market was seriously disrupted; state wholesalers were weakened and destroyed, but the private sector was not yet strong enough to replace them. By the end of the first quarter, however, the private wholesale trade was developing rapidly. Slowly but surely, the state trading monopolies began to break apart.[13] The rapid growth of strong, private wholesale trade and pervasive, private retail street trade was a pleasant surprise that provided a wider range of goods at lower cost than state stores. In addition, significant suspensions and reductions in tariffs in May lowered the price of imports, helped hold overall consumer prices down, and reduced the scope for monopoly pricing.

Table 6-3. Consumer Price Index in Poland, 1989–91

	With same month in previous year equal to 100			With previous month equal to 100		
Month	1989	1990	1991	1989	1990	1991
January	183.2	1,108.0	194.9	111.0	179.6	112.7
February	170.3	1,283.0	180.0	107.9	123.8	106.7
March	174.2	1,233.0	181.8	108.1	104.3	104.5
April	177.8	1,203.0	171.0	109.8	107.5	102.7
May	185.4	1,177.0	167.8	107.2	104.6	102.7
June	191.3	1,151.0	172.4	106.1	103.4	104.9
July	203.9	1,094.0	168.3	109.5	103.6	100.9
August	282.7	848.5	167.6	139.5	101.8	100.6
September	369.2	658.0	167.1	134.4	104.6	104.3
October	557.1	456.0	164.8	154.8	105.7	103.2
November	657.0	385.9	162.7	122.4	104.9	103.2
December	739.6	349.3	160.4	117.7	105.9	103.1

Source: For 1989 and 1990, Central Statistical Office 1991, April, issues 1–3, table 1, p. 14; December, issue 11, table 29, p. 49. For 1991, Central Statistical Office 1992, March, issue 2, table 26, p. 60.

Unfortunately, other influences dominated the movement of prices, which increased almost 8 percent in April, largely as the result of the government's effort to phase out subsidies faster than it had promised at the beginning of the year.[14] In 1990 and particularly in 1991, administrative prices rose several times. Although the government had chosen a shock therapy, it did not increase all prices by the required amount on January 1. Instead, it opted for a large increase at the beginning of the year, followed by staggered increases throughout 1990.

Probably the most startling result in the first quarter of the program was the sharp fall in real wages. Real wages were only 57 percent of the December 1989 level in January 1990 and fell again in February (see table 6-4). Such a dramatic decline in real wages was unexpected, coming as it did before unemployment increased or any state firms went bankrupt. Why did this happen?

In part, it may have occurred because firms paid high bonuses in the last months of 1989, both in anticipation of future wage controls and in an effort to raise their base wage, which would be used to calculate the tax-free wage increases in 1990. Real wages rose again sharply in March—the traditional month for paying the annual bonus—and again in the second half of the year, even though demand and output stayed low. The most plausible explanation is that workers voluntarily gave up wage increases at the very beginning of 1990 to ensure survival of their firms. This view is supported by direct evidence from a sample of state firms.[15] In addition, the financial situation of state enterprises was rather good: their profits were high, and they could have afforded higher real wages. The excess wage tax was more of a constraint on state firms at the end of 1990 and at the start of 1991.[16]

Table 6-4. Real Wages in Poland, 1990–91
(index: previous month = 100)

Month	1990	1991
January	56.7	88.6
February	92.9	105.4
March	131.1	99.2
April	87.6	96.2
May	92.7	95.3
June	98.9	97.4
July	106.9	104.5
August	103.1	99.0
September	102.8	98.7
October	107.5	105.4
November	106.7	101.7
December	97.3	105.4

Note: Real wages include bonus payments for the so-called six branches of material production: industry, construction, transport, communications, trade, and municipal services. They do not include the budget sphere or the service sector.
Source: For 1990, Council of Ministers 1991a; for 1991, Central Statistical Office 1992, March, issue 2, table 1, p. 16.

A striking and surprising fact is that no major state firm went bankrupt at the beginning of the Balcerowicz Plan—bankruptcies remained surprisingly low through mid-1993—despite the huge increase in nominal interest rates (see table 6-5) and the contraction in real credit. There are several explanations for this result. First, the large nominal devaluation of the zloty made many state firms price competitive at home and abroad. Second, state enterprises stockpiled cheap raw materials at the end of 1989 and, under Polish accounting rules, sold their production at a large profit in 1990. Third, very high inflation at the end of 1989 sharply reduced the real value of debts, so higher interest rates did not have a large immediate effect on a firm's financial results.

Early Budget Results

The state budget was obviously a central element of the stabilization program. The original budget law for 1990, passed in January, assumed a balance of revenues and spending in both the central budget and the state budget, which was the sum of central and municipal budgets. The key measures were a reduction in tax relief, an increase in tax receipts, and a large reduction in subsidies for enterprises. The share of enterprise subsidies in spending was intended to fall from 29 percent in 1989 to 17 percent in 1990.

According to the original 1990 budget law, spending and income were to be precisely balanced. However, in December 1989 and January 1990, when this law was discussed, concern was expressed about possible errors in the underlying assumptions about the level of production and the

Table 6-5. Refinance Interest Rate in Poland, 1990–91

Month	1990	1991
January	432.0	55.0
February	240.0	72.0
March	120.0	72.0
April	96.0	72.0
May	66.0	59.0
June	48.0	59.0
July	34.0	51.2
August	34.0	44.2
September	34.0	41.9
October	39.0	40.0
November	47.0	40.0
December	55.0	40.0

Source: Central Statistical Office 1992, January, issue 12, table 1, p. 10.

rate of inflation. For this reason, in January 1990, the Sejm authorized the government to alter the budget if these assumptions proved to be incorrect. This fiscal authority proved to be very useful before the end of the year.

The government expected a temporary deficit at the beginning of 1990 and was allowed to finance this by borrowing from the banking system (this loan could not exceed 4 percent in the first quarter and 2 percent in subsequent quarters of planned spending). In the first quarter of 1990, the government covered its temporary deficit with bank credit, in the form of a Zl 2 trillion loan from PKO BP (the state savings bank). In fact, as table 6-6 shows, the central budget performed much better than expected during the first half of 1990, and the loan was repaid by the end of the second quarter. Initial fiscal results were extremely favorable.

Table 6-6. State Budget of Poland, 1990–91
(trillions of zlotys, rounded to one decimal place)

	Income		Spending		Surplus	
Period	1990	1991	1990	1991	1990	1991
January	11.9	13.2	11.0	12.2	0.9	0.9
January–February	24.7	30.6	23.0	31.4	1.6	−0.7
January–March	37.7	47.7	35.9	52.7	1.8	−5.0
January–April	55.1	64.3	49.9	73.0	5.1	−8.7
January–May	71.8	81.7	64.6	89.5	7.3	−7.7
January–June	87.3	95.6	80.8	108.8	6.5	−13.2
January–July	102.6	114.2	94.1	128.5	8.5	−14.3
January–August	117.2	130.2	108.0	148.9	9.3	−18.7
January–September	133.1	146.3	124.3	168.7	8.7	−22.4
January–October	151.9	166.6	141.9	192.1	10.0	−25.4
January–November	170.7	184.6	161.9	212.5	8.8	−27.9
January–December	196.2	210.6	193.8	241.9	2.4	−31.3

Source: For 1990, Central Statistical Office 1991, April, table 18, p. 34; for 1991, Central Statistical Office 1992, March, table 15, p. 45.

Table 6-7. Membership of Deputies in Parliamentary Clubs in Poland's Sejm, 1990–91

Club	December 31, 1990		February 15, 1991		August 1991	
	Number of members	Percent of total	Number of members[a]	Percent of total	Number of members	Percent of total
Christian Democrats	0	0.0	0	0.0	2	0.4
Christian Social Union	8	1.7	8	1.7	8	1.7
Citizens' Parliamentary Club	155	33.7	111	24.1	106	23.1
Club of Independent Deputies	10	2.2	9	2.0	9	2.0
Club of Military Deputies	7	1.5	7	1.5	7	1.5
Democratic Party	22	4.8	22	4.8	21	4.6
Democratic Union	0	0.0	46	10.0	46	10.0
Ecology Club	0	0.0	0	0.0	5	1.1
Parliamentary Club of the Democratic Left	104	22.7	104	22.7	104	22.7
Parliamentary Club of the Polish Social Democratic Union	41	8.9	40	8.7	0	0.0
Parliamentary Club of Workers	0	0.0	0	0.0	41	8.9
Polish Peasant Party (led by Jan Zych)	73	15.9	73	15.9	72	15.7
Polish Peasant Party (led by Tadeusz Kaszubski)	4	0.9	4	0.9	4	0.9
Polish Social Catholic Union	4	0.9	4	0.9	5	1.1
Solidarity of Workers	0	0.0	0	0.0	6	1.3
Union PAX	10	2.2	10	2.2	10	2.2
Others not registered	21	4.6	21	4.6	20	4.4
Total number of club members	795	100.0	459	100.0	466	100.0
Total number of seats	460	100.0	459	100.0	460	100.0

a. The number of club members does not add up to 459 because some members belonged to more than one club.
Source: Sejm 1991.

The first quarter of the Balcerowicz Plan was in many ways a remarkable success. Shortages were eliminated, inflation was reduced, the budget was balanced, and the zloty was made fully convertible for current account transactions. If anything, this sweeping economic success came more easily than expected. Although both output and real wages fell much more than expected, neither resulted in strong social protests. Most important, the basic coalition supporting the program remained intact.

Political Realignments and the War on the Top

The continuing debate over economic problems gradually caused the disintegration of the original seven parliamentary groupings—known as clubs—and the creation of new clubs as well as new parties. A crucial issue in this political development was the opinion of different groups about who should be president and about the "war on the top."

The first break in the Citizens' Parliamentary Club came as early as mid-December 1989, when four of its deputies joined three United Peasant Party deputies to form a new peasant party, known as the Polish Peasant Party "Wilanowski," which after some maneuvering joined the Polish Peasant Party.[17] After dissolution of the Polish United Workers Party and the creation of two new postcommunist parties, the Communist Parliamentary Club changed its name to the Parliamentary Club of the Democratic Left. At the end of February 1990, six deputies from this club organized a club of independent deputies, and in March another group formed the Polish Social Democratic Union (see table 6-7 for the number of seats in the Sejm that were aligned with different clubs as of December 1990). Although differences inside the parliamentary clubs developed rapidly, this did not brake the economic reforms. Without doubt, some deputies became more radical in their opposition to the government as the perceived social costs of the Balcerowicz Plan increased. Beginning in mid-1990, the economic news was consistently bad: rising unemployment, falling production, and persistent inflation.

The Citizens' Parliamentary Club was initially unified and strengthened by its trade union roots, but after the first quarter of 1990 these roots began to block difficult reforms. Some Solidarity representatives in the club tried to distance themselves from the economic policy of Mazowiecki. Some presented antigovernment views on economic themes, although officially they did not declare their opposition (this was true of the group led by Ryszard Bugaj, for example). These parts of the club were moving to the left, approaching the position of former communist parliamentary clubs and the Polish Peasant Party.

The unifying factor in Solidarity had always been its fight against the communist regime. During the 1980s and especially in 1989, Solidarity appeared to be a monolith, but differences began to emerge over whether the movement should participate in the roundtable talks and then over the election of Jaruzelski and the formation of a Solidarity-backed government. These divisions deepened when it was realized that someone from Solidarity would soon replace Jaruzelski as president.

Immediately after the June 1989 election, further differences were evident inside the Solidarity movement.[18] One of the most critical issues was the role and future of the citizens' committees, in particular their independence and the nature of their relation with leaders of the Citizens' Parliamentary Club and Solidarity.[19] In early spring, a major discussion took place inside Solidarity about the development of the political system, the role of elites, development of the party system, and the role of citizens' committees. The timing of this discussion is important, occurring, as it did, after significant social costs were incurred during the first quarter of the Balcerowicz Plan. Some leaders of the Citizens' Parliamentary Club suggested creating a Solidarity party that would constitute a bloc or political umbrella to support political and economic transformation.

Walesa and Kaczynski opposed this idea (Bochwic 1991). Walesa was concerned about the political alienation of society, which in his view was becoming the object of political games, not an active participant. He used this argument in favor of accelerating institutional changes such as a clear party system, new parliamentary and presidential elections, and privatization.

The economic and political background for the war on the top, which was announced by Walesa and his close associates, are very important. After the first quarter of 1990, strong concerns were voiced in the Sejm about rising unemployment, the deep recession in industrial output, and the steep fall in measured real wages. In the second quarter, a wave of strikes occurred in local communications and railways, and farmers began to mount serious protests. Private businesspersons in small-scale handicrafts also expressed their disappointment with the policies. Growing social disillusion was further demonstrated by the low turnout—42 percent—in the municipal elections in May.

Two quite different interpretations explain the war on the top. One view is that the root cause was pure personal ambition: Walesa felt excluded from the new political elite (Bochwic 1991). The other is that Walesa and his associates saw that reform needed a catalyst and believed that leaders of the Citizens' Parliamentary Club were trying to block political development and retain control of policy for the new political elite.

Whichever explanation is correct, the result is clear: Solidarity started to break up, and the war on the top promoted the creation of new political parties. In spring 1990, the Central Alliance was created, followed by the Citizens' Movement for Democratic Action. The Central Alliance was closely allied with Walesa, while the Citizens' Movement for Democratic Action was led by a group closer to Mazowiecki.[20] Although these changes, combined with the reorganization of former communist groups, did have an impact on economic policy, in 1990 the impact was not ruinous.

The Former Communists

The strongest member of the communist coalition had always been the Polish United Workers Party, but this party was thoroughly discredited by the string of political and economic failures that culminated in the debacle of the June 1989 election. Despite its overwhelming rejection at the polls, this party was able to reform itself and gradually edge its way back to political influence.

During its congress of January 27–28, 1990, the Polish United Workers Party dissolved itself, creating two new parties: Social Democracy of the Polish Republic, led by Aleksander Kwasniewski with Leszek Miller as general secretary, and Social Democratic Union, led by Tadeusz Fiszbach. The Social Democratic Union was notable for its declared intention not to receive any property that had belonged to the old Communist Party, but it was the Social Democracy of the Polish Republic that became the most important postcommunist party. It fielded its own candidate in the 1990 presidential election, and, in partnership with the Communist Trade Union in the Union of the Democratic Left coalition, obtained the second highest number of votes in the 1991 parliamentary election.

Despite having been compromised by decades of cooperation with the communists, another group—the United Peasant Party—transformed itself into the Polish Peasant Party and enjoyed strong support in the villages. It continues to use the symbols and traditions of the Polish independent farmers' movement and has remained an important force in organizing farmers' protests.

Economic Policy Adjustments

The economic results for the second quarter of 1990 were widely viewed as disappointing because there was no sign of an imminent recovery in industrial output. Production declined sharply at the beginning of the program and stayed low. Although most of the decline occurred in January and February, production also fell in April and July, but the fall in July was seasonal. Output increased in August and September, calculated on a month-to-month basis, but flattened out again in October and November. Official unemployment statistics were even more bleak. The rate of unemployment rose from 0.3 percent of the labor force in January 1990 to 3.1 percent in June and 6.1 percent in December, although these statistics should not be taken at face value.[21] In all likelihood, the initial increase in unemployment was due more to voluntary quits and new entries into the labor force than to job losses.

The perception of many Sejm deputies was that the government's policies were unnecessarily harsh. The summer of 1990 saw the first serious debates in the Sejm questioning the government's economic policy. Deputies argued that the social costs of the new policies were too high and should be reduced by increasing government spending. In light of the higher-than-expected government surplus and the continuing war on the top, this political pressure was hard to resist (Dabrowski 1991).

The government's economic team was sensitive to these arguments, and at least some of its members felt that the Polish recession was unnecessarily deep. As a result, in June the government used the discretionary budget powers, granted by the Sejm in January, to advance preferential credits to farmers and increase the budgetary support for housing. Furthermore, steps were taken to ease monetary policy, and the central bank's refinance interest rate—the benchmark rate for Polish financial institutions—was cut to 34 percent a year. The popiwek rules were also relaxed; for the month of June, wages were allowed to rise by the full amount of the increase in prices (the coefficient of permitted indexation was one).

These policy changes had, at most, a small effect on the level of industrial output (see table 6-8). Unfortunately, inflation also increased directly toward the end of 1990 (table 6-3). The renewed increase in inflation was attributed to the loosening of policy, and the government's economic team promptly took disinflationary measures again. These included increasing the refinance interest rate steadily between October 1990 and February 1991 (table 6-5).

After the changes in June, some of which were very controversial, and the September revision in the budget law, state budget incomes and spending for the whole of 1990 were supposed to equal Zl 202.4 trillion. Very quickly it became evident that government revenues would not rise above the original 1990 forecast, and spending plans for wages covered in the budget, social insurance, and subsidies to enterprises had to be curtailed. According to the Ministry of Finance, for the whole of 1990, state budget incomes were only 95 percent of the level anticipated in the September budget law. In 1990 these budgetary problems were manageable, and the government had sufficient political support to make the required adjustments. In 1991, however, they formed the basis of a much more serious crisis.

This instability in macroeconomic policy probably undermined the government's anti-inflation credibility. Yet adjustments to the policy were not fatal, and the Balcerowicz team was able to reassert its anti-inflation priority. Political pressure remained quite mild during 1990, in large part because of the way new economic circumstances affected Polish society.

The Social Impact of Reform, 1990

The adjustment program had important social effects, although it remains very controversial whether they constituted net gains or losses for

Table 6-8. Measures of Industrial Production in Poland, 1989–91
(indexes)

Month	Same month in previous year equal to 100			Previous month equal to 100		
	1989	1990	1991	1989	1990	1991
January	110.4	69.5	92.0	104.4	68.5	82.4
February	101.5	69.7	93.9	97.1	97.9	100.8
March	101.5	69.3	95.1	101.5	100.9	100.1
April	99.7	71.5	87.4	95.5	98.5	91.7
May	98.8	72.0	85.1	99.5	100.3	98.4
June	95.2	72.7	83.8	103.1	104.9	102.2
July	97.5	76.5	81.6	83.7	87.8	87.9
August	93.8	82.1	80.6	100.2	107.6	105.9
September	97.8	79.0	77.0	113.6	108.0	103.5
October	94.3	80.5	78.4	97.7	100.4	101.5
November	90.0	82.1	82.2	97.3	100.0	105.9
December	103.4	75.7	75.6	111.7	103.2	96.0

Source: For 1989 and 1990, Central Statistical Office 1991, April, issues 1–3, table 1, p. 16; for 1991, Central Statistical Office 1992, March, issue 2, table 1, p. 20.

society, if the results can even be evaluated at such an aggregate level. This section examines social attitudes to the reform program and considers how the program affected different social groups. This assessment helps provide a link between economic and political events in 1990 and 1991.

Public Opinion

Support for government policy was initially considerable but declined steadily during 1990 and 1991 (see table 6-9). The net approval rating moved from plus forty seven points in February 1990 to minus three points by August 1991, an enormous swing in opinion. Why did the Balcerowicz program lose its popularity?

Part of the answer lies in how different social groups responded to the question of whether government policy created a "possible exit" from the economic crisis. According to the Center for Opinion Poll Research, there was consistently more pessimism about government policy expressed by people twenty-five to twenty-nine years old; people living in villages and small towns, particularly in the central-eastern region of Poland; people with only a basic education (schooling up to fifteen years of age); farmers; people who considered their own situation to be bad; people who declared themselves to be leftist and who were members of the All-Poland Alliance of Trade Unions;[22] and people who were sure that the general situation in Poland was moving in an undesirable direction (Center for Opinion Poll Research 1991a, 1991b, 1991c).

Groups that were more optimistic in 1990–91 included people between forty and forty-nine and over sixty years old, people living in big cities or the southern region of Poland, people with a university educa-

Table 6-9. Responses to the Question "Do You Think Government Policy Creates the Possibility of Exiting from the Economic Crisis?" Poland, 1990–91

(percent)

Month and year	Yes	No	Difficult to say	Net approval[a]
1990				
February	64	17	19	47
May	58	21	21	37
June	58	24	17	34
July	51	30	19	21
September	56	29	15	27
October	48	31	21	17
November	43	38	19	5
1991				
January	43	11	45	32
February	45	23	32	22
March	48	27	25	21
April	67	26	8	41
May	47	39	14	7
June	41	50	9	−9
July	38	57	5	−19
August	47	50	3	−3

Note: Percentages do not add up to 100 because people who did not answer were not included. The survey was conducted in March, April, August, and December 1990.

a. Calculated as the percentage answering yes minus the percentage answering no.

Source: Center for Opinion Poll Research, Information Service 1991d, April and August.

tion, members of the intelligentsia, managers, people with a good financial position, people who declared themselves to be right-wing, people who said they were members of Solidarity, and people who thought that general developments in Poland were moving in a good direction.

These results are not surprising, because they show that people who were doing well supported the economic policies more than those who were doing poorly. The fall in overall popularity of the program is accounted for by the growing dissatisfaction of people who perceived themselves to be losing out. Over time, it became clear who were the winners and who were the losers (see table 6-10).

Wealth was regarded as the most important defining criterion. According to the persons interviewed, the reform program meant that poor people lost and rich people won. The biggest losers were perceived to be farmers, blue-collar workers, pensioners, and employees in state-owned and cooperative enterprises. The winners were considered to be people who operated on the borders of legality and the old and new so-called nomenklatura.[23] People working in the private sector were also considered to be major winners.

Table 6-10. Responses to the Question "Who Wins and Loses in the Economic Reform?" Poland, 1991

Questions and answers	Percentage of respondents who provided this answer
In your opinion, who wins in the economic reform?	
Rich, nouveau riche, people with a lot of money	28.0
Resourceful, enterprising, and hard-working people	13.0
Private sector, private entrepreneurs	12.0
Speculators and unemployed	11.0
Trade, small street trade, private trade	5.0
Society, all of us, the nation	5.0
Previous nomenclature, new nomenclature, communists	4.0
New nomenclature, those who have power now	4.0
Government	3.0
People with high positions, directors	2.0
Nomenclature companies	1.0
Foreign countries, foreign capital	1.0
People who are active on the border of legality	1.0
People who have connections abroad	0.8
Intermediaries	0.6
Nomenclature as a whole	0.4
Workers, farmers, people who live in villages	0.4
Church, priests	0.3
Solidarity	0.2
Budget sphere	0.1
Monopolists	0.1
Nobody	0.5
Hard to answer	17.0
Who loses in the economic reform?	
Poor people and the poorest	22.0
Farmers and agriculture as a whole	20.0
Blue-collar workers	18.0
Working people, ordinary citizens	12.0
Pensioners, old people	10.0
Workers in the state sector	7.0
Society, the nation, the state	6.0
Unemployed	4.0
State-owned enterprises	2.0
Budget sphere	1.0
Intelligentsia, white-collar workers	1.0
Young people, school graduates	1.0
People with average wages, the middle class	0.9
State treasury	0.6
Families with a lot of children, divorced people	0.4
Education, science, culture	0.4
Industry	0.3
Health service	0.2
Residents of towns	0.1
Nobody	1.0
Hard to answer	12.0

Source: Center for Opinion Poll Research, Information Service, 1991d, April.

Opinion poll research shows growing social dissatisfaction with the economic reforms and declining confidence in the economic measures proposed by the government; for example, a declining proportion of people believed that unemployment was necessary for the country. These are the kinds of changes in attitudes that might be expected to cause a political crisis and necessitate a change in economic policy, yet the policy survived. Why?

Part of the answer has already been mentioned. Opinion polls show important divisions within many social groups: views varied significantly according to age, location, and level of education. But what explains these patterns, and how did they affect organized opposition to the Balcerowicz reform program? How did the economic reform affect existing interest groups?

The Private Sector

In principle one might expect the private sector to support the stabilization program. Compared with other former communist countries, Poland had a strong private sector, which comprised almost all of agriculture as well as parts of urban services and industry. At the same time, communist government policies constrained the private sector, and the Balcerowicz reform program promised to remove those constraints. The initial expectation was that these groups would support the reforms. However, the first results of the program for the private sector were not entirely favorable. The problems were particularly acute in agriculture, which explains why farmers were hostile to the program, but much of the urban-based private sector had to make large adjustments as well.

AGRICULTURE. Farmers are the only group that, when hurt by the economic reform program, was able to mobilize almost immediate effective opposition and obtain a long series of concessions from the government. Alone among all communist countries, Poland kept agriculture based on private property. In 1989, 77 percent of the arable land was private, and private farms produced 78 percent of total output (Central Statistical Office 1990, p. 190). Polish agriculture is, however, characterized by an antiquated structure with a very small average farm size. More than 27 percent of Poland's work force is employed in agriculture, and although productivity varies considerably by region, on the whole it is much lower than in Western Europe.

The first disagreements between agricultural representatives and the government occurred in the fall of 1989 over credit policy.[24] The Rakowski government freed the prices of agricultural products in August and kept those of investment goods and consumer durables artificially low by continued subsidies. Therefore, agricultural profitability was very high in the last months of 1989. From the farmers' point of view, the Balcerowicz Plan worsened their financial position, even though it eliminated shortages and improved access to productive inputs.

In January 1990, farmers' groups—some of which were closely connected to the Communist Party—called for establishing minimum guaranteed purchase prices for basic agricultural products, subsidies for milk, cheap credits for agriculture, and help for Polish agriculture with regard to foreign trade. In March, in response to growing pressure, the Council of Ministers set a low, fixed interest rate on loans of working capital to farmers. In addition, restrictions on agricultural exports were to be gradually removed and intervention purchases by the Agricultural Market Agency were approved for some commodities. Subsidies on fertilizers and pesticides were also retained for the first half of 1990, even though subsidies for industry had been cut drastically. These were merely the first in a long line of government concessions.

In April, the Farmers Solidarity demanded immediate intervention in the form of a purchase of potatoes for export and processing. In May, the Farmers Trade Union refused to pay farmers' contributions into their state-run pension fund. On June 29, police intervened to remove all the farmers—and several Sejm deputies—who were occupying the Ministry of Agriculture. This confrontation resulted in the resignation of the agriculture minister, a representative of the United Peasant Party. Repeated demonstrations followed, and again the government took steps to help farmers.[25] In October, when the income tax deductions for investment were generally abolished, dairies retained these deductions, and in November, the Council of Ministers decided to subsidize some agricultural exports in order to eliminate surpluses. Even though the government repeatedly made concessions, the farmers increased their demands, encouraged by representatives who had belonged to the former communist coalition. In the ensuing competition for support among farmers, Solidarity farmer organizations also became critical of the government.

PRIVATE INDUSTRY AND SERVICES. Compared with farmers, the urban private sector did not launch a unified response to the economic reform program. There was certainly a rapid expansion of new private firms, and people who participated in this growth tended to have favorable attitudes toward the Balcerowicz Plan. Most important, despite the losses for some private entrepreneurs, the new private sector became a way to escape the state sector (Eastern Europe Research Unit 1991). At the same time, parts of the "old" private sector—firms in existence before 1989—were hurt by the economic reform program. The most successful companies were engaged in trade, where profits were extraordinarily high. Retail street trade expanded rapidly, as did private wholesale trade.[26]

Private manufacturers had a much harder time, because demand fell as interest rates rose sharply. Foreign competition also grew, and although the large real devaluation of the zloty gave Polish firms an initial advantage, this steadily disappeared as the exchange rate remained fixed (until May 1991) while prices rose. As a result, the number of private companies in industry and construction actually fell during the first quarter of 1991. Who exactly lost out?

Under the communist system some small private manufacturing companies prospered by taking advantage of the economy of shortage, the supplier's market, and the lack of foreign competition. These companies were in the enviable position of being able both to use subsidized raw materials and to set their own prices freely. These businesspeople even had their own procommunist political organization, the Democratic Party, which had switched its parliamentary support to the Mazowiecki government in the summer of 1990. Under the stabilization program, these businesses suddenly faced foreign competition and limited demand. Paradoxically, the arrival of a free market brought an end to the prosperity of many established small private family businesses.[27] Although the private sector is a useful economic escape route for individuals, the reform program did not mobilize it effectively, and it remains informal, small-scale, and antigovernment.

THE STATE AND COOPERATIVE SECTORS. Arguably, workers in state-owned companies lost the most due to the stabilization program, although, ironically, they gave strongest support to Solidarity both in 1980–81 and during the underground period of 1981–89. They also initially supported the Solidarity government and its reform program. Stabilization revealed the economic weaknesses of state-owned firms, while democratization removed their privileged political position. On top of these problems, exports to the former Soviet Union and military production fell sharply. Nevertheless, it is difficult to determine who were the winners and losers in the state sector. Employees of companies undergoing privatization or already privatized were in a much better position than those working in other state firms.

The troubled condition of many state-owned enterprises is reflected in research indicating that employees of state companies were dissatisfied with the social costs of the economic program and with the uneven distribution of these costs (Institute of Economic Sciences, Polish Academy of Sciences 1991). Despite the general consensus on the need to introduce a market economy, frustration was widespread, although the hostility of workers toward the reforms was not accompanied by demands for a return to communism.

The geographical location of companies also matters. Some regions have only one type of economic activity, such as coal mining in the Walbrzych region. Some face high unemployment because they contain industrial branches that need to be restructured. In some small towns, just one factory employs most of the population, and the failure of such a factory jeopardizes the existence of the whole town. In contrast, in most big cities, a thriving private sector offers alternative employment.

Because of these varied results, for the first few months of the stabilization program, industrial workers and their trade unions exerted little political pressure. This began to change in the third quarter of 1990, and workers' demands have grown steadily since. These demands were particularly evident after the 1990 presidential campaign, when workers sought to loosen the popiwek rules and devalue the zloty, and during the 1991 parliamentary election. All the same, this political challenge to the reform program took a long time to develop.

Privatized companies definitely had advantages over state-run companies, although there are significant differences according to how the company was privatized. Some companies were initially liquidated and then transferred to workers' ownership in a leveraged buyout. By the end of 1991, this form of privatization had been used by several hundred enterprises in various branches of industry. The employees and managers of these companies became effectively self-employed, and their future was more clearly defined. Even though they ran the real risk of bankruptcy for the first time in forty years, people working in these firms may be considered among the winners.

Other companies were large enterprises transformed into joint stock companies by a process known as commercialization, which begins with 100 percent ownership by the state. This process affected more employees than the leveraged buyout. By the end of July 1991, there were 184 such firms, many of which changed their legal form simply to receive tax advantages (the excess wage tax was partially lifted for partially privatized firms). Of the 122 companies that submitted a financial report by the end of July, 95 were profitable and 27 had losses. For employees of unprofitable firms, privatization was likely to mean problems and perhaps even unemployment.

Not all workers in state enterprises were losers. Many lost, but others won. It is not enough to know a firm's sector in order to know if its workers were losers; also important are the region, the size of the town, and an individual worker's characteristics. This differentiated impact on workers in state enterprises delayed the organization of effective opposition.

PENSIONERS. There were also losses for people whose income depended on the state budget, particularly pensioners. The Mazowiecki government, and particularly Minister Kuron, certainly made a serious effort to protect the relative living standards of pensioners. Nevertheless, the average pension masks a significant variation in what individual pensioners receive, because the value of a pension depends on when a person retired. Kuron attempted to change this in 1990, but the Ministry of Finance was opposed to changes that would impose a burden on the budget, and the draft legislation was not discussed. At the same time, the number of retirees grew steadily, as people chose to retire rather than become unemployed. As a result, the financial situation of the Social

Benefits Bureau, which pays pensions, had been worsening for some time and reached a crisis in the second half of 1991.

The inequality of pensions was seized upon by the All-Poland Alliance of Trade Unions, which organized increasingly frequent demonstrations. Protests increased in the second half of 1991, when the government did not comply with the law requiring indexation adjustments to pensions. Overall, however, pensioners did not constitute an effective brake on reform.

CONCLUSION. Three points stand out in the pattern of winners and losers from the Polish reform program. First, despite an initial honeymoon period in which support for the program was widespread, dissatisfaction grew quickly. Second, the effects of the Balcerowicz Plan tended to divide existing social groups, with some members winning and others losing. Because of the new divisions within social groups, in most cases—except agriculture—dissatisfaction was not turned into effective opposition to the program. Third, most groups did not begin the Balcerowicz program with effective organizations. The notable exceptions were workers, who were neutralized by the Solidarity leadership, and farmers, who made a great deal of trouble. It is remarkable that there was *so little opposition* during the program's first year. As 1991 showed, however, once political competition reemerged in Poland, new social grievances were quickly articulated.

The Reemergence of Political Competition, 1990–91

Politics again played a critical role in the third phase of the Polish economic reform. Instead of providing an impulse for radical economic reform, however, as occurred in 1989 and early 1990, political events now constituted a barrier. This section shows that new electoral rules were the result of growing political competition in the Sejm, and, once adopted, they created incentives to form a large number of new parties. The electoral system of proportional representation was both a cause and an effect of political fragmentation and the absence of a dominant bloc in the contract Sejm of 1989. Proportional representation meant that parties had no major incentives to coalesce, although the most important aspects of political fragmentation existed before the new electoral law was adopted.

From the beginning of 1990, the feeling was growing that the political transition, and the introduction of more democracy, should be speeded up, particularly in light of the collapse of communism throughout Eastern Europe. A leading example of this new political direction was the slogan "acceleration," adopted by the Central Alliance when it was officially created in June 1990 and by the citizens' committees. The issue of how to accelerate remained controversial, however, and early proof of this point was provided by the debate over the new electoral law.

The first changes in this direction, proposed in the early fall of 1990, allowed the president to be elected directly for a maximum of two five-year terms. The Sejm also cut short the term of President Jaruzelski and decided that all matters concerning parliamentary elections should be resolved by the end of the first quarter of 1991 and that a new presidential election should be held no later than December 1990.

Far more controversy was generated during the long, and at times dramatic, debate concerning the electoral law for Parliament. Some argued that democracy required the representation of even small political parties in the Parliament. Others argued that if the Sejm were too divided, it would be unable to support a stable executive, which would hurt the chances for continued economic and political transformation.

When the electoral law was discussed in June 1990, the Citizens' Parliamentary Club proposed removing the fixed division of seats that had been adopted at the roundtable, which would have generated a majority voting system. This proposal was rejected by the Sejm. The first draft electoral law (dated August 12, 1990) was prepared by representatives of the former procommunist peasant party (the United Peasant Party), and its basic idea was that voting would be for a list of candidates, although voters could express a preference for particular candidates. This would have produced a typical proportional system of representation, and this idea was supported by, among others, the former communist parliamentary clubs. These groups thought they would get too few votes to win many seats in a majority voting system system.

In September 1990, the Citizens' Parliamentary Club proposed a mixed system with some proportionality and some majority voting. It sought to make strong political parties more likely.

During this debate, an unexpected political configuration emerged when right-wing members of the Citizens' Parliamentary Club and former communists both supported proportional representation. This first round of debates finally came to an end on October 25, when the proportional voting system was chosen and sent to a special commission for detailed work.

At the beginning of 1991, the issue was reopened, although opposing sides were taken by the two leading political institutions: President Walesa, who had been chosen in a free election, and the Sejm, which had been selected according to the roundtable agreements. In fact, the first legislative initiative of the president was to propose an electoral law with proportional voting but some elements of a majority system. This proposal was clearly less favorable to small parties than the scheme adopted by the Sejm. On May 10, the Sejm passed its own electoral law, which had both proportional and majority elements, but on June 11, President Walesa announced that he would veto it. He argued that the proposed system was too complicated and would not elect a Sejm with a stable parliamentary majority, therefore making stable and strong governments impossible.

This presidential veto was accepted by the Sejm, which then prepared an electoral law incorporating some of the president's suggestions, including allowing church participation in election campaigns. This new election law was passed by the Sejm, although the Senate tried unsuccessfully to amend it. After further political struggle between the Sejm and the president, this version became law, and the church played a significant role in the 1991 parliamentary elections.

The political conflict over electoral law, as well as the outcome in favor of proportional representation, was the unintentional result of the roundtable agreements. The contract Sejm and the electoral law of 1989 were designed to allow the Communist Party to retain executive power. Instead, they allowed the erstwhile opposition to gain rapid control of the executive. The contract Sejm became the means through which former communists were able to remain in the legislature at a time when their social support was at its lowest and then prepare to launch themselves when conditions became more propitious. The contract Sejm also strengthened the anti-Walesa forces within Solidarity.

These developments naturally influenced the direction of the party system. Until the roundtable, a dichotomy clearly defined two implacably opposed sides. On one side was the Communist Party with its assorted allies: the Democratic Party, the United Peasant Party, some Christian parties, and the Patriotic Movement for National Rebirth, as well as the procommunist trade union. In opposition was Solidarity, a social movement unifying people with very different philosophies: Christians, conservatives, liberals, social democrats, and even some anarchists. Yet, almost as soon as the roundtable agreements were concluded, cracks began to appear in the two monoliths. The first splits occurred primarily in the Parliament, but these developments also spread to political parties active outside Parliament. These changes came clearly into the open after the adoption, on July 28, of a new law governing the activity of political parties. Once a legal framework was in place, new parties were created and soon covered the whole political spectrum.

The range of political parties can be rather confusing. Some parties emphasize their long history of fighting against the communist system, others emphasize their roots in the tradition of prewar parties. Some have even attempted to rebuild the political map of the Second Polish Republic, which existed between the two world wars. Despite its complexity, the system of political parties can be easily understood once the history of the most important parties is understood. This system is, of course, of utmost importance because it determined the pattern of coalitions for and against the economic reform program.

Various issues contributed to the split within Solidarity: personality (the question of whether Walesa should become president), the optimal speed of all changes, and the attitude that should be taken toward the communists. On these three issues, the Central Alliance wanted Walesa

Table 6-11. Results of the 1990 Presidential Election in Poland

Round and candidate	Percent of votes cast
First round, November 25[a]	
Valid votes	98.5
Candidates	
R. Bartoszcze	7.2
W. Cimoszewicz	9.2
T. Mazowiecki	18.1
L. Moczulski	2.5
S. Tyminski	23.1
L. Walesa	40.0
Second round, December 9[b]	
Valid votes	97.7
Candidates	
S. Tyminski	25.8
L. Walesa	73.4

Note: In the first round, Tyminski received the most votes in relatively undeveloped agricultural regions, and Walesa received the most votes in large towns and the least votes in small agricultural regions in eastern Poland.
a. 60.6 percent of the electorate voted.
b. 53.4 percent of the electorate voted.
Source: State Election Commission 1990.

as president, all reforms accelerated, and measures passed against the former communist nomenklatura. On all three issues, they were opposed by a group inside the Citizens' Parliamentary Club that supported Mazowiecki. This struggle culminated in the war on the top in mid-1990 and the presidential election in November and December of that year, when the issues concerned personalities more than programs.

The results of this election were quite unexpected (see table 6-11). Although some opinion polls showed rising popularity for a previously unknown Canadian businessman, Stanislaw Tyminski, attention was focused primarily on Mazowiecki and Walesa. Mazowiecki did not survive past the first round, however: he received only 18 percent of the vote compared with Tyminski's 23 percent.

Various explanations were offered for Mazowiecki's poor performance. Some observers said it was a clear signal of social disappointment with the results of the reform program, exacerbated by the split within Solidarity, which people did not understand. Some voters were drawn to the image of Tyminski as someone from outside Polish political life with supposedly good connections to foreign business. Tyminski's campaign accused the government of corruption and of betraying the ideals of August 1980. He also made vague promises about benefits he could obtain for Poland. In all probability, disillusioned people voted for the myth of the West rather than for Tyminski himself.

From a short-run perspective, the war on the top disrupted the Polish political scheme and put pressure on the economic reform. From a longer perspective, this "war" acted as a catalyst for the creation of parties. The difference between parties and their programs became clearer than it was in 1989–90. This may have strengthened the former Solidarity parties and weakened the former communists. Once Walesa was elected, he became a strong force in support of the program.

The decisive break in the Citizens' Parliamentary Club came in June 1991, when a new parliamentary club (the Democratic Union) was organized and joined by seventy-nine deputies. At the end of June, several other people, including Ryszard Bugaj, founded the Solidarity of Workers (table 6-7 presents changes in the balance of groups within the Sejm between February and August 1991).

These political realignments took place during 1990 and 1991 and began to affect economic policy in 1991. If the Polish economy had recovered smoothly after the hard year of 1990, political pressure would probably have remained at manageable levels. Unfortunately, however, 1991 brought still further bad economic news for the government.

New Economic Problems, 1991

At the beginning of 1991 one further element of the economic reform program fell into place: in April, Poland signed an agreement to reduce and restructure debt owed to the Paris Club.[28] It was agreed that by March 31, 1994, the debt would be written down by 30 percent and a further 20 percent might be canceled later (any creditor can negotiate a bilateral debt reduction, and in 1991 both the United States and France said they were willing to do this). Future debt reduction was made contingent on Poland continuing to meet economic performance targets set by the IMF, and in April 1991 the IMF agreed to extend a three-year adjustment loan for about $1.6 billion. By fall, Poland's ability to borrow from the IMF had been suspended for failure to meet the specified criteria. What went wrong in 1991?

The contrast between the economic results of 1990 and 1991 is striking. In 1990 Poland achieved many of the targets set by the IMF, and the effects of the slight relaxation of policy in the second half of the year were minor. In 1991 the budget deficit grew rapidly, and the necessary adjustments became politically untenable.

In retrospect, despite the radical policy changes in 1990, one major policy problem was not addressed: the dependence of the budget on the taxation of state enterprises. Taxation on state enterprises was actually more important in the 1991 budget law than it had been in 1989 (see table 6-12), and the government had difficulty finding alternative sources of revenue. Plans were made to introduce a personal income tax and a value added tax, but these could not realistically become significant at least until the beginning of 1992 and 1993, respectively (at least one

Table 6-12. Structure of Budget Revenues in Poland, 1989–91
(percent shares)

Budget category	Results, 1989	Law, 1990	Law, 1991
Payments from enterprises and other economic units	79.5	85.0	84.0
Turnover tax	28.4	27.1	26.9
Corporate income tax	32.6	31.4	37.2
Dividend	5.5	8.8	8.4
Wage tax	10.9	9.8	6.0
Excess wage tax (popiwek)	n.a.	4.6	1.0
Other	2.0	3.3	1.2
Tariffs	n.a.	n.a.	3.3
Payments by financial and insurance institutions	8.6	5.3	5.4
Taxes and payments by private enterprises and individuals	7.0	5.6	3.8
Other income	3.8	4.0	1.5
Transfer from local government	1.1	n.a.	n.a.
Income from the sale of state property	n.a.	n.a.	5.2

n.a. Not applicable.

Note: The definitions of some categories changed between the 1990 and 1991 budget.

Source: For the 1989 results and 1990 law, Council of Ministers 1990, p. 5; for the law of 1991, Council of Ministers 1991b, pp. 10, 22.

member of the economic reform team has argued that the reform of taxation could have proceeded faster; see Dabrowski 1991). For 1991 the popiwek rules were changed, so that the permissible wage increase was based on average wages rather than on the size of the firm's wage fund (generally, the wage fund is simply the number of workers multiplied by the average wage).

The budget showed a small surplus in 1990 because the good financial results of state enterprises meant they paid a high level of taxes. A small deficit was forecast for 1991, but this was based on rather optimistic assumptions: a 5 percent increase in output, a 4 percent increase in GDP, and only 32 percent inflation.[29] Instead, 1991 saw a real budget crisis when the profitability of state enterprises declined. This collapse of revenues created the need to cut budget spending. As government revenue fell precipitously, unemployment rose steadily. Spending on social insurance and housing was higher than the limits set in the 1991 budget law, and the number of people retiring increased rapidly, because it was better to collect a pension than unemployment insurance.

The cumulative budget deficit widened throughout 1991 (table 6-6). By the end of the first half year, it was clear that attaining the levels of revenue projected in the budget law would be extremely difficult. Up to and including June, budget revenues were almost 34 percent of the level intended for the whole year and equaled only 37 percent of spending.

Table 6-13. Changes in the Structure of Current Spending in Poland, 1986–90
(percent shares)

Spending category	1986	1987	1988	1989	1990
Current spending					
(percentage of total spending)	42.0	43.6	43.5	45.2	54.4
Health and social support	10.3	10.9	10.9	11.9	16.9
Basic education	8.0	8.3	8.0	10.4	11.4
Higher education	1.8	1.7	2.1	2.5	3.2
Administration and justice	2.8	3.0	3.0	3.3	4.0
Police	2.5	2.5	2.4	2.6	3.0
Army	7.7	7.8	7.4	6.3	7.0
Treasury enterprises	5.6	6.2	5.9	4.7	6.0

Source: Government documentation for the proposed changes in the budget law, submitted to the Sejm in August 1991.

The proportion of government spending going to health care and other social support also increased from almost 12 percent in 1989 to 17 percent in 1990 (see table 6-13). This increase was financed in large part by lower subsidies to enterprises, which fell from 29 percent in 1989 to 17 percent in 1990 (see table 6-14). The situation worsened considerably in 1991, when a substantial budget deficit developed and spending had to be cut. The effects included a lower standard of living for the state-financed intelligentsia as well as cuts in public health care services and in the number of lessons taught at schools, increasing the burden on teachers at universities. The losers in this sector did not demand more resources from the government during 1990–91. Instead they pressed for accelerating the pace of organizational changes. Workers in health care, for example, protested in the second and third quarters of 1991, demanding the reorganization of medical services, an end to the constitutional guarantee of free medical care, and greater independence for health providers. Many of the losers in the budget sphere were doctors and teachers, whose response was often to demand more rather than less change. Making budget cuts remains problematic, but ironically the problems tend to increase rather than decrease pressure for more fundamental economic change.

The Ministry of Finance took immediate measures to control the size of the deficit. Stronger controls over spending were imposed, and indexation payments on pensions and wages for employees in the budget sphere were delayed. To cut budget spending further, the Ministry of Finance submitted a revised budget law to the Sejm in August.[30]

The Bielecki government was strongly criticized when it presented these proposals to Parliament. Some communist deputies even suggested that the government should be voted out of power. Bielecki responded by offering his government's resignation, which was ultimately declined:

Table 6-14. Changes in the Structure of State Budget Spending in Poland, 1986–90

(percentage of total spending)

Spending category	1986	1987	1988	1989	1990
Current spending	42.0	43.6	43.5	45.2	54.4
Social insurance (pensions and unemployment benefits)	8.8	4.2	4.3	7.0	8.5
Subsidies to enterprises	29.8	30.8	33.2	28.6	17.0
Investment and repairs	5.3	15.8	15.8	12.1	11.2
Subsidies to the Fund for Foreign Debt Repayment	0.0	0.0	0.0	3.2	4.5
Transfers to banks	4.1	5.6	3.2	2.8	4.1
Transfers to the Social Insurance Fund and Fund for the Development of Science and Technology	0.0	0.0	0.0	1.1	0.0
Purchase of treasury bonds	0.0	0.0	0.0	0.0	0.3

Source: Government documentation for the proposed changes in the budget law, submitted to the Sejm in August 1991.

Parliament wanted to embarrass the government, not bring it down. Eventually the Sejm passed the government's budget law.[31]

Although it survived the budget battle, the government's economic team now found that the political situation was quite different from what it had been at the end of 1989. It was now much harder to adjust economic policy, because the government was viewed as too weak to last beyond the parliamentary elections.

Throughout 1991, there was also growing parliamentary opposition to the Bielecki government, which did not have a majority in the Sejm. This opposition culminated in serious conflict between government and Parliament over a whole range of issues: changes in the budget law for 1991, the mass privatization program, the new pension law, the proposed banking law, proposals of special economic powers for the government, and suggestions for strengthening the executive powers of the president and the government. Beginning in late summer 1991, the Sejm blocked the government's attempts to appoint a new president for the National Bank of Poland.

By now, the former communist forces felt they had regained some legitimacy and, as the parliamentary election approached, became increasingly willing to oppose the government on economic policy, which they had not really done since the fall of 1989. As the social costs of the economic transition became more apparent, the former communists tried to legitimize themselves by strongly opposing the Bielecki government. This effort was undoubtedly helped by splits within the Citizens' Parliamentary Club, which made opposition to the government seem acceptable within many Solidarity circles. At the same time, some Solidarity representatives in Parliament also began to oppose the government's economic proposals, reasoning that they should stay faithful to their trade union roots and help protect people.

The emergence of this political competition made life increasingly difficult for the Bielecki government, which would have preferred to reform important political institutions, especially the legislature. It was now too late. The institutions and political rules had been established by the roundtable and confirmed by the new electoral law. These rules could not now be changed.

Poland experienced significant economic problems in 1990, although arguably the problems mounted in 1991, as well as social protests and discontent in both years. But it was the organization of politics that changed the most between the two years. The consequences of these changes became fully evident in the fall 1991 parliamentary election. The political contract of 1989 that had helped initiate the economic reforms was now beginning to block them. This was the price of having a contract Sejm.

From the beginning of 1991, Bielecki's administration was beset by strikes and protests supported by all of the farmers' organizations. Farmers were particularly opposed to the low tariffs, which supposedly opened the Polish market to an inflow of subsidized food from Western Europe, and accused the government of insufficiently stimulating agricultural exports to the Soviet Union. In July, Farmers Solidarity declared that, beginning on August 15, farmers would pay their taxes in kind by delivering their products directly to local tax offices. On August 1, the government responded by introducing a new import tariff of 25 to 35 percent on agricultural and other products. The result was a substantial increase in the domestic price of Polish food, but this did not satisfy the farmers.

Further government concessions did not weaken the pressure of the farmers' lobby, whose demands for higher tariffs, preferential credits, and minimum guaranteed prices for agricultural products grew during the summer as the parliamentary elections approached. Some political groups echoed these demands as a way to obtain more rural votes. By fall, all agricultural groups were hostile to the stabilization program and differed only in the sharpness of their criticism. They all demanded minimum guaranteed prices, tariff protection of the agricultural market, and preferential credits. They all rejected the government's support for modernizing and enlarging farms and for transferring a large part of the work force to agricultural services.

On October 4, twenty-three days before the elections, the Sejm passed a law obliging the government to introduce temporary minimum prices for milk and corn, which would be binding until October 30, and to grant agricultural credits with an interest rate that would be three-quarters of the National Bank of Poland's refinance rate. Similar legislation had failed to pass the Sejm on two previous occasions but succeeded this time, despite firm government opposition.

The Bielecki government also came under pressure from workers' representatives, who, after the presidential election, demanded elimination of the popiwek, devaluation of the zloty, and reduction of interest rates (Balcerowicz 1992). Members of the Sejm, trade unionists, and managers of large state firms argued also that the government should introduce an industrial policy, although it remained unclear what this meant beyond increasing subsidies to state firms.

The Political Barrier, 1991–92

Elections under the new law were held on October 27: 6,980 candidates ran for the 460 seats in the Sejm, reflecting the fragmentation of the system. After the elections, the Sejm had twenty-nine political parties, most of which would not have been able to overcome a 5 percent threshold. The election law clearly favored small parties and coalitions.

The results of this election were rather surprising in several respects (see table 6-15). First, turnout was low—only 43 percent—even though the president and the Catholic Church had appealed for people to vote. The low turnout meant that almost no party received the level of support it had expected, except for the former communists who had counted on hardcore support of around 10 percent of the electorate. The Democratic Union, the biggest political movement created from Solidarity, and the Union of the Democratic Left, the former communists, received close to the same number of votes.

The parliamentary election marked the end of partial democracy based directly on the roundtable rules and the beginning of a period of great political uncertainty. The details of this period highlight the difficulties of establishing strong executive government in Poland. They also illustrate which of the various parties were willing and able to cooperate with one another.

According to the constitution, the president of Poland nominates the prime minister, who must win the support of a majority in the Sejm before forming a government. On November 8, 1991, President Walesa nominated as prime minister Bronislaw Geremek, a leader of the Democratic Union, which had received the largest number of votes in the election. However, Geremek gave up his attempt to form a government after only one week, because he was unable to obtain sufficient support in the Sejm.

The best chance to form a government clearly lay with a potential coalition of four parties that had common roots in the Solidarity opposition movement and had not been closely connected with the first two noncommunist governments.[32] Together, these four parties had 121 seats

Table 6-15. Results of the October 1991 Parliamentary Election in Poland (number of seats, unless noted)

Coalition	Percent of vote for Sejm	Current Sejm	Previous Sejm	Senate	Parliament
Catholic Election Movement	8.73	49	3[a]	9	48[b]
Central Alliance	8.71	44	Unclear	9	53[b]
Christian Democrats	2.36	5	10+5[c]	0	5
Confederation of Independent Poland	7.50	46		4	50[b]
Democratic Party	..	1	21	0	1
Democratic Union	12.31	62	46	21	83[b]
"For Wielkopolska and Poland"		1	0	0	1
German Minority	1.17	7	0	0	7
Krakow Coalition "Supporting the President"	..	1	0	0	1
Liberal Democratic Congress	7.48	37	4	6	43[b]
Orthodox Electoral Committee	..	1	0	1	1
Party of Christian Democrats	1.11	4	28	3	7
Peasant Alliance	5.46	28	16[d]	5	33[b]
Peasant Election Coalition, "Piast"	..	1	0	0	1
People's Unity	..	1	0	0	1
Podhale Union	..	1	0	0	1
Poland West Union	0.23	4	0	0	4

Polish Beer-Lovers Party	3.27	16	0	0	16
Polish Peasant Party	8.67	48	73e	7	55b
Silesian Autonomy Movement	0.35	2	1	0	2
Social Democratic Movement	..	1	0	0	1
Solidarity of Workers	2.05	4	3	0	4
"Solidarnosc"	5.05	27	0	11	38b
"Solidarnosc 80"	..	1	1	0	1
Union of Democratic Leftists	11.98	60	102f	4	64b
Union of Real Politics	2.25	3	0	0	3
Wielkopolski Union	..	1	0	0	1
Women's Union	..	1	0	0	1
"X" Party	0.47	3	1	0	3
Others having only one seat	n.a.	n.a.	n.a.	21	21

n.a. Not applicable.

.. Negligible.

a. National Christian Union.

b. Strongest coalitions in Parliament.

c. Union PAX and Polish Social Catholic Union.

d. Polish Peasant Party–Solidarity.

e. Polish Peasant Party.

f. Parliamentary Club of the Democratic Left.

Source: Rzeczpospolita 1991, November 4, 7; anonymous 1991.

in the Sejm. As events developed, another three parties supported the coalition government, although they did not receive ministerial posts: the Polish Peasant Party, with forty-eight seats; the Party of Christian Democrats, with four seats; and Christian Democracy, with five seats. This gave the government coalition of seven parties a total of 178 seats in the Sejm.[33]

After the election, the seven coalition parties nominated Jan Olszewski for prime minister. Olszewski received the necessary support in the Sejm on December 6, and although the creation of a new government was not without drama, ultimately he unified his coalition enough to obtain approval for his cabinet on December 23.

The most important issue initially dividing supporters of the Olszewski government was economic policy and, in particular, their attitude toward the Balcerowicz Plan. The Balcerowicz Plan at this time was taken to mean faster privatization, tough anti-inflationary monetary policy, fiscal austerity, and the newly signed agreement with the European Community. The full set of these measures was supported by the Liberal Democratic Congress, by the Democratic Union, and sometimes by representatives of the Central Alliance. In contrast, most formal members of the government coalition were hostile to the Balcerowicz Plan and favored more support for state-owned enterprises and expanded aggregate demand. So the Olszewski coalition government was, in principle, opposed to the continuation of the Balcerowicz Plan yet found it very difficult to abandon Balcerowicz's policies. In the first half of 1992, monetary policy was not loosened significantly, and, if anything, fiscal austerity became more effective. Why was it difficult in practice to renounce the Balcerowicz Plan?

Part of the answer lies in Poland's new relationship with the West and the opportunities and constraints this brings. The agreement on Poland's association with the European Community was signed on December 16, 1991. This agreement defined the principles of cooperation in a number of spheres, including politics, trade, finance, and culture. It recognized Poland's desire to become a member of the European Community, although it did not guarantee that an application for membership would be approved. It established a timetable for creating free trade between Poland and the European Community over the next ten years, although some unresolved trade issues remain, particularly concerning textiles and agriculture.

Member countries of the European Community had already committed significant financial assistance to support structural changes, modernize the financial sector, help retrain the unemployed, and develop small businesses. The signing of the agreement offered the prospect, although not the promise, of further financial support.

Most important, in combination with the debt reduction settlement, the agreement appeared to confirm that Poland was on the right economic track and, without imposing explicit constraints on economic policy, did express the expectations of Poland's western partners. This had the important effect of determining what policies were seen as reasonable and responsible *within* Poland.

But the reasons for continuing Balcerowicz's policies also lay with public opinion and with the nature of political institutions at the end of 1992. Some people clearly gained from the reforms and supported the Balcerowicz Plan. These people were not well organized politically up to mid-1991, but by the beginning of 1992 new organizations had begun to mobilize them. Second, the people who perceived themselves as losers from the reforms were also becoming better organized. The losers usually sought only to block further changes: they and their political representatives did not produce a coherent or workable set of economic policies that would in any way substitute for the Balcerowicz Plan, particularly given the current configuration of political institutions.

Beyond the Point of No Return?

The results of the parliamentary election did not seem to favor the Balcerowicz Plan. Only 20 percent of the voters supported the Democratic Union and the Liberal Democratic Congress, the two main parties openly supporting the plan and the only two not promising a quick improvement in the economic situation. It is fair to say that support for the plan did not win many votes.

Relatively more support was received during the election campaign by parties opposed to the Balcerowicz Plan, including support for the unclear idea of a political third path proposed by the Catholic Election Movement and the Confederation of Independent Poland. Although these two parties and the Central Alliance offered typical rightist views on political issues (they wanted, for example, tough measures to achieve "decommunization"), they held leftist views on economics. They wanted to support state enterprises, to have more equality of incomes, and to extend the welfare state. In fact, although all of these parties strongly criticized Balcerowicz, none presented a clear, comprehensive, alternative economic program.

However, it is too simplistic to interpret the election results as a rejection of market reforms. Opinion polls addressing the important issues did not show significant protest against economic reform. They showed high levels of support for the persons of Balcerowicz and Bielecki (the liberal prime minister), and Bielecki received more votes than any other candidate in the parliamentary election. These feelings were not translated into a proreform political coalition.

Given this situation, having even small parties represented in Parliament might reduce the danger of extraparliamentary opposition. Fragmentation of political groups was probably unavoidable because radical economic and political reforms cause social disruptions and politicians on all sides were still identifying their constituencies. After the elections, no proreform coalition enjoyed a majority in the Sejm.[34] At the same time, the strength of Parliament meant that a weak executive would have trouble making any significant change in policy. This was good for fiscal and monetary policy, for which a clear strategy had already been established, but bad for attempts to privatize large state firms, which had not yet had a decisive breakthrough.

Conclusions

By the end of 1991, what remained of the Balcerowicz Plan after the fixed exchange rate was abandoned, the excess wage tax rules were relaxed, and inflation remained high? Despite these apparently significant changes, the Balcerowicz Plan remained very influential and intact in at least three forms: as a long list of irreversible achievements, as a set of priorities, and as a way of making economic policy.

The major achievement of the Balcerowicz Plan was to destroy the final remnants of the old economic system. Shortages were eliminated, foreign trade was liberalized, the currency was made almost completely convertible, most retail trade was privatized, output prices were freed, and the cost of energy was raised to world levels. These were the prerequisites of a market economy, and although the last two communist governments took some steps in this direction, Balcerowicz struck the decisive blow. It is extremely unlikely that these policies can be undone, and they will therefore remain the basis for developing a genuine market economy.

Balcerowicz's main macroeconomic priority was to bring inflation down to a Western European level. Although not fully achieved, this goal remained the central element of government policy even after Balcerowicz's resignation. Changes in supporting policies toward, for example, the exchange rate, do not, therefore, signal the abandonment of this priority; rather they are adjustments required to keep it on track. The main priority for microeconomic policy is still to privatize most state industry.

Balcerowicz's most influential legacy is perhaps that his policies set a very high standard of professionalism for their level of preparation and the level of support they received throughout the West, especially, but not only, with multilateral financial institutions. A new, young technocratic elite emerged to occupy key positions, particularly in the ministries of finance and privatization. Any successor to Balcerowicz who presents a policy that does not match these high standards of quality will face considerable criticism in the government, the Sejm, and the broader political debates of Poland.

This threefold definition of the Balcerowicz Plan identifies several constraints on the choices of subsequent governments. First, the policies of Balcerowicz irrevocably opened Poland to the West. To close the Polish economy again is unthinkable, and although this idea has been proposed by some parties, it has no real political credibility.

Second, although some social groups perceive the reform negatively, they do not agree on the requirements for an alternative set of policies. Furthermore, many people directly benefited from the reforms. Even if a coherent set of alternative policies existed, it would not necessarily have strong support either in the country or in the Parliament.

Third, the executive remains weak and, under the current configuration of parties, does not have the ability to control the legislative process and timetable.[35] Deputies who can identify weaknesses in the government's legislation may use this to embarrass the government and obstruct its proposals almost without limit. As a result, the Bielecki government found it hard to speed up the reform process by introducing mass privatization or constitutional reform, while the Olszewski government found it difficult to loosen macroeconomic policy. Furthermore, on some economic issues, Olszewski's team had to rely on support of the Liberal Democratic Congress and the Democratic Union, which were not part of the government coalition and could thus lobby in favor of tight monetary and fiscal policies.

The Bielecki government resigned formally on December 5, 1991. Although Bielecki continued in office to the end of that month, while a new coalition government was formed, Leszek Balcerowicz's term as Poland's finance minister effectively ended. Despite remarkable economic successes, his reform program had generated too much political opposition for him to continue. Why did this happen, and what does it imply both for the future of the Polish program and for similar programs elsewhere?

The Balcerowicz program was designed first and foremost to deal with a serious economic crisis. Details of the program were debated, but the rapidly accelerating inflation beginning in the summer of 1989 eliminated all alternatives to a tough anti-inflation policy (for example, the economic ideas advanced by Solidarity during the roundtable negotiations were no longer relevant). The rapid political changes taking place in the spring and summer of 1989 meant that Poland had both the political coalition and the social support needed to step back from the brink of hyperinflation.

External support from multilateral institutions and independent economists was particularly important in this initial phase. These outside forces offered valuable economic advice and immediate financial support to the program and, perhaps most important, helped define what kind of economic policies were credible and deserved political support. The fact that Balcerowicz was highly respected in the West was initially a major political asset for him and for the Mazowiecki government.

The shock therapy could not avoid creating losers, and these losers inevitably protested. Given the massive changes wrought by the program, it is impressive that there was so little effective social opposition during 1990. This can be attributed to the absence of prior organization (except Solidarity and the farmers), to the fragmentation of interest groups, and to the lack of effective mobilization of winners in support of the program. Individuals and subgroups (in, for example, particular localities) rather than well-defined social groups won or lost in the initial phase of reforms. The formation of new social groups on the basis of their advantages and disadvantages in the market economy only began with the emergence of new political parties during the 1991 parliamentary elections.

Did the Balcerowicz team miss chances to build a supportive political coalition (by, for example, accelerating institutional changes)? With the advantage of hindsight, the answer is yes. Faster progress should have been made in reorganizing large state firms and restructuring the banking system. Even better, some form of mass privatization, involving the free distribution of shares to all citizens, could have created a strong political umbrella for more painful economic adjustments.

But these criticisms are unfair. Stabilizing the Polish macroeconomy was a full-time job, and there were not enough new technocrats to work on all the worthy issues. Balcerowicz consciously chose the macroeconomy as his priority because he wanted to take the critical and irreversible step toward establishing a market economy: the elimination of shortages. He also preferred to leave politics to the politicians.

Perhaps more seriously, the Balcerowicz team also made technical errors, particularly by failing to address the structural weaknesses of the budget during 1990, when it still had a strong political position. The team made no serious effort to speed up the introduction of new taxes or to break the link between wages in the budget sphere and in the rest of the economy. The decline in the profits of state enterprises in 1991 was widely predicted and probably expected by the government, but there is little sign that the Ministry of Finance was prepared when the crisis finally came.

Nevertheless, Balcerowicz's problems only spiraled out of control once the political rules set by the roundtable agreements ceased to provide impetus to the program and became its most serious barrier. In part, this can be attributed to the perception that the costs of reform were too high, a perception supported by the government's own dubious statistics. Also important were deep-rooted ideological differences within Solidarity, the jostling for political advantage among Solidarity leaders, and the desire of the former communist forces to legitimize themselves again. Quite suddenly, new political parties, movements, and clubs began to articulate and reinforce the frustrations of Poland's splintered interest groups. The honeymoon period of the Balcerowicz program was over by the beginning of 1991.

The 1990 election of Walesa as president can, in retrospect, be viewed as strengthening the program, even though his campaign caused some nervousness in both the Ministry of Finance and governments of the West. The way in which competition inside Parliament played out during 1991 was what really damaged the program. In particular, the Bielecki government lacked a majority in the Sejm and was unable to take decisive measures either on the economy or on the important issue of relations between the executive and the legislature.

The final political result of the divisive struggles during 1991 was a parliamentary election with no decisive winner. It is now very difficult to form a stable government in Poland, and the current electoral rules suggest that this problem will remain for a considerable time. Yet if new social grievances could not have been voiced in Parliament, they probably would have been ultimately expressed in a way that confronted the program even more directly.

Did democracy help or impede the reform program? There is no simple answer. The partial democratization of the roundtable swept Solidarity to power and helped establish impressive social support for an economic reform program that is well described as a shock. As time passed, however, it became increasingly evident that the roundtable-based rules of the new Polish democracy had complicated effects. The Polish political and party system is still at an intermediate stage of development. It is not fully democratic (in which different parties represent the interests of concrete social groups and offer clear, alternative programs), but at least such a system is now emerging.

Appendix 6-1: Glossary of Poland's Major Parties, Political Movements, Coalitions, and Parliamentary Clubs

Movements and Parties with Opposition Roots

Catholic Election Movement (Wyborcza Akcja Katolicka, WAK), created in 1991 for the parliamentary election; the most important member of this coalition is the National Christian Union

Central Alliance (Porozumienie Obywatelskie Centrum, POC or PC), created in May 1990

Citizens' committees (Komitety Obywatelskie, KO); one committee was created unofficially in 1987 by Walesa; a network of committees was formed in the spring of 1989 to organize Solidarity's June 1989 election campaign

Confederation of Independent Poland (Konfederacja Polski Niepodleglej, KPN), created unofficially in 1979

Democratic Union (Unia Demokratyczna, UD), created in December 1990

Liberal Democratic Congress (Kongres Liberalno-Demokratyczny, KL-D), created in 1990

National Christian Union (Zjednoczenie Chrzescijansko-Narodowe, ZCHN), created in 1989

Peasant Union (Porozumienie Ludowe, PL), created in 1991 from Solidarity of Farmers (Solidarnosc Rolnikow Indywidualnych)

Polish Socialist Party (Polska Partia Socjalistyczna, PPS), created in 1892 but operated in London during the communist period and returned to Poland unofficially in 1987

Solidarity 80 ("Solidarnosc 80"), a splinter movement that emerged from Solidarity and did not accept the roundtable agreements

Solidarity of Workers (Solidarnosc Pracy, SP), created in 1991

Solidarity Trade Union (NSZZ "Solidarnosc" or "Solidarnosc," "s"), created in August 1980

Movements and Parties with Communist Roots

All-Poland Alliance of Trade Unions (Ogolnopolskie Porozumienie Zwiazkow Zawodowych, OPZZ), created in 1984 as a procommunist trade union movement

Democratic Party (Stronnictwo Demokratyczne, SD), created in 1939

Polish Social-Democratic Union (Polska Unia Socjal-Demokratyczna, PUS), created in January 1990, from the Polish United Workers Party

Polish Peasant Party (Polskie Stronnictwo Ludowe, PSL), created in 1990 primarily from the United Peasant Party, which was created in 1949 and was closely linked to the Communist Party

Social Democrats of the Polish Republic (Socjaldemokracja Rzeczpospolitej Polskiej, SDRP), created in January 1990, from the Polish United Workers Party and the Communist Party

Union of the Democratic Left (Sojusz Lewicy Demokratycznej, SLD), created in 1991 for the parliamentary election as a coalition of Social Democrats of the Polish Republic and All-Poland Alliance of Trade Unions

Other Movements and Parties

Christian Democrats (Chrzescijanska Demokracja, ChD), created in 1990

Christian Social Union (Unia Chrzescijansko-Spoleczna, uChs), created in 1989 as a reorganization of Chrzescijanskie Stowarzyszenie Spoleczne, which was founded in 1957

German Minority (Mniejsznosc Niemiecka, MN), created in 1991 as an election coalition

National Party (Stronnictwo Narodowe, SN), created unofficially in 1955; a strongly nationalist movement

Party of Christian Democrats (Partia Chrzescijanskich Demokratow, PChD), created in 1990

Polish Beer-Lovers Party (Polska Partia Przyjaciol Piwa, PPPP), created in 1990; this name was kept by the "big beer" faction after the Polish Beer-Lovers Party Parliamentary Club split in 1991

"Polish Economic Program" ("Polski Program Gospodarczy," PPG), created by deputies of the "small beer" faction, which broke away from the Polish Beer-Lovers Party in 1991; closely associated with big private businesspeople

Polish Social Catholic Union (Polski Zwiazek Katolicko Spoleczny, PZKS), created in January 1981

Polish West Union (Polski Zwiazek Zachodni, PZZ), created in 1991 as an election coalition

Union of Real Politics (Unia Polityki Realnej, UPR), created in 1987; strongly conservative on all issues

Union "PAX" (Stowarzyszenie "PAX"), a Catholic movement created in 1952, which was active throughout the communist period

"x" Party (Partia "x," x), created in 1991 by Tyminski supporters

Parliamentary Clubs (with names different from broader parties or movements)

Citizens' Parliamentary Club (Obywatelski Klub Parlamentarny, OKP)

Club of Independent Deputies (Klub Niezaleznych Poslow, KNP)

Club of Military Deputies (Klub Poslow Wojskowych, KPW)

Parliamentary Club of the Democratic Left (Parlamentarny Klub Lewicy Demokratycznej, PKLD)

Parliamentary Club of Social Democratic Union (Parlamentarny Klub Unii Socjaldemokratycznej, PKUS)

Parliamentary Club of Workers (Parlamentarny Klub Pracy, PKP)

Notes

1. This was made quite clear when the government's economic and political proposals were defeated in the referendum of November 29, 1987. According to the public statements of ministers, this defeat made the government unwilling to impose the high costs of reform.

2. According to the rules, in order to be elected, a presidential candidate had to receive an absolute majority, more than 50 percent of the valid votes cast. There were 537 valid votes (for, against, and abstaining), which meant that Jaruzelski needed more than 268.5 votes. He received 270.

3. For example, Maciej Letowski expressed support for the idea of a Solidarity government in *Lad*, a weekly newspaper linked to the Christian wing of Solidarity (see Letowski 1989).

4. Mazowiecki (1989) argued in favor of gradual political changes, stating that Solidarity would have to remain in opposition until the free elections agreed to during the roundtable talks were held in 1993.

5. The major roles in the economic reform were played by people who had not been part of the Solidarity roundtable team, with two exceptions: Jerzy Osiatynski and Witold Trzeciakowski. Osiatynski became head of the Central Planning Office in 1989 but began to distance himself from the economic policy after the first quarter of 1990. Trzeciakowski had been chief of the Solidarity economic roundtable group and, in 1989, became head of the Economic Council—an advisory group that provided expert opinions—but he did not play a decisive role in creating the economic program.

6. Poland's currency is the zloty.

7. A billion is 1,000 million; and a trillion (also known as the Polish billion) is 1,000 billion.

8. This is the explanation offered by Kuron. An alternative view, expressed by Kuczynski (1992), is that Mazowiecki wished to demonstrate that he could act independently as prime minister and could appoint anyone he wanted to run economic policy.

9. Ministry of Finance 1989. The ideas expressed are impressively detailed, given that Balcerowicz had officially been in power only eleven days.

10. Although the government's first set of proposals concerning the privatization of state enterprises was criticized so much that it was not even formally submitted to the Sejm, this was not then regarded as a major setback.

11. Poland's hard currency reserves more than doubled during 1990, from $3.6 billion (at the end of 1989) to $8 billion (at the end of 1990). Despite all the setbacks in 1991, reserves were still $6.4 billion on November 31. The enormous improvement in Poland's current account is an unmistakable success of the stabilization program.

12. The budget law explicitly assumed inflation for January and February 1990 of 45 and 15 percent, but the outcomes were almost 80 and 24 percent, respectively; see Council of Ministers 1990, p. 7.

13. Strong monopolies had previously existed in trade, particularly Spolem for the processing and retailing of food and WPHW for consumer durables such as furniture, radios, and televisions. Officially, these monopolies were cooperatives, but in practice they were run by the state. There had been some delay in breaking up these monopolies because the government's Law on Cooperatives, which was ready on October 9, 1989, ran into criticism from representatives of these monopolies. However, these organizations were widely regarded as nomenklatura, and they could not mount credible opposition. The law that initiated the breakup of trade cooperatives was passed by the Sejm on January 20, 1990.

14. In addition, on January 26, 1990, the Economic Committee of the Council of Ministers decided to increase required payments for social insurance from 38 to 43 percent of gross wages. The goal was to help finance the indexation of pensions, but the immediate effect was probably to push prices somewhat higher.

15. Dabrowski, Federowicz, and Levitas 1991. For the first six months of 1990, only 10 percent of the state enterprises sampled increased their wages by the full amount allowed under excess wage legislation. Most of the firms increased their wages less than 85 percent of the increase allowed. Dabrowski, Federowicz, and Levitas (1991) found two main reasons for this behavior: cash flow problems and fear of the future. Many firms reduced real wages and increased their financial reserves.

16. Supportive evidence is provided by the decision of some state enterprises to convert into joint stock companies, which under the budget legislation for 1991 reduced their popiwek. At the end of 1990, many joint stock companies were created, apparently to reduce the burden of popiwek.

17. The fact that the Citizens' Parliamentary Club could not survive indefinitely became fully evident during the presidential election at the end of 1990, although at the time of the new parliamentary elections in 1991, 106 deputies and 59 senators still belonged to it. Divisions continued to develop in both the Citizens' Parliamentary Club and the postcommunist parties, where the splits were over personality much more than over policy.

18. These differences began when the national list was withdrawn after the first round of elections and the opposition accepted changes designed to make the results of the parliamentary election consistent with the roundtable agreements.

19. Citizens' committees were informal structures created by Solidarity activists at the time of the roundtable. Their most important role was before and during the June 1989 election.

20. These are the roots of the main parties emerging from Solidarity, although after Mazowiecki's poor performance in the presidential election, many leaders of the Citizens Movement for Democratic Action formed a new party, the Democratic Union.

21. First, under the Polish system in 1990, individuals could register as unemployed, even if they had never worked. For this reason, measured unemployment would be expected to increase at the end of the school year. Second, overemployment or hidden unemployment existed in the communist economy. In 1990, for the first time, managers could and did fire workers. Third, anecdotal evidence suggests that many of the unemployed were actually working as street traders or elsewhere in the rapidly growing private sector. Unfortunately, no good estimates describe the size of that phenomenon. Fourth, relatively little of the increase in unemployment was due to the "group layoffs" usually associated with closure of a firm. The numbers on this point are quite clear (Central Statistical Office 1991, December, table 10, p. 28). Group layoffs accounted for 6 percent of total unemployment in the first quarter of 1990, rising to 10 percent in the second quarter, 14 percent in the third quarter, and 16 percent in the final quarter of that year.

22. The All-Poland Alliance of Trade Unions was originally formed as a procommunist trade union. Although it had become much more independent by 1989, it is still regarded as closely aligned with the former communists.

23. The old nomenklatura were people under the communist regime who were appointed to their position by the communists. The new nomenklatura were people who had recently risen to power or wealth due to political connections. Of course, it is not easy to decide who is and is not either kind of nomenklatura.

24. Just after free prices were introduced for agricultural products, Jozef Slisz, representing Farmers Solidarity, declared the creation of a new farmers' party aimed at defending the interests of farmers. Members said they were responding to insufficient reform of the agricultural market and to the constantly worsening situation of their sector.

25. On July 11, 1990, farmers, with support from the Farmers Trade Union, blocked important roads throughout Poland. Another surge of protests occurred in October 1990 when sugar processing enterprises were not able to buy up the entire harvest of sugar beets.

26. Street traders had a major cost advantage over shops, which had to pay rent. Rents generally rose sharply after the amended law of municipal self-government forced them to become financially independent.

27. On April 7, 1990, the leaders of the Democratic Party advised its members to leave the government coalition because of the official policy toward the private sector. In contrast to the agriculture minister, who resigned after the farmers' protests of June 1990, the Democratic ministers declined to leave their posts.

28. Poland's hard currency debt was $40.8 billion at the end of 1989 and around $45 billion by September 1991 due to the capitalization of interest payments. Of this amount, about two-thirds ($23.9 billion) were owed to other governments, collectively known as the Paris Club.

29. The budget law for 1991 authorized revenues of Zl 289.2 trillion, expenditures of Zl 293.5 trillion, and a deficit of Zl 4.3 trillion. This deficit was supposed to be financed by the surplus carried over from the central budget in 1990, proceeds from extrabudgetary funds being liquidated, and the issue of treasury bonds.

30. The new proposal would have set budget spending at Zl 251 billion, compared with Zl 293.5 trillion in the original 1991 law. Budget revenues were set at Zl 227 trillion, down from Zl 289.2 trillion. The forecast deficit was Zl 24 trillion, which would have been between 2.5 and 3.0 percent of GDP.

31. The government had to submit yet another revised budget law in December 1991 because its August version turned out to be too optimistic.

32. These parties were the Central Alliance, with forty-four seats in the Sejm; the National Christian Union, the most important element of the Catholic Election Movement, which had forty-nine seats; and the Peasant Alliance and the Peasant Alliance "Solidarity," which together had twenty-eight seats.

33. The coalition also received support from other parties on some issues. An additional three parties—known as the "small coalition"—did not support the Olszewski government in general but did vote in favor of its fiscal austerity measures. These were the Liberal Democratic Congress, the Democratic Union, and the Polish Economic Program. Their support of the government's economic policies was crucial.

34. The three parties most supportive of the Balcerowicz program immediately after the election were the Democratic Union, the Liberal Democratic Congress, and the Polish Economic Program, with sixty-two, thirty-seven, and sixteen seats, respectively. This gave them a maximum of 115 seats in the Sejm, exactly one-quarter of the total 460 seats.

35. A notable exception was the package of laws passed in December 1989 constituting the legal basis of the Balcerowicz Plan. The legislative process in this case followed a special fast path, organized under a special commission of the Sejm. This was a temporary arrangement that was only possible with the agreement of all major groups in Parliament.

References

Anonymous. 1991. "The Final Results of the Parliamentary Elections." *Gazeta Wyborcza,* November 2–3.

Balcerowicz, Leszek. 1992. *800 dni. Szok kontrolowany.* Warsaw: Polska Oficyna Wydawnicza BGW.

Beksiak, Janusz, Tomasz Gruszecki, Aleksander Jedraszczyk, and Jan Winiecki. 1989. "Outline of a Programme for Stabilisation and Systemic Changes." September. Reprinted in *The Polish Transformation: Programme and Progress*. New Series 1. Centre for Research into Communist Economies, London, 1990.

Bochwic, Teresa. 1991. *Odwrotna strona medalu z Jaroslawem Kaczynskim*. Warsaw: Oficyna Wydawnicza MOST, Wydawnictwo VERBA.

Center for Opinion Poll Research, Information Service. 1991a. "Serwis informacjny [Public Opinion about Economic Transformations]." Warsaw, October. Processed.

_____. 1991b. "Public Opinion about Key Institutions, Social-Political Organizations, and Important People in Political Life." Warsaw, December. Processed.

_____. 1991c. "Social Perceptions of Change in Poland." Warsaw, March. Processed.

_____. 1991d. "Survey of Opinions about the Stabilization Program." Survey conducted in April, August, September, October. Warsaw.

_____. 1992. "Survey of Opinions about the Stabilization Program." Survey conducted in January. Warsaw.

Central Statistical Office. 1990. *Statistical Yearbook*. Warsaw.

_____. 1991. *Monthly Statistical Bulletin*. Warsaw, April, December.

_____. 1992. *Monthly Statistical Bulletin*. Warsaw, January, March.

Council of Ministers. 1990. "Sprawozdanie z realizacji budzetu panstwa w pierwszym polroczu 1990 roku [Report about the Results of the State Budget in the First Half of 1990]." Warsaw, September.

_____. 1991a. "Raport o stanie panstwa—1991 [Report on the Situation of the State—1991]." Warsaw, December 21.

_____. 1991b. "Ustawa o zmianie ustawy budzetowej na 1991 r. i o zasadach wykonywania budzetu panstwa w 1991 r. [Amendment to the Budget Law for 1991 and Report about the Rules for the State Budget in 1991]." Warsaw, August.

Dabrowski, Marek. 1991. *W strone rynku, Przemyslenia z lat 1989–1991*. Warsaw: Dom Wydawniczy ANKAR.

Dabrowski, Janusz M., Michal Federowicz, and Anthony Levitas. 1991. "Przedsiebiorstwa panstwowe w roku 1990—Wyniki badan." Transformacja Gospodarki 11. Instytut Badan nad Gospardarka Rynkowa, Warsaw, styczen.

Domaranczyk, Zbigniew. 1990. *100 dni Mazowieckiego*. Warsaw: Wydawnictwo Andrzeja Bonarskiego.

Eastern Europe Research Unit, Institute of Philosophy and Sociology, Polish Academy of Sciences. 1991. "The Poles of 1990: Conflicts and Change. Report of Empirical Research." Unpublished ms., Warsaw. Processed.

Gomulka, Stanislaw. 1991. "Tworcza destrukcja." *Zycie Gospodarcze* 18 (May), pp. 1, 6–7.

Institute of Economic Sciences, Polish Academy of Sciences. 1991. "Expertise on the Social Aspects of Privatization." Research of the Institute of Economic Sciences of the Polish Academy of Sciences, the Social Economy Institute of the Warsaw School of Economics, and the Sociology Institute of Lodz University. Materials prepared for a conference on the social aspects of the ownership transformations, the Institute of Philosophy and Sociology of the Polish Academy of Sciences, Warsaw, August. Processed.

Kuczynski, Waldemar. 1992. *Zwierzenia zausznika*. Warsaw: Polska Oficyna Wydawnicza BGW.

Kuron, Jacek. 1991. *Moja zupa*. Warsaw: Polska Oficyna Wydawnicza BGW.

Letowski, Maciej. 1989. "Tak jak jest, bye nie moze [It Cannot Be Like Now]." *Lad* 34, pp. 2, 6.

Lipton, David, and Jeffrey Sachs. 1990. "Creating a Market Economy in Eastern Europe: The Case of Poland." Brookings Papers on Economic Activity 1. Brookings Institution, Washington, D.C.

Mazowiecki, Tadeusz. 1989. "Spiesz sie powoli [Slow and Steady Wins the Race]." *Tygodnik Solidarnosc* 7.

Michnik, Adam. 1989. "Wasz prezydent, nasz premier [Your President, Our Prime Minister]." *Gazeta Wyborcza,* July 3, p. 1.

Ministry of Finance. 1989. "Memorandum on the Economic Reform Program in Poland and the Role of Foreign Financial Assistance." Warsaw, September 23. Processed.

Rzeczpospolita. 1991. November 4, 7.

Sachs, Jeffrey, and David Lipton. 1989. Unpublished memorandums provided through private correspondence. Processed.

Sejm. 1991. "Niektore dane statystyczne o pracy Sejmu i jego organow w okresie od 4 lipca 1989r do 31 pazdziernika 1991 [Some Statistical Data about Sejm Activity and Its Sections from July 4, 1989, to October 31, 1991]." Warsaw, November.

State Election Commission. 1990. "Wyniki wyborow prezydenta, pp. 25.11–9.12.1990 [The Results of the Presidential Election, pp. 25.11–9.12.1990]." Warsaw.

7

Chile: Sustaining Adjustment during Democratic Transition

Genaro Arriagada Herrera
and Carol Graham

CHILE'S RECENT ECONOMIC PERFORMANCE, WHICH IS AMONG THE BEST in Latin America, is frequently used as a prototype of structural adjustment policy implemented by a strong military dictatorship and then bequeathed to a democratic successor. Yet the Chilean case is more complex than it looks at first glance. The authoritarian nature of the military regime is often cited as the reason for Chile's successful implementation of dramatic economic reforms, yet many reforms of the social security, public health, and education systems and decentralization of municipal governments would not have been possible without the preexisting and relatively efficient public sector, a phenomenon rare in Latin America. Chile's public sector provided a sound basis for reform as well as safety nets to protect the poorest sectors during the process. The surprisingly peaceful transition to democracy, meanwhile, was due largely to Chile's strong democratic traditions and well-developed party system, also the exception in the region.

Chile's 1980 constitution called for holding a plebiscite by 1988 on whether to prolong Augusto Pinochet's rule another eight years. When the no vote won in October, elections were called for December 1989 and

The authors thank Alan Angell, Vittorio Corbo, Stephan Haggard, and Steven Webb for their helpful comments.

a delicate and often difficult dialogue and series of negotiations were initiated between the military government and the civilian opposition. Agreement was reached—albeit with substantial tradeoffs—in four fundamental arenas: economic management, the political system, relations between civil society and the military, and relations between the state and society, particularly trade unions. For the opposition, this agreement meant trusting that the military would allow free elections and would transfer power in the event of an opposition victory; for the military and its supporters on the right, it meant trusting that an opposition victory would not result in populist economic chaos or in persecution of the military. This basic consensus represented a substantial moderation of the polarization that characterized Chilean society in the early 1970s.

Two features distinguish the Chilean transition and the implicit social pact underlying it. First, although the consensus achieved was quite strong among political leaders and elites, particularly in the arena of economic management, it was far less so among the rank and file of the parties. Opinion polls recorded surprisingly low public acceptance of or support for the economic reforms, particularly among low-income groups.[1] This is explained, in part, by the authoritarian nature of the regime implementing the reforms; it had no desire to educate or "sell" them to the public.[2] In addition, income distribution worsened during the period of adjustment: although the restructuring of public social expenditure effectively targeted and protected the poorest segments of society, many people at the margin lost access to what had been one of the most comprehensive social welfare systems on the continent.[3] Leaders of the democratic opposition were aware that, regardless of popular sentiment, they had to contend with a balance of social forces, including important private sector groups and middle-class strata as well as the military, with a stake in preserving the economic model implemented by the Pinochet regime. Reversing any of the model's major tenets would endanger the entire transition.

Second, the Chilean transition is distinguished by the relative strength of the military and its supporters on the right. Unlike many other transitions in Latin America, where the military abandoned power in the midst of economic crisis, the Chilean military turned over power according to a preestablished timetable and during a period of sustained economic growth. This strengthened its position during the transition and allowed it to retain an unusual amount of control over the political system, as well as to institutionalize certain aspects of economic management.

This chapter seeks to explain the process behind Chile's successful transition and, in particular, the implicit social pact in which the democratic regime maintained the military's structural economic reforms. To do so, it briefly considers the factors leading to the system's breakdown in 1973 and describes the economic model implemented by the military regime as well as the political system it established. This system preserved certain political and economic choices through a series of authoritarian enclaves ensured in the 1980 constitution.[4] The gradual formation of a national consensus is the primary focus of the chapter, which examines the organization of the opposition for the 1988 plebiscite and the 1989 elections through the new government's first two years in office, ending with the June 1992 municipal elections. With a particular focus on economic management, the analysis examines how Patricio Aylwin government preserved the successful elements of the structural adjustment that began under military rule as well as how it attempted to correct its flaws. The ultimate aim is to understand the political economy of implementing and sustaining structural economic reforms in new democracies.

From Polarization to National Reconstruction: Political Breakdown and the Origins of a New Consensus

The consensus reached in each of the four major arenas during the transition process was profoundly affected by the extremes reached under both Salvador Allende and Augusto Pinochet: in each case, various actors sought utopian or highly ideological solutions (this process is described well in Angell 1993, a recent political history of Chile). First, political parties, particularly of the left, attempted to implement an ideologically uniform solution, regardless of social costs. Then, the military government stepped in to eliminate the ideologies and social sectors deemed responsible for the resulting chaos: communism, the left, and organized labor. In striking contrast, the transition and the subsequent democratic regime brought an acceptable, if not perfect, resolution in all four arenas.

The Economic Model

Management of the economy was only one component of the process of national reconstruction and consensus-building, but it was clearly a central one. It played a critical role in precipitating the breakdown of democracy, raised controversy, particularly over social costs, and generated a surprising amount of consensus at the time of the transition.

The economic chaos at the end of the Allende years was one of the primary reasons for the polarization of the political system and, ultimately, for the military coup. By mid-1972, the government had brought the entire banking system under state control and had expropriated or occupied more than 500 manufacturing companies. The extent of the process created much more than a breakdown of economic consensus: the violations and threats to private property brought Chilean society to the brink of civil war and, coupled with spiraling inflation, created the conditions for the breakdown of the political system.

Irresponsible monetary expansion and rapidly growing fiscal deficits resulted in unprecedented inflation rates. Inflation was 119 percent from December 1970 to December 1971, 138 percent in the next year, and 314 percent in the twelve months preceding August 1973. Although the economy experienced a boom induced by government spending in 1971, with growth at 8.3 percent, growth slowed to 1.6 percent in 1972 and fell 5.7 percent in 1973. At the same time, production collapsed due to a combination of security threats, widespread strikes, rampant shortages, and the massive retrenchment of investment. By mid-1973, economic chaos was probably the most important factor contributing to initial support for military intervention and lasting support for the military regime, even during times of severe economic crisis.

The military regime that came to power in 1973 did not initially espouse the neoliberal economic policies implemented in 1975; indeed the lack of state control was anathema to many elements of the Prussian-style Chilean military. Substantial debate took place within the regime about whether to implement a shock-style program, with hard-liners on the economic team eventually winning Pinochet's favor.[5] At the same time, many economists rejected the authoritarianism of the military as well as the human rights violations that constituted one of the regime's most distinctive political features.[6]

Nevertheless, some agreement existed between these two groups. On the one hand, the military used the support of highly skilled technocrats to justify authoritarian rule. On the other, the regime's proponents, including many economists, tirelessly insisted that dictatorship was necessary to implement the economic and social transformations needed. According to Rolf Luders, vice president of one of Chile's most powerful economic groups and finance minister in 1982, "It is possible that in order to conduct as radical a change as has been implemented in Chile it was necessary to have an authoritarian political structure" (Luders 1980, p. 77). In the same vein, Pablo Barahona, economics minister and one of the most prominent economists of the regime, stated, "I have no doubts that as of 1973 and for many years before in Chile an authoritarian government—absolutely authoritarian—that could implement reform despite the interests of any group, no matter how important it was, was needed" (Barahona 1980, p. 13).

Neoliberal economists of the regime argued that previous development strategies had failed and blamed the economy's failure to grow adequately, accelerating inflation, and a chronic balance of payments crisis on excessive government and a combination of Keynesian and import-substitution policies and distortions in the price system (Ffrench-Davis 1991). They also argued that public social expenditure should be targeted only to the very poorest people who could not provide for themselves.[7]

Structural changes included privatization of key public enterprises and creation of the social security system. Between 1974 and 1989, the government privatized 550 state-owned enterprises (Luders 1991). Domestic capital markets were liberalized, contributing to large increases in real interest rates and fears of massive inflows of capital.[8] Nominal tariffs were reduced to 10 percent by June 1979, and the exchange rate was fixed. This, reinforced by inflows of capital, created a price substitution effect that favored imports over domestic production. The rapid pace of trade liberalization may have forced many firms out of business unnecessarily and increased unemployment. Neither foreign nor domestic private investment, meanwhile, compensated for the fall in government outlays after 1974. The import boom focused on consumer durables rather than capital goods.[9] Total foreign debt increased substantially, most of it contracted with private banks at variable rates. During 1980–81, total debt represented 50 percent of gross domestic product (GDP), and in 1982 amortizations plus interest payments were approximately 85 percent of Chilean exports, compared with 42 percent for 1975–80. Because the bulk of the debt was private, however, both domestic authorities and international institutions failed to attribute sufficient importance to it (Zahler 1983).

From 1977 to 1981, growth was consistently between 5 and 10 percent (see table 7-1). Then, in 1982 with the international recession and devaluation of the overvalued peso, GDP fell 14 percent and unemployment skyrocketed to 24 percent. The financial sector entered a major crisis, and in January 1983, the government took over 70 percent of the Chilean financial sector, intervening in sixteen financial institutions (Zahler 1983). It also bought back approximately fifty of the enterprises that had been privatized in the 1970s (Luders 1991).

Even before the 1982 crisis, employment and real wage rates bore the brunt of the stabilization policies, with real wages losing 25 percent of their value between 1974 and 1981 (see, for example, Cortázar 1982; Ffrench-Davis and Muñoz 1990). Indeed, the problem was so grave that in 1982 government-run emergency employment programs employed up to 13 percent of the labor force—500,000 workers—at wages between half and one-quarter of the minimum.[10] Not surprisingly, the economic collapse coincided with the first significant worker protest against the regime in 1982. Yet the scale and duration of the employment programs suggest that they did supplement the income of the poorest sectors and reduced the potential for social unrest, as even their harshest critics note.

After the crisis of 1982–83, and a drift in economic management, the economic team changed, most notably by the entrance of Hernán Büchi as finance minister in 1985 (for details on this period, see Corbo and Solimano 1991). From 1984 on, the government implemented a set of policies to encourage structural change in favor of exports, savings, and investment (see tables 7-2 and 7-3). Several protective tariffs were rein-

Table 7-1. Selected Macroeconomic Indicators for Chile, 1971–91
(percent)

Year	Growth in GDP	Unemployment	Inflation	Index of real wages
1971	9.0	5.5	26.7	119.3
1972	−1.2	3.7	108.3	108.2
1973	−5.6	4.6	441.0	80.0
1974	1.0	9.7	497.8	64.8
1975	−12.9	15.6	379.2	62.1
1976	3.5	18.6	232.8	63.0
1977	9.9	17.4	113.8	71.1
1978	8.2	17.1	50.0	75.7
1979	8.3	16.7	33.4	82.0
1980	7.8	15.8	35.1	89.4
1981	5.5	26.3	19.7	97.5
1982	−14.1	23.7	9.9	97.1
1983	−0.7	22.5	27.3	86.4
1984	6.3	18.5	19.9	86.7
1985	2.4	16.6	30.7	82.9
1986	5.7	13.9	19.5	84.5
1987	5.7	12.9	19.9	84.3
1988	7.4	12.2	14.7	89.8
1989	10.0	9.3	17.0	91.5
1990	2.2[a]	5.1	27.3	—
1991	5.5[a]	5.7	18.7	—

— Not available.
a. Growth in GNP.
Source: Flano 1992; Luders 1991.

troduced, with the rate reaching as high as 35 percent before being gradually reduced, and regulation of the financial sector was tightened. The decrease in foreign resources was offset by a combination of expenditure policies, favorable renegotiation of the foreign debt, and active promotion of debt-equity swaps. As a result, total debt service declined from 43 percent of exports in 1985 to 20 percent in 1988. A realistic exchange rate was maintained through successive devaluations to encourage the use of resources in producing tradable goods. This implied a real devaluation of 50 percent between 1982–83 and 1987. Exports other than copper grew at an annual rate of 13 percent from 1986 to 1988 (Corbo and Solimano 1991). Finally, increases in the price of copper and reductions in the price of oil and in the London interbank offer rate had favorable economic effects (Luders 1991). Growth steadily picked up, averaging 6 percent between 1985 and 1989; unemployment dropped to 9 percent in 1989 and 5 percent in 1990. During the 1985–90 period, the bulk of government subsidies went to the private sector, with a strict policy maintained in the face of popular and labor demands; income distribution continued to worsen (Ffrench-Davis and Muñoz 1990).

Table 7-2. Growth of the Gross Domestic Product in Chile, 1950–89
(percent)

Year	Annual growth in GDP	Investment as share of GDP	Annual growth rate			Share in GDP		
			Manufacture	Agriculture	Exports	Manufacture	Agriculture	Exports
1950–61	—	—	4.8	1.8	2.6	22.2	11.8	12.3
1961–71	4.6	20.2	6.0	2.9	3.2	25.4	9.6	12.0
1971–74	0.3	15.9	−1.6	−1.8	8.4	27.2	8.3	9.9
1974–81	2.6	15.7	−1.0	1.8	9.4	22.0	8.6	20.2
1981–89	2.6	15.4	2.6	3.1	7.3	19.3	8.8	28.1

— Not available.
Source: Ffrench-Davis 1991; Ffrench-Davis and Muñoz 1990.

Table 7-3. Proportion of Fixed Gross Investment in
Gross Domestic Product, Chile and Latin America, 1980–89

Year	Latin America	Chile	Chile/Latin America
1980	22.7	16.6	73.1
1981	22.5	18.5	82.2
1982	20.0	14.0	70.0
1983	16.6	12.0	72.3
1984	15.9	12.3	77.3
1985	16.2	13.8	85.2
1986	16.8	14.1	83.9
1987	16.8	15.5	92.3
1988	16.5	16.0	97.0
1989	16.4	17.2	104.9

Note: In 1990, foreign investment equaled 4–5 percent of GDP, and public investment equaled 5–6 percent.

Not available.

Source: Ffrench-Davis 1991; Ffrench-Davis and Muñoz 1990.

The economic turnaround was thus due to many factors: international trends, longer-term structural changes, the adoption of a much more aggressive export promotion strategy, and a more active regulatory framework. Many of the enterprises bought back by the state were privatized again, but the second round of privatizations was managed much more closely, with mechanisms to avoid the concentration of ownership and heavy indebtedness.[11]

The resumption of high growth rates coincided with three developments that facilitated a rapprochement between the government and the opposition. The first was a shift within the regime toward a more pragmatic and less ideological formulation of political economy. The second was the crisis of the socialist economies in the latter part of the 1980s, leaving the left sector of the Concertación without an alternative economic paradigm (interview with Nicolás Eyzaguirre, June 24, 1992). The third was the dramatic collapse of the populist heterodox economic experiments undertaken in countries whose transition to democracy immediately preceded Chile's: Alan García in Peru, José Sarney in Brazil, and Raúl Alfonsín in Argentina. A consensus gradually developed on economic policy, and although in the early 1980s the opposition criticized the neoliberal model in general, by the late 1980s their criticisms centered much more on questions of emphasis or technique.[12]

Wide differences remained, however, over issues of social welfare and distribution. Income distribution was more concentrated in 1990 than in 1970, and although social welfare expenditure per capita for the poorest sectors increased, many people at the margin lost access to services. In addition, the quality of public health and education services, as well as public infrastructure, declined dramatically during the military years.

Partial privatization of the public health, education, and pension schemes meant that persons who could not afford private services were left with lesser-quality public ones, which were receiving declining amounts of public investment. Although basic consensus gradually formed on Chile's economic model, caution is necessary prior to labeling it a miracle. In addition to social welfare and equity costs, growth rates for the 1973–90 period, at an average of 2.6 percent, were actually on par with Chile's average growth rate of 3.5 percent since 1920.[13]

The Political System

Compared with the rest of Latin America, Chile's political system was an exemplary democracy for the forty-one years from 1932 to 1973. Nonetheless, as of the 1950s, the politics of consensus underlying Chilean democracy began to deteriorate. The political center became more rigid as the Christian Democratic Party, which at the time was highly ideological and sought to transform society unilaterally, grew in importance (for an excellent account of the role of the ideological center in the breakdown of Chilean democracy, see Valenzuela 1986; for a comparison of the Christian Democratic Party with parties in Latin America that shared similar sectarian traits, see Graham 1992). The left, meanwhile, became increasingly inflexible. It was composed of a strong and electorally powerful pro-Soviet Communist Party—in 1970 Chile's Communist Party was the third most important in the West, after that of Italy and France—and of increasingly radical socialists, who, influenced by the Cuban revolution, rejected "bourgeois democracy" and supported armed struggle. The right, during those same years, also became less tolerant. In 1965, following a dramatic electoral setback, the National Party was formed to replace the Liberal and Conservative parties. The right began to see democracy as a hindrance to the application of scientific and technical formulas for governance and as leading to an alliance between politicians and the masses that was vulnerable to both Marxism and populism. The country became divided into irreconcilable political thirds.

During the next seventeen years, the military aggravated this polarization. To varying degrees, the regime's ideology firmly rejected liberal democracy and embraced brutal anticommunism, an extremist neoliberal economic approach, and two antidemocratic recourses of the military: the national security doctrine and French counterinsurgency techniques. This resulted in systematic violation of human rights, proscription of political parties and major trade unions, intervention on university campuses, academic and press censorship, and a permanent state of emergency.

In 1980, at the height of the economic boom, the regime presented its new constitution for popular approval. In a widely criticized plebiscite, the regime sought to extend its stay in power for the next sixteen years, expecting that the boom would continue and that Pinochet would win in 1988. Yet the disastrous "crash" of 1982 and the extensive and effective organization of the opposition in 1988 led to the unforeseen defeat of Pinochet and the democratic transition. As early as 1980, however, the military devised a series of constitutional safeguards that guaranteed its influence well beyond its tenure in power.

The first of these authoritarian enclaves was the procedure for constitutional reform. An extraordinarily rigid system was established, making it impossible for the new government to introduce modifications without the blessing of some supporters of the military regime. Different quorums were established for various kinds of reforms, with the most rigid being those pertaining to the Constitutional Tribunal, the armed forces, the National Security Council, and the constitution itself.[14]

A second enclave was the electoral system, which was designed to allow the right—a minority—to secure representation in Congress way beyond its share of the popular vote. The presidential system was quite standard: if no candidate received more than 50 percent of the national poll, a runoff ballot was held. The congressional system was far less straightforward, however. To begin with, there were nine designated and twenty-six elected senators (this number was raised from twenty-six to thirty-eight by the 1989 constitutional reforms). Designated senators were appointed by the Supreme Court, the National Security Council, and the president (in this case, Pinochet). Each constituency returned two elected members to the Senate and to the Chamber of Deputies, although each voter only had one vote. Parties were allowed to form alliances to present lists of two candidates per constituency. If a party alliance gained more than twice the votes of the next most-voted list, it took both seats. If it gained less than that, it returned only one member and the next most-voted list took one. This favored the weaker parties of the right.[15] The system also established arbitrary district electoral boundaries to facilitate the representation of supporters for the previous regime at the expense of the Concertación.[16] To pass legislation in Congress, the Concertación government had to gain the support of opposition or appointed senators, despite its large electoral majority.

A third enclave was the autonomy of the military apparatus within the constitutional regime, which grew out of the extensive military penetration of civil society during the Pinochet regime. Almost half of the total number of cabinet members by 1986 were members of the armed forces (56 of 118). In August of 1986, in all thirteen of Chile's regions, the highest ranking government official was a military officer on active duty. Only one of the presidents of the eight most prestigious universities was an academic; the rest were active or retired officers. The military's independence under the democratic regime was based on the entrenched status of the commander in chief: Pinochet remained commander in chief for eight years, and the presidential prerogative to appoint military officers or paramilitary police was removed. The armed forces also maintained influence by designating leading members of key institutions.

The compromises underlying the transition categorically rejected all efforts at military reform. The Chilean military retained a strong position since, unlike that in other countries, it had not been defeated militarily or socially and had the strong support of the most powerful conservative and economic sectors of society. Under the new government, proposals surfaced to give the president control over appointments as well as to end the durable status of the commander in chief. The latter was scheduled for 1997, when Pinochet's term expires, to avoid personalizing the issue.

The fourth enclave was the Supreme Court, whose power lay in the Constitutional Tribunal. Three of the seven members of the tribunal were named by the Supreme Court and two by the National Security Council. Five of the eight members of the National Security Council were either judges or military officers. Moreover, the Supreme Court appointed three members of the Senate (two former justices and the equivalent of the head of the U.S. General Accounting Office). During the last nine months of his government, Pinochet appointed nine of seventeen members of the Supreme Court through dubious mechanisms.

In purely institutional terms, the political system bequeathed to Aylwin could easily be called "dismantled presidentialism." Many of the powers commonly held by presidents were impounded and disbursed to bureaucratic state entities, which were granted both autonomy and tutelage over the political system: the military, appointed senators, and the Supreme Court.

The parties of the Concertación government sought to counter the effects of these enclaves with an approach more common to parliamentary or semipresidential regimes than to presidential systems. With the obvious exclusion of appointed senators, President Patricio Aylwin's government represented less a division of powers (presidential system) than a unity of powers, whereby parties holding a majority in Congress were also members of the executive branch, thereby limiting the conflict between them. Indeed, even without the authoritarian enclaves, it is unlikely that Chile would have been stable if, as is common in presidential regimes, the transition had been initiated by a minority government founded on presidential prerogative. In addition, tensions among the parties in the governing coalition were rare, a consensus that leaders of the main parties in the Concertación placed strong emphasis on maintaining. It was also reinforced by the strong showing of the Concertación in the 1992 municipal elections.

The process of gradually dismantling the authoritarian enclaves and establishing indisputably democratic norms and principles was fundamental to the transition and one of the most important subjects of debate between supporters of the authoritarian regime and those of the Concertación government. At the time of this writing, progress had been made in two arenas. The first was the reform of the National Television Council, whose members were previously appointed by the president, the Council of University Rectors, the armed forces, and the Supreme Court. The new composition included eight representatives elected by an absolute majority of the Senate and a presiding officer appointed by the president.

Much more important was municipal reform, which replaced appointed mayors with freely elected ones. In all but the fifteen most populous municipalities of the nation, the mayors were Pinochet appointees until June 1992 (for details on the municipal system and municipal reform under the Pinochet regime, see Graham 1991b). On June 28, more than two years after the transition, council members in the central government were elected in 334 municipalities, and they, in turn, selected the mayors.

A series of constitutional reform packages was due to be presented and discussed in Congress at the time of this writing. Although many transition processes have been initiated with the election of a constituent assembly or the appointment of a commission charged with drafting a new democratic order, in Chile, the transition was conducted through a series of negotiations and succeeding pacts within the existing political system. This type of transition postponed full democracy and exposed the political system to interminable debates and negotiations over institutional issues; it also avoided a climate of instability and prevented the military and the right from gathering under a single political umbrella.

The new government's ability to govern effectively despite the authoritarian enclaves vividly demonstrates the extent to which the transition process forged a national consensus. It is unlikely that in 1980 any members of the opposition believed that the constitution would generate a viable political system or that consensus would be reached with members of the Pinochet government in 1989. In the short term, the enclaves may have played an important role in maintaining the confidence of the right and the military. In the long term, most will have to be reformed if the democratic system is to succeed. As the political system becomes more established, and individual parties begin to assert their identity more, the continued existence of the enclaves could become a substantial obstacle to effective government.

Relations between Civil Society and the Military

Historically, with the exception of a brief military interregnum from 1927 to 1931, the Chilean armed forces did not intervene in the political system, maintaining a strictly professional role and little contact with civilian society. Mutual disdain meant that the military's adhesion to the democratic system did not stem from training in democratic values, but rather from military acceptance of a political reality. Civilian control over the military began to erode gradually with an attempted coup under the Eduardo Frei administration and accelerated under the Allende government, particularly as parties to the left of the Popular Unity coalition promoted insurrectionary activities.[17] The 1973 coup replaced the "civilianism" that characterized relations from 1930 to 1973 with a high degree of militarism, in which the armed forces dominated almost all civilian institutions: Congress, universities, trade unions, and political parties (for an account of civilian-military relations during the Pinochet period, see Arriagada Herrera 1988; Valenzuela and Valenzuela 1986).

By the early 1980s, at least legally, military proscription of civil society lessened somewhat. Labor unions, for example, were legalized, although opposition activities, such as the 1983 labor protests, were still repressed, and, indeed, the number of arrests rose markedly from 1983 to 1986 (for a detailed account of repression during this period, see Arriagada Herrera 1988; for the role of unions during the 1980s, see Angell 1991). Until a new law was passed in 1987, political parties could not legitimately own property, raise funds, or engage in political organizing (Puryear 1991). From the 1985 formation of the National Accord by several opposition parties, including members of the moderate right, until the 1988 plebiscite, civil-military relations improved somewhat, and sporadic but continual dialogue took place between the military and the opposition.

The turning point was clearly the opposition's victory in the October 5, 1988, plebiscite and the government's recognition of the results. Sectors within the armed forces that staked their institutional legitimacy on the 1980 constitution rather than on the persona of Pinochet ultimately tilted the balance. Public acceptance of the opposition victory by prominent leaders of the right, such as the president of National Renovation and the chief of staff of the Air Force, played a decisive role. International support for voter registration and the holding of a free election, meanwhile, clearly signaled that the regime would become an international pariah if it violated the results, which was hardly in keeping with an economic strategy that relied heavily on international trade.

With the defeat of Pinochet in the plebiscite, both the military regime and the civilian opposition recognized the need for a political compromise. The government realized that without Pinochet as head of state, the excess presidentialism envisioned in 1980 was dangerous and would have to be reduced. The opposition, meanwhile, felt reforms were needed to meet objectives such as reducing the relative weight of designated senators, changing the composition of the Security Council, ending the legal proscription of the communists, and incorporating international treaties on human rights into the constitution.

At this point, the government initiated a dialogue with representatives of the political parties and negotiated a series of constitutional reforms. These reforms were then approved by 86 percent of the vote in a national plebiscite held on July 30, 1989. Although the changes made to the constitution were quite limited, the *process* of negotiating had important real and symbolic effects. It diminished the mutual distrust between the military regime and the opposition and signaled Pinochet's willingness to turn over power. In addition, since the legitimacy of the 1980 constitution had always been questioned by the opposition, the regime hoped that the negotiation process would increase its credibility and therefore reduce the challenges to it after the transition (interview with Carlos Caceres, June 26, 1992). Opposition to negotiating clearly came from within the ranks of the military and at times from Pinochet himself. The primary opposition came from civilian rather than military elements of the regime, however, and Carlos Caceres, former interior minister, resigned at least once in the face of such opposition, only to be reinstated and eventually prevail.

The process of negotiation is one of the distinctive features of the Chilean transition. This process was the result of several factors that were critical and very specific to the Chilean context. First, the economic performance of the military regime was relatively strong, which put the military in a strong bargaining position. Second, and related to the first, the Chilean armed forces, in contrast to those of neighboring countries, continued to have the strong support of the majority of parties on the right and of the entrepreneurial class. Third, when the transition was initiated, the Chilean military, in contrast to the Greek or the Argentine militaries, had not suffered any kind of military defeat. On the contrary, the military clearly asserted that it had been victorious in a countersubversive war that had defeated communism. Although the opposition legitimately saw the *poder moderador* as undemocratic and a constraint to government, in the short term, it was probably critical to guaranteeing the military and the right's cooperation with the democratic transition process.

Relations between Society and the State

Chile traditionally had a highly organized civil society, and organized labor was an influential actor. By 1945, 14 percent of the work force was affiliated with a union; in the 1960s, this rose to 19 percent. Including organized peasant and public sector associations, close to 30 percent of the work force was unionized by 1970, more than in the majority of industrial western democracies (for a detailed account of the role of unions in Chile before Pinochet, see Angell 1972). Unions grew more aggressive during the Frei years and mobilized intensively during the Allende years, as parties of the left and the Christian Democratic Party played an increasingly important role in the activities of the unions and their demands became more political than economic in nature. More than 3,000 strikes took place in 1972 alone. The mobilization of unions was complemented by that of student organizations, professional organizations, and even groups of small and medium-size businesses.

With the military coup, the situation shifted from one extreme to the other: trade unions were dissolved and labor leaders repressed or exiled. Only when the persecution of Chile's trade unions produced severe conflict with other countries, heightened by threats of the AFL-CIO in the United States to sponsor an international boycott against Chilean products, did the regime introduce a new set of labor laws. The legislation, approved in 1979 and known as the Labor Plan, authorized the existence of unions, but only at the company level. It also created a system of free association, so that several unions could exist and negotiate separately within a single company. Workers in key services and the public sector were forbidden to engage in collective negotiation at all. The right to strike was limited, and the negotiation process tilted in favor of business owners.[18] Companies or sectors were not allowed to join forces and form associations, federations, or confederations.

The labor movement also lost strength due to the severity of the economic shocks that occurred in the 1980s: unemployment reached 30 percent at the height of the crisis in 1983. In addition, sectors that eventually benefited from structural adjustment because they were oriented toward nontraditional exports lacked a tradition of labor organization, such as the largely white-collar financial sector, or faced structural factors that made it difficult for labor to organize, such as agricultural sectors that relied heavily on seasonal labor or were geographically disperse. Sectors where labor was traditionally strong, such as mining and industry, decreased in importance (interview with Manuel Barrera, January 15, 1992). The repressive nature of the military regime, coupled with economic restructuring, permanently changed the nature of relations between unions and the political system in Chile.

More important than economic trends was the extent to which, by the late 1980s, unions perceived themselves as, first and foremost, important actors in the process of national reconstruction. Unions recognized that democracy was essential to obtaining their other objectives, as the Pinochet years so painfully demonstrated (Alburquerque 1991; interviews with José Cisternas and Federico Mújica, January 21, 1992). Manuel Bustos, respected leader of the Central Workers Confederation who spent many years in internal exile, emphasized such a role throughout the transition period and under the new government. Like key actors in the political system, the organizations of civil society, and unions in particular, explicitly recognized the dangers and costs of extreme positions. They began to place a strong emphasis on negotiating and seeking consensus.[19]

Organization of the Opposition and the 1988 Plebiscite

Besides engaging in an ideological debate over the breakdown of democracy, many sectors sought to learn from the experience in order to reconstruct a new national project.[20] Gradually, intellectual groups with the greatest influence on parties opposed to the military regime came to perceive the crisis of 1973 as a collective responsibility and the result of a breakdown in the consensus on which society was based. Efforts were made to identify new approaches and policies.

First, ideological extremes were moderated. Many leaders of the left were exiled either forcibly or voluntarily during the military years; this brought them into extensive contact with their less militant counterparts in Europe (the issue of exile in Chilean politics is discussed in detail in Angell and Carstairs 1987). Only the Communist Party, which ironically had been less radical than the socialists during the Allende years, remained committed to armed struggle by the mid-1980s. The left's thinking was further tempered by the collapse of the Eastern bloc in the late 1980s.[21] The Christian Democratic Party reevaluated its single-party stance and began to emphasize coalition politics.

Second, the political system that had collapsed in 1973 was criticized for not requiring a majority to govern and for failing to facilitate the formation of stable governing majorities, all of which enabled minority will to be imposed (Aylwin, cited in Arriagada Herrera 1978). The political structures were accurately characterized as a "double-minority presidential system," since the president could be elected with the support of only a minority of the electorate (Arriagada Herrera 1984).[22] More important, the president could use exclusive legal initiative to control some of the most important matters discussed in Congress. Both in government and in the private sector for several decades prior to the Allende years, basic political and economic consensus had been absent in Chilean society (Foxley 1985).

Even among some of the harshest critics of the military regime and its economic policies, consensus grew on why the political and economic status quo prior to the coup was unsustainable and on what should be done to correct it. This trend was strengthened in the late 1980s by chaotic economic events in neighboring countries (Graham 1991a). Critical to this process was the talent of the political and economic leadership of the opposition, which grew in part out of Chile's tradition of highly skilled social scientists and in part from the experiences of these leaders during the military years.

Opposition Leaders, Research Institutions, and Convergence of Economic Thinking

Key to the ability of the opposition leaders to organize and develop a strategy for governing was the work conducted by a host of research institutions in Chile, which produced and published some of the finest social science research in Latin America. These institutions, which received substantial international support, supplied the opposition's social scientists with a safe haven and a forum in which to criticize the government (Angell 1989). During the military years, their work tended to stress the technical errors and high social costs of the regime's economic policies (Feinberg 1992).

Despite their public differences, Chile's researchers and military agreed on some basic issues of macroeconomic management, particularly regarding the money supply and inflation, and had done so since the Frei years. With the opportunities presented by the plebiscite and even more so by the elections, the economists of the Concertación began to direct their skills toward defining concrete policy options.

During the military years, the opposition used three kinds of economic criticism. First, economic issues were used to mount veiled political criticism of the regime. Second, criticism on technical grounds was leveled at issues such as the fixed exchange rate and the social effects of the regime's stabilization policies. By the late 1980s, however, most of these policies had been corrected. Third, criticism was directed toward areas in which key changes occurred, and a learning process took place among many opposition economists, particularly concerning the role of the market and the potential of Chilean entrepreneurs, neither of which had been respected by opposition economists prior to the Pinochet years (interview with Joseph Ramos, January 1992). Before 1982, for example, one sector of economists within the opposition was convinced of the merits of an open economy, while the other was not. After 1982, however, total agreement was reached on this point. In mid-1985, opposition criticism centered on the level of debt payments. In 1988, the focus was on the manner in which privatizations were handled, with many contending that firms were being sold to former functionaries on highly favorable terms (interviews with Juan Andrés Fontaine, June 25 and 26, 1992, and Jorge Rodríguez, June 25 and 26, 1992).

Economists in various think tanks also played an important role in the democratic transition and through that process gained increased contact with and respect from political leaders (interview with Juan Eduardo Coeymans, June 25, 1992). "They constituted the network of 'political intellectuals' who had come to know and respect each other as such as well as to share a common faith in democracy" (Feinberg 1992, pp. 51–52).

Of particular prevalence were the CED (Center for Development Studies) and CIEPLAN (Corporation for Economic Research on Latin America), both of which had close ties to the Christian Democratic Party, and many of whose leading figures were closely connected first with the campaign for voting no in the 1988 plebiscite and then with the Aylwin campaign for the presidency (Hojman 1990). Particularly after 1985, under the leadership of Edgardo Boeninger, the CED was a key forum for political and economic discussion among different political sectors (its role and the process of dialogue are detailed by Puryear, forthcoming; Boeninger later became interior minister and secretary of the presidency in the Aylwin government). Even elements of the right, represented in the universities and its primary think tank, the Center for Public Studies, participated in this dialogue. CIEPLAN, meanwhile, through a series of community dialogues, disseminated its research and made contact with diverse sectors of society, which ultimately proved invaluable when it came time to formulate the opposition's economic program (for details, see Puryear, forthcoming). The president of CIEPLAN, Alejandro Foxley, was the opposition's leading spokesperson on economic affairs and became economics minister under the new government.

The role of the CED and CIEPLAN was matched by that of the socialist-linked think tanks and by the return from exile of several prominent socialist economists and leaders. FLACSO (Latin American Faculty of the Social Sciences) provided a wealth of research on democratic transitions. The Program of Employment and Labor focused on poverty and employment and organized training sessions for labor leaders. Perhaps most influential for developing a new-left position on economic policy was the economic commission of the new Socialist Party, whose director, Carlos Ominami, subsequently became finance minister. VECTOR, a small institution whose board of directors was headed by socialist leader Ricardo Lagos, also provided a center for the discussion of economic policy. These institutions and discussions both generated and reflected a growing consensus on economic policy. Indeed, the term "Chicago Boy," which referred to the link between the University of Chicago and the Catholic University, lost some relevance with time because it excluded some of the most representative members of the military regime, such as Hernán Büchi and José Piñera, and included some of the regime's most visible opponents, such as Ricardo Ffrench-Davis. The returning exiles, meanwhile, had been "converted into Felipe Gonzáles–style socialists" (interview with Jorge Rodríguez, June 25 and 26, 1992). A whole generation of economists who remained at home during the military years had been trained in the neoliberal school regardless of their political affiliation (interview with Nicolás Eyzaguirre, June 24, 1992). Although the formation of basic consensus on economic management among leaders of the opposition was replicated in various policy sectors, it was particularly important to providing assurances that the opposition would sustain the macroeconomic policies of the military regime.

Consolidation of the Opposition and the Plebiscite

As of 1985, and particularly toward the end of 1987, Chile faced a curious and difficult political stalemate in which two antagonistic forces with similar levels of support—the military and the opposition—confronted each other unsuccessfully. Neither could impose its conditions on the other, nor was either side willing to negotiate or accept a compromise.

Pinochet's power was military and governmental: absolute military power over a united armed forces and a strong executive were concentrated in one man. The regime also had the backing of significant sectors of the right. These sectors perceived the reform processes of the Frei and especially the Allende governments as an extraordinary threat that put into question both their property and their loyalty to the Chilean state. The Pinochet regime satisfied their aspirations in a way no other government ever had.

In the face of a highly militarized state with the support of conservative groups of entrepreneurs, artisans, professionals, independent workers, and intellectuals, the opposition's power was based on the support of "moral" elements (such as the Catholic Church and human rights attorneys) and civil society more generally: intellectuals and artisans; the limited independent press, primarily radio and magazines; the workers' movement; professionals; and students. Most important, the opposition was firmly rooted in a strong and well-organized party system, composed of Christian democrats, socialists, and communists, and had the support of strong students' and workers' movements.

The consolidation of the opposition had its roots in the severe economic crisis of the early 1980s and the labor unrest that began in 1983 and grew in size and strength with the participation of political parties. The protest, which began as unrest in the Copper Workers Union and then produced a failed national strike led by the National Workers Command, developed into a broader political movement that eventually embraced political parties as well as *pobladores*—shantytown dwellers. There were limits to what the movement could attain, "when the workers were facing not only the threat of police repression but extreme unemployment and the consequent inability to feed their families" (Arriagada Herrera 1988, p. 60). Yet the protests did demonstrate the regime's vulnerability, revive opposition parties, and launch a longer-term process of organized opposition.

The protests also led to a collaboration between unions and most of the opposition parties. In August 1983 leaders of the three major political currents reached a political accord for the first time in two decades. Six groups—one from the right, the Republican Party; three from the center, the Radical, Social Democratic, and Christian Democratic parties; and two from the left, the Socialist and Popular Socialist Union parties—united as the Democratic Alliance for the purpose of promoting democratic principles (for a detailed account of this process, see Arriagada Herrera 1988). This accord was not without rifts, but it began a cautious and erratic dialogue with the government that eventually produced the National Accord for the Full Transition and then, in 1986, united the opposition behind the campaign to vote no in the plebiscite (Angell 1989).[23]

By the end of 1986 the opposition began to propose ways of overcoming the stalemate using a mechanism created by the military regime itself:

the plebiscite. For the first time in fifteen years, Pinochet and the democratic opposition agreed to fight under common rules.

The opposition began to form committees for free elections, which, for most of 1987, sought to substitute the plebiscite with competitive elections. The military regime refused all proposed changes, however, and in February of 1988, the opposition formally accepted its terms and formed the *Comando por el No*, which sought to constitute and maintain a broad alliance of parties. The result was a coalition of seventeen parties ranging from the democratic right to diverse socialist factions, with the Christian Democratic Party as the major force in the center. This coalition, the *Concertación de los Partidos por la Democracia*, with Patricio Aylwin as president, sought to overcome the sectarian divisions of the past and to forge a consensus based on mutual respect and united behind a clear objective.

At this time, polls showed that neither Pinochet nor the military regime was popular: the majority of Chileans felt that the authoritarian regime was socially unjust and rejected its dictatorial nature and violation of human rights. Nevertheless, fear of its invincibility had created a popular inertia of sorts. Too many times the Chilean opposition had believed the regime was weakening. Even more doubtful seemed the hope that a dictatorship could be defeated by a vote.

For the majority of the population—the common people who had lived through the military regime without belonging to parties, unions, or human rights organizations—fear largely determined their actions in the political arena. Some feared political repression; others feared that opening the political system would convert the country into a theater of highly radicalized social and political conflicts. Everyone feared socioeconomic instability. From the beginning, analyses of public opinion demonstrated that most Chileans were concerned with order, security, and better material living conditions.

This had enormous influence not only on the opposition's strategy for the plebiscite but also for the subsequent presidential campaign. The Comando rejected launching a negative campaign based on the regime's dictatorial nature and human rights record, choosing instead to communicate a positive message of moderation and compromise that could generate confidence among all sectors of the country, including those supporting the military.

During the campaign, the Concertación was careful to portray—and maintain—an image of unity. Careful and prudent macroeconomic management was stressed. It promised to redistribute income, increase social expenditures, and not attack private property. Although every effort would be made to establish the truth about human rights abuses, the army as an institution would not be tried, and the civil courts would be the appropriate place to redress grievances. The Concertación distanced itself from the Communist Party and from other groups that had advocated the use of violence against the Pinochet government (Angell and Pollack 1990). Its political leaders sought to emphasize the need to rebuild society through consensus, not transform it through extreme efforts.

To the extent that the economy was an issue in the plebiscite, opposition leaders, Alejandro Foxley and Ricardo Lagos in particular, focused on the increase of poverty during the military years and on the declining consumption per capita of the poorest segments of the population. At the same time, they recognized that inflation had decreased and exports increased. The attempts of the vote yes campaign to capitalize on economic improvements with the slogan "Chile: un país ganador" (Chile: a winning country) were far less effective at capturing the attention of a population seeking redress for worsening distribution of wealth and, what was more important at the time of the plebiscite, the return of individual and political rights (interview with Juan Andrés Fontaine, June 25 and 26, 1992).

The opposition's strategy had three objectives, which were successively achieved. The first was to register voters, which translated, for the opposition, into a difficult fight against skepticism, especially among the youngest voters, who doubted that voting in a plebiscite could defeat a dictator. On the one hand, this lack of confidence was heightened by various groups, in particular the Communist Party, which condemned the act of registration as "an improper behavior of a democratic constituency . . . electoral life under fascism is a route that is in the interests of the politicians and of North American imperialism" (Communist Party 1987). On the other hand, extensive public awareness campaigns were launched—and supported from abroad—by groups such as the Campaign for Citizen Participation. Substantial amounts of money flowed to Chile from the United States, Great Britain, the Netherlands, Italy, and several Scandinavian countries. At the time of the 1988 plebiscite, most aid focused on registering and educating voters rather than directing their vote. Thus most political forces saw aid as neutral and positive, leaving the military little choice but to tolerate it (for a detailed account of the role played by the *Participa* campaign, see Jiménez de Barrios 1990; for an account of the role of foreign aid, see Angell 1989).

The second strategy was to implement a system of electoral control that provided at least three poll watchers from the opposition for each of the country's 11,000 voting establishments as well as a system of parallel vote counting. The night of the plebiscite, the Chilean opposition attracted national and international attention by publishing electoral results with surprising precision several hours before the government did.

The third was to win the election. The opposition's campaign worked well, and it won decisively w th 55 percent of the vote. Still, Pinochet's 43 percent was no small achievement, and, surprisingly, the military made virtually no move to overturn the result. In part this was because the private sector and the international community were strongly opposed to tampering with the results: by the time the plebiscite was held, macroeconomic stability had become linked with the maintenance of constitutional order, and democracy had become a prerequisite to full incorporation into the international financial system.

Although the availability of [international] financial assistance was never formally linked to progress made in the redemocratization program, it was clearly understood that, for example, the abandonment of the constitutional timetable would have had dramatic financial consequences. . . . This is not to say that either domestic or foreign businessmen actively pressed to speed the pace of political transition. On the contrary, business leaders . . . favored General Pinochet in the 1988 plebiscite. . . . [Yet] their concern for economic stability made them favor the maintenance of the constitutional timetable (Fontaine 1992, pp. 13–14).

Most important, "the military argued that the result was a personal defeat for Pinochet, but not for the political and economic system that they had created."[24] Indeed, the military rested its legitimacy as an institution on guaranteeing the constitution it had established in 1980. Significantly, the commander in chief of the Air Force publicly recognized the electoral results prior to meeting with General Pinochet, as did the president of the principal party of the right, Sergio Onofre Jarpa. Moreover, opposition supporters, while jubilant, did not engage in any kind of street unrest or violence after the results were announced. The transition progressed as planned, and elections were scheduled for December 1989. In a country without Chile's strong judicial traditions, it is less likely that the military would have supported the very process reducing its power.

Process of Consensus-Building: The 1989 Campaign and Elections

No other event demonstrates the ability of the Chilean opposition to sustain and indeed consolidate the process of economic reform as well as the 1989 electoral campaign. The new government clearly enjoyed the confidence of both the public and the private sectors from the start. Immediately before the election, after all reliable polls indicated that Aylwin would win with an absolute majority, the stock market rose and the parallel dollar rate fell. The day after the election, the stock market rose 5 percent, and the parallel dollar rate fell again (Angell and Pollack 1990; Hojman 1990).

Private sector confidence in the Concertación's commitment and ability to continue market-based, export-oriented, and fiscally sound economic policy was due to several factors: the nature of the 1989 electoral campaign; the highly qualified nature of the Concertación's economic team; the congruence of opinion on economic management that had developed between moderate socialists, Christian Democrats, and elements of the right; and the military's continued presence as a guarantor of stability—either directly, through the threat of intervention, or indirectly, through the clauses in the constitution that gave the military continued say in matters of government.

The Election Campaign

The election campaign was telling. After the October 1988 plebiscite and opinion polls taken throughout the campaign confirmed the degree of popular support for the opposition, Aylwin behaved "as if the election were a foregone conclusion and as if he were president-elect" (Angell and Pollack 1990, p. 13).

The Concertación's program, a detailed, forty-eight-page document, contrasted sharply with the vague sixteen-page program of the campaign for Hernán Büchi, former finance minister and candidate of the regime. The Concertación's starting point was constitutional reform, including a completely elected Congress, chosen by the traditional Chilean list system of proportional representation. It also called for the direct election of mayors, administrative decentralization, modernization of the state machine, and a stronger role for Congress. The program stressed the need to establish full civil control over the military and pledged to establish the truth about human rights violations since 1973. It also called for prosecution of the most severe violations in civil courts and for annulment of the 1978 amnesty law (Angell and Pollack 1990).

Stressing prudence, the economic program also raised important distributive issues: raising the minimum wage, but keeping it "in line with the possibilities of the economy" (Angell and Pollack 1990, p. 11); reforming the labor code, which severely restricted the bargaining power of unions; and examining policies to address environmental and ecological concerns and the role of women. The program highlighted the needs of the country's 5 million poor—40 percent of the population, according to some estimates. It also noted the need to *incorporar el mundo de trabajo* (include the workers), which implied giving labor issues a higher priority, but stopped short of offering specific proposals for doing so (Hojman 1990). Yet the campaign gave the need for prudent macroeconomic management equal, if not more, weight. Economists tended to have differences of opinion that were very specific and technical—such as differences over the effect of tariffs or the level of interest rates that would generate the optimal level of savings in the economy—rather than differences concerning the central features of the economic model.

In contrast, the Büchi campaign reflected divisions within the right and, ironically, made unrealistic, populist promises. The program set out four objectives for the new government: (a) complete the construction of democracy, (b) implement economic and social policies that would open up possibilities for all, (c) design an education system that would prepare people for liberty and progress, and (d) make Chile a leader in the region. Much was made of the failures of collectivism and the virtues of liberty; the section on human rights simply condemned the violence that, in general, leads to such abuses. Its economic promises seemed to contradict the regime's economic record and approach. According to Angell and Pollack (1990, p. 12), "Here was the austere former finance minister far outdoing the opposition in his promises of a million new jobs, better salaries, [improved] working conditions, private health facilities for all (with state subsidies to help the poor pay fees), a housing target of 100,000 new houses annually, and new initiatives to reduce the weight of personal indebtedness." The independent, right-leaning Francisco Errazuriz, meanwhile, promised free health care and education to all and elimination of the unit of development (the indexation system for mortgages on houses and other forms of long-term borrowing; Hojman 1990).

The opposition's ability to maintain such a prudent approach to macromanagement—even while campaigning—is even more striking when one considers that public opinion about key aspects of the economic model remained quite negative, at least as reflected by opinion polls taken from 1986 through 1991, and particularly in the early years. Polls were taken by CEP in December 1986 and January 1987, by FLACSO in 1988, and by CIEPLAN in October 1990 and February and May 1991. In the arena of privatization, for example, more than 70 percent of the persons polled opted for health care and education managed by the central state, while 20 to 30 percent opted for services administered by municipalities. A surprisingly high 57 percent felt the state should own the most important companies. Meanwhile, almost 80 percent of the respondents believed that foreign investment should be subjected to greater controls or even nationalized. Countering this were the two-thirds who felt that foreign investment was favorable for the country.

The Concertación's strategy in part grew out of the need to avoid a military-business alliance, which would form if private property were threatened in any way. Many transitions to democracy have had to be conscious of what Angel Flisflish calls "the ghost of the reemergence of a coalition between the military and dominating groups over economic policy with expropriatory connotations" (quoted in Arriagada Herrera 1984, p. 53). With the benefit of hindsight, it seems that the military was committed to upholding the 1980 constitution and thus accepting the results of the transition process it had set in place. Prior to the 1988 plebiscite, however, this was by no means clear. After the plebiscite, doubts continued, although they were alleviated somewhat by the process of negotiating constitutional reforms. In addition, there was never any guarantee that a military-business alliance would not form, particularly if the opposition overstepped its bounds in any of the four fundamental arenas.

Key actors within the Concertación's economic team were convinced that few alternatives existed to the economic strategy adopted and that changes under the new government would be in emphasis only. Despite some disagreements within the party rank and file, key members of the economic team, both Christian democrats and socialists, as well as much of the political leadership, were committed to adopting a market-based strategy.[25] Finally, the Concertación's reluctance to criticize the military regime's economic model also stemmed from the need to "sell" the viability of orthodox economic management to a polity that associated it with the authoritarian regime.

As in most campaigns, though, much more attention was paid to political issues on television, radio, and in the press than in normal times. Economic policy was not really an issue in the public campaign, and the competing candidates largely agreed on the need for careful fiscal management, export promotion, low tariffs, new investment, and repayment of the international debt. The main source of debate on the economic front was over fine details and the ability of each side to implement such policies. The Büchi campaign, for example, made much of a statement by Aylwin that a 20 percent inflation rate was not intolerable (Angell and Pollack 1990). Ironically, at the same time, the government was overheating the economy, ostensibly for electoral purposes.[26]

A variety of indicators demonstrated an unsustainable expansion of the economy. Real GDP grew 8 percent in 1988 and 10 percent in 1989. The money supply grew 106 percent in 1988–89. Inflation was 31 percent on an annualized basis between September 1989 and January 1990 compared with 10 percent at the end of 1988. While exports increased 20 percent in 1989, imports increased 46 percent (Flano 1992; Ffrench-Davis 1991).

This overheating was the result of high copper prices as well as policies undertaken prior to the 1988 plebiscite: expansionary monetary policy and tax reductions for the private sector, including reductions of the value added tax and import tariffs. In keeping with the monetarist bent of the regime, the expansion was strictly through monetary measures; public finances remained intact. After the plebiscite and prior to the elections, the regime attempted to adjust: interest rates were raised to 16 percent in real terms, three times the average for advanced industrial economies (Ffrench-Davis 1991). The expansion was most likely designed to affect the plebiscite, which the Pinochet regime hoped to win up until the final hour, rather than the 1989 elections, which the opposition was predicted to win as early as mid-1989. Regardless of the cause, the Concertación government would have to make sharp adjustments on taking office.

The Aylwin team's cautious approach in the campaign, meanwhile, kept popular expectations, which were understandably high, from growing far beyond the capacity of any government to meet them.

The military campaign primarily focused on emotional political issues. Büchi, for example, accused the Concertación of having secret pacts with the communists. These were hardly credible, given Aylwin's strong opposition to the Allende government, as well as the weak position of the Chilean Communist Party in the face of the global collapse of communism. The Aylwin campaign focused instead on the need to improve social justice—especially education, health, and housing programs—on the need to address human rights issues, and on the need for the president to control the military. Its approach to these issues was firm but restrained and was bolstered by consistently high ratings in the polls. The government's support remained below 30 percent and was eroded by the presence of Errazuriz as well (Angell and Pollack 1990).

Negotiations over Constitutional and Other Reforms

The opposition's relatively strong political position was established by the 1988 plebiscite and the commitment of the armed forces to ensuring a smooth transition. In mid-1989, through a process of dialogue—Patricio Aylwin represented the Concertación, and Sergio Onofre Jarpa represented the right—significant changes were made in the constitution and approved in the July 30 plebiscite. The reforms reduced the power of the president in three areas. First, the president's authority over the appointment, promotion, and retirement of armed forces and security personnel was reduced. Rather than having these appointments regulated by supreme decree, as specified by the 1980 constitution, they would be regulated by a constitutional law issued by the Pinochet regime. Second, the president's power of insistence, or co-legislation of laws, was withdrawn. Third, the president's constitutional right to dissolve the Chamber of Deputies once during his term was also withdrawn.

In contrast, the opposition gained some advantages. The relative weight of designated senators was reduced by increasing the number of elected senators from twenty-six to thirty-eight. Nevertheless, after the 1989 elections, designated senators were still able to guarantee a majority in the Senate for the forces of the right (see table 7-4).

Perhaps the most important result was a slight moderation of the extremely rigid procedure for changing the constitution, although the presence of designated senators continued to make it impossible to remove authoritarian enclaves from the system. Also important was the reform of article 8 of the constitution, which proscribed the Communist Party.

Without a doubt, though, the most significant concession made by the Concertación was in the constitutional norms regulating the armed forces. The negotiations did not alter the 1980 constitution's creation of an autonomous and independent military establishment within a consti-

Table 7-4. Party Representation in Congress in Chile, 1989
(number of seats)

Party	Senate	House
Concertación and PAIS	22	72
Democracy and Progress	16	48

Note: See table 7-5 for the composition of coalitions.
Source: Angell and Pollack 1990.

tutional democracy. That autonomy continued to be based on the durable nature of the commanders in chief for an eight-year period. The armed forces and the *carabineros* would continue to appoint four members of the Senate, four of eight members of the National Security Council, and two of seven members of the Constitutional Tribunal. In the 1980 version, civilians maintained control over the appointment of military officers, through a supreme decree signed by the president and the defense minister, as well as over the defense budget. In its final days, however, the military regime passed an organic constitutional law regulating not only appointments and retirements but also a host of other areas such as the budget. The armed forces thus maintained even more autonomy than had been envisioned in 1980. As compensation for these concessions, the number of members of the National Security Council was raised from seven to eight, including the comptroller general, and its role was changed from that of representative to adviser.

Of all the negotiations following the plebiscite, only the ones concerning the board of the autonomous central bank were a clear success for the Concertación. Indeed, this is the arena in which the military seemed willing to make the most concessions, for several reasons. It did not encroach directly on military power or hierarchy. A board appointed by Pinochet and composed strictly of his supporters would be unacceptable in the likely event of an opposition victory and would jeopardize both the governability and viability of an autonomous central bank in the future (interviews with Carlos Caceres, June 26, 1992, and Juan Andrés Fontaine, June 25 and 26, 1992). The opposition, meanwhile, was willing to negotiate in order to avoid having to draft an entirely new central bank law upon entering government, when they would have many other pressing issues to resolve (interview with Nicolás Eyzaguirre, June 24, 1992). Discussions between Caceres and Foxley led to the appointment of an independent bank president—Andrés Bianchi from the United Nations Economic Commission for Latin America—and two members to be chosen, one by the opposition and one by the government. Increasing evidence suggests that insulating key institutions, like the central bank, from political pressure improves economic management and provides the government with an important political escape when unpopular monetary contractions are necessary (see chapter 1 of this volume).

The negotiations were also successful because opposition economists agreed substantially on the benefits of ensuring some degree of autonomy for the central bank. Indeed, much of the debate prior to the agreement was largely political. Opposition economists were understandably concerned about Pinochet's freedom to appoint the entire board five days before the elections. Autonomy per se was thus secondary to the issue of whether the central bank would be a potential tool for Pinochet. Some debated the optimal degree of autonomy and other technicalities of the law; many agreed that as long as the board members were independently elected and mechanisms for coordinating with the Ministry of Finance were adequate, an autonomous bank was desirable (interviews with Nicolás Eyzaguirre, June 24, 1992, and Juan Andrés Fontaine, June 25 and 26, 1992).

The central bank law had been written in 1980, at the height of faith in passive monetary policy and fixed exchange rates. Opponents of the law thought it created a bank that was too autonomous in legal terms, yet not sufficiently strong in financial terms (the central bank has responsibility for the entire public debt). They feared the bank would not be able to respond to external shocks and would have too much responsibility. Moreover, lack of coordination between the Federal Reserve and the Treasury Department, which characterizes the system in the United States, for example, would be far more problematic in Chile's relatively unstable economy, which is particularly vulnerable to external shocks. Indeed, despite the negotiations, the bank and the Ministry of Finance were successfully coordinated under the new government largely because the economics team was highly cohesive, not because the institutional arrangements themselves were adequate.[27]

The 1989 Election Results

The results of the electoral campaign were a clear-cut majority for the Concertación, although its margin in Congress was curtailed by the peculiar electoral system and the presence of nine senators designated by Pinochet. Aylwin received 55 percent, Büchi 29 percent, and Errazuriz 15 percent of the popular vote. In Congress, the obvious victor was the Concertación, led by the Christian Democratic Party, which won 13 of the 38 seats in the Senate and 38 of the 120 seats in the Chamber of Deputies (see table 7-5). The bias in favor of minority parties meant that the socialist umbrella party, the Party for Democracy, failed to elect its leader, Ricardo Lagos, to the Senate (although he subsequently became education minister). It did obtain four Senate and seventeen Chamber of Deputies seats, emerging as the third largest party after the Christian Democratic Party and National Renovation, the party of the moderate right. National Renovation ran on a joint platform with the Independent Democratic Union, which was adamantly pro-Pinochet, and together they obtained almost 45 percent of the national vote (see table 7-6). The defeat of Lagos and the prominent role gained by National Renovation

Table 7-5. Composition of Party Coalitions in Chile, 1989
(number of seats)

Party and coalition	Senate	House
Concertación		
Almeyda Socialist Party (Partido Socialista Almeyda)	1	6
Christian Democratic Party (Partido Democrático Cristiano)	13	38
Christian Left (Izquierda Cristiana)	0	2
Democratic Party of Radical Socialists (Partido Radical Socialista Democrático)	1	0
Humanist Party (Partido Humanista)	0	1
Party for the Central Alliance (Partido Alianza de Centro)	0	1
Party for Democracy (Partido por la Democracia)	4	17
Radical Party (Partido Radical)	2	5
Social Democratic Party (Partido Social Democracia)	1	1
Independents	0	1
Democracy and Progress		
Independent Democratic Union (Unión Democrática Independiente)	2	11
Renovation National (Renovación Nacional)	6	29
Independents	8	8

Note: The Party for Democracy includes members of the Arrate Socialist Party. The Christian Left, the Communist Party, and some socialist parties ran under the PAIS umbrella (some socialists were in both PAIS and Concertación). The electoral returns for the PAIS were quite low, and it has since dissolved.

Source: Angell and Pollack 1990.

were comforting to the business sector. The labor movement also elected three senators and two deputies (Angell and Pollack 1990). The prominent role gained by the center-leaning poles of the spectrum, coupled with the clear economic message issued by the Concertación, generated widespread confidence that continuity in economic management would be maintained. The election results also demonstrated a strong commitment to the democratic process on the part of civil society. Abstention rates, which were as high as 25 percent in elections in 1969 and 1971, were only 5 percent in the 1989 elections.[28]

Politics of Consensus and Macroeconomic Stability under the Concertación Government

Economic policy was not the only arena in which the new government had to establish a viable consensus. The message of reconciliation also had to be put into practice in the arenas of civil-military relations, the political system, and state-society relations. Finding a compromise position in all these areas proved to be one of President Aylwin's strengths. The National Commission for Truth and Reconciliation on human rights abuses, for example, found a solution to the need to redress human rights

Table 7-6. Election Results in Chile, 1989 and 1992

Candidate, party, and election	Percent of the vote
Presidential election, 1989	
Patricio Aylwin (Concertación)	55.18
Hernan Büchi (Democracy and Progress)	29.39
Francisco Javier Errazuriz (Center-Center Union)	15.43
Municipal elections, 1992	
Concertación/Socialist Party	53.25
Parties of the right	29.67
Independents	17.08

Note: See table 7-11 for the composition of political groupings in 1992.
Source: Information from the Chilean Embassy, Washington, D.C.

abuses that was acceptable both to the military and to the victims of abuse or their families.[29] Economic policy was a component of this broader process, and from the start it was clear that the new government would support the trade, exchange rate, and macroeconomic policies of the previous government. At the same time, the Concertación had to address popular expectations and an accumulated social debt.

The extent to which the Aylwin government adopted the economic principles of its predecessors was reflected in three of the four pillars supporting its policies: maintaining a macroeconomic equilibrium, achieving integration into the international economy, and fostering investment and long-term growth. The leaders of the Concertación government were clearly determined to avoid the high inflation rates of most of their neighbors (see table 7-7). With the exception of the Sanguinetti government in Uruguay, all the others (the Alfonsín, García, and Sarney governments)—due to either their own lackluster policies or their inability to reverse previous situations—ended up with economies destroyed by hyperinflation, instability, capital flight, and income repression among the poorest sectors of society. The Concertación clearly had to avoid the politically damaging specter of inflation.

Table 7-7. Inflation in Neighboring Countries during Chile's Transition to Democracy
(percent)

Country	Inflation twelve months after Aylwin's victory	Inflation twelve months after Aylwin took office
Argentina	4,923.8	20,263.4
Brazil	1,783.6	6,233.8
Peru	2,775.3	2,068.4
Uruguay	89.2	95.4
Chile	21.4	23.9

Source: CEPAL 1991.

Macroeconomic management was, if anything, more cautious than that of the previous government. In part due to the Pinochet regime's overheating of the economy, inflation reached 27 percent in 1990, and the Aylwin government was forced to implement contractionary policies its first year in office: growth was only 2 percent in 1990 compared with 10 percent the previous year. The government did manage to achieve a surplus of 1.5 percent of GDP and to increase investment to 20 percent of GNP. Adjustment policies bore fruit the next year, as GNP grew almost 6 percent, inflation dropped to 19 percent, wages increased 5 percent in real terms, unemployment declined to 5 percent, and the budget surplus was maintained. Exports increased 7 percent despite a decline in the price of copper, resulting in a trade surplus of $1.5 billion. Even more striking, all of this was achieved despite the increase in oil prices that occurred as a result of the Gulf War (Chile imports 85 percent of its oil). The previous government's prompt servicing of debt was maintained, and in September 1990 more favorable terms were negotiated with private creditor banks for Chile's $18 billion debt. In 1993 Chile's debt traded at almost 100 percent of its value, while that of most of its neighbors traded at less than half.

The continuity between the Aylwin government's economic policies and those of its predecessors resulted "not only or mainly from the fear of antagonizing the military" (Hojman 1990, p. 41) but also from the gradual convergence of economic thought that included the Christian Democrats and the right, as well as most prominent economists on the left. Some principles, such as controlling the money supply to control inflation, had been widely accepted for several years, as were the potential dangers of a system of fixed exchange rates and views about import/export demand elasticities and the labor market. In other arenas, such as agriculture, the international copper market, financial market regulation, poverty relief measures, and the returns to investment in human capital, there was much more disagreement, even among the Christian Democrats themselves, and the attainment of consensus was a relatively recent phenomenon (Hojman 1990).

Trade policy provides a good example of continuity. Liberalization was attempted as early as 1958, under the conservative President Jorge Alessandri. The Frei administration attempted to rationalize the trading sector by introducing a crawling peg exchange rate and a differentiated tariff system that resulted in a trade surplus. These efforts were sharply reversed when the Allende government imposed strict trade controls. When the Pinochet regime made tariffs as low as the uniform 10 percent of 1979, Christian Democrat economists in the opposition, including Foxley and Ffrench-Davis, disagreed over the rhythm and extent of opening, not the objectives; these differences of opinion continue, to some extent, today (interviews with Juan Eduardo Coeymans, June 25, 1992, and Jorge Rodríguez, June 25 and 26, 1992). After the crash of 1982, trade policy was adjusted, and tariffs were raised as high as 35 percent in 1984 and then reduced to a uniform 15 percent in 1988. More gradual liberalization, coupled with a more realistic exchange rate policy, was a success: exports grew at an annual rate of 20 percent from 1986 to 1989 (table 7-2). The Aylwin government further liberalized trade and lowered the uniform tariff to 11 percent in June 1991 (Flano 1992).

On the privatization front, the Aylwin government entered into arenas that the Pinochet regime had been hesitant to touch. It authorized the privatization of up to 50 percent of the cargo services provided by the state railroad company; the development of joint ventures between CODELCO (the state copper company) and private corporations to exploit state-owned deposits; and the concession of public works infrastructure such as ports, tunnels, and railways to private firms. At the same time, the government rejected privatizing highly profitable public companies, which had, during the military years, resulted in the generous subsidization of certain entrepreneurial sectors (Flano 1992).

Finally, investor confidence in the new government was demonstrated by Chile's 1991 move into the category of a low-risk country according to the classification of the Economist Intelligent Unit, joining Mexico, the Republic of Korea, and Spain (Flano 1992). Chile's rate of direct foreign investment was between 4 and 5 percent of GNP, which is among the highest in the world, and this was coupled with a rising rate of domestic private and public investment (table 7-3). Chile was also cited as next in line after Mexico for a free trade agreement with the United States (Chile's role in the Enterprise for the Americas Initiative and the prospects for a free trade agreement are discussed in Graham 1991a, an article adapted from the author's testimony before the U.S. Congress in May of that year). In the international context of the late 1980s, political liberalization eventually became a prerequisite to consolidating the military's externally oriented model, rather than a threat as was previously assumed.

Indeed, the right's early warnings of impending chaos proved to be less than credible, and even within the right, fears of a return to populism dissipated. Indeed, the question facing economists of all bents was how deep the commitment to the free market model would be in the face of a crisis, which most likely would be precipitated by an external shock. The government had a good buffer against most external shocks: eleven months' worth of reserves, including copper and petroleum price stabilization funds (interview with Jorge Rodríguez, June 25 and 26, 1992). Its management of the Gulf War increases in the price of oil, meanwhile, demonstrated that the Concertación economic team could manage the economy and left the right without a political strategy (interview with Juan Andrés Fontaine, June 25 and 26, 1992).

At the same time, the government moved quickly to address its campaign priorities: first, reform of the labor code and alleviation of poverty;

second, reform of the municipal law and the holding of elections in June 1992.

Labor Reform

The perspectives of labor unions changed dramatically during the Pinochet years. From 1932 to 1973, unions were organized around preserving or bettering the purchasing power of workers, with political objectives at the national level linked to those of the parties of the left (for a detailed analysis of labor unions prior to the Pinochet years, see Angell 1972; for the Pinochet years, see Angell 1991). The ultimate objective was to attain a government predominantly representative of labor interests, which often meant that unions took a confrontational stance against the government and eventually contributed to the democratic breakdown that occurred in 1973 (Alburquerque 1991). The military years dramatically reduced the power of Chile's unions. Union membership in the early 1980s was one-third what it had been the previous decade: while 30 percent of workers were affiliated in 1970, only 12 percent were in the 1980s. Unions then adopted the attainment and preservation of democracy as their primary objective, recognizing that democracy was essential to attaining their other objectives (interviews with José Cisternas and Federico Mújica, January 21, 1992). Like political parties, key to the unions' new strategy was "la renuncia de una utopia que pase por la eliminación de los adversarios" (Alburquerque 1991, p. 4).

The relative power of unions was weakened by structural changes and repression, which coupled political repression with wage repression. The economic transformations that ensued weakened the industrial sectors where unions were traditionally strong and reduced the importance of the mining sector, where unions had their origins. Although union representation remained strong in the mining sector, in large manufacturing firms, in the electric and water services, and in some other service sectors, the percentage of the work force with salaried jobs in the formal sector remained relatively small (interview with Manuel Barrera, January 15, 1992). The union movement criticized the export promotion strategy's reliance on low wages, but the dramatic unemployment rates of the early 1980s made the issue of employment more central to the concerns of the average worker than the level of wages. The export strategy, meanwhile, ultimately provided the solution to the employment issue.

The links between political parties and unions also changed. Previously unions were most closely linked with the socialist and communist parties; since the coup and the persecution of parties of the left, however, the relative importance of the Christian Democrats in unions increased, followed by the socialists and then the communists. This balance remained under the new government. Interestingly enough, though, while the socialists and Christian Democrats had an agreement at the national and government level, at the union level the differences between the two remained. In July 1991, for example, the left within the union at

CODELCO was clearly the most active proponent of the strike against the state-owned copper industry (interview with Manuel Barrera, January 15, 1992).

Addressing the grievances of the labor movement was a priority for the Concertación government, although it clearly fell within the broader parameter of maintaining macroeconomic stability. Prior to the reforms in 1990, the 1980 labor code acted as a disincentive to unionization, since employers could extend collective contracts to nonunionized workers, thereby stimulating free-rider conduct. The code also placed severe restrictions on union financing; failed to recognize the legal existence of workers' centrals; made unionization extremely difficult, requiring a minimum of twenty-five workers and 50 percent of all employees to form a union; and hindered unions' negotiating activities, particularly where strikes were concerned. The main achievements of reform were the elimination of a clause that allowed arbitrary dismissal; an end to the time limit on strikes; the creation of an indemnification system for all levels of workers; the legal recognition of small syndicates; and the approval of new legislation on union organization and collective negotiation, which facilitated the creation of unions and improved the system for financing labor organizations. Perhaps most important was that National Renovation supported passage of the reforms in Congress (Mino Rojas 1992). From a union standpoint, meanwhile, some major issues remained unresolved, such as the absence of state involvement in collective bargaining, the absence of a system for unemployment insurance, the large share (40 percent) of the work force without health insurance in the workplace, the lack of state support for training facilities, and the continued persecution of union leaders in certain industries (anonymous 1992b, 1992c; Echeverría 1990; Walker 1991).

Unions achieved some material gains with the democratic government, and the number of organized workers increased, as did the number of strikes. The percentage of the total work force affiliated with unions reached 16 percent or 700,000 workers by the end of 1991, an increase of 35 percent since the end of the military years. Of these, the mining sector had the highest share of its workers in unions—67 percent—followed by electricity and gas with 64 percent, industry with only 24 percent, and agriculture with 9 percent. More than 75 percent of organized workers were in the CUT (United Workers Confederation). Only a little more than 2,400 workers were on strike at some point in 1991, and approximately 1.2 hours per worker were lost, a rate lower than that of the United States or Great Britain (anonymous 1992d; Programa de Empleo y Trabajo 1992). The minimum wage was increased 15 percent above the consumer price index in 1990 and 6 percent in 1991. Pensions were increased 30 percent in that same period. Unemployment was at 6 percent compared with almost 30 percent at the height of the economic crisis in 1982 (Programa de Empleo y Trabajo 1992).

Still, there were limits to what unions could attain, as demonstrated by strikes in the mining sector. Major strikes occurred in both the Chuquicamata and El Teniente branches of CODELCO in July and August 1991. Demands—and negotiations—remained focused on bread-and-butter issues: wages and benefits. Yet the strikes did have political overtones, as demonstrated by the slogan of some El Teniente strikers: "Yesterday we fought for democracy, today for dignity" (Bachelet 1991; Crawford 1991). Because Chuquicamata is the world's biggest copper mine, and these were the first strikes in the mining sector in eighteen years, their occurrence and duration had some political impact, albeit limited. The unions were disappointed by the government's refusal to intervene in the negotiations and then by a series of financial scandals that discredited leaders of the Chuquicamata movement. Any progress achieved in government-labor relations is likely to be incremental, given the government's commitment to macroeconomic stability, the limits to what unions can attain within a neoliberal parameter, and the commitment of unions themselves to the still ongoing process of democratic consolidation. For the foreseeable future, both government and unions seem committed to maintaining the political consensus that exists on macroeconomic management.

The extent to which union demands would remain within these parameters was demonstrated by a statement by Manuel Bustos in 1992 warning workers against seeking a "statist" solution to the problems of the coal and textile workers:

> We would have to be extremely stupid if we were to propose a change in these economic policies for state-led ones, because we would be threatening the positions of thousands of workers. What we should do is inject a grade of solidarity into this economy that is today gaining potential (anonymous 1992d).

The access of union leaders to the government reassured the union members and demonstrated the extent of consensus on the role of the state.

Social Welfare Policy

The other arena identified for reform was social welfare, and this was the only arena in which a consensus was not attained. In 1987 as much as 44 percent of Chile's population, or 5 million people, were estimated to be living under the poverty line, with 1.8 million in conditions of extreme poverty.[30] Although the poorest segments of the population were protected from the social costs of the adjustment program by emergency employment, targeted school feeding, and mother and child nutrition programs, income distribution worsened and the number of people below the poverty line increased (see tables 7-8, 7-9, and 7-10; for details on these programs, see Graham 1991b). In 1969 the poorest 10 percent of the population held 1.3 percent of national income; in 1989 they held only 1.2 percent. The wealthiest 10 percent, in contrast, held 39.0 per-

Table 7-8. Infant Mortality in Selected Latin American Countries, Selected Years, 1960–89
(deaths per 1,000 live births)

Year	Chile	Bolivia	Brazil	Mexico	Peru
1960	114	167	118	91	163
1965	101	160	104	82	130
1975	79	—	—	50	65
1980	43	131	77	56	88
1985	20	117	67	50	91
1989	19	106	59	40	79

— Not available.
Source: World Bank, various years.

cent in 1969 and 41.6 percent in 1989. Expectations for an improvement in social welfare were substantially raised by the transition to democracy and the priority accorded social expenditure by the new government.

At the same time, the government insisted that social expenditures could only be increased in a noninflationary manner as resources were generated. All revenue generated by the April 1990 tax reform was allocated to social welfare expenditure. The tax increase was equivalent to 2 percent of GNP, or $600 million, and its expenditure on the poorest 20 percent of the population, which only consumed 4 percent of the national total in 1988, had significant effects.[31] The main concessions made to the right were that one-third of the increase came from the value added tax, which is regressive, rather than the income tax, which is progressive, and that the reform lasted only four years, after which it would have to be renewed. The party of the more extreme right, the Independent Democratic Union, criticized the tax on the grounds that it hampered business savings, and therefore investment, and gave the illusion that tax increases automatically enhanced equity (interview with Juan Andrés Fontaine, June 25 and 26, 1992).

Social welfare expenditures grew 10 percent between passage of the tax increase and inauguration of the Aylwin government (Flano 1992).

Table 7-9. Indigent and Poor Households in Santiago, Chile, Selected Years, 1969–89
(percent)

Year	Indigent[a]	Poor[b]	Nonpoor
1969	8.4	20.1	71.5
1979	11.7	24.3	64.0
1988	22.9	26.8	50.3
1989	14.9	26.3	58.8

a. Family income is insufficient to meet basic food needs.
b. Family income is insufficient to meet basic needs other than food: the level of income is less than twice that of indigence.
Source: Programa de Economía del Trabajo 1989.

Table 7-10. Income Distribution in Chile, Selected Years, 1968–88
(proportion of national household income by quintile and Gini coefficient)

Year	First	Second	Third	Fourth	Fifth	Gini coefficient
1968	4.4	9.0	13.8	21.4	51.4	0.426
1978	4.6	9.6	14.1	19.9	51.9	0.448
1988	4.2	7.5	10.8	16.9	60.5	0.525

Source: van de Walle 1989.

Priority was given to creating equality of opportunity. Preventive health care programs, school feeding, and low-income household food supplements were increased, and programs for bettering the quality of education and training of unemployed youth were implemented.[32] Minimum wages, pensions for the retired and handicapped, and income subsidies for poor families were all increased on the order of 50 to 80 percent, and a new housing program, launched in 1990, had completed 24,000 housing provision projects as of this writing. The budget for health was increased 30 percent in real terms in the government's first two years in office and was aimed at primary health care and the poorest sectors (Flano 1992).

An important policy for alleviating poverty was the FOSIS (Social Investment and Solidarity Fund), a social fund proposed by nongovernmental organizations, community organizations, and local governments. The program's main areas of activity were support to microenterprises, youth education and training, improvement of infrastructure in the poorest areas, and social and community development activities, including training for female heads of households and better child care facilities. The FOSIS had a budget of $6 million in 1990, $26 million in 1991, and a projected $30 million in 1992 (interview with Jorge Chateau, January 16, 1992; FOSIS 1990). Although slow to get off the ground, in part because it originally lacked budgetary freedom and relied on planning ministry procedures for funding (which have been amended since), after 1991 FOSIS began to take a more visible and active role in alleviating poverty.

The government could not immediately meet all the expectations raised by the transition, but its well-researched and forward-looking social welfare policy, which expanded Chile's preexisting and extensive social safety net, was an important first step toward addressing Chile's pressing issues of poverty and social welfare. Income distribution had already improved by 1991: the share of the wealthiest 20 percent fell from almost 60 percent in 1989 to 58 percent in 1990 and 55 percent in 1991. These improvements were largely due to the 1990 tax reform. At the same time, poverty fell from 40 percent in 1990 to 38 percent in 1991 (Marcel and Solimano 1993). Yet the government kept its social policy—

as its labor policy—within the parameters of macroeconomic stability and growth.

Nevertheless, sectors of the right criticized the government's social welfare policy: the editorial page of the conservative and influential daily *El Mercurio* called the government's focus on social welfare the silent counterrevolution (interview with Ignacio Walker, January 16, 1992). Such criticism had limited impact. At least in its first two years, the government effectively balanced the country's social and political need to address social concerns, on the one hand, and to balance budgets and maintain the confidence of the private sector, on the other. Given accumulated social grievances and expectations raised by the transition to democracy, a visible government commitment to poverty alleviation was likely to become increasingly important for political as well as social reasons.

Municipal Reform and Elections

In Chile, as in much of Latin America, municipal governments have traditionally been dependent, both financially and administratively, on the central government (much of this section is drawn from Graham 1991b). In theory, the military government's municipal reform laws opened the door to decentralized government. The laws established a certain degree of financial and administrative independence for municipalities, guaranteed certain fiscal transfers to municipalities, and established a common fund through which wealthier municipalities transferred resources to poorer ones. In addition, municipalities were central to implementing safety net programs. Despite the military's legislation, true decentralization did not occur, and authoritarian government structures were merely transmitted to municipalities. During most of the Pinochet regime, mayors were designated by the government. In 1988, a new law was passed in which the mayors of the fifteen most populous cities were appointed by the government, and the rest were appointed by each city's community development council, whose members were also designated. Thus in 1988, more than 300 mayors were appointed by the authoritarian government for a term that lasted until June 1992.

The delay in holding municipal elections was in part a result of the need to reform the municipal law prior to the elections. The prolonged debate over municipal law focused primarily on political parties vying for the formula that best suited their electoral chances. The law approved by the Senate in January 1992 established direct elections for municipal councils, whose size varies according to the population of the city. Councils then elect the mayor if one candidate does not receive a sufficient proportion of total votes. Parties run on joint lists, which guarantee representation of smaller parties, and independents run on pacted party lists (such as the Concertación) without declaring party allegiance (anonymous 1992e). The debate over municipal reform illustrates the extent of political consensus: the differences were greater within party coalitions, and between parties of the right, in particular, than they were between the right and the government. For example, designated senators voted in favor of the government and against some of the right.

Elections were held in June 1992, and the Concertación government obtained 53 percent of the vote (table 7-6). The results were not all that different from those of the 1989 elections, and the right obtained 30 percent of the vote. The Communist Party did surprisingly well, obtaining 7 percent of the vote and one mayoralty, as did the Center-Center Union of populist and former presidential candidate Francisco Errazuriz with 8 percent of the vote. The tendency to vote for parties rather than independents and to maintain a center consensus remained quite strong after two years of government and markedly so compared with voting trends in neighboring countries, where the appeal of nonparty populists had grown substantially. The 1992 municipal elections demonstrated that support for the party system and for the Concertación government was as strong after two years of government as it was at the time of the 1990 transition (see table 7-11).

State Sector Reform

The new government also sought to consolidate rather than simply maintain structural reforms in the state sector. Although the Pinochet regime implemented several key reforms in some sectors such as social security and health, municipal government, and public sector enterprises, other state sectors, such as the judiciary, retained their 1973 institutional framework. The regime's focus on reducing the state did not necessarily enhance its efficiency, however. The military was not particularly interested in reforming the government, because it could bypass institutions and legal norms in order to get things done. If there were delays in the Comptroller General, for example, which must give prior approval for most expenditures made by government ministries, the regime merely replaced the director rather than reform the procedures. It is telling that most of the programs intended to produce rapid results and be highly visible, such as the government's youth training and education reform programs, were set up as quasi-independent agencies precisely to avoid inefficiency in the state mechanism.[33] A related issue is the maintenance of infrastructure, which was sorely neglected during the military years, particularly in public health and education. Ultimately, sound macroeconomic policies must be complemented with equally sound policies in other areas if structural reform is to be achieved.

Conclusions

Two years after the transition to democracy in Chile, a broad national consensus clearly existed in several areas, particularly maintenance of the structural reforms implemented by the military. This consensus is likely

Table 7-11. Results of Municipal Elections in Chile, 1992
(seats won and popular vote)

Grouping and party	Councils	Mayors	Percentage of votes received
Concertación/Socialist			
Christian Democratic Party (Partido Democrático Cristiano)	625	18	28.97
Humanist Party (Partido Humanista)	15	0	0.82
Radical Party (Partido Radical)	140	3	4.91
Social Democratic Party (Partido Social Democracia)	20	0	0.42
Independents	22	0	0.48
Subtotal	822	21	35.60
Party for Democracy (Partido por la Democracia)	165	3	9.18
Socialist Party (Partido Socialista)	170	4	8.46
Independents	1	0	0.01
Subtotal	336	7	17.64
Parties of the Right			
National Renovation (Renovación Nacional)	400	5	13.42
National Party (Partido Nacional)	2	0	0.07
Independents	113	8	4.37
Subtotal	515	13	17.86
Independent Democratic Union (Unión Democrática Independiente)	181	5	10.21
Independents	29	3	1.19
Subtotal	210	8	11.40
Independents			
Liberal Party (Partido Liberal)	4	0	0.24
Communist Party of Chile (Partido Comunista de Chile)	35	1	6.60
Center-Center Union (Unión de Centro Centro)	80	0	8.10
Additional independents	22	0	2.14
Subtotal	141	1	17.08
Total	2,024	50	
Abstention rate			10.20

Note: The parties composing the Concertación in the 1992 municipal elections did not include the Party for Democracy or the Socialist Party. These two parties composed the socialist element of the political grouping. The parties of the right did not run under a coalition umbrella for these 1992 elections.

Source: Information from Chilean Embassy, Washington, D.C.

to continue, at least in the near future. The explanations for that consensus are complex, extending well beyond the debate over whether an authoritarian regime was necessary to implement structural economic reform. The most tangible and replicable lessons from the Chilean case relate to the consolidation of reform and the formation and maintenance of political consensus during the democratic transition.

On the one hand, the Concertación was forced to adopt a consensus-building strategy and to accept certain parameters of economic management for fear of a return to military rule. On the other hand, and far more instructive, the consensus was possible because of political and economic lessons learned by all parties. On the political front, pragmatism and coalition-building replaced confrontation and ideological utopianism. On the economic front, the principles of prudent fiscal management, respect for private property, a liberal trade regime, and minimal state intervention were accepted virtually across the political spectrum. This was the result of Chile's recent success, its neighbors' present failures, and global ideological and political trends. Since the basic principles of the economic model were not challenged by the opposition, which instead focused its efforts on adjusting certain aspects of the model, popular expectations were not raised beyond the new government's capacity to meet them. Finally, consensus began filtering down from political elites to the population as a whole, as the strong showing of the Concertación in the 1992 municipal elections demonstrated.

Equally as important, though, was the view across most of the political spectrum that sound economics had to go hand in hand with increased attention to issues of social welfare and poverty alleviation. This view, coupled with the introduction of democratic government, is likely to enhance the public's understanding and acceptance of the current economic model, freeing it from the taint of authoritarianism and increased inequality. This lesson *can be replicated* by other new democracies in the process of economic adjustment.

Another lesson is the need for a team prepared to govern and manage the economy. If such a team cannot be found at home, then advice should be sought abroad, although it is a less-effective alternative. The Chilean case underscores the importance of international support for academic research in developing countries and the importance of the international context itself. The temptation to employ short-term populist strategies will be substantially reduced if policymakers—and the public—are aware of what has worked and not worked in other countries. In Chile, the chaos in neighboring countries made continued macroeconomic restraint much more politically palatable.

Another factor equally important to Chile's success and far less replicable is the extent to which Chile's successful economic transformation was due to its preexisting, extensive social welfare system and relatively efficient structure of state and local government. These institutions provided an important basis for the military's policies of decentralization and targeted social welfare expenditure, for example. The subsequent successful political transformation, meanwhile, owed a great deal to the existence of a developed party system and leadership and to the wealth of highly skilled social scientists. Caution must thus be taken in drawing conclusions from the Chilean case about the prospects for economic reform in fragile new democracies. If anything, this aspect of Chile's success points to the importance of supporting institutional development in conjunction with economic reform.

Finally, the consensus-building process in Chile cannot be viewed as independent of the global ideological context in which it took place. While consensus is striking in Chile, as is the adoption of Pinochet's free market economic policies by his former opponents, similar changes are taking place across Latin America.[34] The Institutional Revolutionary Party in Mexico, the Nationalist Revolutionary Movement in Bolivia, the Peronists in Argentina, and Change 90 (Alberto Fujimori's party) in Peru all became unlikely advocates of free market economics, as did the socialists in Spain before them. A major difference is that the political consensus that exists in Chile eludes many of these countries, where the appeal of antisystem populists is on the rise. The strength of Chile's institutions and, most important, its party system may well prove far more important than ideological trends in providing the political stability necessary for consolidating economic reform.

Notes

1. This lack of support was noted in three major polls taken in 1986, 1988, and 1990 by CEP, FLACSO, and CIEPLAN, all of which are respected academic institutions. Lower-income groups were an important electoral base for the then-opposition Christian Democrats and socialists. A caveat is the limited utility of opinion polls in the economics sphere. Poor understanding of economics does not seem to prevent people from having strong opinions, and contradictory answers were often expressed in surveys. For example, in a survey taken in Santiago in October 1990 through May 1991, 800 adults expressed support both for protection of industries and for free trade. The most important variables influencing opinions were political leaning, perception of purchasing power, and use of communications media (Halpern and Bousquet 1991).

2. The failure to sell the reforms is even noted by members of the Pinochet government. See, for example, an account by a former functionary of the central bank (Fontaine 1992).

3. The restructuring of the system, the extent of poverty, and the issue of income distribution are discussed in detail in Graham 1991b. Although the poor in Chile are relatively better off than the poor in neighboring countries, an extensive debate still discusses the extent and severity of poverty, with estimates varying from as high as 5 million poor, or 40 percent of the population, to as low as 15 percent. The reality is somewhere below the higher estimate.

4. The term "authoritarian enclaves" was originally coined by Manuel Antonio Garretón and is used in several of his publications, including "La transición chilena, una evaluación provisoria" (Garretón 1991).

5. This process is described in Fontaine 1992. Initially, strong currents favored protectionist policies to build a strong industrial base for national security rather than for opening free trade. In the end, the team of economists from the University of Chicago won out largely because of exogenous events: the severe balance of payments crisis in early 1975 that resulted from the international rise in oil prices. General Pinochet accepted a shock plan at this point, which was implemented by Jorge Cauas as finance minister, Sergio de Castro as economy minister, and a growing team of University of Chicago technocrats.

6. Details of these violations are found in the public findings of the Rettig Commission, which was charged by the Aylwin government with identifying the number of deaths and disappearances, although not the names of those responsible. See National Commission for Truth and Reconciliation 1991.

7. The principle of targeting was espoused and developed by one of the "Chicago Boys"

team, Miguel Kast, and the regime was actually quite effective at protecting the poorest sectors, although not without substantial losses by those at the margin. See Graham 1991b.

8. The difference between the domestic dollar-dominated interest rate and the international rate was 112 percent in 1976, 52 percent in 1977, and 42 percent in 1978. The privatization of the financial sector proceeded more slowly than that of other sectors, and quantitative controls on the import of financial capital and a tendency toward gradual liberalization prevailed, at least until the late 1970s. As a result, the bulk of external debt accrued by Chile during this period was private rather than public. In 1974 the private sector's share of the total foreign debt was 14 percent; by 1981 it was 65 percent (Zahler 1983).

9. In East Asian countries, selective opening up of the economy was combined with export promotion. In Chile, rapid liberalization was combined with a fixed and overvalued exchange rate and high domestic interest rates (Zahler 1983).

10. For detail on these programs, see Graham 1991b. Compensation was regressively distributed at this point: approximately 1.5 percent of gross national product (GNP) was used to hire 500,000 workers, while 3 percent of GNP was used to subsidize less than 10,000 debtors.

11. "During the second round of privatizations, conversely, the government encouraged widespread stock ownership, sold shares to workers and pension funds, and allowed debt-equity swaps. As a result, the second round avoided many pitfalls of the first round and helped to develop the capital market, reduce the foreign debt, and extend public support of the privatization process itself" (Luders 1991, p. 2).

12. They criticized, for example, the limited equity gains of *capitalismo popular,* the practice of giving workers options to buy shares. This conclusion is drawn from interviews with a variety of opposition economists, many of whom are now in the government, including Manuel Marfán and Jorge Rodríguez of the Ministry of Economics, Nicolás Eyzaguirre of the central bank, Joseph Ramos of CEPAL, and Juan Eduardo Coeymans of the Catholic University.

13. Interview with Juan Eduardo Coeymans, June 25, 1992. The economy was positioned for a period of sustained growth in 1992 but remained very vulnerable to falls in the price of copper and increases in the price of oil, as the inflationary effects of the Gulf War–induced increases in the price of oil demonstrated. In addition, despite strides made in diversifying trade from the United States to the European Community and the Far East, the failure to strike a free trade agreement with the United States or increased protectionism in the European Community could still have very negative consequences. In 1989, for example, a U.S. boycott of Chilean grapes cost approximately $300 million or approximately 5 percent of Chile's total export revenues (Graham 1991b). All dollar amounts are U.S. dollars unless indicated otherwise.

14. For this category, modifications had to be approved by a two-thirds' vote of both houses of Congress (31 of 47 senators and 80 of 120 representatives). For most other aspects, modifications required three-fifths of both houses (28 senators and 72 representatives), while for organic laws (separate, complementary laws elevated to the rank of the constitution for these purposes), they required four-sevenths (27 and 69 members, respectively).

15. Angell and Pollack 1990. In the 1989 elections, for example, Andrés Zaldívar and Ricardo Lagos of the Concertación won 29.8 and 29.2 percent of a Santiago poll, respectively; and Jaime Guzmán and Miguel Otero of the right's Democracy and Progress alliance won 16 and 15 percent, respectively. Yet Guzmán rather than Lagos took the Senate seat!

16. Santiago, for example, where the vote no won decisively in the October 1988 plebiscite, saw its representation in Congress substantially reduced. Even though 40 percent of the population resides in this area, it elects only 26 percent of the lower house.

17. The coup during the Frei years was attempted by several units rebelling against the civil neglect of the military's institutional needs. The main proponent of the strategy of insurrection, the Movement of the Revolutionary Left, was not a member of the Popular Unity coalition.

18. After sixty days, workers were obliged to choose between the company's latest offer and dismissal. After thirty days, workers were permitted to return to work individually, and the company, as of the first day of the strike, was authorized to hire new workers to replace the strikers.

19. Rural society and the agricultural sector also experienced important changes during

the military years. The agriculture sector is addressed in recent works by Lorell Jarvis (1985) and David Hojman (1992), among others.

20. These debates grew out of a wealth of works by various social scientists, including Genaro Arriagada Herrara (1988) and Manuel Antonio Garretón (1989). The work of Arturo Valenzuela provides an excellent explanation of the 1973 breakdown (Valenzuela 1986).

21. This section is drawn from interviews in June 1992 with a variety of socialists and Christian Democrats who are now in the government, including Nicholás Eyzaguirre and Jorge Rodríguez.

22. Presidentialism in Chile historically did work, and the 1973 breakdown was the exception rather than the rule. One reason may be Chile's strong party system, which, coupled with agreement among the parties, has been critical to the functioning of presidentialism in the Latin American countries where it has had the most success: Mexico, Uruguay, and Venezuela (this point has been noted by Alan Angell). It is often noted, for example, that Allende won the presidency in 1970 with fewer votes than he attained in the 1964 election, which was won by Frei.

23. The unity of the National Accord, and the opposition's commitment to defeat Pinochet by nonviolent means, were severely tested by a 1986 assassination attempt on the general, which was attributed to the Communist Party.

24. Angell and Pollack 1990, pp. 2–3. The night of the plebiscite, when the results were clear, General Pinochet was purportedly not ready to accept them. All doubt was removed, however, when the interior minister appeared on national television to announce the results and the military's intention to stick by them.

25. This conclusion was drawn from a series of interviews conducted in January and June 1992 with Christian Democrat and socialist members of the Aylwin government's economic team, many of whom were closely involved in formulating the Concertación's strategy.

26. This conclusion was drawn from Graham's conversations and interviews with a variety of government and nongovernment sources in Santiago in January 1992. These include Ignacio Walker, secretariat of the presidency; Manuel Marfán, vice minister of economics; Dagmar Raczynski, senior researcher, CIEPLAN; Juan José Rivas, director of the Youth Training Program of the Ministry of Labor; and Manuel Barrera, director of the Centro de Estudios Sociales. The "overheating" and the adjustments it necessitated were also noted by Alejandro Foxley, finance minister, in a lecture delivered at the Brookings Institution, Washington, D.C., on May 3, 1991.

27. Interviews with several members of the economic team at both the central bank and the Finance Ministry, Santiago, June 1992. The 1980 law stipulated that all five members of the board would be named by the president. Members would be replaced, one at a time, every two years, so that each eight-year presidential term would have some continuity from the term before. The board was required to inform the finance minister, who was given power to suspend resolutions and to determine exchange restrictions. For details on the law as well as the debate at the time, see a special issue of *Cuadernos de Economía* (1989) and especially the pieces by 1992 president of the central bank, Roberto Zahler (Zahler 1989), and Fontaine (1989).

28. Abstention rates were 26, 25, and 18 percent in 1969, 1971, and 1973, respectively, compared with 5 percent in 1989. The abstention rate in the 1992 municipal elections was 10 percent (see table 7-11; anonymous 1992d; information from the Chilean Embassy, Washington, D.C.).

29. The commission's report concluded that the security forces were responsible for 2,200 executions and disappearances and released the names of the victims and the circumstances of their deaths. Families of each of the victims received a payment of $4,600 as well as a monthly payment of $384, at a cost to the government of $27.4 million. It also agreed to compensate the families of 350 deceased soldiers and police and to investigate the deaths of the 752 persons who had "disappeared." At the same time, crimes linked to military officers were not prosecuted (anonymous 1992a).

30. These estimates, which are from the Economic Commission for Latin America, may be high, since other credible sources report lower figures. See Graham 1991b.

31. Ffrench-Davis 1991. A tax increase of 2 percent of GNP in the United States would signify a $100 billion increase (interview with Joseph Ramos, June 25, 1992). A billion is 1,000 million.

32. Interview with Juan José Rivas, January 21 and 22, 1992; see Scholnik 1992. The

youth training program, for example, will reach approximately 20,000 youth each year for four years. In 1990, 220,000 primary school students benefited from the Quality Improvement in Education Program for the 900 schools in the poorest areas of the country, with an additional 416 schools added in 1991 (Flano 1992).

33. In addition, the military passed a permanency of employees law at the end of its term in order to protect its employees from political purges. Although it is not desirable to effect a total turnover of state personnel with a change of government, legally fixing the composition of the state bureaucracy is a major barrier to improving efficiency (interview with Juan José Rivas, January 21 and 22, 1992).

34. The authors are grateful to John Biehl for raising this point in this context.

References

Alburquerque, Mario. 1991. "El sindicalismo a un año del gobierno democrático." Serie Documentos 9. Centro de Investigación y Asesoría Sindical, Santiago, September.

Angell, Alan. 1972. *Politics and the Labor Movement in Chile*. London: Oxford University Press.

_____. 1989. "International Support for Political Democracy in Contemporary Latin America: The Case of Chile." *Foro Internacional* 30 (October), pp. 19–40.

_____. 1991. "Unions and Workers in Chile during the 1980s." In Paul W. Drake and Ivan Jasnic, eds., *The Struggle for Democracy in Chile, 1982–90*. Lincoln: University of Nebraska Press.

_____. 1993. *Chile from Alessandri to Pinochet: In Search of Utopia*. Santiago: Editorial Andrés Bello.

Angell, Alan, and Susan Carstairs. 1987. "The Exile Question in Chilean Politics." *Third World Quarterly* 9:1 (January), pp. 148–67.

Angell, Alan, and Benny Pollack. 1990. "The Chilean Elections of 1989." *Bulletin of Latin American Research* 9:1, pp. 1–24.

Anonymous. 1992a. "Chile Votes for Compensation for Victims." *Washington Post*, January 30.

Anonymous. 1992b. "CUT: Situación social se está agravando." *El Mercurio*, January 18.

Anonymous. 1992c. "Petitorio de 7 puntos entregó la CUT a S.E." *El Mercurio*, January 16.

Anonymous. 1992d. "Posición del presidente del CUT: El país no puede cambiar política económica abierta." *El Mercurio*, June 20.

Anonymous. 1992e. "Rechazada franja de propaganda electoral gratuíta por televisión." *El Mercurio*, January 16.

Anonymous. 1992f. "Trabajadores sindicalizados aumentan un 35% desde que asumió gobierno: Reportaje del Ministro Cortázar." *La Segunda*, January 15.

Arriagada Herrera, Genaro. 1978. "La doble crisis de 1973." *Revista Mensaje* 266 (January–February).

_____. 1984. "El sistema político chileno." *Coleccion Estudios CIEPLAN* 15 (December), p. 173.

_____. 1988. *Pinochet: The Politics of Power*. Boston, Mass.: Unwin Hyman.

Bachelet, Peter. 1991. "El Teniente Miners Extend Strike by Rejecting Offer." *Financial Times,* August 16.

Barahona, Pablo. 1980. Interview with Barahona, former economics minister, in *Cosas,* July 3.

CEPAL. 1991. "Panorama económico de América Latina." Santiago.

Communist Party. 1987. Public declaration. Santiago, July 17.

Corbo, Vittorio, and Andrés Solimano. 1991. "Chile's Experience with Stabilization Re-visited." In Michael Bruno and others, ed., *Lessons of Economic Stabilization and Its Aftermath,* pp. 57–91. Cambridge, Mass.: M.I.T. Press.

Cortázar, René. 1982. "Desempleo, pobreza, y distribución: Chile, 1970–1981." *Apuntes CIEPLAN* 34 (June), pp. 1–19.

Cosas. 1980. November 6, July 3.

Crawford, Leslie. 1991. "Chilean Copper Miners Vote Today on Strike Call." *Financial Times,* June 26.

Cuadernos de Economía. 1989. 77, special issue (April).

Echeverría, Fernando. 1990. "Sindicalismo continuido bajo el autoritarismo." *Movimiento: Revista laboral* (November–December).

Feinberg, Richard. 1992. "Centros de investigación en el Chile democrático." *Norte-Sur* (February–March), pp. 46–52.

Ffrench-Davis, Ricardo. 1991. "Desarrollo y equidad en Chile: Herencias y desafíos en el retorno a la democracia." *Estudios CIEPLAN* 31 (March), pp. 31–52.

Ffrench-Davis, Ricardo, and Oscar Muñoz. 1990. "Desarrollo económico, inestabilidad y desequilibrios políticos en Chile: 1950–1989." *Estudios CIEPLAN* 28 (June), pp. 121–56.

Flano, Nicolas. 1992. "On Solid Ground: Chile's Economy Today." Lecture, Smithsonian Campus on the Mall, Washington, D.C., February.

Fontaine, Juan Andrés. 1989. "Banco Central: Autonomía para cautelar la estabilidad." *Cuadernos de Economía* 77, special issue (April).

———. 1992. "Economic and Political Transition in Chile, 1970–90." Paper presented to the Hoover Institution/AID Project on Economy, Society, and Democracy, Washington, D.C., May.

FOSIS. 1990. "Un compromiso en marcha: Invertir con la gente." *FOSIS Annual Report.* Santiago.

Foxley, Alejandro. 1985. *Para una democracia estable.* Santiago: Editorial Aconcagua.

Garretón, Manuel Antonio. 1989. *The Chilean Political Process in Transition.* Boston, Mass.: Unwin Hyman.

———. 1991. "La transición chilena, una evaluación provisoria." FLASCO Serie Estudios Públicos 8. FLASCO, Santiago, January.

Graham, Carol. 1991a. "The Enterprise for the America's Initiative: A Development Strategy for the Region?" *Brookings Review* 9:4 (fall), pp. 22–27.

———. 1991b. *From Emergency Employment to Social Investment: Alleviating Poverty in Chile.* Brookings Occasional Papers. Washington, D.C.: Brookings Institution.

_____. 1992. *Peru's* APRA: *Parties, Politics, and the Elusive Quest for Democracy.* Boulder, Colo.: Lynne Rienner Publishers.

Halpern B., Pablo, and Edgardo Bousquet. 1991. "Opinión pública y politica económica: Hacia un modelo de formación de percepciones económicas en transición democrática." *Estudios* CIEPLAN 33 (December).

Hojman, David. 1990. "Chile after Pinochet: Aylwin's Christian Democrat Economic Policies for the 1990s." *Bulletin of Latin American Research* 9:1, pp. 25–47.

_____. 1992. *Neoliberal Agriculture in Rural Chile.* London: Macmillan.

Jarvis, Lovell S. 1985. *Chilean Agriculture under Military Rule: From Reform to Reaction, 1973–1980.* Berkeley: University of California Press.

Jiménez de Barrios, Mónica. 1990. "Mobilizing for Democracy in Chile: The Crusade for Citizen Participation and Beyond." Participa Institute, Santiago. Processed.

Luders, Rolf J. 1980. Interview in *Cosas,* November 6.

_____. 1991. "Massive Divestiture and Privatization: Lessons from Chile." *Contemporary Policy Issues* 9 (October).

Marcel, Mario, and Andrés Solimano. 1993. "Developmentalism, Socialism, and Free Market Reform: Three Decades of Income Distribution in Chile." Paper presented at the Brookings conference, the Chilean Economy: Policy Lessons and Challenges, Washington, D.C., April 22–23.

Mino Rojas, Irene. 1992. "Las reformas laborales." In Gonzalo Rivas, ed., *Economía y trabajo en Chile: 1990–1991.* Santiago: PET.

National Commission for Truth and Reconciliation. 1991. *Report of the National Commission for Truth and Reconciliation.* Santiago, March.

Programa de Economía y Trabajo. 1989. *Monthly Bulletin.* Santiago.

Programa de Empleo y Trabajo. 1990. *Encuesta de empleo.* Santiago.

_____. 1992. *Página económica de los trabajadores* (January–February).

Puryear, Jeffrey. 1991. "Building Democracy: Foreign Donors and Chile." Conference Paper 57. Paper presented at Columbia University conference on Crossing National Borders: Invasion or Involvement, New York, December.

_____. Forthcoming. *Intellectuals and Chile's Transition to Democracy.* Processed.

Scholnik, Mariana. 1992. "Inversión social para un crecimiento sostenido." *La Epoca,* January 20.

Valenzuela, Arturo. 1986. *The Breakdown of Democratic Regimes: Chile.* Baltimore, Md.: Johns Hopkins University Press.

Valenzuela, Arturo, and Samuel Valenzuela, eds. 1986. *Military Rule in Chile: Dictatorship and Oppositions.* Baltimore, Md.: Johns Hopkins University Press.

van de Walle, D. 1989. Press conference, September, cited in "Efectos de una apertura sobre la distribución del ingreso," *Estudios* CIEPLAN 33 (December 1991).

Walker, Francisco. 1991. "Algunas observaciones acera las modificaciones pendientes en el Congreso Nacional de los libros del código del trabajo." *Unión y Trabajo* (December).

World Bank. Various years. *World Development Report*. Washington, D.C.

Zahler, Roberto. 1983. "Recent Southern Cone Liberalization Reforms and Stabilization Policies: The Chilean Case, 1974–1982." *Journal of InterAmerican Studies and World Affairs* 25:4 (November), pp. 509–62.

_____. 1989. "La inserción institucional del Banco Central de Chile." *Cuadernos de Economía* 77, special issue (April).

8

Senegal: Stalled Reform in a Dominant Party System

SAMBA KA AND NICOLAS VAN DE WALLE

THE SENEGAL THAT BEGAN ITS PROCESS OF STRUCTURAL ADJUSTMENT in the early 1980s was a country of great contrasts. Covering only 196,000 square kilometers and endowed with a population of only 7.5 million people in 1991, it had nonetheless long enjoyed a high profile in African affairs on account of its "poet-president," Leopold Senghor, its sophisticated elite, and its open political system. Yet, Senegalese democracy was Janus faced. The country's modern face included a multiparty political system and a tradition of political pluralism unrivaled in postcolonial Africa. Although the ruling party exercised de facto control over all associational life from 1964 to 1974, liberalization had progressed since then, and legal opposition and considerable freedom of expression were assured. Because of this tradition of pluralism and Senghor's eloquent rhetoric in international forums, the country enjoyed the reputation of having one of the continent's most progressive political systems.

This modern political system coexisted with another face: in the countryside, in particular, social expressions were more traditional, and Senegalese democracy had done little to improve the welfare of the majority of the people. Senegal remained largely a peasant society: 61 per-

This chapter is based on interviews in Washington, D.C., Paris, and Senegal during 1991 as well as on materials cited. The authors thank the International Center for Economic Growth for funding and Jeff Coupe for research assistance.

cent of the population was involved in the agricultural sector, and poverty, malnutrition, and illiteracy remained endemic. In most social statistics, Senegal continued to lag behind other African states. Traditional and religious ties still played an important role and explained the strength of the clientelist relationships built around national politicians and leaders of the Muslim brotherhoods, called *marabouts*. Indeed, many Senegalese viewed the marabouts as their link both to God and to the state; the polarization generated by modern political parties was mediated by the vertical alliances between patrons and clients.

In contrast to the government's rhetoric and the heady discourse of Dakar intellectuals invoking "African socialism," development policy was characterized by a stagnant and highly protected manufacturing sector, an agricultural sector undermined by drought and wrong-headed policies, and the inexorable growth of a patronage-ridden and inefficient state bureaucracy. In the first two decades after independence, growth in gross domestic product (GDP) averaged at most 2.5 percent a year, barely keeping pace with the country's rapid population growth.

It is in this extremely fragile economy and hybrid political culture that a program of structural adjustment was formulated at the beginning of the 1980s by the Senegalese authorities with the help of the International Monetary Fund (IMF) and the World Bank. Senghor had retired at the end of 1980, and his hand-picked successor Abdou Diouf, a technocrat of impeccable credentials, promised to tackle the country's economic problems. Beyond regaining macroeconomic equilibrium, the program sought to spur long-term economic growth through a series of policy reforms that introduced price mechanisms and reduced the role of government in the allocation of resources. The government pledged to reduce its bureaucracy substantially, deregulate the market for domestic goods, gradually eliminate subsidies, liberalize the labor market, and stop protecting local industries from international trade. In sum, the program asked a long-subsidized economy, a polity trapped in the political logic of crony statism, and a public opinion molded by interventionist ideologies to accomplish an *aggiornamento*.

After a stuttering start, the country seemed to make good progress. President Diouf named Mamoudou Touré, then a high-level administrator in the IMF, to lead the adjustment effort as finance and economy minister, and an ambitious reform program was articulated. The economy improved enough for the IMF to call Senegal a model of African stabilization in 1988. Yet, a couple years later, much of the reform program had stalled, Touré had gone back to Washington, D.C., and external aid and lending agencies like the World Bank and USAID (U.S. Agency for International Development) were vowing to "get tough" with the government. In early 1991, the new prime minister, Habib Thiam, publicly declared his government's intentions to put reform on the back burner.

Why did economic reform prove so problematic during the 1980s? Why did the effort stall after a promising start? Observers of adjustment in Senegal—as indeed of economic reform throughout Sub-Saharan Africa—often emphasize one of two arguments to explain the disappointing results of two decades of adjustment. First, many observers argue that reform failed because the government lacked political will. Senegal's high degree of political pluralism is often adduced to suggest that the government's fear of electoral defeat slowed the pace of reform. Second, other observers argue that adjustment failed because the policy prescriptions of the International Monetary Fund and the World Bank were inappropriate for the African environment. In their estimation, the government did not implement more of the reform program because what it did implement proved disastrous.

Both of these arguments hold a kernel of truth but are ultimately not that useful for understanding the problems of adjustment in a country like Senegal. The political will argument assumes the government wanted adjustment but was afraid to carry it out because of societal pressures. In fact, state elites in Africa are rarely motivated by specific policies. Rather, they seek to maximize their chances of political survival and therefore base their policy decisions on perceptions of political risk. This is not to suggest that ideas do not matter; indeed, this chapter argues that a pervasive distrust of the private sector and a concomitant belief in the state's developmental functions conditioned all economic policy decisions during the adjustment period. Clearly, the ideological orientation of state elites shaped policy choices.

The commitment of state elites to adjustment policies was, nonetheless, a function of their assessment of how reform would affect political stability in the short to medium run. This was, in turn, a function of the credibility of reform and popular confidence regarding its sustainability. A small substratum of the state elite staked its professional future on adjustment. These were typically officials who ran the ministry policy units or the aid-funded technical assistance programs; typically trained in the West and having benefited from several adjustment workshops and seminars, they internalized the values of adjustment, whether by genuine conviction or professional opportunism. Most state officials were poorly informed about the strategy and objectives of adjustment, however, and did not stand to gain personally from it. The top of the state apparatus perceived adjustment as a highly risky undertaking with little or no immediate payoff. They did not lack political will so much as they were unconvinced that undertaking reform maximized their political welfare.

An analysis of the case of Senegal broadly confirms this contention. The regime did not espouse adjustment wholeheartedly because the reform package was not completely credible and muddling through within the current policy regime ultimately seemed the safer strategy. It is true, nonetheless, that Abdou Diouf came to power with reformist ambitions.

Indeed, he based his political legitimacy on his reformist credentials. He put together a team of technocrats that he hoped would be able to implement the reform program and sought to weaken the old-style politicians of the Senghor regime who constituted one of the main obstacles to reform. This led to the high point of economic reform, the period during which Touré was in charge of adjustment (1985–88) and unambiguously enjoyed Diouf's support. During that time, what some Senegalese intellectuals have called *le débat sur la technicité* tipped the balance in favor of reform. Helped by a brief improvement in the international environment and a strong economy, Touré convinced a majority of the political class that implementing the reform program was desirable. Although the reform package was credible, reformers within the government were never able to build a substantial coalition on behalf of it. After 1987, when the economy's downturn combined with increasing social unrest, the balance shifted in favor of the forces opposed to reform, effectively ending the reform interlude.

Profound doubt about the political merits of adjustment was justified intellectually, since many experts inside and outside Senegal did not believe in the program's capacity to lift the economy out of its endemic crisis. This is the second view that is emphasized in discussions of adjustment; it, in turn, has two variants. The first, which might be called the heterodox position, criticizes the adjustment strategy advanced by the twin sisters in Washington, D.C., but argues (more or, often, less explicitly) that there is an alternative path to adjustment (see Commander, Ndoye, and Ouedrago 1989; Diouf 1992; Duruflé 1988). The second, or pessimistic position, essentially doubts the capacity of the Senegalese economy to undertake sustained autonomous development. It argues that Senegal's problems are too significant and its resources too slight for adjustment to be possible, at least without massive infusions of foreign capital for years to come.

This study is not the appropriate forum for analyzing the economic merits of structural adjustment policies as presently conceived or for assessing Senegal's long-term development potential. For its purposes, this skepticism about adjustment is relevant because of its implications for domestic politics. Throughout the 1980s, the credibility of the reform effort was consistently undermined not only by the heterodox and pessimistic arguments made by local and international experts and scholars, but also by members of the community of external aid and lending agencies itself. These arguments fueled pervasive skepticism within the state apparatus about the reform program and its likely sociopolitical consequences. The actions of the external aid and lending agencies and the early effects of adjustment measures could not alter these negative attitudes within the political class.

This study measures the formal and informal political and institutional constraints facing authorities implementing the structural adjustment program in the 1980s. Embedded in an appreciation of economic institutions and realities, this political analysis argues that Senegal's inability to resort to devaluation because of its membership in the Franc Zone had important political implications. Moreover, the government's declining extractive capabilities and the resulting budgetary pressures conditioned its commitment to the reforms and their sustainability.

This analysis of the politics of adjustment develops several themes. First, it assesses the impact that pressure exerted by interest groups had on reform. The program's distributional consequences reduced the relative welfare of the social groups supporting the ruling party, the Socialist Party. These interest groups demonstrated a will to organize and acted in concert to promote and protect their collective interests. Their mobilization was facilitated by a multiparty system that allowed vested interests to be marshaled rapidly into opposition. The question, then, is the extent to which the program triggered opposition and demand for preserving the status quo or generated an organized movement of groups supporting liberalization. The proreform team in the government was never able to create a social coalition to sustain the reform process.

Second, one of the key comparative features of adjustment in Senegal is that it accompanied a process of political liberalization. National elections were held in 1983 and 1988, in the context of a stated desire on the part of President Diouf to see the peaceful emergence of multiparty democracy. What was the impact of democratization on adjustment and vice versa? Diouf believed the two processes were largely compatible, insofar as the forces most hostile to adjustment—the old guard in the Socialist Party—would be weakened by democratization. For the same reasons, he also believed that consolidating and maintaining his own power would be served by economic and political reform. The paradox is apparent: the regime's democratization in the 1980s never threatened Diouf's hold on the presidency.

Third, the program entailed bureaucratic reordering. Formulating and implementing a structural adjustment program was concomitant with the rise of technocrats to positions of leadership. The nature of the program increased their autonomy and power, since they had the scarce professional and technical skills the program required. The old administrative elite, however, lost status, discretionary powers, and income as a result of reform. This chapter investigates how old habits and jealousies among bureaucrats slowed or reversed implementation of the program, how well technocrats organized themselves to orient the government's actions, and how much the president tried to insulate and protect his technocrats in order to allow them to implement the difficult process of adjustment.

Finally, it investigates the role of external aid and lending agencies in the adjustment process. These agencies provided increasingly important resources to the Senegalese economy. Did their support abet or hinder the adjustment process? Although its role is ambiguous, aid clearly represented an important net resource for the state, which was strengthened, regardless of its commitment to reform. In addition, the need to ensure the continuous flow of aid from external agencies led the government to exaggerate threats to its stability.

This chapter is organized as follows: it begins with a review of the basic features of the Senegalese political economy in the years after independence followed by discussion of the adjustment program and the implementation record. The reasons why the program was not fully implemented are then assessed. Throughout, an avowedly political economy approach keeps explicit at all times the political implications of economic policies and clarifies the economic impact of political choices.

The Political Economy of Postcolonial Senegal

The current crisis has deep historical roots, and a short review of Senegal's economic history after independence is needed to understand more recent events. Senegal derived advantages from its central position in the French colonial system that left it ill prepared to handle the economic dilemmas of independence. Dakar had long served as the administrative capital of *Afrique Occidentale Française*, the federation of France's West African colonies, and as a result Dakar and its hinterlands had been favored in French investment programs. Dakar itself emerged as probably the most important commercial center on Africa's western coast and possessed an important non-African population, significant industry (Boone 1992), and an impressive communications infrastructure. Indeed, Senegal's gross national product (GNP) per capita in 1950, estimated at some $238 (in 1974 terms), was among the highest in Sub-Saharan Africa, topped only by that of the Republic of Congo, Côte d'Ivoire, Ghana, and Zambia.[1] On the face of it, the fledgling republic benefited from key economic advantages: France left Senegal with probably the best infrastructure in West Africa, a well-trained labor force, and a significant import-substitution industrial sector that had long benefited from a large, heavily protected market in French West Africa.

Economic Performance after Independence

The end of the colonial federation also dictated drastic adjustments for Senegal. With the end of preferential access to the rest of the French empire, the productive capacity of most manufacturing businesses was underused. Firms had to adjust to a smaller domestic market and the vicissitudes of international competition. In addition, Senegal was left with an oversized public administration and a public sector wage bill that the country could ill afford.[2] The population of a little more than 3 million persons at independence could not justify a central bureaucracy of 10,000 civil servants, based for the most part in Dakar and enjoying French civil service–scale salaries.[3]

Finally, the country needed to wean itself away from dependence on what had been the mainstay of the colonial economy, the groundnut sector. France had assiduously promoted the crop starting in the last quarter of the nineteenth century, and growth had been rapid if irregular: output reached 200,000 tons by 1914, 600,000 tons in 1937, and 1 million tons in 1965 (Amin 1973). By independence, roughly half of the land cultivated in any given year was devoted to groundnuts, a remarkably high percentage for a cash crop. France agreed to continue paying highly advantageous prices for Senegalese groundnuts after independence. During the 1960–67 period, groundnuts represented some 78 percent of all export revenues and constituted the largest single source of government revenues, while sales from oil mills represented 40 percent of industrial activity (Youm 1991, pp. 23–24). The elimination of export price supports by France in 1968, in the context of French participation in the Common Agricultural Policy of the European Economic Community, resulted in a decrease of some 25 percent in the country's terms of trade and began the progressive decline of the groundnut sector.[4]

Little or no growth could be expected from groundnuts, however, without a technological revolution: the crop's growth had been fueled almost entirely by increasing acreage, rather than by the use of yield-enhancing inputs. By the early 1960s, little new suitable land was still available (Bonnefond and Couty 1991), and increasing population pressures made food crops more attractive to farmers, who responded by leaving the groundnut economy. Higher productivity was needed to spur further growth but would be economical only in the higher-potential areas on the southern edge of the groundnut basin. Increasingly inadequate rainfall as well as the depletion and erosion of soils were, in fact, tending to decrease average yields. All in all, in the years following independence, the government could no longer realistically expect significant growth in what had been the mainstay of the colonial economy.

The government faced several challenges in the period following independence: it needed to (1) diversify production away from groundnuts, (2) make its industry more competitive, and (3) reduce the burden of the state on the economy. Clearly, without these adjustments, sustained economic growth would prove highly problematic. Indeed, the government's inability to address these problems, along with several trade shocks during the 1970s and the recurrence of drought, ensured the slow but steady decline of the economy during the first two decades after independence. There is considerable disagreement over most Senegalese economic statistics, but estimates of the evolution of GDP for the 1960–85 period suggest an average annual growth rate of around 2.5 percent. Given an annual population growth of some 2.9 percent, individual incomes declined during this period.

Through the 1970s and early 1980s, the country's industrial cost structure continued to make Senegalese products noncompetitive outside the Franc Zone and helped produce a chronic trade deficit. The average annual trade deficit in goods and services totaled some CFAF36.4 billion between 1970 and 1980, while total exports exceeded CFAF200 billion only once during this period, in 1977.[5] Dependence on imports was particularly notable in the area of foodstuffs. France had encouraged the importation of cheap rice from its colonies in Indochina, and rice became a staple of the diet, particularly in urban settings, despite being all but absent from traditional farming systems. By 1974, the cost of imported rice had reached CFAF18 billion, and imported food accounted for 5–10 percent of the value of all imports (Craven and Tuluy 1981; Youm 1991, p. 25).

Successive governments grappled with these structural problems. To decrease real wages in the public sector to levels consistent with post-colonial fiscal realities, the government imposed a wage freeze on public sector employees from independence until 1968. Throughout the 1970s and early 1980s as well, the real wages of public servants were allowed to fall close to one-third (Berg 1990, p. 12). This freeze sharply lowered the real urban wage because the private sector followed the lead set by the state on salaries (see table 8-1). The common perception that post-colonial economic policies have routinely favored urban workers at the expense of the countryside (Bates 1981; Lofchie 1975) is thus, in the case of Senegal, something of a simplification. Between 1960 and 1983, average urban income was halved, while rural incomes decreased a more modest 22 percent.[6] The perception is accurate, however, in the sense that the government was never able or willing to contain growth of public sector employment, in part because of pressures to deal with the problem of unemployment. As indicated in table 8-1, the central bureaucracy grew from some 10,000 employees at independence to 37,700 in 1970 and 59,300 in 1980.[7] As a result, the public sector wage bill still accounted for close to 60 percent of government recurrent expenditures in 1980, despite the reduction in the real wage of the individual civil servant.

Public sector direct involvement in production was for the most part limited to agriculture. The government allowed private French and Middle Eastern interests as well as increasingly aggressive local businessmen to dominate most industrial sectors, albeit in the context of considerable influence peddling, rent seeking, and favoritism (Boone 1992). Direct public sector involvement was focused on agriculture, reasonably perceived as an area of critical importance in which market imperfections justified an important role for the state. An impressive apparatus of

Table 8-1. Civil Service Employment in Senegal, 1970–90

Fiscal year	Government wage bill (billions of CFA francs)	Total employment (thousands)	Average monthly earnings (CFA francs)	
			Thousands	Deflated
1970	20.8	37.7	46.0	107.9
1971	21.6	38.5	46.8	105.6
1972	23.3	39.7	48.9	103.8
1973	25.5	40.6	52.3	99.9
1974	32.0	42.7	62.5	102.4
1975	37.0	45.9	67.2	83.5
1976	40.8	—	—	—
1977	41.8	52.7	66.1	73.0
1978	48.4	51.8	77.9	89.6
1979	68.5	56.9	100.3	90.8
1980	79.4	59.3	111.6	100.0
1981	83.3	63.0	110.2	93.2
1982	92.7	66.3	116.5	84.0
1983	100.4	67.7	123.6	79.8
1984	106.6	67.0	132.6	76.6
1985	111.8	68.8	135.4	69.2
1986	119.8	68.1	146.6	70.5
1987	122.3	67.1	151.9	76.3
1988	125.2	66.5	156.9	80.3
1989	126.8	63.6	167.7	85.5
1990	129.5	63.7	—	—

— Not available.
Source: Berg 1990, pp. 4, 194; World Bank staff estimates.

public institutions was developed in the years after independence, including ONCAD (National Office of Cooperation and Assistance for Development) and its successor agency the National Company for Rural Procurement, the Company for Agricultural Development and Dissemination, SAED (Society for the Development and Management of the Delta), the Company for the Development of Casamance, and SODEFITEX (Company for the Development of Textile Fibers).[8] These organizations sought to intervene in every aspect of the rural economy.

The state's deployment of resources generated by the agricultural and the mining sectors is at the heart of the political economy of Senegal. Over the past thirty years, the government has invested financial and human resources to improve the productivity of the two main commodities, groundnuts and phosphates. An average of 10 percent of all public investment was devoted to the rural economy during this period (Touré 1985, p. 12). The government pushed for the extension of new crops such as cotton, maize, and cowpeas. Specialized public agencies distributed credit, seeds, subsidized fertilizers, and equipment to about 1,700 state cooperatives in villages throughout the country (Barker 1985; Delgado and Jammeh 1991; Waterbury and Gersovitz 1987). It invested heavily in infrastructure for irrigated agriculture, notably along the Senegal River (Freud 1988).

The government also taxed agriculture, notably by paying farmers well below world market prices. Thus, producer prices for groundnuts averaged only 43 percent of unit export prices during the 1970s.[9] Policymakers argued that taxing agriculture was justified because it funded investments that increased productivity and thus increased or maintained net producer incomes. Using smallholder surpluses to finance public institutions spearheading agricultural development conformed to the dominant development fashions of the day and was eagerly promoted by external aid and lending agencies as well as the government. These institutions and the taxes meant to pay for them would have justified themselves had they engineered significant improvements in agricultural productivity or even prevented its erosion. The fact is, however, that government intervention in agriculture did not generate sustainable increases in either yields or aggregate production.

In particular, the government was only partly successful in diversifying its exports away from groundnuts. By 1982, groundnut products were still the single largest export, accounting for 25 percent of all exports, while phosphates and fishing accounted for 11 and 18 percent, respectively. (Senegal is the seventh largest producer of phosphates in the world, with annual sales of 15 million tons.) Within agriculture, groundnuts retained its central position, although peasants tended to devote an increasing share of their land to food crops. Projects to promote the large-scale irrigated cultivation of crops like rice yielded disappointing results despite cost overruns that rendered them largely uneconomical.

To be fair to the government, it must be said that agricultural policy was conducted in the context of highly variable and declining rainfall. The level of rainfall fell from an average of 799 millimeters a year in 1961–65 to 448 millimeters a year in 1981–85: drought conditions reigned in 1968, 1970, 1972, 1973, 1978, 1980, 1984, and 1985 (World Bank 1989b, p. 49). The effects of this natural calamity were related to and compounded by human activities that accelerated the deterioration of an already fragile ecosystem, notably through deforestation, overgrazing, and improper crop rotation.

The policy of spearheading the development process with an expansive and intrusive public sector was never an economic success, leading eventually to the current crisis. It was much more successful in political terms, as these institutions helped the regime consolidate its power and then maintain political stability.

The Politics of State-Led Growth

After independence, the state extracted revenues from commodity production to buy support from rural elites, the civil service, and, to a lesser extent, the labor union hierarchy and the security and defense apparatus.

The relative strength of these groups and of religious and political patrons was reflected in their differential access to state resources and rents.
At the same time, economic stagnation put increasing pressure on the
state to limit transfers to them.

Politics was conditioned, first, by the presence of three somewhat
overlapping groups, all based essentially in Dakar: civil servants, members of trade unions, and students. The civil service constituted the social
base of the regime and was its primary clientele. Its political power can
be traced back to the middle of the nineteenth century when France
enfranchised a small number of urban African elites and then granted full
political rights to the country's four biggest towns (Dakar, Gorée, Ru-
fisque, and Saint-Louis) as *communes de plein exercise*. As independence
approached, the main beneficiaries of this policy of assimilation were the
African civil servants, since the public sector was the leading avenue of
social promotion for educated elites (Crowder 1962).

Leaders of the nationalist movement made generous promises in order
to win the support of what was the most cohesive and powerful social
category in the political system. After independence, civil servants continued to receive high salaries and extensive entitlements, such as health
care, housing assistance, and so on. In exchange for these benefits, the
bureaucracy became a client of the ruling party, and high-level administrative posts became politicized. The overlap of party and state allowed
state elites to use administrative institutions to distribute rents, patronage, and other resources in exchange for loans, illicit investments,
and profits. They also controlled and benefited from the inflows of foreign aid.

Senghor used the resources of the state to consolidate power and then
reward supporters, co-opt opponents, and play political factions against
one another. Such political strategies necessarily fueled state growth and
conditioned the choice of a state-led development strategy. In addition,
the civil service's influence on policy was reinforced by the size of the
public sector inherited from the colonial period, the fact that it was
concentrated in Dakar, and its organization in the trade unions. Public
sector employment, defined as the civil service plus noncommercial public enterprises, comprised 52 percent of total employment in the formal
sector in 1960 and still 45 percent in 1980.[10]

The state's relationship to organized labor was more complex. Senegal
had a long tradition of labor movement activities, and unions had played
a key role during the decolonization period. However, the postcolonial
state soon excluded the most militant and confrontational unionists from
labor leadership. In 1968, widespread discontent in its rank and file led
the National Union of Senegalese Workers to break ranks with the ruling
coalition and call for a national strike to protest the decline in living
standards of its membership. The government dissolved that union,
banned all independent union activity, and created the National Confed-

eration of Senegalese Workers (Confédération Nationale des Travailleurs Sénégalais, or CNTS) as the official trade union linked to the ruling party. In keeping with the state's general strategy of repression coupled with co-optation, the CNTS was guaranteed ministerial posts, as well as the vice presidency and ten deputies in the National Assembly, in exchange for helping maintain social peace. The union was also assured of representation in major bodies such as the Economic and Social Council (Conseil Économique et Social) and the boards of parastatals. In turn, it adopted the policy of *participation responsable,* under which it discouraged strikes and promoted rank-and-file support for the single party. The CNTS came to represent some sixty or so individual unions, with a membership between 50,000 and 60,000 workers. Its presence in the government allowed it to promote favorable labor legislation, as well as to lobby for subsidies on basic consumer items such as sugar, rice, and bread.

The students—bureaucrats in the making—also received the attention of the government and were the third important group in urban politics, in part because of their sheer numbers in a country where more than half the population was below twenty years of age. Moreover, the University of Dakar, initially designed to serve all of Francophone West Africa, was now essentially Senegalese and increasingly radicalized on political and economic issues. Students received scholarships, free tuition, subsidized meals and rooms, as well as guaranteed jobs after graduation. Despite this, the government never succeeded in incorporating the majority of students in official youth organizations. On the contrary, schools were often disturbed by sporadic demonstrations and strikes. In fact, the student riots of 1968 posed the most serious threat to governmental stability in the decades after independence.

Before independence, politics had been largely circumscribed to these urban groups. The first generation of nationalist leaders, men like Blaise Diagne and Lamine Guèye, hardly bothered seeking support in the countryside. Leopold Senghor's rise to power was due, at least in part, to his early grasp of the importance of rural support (Coulon 1990). As the franchise was progressively extended to the countryside, his party's superior organization there ensured him electoral victory. To consolidate his power and ensure political stability, Senghor sought alliances with rural elites and, in particular, with leaders of the Islamic brotherhoods, or marabouts, who dominate rural society.

In Senegal, Islamic brotherhoods carry significant political weight (for a much more complete introduction to them, see Copans 1988; Coulon 1981; Magassouba 1985; O'Brien 1975). More than 90 percent of the population in Senegal embrace Islam, although less than half did so at the turn of the century. The main vehicle for propagating Islam during the twentieth century has been the Islamic brotherhoods. Today, most Muslims are affiliated with one of the three major brotherhoods: the Tijaniyya, the Mourides, and the Qadiriyya, each distinguished by slight differences in conduct and ritual, but all practicing the Sufi form of Islam. Although there are literally hundreds of marabouts, the brother-hoods are hierarchically organized and led by *khalifes* who can trace their origin to the founder of the brotherhood.

The marabouts' political role started in the colonial period and in-creased during decolonization. The French colonial administration pro-moted the authority and power of the brotherhood leaders as an instru-ment of social control, and marabouts feared that independence would rupture the country's relations with France. They sought to guarantee French economic and political interests in the country. Their stance helped weaken the most intransigent militant leaders within the national-ist movement. In the early years of independence, these religious leaders sided with Senghor against Prime Minister Dia and his team of techno-crats, accusing them of introducing rural policies that sought to liberate small producers from the rural elite. The state under Senghor and Diouf continued to use the marabouts as intermediaries in the countryside and as instruments of social control. The marabouts were important bene-ficiaries of state action, obtaining free distribution of or subsidies for seeds, fertilizers, and equipment. They had easy access to capital, with little pressure to pay back loans, and were able to import duty-free goods. They also served as intermediaries between the state and the peas-antry: as patrons, they could guarantee jobs for their followers in the state administration, which they were allowed to influence; and they secured strategically placed development projects such as roads, wells, schools, and industries for their client areas (Copans 1988; Coulon 1981; Gellar 1982; O'Brien 1971, 1975; Schumacher 1975).

The state's generosity toward the marabouts had economic and politi-cal foundations. First, the marabouts controlled large groundnut estates of their own and enjoyed the free labor of their followers, called *taalibe*. A *zakat,* or tithe, also brought them a share of the harvest from the private farms of other followers. O'Brien (1977, p. 223) estimates that the khalife general of the Mourides received well over $100,000 annually from groundnuts during the 1970s. His own farms totaled more than 750 hectares (Copans 1980, pp. 243–44). In addition, the marabouts exercised considerable influence over the economic decisions of the taa-libe, notably the crops selected at the beginning of each year. As many as two-thirds of all groundnut producers were affiliated with the Mouride brotherhood alone, which accounted for as much as two-thirds of the crop every year. Thus, the approval of the marabouts was critical to the success of any agricultural program (Barker 1985; Markovitz 1970; Wa-terbury and Gersovitz 1987). Second, marabouts could deliver the rural vote. In a country where 70 percent of the population was rural and illiterate and where policies were discussed in a foreign language and decided by a westernized elite, marabouts provided the link to the masses. Even though they did not make policies, their support for a leader or a political party generally decided the election. As the regime democratized after 1976, their political importance grew.

The influence of the marabouts, the civil service, and the unions in the allocation of resources was considerable; that of the small agricultural producer and the embryonic Senegalese entrepreneur was not. As discussed, government agricultural policy emphasized large parastatals that were supposed to promote intensive production, not incentives for individual farmers. State institutions were allowed to fall under the control of rural elites. The government's treatment of smallholder agriculture led to what has been called the *malaise paysan*, a wave of rural discontent that grew after 1968.

Farmers were not, however, completely powerless to affect government decisions. Peasants began withdrawing from the production of cash crops and turning toward subsistence crops. They boycotted the official structures in favor of parallel markets and refused to pay the debts they had accumulated toward the state. Even the usually conservative religious leaders joined the peasant movement. In 1970, for example, the marabouts openly undermined the state's authority by refusing to bless the groundnut seeds and then blessing only those of the food crops millet and sorghum. The peasantry's actions denied the state the resources to carry out its policies. In a response that has not varied since, the government briefly increased groundnut prices, forgave peasant debts, and promoted the construction of schools, health care facilities, and water wells in the most sensitive areas. In addition, it increased its assiduous courting of the marabouts. Debt forgiveness was the most important of these measures, given its fiscal implications: in 1981/82, for example, the government canceled CFAF30 billion of farmers' debt, which would not have been paid anyway.[11]

As Barker (1985, p. 64) perceptively notes, the lack of durable changes in relative prices reflected the political weakness of small producers. Indeed, besides keeping producer prices low, authorities also sought to maintain a rural power structure characterized by the domination of religious leaders, local notables, and party bosses. Thus, small farmers had no institutional leverage to lobby for more timely technical services or better prices. In 1972, the government introduced some reforms in rural administration that officially sought to give rural populations a larger role in local administration. Issues of law and order, rural community budgets, rural taxes, and land allocation were to be discussed in locally elected councils, thus increasing popular participation. These rural councils were nonetheless placed under the supervision and tutelage of the local administrative authority—the *sous-préfet*—obliging the local population to operate within a policy framework set by the government. Furthermore, the reforms served to strengthen the hand of the rural elites, whose influence and power undermined open debate, and further stifled the possibility of political pluralism and change.

Finally, state policies prevented the emergence of an autonomous national business class. At independence, French businessmen owned more than 95 percent of the firms in the modern manufacturing sector, which included some ninety-five businesses in 1963. The French monopolized the modern banking sector and import-export trade as well. Senegalese entrepreneurs were left to compete with the Lebanese community for retail trade and small-scale businesses in the service sector.[12] During the 1960s, government policies did not challenge the dominance of the French firms, which remained undiminished. As late as 1967, for example, Senegalese businessmen obtained only about CFAF700 million of loans made by the banking sector, some 3 percent of a total of CFAF22 billion loaned that year (Bathily 1989). Government import-substitution policies favored French interests, notably in the allocation of investment incentives (Lo 1991, p. 65).

The progressive Africanization of the economy during the 1960s and 1970s did not strengthen the business class (Boone 1990, pp. 433–37). French withdrawal was followed by state control, an expanding public sector, and growing politicization of the opportunities left for the private sector. Thus, in the agricultural sector, state interventionist policies drove Senegalese intermediaries out of the niche left them by the colonial administration. In 1968, Senegalese businessmen formed the National Union of Senegalese Economic Groups to protest government policies and demand access to import opportunities, loans guaranteed by the state, control of the Chamber of Commerce, and protection for their nascent enterprises (Bathily 1989). These protests, as well as the labor and student unrest in 1968, led the government to nationalize several important private businesses and utility companies. The 1970s thus witnessed the progressive emergence of a more aggressive industrial policy on the part of the state and implementation of most of the union's demands. Industrial policy was used as a political instrument, however, rather than as a development strategy. The ruling party used the parastatals to finance its activities and to find jobs for many of its adherents. Relations between government and business were characterized by clientelism and cronyism, with access to loans, licenses, subsidies, and government contracts being greatly facilitated for persons claiming family or political ties to the ruling elite. When the first opposition parties put the interests of the Senegalese business class at the forefront of their electoral platforms, the state treasury became even more generous to Senegalese *hommes d'affaires*, many of whom had more political connections than business acumen. Given these circumstances and the chronic overvaluation of the CFA franc, it is little wonder that the profitability of private enterprises depended on the absence of internal competition and the efficacy of import controls (Boone 1991).

The private sector was weakened by its dependence on the state. Given its need for a dynamic business sector to promote growth, exports, and tax revenues, the Senegalese government was surprisingly reluctant to foster an autonomous capitalist stratum after independence. This reluctance was motivated in part by the fear that an independent business class would use its power to undermine the regime in power and the understanding that manipulating economic policies in a clientelist fashion would be politically advantageous as well as profitable for friends and kin. In addition, industrial policy was influenced by ideological motives. The appeal of socialist rhetoric played its role here, but even first-generation technocrats who paid only lip service to African socialism had a profound distrust of the ability of the market to value and allocate resources. At least in part because the private sector was widely associated with French and other foreign interests and thus genuinely unpopular, state elites were comforted in their view that full sovereignty and economic development required significant state regulation of the economy.

Democratization of the Regime after 1976

The Senegalese constitution, which has been amended several times since independence, provides for a presidential system of government. The president is elected by direct universal suffrage for a five-year term, as are members of the National Assembly. Half of the 120 members of the National Assembly are elected on the basis of a nationwide system of proportional representation, and half are elected on a winner-take-all system of departmental lists.

The period after independence witnessed the centralization of power in the presidency and the weakening of the legislature. During the 1964–74 period, the party and the state were progressively fused and the power of the president reinforced, all in the name of national construction (Lo 1987). President Senghor emerged from his power struggle with Mamadou Dia in 1962 with the firm intention of centralizing power and making future challenges to his preeminence impossible. He eliminated the prime minister's office and began centralizing authority within the office of the presidency, taking decisionmaking authority away from most ministries. Two technocrats gained prominence by assisting Senghor's attempts to centralize power: Jean Collin and Abdou Diouf. Jean Collin, a French colonial administrator who had taken Senegalese nationality at independence, used his position as secretary general of the presidency between 1962 and 1964 and then in various cabinets to help Senghor centralize power. An able administrator and brilliant player of bureaucratic politics, he emerged as the second most powerful man in the Diouf regime in the mid-1980s.[13] Abdou Diouf, a young technocrat trained in France, entered the government in May 1963 as head of the president's cabinet before replacing Collin in the post of secretary general of the presidency in February 1964. He held this post until his nomination as Senghor's prime minister in 1970, with an interlude as planning minister.

Some parties were banned, while others were pressured into rallying the Progressive Senegalese Union (Union Progressiste Sénégalaise), so that by the 1968 elections, the party ran uncontested. This period also saw the rise of the "barons" within the party, conservative politicians closely tied to clientelist networks, and the decline of the progressive technocrats, most of whom had sided with Dia. Although such labels should be taken with a grain of salt, it seems clear that despite his lofty rhetoric, Senghor ruled increasingly through the skillful manipulation of clan politics within the single party and state in a process that enhanced the importance of the old guard of clientelist leaders who had strong bases of rural support (Foltz 1977).

The ideology of national construction was formally abandoned in 1975, and new political parties as well as new autonomous unions were legally recognized. Since then, there has been a cautious and progressive process of democratization, with constitutional changes in 1976 and 1979. The regime has come to allow real political pluralism, without threatening the preeminent position of the former single party, renamed the Socialist Party in 1976 (Coulon 1990; Fatton 1987; Mbodji 1991).

The democratization of the regime after 1975 coincided with a return to favor of technocrats in a process clearly abetted by the regime's economic problems and the sense that the old clientelist politics were undermining the search for economic solutions. Senghor began promoting a younger generation of civil servants with foreign degrees who clearly intended to solve the country's economic ills and exhibited considerable impatience with the old, less educated barons. The symbol of this generation came to be Abdou Diouf, by then Senghor's undisputed *dauphin*. Diouf's growing influence within the state and within the ruling party during the 1970s came from his technocratic credentials. Although that image was oversold to the public in order to attract young technocrats, rejuvenate the political system, and convey a more credible image of the country to external aid and lending agencies, his appointment as prime minister was clearly part of a strategy for improving the government's management of the increasingly vulnerable economy. Throughout the 1970s, he was the economic adviser to a poet-president whose understanding of economic issues was at best limited. When President Senghor resigned at the end of 1980, and Diouf became president, this younger generation of well-trained, ambitious civil servants was in a good position to fight for control of the party and the government.

The Onset of Crisis

Given the nation's structural economic problems and political pressures, it is remarkable that the country managed to avoid recourse to the IMF as long as it did. Fundamental economic problems were masked by several factors. First, the continuation of French preferential treatment for groundnut exports artificially sustained the country's terms of trade in the years immediately after independence. Its termination in 1968 contributed to Senegal's first fiscal crisis in the early 1970s, but the government was able to take advantage of Franc Zone rules in order to avoid fiscal retrenchment and stabilization (Plane 1990). The French treasury intervened to cover Senegal's deficits, although the government did accumulate arrears on various payments.

The commodities boom of 1974–77 saved the economy from this crisis and further delayed reform. In 1974, the price of phosphates increased 274 percent and that of groundnut oil, 132 percent. During the next three years, the price of phosphates remained steady, while that of groundnut oil increased. Overall, Senegal's terms of trade improved dramatically during this period, even though the first oil shock had significantly raised the energy bill (Gersovitz 1987, p. 38). The government suddenly found itself with impressive surpluses; in the single fiscal year 1976–77, state marketing of groundnuts and phosphates generated a surplus of CFAF10 billion for the national budget (Touré 1985, p. 37). The government did not use these windfall revenues to promote investment or to slow the growth of debt accumulated during the previous decade. Instead, it increased government consumption 78 percent between 1974 and 1977, the industrial minimal wage 82 percent in 1974, and the producer price for groundnuts 30 percent in 1974 and 38 percent in 1975 (Youm 1991, p. 26).

With the blessing and financial assistance of the external aid and lending agencies, Senegal also embarked on another round of public sector investment, financed in part with the petrodollars that international banks were all too willing to lend. The pace of parastatal growth quickened, with investments of dubious value and the increasingly careless management of resources. The result was the accumulation of public debt, much of it in the parastatal sector. Thus, ONCAD possessed debts of more than CFAF90 billion by the early 1980s (Caswell 1984); SOSAP, a parastatal for fisheries, had debts of CFAF12 billion; and SAED had debts of CFAF10 billion. The nation's total external public debt was estimated at $1.3 billion, or 45 percent of GDP, in 1980.

The government evidently believed that the commodities boom would continue and that cyclical downturns could be overcome with the help of external aid and lending agencies, whose assistance to Senegal had increased rapidly since the Sahel drought. Indeed, as Lewis (1987, pp. 282–90) has shown, during the 1970s, international transfers more than compensated the decline in domestic investment. The government's optimism initially seemed well founded, since the mid-1970s also saw an average annual rate of growth in GNP of 4.5 percent, the highest since independence. Unfortunately, the boom in phosphates and groundnut oil collapsed in 1978, a severe drought occurred that year, and the second oil shock hit the economy in 1979. The economy found itself in another financial crisis. By 1981, the current account deficit had reached one-

Table 8-2. *Macroeconomic Indicators for Senegal, 1981–90*

Indicator	1981	1982	1983	1984	1985	1986	1987	1988	1989	1990
	(in billions of current CFA francs)									
Gross domestic product	674	849	945	1,022	1,151	1,304	1,382	1,483	1,478	1,590
Primary	120	184	203	173	217	291	300	333	282	327
Secondary	107	127	146	174	205	228	247	273	272	292
Tertiary	447	537	595	674	736	785	836	877	921	971
Resource balance	−130	−104	−116	−97	−130	−71	−78	−75	−78	−64
Imports[a]	347	395	427	484	474	416	423	448	474	474
Exports[a]	216	291	311	387	344	346	346	373	396	410
Net official transfers	48	60	60	61	60	61	64	61	72	75
Fiscal balance[b]	−70	−77	−78	−54	−50	−47	−60	−64	−70	−8
Expenditures	222	253	270	258	269	298	311	310	330	309
Revenues	152	176	189	204	219	251	251	246	260	301
	(as a percentage of gross domestic product)									
Gross domestic investment	11.9	11.3	11.9	11.7	9.8	11.0	11.7	12.5	10.8	12.7
Fiscal balance[c]	−9.3	−8.7	−7.9	−5.0	−4.1	−3.5	−4.2	−4.4	−4.6	−0.5
Resource balance	−19.3	−12.3	−12.3	−9.5	−11.2	−5.4	−5.6	−5.0	−5.3	−4.0
Imports[b]	51.4	46.5	45.2	47.4	40.9	31.9	30.6	30.2	32.1	29.8
Exports[b]	32.1	34.2	32.9	37.9	29.7	26.5	25.0	25.2	26.8	25.8
Inflation rate										
European current price index	11.3	12.5	9.4	8.5	8.0	6.2	−2.2	−0.4	0.1	4.7
African current price index	5.9	17.4	11.6	11.8	13.1	6.1	−4.1	−1.8	0.4	0.3
Exchange rate (CFA francs per U.S. dollar)[d]	272	329	381	437	449	346	301	298	319	272

Note: Errors are due to rounding.

a. Trade figures include goods and nonfactor services.

b. On cash basis, before debt rescheduling. Dates refer to fiscal (for example, 1981 refers to fiscal 1981/82).

c. Annual average.

d. Provisional estimate.

Source: Estimates of the World Bank staff; World Bank 1989a, 1989b; International Monetary Fund, various years.

fifth of GDP, while the government's budget deficit now totaled 9.3 percent (see table 8-2). Between 1977 and 1982, real GNP is estimated to have declined an annual average of 5.3 percent.

The Adjustment Experience, 1980–91

The government's initial response to the crisis was indecisive and mixed. Segments of the state elite evidently believed the problems were cyclical and could be overcome with fresh infusions of capital from external aid and lending agencies in a pattern already well established (Lewis 1987, pp. 289–99). Thus, despite its difficulties, the government canceled farmers' debts again in 1978 and allowed public sector wages to increase some 36 percent in 1979, with further negative consequences for the deficit.

Abdou Diouf and Reform

Officially, the government responded to this crisis with a short-term stabilization plan in December 1979, the Medium-Term Economic and Financial Recovery Plan (EFRP), which covered the 1980–84 period and provided the framework for several early adjustment efforts by external aid and lending agencies. A first structural loan was signed with the World Bank in December 1979, and an extended fund facility credit was negotiated with the IMF in August 1980 (Senegal's relationship with the World Bank is exhaustively reviewed in a 1989 report by the Bank's Operations Evaluation Department; see World Bank 1989b). The government promised to reduce the current account deficit from almost 16 percent of GDP to between 6 and 7 percent, to increase net public savings from 15 percent of public investment in 1981 to 25 percent in 1985, to raise the overall level of investment from 16 percent in 1981 to 18 percent in 1985, and to achieve a 4 percent annual growth of GDP (Duruflé 1988; World Bank 1989b, pp. 20–22).

It is in this climate of economic uncertainty at the end of 1980 that Senghor resigned in favor of Diouf. In his first speech as president in January 1981, Diouf acknowledged the need for major economic and political changes in the country and made explicit the reformist ambitions of his presidency. As prime minister since 1970, Diouf appreciated the severity of the economic crisis and the unsustainability of current policies. He had played a large role in drafting the EFRP (Lewis 1987, p. 302). The slogan "Moins d'Etat, Mieux d'Etat" (Less State, Better State) reflected Diouf's heartfelt belief as a technocrat in the possibility of creating a more efficient developmental role for the state. That is not to say that he fully espoused the economic liberalism of the U.S.-based institutions. The ideal state for Diouf and his allies was still a highly *dirigiste* state, but one without the cronyism and political expediencies of the old single-party model.

He was well aware of the obstacles to reform, however. The political and administrative leadership was deeply divided over the speed of reform, not only because of its uncertainties, but also because many benefited from the current policies. Moreover, the inefficient and slow-moving Senegalese administration was a poor instrument for change. As the appointed heir to Senghor, Diouf found it difficult to control the political game and rein in the old regime's barons, who had independent power bases, particularly within the Socialist Party. Insofar as Diouf had a power base, it lay within the state apparatus, not the ruling party.

Diouf's dilemmas were exemplified by the failures of the EFRP. The government was not able to redress the economic situation, despite the financial support of the external aid and lending agencies. Part of the blame lay in the bad weather of 1980 and 1981, which led to terrible groundnut crops and greater food imports. In addition, public debt turned out to be much higher than originally admitted, and the government proved incapable of balancing expenditures and revenues (table 8-2). In fact, fiscal revenues declined 10 percent in real terms between 1979 and 1984 (Duruflé 1988, p. 31). Furthermore, the government lost ground in the months preceding the elections in February 1983 as urban salaries rose considerably.[14] The IMF had already discontinued the extended fund facility credit in January 1981 and replaced it with one-year standby agreements. The World Bank canceled the second tranche of its first structural adjustment loan (SAL I) in June 1983 because of noncompliance.

The process of democratization that Diouf put in motion in 1981 must be understood in this context. The progressive and controlled democratization of the regime served the interests of economic reform in several ways. First, as a long-standing demand of the opposition, democratization would provide Diouf with greater legitimacy and deflect attention away from the economic crisis. Senghor opposed the democratization measures, so Diouf's initiative was welcomed and helped defuse political polarization and opposition to the economic program taking shape. Confident that there was no policy alternative to economic reform and—perhaps more important—that he could maintain control over the political game, Diouf may have felt that the greater pluralism of multiparty democracy would serve as a useful pressure valve and help channel discontent.

Second, Diouf believed that democratization would serve the interests of economic reform by forcing the state to be more accountable and disciplined. Democratization was thus a weapon against the old Senghor barons whose clientelism and corruption Diouf believed to be responsible for the crisis. Democratization would free him from the grips of the Socialist Party. In plebiscitary fashion, democratization would bestow enough power on the presidency and legitimacy on Diouf himself to enable him to accomplish reform without recourse to the web of Socialist Party networks on which Senghor had based his own power.

In this context Diouf moved to liberalize the political system despite foot dragging from the party bosses. There were already four political parties: the ruling Socialist Party; the Senegalese Democratic Party, a liberal democratic party; the African Independence Party, Marxist in orientation; and the conservative Senegalese Republican Movement. On the day of his inauguration, the new president promised to remove all legal restrictions on political parties. Twelve new parties soon emerged, covering the political spectrum, although none had a solid power base (see table 8-3). The only party that proved capable of gaining significant electoral support was the Senegalese Democratic Party, led by the attorney Abdoulaye Wade. Gaining roughly one-fifth of the vote in 1978 and 1983, it alone received support from different segments of society. Other parties received support largely from urban intellectuals.

The failure of the EFRP indicated the obstacles to economic reform. Diouf knew he could not undertake the necessary structural reforms of the state and of the Socialist Party without a popular mandate, which he sought in a general election held in February 1983 (Hesseling 1985, pp. 292–300; O'Brien 1983). These elections, which he promised would be the freest in Senegal's history, were risky. His promises of political liberalization had, as he had gambled, gained him the goodwill of the public, and he won the presidential race with an impressive 84 percent of the vote, beating five rivals. The multiparty system in fact split the opposition, especially the extreme left, and helped inflate the Socialist Party's dominance, which officially won 80 percent of the vote and 111 out of 120 seats. For the first time, the party proved less popular than Diouf himself. Despite the low turnout and allegations of fraud (only 58 percent of registered voters actually voted; see Coulon 1990, p. 426), the elections strengthened Diouf's position and provided him with a popular mandate and considerable legitimacy to begin serious economic and political reforms.

Armed thus, he abandoned the EFRP and replaced it with the Economic Adjustment Plan in the Medium and Long Term (PAML), which was announced in mid-1984. Diouf moved quickly to increase his personal control over the administration. First, he eliminated the post of prime minister through the constitutional revision of 1983 and introduced several other institutional changes to limit the power of the National Assembly and reinforce the presidential character of the Senegalese system. As he explained, eliminating the Prime Ministry would "lessen the number of intermediaries and accelerate decisionmaking and provide the presidency with a direct understanding of the problems of the Senegalese people" (authors' translation, quoted in Wane 1990, p. 84).

Second, the most unpopular barons were eased out of the government and replaced with men and women with obvious technical qualifications. Among the new ministers were well-known opposition leaders as well as experts familiar with international organizations. Technocrats increased their number within the government but also improved their position in

Table 8-3. Political Parties in Senegal, in Order of their Founding, 1947–88

Party	Description	Date founded
Socialist Party (Parti Socialiste)	Democratic socialist; member of the Socialist International	October 27, 1947
Senegalese Democratic Party (Parti Démocratique Sénégalais)	Center right	Founded August 8, 1974
African Independence Party (Parti Africain de l'Indépendance)	Split of the old African Indendence Party of 1957; Marxist-Leninist	Recognized August 1976
Republican Movement of Senegal (Mouvement Républicain Sénégalais)	Conservative	Founded February 7, 1979
National Democratic Rally (Rassemblement National Démocratique)	Nationalist and pan-Africanist	Legalized June 18, 1981
Socialist Workers Organization (Organisation Socialiste des Travailleurs)	Trotskyist	Founded July 4, 1981
Democratic League / Movement for the Workers Party (Ligue Démocratique / Mouvement pour le Parti du Travail)	Marxist-Leninist	Legalized July 9, 1981
And-Jëff / Revolutionary Movement for New Democracy (And-Jëff / Mouvement Révolutionnaire pour la Démocratie Nouvelle)	Marxist	Legalized July 9, 1981
Party of Independence and Labor (Parti de l'Indépendance et du Travail)	Split of the old Party of African Independence	Founded July 9, 1981

the ranking order of the ministers, an important indication of their growing influence in decisionmaking. Technocratic skills and the ability to generate alternative analysis became an important criterion for positions of leadership, rather than simply one's position within the Socialist Party. The promotion of independent technocrats indicated Diouf's intention to free himself from the ruling party. In addition, of course, these technocrats tended to be less well known and typically lacked their own power base, making them more dependent on the presidency.

Third, Diouf sought to improve the internal capacities of government by initiating several administrative reforms. He reinforced data collection and policy analysis capabilities to improve the government's infor-

Party	Description	Date founded
Union for a People's Democracy (Union pour la Démocratie Populaire)	Left	Founded July 20, 1981
Senegalese People's Party (Parti Populaire Sénégalais)	Pragmatist	Founded October 12, 1981
African Party for the Independence of the Masses (Parti Africain pour l'Indépendance des Masses)	Leftist	Founded July 30, 1982
Party for the People's Liberation (Parti pour la Libération du Peuple)	Split of the National Democratic Rally	Founded August 31, 1983
Union for Senegalese Democracy-Renewal (Union pour la Démocratie Sénégalaise-Renouveau)	Split of the Senegalese Democratic Party	Founded 1985
Party for Senegalese Democracy-Renewal (Parti Démocratique Sénégalais-Renouveau)	Split of the Senegalese Democratic Party	Founded 1985
Movement for Socialism and Democracy (Mouvement pour le Socialisme et Democratie)	Fusion of two former political parties: Movement for People's Democracy (Mouvement pour la Democratie) and Workers' Communist League (Ligue Communiste du Travail); autonomous socialism and Troskyist	Founded 1988

mation base and economic expertise. A team of young analysts and statisticians supervised by Mamoudou Touré was charged with producing periodic, well-documented reports on the economic conditions of the country, first at the Ministry of Planning and later at the Ministry of Economy and Finance. Policy analysis units were created or reinforced in other ministries as well.

The government also created several coordinating committees to promote communication among ministries and speed up decisionmaking. The most important of these was the Interministerial Committee of Supervision, composed of the minister of state; the general secretary of the presidency; the ministers of planning, economy and finance, rural development, industry and crafts, and trade; and the director of the central bank. The Committee for Implementation of the Structural Adjustment

Program (CSPA) was created in early 1985 to be the general coordinating body of the adjustment program. Constituted of five high-level technocrats and financed under a United Nations project, the CSPA provided technical support to the Interministerial Committee of Supervision, through its chair, a full-fledged member of the full committee. The interministerial committee met every three months, with the head of state as its chair, to evaluate implementation of the structural adjustment program. Their conclusions were to be implemented by the CSPA. This particular arrangement was intended to insulate the CSPA from the Senegalese administration and professional politicians.

The CSPA, which soon became the main interlocutor with external aid and lending agencies, worked with special cells created within the ministries as part of the structural adjustment program. In time, it diverted power from established agencies, which tended to act like private interest groups engaged in lobbying. The rest of the civil service soon resented the extra resources and perks granted to these special units.

In brief, 1983–85 witnessed Diouf striving to create the necessary conditions within his government for a concerted reform attempt. The reformist team of technocrats he assembled brought about the adjustment he sought and helped him consolidate his power free from the grasp of the Socialist Party.

The Adjustment Program, 1984–91

Debates about the adjustment process in Senegal have concerned not only the program's design, internal logic, and impact on the economy but also the degree to which certain measures were actually carried out. Some observers in and out of Senegal have blamed the economy's ills on the PAML. Yet, a report commissioned by USAID argues that the government achieved some macroeconomic stabilization but largely failed to carry out the structural adjustment program. It concludes that, "despite many positive changes, little real adjustment took place in Senegal over the decade, and many of the policies set out in government statements of loan agreements were weakly implemented" (Berg 1990, p. xv). Is such a negative assessment warranted? To what extent have Senegal's continuing economic problems arisen because of, rather than despite, the adjustment program? Parts of the program were clearly implemented on schedule and satisfactorily. Nonetheless, implementation was highly uneven, varying across areas in revealing ways, and slowed considerably after an initial burst of action in 1986–88.

In all but one respect, the PAML consisted of a fairly conventional package of reform measures. The following brief discussion starts with the measures in the program that aimed for short-term stabilization and then analyzes the policy reforms whose objective was longer-term, sustained economic growth and structural transformation of the economy. This analysis is not comprehensive and only covers elements of the reform program relevant to the political analysis that follows (it does not, for example, discuss the government's relatively successful restructuring of the banking sector or reform of the public enterprise sector).

STABILIZATION. Stabilization measures, such as limiting government expenditures and placing tighter controls on credit, were pursued more consistently than any other part of the program. Government expenditures were cut from 32 percent of GDP in fiscal 1981/92 to 21 percent in 1989/90. The growth of credit fell from an average of more than 20 percent annually during the 1970s to some 5 percent in 1989. Effort was made to limit the share of the wage bill in overall government expenditures. Real wages in the public sector were allowed to decrease 15 percent between 1980 and 1989, and the size of the civil service was held more or less constant from 1986 to 1991.

These measures are standard fare for reform supported by the IMF and World Bank. The program did not include a devaluation of the currency, however, because this was precluded (through 1992) by Senegal's membership in the West African Monetary Union. As a member of the Franc Zone, Senegal shared a currency, the franc of the Communauté Financière Africaine (CFA franc), with the other fourteen members. The CFA franc was pegged to the French franc at the rate of 50:1, a parity that had not changed since 1948. The members of the Franc Zone keep their reserves in the French treasury, in exchange for which France agrees to guarantee convertibility of the currency. The developmental merits of the Franc Zone have long been a source of debate (Guillaumont and Guillaumont 1984, 1988; Martin 1986; Vallée 1989; van de Walle 1991). The member states clearly have little control over the parity of the CFA franc with other currencies. Recent years have witnessed both high levels of exchange rate variability and, for many of the countries in the zone, high levels of overvaluation (table 8-2). This has led to repeated calls for devaluation (Vallée 1989), which have been steadfastly resisted by both France and all the member states. Because the government was not able to effectuate a nominal devaluation, it had to pursue a depreciation of the real exchange rate through fiscal and commercial policy alone. The exact level of overvaluation in Senegal during this period is subject to some dispute, and estimates are sensitive to the methodology used (for discussions, see Devarajan and de Melo 1987; Krumm 1987). The level of overvaluation was perhaps 15–25 percent in the late 1970s, followed by improved competitiveness in the early 1980s. This improvement was due to a variety of factors, including the strong appreciation of the dollar between 1979 and 1985, three devaluations of the French franc between 1981 and 1983, and the loss of competitiveness of African economies outside the Franc Zone (these successive devaluations of the French franc resulted in no less than a 25 percent depreciation relative to the deutschmark). By the second half of the 1980s, these external forces began exerting an opposite, negative influence on Senegalese competitiveness. In particular, repeated devaluations in neighboring African countries undermined the country's equilibrium exchange rate. By 1991, many observers argued that a depreciation of between 30 and 50 percent was necessary to restore Senegal's competitiveness (Economist Intelligence Unit 1991, p. 11).

As a result of the measures undertaken under the PAML, the current account deficit was cut from 17 percent of GDP in 1983/84 to less than 10 percent in 1988/89. Similarly, the fiscal deficit was cut from 9 percent of GDP in fiscal 1982/83 to less than 4 percent in 1986/87, before rebounding to almost 5 percent in 1989/90 (if one takes into account foreign grants, these numbers are 8 and 2 percent, respectively; see Berg 1990, p. 6). Modest growth in GDP per capita of almost 2 percent in 1986–88 and a decrease of the official inflation rate from 11 to −2 percent between 1981 and 1988 led some observers to argue that these stabilization measures had put Senegal on the right track to achieve sustained growth. In fact, this progress toward macroeconomic stabilization was fragile. Budgetary growth was limited, by the sheer scarcity of capital, to growth rates of the past. Much of the improvement in the trade balance during the mid-1980s resulted from the appreciation of the U.S. dollar with respect to the French franc. The CFA franc's depreciation from CFAF209 to the dollar in 1980 to CFAF437 in 1984 provided the economy with a respite and a temporary improvement in the current account.[15] The dollar's decline after 1985 similarly worsened the trade deficit, however, and by 1990, Senegalese exports totaled CFAF410 billion, while imports remained at levels comparable to the mid-1980s, CFAF474 billion.

The government maintained high domestic prices for several consumer goods, which constituted an increasingly important source of revenue. By 1990, rice imports brought in CFAF15 billion in revenues annually, while the import tax on oil accounted for more than 12 percent of all revenues (imported petroleum products accounted for 22 percent of all government revenues, if value added taxes and nontax receipts are added to the revenues from import duties). In general, that year, taxes on international trade accounted for 40 percent of all revenues. In effect, then, fiscal stabilization depended in large part on a tax policy at odds with the reform program's objective of trade liberalization.

Finally, at least some of the stabilization progress must be understood in the context of finance by external aid and lending agencies and debt forgiveness and rescheduling. Indeed, it is difficult to overstate the impact of foreign transfers to the economy. During the period 1980–87, international aid grew 18 percent a year, so that Senegal received some $642 million in aid in 1987, equivalent to more than $100 per person, or one-fifth of GDP. This was almost as much as total government revenues, which were about $750 million, and made Senegal the leading recipient of aid per capita in Africa.[16]

In addition to IMF and World Bank assistance, the country received extensive bilateral assistance. The United States and France both developed independent structural adjustment programs parallel to and coordinated with the World Bank effort. French support of the state budget alone totaled some CFAF131.5 billion in loans between 1978 and 1989 (Berg 1990, pp. 151–53). U.S. aid commitments totaled $472 million between 1978 and 1987. In addition, a host of other bilateral aid and lending agencies were active in Senegal. In total, during the period 1981–88, commitment of medium- and long-term loans and grants averaged $600 million a year, equivalent to 16 percent of GDP.

Much of this aid came in the form of loans, and Senegal's external debt steadily climbed throughout the 1980s. Total public debt outstanding almost tripled, reaching $4.13 billion at the end of 1989 (World Bank 1991a), up from $1.284 billion in 1980. Indeed, Senegal successfully negotiated debt reschedulings with the Paris Club in October 1981, November 1982, December 1983, January 1985, November 1986, November 1987, January 1989, and June 1991. Senegal was also the leading beneficiary of French debt forgiveness, with the cancellation of F2.0 billion of Senegalese debt in May 1989, during the Francophone World Summit held in Dakar.

STRUCTURAL ADJUSTMENT. Concurrent with these stabilization measures, the government agreed to undertake measures designed to bring about a higher average rate of economic growth in the long term. In the public sector, reforms sought to liquidate, privatize, and rehabilitate many of the eighty-five existing public enterprises that had been soaking up 40 percent of all gross fixed capital formation. In addition, two sectoral reform programs were developed to spearhead the adjustment program by improving competitiveness and the incentives' structure. These were the New Agricultural Policy and the New Industrial Policy.

The New Agricultural Policy (NPA) was promulgated in 1984 and given added momentum by measures spelled out in the Seventh Five-Year Plan in 1985 and the National Cereals Plan in 1986. The plan was designed to reduce the government's role in production and marketing activities, including the liberalization of input markets, the gradual elimination of subsidies on fertilizers, as well as the transfer of functions from state agencies to private ones or to agricultural producers themselves. The movement begun by the dissolution of ONCAD in 1980 was thus accelerated. In addition, reform measures sought to lessen dependence on imported rice and wheat by promoting domestic output of coarse grains. Finally, the state's monopoly on cereal imports was eliminated.

On one level, the NPA was designed to address the near collapse of traditional state marketing structures. In 1984/85, only 238,000 tons of groundnuts out of the estimated 500,000 tons produced were sold to the parastatal SONACOS; instead, farmers took their crops to parallel marketing structures, which paid better prices. Groundnut production rose 20 percent in 1985/86, but the season was disastrous for the oil mills, which in 1988/89 still operated at only 30 percent of their capacity (*Le Soleil,* March 11, 1985, April 9, 1986; *Sud-Hebdo,* no. 61, July 12, 1989; World Bank 1987a, p. 8). Reforms in 1985 and 1986—notably the decision to raise official prices in 1986 as well as to distribute 60,000 tons of free seeds—were thus essentially geared to preserve the official market for cash crops and prevent the parallel market from growing further.

Implementation of the NPA proved problematic. On the one hand, fertilizer subsidies were eliminated progressively between 1986 and 1989, marketing was partially liberalized, the government stopped setting prices for major food crops, and a number of public enterprises were restructured. On the other hand, the government, which came to accept the general principle that domestic prices should be linked to world prices, proved reticent about price liberalization and continued to administer the price of groundnuts, cotton, rice, sugar, and edible oils. By 1988, the depreciation of the dollar and lower world commodity prices led to a net loss for the government on groundnut prices. The government backtracked from its previous commitment to improve farmer incentives and reduced groundnut prices 22 percent, from CFAF90 to CFAF70 per kilogram. It argued, with some justification, that it could not afford yearly subsidies equal to 1.4 percent of GDP.

Pressures from rural elites who had most benefited from the old policies kept delaying implementation of reform policies. For example, in 1989, farmers received a special payment equivalent to CFAF2 per kilogram of groundnuts sold to SONACOS the preceding season. In addition, they were offered the option of swapping bad or pest-damaged groundnut seeds for good-quality seed held by SONACOS and normally only available for cash payments (Economist Intelligence Unit 1989). Marabouts were similarly responsible for pressuring the government to authorize SONACOS to distribute groundnut seeds in 1987, despite a commitment to end this subsidy program, and for keeping alive the issue of fertilizer subsidies.[17]

As early as 1988, major external aid and lending agencies started pressuring the government to quicken the pace of change. This led to a general declaration of government policy for agriculture in December 1989 and negotiations for an agricultural sector adjustment loan in 1990 and 1991. These negotiations became quite acrimonious in 1991, as the government refused to accept a series of conditions from external agencies, notably policies governing the price of rice and fertilizer subsidies.

At the end of 1991 one could hardly speak of a structural transformation of agriculture. The past five years had witnessed some growth in the production of food and cash crops, but this appeared to be due, at least in part, to the return of normal levels of precipitation after the drought at the beginning of the decade. For example, groundnut production grew from a low of 500,000 tons in the drought year 1984/85 to 950,000 tons in 1987/88 but still averaged less than the 1 million tons produced annually in the late 1970s. Input use had actually fallen since the beginning of the decade as a result of the reduction of subsidies on fertilizer and pesticides, and output growth had come entirely from increased acreage. Most of the progress in food crops had occurred because farmers were opting out of the traditional cash crops and thus could not be considered evidence of an aggregate increase in production. There was little evidence of productivity growth, and rainfall remained the principal determinant of changes in output (Berg 1990, p. 105).

Industrial reform initially took a back seat to agricultural reform, but a fundamental revision of industrial policy was a condition of the World Bank's second structural adjustment loan in early 1986 (see Berg 1990 for an excellent account of the New Industrial Policy; see also Boone 1991; Thioune 1991). The New Industrial Policy (NPI) was drafted by the Ministry of Industrial Development and Small Industries, with the help of an adviser from the United Nations Industrial Development Organization and in close consultation with the World Bank. There was little or no consultation with industry itself, which learned about the program only weeks before it was promulgated. Besides the measures included in the privatization program, it emphasized the liberalization of trade policies to lower the level of protection benefiting national firms. This included ending quantitative restrictions, reducing and harmonizing tariffs, eliminating special tariffs for specific industries, eliminating *mercuriales*, and liberalizing import licensing procedures.[18]

By the mid-1980s, the industrial sector was composed essentially of import-substitution light industries located on the coast near Dakar. They were highly concentrated, with each industrial or manufacturing branch dominated by one or two companies, most of which were hopelessly noncompetitive with foreign goods. Given overvaluation of the currency, the uncertain state of the economy, and high costs of labor, private businessmen had little incentive to invest in long-term projects. Instead, they survived by lobbying for protection and subsidies from the state and by engaging in short-term speculative activities and extensive rent seeking.

Trade liberalization was of course feared by the industrial sector, which had grown used to this extensive protection. Thus, the NPI also included a second set of measures, which came to be known as the *mésures d'accompagnement,* or accompanying measures, designed to help firms adjust to the stiffer competition. These included measures to decrease production costs by lowering excessive labor and energy costs, as well as financial assistance for firms seeking to restructure, a new investment code, and an increase in the export subsidy available to firms seeking to sell part of their production abroad. Extensive reform of the labor code was also foreseen to eliminate rigidities in labor markets that raised labor costs and lowered productivity. These measures were intended to help firms weather the shock of competition and prepare the ground for future growth.

Implementation of the NPI was uneven (Berg 1990; Thioune 1991). Quantitative restrictions were eliminated for a wide range of products on schedule, although they remained in place for a small number of important imports (cement and sugar, among others) for which special arrangements exist between the government and individual firms. Tariff protection was reduced, first in July 1986 and again in July 1988, and the tariff structure was simplified. As a result, the average effective protection rate declined from 165 percent in 1985 to 90 percent in mid-1988, and customs duties were spread more uniformly over a larger number of goods. However, 38 percent of all imports remained exempted from the payment of customs duties, because of investment code privileges, dispensations for government purchases, and special agreements between the state and individual businesses. The undeniable success of tariff reduction was partly overturned after 1988. Prodded by the need for revenue and the lobbying of businesses unable to compete in the new environment, the government reintroduced protection measures. By August 1990, the average effective protection rate had once again reached 98 percent.

In any event, the record on tariff reduction remained positive, although implementation of the accompanying measures was less satisfactory. Measures designed to decrease the costs of inputs were not implemented, for example, or were not implemented effectively. For example, in 1991, energy costs remained unduly high largely because of import taxes charged on imported oil. The state never passed on to domestic consumers the decline in the world price of oil after 1984, largely because this tax provided more than 12 percent of the government's revenues by 1990.[19]

The government held the number of civil servants roughly constant during the 1985–90 period at around 67,000 employees (see table 8-4). The government's wage bill continued to rise, however, despite a wage freeze, largely because of the liberal use of internal promotions (Berg 1990, pp. 194–95; Terrell and Svejnar 1990). Labor costs remained much too high for Senegal to be competitive. The NPI's proposal to change labor legislation in order to make hiring and firing more flexible was defeated in the National Assembly in June 1987, after intense lobbying by the trade unions, and the bill that was eventually passed constituted a much more modest improvement on existing legislation. The World Bank initially backed off the issue when the government pleaded that political realities made such a reform impossible. After a hiatus, the Bank reintroduced the issue in negotiations and made lower labor costs and increased productivity a major objective of the structural adjustment loan (SAL IV) signed in 1990. By that point, the government appeared to

Table 8-4. The Impact of Civil Service Reform in Senegal, 1981–90

Fiscal Year	Total employed in the civil service	Wage bill (billions of CFA francs)	Wage bill as a percent of current expenditure	Wage bill as a percent of total expenditure	Wage bill as a percent of GDP
1981/82	63,011	83.3	50.4	39.2	11.0
1982/83	66,310	92.7	49.7	36.5	10.4
1983/84	67,718	100.4	48.9	40.5	10.3
1984/85	67,034	106.6	49.1	41.9	9.7
1985/86	68,843	111.8	50.7	42.0	9.2
1986/87	68,131	119.8	51.5	41.9	8.9
1987/88	67,100	122.3	50.0	42.4	8.5
1988/89	66,549	125.1	50.5	41.0	8.5
1989/90	63,641	126.8	49.1	38.4	8.1
1990/91	66,549	125.1	55.8	43.6	8.1

Source: World Bank 1990a; estimates of World Bank staff.

recognize that, to succeed, structural adjustment required improvements in the labor situation. In the first decade of adjustment, the civil service wage bill had only decreased 2 percent in real terms, suggesting that a more concerted effort was necessary to make progress on this front. SAL IV foresaw the reduction of the civil service by some 8,642 staff members.[20] However, in the uncertain political climate of 1990 and 1991, it was not clear that the government was any more willing to tackle this delicate issue than it had been before. Despite some undeniable initial progress, in which a little more than 2,000 civil servants left public employment voluntarily, only limited further movement on these measures had occurred at the time of this writing.

Another accompanying measure, the increase of export subsidies, was also not satisfactorily implemented. Given the increasing level of currency overvaluation and the impossibility of resorting to devaluation, policymakers viewed export subsidies as a useful instrument for promoting exports. These had been resorted to as early as 1980 as part of the EFRP, but the NPI increased and extended them to new products in August 1986. Various restrictions, administrative delays, and red tape greatly reduced their usefulness. Few exporters received these payments, which were, in any event, too small to compensate the overvaluation of the currency (the subsidy is calculated as 25 percent of domestic value added, rather than the free on board value of the product; on the ineffectiveness of tariff policy to overcome overvaluation, see Salinger and Stryker 1991).

The final accompanying measure of some importance, the creation of a fund to assist in industrial restructuring, also proved unsatisfactory. The World Bank included some funding for this purpose in an industrial restructuring credit of $25 million signed in late 1987. This credit did not, however, start functioning until October 1988 and did not give out a single loan until mid-July 1989, three years after the first phase of trade liberalization had been completed. Commercial banks were asked to provide loans on APEX funding (the Agricultural Promotion Export Fund) through the central bank, although they had little or no experience in industrial lending and were in the midst of their own protracted financial crisis. Various delays again conspired to limit the impact of this fund.

Public enterprise reform was more encouraging (see Berg 1990, p. 31–33; World Bank 1990a, pp. 31–32). After an extremely slow start, much progress was achieved. Of the eighty-five public and parastatal enterprises in the state portfolio before reform, nineteen had been privatized and another eleven liquidated by October 1991. Further, considerable progress was made in restructuring public enterprises, introducing management autonomy, streamlining the institutional and legal framework, improving operations, and settling cross debts among enterprises and between enterprises and the government. Nevertheless, some of the biggest and costliest parastatals had been left untouched, and direct budgetary support for the public enterprise sector still amounted to 5 percent of current government expenditures, some CFAF11.8 billion in fiscal 1990/91, albeit down from CFAF14.4 billion in 1988/89.[21]

An overall evaluation of the NPI is difficult, in part because the quality of the data is extremely uneven and in part because it is difficult to establish the counterfactual, namely, what would have happened in the absence of the NPI, on the one hand, or what would have happened had the NPI been fully implemented, on the other hand. It seems clear that the industrial sector's crisis worsened after 1986. Estimates suggest that industrial production may have declined 12 percent between 1986 and 1988 and that as many as thirty industrial enterprises may have gone bankrupt between 1986 and 1991 (*Wal Fadjiri,* no. 251, March 7, 1991). Total net industrial employment in the formal sector may have decreased as much as 10 percent during the 1980s.[22] At the same time, much of the sector's crisis could not be blamed on the NPI but rather on the overvaluation of the CFA franc and the prevailing conditions of economic austerity.

Explanations of the Scope and Speed of Adjustment

This section analyzes the reasons why the government did not fully implement the reform program, focusing first on structural economic issues. Without providing yet another economic assessment of the program (Commander, Ndoye, and Ouedrago 1989; Duruflé 1988; Kassé 1990), it examines the political implications of issues relating to the program's design and internal economic logic. Second, it analyzes the importance of several political factors in shaking the government's commitment to reform: the role of the urban riots of 1988 and 1989 and the fears they created about political instability as well as the weight of interest groups in influencing the course of the reform program.

Economic Constraints

As in other African programs, the reform strategy in Senegal was that deregulation, liberalization, and privatization would reduce government consumption and spur private sector investment, improve external competitiveness, and promote export-led growth. The government needed to address three problem areas for the program to succeed: (1) the program had drastic revenue implications, (2) membership in the Franc Zone precluded devaluation of the currency as an instrument to increase competitiveness, and (3) the sources of future growth had to be identified and promoted successfully. Each of these constraints posed critical political dilemmas for the government, and it is important to see how the government tried to address them. Each is addressed in turn.

THE REVENUE SQUEEZE. Economic liberalization was likely to have short-term implications for government revenues, since more than 40 percent of all government revenues came from taxes on international trade. A liberalization program thus had to choose among (1) increasing other types of revenues, notably income taxes; (2) reducing government expenditures, cutting down on fraud, and improving revenue mobilization; and (3) finding capital to finance government deficits. In practice, the program counted on all three to balance the budget: improvements in tax administration would increase other tax revenues, expenditure would be cut, and the external aid and lending agencies supporting the program would provide substantial capital. In addition, it was believed that lower marginal tariff rates and a wider base would decrease fraud and improve tax yields. In short, the PAML's design did not anticipate that fiscal shortfalls would become a major constraint on implementing the program fully.

In the short run, the PAML developed optimistic projections of revenue growth and expenditure cuts to obscure the likelihood of deficits. In the longer run, economic growth resulting from the program was predicted to increase tax receipts and end the need for outside capital. In estimates made to the Paris Club in 1987 and accepted by the external aid and lending agencies, for example, industry and mining were forecast to grow more than 6 percent a year as a result of the NPI, a rate that had no precedent in the country's recent history and that assumed virtually no lag for the NPI to have a favorable impact on the industrial sector (World Bank 1989b, p. 27). These unrealistic predictions were not questioned because the government sought to avoid having to cut government expenditures even more than promised. For its part, the World Bank did not want to jeopardize the trade liberalization reforms, which it viewed as the most important component of the program, and needed to present a coherent program to its board of directors.

Nowhere were the fiscal implications of the program more dramatic than in the NPI. It is true that eliminating quantitative restrictions, reducing tariffs, and widening the tax base did not decrease customs revenues, because the reforms rationalized the tariff structure and eliminated opportunities for tax evasion. In fact, taxes on foreign trade increased from CFAF79 billion in 1984/85 to CFAF92 billion in 1989/90. Nevertheless, overall government revenues decreased during this period, from 20 percent of GDP in 1981/82, to 19 percent in 1986/87, and to 16 percent in 1989/90 (table 8-2), putting tremendous pressure on the government to control its expenditures. Liberalization made sense only if the accompanying measures were also implemented, since they were designed to allow the economy to respond to external competition. Without them, the overvalued exchange rate and the industrial sector's outdated capital stock, high input costs, and other production inefficiencies made a rapid growth in exports an unrealistic response. (The NPI was designed in 1984 and 1985, when the real exchange rate was arguably in equilibrium; by the time it became operational, however, the currency was rapidly appreciating.) These measures were never implemented, in part because the government and external aid and lending agencies had underestimated the difficulty of administering them (this was notably the case for the Restructuring Fund, for which the banking sector was ill equipped) and in part because their fiscal implications were prohibitive and would derail the IMF-backed stabilization plan. Because the government was never able or willing to reduce its expenditures, it remained dependent on revenues that undermined the competitiveness of the economy. The tax on energy imports exemplifies this dilemma. In the abstract, the external agencies opposed this state of affairs, but in practice, they recognized that the government had to improve dramatically its capacity to mobilize revenue, a process that could not realistically bear fruit in the short term.[23]

With the benefit of hindsight, it is clear that the NPI's liberalization measures were bound to have a powerful effect on the long-overprotected economy and to prove politically unsustainable without the prior, or at least concurrent, implementation of measures to ease transitional problems. Would some other sequence of reform have been preferable? It seems obvious that undertaking deregulation and liberalization without refashioning fiscal policy was a recipe for disaster. It proved a lot easier for the government to reduce import tariffs than to cut the wage bill. Compounded by the overvalued exchange rate, this meant that the domestic economy was opened up before Senegalese industry could respond. The impact of these reforms on the fabric of Senegalese industry then provided enough ammunition to the opponents of reform to reestablish protection in 1989. Indeed, when the inevitable crunch came, the IMF sided with the revenue imperative in the name of budgetary stabilization. Yet, absent even more foreign aid than the external agencies were already providing, the adjustment program they backed was doomed if the government did not actively promote a supply response by the private sector.

ADJUSTMENT WITHOUT DEVALUATION. This conflict between the fiscal requirements of stabilization and the resource needs of the economy was exacerbated by Senegal's membership in the West African Monetary Union, which precluded devaluation. The main vehicle of adjustment, in other words, had to come from fiscal contraction and trade policy. Theoretically, nominal devaluation is not necessary to bring about real depreciation (Devarajan and de Melo 1987; Krumm 1987), which occurs when the domestic rate of inflation falls below the rate of inflation in the economies of the country's trading partners. In practice, however, no country in Sub-Saharan Africa has been able to bring about a substantial and sustained real depreciation of its currency without resorting to several successive nominal devaluations. Senegal's experience during the 1980s illustrates this fact: after a decade of attempts at economic reform and austerity, the level of overvaluation of the CFA franc was as high as it had been in the late-1970s. Indeed, overvaluation increased at the end of this period, according to some estimates (Economist Intelligence Unit 1991, p. 11; Salinger and Stryker 1991).

Given stagnant productivity, overvaluation prevented Senegal from improving its ability to compete. By some estimates, labor costs in Senegal were still 60 percent higher than in Malaysia and 370 percent higher than in Indonesia in 1990 (Berg 1990, p. 12). At such levels of overvaluation, domestic production had to be protected to survive and exports subsidized to be competitive, a fact used to justify a wide variety of government interventions that the state was poorly equipped to carry out and that resulted in extensive rent seeking and fraud. In the meantime, domestic production continued to be devastated by foreign goods.

Evidence from the rest of Africa suggests that devaluation offers at least two major advantages to a government seeking to engineer a major restructuring of the economy. First, it is among the least problematic economic reform measures to implement. Although much of its effect is likely to be short-lived without accompanying measures—notably measures that control inflation—devaluation itself can be accomplished at the stroke of a pen. By forgoing devaluation, in other words, the Senegalese government put the burden of adjustment on policy instruments that are inherently harder to wield.

The second related advantage of devaluation is more strictly political. It offers an indirect but effective way of attacking the purchasing power of the urban bourgeoisie and in particular of public sector wage earners. By shifting relative prices in favor of the traded goods sector, devaluation in effect lowers the real salary of wage earners. Franc Zone countries like Senegal forgo that choice and thus have to lower the nominal wage bill. That this is politically much harder seems clear if one examines the experience of adjustment in Sub-Saharan Africa. After a decade of adjustment, Franc Zone countries like Senegal have barely made a dent in their civil service wage bills, while countries outside the zone have typically cut the purchasing power of civil servants by more than half. Yet the Franc Zone countries have, if anything, faced more urban labor unrest than other countries (Bratton and van de Walle 1992).

The overvaluation of the CFA franc has long been widely admitted, yet the implications of devaluation, whether it is achieved by pulling out of the West African Monetary Union or by renegotiating new parities with France and other member states, are so complex and sensitive that it has hardly been mentioned in policy debates on adjustment at least until recently.[24] During the 1980s, the government's unwillingness to consider devaluation clearly suggested that the advantages of the Franc Zone outweighed its economic costs, including a much more difficult adjustment process (for an analysis of this issue, see van de Walle 1991). First among these advantages was the link with France, which the government did not want to jeopardize. France remained the leading bilateral supporter in Senegal, and its willingness to respect Franc Zone arrangements provided Senegal with significant balance of payments support.[25] In addition, extensive historical and individual ties existed between the two countries, including those that the politically influential French community in Senegal continued to maintain with France (persistent rumors suggest that French businessmen in Dakar have long helped finance the ruling Socialist Party). In a period of economic uncertainty, the security provided by such ties was very appealing to the government. Moreover, overvaluation favored the import-intensive consumption of social groups that supported the government and served, for example, to inflate the purchasing power of the civil service, which remained unrivaled in the region.

THE ISSUE OF SUPPLY RESPONSE. The third constraint on economic reform was the absence of any obvious source of rapid, sustained economic growth to spearhead adjustment. The theory of structural adjustment posits short-term sacrifices in exchange for higher rates of growth in the medium to long run. The PAML's credibility and political sustainability depended on the government's ability to find a plausible source of sustained growth in the economy. The more thoughtful studies by external aid and lending agencies argued that the government should not try to plan where the future growth should come from but should only "create a policy and institutional environment that is conducive to entrepreneurship and investment" (Berg 1990, p. 223). If it did so, the argument went, growth would follow. This faith in the market was not shared by the Senegalese, apart perhaps from a small number of technocrats. Most sought a more precise prescription before backing reform.

After all, where would growth come from? Industry was, in theory, the most plausible candidate in the minds of most Senegalese, but its crisis in the mid-1980s, even before the NPI was implemented, indicated daunting structural problems. The conventional wisdom among external aid and lending agencies suggested that a viable development strategy had to be based on the revitalization of agriculture. But was this the case? For much of the Senegalese political class, the desertification of the north and repeated droughts elsewhere, the complete failure of two decades of attempts at intensification, the decline of international commodity prices, and the general backwardness of the sector were all factors that left agriculture a less-than-convincing candidate to spearhead an economic renaissance.

Indeed, many outside observers viewed agriculture's future with deep pessimism. Bonnefond and Couty (1991, p. 43), for example, argue that "there will be no [agricultural] development for Senegal without a long-lasting deficit in the balance of payments . . . [and] extensive financial assistance." Given the increasing unwillingness of external aid and lending agencies to continue providing new finance to the government, such a view was tantamount to denying Senegal's ability to overcome its crisis. Whether such pessimism was warranted is irrelevant. The important point is that the external agencies pushing for adjustment and their allies in the government never succeeded in overcoming this pervasive pessimism by developing a credible positive scenario for the country's future. Most observers agreed that there was still "an urgent need to evolve a new long-term economic development strategy with the capacity to replace the old groundnut export system" (Delgado and Jammeh 1991, p. 4). Sadly, a decade of reports, independent studies, and adjustment programs by external agencies did not produce a credible vision of the likely benefits of adjustment.

In any event, the Senegalese political class never accepted the broad argument that the proper incentive structure would produce growth and a secure fiscal base for the state. This should not be surprising, given thirty years of seemingly inexorable economic decline and the failure of successive policy fads. The important point is that pessimism regarding the country's long-term economic potential may have created the expectation that the adjustment process could not succeed and thus created the unwillingness to invest in it. Adjustment was unlikely to succeed, then, without major changes in those expectations.

The Role of the External Aid and Lending Agencies

International aid played a highly paradoxical role in the adjustment process during the 1980s. On the one hand, the flow of aid constituted a stable source of state revenue that helped sustain the policy mix and made reform less urgent. On the other hand, much of the aid was explicitly tied to economic reform in the form of conditionality. The external agencies argued that aid provided the government with the margin of security it needed to proceed with difficult reforms in an uncertain environment. In political terms, assistance eased the pain of redistributive reforms by allowing the government to provide key constituencies with compensatory payments during the adjustment process. Aid thus helped induce the government to undertake economic reform.

The external agencies had a highly ambiguous impact on the adjustment process, comforting to both the opponents and supporters of reform. Aid was unambiguously a resource for the state, however, and it had long been perceived as a useful instrument with which to lessen the economic and fiscal constraints facing the state. In the 1980s, Senegal clearly sought external support to deal with the economic crisis. Indeed, support from external agencies weighed heavily in Diouf's decision to commit his government to reform. It was certainly a factor in his appointment of Touré to head the adjustment effort in 1985. On the whole, this strategy met with remarkable success.

What were the implications of international support, both for economic adjustment and for the politics of adjustment? Berg (1990), for example, argues that aid undermined the incentives state elites had to pursue adjustment, because external agencies proved unwilling to impose sanctions for noncompliance. In this argument, the macroeconomic situation was more or less sustainable thanks to aid. In effect, a leader like Diouf asked why the country should opt for reform, when there are no costs to maintaining the status quo.

Berg argues that adjustment was delayed in Senegal because it did not garner "local ownership" and remained after ten years essentially a venture of the external agencies. The result was limited and uneven progress in implementing reform policies: where an external agency took the lead and provided financing, there was progress; where the government was meant to take the initiative, there was none. Traditional conditionality of external agencies was fatally flawed, according to this analysis, because it assumed that conditionality was effective and that financial assistance was provided only to governments reasonably committed to the process of reform. In fact, neither assumption was warranted. As Collier (1991, p. 163) wittily puts it, "Highly detailed conditionality is either a political fantasy (a game played by African governments without the intention of adherence) or a bureaucratic fantasy (fussy interventions from an extremely remote center of decision, reminiscent of the way Philip II ran the Spanish Empire)."

The impact that external agencies had on adjustment in Senegal in the 1980s was nonetheless complex. Their financial and technical resources clearly provided them with some leverage in policymaking. External agencies and their allies within the state apparatus functioned as a powerful lobby that influenced the decisions of top policymakers, if not routinely at least occasionally. It is easy to point to reform measures within the NPA and NPI that would never have been implemented without external agency pressures on the state. An analysis of the World Bank's conditions for structural adjustment loans shows a pretty good rate of implementation, particularly between 1985 and 1989, once delays due to administrative difficulties are taken into account. Indeed, external agency conditionality was simultaneously too rigid and too lax. Each structural adjustment loan included dozens of conditions, many of which were unrealistic.[26] External agencies effectively set the policy agenda in Senegal during the 1980s. The economic values associated with reform, such as the virtues of the market and the need for less state intervention, were internalized by many government officials and, by the early 1990s, framed most policy debates.

Still, external agencies did not sanction the Senegalese government for noncompliance. Other than expressing their unhappiness and making occasional threats to withdraw from the country, they continued to increase their commitments in Senegal throughout the 1980s. In addition, they consistently accepted excessively optimistic forecasts of Senegal's performance (World Bank 1989b), allowing the government to avoid choices even more difficult than the ones they were making within the adjustment program. The government was allowed to delay necessary reforms and, in effect, to accumulate extra debt.

Ultimately, aid represented a net resource for the government, but an often troublesome one that could never be fully taken for granted. Even if the government could escape from agreed-upon conditionality through delays, obfuscation, and the invocation of special circumstances, it could not afford to disregard completely the promises it had made and was forced to make some concessions to placate, if not satisfy, the external agencies. Given the government's reliance on external finance, even a temporary interruption of aid would pose real risks for the government. This was particularly true of the IMF and World Bank because—under Paris Club arrangements—other external agencies waited for their approval before providing new credits or rescheduling old ones. A conflict with one of the twin sisters could result in a dramatic decline in the total level of aid.

The various economic constraints reviewed here and the likelihood of continued support from external agencies convinced much of the political class that the benefits to be gained from implementing the reform program fully were much smaller than the dangers posed for social stability—namely the political risks of undertaking major layoffs in general and in public enterprises. Why risk destabilizing the precarious political balance when doing so was unlikely to result in significant growth? This was the cost-benefit calculation that weakened the political class's commitment to the reform process and conditioned the response of Diouf's government to the domestic political pressures that increased in 1988 and 1989.

Lobbies for and against Adjustment

Diouf's government faced difficult economic constraints as it implemented the PAML. Whatever the flaws in the economic design of the program, these constraints clearly undermined the political sustainability of adjustment. Even the generous support of the external aid and lending agencies—and aid conditionality was far from toothless—could not obviate the need for severe deflation and fiscal retrenchment if the program was to succeed. The failure of past attempts to jump start the economy and pervasive pessimism about the country's development potential undermined the political class's commitment to adjustment, moreover, and created an expectation of failure in many quarters.

These were daunting problems for the government, but, at the same time, Diouf and his allies began adjustment with significant assets: his technocratic team was competent and dedicated and enjoyed the confidence of the external aid and lending agencies. In addition, the mid-1980s witnessed as favorable an environment for growth as had existed in decades, with a strong upturn in the world economy and the return of decent rains. Finally, Diouf enjoyed considerable popularity and a capital of goodwill on the part of both the general public and several traditionally volatile groups such as students and unions. After the elections of 1983, he possessed a strong electoral mandate to push ahead with economic reform.

The program's political sustainability depended on two interrelated factors. First, of course, it depended on rapid economic results, without which the reforms would appear ineffective and the regime would lose the expectations game. Second, sustainability depended on the regime's ability to overcome the opposition of interest groups that stood to lose the most from the reforms. The state needed to mobilize groups favorable or at least not hostile to reform, and it needed to undermine, co-opt, or marginalize groups hostile to it. On paper, these groups were easily identifiable. Two social actors stood to gain most from successful adjustment: the peasantry and the private business class. Labor and the civil service were the likely losers, as were the rural elites and religious leaders who benefited the most from the old agricultural policies. Within the state elite itself, the technocratic element was likely to gain and the old-line political appointees to lose.

Coalition-building was particularly important for Diouf for two reasons. First, in his first years in office, he had distanced himself from the Socialist Party and antagonized many of Senghor's barons in order to consolidate his power and promote his reform agenda. Second, the regime's democratization after 1976 resulted in an explosion of associational life: farmer organizations, trade unions, and business associations increasingly voiced demands for their constituencies and were poised to play an important role in mobilizing support for or opposition to Diouf's policies.

An investigation of the political role of these different groups and of their relationship to the state is necessary to understand why the adjustment program did not fully succeed. What social groups supported the program? How did the state try to mobilize support on behalf of adjustment? How did it try to overcome opposition? After examining adjustment politics in the countryside in the context of the NPA, this section explores the role of organized labor in the context of the NPI and discusses the relationship between the state and private business.

THE PEASANTRY. The first structural reforms announced and implemented by the government in 1984 focused on the agricultural sector. Agricultural reform was urgently needed, it had been on the policy agenda longer than any other sector, external agency conditionality emphasized it (Lewis 1987, pp. 308–12), and last but not least, the government understood that political opposition to reform would be less difficult to overcome in agriculture than in industry. Contrary to other sectoral policies, the new agricultural reforms were designed to increase the welfare of domestic producers in the short run, despite the progressive elimination of input subsidies. In addition to increases in producer prices, the NPA aimed to empower smallholders to take over tasks formerly undertaken by state institutions, a policy that came to be known as *responsabilisation*. The NPA privatized or liquidated rural development agencies and allowed farmers to make more market-based decisions and to increase their power and initiative in relation to state developmental administrations. On both counts, therefore, one would expect farmers to have supported the NPA and to have mobilized on behalf of reform. It is thus important to explain why farmers never did so.

As a result of the NPA and of the actions of various nongovernmental organizations working in the countryside, new institutional structures emerged to take over functions previously performed by the parastatals. The new structures included 4,500 government-organized *sections villageoises*, or village-sections, created by the Ministry of Rural Development in the mid-1980s to replace the largely discredited cooperatives. Their size and importance varied, but they all played an increasing role in the production, transport, and marketing of agricultural products. Their members gained access to inputs and credit from the National Bank of Credit, whose creation in 1986 was part of the structural reform program. The village-sections faced the same problems as the village cooperatives before them, however, and came to be seen by their members as an artificial instrument of the state, rather than as a tool of empowerment.

The government also legislated changes to democratize local government structures. The power of the president of the rural council was somewhat reduced shortly before the November 1990 elections of local councils, and legislation made the seats formerly attributed to the cooperatives subject to universal suffrage. Despite these significant changes, the most dynamic elements of the Senegalese population—youth and women's associations—were not adequately represented in the rural councils, which came to be controlled by the local representatives of the Socialist Party.

Farmer groups created by private initiative during this same period generated more enthusiasm. The most dynamic sectors of the rural populations were organized in producer groups, *groupements de producteurs*, such as the strong ones that are managing lands and water resources freed by former rural agencies in Casamance and in the river valley. Particularly striking was the growth of economic interest groups, or *groupements d'intérêt économique*, new legal entities promoted as part of the NPA policy on responsibility. By 1990, nearly 5,000 economic interest groups were registered, and some village-sections were asking for a change in status. The major advantage offered by these groups was access to credit. Major banks lacked branches in rural areas and only gave loans to big agribusiness and companies that produced inputs. In recent years, however, a few economic interest groups or unions of them, such as the Groupement Économique du Nord, were able to get loans from commercial banks and even direct assistance from external aid and lending agencies.

These groups were strengthened by the assistance of nongovernmental organizations that provided them with organizational skills and material support. The council of nongovernmental organizations as well as the Federation of Nongovernmental Organizations—an umbrella of about 100 private voluntary organizations—were in the process of increasing their role and influence in rural areas, especially in the river valley and the groundnut basin. They saw economic interest groups as useful vehicles for realizing their own objectives. These new rural structures were also reinforced by the participation of farmers who were former bureaucrats, agents of rural development agencies, or returned immigrants from Europe. These new farmers were well informed about organizational techniques and exhibited more entrepreneurial initiative than traditional farmers. Thus, during the 1988 season, despite financial and transport difficulties, farmers—both as individuals and in groups—sold about 45 percent of the fertilizer distributed and collected about half of the agricultural production (Cissoko 1989, p. 62; *Sud-Hebdo,* no. 61, December 7, 1989).

Yet the growing institutional capacity of farmer organizations did not substantially increase their influence on agricultural policies for several reasons. First and most obvious, farmers are difficult to organize: they are dispersed geographically, the majority are illiterate, their work is seasonal, and they are extremely poor. Decades of low agricultural prices, inadequate rural investment, and a series of droughts weakened their capacity to self-finance agricultural production and left them highly vulnerable. In the absence of efficient input and output markets, farmers depended on traditional clientelism and state organizations regardless of their exploitative nature. The new institutions spread unevenly, and many villages were not affected by them at all.

Second, farmers were not a homogeneous group, and rural society had become increasingly stratified. It included a large number of small producers but also a class of rural elites and marabouts. The state traditionally pursued the classic policy of co-opting rural elites with discretionary benefits and privileges (Bates 1981). The marabouts, in particular, were the principal beneficiary of the agricultural parastatal system. The NPA assailed this system of selective benefits and reduced the welfare of the marabouts much more than that of small producers. The influence of marabouts on agricultural policy should not be exaggerated, however. The wide variety of economic and class interests represented in brotherhoods often prevents them from presenting a united front to the government when pressing claims. In addition, experience has shown that the Senegalese government can compensate the marabouts' losses by giving away government-protected land or by helping them expand their interests in the real estate, trade, or industrial sectors.[27] Nonetheless, the NPA never altered the traditional power relations in the countryside, despite the creation of new institutions for empowering smallholders.

The political weakness of small farmers was reflected and reinforced by their poor representation in the political leadership even after the formal political process was broadened in 1981. The ruling party never sent farmers to the National Assembly or its executive committee. Farmers played no role in formulating the NPA and continued to be absent from policymaking in general. Although the new structures began empowering them, smallholders remained too fragmented and localized to have a voice on the national stage. A deep mistrust continued to pervade peasant attitudes to the state apparatus, given two decades of drought, the hegemonic aspirations and incompetence of the state, and constant shifts in policy. After years of *malaise paysan*, two years of reform were not enough to restore trust in the government. The reduction or termination of various subsidies, as well as the increase in producer prices and the reduction of state intervention, only deepened the suspicion that the NPA was some new trick on the part of the state.

The opposition parties included farmers' demands for higher subsidies and producer prices in their electoral platforms during 1988. One opposition party—the Senegalese Democratic Party—went further and promised free distribution of inputs for two years during the 1988 elections. This gained it some support, but most opposition parties lacked the means to campaign effectively in rural areas, where the supremacy of the Socialist Party was ensured by the complicity of state and parastatal structures. In addition, the leadership of the opposition parties remained essentially urban. Such electoral promises did exert pressure on the state, however; there are indications, for example, that the government waited until after the elections in 1988 to announce the decrease in groundnut prices (although it did not consult farmer groups before doing so).

Of course, many, if not most, officials representing the Socialist Party in the countryside were not highly supportive of the NPA to begin with, since it threatened their power and discretionary sources of income. To promote reform, Diouf had marginalized the Socialist Party and lessened its importance in the higher echelons of the state apparatus. However, he needed the party, which still dominated state structures at the local level, to mobilize farmers on behalf of agricultural reform. Reform-minded technocrats designing policies in Dakar lacked the rural contacts and knowledge needed to mobilize support for their policies, even if they had been inclined to do so. Their attitudes to the countryside remained paternalistic, if not condescending, and they never thought to seek allies in the rural areas.

ORGANIZED LABOR. Farmers' attitudes to economic reforms, however negative, posed fewer risks for the government than the reactions of urban groups such as labor unions and students. In Senegal, 39 percent of the population is urban, and there are at least 1,800 persons per square kilometer in the Cap Vert peninsula, where most of the modern labor force and civil servants live. Given their concentration in Dakar, these urban groups influenced policy to a degree not justified by their numbers alone. The government did not fear individual union strikes or student demonstrations. Although troublesome, these kinds of actions had become too commonplace to upset political stability and threaten the regime. The government feared, instead, the kind of general strike that had closed down the country in 1968.

Given their material interests in maintaining subsidies, state regulation, and industrial protection, unions were likely to oppose structural adjustment. Students were likely to oppose the PAML, since reforms would cut funding in the university budget for housing, meals, and stipends, as well as for library books and other recurrent expenditures. Adjustment also reduced graduate students' expectations of employment, particularly in the civil service, a major issue given the rising unemployment rates.

From 1981 to 1987, President Diouf enjoyed something of a honeymoon with these usually volatile urban groups. His early strategy was to make concessions, on the one hand, and to weaken them through various manipulations, on the other. First, his promises of political liberalization were welcomed and seemed to indicate the beginning of a new dialogue with the groups Senghor had spurned and at times repressed. Several opposition figures actually joined the government.

Trade union pluralism, which was reintroduced after 1976, also increased factionalism and encouraged reorganization, weakening the unions. These struggles were diligently manipulated by Jean Collin, secretary general of the presidency and Diouf's point man on union issues (Bergen 1992). In some cases, such as that of the French-owned Senegalese Sugar Company (Compagnie Sucrière du Sénégal), the largest employer in Senegal with 6,600 workers, unified union action was prevented by the membership's split along religious lines. In addition, Diouf indicated his willingness to engage in a dialogue with the unions, and the union leadership was willing to adopt a wait-and-see attitude toward the new government and the talk of a reform program.

The government chose to avoid a frontal attack on these groups in the early years of the PAML. Although the public sector was hurt by the general deflationary trend, issues such as reforms of the civil service, education, and the labor code were not addressed in a sustained manner until 1987. The government seemed to have adopted a strategy of delaying the most difficult reforms while front-loading the easy ones.

The resulting grace period was most obvious in the education sector, where Diouf met most of the demands of teacher, parent, and student groups (Diop and Diouf 1990, pp. 188–92). Thus, after he came to power, the atmosphere at the university and other schools was relatively calmer than that of the late 1970s. Elsewhere, periodic strikes were called by individual unions—notably by the unions affiliated with the National Confederation of Senegalese Workers in the areas of textiles, fishing, and transport—but all in all, labor peace prevailed. This period saw the rise of the autonomous unions, an evolution that would have important subsequent repercussions. These unions were independent of the CNTS and had broken from the government union either because of personality clashes and factional disputes or because of the view that the CNTS was not militant enough on behalf of the rank and file. The militancy of the autonomous unions and the concessions these unions were able to obtain from the government convinced many workers to move away from the CNTS. By 1991, employment losses in the private and public sectors, as well as defections to rival unions, reduced the CNTS from between 65,000 and 70,000 members to no more than 40,000, and perhaps even fewer according to various sources (Bergen 1992; see also *Le Soleil,* August 12 and October 17, 1991). In the electricity sector, for example, the CNTS-affiliated union captured only 20 percent of the delegates in the 1990 elections, largely because of the inroads made by the Single Union of Electrical Workers (Syndicat Unique des Travailleurs de l'Electricité, or SUTELEC). This union, founded in 1981, rapidly displaced the CNTS's progovernment union in that sector. It claimed 1,600 members out of the 2,000 workers in the energy parastatal SENELEC, and its strikes disrupted the distribution of energy sporadically during and after 1988. Similarly, the Democratic Union of Senegalese Workers (Union Démocratique de Travailleurs Sénégalais), which had broken with the CNTS in 1987, managed to weaken the hold of the CNTS on workers in the manufacturing sector. These defections fueled the militancy of the CNTS, which distanced itself somewhat from the government.

By 1987, the increasing austerity and stringency of the stabilization measures being carried out spelled the end of the honeymoon in the education sector. Students boycotted classes in 1987, complaining that their grants had not been paid for an exceptionally long period of time and that the working and living conditions at the university were deteriorating (*West Africa,* March 2, 1987, pp. 111–12). During the entire 1987/88 school year, schools were closed. At the university, the academic year was nullified, and at secondary schools, only 15 percent of the students, mostly from private schools, took the high school examination in mid-July. In the end, public concern brought Diouf to meet and negotiate an end to the student strike with the Student Committee of Senegal. The government agreed to provide more classrooms, more scholarships, and subsidies for transport. Jean Collin was appointed chair of a committee to oversee the return to class for the 1988/89 school year (*Africa Confidential,* October 21, 1988). Students soon struck again, however, claiming that the government had not honored the agreement (*Le Soleil,* March 8, 1989). Throughout 1990 and 1991, sporadic strikes paralyzed the school system.

Union militancy also picked up in 1987 in reaction to the budget cuts in the agricultural parastatals and the social ministries of health and education. The Single Union of Health Care Workers (Syndicat Unique des Travailleurs de la Santé) was among the first to react to the increasing unemployment. It had already gone on strike in 1984 and 1985 to call attention to the declining percentage of the national budget devoted to health spending.[28] In September 1988, hospital staff went on strike for two days a week and threatened to strike every other week if their demands for more funds for the health sector were not met. In a compromise, Diouf agreed to negotiate with the union and promised to improve working conditions and increase funding (*Africa Confidential,* October 21, 1988).

SUTELEC, in particular, was very active in organizing an umbrella organization for autonomous unions. Composed of six autonomous unions, the National League of Autonomous Unions (L'Union Nationale des Syndicats Autonomes) was constituted in May 1990 to counterbalance the progovernment CNTS (*Le Soleil,* August 12 and October 17, 1991). Growth of the autonomous union movement had repercussions for the relationship between the government and the CNTS, which had hardened its stand on adjustment to maintain credibility with its members. As early as 1986/87, the CNTS had refused to sanction the economic program. Madia Diop, the CNTS strong man, even denounced the layoffs foreseen under the adjustment program, although he did not call for a general strike against government policies (see Diop and Diouf 1990, pp. 182–83).

It was over the issue of changes in the labor code that the CNTS chose to highlight its differences with government policies. The World Bank and the employers saw the old labor code as a major constraint in two respects: enterprises had to go through the government recruitment services to hire workers, and firing an employee was extremely difficult.

The World Bank and the employers wanted to eliminate such rigidities, making it possible for companies and labor to adjust quickly to market conditions. Changes in the labor code were supposed to be introduced before August 31, 1987, as a condition for the release of the second tranche of SAL II. In a speech to the Economic and Social Council at the end of March 1987, President Diouf rejected external aid and lending agency demands for a fundamental overhaul of the labor code but accepted flexibility in the hiring of temporary employees.[29] A few weeks later, the CNTS denounced the president's policy, arguing that it reduced worker protection. CNTS members demonstrated outside the National Assembly the day the new amendments were to be debated. The National Assembly rejected the new laws on flexibility, even for temporary workers, at the risk of losing the World Bank structural adjustment loan. It did, however, abolish the government employment services' monopoly on recruitment, opening the way for private employment agencies. Soon after that "victory," the CNTS publicly endorsed the candidacy of the ruling party and the president for the elections to be held six months later. Nonetheless, in October 1989, months after the elections and after heated debate, the National Assembly approved a new investment code that, in effect, overrode the legislation restricting the right of employers to take on workers in short-term contracts or to lay them off for commercial reasons. At the time of this writing, the government was still fighting to introduce those provisions in the labor code.

In the months following the 1988 elections and Dakar riots, the CNTS's stand against reform became more pointed, and it began seeking a rapprochement with the autonomous unions. The possibility of a broad union front allied to the opposition confirmed the worst fears of the government. During the March 1989 Congress, Abdou Diouf reminded union leaders that the CNTS was affiliated by law with the Socialist Party and that its increasing opposition to the policies of the government was out of line. This warning was disregarded by the leadership, which soon formed an alliance with the Marxist Party of Independence and Labor (Parti de l'Indépendence et du Travail), whose militant opposition to the structural adjustment program was well known and whose influence in the union movement was growing. The traditional May Day rally was canceled in 1988 because a state of emergency was imposed in the aftermath of the elections, and the May Day rally the following year promised to be a big show of labor strength. In obvious defiance of the government and much to the annoyance of the Socialist Party, leaders of the CNTS marched with those of the Party of Independence and Labor at the head of the rally that day.

These union activities led the government to delay or reject elements of the reform program in violation of external agency conditionality. The agencies protested but broadly accepted the government's pleas that the threat of a general strike justified a slowdown in implementing the ad-

justment program. The CNTS's show of strength gained some concessions; the union took credit for the government's decision to lower the
price of foodstuffs, including rice, sugar, and oil in 1988. It now claimed
the April 1990 wage hike—CFAF6,000 across the board—in blatant
disregard of external agency conditionalities. In the spring of 1989, the
government had introduced a 5 percent across-the-board tax in order to
face its budgetary problems. Joint union protests led the president to
overrule his finance minister and rescind his own decree in November
1990, on the eve of municipal elections. Two months later, the government introduced a more progressive income tax. The minister of finance
was subsequently replaced.

The teacher unions also increased their militancy in reaction to growing austerity. As their jobs and benefits were threatened and working
conditions worsened, the Autonomous Union of High School Teachers
(the Syndicat Autonome des Enseignants du Supérieur), the Democratic
Teachers Union (the Union Démocratique des Enseignants), and the Single Union of Senegalese Teachers (Syndicat Unique des Enseignants du
Sénégal) reacted to the threats to their jobs, benefits, and the worsening
working conditions by resorting to demonstrations and strikes. The most
important developments took place in 1989, when, after negotiations
between authorities and teachers' organizations failed, the unions organized a series of strikes that paralyzed the school system for seventy days.
Finally, the government conceded to prevent the loss of a second successive academic year (the first was lost due to a student strike; Diop and
Diouf 1990, pp. 242–44). Thus, despite the World Bank's pressure to
control salary levels, the government agreed to a 40 percent rise in
teacher salaries, special research grants, and a doubling of housing
allowances.

In sum, the pressure exerted by both autonomous as well as government unions was successful in slowing down the implementation of the
economic structural adjustment reforms. One should not exaggerate
union power, however, and it is important to realize the limits of its role
in derailing adjustment policies. Union pressures did not prevent the
union rank and file from being the big economic losers of the 1980s.
Indeed, wage earners may have lost as much as 40 percent of their
purchasing power during the adjustment period, while unions saw many
of their members lose jobs and face increasing insecurity (Bergen 1992).
In early 1991, 24 percent of the economically active population in Dakar
was unemployed, and, with 100,000 new entrants to the job market
every year, the downward pressure on wages seemed irresistible.

Despite its growing independence from the government, the CNTS leadership remained essentially loyal to the Socialist Party and to government
policies throughout this period. Given the worsening economic conditions, union opposition could have been considerably more destabilizing
than it was. While trying to keep up with the growing militancy of the

rank and file, Diop and the CNTS leadership consistently sided with the government on the most important issues and remained faithful to the ideals of *participation responsable*. In other words, the CNTS strategy remained one of trying to channel and diffuse worker discontent in order to maintain political stability.

The appearance that the CNTS had become significantly more independent from the government was ultimately useful to Diouf, not only because it helped maintain the union's credibility, but also because it provided an effective excuse for the government's failure to comply with external agency conditionality. The external aid and lending agencies proved to be highly sensitive to the issue of union activity and tolerated more slippage in this area than in any other. On the one hand, this allowed Diouf to slow the speed of implementation and maintain the appearance of standing up to the international organizations. This was politically valuable, particularly in the months preceding the 1988 elections. On the other hand, union activities allowed Diouf to convince the external agencies that political instability and Diouf's electoral defeat were real risks if reform proceeded too fast.

BUSINESS GROUPS.   Unlike students and unions, the business sector was not opposed to reform per se. The liberalization of trade foreseen by the NPI probably threatened the survival of three-quarters of the enterprises established in Senegal. Much of the business sector was composed of classic rent-seeking entrepreneurs who depended on both contacts within the state and government intervention in the economy to make profits. In so doing, they responded to the environment created by state actions. By the mid-1980s, however, fraud, economic austerity, and the breakdown of the banking sector had undermined the old system to the point that businessmen were open to reform. The private sector welcomed the prospect of labor market liberalization, arguing that the current labor code increased their costs and reduced their ability to respond to market forces. It supported all accompanying measures. Businessmen were also likely to benefit from the privatizations, which promised to strengthen the private sector as a whole.

Business influence on policy had traditionally relied on the alliances, family ties, and intermarriages among businessmen, important civil servants, religious leaders, and politicians. Many businessmen were politically active, and their significant contributions to the Socialist Party played a major role in President Diouf's election in 1983 and 1988. The early years of the NPI witnessed the emergence of several business groups, which came to represent different interests in a less personalistic manner. The foremost group was the National Council of Senegalese Managers (Conseil National du Patronat Sénégalais, or CNPS), which was formed in 1986 after the government launched the new industrial policy without consulting the business sector. The CNPS was dominated by the French employers' union SPIDS, which represents most of secondary industry. CNPS's concerns were raised in letters sent to the authorities and in regular meetings with senior political leaders including the head of state, who met with the CNPS twice a year, and key administrative personnel.

In addition, smaller businesses were represented by the National Union of Merchants and Manufacturers of Senegal (Union Nationale des Commerçants et Industriels du Sénégal, or UNICOIS), an association whose size and influence increased during the NPI, thanks to the liberalization program. Dominated by the Mourides, UNICOIS lobbied on behalf of the brotherhood's increasing investments in trade and small industry.

As mentioned, NPI measures passed in 1986 and 1987 eliminated quantitative restrictions on imports, lowered tariffs, and deregulated import licensing. The number of import licenses dramatically increased as a result, many of them going to Mouride businessmen. These reforms had highly negative effects on the big French companies and the Lebanese commercial houses, which were furious about losing their cozy monopolies. Manufacturers, notably in textiles, simply could not compete with imports. They complained bitterly about the imbalance between the constraining measures implemented under the NPI, the speed of the tariff reduction, and the slow progress made in changing the business environment, which was characterized by a rigid labor market, high interest rates, and multiple administrative bottlenecks. The CNPS, in particular, demanded the reintroduction of protection and a reduction in smuggling.

In contrast, liberalization dramatically helped the more efficient and less regulated small indigenous companies (see Ebin 1992 for a fascinating analysis of one of the bigger firms operating in Sandaga during this period). Reform resulted in Senegalese traders developing their activities in the electronic, equipment, clothing, and footwear sectors. The Sandaga market in Dakar was transformed into a quasi–free trade area as a result of these reforms and the increasing amount of fraud that occurred during this period. The Sandaga traders, frustrated by the slow speed of reform, pushed UNICOIS to lobby on behalf of liberalization.

After a period of speedy implementation of the NPI, the government abruptly reintroduced protective tariffs in August 1989. The decision to rescind much of the NPI sparked anger from the traders, who went on strike in September 1989 and continued to protest the government's decisions. These pressures led the government into a balancing act between the interests represented by the CNPS and those represented by UNICOIS. The return of protection signaled a victory of the old alliance of rent-seeking businesses and conservatives within the Socialist Party who had opposed reform all along. Not willing to displease the Mourides, nonetheless, the government allowed the Sandaga Market to continue flourishing by failing to clamp down on import fraud. The business sector seeking liberalization was ultimately unsuccessful, however, because the government was preoccupied with the country's deteriorating public finances and with the threat of factory closings and political instability.

By 1991, large sections of domestic manufacturing were bankrupt, and the credibility of the reformers and of their program of free trade had been seriously undermined. Elements in both CNPS and UNICOIS favored industrial reform, albeit for very different reasons, and, under the right circumstances, could have been mobilized to support reform efforts. The government failed to reach out and seek allies among these groups, however, in part because the old clientelist networks linking individual businessmen to the state and party undermined reform. License exemptions, fraud, and tax evasion continued as before. In part, reform failed because fiscal exigencies undermined the government's commitment to liberalization. But in addition, the government failed to seek alliances with business on behalf of the NPI because many of the reformist technocrats within the government considered private business as corrupt and parasitic. Indeed, once again, business leaders were never consulted, let alone involved in a systematic fashion, regarding the NPI reform. Ironically, the antireform element within the state was much more familiar with the private sector, through rent-seeking and clientelist networks, than the free market reformers. Like the cartoon character who loves mankind but hates people, they promoted trade liberalization without wanting domestic firms to succeed.

The Politics of Nonreform, 1987–91

As reform failed to deliver economic results and abate the conditions of austerity, the government was increasingly put on the defensive. After almost a decade of official commitment to economic stabilization and restructuring, most *Dakarois* felt that the country had gained little except declining purchasing power, deteriorating social services, and rising unemployment (Sommerville 1991). Most blamed the PAML for these ills rather than the policies of the previous quarter century. Constituencies likely to oppose reform were increasingly well organized and, like the union movement, able to mobilize against government policies. This opposition did not actually threaten the regime's stability, but it was bothersome and eroded its popularity. Diouf had undermined the power and legitimacy of the Socialist Party and, in the process, antagonized its stalwart members. This initially strengthened the reformers but in time meant that the one political organization capable of carrying Diouf's message to the country was largely opposed to reform. Open support for the program was increasingly limited to the small cadre of technocrats charged with implementing it. Diouf and his allies had simply never been able to create a coalition for reform among the groups who stood to gain

from it. The last section of this chapter focuses on these economic constraints and coalitional dynamics because they provide the context for
understanding key events after 1987 that signaled the end of reform.

In mid-April 1987, the government faced an unexpected challenge
from its own police force. Police resentment surfaced when disciplinary
and then legal action was taken against seven officers who had tortured a
suspect in custody. The police force went on strike, demanding the return
of their colleagues. The government responded forcefully by suspending
the entire police force, more than 6,000 agents, just months before presidential and parliamentary elections (Diop and Diouf 1990, pp. 285–93).
Some of the police were reintegrated after pledging loyalty to the government (Le Soleil, April 16, 29, and 30, 1987). The police strike, motivated in part by deteriorating purchasing power and generally poor
working conditions, underscored the dangers posed by the economic
crisis to state institutions themselves.

The legal opposition capitalized on growing popular opposition to
economic austerity in the months preceding the 1988 campaign. In a
skillful campaign, Abdoulaye Wade and his Senegalese Democratic Party
exploited popular discontent by promising that if elected, he would cut
the retail price of rice from CFAF160 a kilo to CFAF60 and provide free
fertilizers to farmers for two years. His party was no match for the
Socialist Party, despite the growing discontent. The Mouride hierarchy
had declared its support for Diouf and virtually ensured him strong
majorities in the countryside (see anonymous 1988a). In any event,
Wade's party could not match the Socialist Party's control of the media,
its much stronger organization outside of Dakar, and its ability to tap
public funds for electoral purposes. Nonetheless, its constant slogan,
"SOPI!" (meaning "Change!" in Wolof), captured the public's imagination. Large crowds attended opposition rallies, demonstrating their dissatisfaction with government policies.

The opposition challenged the legality of electoral procedures and
accused the government of planning to steal the election. Tension
mounted throughout the campaign, with increasingly strident protests by
university students and trade unions (Diop and Diouf 1990, pp. 295–
301, 311–13). The CNTS became more aggressive as it rightly believed
the government would be more likely to make concessions now than
after it had renewed its mandate. It pressed the government to reduce the
price of basic foodstuffs and of energy and electricity, as well as to
increase salaries and create new jobs to compensate for those lost under
the economic restructuring program (Africa Contemporary Record, vol.
20B 130, 1987/88).

The election proceeded amidst considerable tension. In the official
results proclaimed by the Supreme Court several days later, Diouf received 72 percent of the vote and the Socialist Party was attributed 103 of
120 seats, since it had gained a little more than 71 percent of the vote (see

table 8-5). The Senegalese Democratic Party officially received 25 percent of the vote and 17 seats. Wade himself won 26 percent. A little less than half of the eligible population voted. Most outside observers accepted these results as a reasonable reflection of the actual popular vote, albeit in the context of voter intimidation, some fraud on behalf of the Socialist Party, and the usual practice of marabout-directed voting in the countryside. (See, for example, Young and Kante 1991; O'Brien 1992 argues, however, that Wade actually did win the election, but this is a minority view. Copans 1988 describes well how, in much of the peanut basin, the local marabout votes on behalf of his followers, thus controlling a large number of votes, usually for the Socialist Party). The opposition contested the results, and Wade claimed to have won the presidency. This was widely believed by urban youth in Dakar, who went on a rampage to protest. The day following the elections, official cars were burnt, government buildings and gas stations were sacked, and the private properties of well-known individuals connected to the regime were looted. The government declared a state of emergency, called in the army to maintain order, imposed a curfew, and arrested the main opposition leaders, accusing them of instigating the riot. Wade himself was arrested and tried for his role in these events; on May 11, he received a suspended sentence of one year but was amnestied almost immediately by Diouf and allowed to take his seat in Parliament.

The state of emergency enabled the government to restore order, but tensions remained high in Dakar for the following months. During April and May 1988, groups of women organized demonstrations in which they protested against the austerity measures by banging empty pots and shaking rice bags. The authorities were surprised and shaken by the depth of popular discontent and dissatisfaction with the economic restructuring program. Indeed, it was not the first time that opposition parties had whipped up popular dissatisfaction and alleged fraud after an election (Hesseling 1985). But the enthusiasm demonstrated by disaffected urban youth for the opposition and the violence occurring after the elections were a new source of preoccupation for the authorities.

This propensity to violence was confirmed by two more episodes. First, late 1988 witnessed growing dissatisfaction among farmers. Cotton farmers in the south were increasingly unhappy with marketing conditions. Unlike groundnut farmers, however, cotton farmers did not have the option of turning to the parallel market, so they protested instead. For the first time in the postcolonial history of Senegal, cotton producers defied the government openly by demanding a 150 percent increase in prices or a 60 percent reduction in input costs. From December 1988 to June 1989, the region of Velingara witnessed farmer protests and a boycott of the cotton parastatal SODEFITEX. Farmers organized themselves using methods so far only seen in urban unions. As a consequence, cotton sales fell from 42,000 to 28,000 tons.

Table 8-5. Official Results of the Presidential and Legislative Elections in Senegal, 1978–88

Candidate and party	1978		1983		1988	
	Percent of votes	*Number of seats*	*Percent of votes*	*Number of seats*	*Percent of votes*	*Number of seats*
Presidency						
Leopold Senghor (Socialist Party)	82.5	n.a.	n.a.	n.a.	n.a.	n.a.
Abdou Diouf (Socialist Party)	n.a.	n.a.	83.5	n.a.	72.3	n.a.
Abdoulaye Wade (Senegalese Democratic Party)	17.4	n.a.	14.8	n.a.	25.8	n.a.
Oumar Wone (Senegalese People's Party)	n.a.	n.a.	0.2	n.a.	n.a.	n.a.
Mamadou Dia (Movement for People's Democracy)	n.a.	n.a.	1.4	n.a.	n.a.	n.a.
Majmout Diop (African Independence Party)	n.a.	n.a.	0.2	n.a.	n.a.	n.a.
Babacar Niang (Party for the People's Liberation)	n.a.	n.a.	n.a.	n.a.	0.8	n.a.
Landing Savane (And-Jëff/ Revolutionary Movement for New Democracy)	n.a.	n.a.	n.a.	n.a.	0.3	n.a.

More immediately threatening were the riots in April 1989, when increasing tensions with Mauritania over land right disputes along the Senegal River led to an outbreak of ethnic violence (Diop and Diouf 1990, pp. 387–404). Reports of widespread atrocities against the Senegalese in Mauritania that winter aroused anti-Mauritanian sentiment in Dakar, where Mauritanians have traditionally controlled a share of the petty trading sector. In April, violence erupted when gangs of Senegalese youths looted shops and lynched Mauritanians. Unemployed adults took advantage of the disturbance to plunder shops for their essential needs, and what began as violence targeted specifically at Mauritanian merchants turned into random violence (*Wal Fadjiri*, no. 158, April 28, 1989, p. 160). In the end, tens of thousands of people had to be protected and evacuated by the army in both countries.

Candidate and party	1978		1983		1988	
	Percent of votes	*Number of seats*	*Percent of votes*	*Number of seats*	*Percent of votes*	*Number of seats*
Legislature						
Socialist Party	81.7	82	79.9	111	71.3	103
Senegalese Democratic Party	17.8	18	14.0	8	24.7	17
African Independence Party	0.4	0	0.3	0	n.a.	n.a.
National Democratic Rally	n.a.	n.a.	2.7	1	n.a.	n.a.
Movement for People's Democracy	n.a.	n.a.	1.2	0	n.a.	n.a.
Democratic League/ Movement for the Workers Party	n.a.	n.a.	1.2	0	1.2	0
Party of Independence and Labor	n.a.	n.a.	0.6	0	0.8	0
Senegalese People's Party	n.a.	n.a.	0.2	0	n.a.	n.a.
Party for Senegalese Democracy- Renewal	n.a.	n.a.	n.a.	n.a.	0.4	0
Party for the People's Liberation	n.a.	n.a.	n.a.	n.a.	1.2	0

n.a. Not applicable.
Source: Hesseling 1985 and accounts in *Le Soleil, Sub-Hebdo,* and *Wal Fadjiri.*

One of the immediate consequences of the departure of the Mauritanian petty traders was that their market share was recaptured by the
Senegalese, providing the government with some relief from pressing
unemployment. In fact, authorities seized the occasion to encourage unemployed and redundant civil servants to invest in the commercial sector.
The violence of this second riot also reminded the government of how
precarious social peace had become.

These episodes concerned the government more than growing union
militancy or the opposition's speeches. Diouf's comfortable margin of
victory in the 1988 elections indicated that he need not worry about
being voted out of office. Traditional tactics could be used to divide, co-

opt, and undermine the opposition and the unions. The violence in 1988 and 1989 came, however, from marginalized and disaffected groups outside the usual political spectrum, for whom traditional methods of social control had proved ineffective.

The government responded to these crises in several ways. First, it became more tolerant of the CNTS's independence, hoping a more credible union would be able to channel and contain discontent. This strategy forced the government to take a series of steps that undermined implementation of the program agreed to with the World Bank. For example, the government responded to the opposition's electoral promises by lowering the price of rice from CFAF160 to CFAF130, the price of groundnut oil from CFAF400 to CFAF350, and the price of sugar from CFAF355 to CFAF300 in view, said the president in his 1988 May Day speech, "of the difficulties faced by families to make ends meet." However, he added, "it is the maximum that can be done," and he pleaded that the Senegalese Democratic Party's campaign promises of further reductions were simply not realistic (Foreign Broadcast Information Service 1988).

The riots convinced the authorities that the problem of unemployment had to be addressed. The government considered creating a civilian form of national service to be administered by the Ministry of Armed Forces and increased support for sports programs, hoping to gain popularity with the young or at least keep them off the streets. More strategically, the president pledged that the social dimension of adjustment would receive greater priority in the future. Specifically, the government reversed its policy of cutting the civil service and began implementing a voluntary retirement scheme promising that "there will be no question of sacking people against their will." This again implied slippage in the implementation of the PAML, but Diouf convinced external aid and lending agencies in September 1989 to mobilize some $50 million to $60 million for a plan to create jobs (Economist Intelligence Unit 1989, p. 4).

The government dealt with farmer demands similarly in the south. In the short run, it refused to make concessions on its cotton pricing policies but accepted a moratorium on producer debt and promised free fertilizer and equipment to the most productive farmers (Sud-Hebdo, no. 59, June 29, 1989). More profoundly, these episodes eroded its commitment to the NPA reforms. By 1991, the government was openly criticizing the objectives of the World Bank's agricultural policy, particularly input subsidies. In his first speech to the National Assembly as prime minister, Habib Thiam complained about the decline in fertilizer consumption: "It is not possible to develop agriculture without subsidies," especially for a country facing ecological challenges such as drought and soil erosion. In a direct barb at the external agencies, he added, "It is such a serious problem, it should not be left to the experts" (Thiam 1991). This signaled a further relapse into the inefficient but stable system of low incentives coupled with selective, politically motivated benefits.

Diouf's second general strategy was a belated attempt to use the Socialist Party as his political instrument. Diouf had largely written off the party up to that point, preferring to consolidate his power by controlling the state apparatus. This policy had been justified in part by the Socialist Party's conservative and ossified nature, and the 1983 and 1988 elections had revealed the extent to which the barons had been discredited. The party had given Diouf little support for reform. The old professional politicians who could have increased the political viability of the economic program remained entrenched in their local fiefs and organized political obstruction of the program.

Diouf now realized, however, that the party remained the only organization at his disposal to ensure social control, the stability of his power, and—albeit now a less pressing concern—economic reform. He thus sought to revitalize it. This proved hard to accomplish. Even after the 1988 elections further discredited the barons, the new and younger militants promoted by Diouf did not capture the top positions in the party. Diouf now launched a frontal attack on the barons. In March 1989, he abolished the central committee and the politburo and appointed a new ten-member committee constituted by his own men (*Le Soleil,* February 16 and March 6, 1989). The new committee oversaw registration and recruitment, trying to help newcomers capture senior positions in local cells of the party. By July 1989, however, Diouf was forced to acknowledge his failure to rejuvenate the party. The barons were called in to form a new commission for settling internal disputes. Diouf implicitly accepted the need to seek accommodation with the old guard, even if it meant sacrificing policy objectives in the short term.

The third element of Diouf's strategy was to seek a rapprochement with the opposition. In the aftermath of the February elections, Diouf was forced to realize that the ruling party did not represent most of the existing social interests. The narrow social base of the members of Parliament meant that large portions of the politicized public remained outside the arena where they could be co-opted. Diouf understood that he could not afford to allow leaders like Wade to continue taking pot shots at him from the sidelines; the continuation of the austerity program required the passive acquiescence of the opposition, if not its active support. Thus, the government made overtures to opposition leaders, most of whom were soon amnestied from the sentences leveled at them after the 1988 elections. After a rocky start, a series of informal negotiations were undertaken between the Socialist Party and several of the leading opposition parties. In April 1991, Diouf constituted a coalition government in which the Senegalese Democratic Party and the Party of Independence and Labor joined the Socialist Party. Habib Thiam, an old friend of Diouf's whose lack of enthusiasm for economic liberalization was well known, became prime minister, a post he had occupied from 1981 to 1983. Abdoulaye Wade joined the government as its number two minister but without any specific attribution. It was widely believed at the time that Diouf had made specific promises to convince Wade to join the government, although both men denied it. Some broad programmatic agreement is likely to have been reached because Wade and the other four opposition ministers did not deviate from official government positions once they joined the government.

What were the implications of cohabitation for adjustment? It seems clear that the granting of ministerial positions effectively tempered the opposition's criticism of official economic policies. In exchange for this new consensual approach, the government precluded rapid movement on the most controversial aspects of the adjustment program. Some observers feared that the consensus between the Socialist Party and the Senegalese Democratic Party would only serve to discredit Wade as an opportunist and further alienate the disaffected youth from electoral politics. The stand of the Party of Independence and Work against adjustment is well documented; that of the Senegalese Democratic Party is less clear. On the one hand, the Senegalese Democratic Party drew most of its supporters from sectors of the economy where adjustment had had negative effects. On the other hand, it had always claimed that it understood the rationale of the structural adjustment program and was equipped to implement it better than others who were more compromised by the old institutional structures (Wade 1989).

The appointment of Habib Thiam was the logical consequence of Diouf's strategy for dealing with the heightened political threats he faced after 1988. The elimination of the prime minister's position in 1983 had signaled Diouf's commitment to grapple directly with the country's economic woes. After 1988, Diouf lessened his commitment to the reform process and began criticizing the external aid and lending agencies in his speeches. He distanced himself from the reform effort within the government and increasingly sided with the politicians and against the technocrats. This process was complete when he reestablished the Prime Ministry and named Thiam to head the coalition government. He could now step away from everyday policy issues and let the prime minister share the blame for unpopular decisions. In addition, the appointment of Thiam, an old Socialist Party warhorse with good party contacts, was widely perceived as an attempt to reassure the conservatives in the party that the pace of reform would be slow. Thiam's first public statements indicated he was at least ambivalent about reform and would contest external agency conditionality much more strenuously than his predecessors.

Thus, by 1991, economic reform had lost most of its domestic political momentum. Continued financial support from abroad was much too important for the government to antagonize the external agencies openly, however. The reform program proceeded, and concessions continued to be made to assuage external agency demands. Nonetheless, reform proceeded much more cautiously than before, and Diouf did not take any risks on behalf of the reform process.

Why, it may be asked, did the reformist team that Diouf had assembled back in 1983 not fight to maintain the program? Many technocrats had staked their careers on reform and had risen to important positions in the state bureaucracy; why were they not able to maintain some momentum for reform? First, the reformist technocrats who were brought in to lead the reform effort in the early 1980s were for the most part political innocents with little or no experience in party politics. They never sought to create a political base or to defend the program in political terms. Only the president and a handful of technocrats could claim to be politicians, and few had the savvy and foresight to gain political experience and power. Most failed miserably in local elections. The absence of this political base was, if anything, an advantage as long as they enjoyed the trust and support of the highest echelons of the state, since it insulated the team from the rough and tumble, pressures, and compromises of politics. Over time, however, it meant that their success and political survival depended on the continued support of Diouf himself.

The president made few sustained efforts to sell adjustment. In the mid-1980s, with the help of Jean Collin, Diouf nominated young militants who espoused his views in the Group of Study and Research (Group d'Étude et de Recherches, or GER). The GER had full membership in the central committee and was represented in the party politburo. The new members were instrumental in focusing the party's debate on economic issues. Thus, in 1985 and 1986, architects of the structural adjustment program presented their views to all levels of the Socialist Party (to get the flavor of these exercises, see, for example, Kane 1986; Touré 1985). These discussions involved techniques and jargon well beyond the comprehension of the average party member and rarely addressed the everyday concerns of the rank and file. No effort was made to convey the ideas behind the adjustment program. Ironically, Diouf and Collin did not seem to realize that the democratization reforms promulgated by the government had changed the rules of the game and made the old elitist paternalism outmoded.

Second, the technocratic team was undermined by bureaucratic politics. In the early phases, Touré's credibility as well as the technical competence and integrity of the architects of the program established their reputation. The CSPA, by improving administrative efficiency through its coordinating functions, gained some influence and power. In the process, however, it began to annoy the rest of the administration in the regular ministerial structures. The CSPA's ability to avoid normal channels, refer issues to the cabinet and presidency, and use its privileged links with the external aid and lending agencies to push dossiers was increasingly resented. A war of attrition emerged between the adjustment structures and the old administrative elite, even within the Ministry of Planning, where the CSPA was initially housed. Consequently, in April 1988, the CSPA was placed under Collin within the presidency, elevating its status but simultaneously reinforcing the administration's mistrust of it.

The departure from the government in March 1988 of the two architects of the program, Mamoudou Touré and Cheikh Hamidou Kane, left the adjustment team without a spokesperson who had a strategic understanding of the program and enough prestige to counter attacks on the adjustment structures. Reports suggested that Collin had forced Touré out for trying to cut government subsidies to the Sugar Company of Senegal, long an important contributor to the coffers of the Socialist Party (*Africa Confidential,* May 27, 1988).

In fact, relocating the CSPA to the presidency concentrated decisions in the hands of Collin, who became prime minister de facto. By the end of 1989, he controlled twenty-two out of twenty-six major national services, with the president in charge of the other four, and made all important expenditures decisions and key appointments. Now a bureaucratic patron in his own right, Collin gave key players his protection and help, leaving cabinet ministers with reduced influence over their subordinates. Most of his clients were precisely the persons who had problems with their ministers and were not necessarily partisans of structural adjustment. The minister of state became the arbiter of conflicts between agencies and between the government and pressure groups, which negotiated directly with him rather than with the minister in charge. Even though he agreed with many of the objectives of structural adjustment, Collin was motivated by the accumulation of bureaucratic power and did not always favor quick implementation of structural policies. Some of his decisions, in fact, tended to support conservative forces whose interests lay squarely with the status quo—preserving market distortions related to the patron-client relationship or protecting inefficient industries. Nonetheless, when Diouf finally forced Collin into retirement in March 1990—his departure appears to have been a condition of the national unity talks with the opposition—the CSPA lost a powerful patron, which weakened it considerably.

Other factors also undermined the prospects for reform. Internal divisions and personal rivalries among several members of the reform team appeared precisely when the program was losing momentum and its opponents in the unions and party were colluding to fight against reforms. Institutional instability at the ministerial level also generated confusion. Between April 1983 and April 1991, there were five major cabinet reshuffles—April 1983, January 1985, April 1988, March 1990, and April 1991. The ministerial turnover did not spare "adjustment" of the finance, planning, rural development, and industry portfolios. Ministers came and went every two years on average, as did their teams. Each reshuffle was accompanied by an internal reordering, with functions absorbed or new ones created. For example, data production and forecasting and planning agencies were separated at one point before being absorbed by the Ministry of Planning, itself later incorporated into the new Ministry of Economy, Finance, and Planning. In the rural sector, the opposite trend was observed. Farmers' organizations, which were supervised by the Ministry of Rural Development in the early phases, were placed under the jurisdiction of five ministries, which perform similar functions.

In sum, the institutional reforms associated with the reform program and the ministerial ballet accompanying them created greater disruptions in services than coordination of actions. The continuous reordering of organizational responsibility created administrative discontinuity, strengthened parallel networks, and delayed implementation of the program. Fighting among bureaucracies left the government little energy to face the societal pressures placed on the program.

Conclusions

This study has tried to explain why the economic reform program in Senegal during the 1980s was never fully implemented. The new team that came to power in 1981 with Abdou Diouf based its political legitimacy on technocratic competence and the urgent need to promote economic and political reform. After receiving a convincing electoral mandate in 1983, Diouf's government presented an economic reform program in line with reforms advocated by the IMF and the World Bank. From roughly 1983 to 1988, the government exhibited a strong commitment to the program, which proceeded reasonably well. After 1988, however, the program lost momentum, and by the end of 1991, the reform impulse appeared to have died, even if the economic crisis and external agency pressures kept reform on the agenda.

The common wisdom suggests that Senegal's economic stagnation is linked to its being one of the most democratic regimes in Africa. In this view, the presence of political pluralism weakened the state's will to undertake economic reform. Social pressures were indeed to blame for the failure of reform. The mobilization against the PAML by the workers' unions, the employer federations, and, to a much lesser extent, farmer organizations pressured the state to return to the preadjustment policies of subsidies, regulation, and trade protection. Regular and reasonably honest elections obviously pressured the government to lessen the bite of economic austerity.

Yet, Diouf's victory in the 1988 elections by virtually the same share of the vote received in 1983 demonstrates well the limits of this kind of analysis. Electoral defeat was simply never the biggest concern of Diouf and his allies, and this study has argued that the effect of interest group pressures must be put into a larger context if the failure of reform is to be understood. First, the program failed to address critical economic constraints on adjustment. The program's fiscal contradictions, the difficulty of achieving adjustment without devaluation, and the problematic nature of the response of aggregate supply to reforms all returned to haunt the government. Perhaps as important, pessimism about the economy shaped expectations; it lessened the credibility of reform to economic actors and undermined the commitment to reform of a political class already skeptical of the virtues of economic liberalism in the local environment.

Moreover, the effect of interest group pressures must be understood in the context of President Diouf's consolidation of power. In the early 1980s, the logic of economic and political liberalization coincided with Diouf's own political needs. Political pluralism and economic reform helped him discipline and weaken the old guard within the Socialist Party and introduce to politics a new generation of men beholden to him. Democratization held relatively few risks as long as he maintained the support of the marabouts, even while he pretended otherwise in negotiations with the external aid and lending agencies.

The violence of 1988 and 1989 changed the rules of the game, however, by suggesting that the traditional methods of social control were not effective on marginalized elements of the population, which were controlled neither by the marabouts nor by the unions and the political parties. It signaled to the government the need to take a much more cautious approach to economic changes.

Finally, the government lacked a viable political strategy of implementation. Because his top priorities were his own political needs rather than the needs of reform, Diouf never attempted to create a coalition on behalf of reform. In particular, the Socialist Party was never mobilized to sell the program, and the technocrats did not compensate for this oversight. They were not active in party politics, were nonexistent in the Parliament, and did not seek out allies among groups of farmers or businessmen who stood to gain from a successful reform program. Lacking any political strategy, they trusted Diouf to continue backing them. With the departure of Mamoudou Touré and Cheikh H. Kane, the two principal architects of the structural adjustment program and its most forceful advocates, the program and its technocratic allies succumbed to the changing political context as well as their own internal divisions and personal rivalries. Some senior civil servants and politicians played the reform card fully. Most sat on the fence, along with Diouf, giving reformers their chance but reserving judgment until the program had proven it entailed fewer risks than the status quo. As the difficulties and contradictions increased, the fence-sitters increasingly abandoned reform.

The external aid and lending agencies were just as shocked as the government by the riots of 1988 and 1989 and relaxed conditionality somewhat for the sake of political stability. By 1991, they were growing impatient again, and the end of the Cold War led many to rethink their priorities in Africa. There remained no ready alternative to their program of adjustment, which did not disappear from the policy agenda. Nonetheless, the April 1991 appointment of Thiam as prime minister—a technocrat from the old school with good connections to the old-style patrons of Senegalese politics and an avowed critic of economic liberalism—indicated the extent to which economic reform had been dislodged by the exigencies of Senegalese politics.

Notes

1. Morawetz 1977, pp. 77–78. All dollar amounts are U.S. dollars.

2. Some observers have noted similarities with the situation of Austria and Vienna after the breakup of the Austro-Hungarian Empire; see the references to Senegal's "Vienna problem" in Berg 1990, p. 1.

3. Complete wage parity between African and French employees had been reached with passage of the Lamine Guèye Law of 1950. As a result, in the early 1960s civil servants had seven times the average household income of peasants and twice the wage of skilled industrial workers (see O'Brien 1975, p. 219).

4. Since the late 1960s, the European Economic Community's Common Agricultural Policy has promoted other vegetable oils, such as sunflower seed oil, with subsidies that make them much cheaper than peanut oil. As a result, peanut oil has lost considerable market share, passing from more than 80 percent of total consumption in France in 1960 to less than 30 percent by the mid-1980s. See anonymous 1986 p. 1460.

5. Senegal's currency is linked to the *Communauté Financière Africaine*. See table 8-2 for the value of the CFA franc relative to the U.S. dollar. A billion is 1,000 million.

6. See Bonnefond and Couty 1991, p. 41. The authors suggest that the income differential between urban and rural areas remains 5:1, down from 7:1 at independence. This evolution reflects, in part, the rapid rate of urbanization through which the rural poor have migrated to the cities, decreasing the average urban income; urbanization proceeded by 3 percent between 1965 and 1980 and by 4 percent during the 1990s. By 1989, 38 percent of the population lived in towns or cities (World Bank 1991a).

7. Terrell and Svejnar (1990, p. 23) estimate that employment in the public sector—defined as the civil service and noncommercial public enterprises—grew from 46,100 in 1960 to 61,800 in 1970 and to 88,400 in 1980.

8. The official names of these agencies in French are the Office National de Coopération et d'Assistance pour le Développement, Société Nationale d'Approvisionnement Rural, Société de Développement et de Vulgarisation Agricole, Société d'Aménagement et d'Exploitation des Terres du Delta, Société de la Mise en Valeur de la Casamance, and Société de Développement des Fibres Textiles.

9. See World Bank 1989b, p. 93. Taking into account the various subsidies granted to smallholder farmers, the implicit tax on their production is estimated at CFAF98 billion in constant 1980 prices between 1967 and 1985, roughly 5 percent of agricultural GDP (see Delgado and Jammeh 1991, p. 7). In addition, the government collected fiscal resources generated by industries related to agriculture (see *Sud-Hebdo*, no. 61, July 12, 1989; Jammeh 1987 for a full discussion).

10. See Terrel and Svejnar 1990, p. 23. In 1982, according to the Ministry of Planning, the total work force included 2.917 million persons, of which 35 percent were in the formal sector, 54 percent in the traditional rural sector, 11 percent in the urban informal sector, and 12 percent unemployed.

11. For example, in 1979, only 558 out of 1,700 cooperatives reimbursed 65 percent of their debt (*Ande-Sopi*, May 1979, p. 2).

12. In the mid-1960s, the community of 35,000 to 40,000 Lebanese controlled 25 percent of the retail trade, 20 percent of the wholesale trade, and 40 percent of the semi-wholesale trade (Boumedouha 1990).

13. Collin returned to the presidency as secretary general from 1981 to 1989 under Diouf, when his power reached its peak (see Diop and Diouf 1990, pp. 106–11).

14. The minimum wage went from an index of 100.0 in 1979 to 141.4 in 1983, while the average civil service salary climbed to 146.5 from the same base over the same period, thanks largely to internal promotions and job redefinitions (see Duruflé 1988, pp. 34–35).

15. In addition, the trade balance benefited from the relatively low prices prevailing for rice and oil, two of the biggest imports, during the 1980s.

16. These totals do not include French budgetary support through the treasury, which totaled an estimated $100 million. See anonymous 1988b, p. 1951.

17. In a cabinet meeting held in May 1989, the government decided to seek aid to subsidize fertilizers and increase fertilizer consumption, which had decreased from 100,000 tons to 15,000 tons a year in the past five years.

18. Mercuriales are administratively derived values for goods, which are used to derive the appropriate tariff for imports. The tariff is then assessed on the basis of that value rather than on the actual invoice price. Theoretically used to prevent dumping, mercuriales have, in fact, been used to increase the tariffs on goods, since the derived value is invariably higher than the invoice value.

19. According to Berg (1990, p. 132), electricity costs in Senegal were 60–65 percent higher than in nearby Côte d'Ivoire in 1987.

20. According to staff of the World Bank, this included 4,300 staff reductions through a voluntary departure program to be financed in part by the Bank loan; in addition, scheduled retirements would decrease staffing by 2,663 persons, 1,309 civil servants would leave as a result of the privatization program, and 370 irregular employees would also be terminated.

21. In addition, public enterprises continue to benefit from a wide assortment of indirect state subsidies, such as tax exemptions, forgone interest payments, and subsidized interest rates.

22. The government's own data estimate that 3,317 permanent and 1,236 temporary jobs were lost between 1985 and 1988, from a total of 41,843 jobs in the formal industrial sector at the start of the structural adjustment program; see Bergen 1992. The opposition press and some outside observers argue that job losses were as high as 20,000 during this period, but it is not clear whether these figures are gross or net (see Boone 1991; *Wal Fadjiri,* no. 251, March 7, 1991). The World Bank modestly estimates that 8,500 jobs were lost, or about 6 percent of total employment in the modern sector in 1986.

23. Here, a distinction needs to be made between the IMF, whose priority was short-term balance of payments objectives, and the World Bank, whose primary concern was the longer-term objectives of the NPI. The World Bank apparently lobbied its sister organization for more flexibility on the revenue side and a cut in the tax on oil, but to no avail. The government sided with the IMF, albeit for different reasons.

24. As monetary integration increases, France's obligations within the European Community are likely to impose some reforms on the operation of the Franc Zone; see Guillaumont and Guillaumont 1989.

25. In 1985, Senegal's negative position in the operations account at the French treasury stood at $207 million, and it remained as high as $162 million in 1990.

26. To cite just one example, SALS II and III included much too rapid a rate of privatization, given the difficulty involved in valuing assets, evaluating bids, and closing deals; for similar criticisms of Bank conditionality, see Duruflé 1988; Lewis 1987; World Bank 1989b. In fairness to the Bank, these criticisms were taken into account in designing SAL IV, which was considerably more circumspect about the possibility of rapid reform.

27. For example, in May 1991, it was revealed that in complete contradiction to the official forestry and ecological policies, the government had cleared some 45,000 hectares of forest in the Kelkhom region and given them to an important marabout for his personal cultivation (*Sud-Hebdo,* June 1991; *Wal Fadjiri,* no. 267, June 27, 1991).

28. The health budget dropped from 9 percent of the national budget in 1970 to less than 6 percent in 1985 and continued to decrease, reaching some 5 percent in the 1987–89 period; see Berg 1990, pp. 181–83.

29. In 1982, one-third of the persons employed in the formal sector held a permanent job, and that proportion probably decreased further by 1987 (Terrell and Svejnar 1990, p. 22).

References

Africa Confidential. 1988. May 27, October 21.

Africa Contemporary Record. 1987–88. Vol. 20B 130.

Amin, Samir. 1973. *Neo-Colonialism in West Africa.* New York: Monthly Review Press.

Ande-Sopi. 1979. May.

Anonymous. 1986. "La CEE et le déclin de l'arachide au Sénégal." *Marchés Tropicaux.* May 30.

Anonymous. 1988a. "Sénégal: Le vote des religieux." *Jeune Afrique* 1416. February 24.

Anonymous. 1988b. "Un des pays les plus aidés de l'Afrique Noire." *Marchés Tropicaux.* July 15, p. 1951.

Barker, Jonathan. 1985. "Gaps in the Debates about Agriculture in Senegal, Tanzania, and Mozambique." *World Development* 13:1 (January), pp. 59–76.

Bates, Robert. 1981. *Markets and States in Tropical Africa.* Berkeley: University of California Press.

Bathily, Abdoulaye. 1989. "Senegal's Structural Adjustment Program and Its Economic and Social Effects." In Onimode Bade, ed., *The IMF, the World Bank, and the African Debt,* vol. 2, *The Social and Political Impact.* London: Zed Books.

Berg, Elliot. 1990. *Adjustment Postponed: Economic Policy Reform in Senegal in the 1980s.* Report prepared for USAID/Dakar, October. Washington, D.C.: Elliot Berg and Associates.

Bergen, Geoffrey. 1992. "Labor, Democracy, and Development: Unions in the Political Economy of Senegal." Ph.D. diss., Department of Political Science, University of California at Los Angeles. Processed.

Bonnefond, Philippe, and Philippe Couty. 1991. "Agricultural Crisis: Past and Future." In Christopher Delgado and Sidi Jammeh, eds., *The Political Economy of Senegal under Structural Adjustment,* pp. 31–45. New York: Praeger.

Boone, Catherine. 1989. "The Making of a Rentier Class: Wealth Accumulation and Political Control in Senegal." *Journal of Development Studies* 26:3, pp. 425–50.

———. 1990. "State Power and Economic Crisis in Senegal." *Comparative Politics* 22:3 (April), pp. 341–58.

———. 1991. "Politics under the Specter of Deindustrialization: 'Structural Adjustment' in Practice." In Christopher Delgado and Sidi Jammeh, eds., *The Political Economy of Senegal under Structural Adjustment,* pp. 127–49. New York: Praeger.

———. 1992. *Buy Cheap, Sell Dear: Merchant Capital and the Roots of State Power in Senegal.* New York: Cambridge University Press.

Boumedouha, Said. 1990. "Adjustment to West African Realities: The Lebanese in Senegal." *Africa* 60:4, pp. 538–49.

Bratton, Michael, and Nicolas van de Walle. 1992. "Popular Protest and Political Reform in Africa." *Comparative Politics* 24:4 (July), pp. 419–42.

Caswell, Nina. 1984. "Autopsie de l'ONCAD: La politique arachidière au Sénégal, 1960–1980." *Politique Africaine,* Paris, 14, pp. 39–73.

Cissoko, Cheikh A. K. 1989. "La nouvelle politique agricole." *Parti Socialiste: Les cahiers de l'université d'été du Parti Socialiste,* Dakar (September).

Collier, Paul. 1991. "Africa's External Economic Relations, 1960–1990." In Douglas Rimmer, ed., *Africa, 30 Years On.* London: James Curry.

Commander, Simon, Ousseynou Ndoye, and Ismael Ouedrago. 1989. "Senegal 1979–1988." In Simon Commander, ed., *Structural Adjustment and Agriculture: Theory and Practice in Africa and Latin America*, pp. 145–74. London: Overseas Development Institute.

Copans, Jean. 1988. *Les marabouts de l'arachide: la confrérie et les paysans du Sénégal*. Paris: Le Sycomore.

Coulon, Christian. 1981. *Le marabout et le prince: Islam et pouvoir au Sénégal*. Paris: Editions Pedone.

_____. 1990. "Senegal: The Development and Fragility of Semidemocracy." In Larry Diamond, Juan J. Linz, and Seymour Martin Lipset, eds., *Politics in Developing Countries: Comparing Experiences with Democracy*, pp. 411–48. Boulder, Colo.: Lynne Rienner Publishers.

Craven, Kathryn, and Hasan A. Tuluy. 1981. "Rice Policy in Senegal." In Scott R. Pearson, Josiah D. Stryker, and Charles P. Humphreys, eds., *Rice in West Africa*. Stanford, Calif.: Stanford University Press.

Crowder, Michael. 1962. *Senegal: A Study in French Assimilation Policy*. Oxford, Eng.: Oxford University Press.

Delgado, Christopher, and Sidi Jammeh, eds. 1991. *The Political Economy of Senegal under Structural Adjustment*. New York: Praeger.

Devarajan, Shantayanan, and Jaime de Melo. 1987. "Adjustment with a Fixed Exchange Rate: Cameroon, Côte d'Ivoire, and Senegal." *World Bank Economic Review* 1:3, pp. 447–88.

Diop, Momar, and Mamadou Diouf. 1990. *Le Sénégal sous Abdou Diouf*. Paris: Karthala.

Diouf, Makhtar. 1992. "La crise de l'adjustement." *Politique Africaine* 46, pp. 63–85.

Duruflé, Gilles. 1988. *L'ajustement structurel en Afrique: Sénégal, Côte d'Ivoire, Madagascar*. Paris: Karthala.

Ebin, Victoria. 1992. "A la recherche de nouveaux 'poissons': Strategies commerciales mourides par temps de crises." *Politique Africaine* 46, pp. 86–99.

Economist Intelligence Unit. 1989. *Country Report Senegal* 3. London.

_____. 1991. *Country Report Senegal* 1. London.

Fatton, Robert. 1987. *The Making of a Liberal Democracy: Senegal's Passive Revolution, 1975–1985*. Boulder, Colo.: Lynne Rienner Publishers.

Foreign Broadcast Information Service. 1988. *Daily Report Africa*. May 3.

Foltz, William J. 1977. "Social Structure and Political Behavior of Senegalese Elites." In Steffen W. Schmidt, James C. Scott, Carl Lande, and Laura Guasti, eds., *Friends, Followers, and Factions*, pp. 242–50. Berkeley: University of California Press.

Freud, Claude. 1988. *Quelle coopération? Un bilan de l'aide au développement*. Paris: Karthala.

Gellar, Sheldon. 1982. *Senegal: An African Nation between Islam and the West*. Boulder, Colo.: Westview Press.

Gersovitz, Mark. 1987. "Some Sources and Implications of Uncertainty in the Senegalese Economy." In John Waterbury and Mark Gersovitz, eds., *The Political Economy of Risk and Choice in Senegal*. London: Frank Cass.

Guillaumont, Patrick, and Sylviane Guillaumont. 1984. *Zone Franc et développement africain.* Paris: Economica.

_____, eds. 1988. *Stratégies de développement comparées: Zone Franc et Hors Zone Franc.* Paris: Economica.

_____. 1989. "The Implications of European Monetary Union for African States." *Journal of Common Market Studies* 28:2, pp. 139–53.

Hesseling, Gerti. 1985. *Histoire politique du Sénégal.* Paris: Kartala.

International Monetary Fund. Various years. *Government Finance Statistics Yearbook.* Washington, D.C.

Jammeh, Sidi. 1987. "State Intervention in Agricultural Pricing and Marketing in Senegal." Ph.D. diss., Johns Hopkins University, Baltimore, Md.

Kane, Cheikh Hamidou. 1986. "La nouvelle planification du développement économique et social." Parti Socialiste, Dakar, April 26.

Kassé, Moustapha. 1990. *Sénégal: Crise économique et ajustement structurel.* Ivry-sur-Seine, France: Editions Nouvelles du Sud.

Krumm, Kathie L. 1987. "Adjustment in the Franc Zone: Focus on the Real Exchange Rate." CPD Discussion Paper 1987-7. World Bank, Washington D.C.

Lewis, John. 1987. "Aid, Structural Adjustment, and Senegalese Agriculture." In John Waterbury and Mark Gersovitz, eds., *The Political Economy of Risk and Choice in Senegal.* London: Frank Cass.

Lo, Magatte. 1987. *Syndicalisme et participation responsable.* Paris: L'Harmattan.

_____. 1991. *Sénégal, le temps du souvenir.* Paris: L'Harmattan.

Lofchie, Michael F. 1975. "Political and Economic Origins of African Hunger." *Journal of Modern African Studies* 16:3, pp. 451–75.

Magassouba, Moriba. 1985. *L'Islam au Sénégal: Demain les mollahs?* Paris: Karthala.

Markovitz, Irving Leonard. 1970. "Traditional Social Structure, the Islamic Brotherhoods, and Political Development in Senegal." *Journal of Modern African Studies* 8:1, pp. 73–96.

Martin, Guy. 1986. "The Franc Zone, Underdevelopment, and Dependency in Francophone Africa." *Third World Quarterly* 8:8, pp. 205–35.

Mbodji, Mohamed. 1991. "The Politics of Independence: 1960–86." In Christopher Delgado and Sidi Jammeh, eds., *The Political Economy of Senegal under Structural Adjustment,* pp. 119–26. New York: Praeger.

Morawetz, David. 1977. *Twenty-Five Years of Economic Development, 1950 to 1975.* Baltimore, Md.: Johns Hopkins University Press for the World Bank.

O'Brien, Donal Cruise. 1971. *The Mourides of Senegal.* Oxford, Eng.: Clarendon Press.

_____. 1975. *Saints and Politicians.* Cambridge, Eng.: Cambridge University Press.

_____. 1977. "Ruling Class and Peasantry in Senegal, 1960–1976." In Donal C. O'Brien, ed., *The Political Economy of Underdevelopment.* Beverly Hills, Calif.: Sage Publications.

_____. 1983. "Les élections sénégalaises du 27 février 1983." *Politique Africaine* 11, pp. 7–12.

_____. 1992. "Le contrat social sénégalais à l'épreuve." *Politique Africaine* 46, pp. 9–20.

Plane, P. 1990. "La genèse de la crise financière extérieure de l'Union Monétaire Ouest-Africaine, 1970–1985." *Politique Africaine* 35, pp. 105–19.

Salinger, B. Lynn, and J. Dirck Stryker. 1991. "Exchange Rate Policy and Implications for Agricultural Market Integration in West Africa." Associates for International Resources and Development, Cambridge, Mass. Processed.

Schumacher, Edward J. 1975. *Politics, Bureaucracy, and Rural Development in Senegal.* Berkeley: University of California Press.

Le Soleil. Various years, 1985–91. Dakar. March 11, 1985. April 9, 1986. April 16, 29, 30, 1987; February 16, March 6, 8, 9, 1989; August 12, October 17, 1991.

Sommerville, Carolyn M. 1991. "The Impact of the Reforms on the Urban Population." In Christopher Delgado and Sidi Jammeh, eds., *The Political Economy of Senegal under Structural Adjustment,* pp. 161–74. New York: Praeger.

Sud-Hebdo. Various years, 1989–91. Dakar, no. 59, June 29, 1989; no. 61, July 12, 1989; no. 61, December 7, 1989; no. 162, June 20, 1991.

Terrell, Katherine, and Jan Svejnar. 1990. "How Industry-Labor Relations and Government Policies Affect Senegal's Economic Performance." World Bank, Washington, D.C., January.

Thiam, Habib. 1991. "Discours de politique générale." Assemblée Nationale, Dakar, June. Processed.

Thioune, Assitan. 1991. "Les réformes de politique économique au Sénégal: 1986–1990." USAID, Dakar. Processed.

Touré, Mamoudou. 1985. *Politique d'ajustement économique et financier.* Dakar: Parti Socialiste du Sénégal.

Vallée, Olivier. 1989. *Le prix de l'argent CFA: Heurs et malheurs de la Zone Franc.* Paris: Karthala.

van de Walle, Nicolas. 1991. "The Decline of the Franc Zone: Monetary Politics in Francophone Africa." *African Affairs* 90 (July), pp. 383–405.

Wade, Abdoulaye. 1989. *Un destin pour l'Afrique.* Paris: Kartala.

Wal Fadjiri. Various years. Dakar, no. 158, April 28, 1989; no. 251, March 7, 1991; no. 267, June 27, 1991.

Wane, Abdoul Baila. 1990. *Collin, l'africain.* Dakar: Les Editions Republicaines.

Waterbury, John, and Mark Gersovitz, eds. 1987. *The Political Economy of Risk and Choice in Senegal.* London: Frank Cass.

West Africa. 1987. March 2.

World Bank. 1987a. "Senegal: An Economy under Adjustment." Report 6454-SE. Washington, D.C., February 13.

_____. 1987b. "Senegal: A Review of the Three-Year Public Investment Program, 1987/88–1989/90." Report 6450-SE. Washington, D.C., February.

_____. 1989a. "Republic of Senegal: Parapublic Sector Review." Report 7774-SE. Washington, D.C., May 1.

_____. 1989b. "The World Bank and Senegal, 1960–87." Report 8041. Operations Evaluation Department, Washington, D.C., August 31.

_____. 1990a. "Program Performance Audit Report, Senegal Second and Third Structural Adjustment Credit." Washington, D.C., May 31.

_____. 1990b. "Senegal: Report and Recommendations to the President of the International Development Association to the Executive Board of Directors for SAL IV." Washington, D.C., January 17.

_____. 1991a. *World Development Report 1991*. New York: Oxford University Press.

_____. 1991b. *World Tables 1991*. Baltimore, Md.: Johns Hopkins University Press.

Youm, Prosper. 1991. "The Economy since Independence." In Christopher Delgado and Sidi Jammeh, eds., *The Political Economy of Senegal under Structural Adjustment*. New York: Praeger.

Young, Crawford, and Babacar Kante. 1991. "Governance, Democracy, and the 1988 Senegalese Elections." In Goran Hyden and Michael Bratton, eds., *Governance and Politics in Africa*. Boulder, Colo.: Lynne Rienner Publishers.

9

Mexico: Radical Reform in
a Dominant Party System

Robert R. Kaufman, Carlos Bazdresch,
and Blanca Heredia

THE MEXICAN DEBT CRISIS OF 1982 TRIGGERED A PROLONGED EFFORT to
achieve stabilization and structural adjustment that has continued into
the early 1990s. This chapter focuses on an important turning point in
this effort: the Pact for Economic Solidarity (the pact), which was
launched during a major inflationary crisis in December 1987. This
analysis covers the program from its inception to the end of President
Miguel de la Madrid's term of office in December 1988.

This phase of the program constituted only one episode in an ongoing
process, but it warrants special attention for several reasons. First, the
pact featured concerted wage and price controls aimed at halting inertial
inflationary pressures. This turn toward an explicit new incomes policy
added a heterodox component to earlier stabilization plans, which had
relied more exclusively on fiscal and monetary instruments. In conjunction with continuing fiscal austerity, the incomes policy appeared to play
an important role in bringing inflation under control and thus helped set
the stage for a resumption of growth in the 1990s.

Second, the pact was accompanied by major new steps toward trade
liberalization. These included lowering maximum tariffs to 20 percent

The authors thank Armando Baqueiro, Vittorio Corbo, Stephan Haggard, Adriaan Ten
Kate, and Steven Webb for advice and comments at various stages of drafting this chapter.
Funding for the chapter was provided by the International Center for Economic Growth.

and the average tariff to about 10 percent, as well as a sharp reduction in the coverage of quantitative restrictions and the virtual elimination of official reference prices. Such measures represented a sharp acceleration of trade reforms already initiated during the crisis of 1985–86 and were pivotal in consolidating the opening of the Mexican economy.

Third, in negotiating the pact, the government strongly reaffirmed its commitment to fiscal discipline. Fiscal austerity had been a more or less ongoing feature of Mexican macroeconomic policy since de la Madrid's inauguration in December 1982. During 1988, however, the effort to control expenditures intensified, becoming a key component of the pact, notwithstanding the political pressures associated with a difficult presidential election campaign.

This chapter traces how two sets of factors influenced the content, timing, and implementation of these decisions. At the most immediate level, the successful implementation of a concerted incomes policy was the product of attempts by a relatively cohesive government elite to adapt long-term reform goals to constraints imposed by changing economic circumstances. General objectives of macroeconomic stability and economic liberalization were pursued more or less consistently throughout de la Madrid's administration. The way these objectives were implemented, however, was shaped by trial-and-error adjustments to a series of economic crises occurring throughout the six-year presidential term.

At a second level, the analysis focuses on broader political forces in Mexico and within the international system. The pact was framed and implemented in the context of rising concern about the stability of the Mexican political system and reflected important shifts in power both within the Mexican state bureaucracy and in the larger society. Special attention is paid here to the growing dominance of market-oriented technocrats within the bureaucracy and to the reconstruction of cooperative relations with business groups and international creditors.

The study is divided into five sections. The first deals with the political and economic antecedents of the pact, especially during the first five years of de la Madrid's administration. The second analyzes the inflationary crisis of 1987 and the decision to initiate the pact. The third and fourth sections describe the implementation of the pact during 1988, focusing on the evolution of macroeconomic and trade policies during this period and on the institutional mechanisms through which such policies were carried out. The fifth section analyzes the political institutions and social structures that account for the relative success of the program.

Unlike other countries examined in this book, the Mexican system is not undergoing a quick transition from authoritarian rule to competitive electoral politics, and, therefore, few direct conclusions can be drawn from this case about the effects of such transitions on economic reform. Although some steps toward political liberalization have been taken since the 1970s, government elites have maintained considerable control over the pace and timing of both economic and political initiatives. During the period under discussion, these elites attached the highest priority to economic adjustments and tended to deemphasize political reforms or allow them to run on a separate track.

In a number of other respects, however, the Mexican experience is relevant to themes raised in this book, including the importance of the security and time horizons of decisionmakers, the role of political support in the implementation of reforms, and the political significance of how these reforms are packaged. First, we argue that the initiation of extensive reforms in Mexico depended heavily on the elite's control of the official party and corporatist apparatus. Substantial insulation from political opposition enabled the government to undertake its program even in the face of electoral-cycle pressures associated with the change of presidential administrations.

The Mexican case also demonstrates the importance of forging channels of support and communication with strategic groups in the private sector. Since the early 1970s, relations between the state and important business sectors had been marked by considerable tension and confrontation. Successful implementation of the pact depended on the capacity of government to reestablish mutual trust and cooperation, built largely around shared interests in maintaining the stability of the political and economic system.

Although many factors facilitated this reconciliation, the packaging of reform helped smooth the way for leaders in the private sector to offer a cooperative response. Specifically, business groups were less inclined to oppose trade liberalization because it was included as a component of the pact and was presented as essential to reducing inflationary pressures.

Finally, the Mexican case raises questions about the longer-term compatibility of economic reform and political democratization. The alliance constructed by the government, although crucial for the success of the pact, did not extend far beyond the representatives of the very large firms and conglomerates that dominated substantial portions of the Mexican economy. Smaller private firms, along with labor and peasant organizations, were subject to more extensive political control, and opposition parties had little real chance to defeat the official candidate in the 1988 presidential campaign.

Important changes in the political system were initiated as the Mexican economy began to revive. Under President Carlos Salinas de Gortari, the government stepped up its efforts to modernize the PRI (Institutional Revolutionary Party), reform election procedures, and expand opportunities for opposition parties to contest state and municipal elections. There was substantial continuity, however, in the centralized features of the system that initially facilitated reform. These included highly concentrated presidential authority, the dominance of the PRI over national elections, and extensive government control over organized labor.

Antecedents of the Pact, 1982–87

Since the 1930s, the Mexican political system has been characterized by the electoral dominance of an official party, the PRI, by a very strong presidency, and by the use of government and party resources to co-opt and constrain the activities of organized economic interests, particularly labor unions (for general discussions of the Mexican political system, see Carpizo 1978; Collier and Collier 1991; Cornelius, Gentleman, and Smith 1989; Cosío Villegas 1973; González Casanova 1977; Hansen 1971; Loaeza 1988; Molinar Horcasitas 1991; Reyna and Weinert 1977). Beginning in the early 1970s, a degree of political liberalization began to provide wider latitude for debate among political and economic interests, and electoral reforms in 1977 offered somewhat greater opportunities for opposition political parties. Nevertheless, throughout the 1980s, the president and the executive bureaucracy dominated the system. Congress, state and local government, the courts, and other institutions of the federal constitutional system played far less significant roles.

Within this highly centralized structure of authority, however, substantial political contestation has occurred. Among government technocrats, the most important cleavage has been between orthodox groups that have emphasized relatively market-oriented approaches to macroeconomic management and developmentalist factions urging a more activist role for the state. The orthodox financial bureaucracy was based historically in the Bank of Mexico and the Ministry of Finance (Maxfield 1990), although its influence later expanded to the Ministry of Budget and Planning and other parts of the state apparatus. Prior to the 1980s, this group reached the peak of its influence during the so-called period of stabilizing development, from the mid-1950s to the late 1960s, when import-substituting strategies and cautious fiscal and monetary policies combined to produce relatively low inflation and high growth.

Developmentalists became influential during the 1970s, as the Mexican state took a more activist role in stimulating growth and addressing problems of equity. Until the early 1980s, their most important bureaucratic stronghold was the Ministry of National Wealth and Public Industry. They were weakened substantially after 1982, when this agency was reorganized into the Ministry of Trade and Industrial Development (SECOFI), and virtually all of the hard-line protectionists were pushed out of positions of authority. Even after that time, however, SECOFI continued to provide a base for critics of full import liberalization (on policy debates in the 1970s, see Bazdresch and Levy 1991; Solís 1981; Tello 1979).

Within the larger political system, relations between the state and economic interest groups ran roughly parallel to the factional conflicts evolving within the government apparatus. The stabilizing development period was marked by close relations between the state and most segments of the business community, as well as by rising real wages for the relatively small portion of the working class represented by the official union movement. Major problems of social inequality and political exclusion remained, however. During the 1970s, the government attempted to address these issues with populist measures and social reforms, and politics within the Mexican system became far more confrontational.

Business groups became increasingly politicized, especially during the populist administration of Luis Echeverría (1971–77). Business elites previously inclined to rely on private contacts with officials increasingly protested what they viewed as abuses of state power (Arriola 1988; Maxfield and Anzaldúa 1987). Concerns about discretionary presidential authority were reinforced by a sudden decision to nationalize the banking system at the end of José López Portillo's administration in 1982. One important outgrowth of these concerns was the formation in the mid-1970s of a powerful new business peak association, the Coordinating Council of Entrepreneurs, which sought to establish a more independent role for the private sector within the political arena. During 1987 and 1988, the powerful heads of the council played a major role in initiating and implementing the Economic Solidarity Pact. A large network of state-sponsored business chambers also became more militant and independent during the 1970s and 1980s (Shafer 1973).

Although so-called popular sector groups were the intended beneficiaries of the 1970s' reform initiatives, they were generally less powerful than business elites and middle-class groups. The official union movement gained in strength and independence during the 1970s, and some labor federations began to act with greater militancy prior to the crisis of the 1980s. But the labor movement as a whole remained closely tied to the governing party and to the state, and its influence eroded substantially during the 1980s, as prolonged recession and growth of the labor force weakened labor markets (Bizberg 1990a, 1990b; Carr 1986; Middlebrook 1989; Reyna, Zapata, and Fleury 1976; Trejo Delarbre 1990). Other popular sector groups—student movements, neighborhood associations, and dissident political organizations—formed after the 1970s and were generally tolerated as long as they did not become too large.

Demands from both business and popular sector groups often pulled the system in conflicting directions, straining the resources of the Mexican state. During the 1970s, successive administrations sought to cope with these challenges through accelerated programs of public investment, subsidies and protection of the business sector, and expanded social services. Given the limited tax base of the Mexican system, however, these policies could not be sustained over the long run. By the early 1980s, the economy was burdened with very high fiscal deficits, a badly overvalued peso, and a large foreign debt. This left the system extremely vulnerable to the decline in petroleum prices and the sharp rise in international interest rates that hit the system in 1981 and 1982.

Initial Efforts at Stabilization under de la Madrid, 1982–85

The debt crisis in August 1982 brought important changes to the situation confronting the Mexican government (for the origins of the 1982 debt crisis, see Bazdresch and Levy 1991; Buffie and Sangines Krause 1989; Ros 1987). First and most important, authorities could no longer ignore the very large macroeconomic disequilibrium that had developed during the past decade. In a last-ditch effort to expand its room to maneuver, the outgoing administration of López Portillo nationalized the private commercial banking system in September 1982, exacerbating the already serious tensions between the government and the private sector (Hernández Rodríguez 1988a; López Portillo 1988; Tello 1984). Reducing these tensions constituted a major challenge for the incoming administration of Miguel de la Madrid.

The debt crisis and the threat of falling into a moratorium on payments also weakened the hand of the Mexican government in negotiations with multinational financial institutions and foreign commercial creditors.[1] In many respects, to be sure, the International Monetary Fund (IMF) and the World Bank offered advice that coincided closely with the views of the incoming administration itself. From this point forward, however, the influence of the international financial institutions increased considerably.

Finally, the crisis expanded opportunities for market-oriented technocrats to increase their influence within the state apparatus. Key appointments under de la Madrid went to officials from the financial bureaucracy, and advocates of expansionist policies were removed from major positions of influence (Hernández Rodríguez 1988b). A major shift in factional alignments, this response implied that, much more than in the past, the administration as a whole would adopt a common perspective about the urgency of fiscal and monetary retrenchment. Most new officials also shared the broad view that at some point trade and regulatory policies would have to be revised to provide greater scope for market forces (see Poder Ejecutivo Federal 1983). In this area, however, there was less consensus on the scope and design of the prospective reforms.

The steps taken during the first years of de la Madrid's administration reflected these initial priorities (Kaufman 1990). The primary emphasis was on stabilization and the normalization of relations with external creditors. An IMF agreement concluded in November 1982 provided the basis for an extraordinary effort to achieve fiscal adjustment. Between 1982 and 1984, the public sector borrowing requirement (the financial deficit in table 9-1) was cut from almost 17 percent to less than 9 percent

Table 9-1. Public Expenditures as a Percentage of Gross Domestic Product in Mexico, 1977–90

Expenditure	1977–82ᵃ	1982	1983	1984	1985	1986	1987	1988	1989	1990
Deficit										
Financial	9.9	16.9	8.6	8.5	9.6	16.0	16.0	12.3	5.5	3.5
Economic	8.7	15.6	8.1	7.1	8.0	14.9	15.0	10.7	4.9	2.3
Primaryᵇ	4.3	7.6	-4.0	-4.6	-3.3	-1.7	-4.7	-6.0	-7.7	-7.5
Operational	4.8	5.5	-0.4	0.3	0.8	2.4	-1.8	3.6	1.7	-1.8
Revenue										
Total public sector	26.6	28.9	32.9	32.2	31.2	30.4	30.5	29.9	28.9	30.0
Oil	6.4	9.9	14.2	13.0	11.5	9.0	9.8	7.6	6.7	7.7
Tax	10.1	9.9	10.2	10.3	10.2	11.3	10.7	11.9	11.8	11.6
Value added tax	2.4	2.2	2.8	2.7	2.8	2.7	3.2	3.5	3.3	3.6
Income tax	5.4	4.7	4.1	4.1	4.1	4.3	4.0	4.9	5.1	4.9
Expenditure										
Total public sector	35.3	44.5	41.0	39.3	39.2	44.9	44.9	39.1	33.6	32.2
Budget	33.0	41.8	39.0	37.7	37.5	42.6	43.6	38.0	32.7	30.0
Programmable	25.0	26.0	22.2	20.9	21.7	22.3	23.1	18.1	16.8	16.8
Social (percentage of programmable)	—	33.8	28.0	27.6	31.1	30.7	30.6	32.0	35.6	—
Nonprogrammable	7.9	12.0	13.3	15.7	16.5	14.9	22.6	20.0	15.8	13.1
Interest										
Total	4.4	8.0	12.1	11.7	11.3	16.6	19.7	16.7	12.6	9.8
Internal	2.8	4.9	7.7	8.0	7.8	12.1	15.4	13.1	9.2	—
External	1.6	3.3	4.6	3.9	3.7	4.4	4.4	3.6	3.5	—

— Not available.
a. Simple arithmetic average.
b. Economic deficit minus total interest.

Source: Banco de México, *Indicadores económicos*, 1991, p. D, December 1988, October 1989, October 1991; Banco de México 1992; Secretaría de Hacienda y Crédito Público, Dirección General de Planeación Hacendaria, 1977–86; Lustig 1992, table III.5.

of gross domestic product (GDP), in spite of a sharp drop in petroleum revenues. On the external front, the government concluded debt rescheduling agreements with its creditors and established FICORCA, a program through which the government provided financial relief to dollar-indebted private firms that were gravely affected by exchange rate losses.

Trade reform and other structural adjustments were much less salient during the early 1980s. Both Mexican officials and external lending agencies assumed that stabilization should precede any major attempt at economic restructuring. This perspective changed during the mid-1980s, however, as a new series of difficulties undermined the stabilization effort.

Serious problems began to appear as early as 1984. First, the terms of trade dropped severely between 1982 and 1985. Moreover, the very tight conditions attached to the initial debt agreements provided little breathing space for the stabilization effort to succeed; the rescheduling of external debt had not yielded enough "fresh money," either from concerted lending agreements or a return to the voluntary capital market. Consequently, continued servicing of the debt required a brutal compression of domestic demand and a major drain on fiscal resources. After two years of severe fiscal austerity, there were only limited signs of economic reactivation, and inflation continued at around 60 percent through 1984 and 1985 (see table 9-2). In this context, the perception grew within the government that something had to be done. Controls on public spending were relaxed somewhat at the end of 1984 and continued to ease during the mid-term election campaign of 1985.

In 1985, the situation deteriorated further. Popular protest following the devastating earthquake that hit Mexico City in September was a disturbing indication of widespread political alienation. Meanwhile, the public sector borrowing requirement began to widen again in 1985, approaching 10 percent of GDP, and relations with the IMF grew increasingly acrimonious. On September 19 (coincidentally, the day of the earthquake itself), IMF officials announced that they were suspending disbursements on the Extended Fund Facility agreement with the government.

At the core of the dispute were sharp differences over how to interpret the causes of the growing fiscal deficit. The IMF tended to blame election-year spending, but the inflation premium paid on the servicing of the domestic public debt was also a significant source of pressure on the budget, as was the decline in petroleum revenues. These critical variables lay beyond the government's control. For the next nine months, attempts to renegotiate the Extended Fund Facility agreement were locked in a tense stalemate over the question of how much this factor should be discounted in setting fiscal targets.

During the first part of 1986, the crisis escalated even further. The international petroleum market collapsed at the beginning of the year,

Table 9-2. *Prices and Wages in the Mexican Economy, 1977–90*
(percentages unless otherwise noted)

Indicator	1977–82	1982	1983	1984	1985	1986	1987	1988	1989	1990
Export oil prices (dollars per barrel)	25.2a	26.7	26.7	26.9	25.3	11.9	16.0	12.2	15.6	19.1
Nominal exchange rate (pesos per dollar)										
Free	28.8b	57.2	150.3	185.2	310.3	637.9	1,405.8	2,289.6	2,483.4	2,838.4
Controlled	—	57.4	120.2	167.8	257.0	611.4	1,366.7	2,250.3	2,453.2	2,830.7
Nominal interest rate	—	57.4	53.8	49.2	74.2	105.6	133.0	51.5	44.7	35.0
Change in the nominal minimum wage										
December–December	285.1c	73.8	44.2	56.7	54.0	102.6	145.0	31.9	24.9	19.1
Average	261.3c	40.4	67.9	54.2	55.6	70.6	117.6	87.6	12.7	14.9
Change in the nominal manufacturing wage										
December–December	314.0c	64.1	53.8	57.5	58.1	95.6	149.8	59.9	29.5	32.7
Average	357.6c	60.2	56.1	53.8	53.3	75.2	127.4	111.4	30.8	30.3
Change in the inflation rate										
December–December	458.9c	98.8	80.8	59.2	63.7	105.7	159.2	51.7	19.7	29.9
Average	360.2c	58.9	101.9	65.4	57.7	86.2	131.8	114.2	20.0	26.7
Real exchange rate (70 = 100)	116.1b	124.2	135.2	110.9	106.8	155.9	169.8	140.3	127.6	123.4
Real interest rate	—	−1.5	−48.2	−16.2	16.5	19.3	1.2	−62.7	24.7	8.3
Change in the real minimum wage										
December–December	−28.6c	−12.6	−20.2	−1.6	−5.9	−1.5	−5.5	−13.1	4.3	8.4
Average	−19.9c	−11.6	−16.8	−6.8	−1.3	−8.4	−6.1	−12.4	−6.1	−9.2
Change in the real manufacturing wage										
December–December	−22.9c	−17.5	−14.9	−1.1	−3.4	−4.9	−3.6	5.4	8.2	2.2
Average	−0.5c	0.8	−22.7	−7.0	−2.8	−5.9	−1.9	−1.3	9.0	2.8

— Not available.
a. Average 1978–82.
b. Simple arithmetic average.
c. Accumulated increase during the period.
Note: Increases in the real minimum and manufacturing wage correspond to increases in the index of real wages, defined as the index of nominal wages divided by the consumer price index. Real interest rates are the nominal interest rate minus the average inflation rate.
Source: Lustig 1992, tables I.5 and II.2; Banco de México, *Indicadores económicos,* December 1991.

deepening the recession that had resumed during the last half of 1985 and adding still another crushing blow to the Mexican process of adjustment. Oil prices dropped nearly 50 percent, causing government revenues to plunge and sending the public sector borrowing requirement soaring to 16 percent of GDP, near the heights reached in 1982. On the political front, relations with the United States were increasingly embittered by conflicts with the Reagan administration over Central American policy and by congressional and press criticisms of alleged fraud in the 1985 and 1986 mid-term elections (Aguilar Zinser 1988).

Confrontation and Reconciliation with Creditor Groups, 1985–86

The Mexican policy response to this new round of crises was conditioned in fundamental ways by how these external economic and political conflicts were resolved. Until about the second half of 1986, there appeared to be very little agreement between Mexico and its creditors about why the policies initiated in 1982 had failed and about what needed to be done. The view of most creditor groups, implied in the IMF's position on the fiscal deficit, was that the adjustment process had not gone far enough and that both a stronger fiscal effort and a push toward trade liberalization and privatization were needed. The Baker Plan, announced in September 1985, promised fresh financing for countries following that route. In the absence of a mechanism for compelling commercial banks to resume voluntary lending, however, this served primarily to reinforce the creditor calls for structural adjustment.

As of mid-1985, the Mexican government's view crystallized around the following points. First, previous stabilization efforts had not been backed sufficiently by new external financing. Second, the government agreed that structural adjustments were indeed necessary but insisted on its right to implement these in its own way and its own time (as budget and planning secretary, de la Madrid had himself championed trade reform measures in 1978 and 1979). Although gradual liberalization measures were introduced in 1985, the shock treatments advocated by many orthodox economists in the United States and Mexico were not viewed as politically viable. Finally, the increase in the public deficit, defined by the public sector borrowing requirement, was attributed primarily to the inflation of interest payments charged on the domestic debt, as well as to sharp fluctuations in the international price of oil.

By mid-1986, Mexico's standoff with the IMF on these issues appeared to be leading to a unilateral suspension of the debt service and to a confrontation that all sides had hoped to avoid. This prospect, however, led both the United States and Mexico to search for new ways to back away from the brink.

Regardless of conflicts over other issues, the Reagan administration did not want a new financial crisis in Mexico, and it pressed the IMF to accede to the principal demands of the Mexican negotiating team. In an agreement finally concluded in July 1986, the standard for fiscal performance was defined primarily in terms that corrected for the impact of inflation on interest payments to domestic creditors (the operational budget) and acknowledged the impact of fluctuations in the price of oil (Gurria Treviño 1988, p. 97). This was followed in August by a statement from President de la Madrid in Washington, D.C., that Mexico would no longer press the Contadora effort to negotiate a peace settlement in Central America and that new initiatives would be left to the combatants themselves (on the evolution of Mexico's policy toward Central America and its effects on U.S.-Mexican relations, see Castañeda and Pastor 1989, pp. 229–38).

Agreements in these areas untied negotiations with commercial creditors and opened the way for a significant new infusion of external financing. During 1987, new debt servicing agreements, reached in conjunction with the IMF and backed by the U.S. government, led to an inflow of more than $4.5 billion in commercial bank financing.[2] These funds, in conjunction with a large trade surplus, allowed a large buildup of reserves, which—as we shall see—provided a crucial cushion for exchange rate policies initiated under the Economic Solidarity Pact.

The Evolution of Trade and Stabilization Policies, 1986–87

By the end of 1986, the preceding round of crisis and reconciliation with creditors had led Mexican officials to make several important new assumptions about the relation between stabilization and trade reform and at least three major shifts in policy emphasis. In response to the evident failure of the earlier stabilization program, the first major shift was to attach a much higher priority to trade reform—now viewing it as a step that had to accompany, rather than follow, stabilization. In conjunction with a World Bank loan, a new program was launched that substantially reduced the coverage of import licenses from more than 90 percent of production in 1985 to only 47 percent in 1986 (see table 9-3), increased reliance on tariffs as a means of regulating imports, and introduced a schedule of phased reductions in tariff levels (Ten Kate 1990, p. 53).

The design of these measures reflected a preference for a gradualist approach to liberalization. The schedule of tariff reductions, outlined in negotiations between SECOFI and representatives of the private sector, was to take place over a period of four years and offered substantial protection in the meantime. A sharp depreciation of the peso accompanied these measures, moreover, and significantly reduced the initial costs of trade liberalization to import-substituting industrialists. The gradualist reforms of the mid-1980s, however, laid the groundwork for the more sweeping reforms implemented in conjunction with the pact. The depreciation of the peso provided a cushion of undervaluation that

Table 9-3. Measures of Trade Liberalization in Mexico, 1985–90
(percent)

Indicator	1985	1986	1987	1988	1989	1990
Domestic production						
Covered by import licenses	92.2	46.9	35.8	23.2	22.1	19.0
Covered by official reference prices	18.7	19.6	13.4	0.0	0.0	0.0
Average product weighted tariff	23.5	24.0	22.7	11.0	12.8	12.5

Source: Lustig 1992, table V.3.

permitted subsequent use of the nominal exchange rate as an anchor of the pact (Ten Kate and de Mateo 1989). The reduction in the coverage of quantitative restrictions weakened the discretionary resources available to SECOFI, still an important center of opposition to outright trade liberalization, and eroded the bridges between protectionists inside and outside the government.

The second major change in policy was to reduce the priority attached to achieving price stability. Basic commitments to fiscal discipline remained strong, but comparatively high levels of inflation were viewed as a necessary cost of the exchange rate policy linked to the trade reform. The third new emphasis was on renewing growth. After mid-1986, the government began to ease monetary policy in an effort to encourage private sector investment. Available credit, though still very tight, was expanded, and real interest rates were reduced substantially during 1987.

The Inflation Crisis of 1987 and Initiation of the Pact

These policy changes were the backdrop to the inflation crisis of late 1987 and the initiation of the Economic Solidarity Pact. In several major respects the economy appeared to be doing relatively well in 1987 (see tables 9-4 and 9-5). Growth rates turned positive (1.5 percent), after declining almost 4 percent in 1986, and the current account balance grew from a deficit of $1.7 billion in 1986 to a surplus of $4.0 billion the following year. The annual rate of inflation in 1986 climbed to 86 percent, and quarterly rates averaged around 25 percent during the first nine months of 1987 (table 9-2). This was high, but acceptable, given other priorities. In the last three months of 1987, however, a sudden escalation of prices brought inflation to more than 34 percent for the quarter, and stabilization moved to the top of the policy agenda.

The cause of the high long-term inflation preceding this upsurge is the subject of some dispute. Critics of the government attribute it primarily to deficient and inconsistent fiscal policies, pointing especially to the expansion of public deficits after 1985. More disaggregated measures,

Table 9-4. Annual Real Growth Rates in the Mexican Economy, 1977–90
(percent)

Indicator	1977–82[a]	1982	1983	1984	1985	1986	1987	1988	1989	1990
Gross domestic product	6.6	-0.5	-4.2	3.6	2.6	-3.8	1.5	1.7	2.9	3.9
Consumption										
Total	6.8	1.2	-4.2	3.8	3.1	-1.5	-0.2	1.6	5.0	4.7
Private	6.6	1.1	-5.4	3.3	3.6	-2.1	-0.1	2.2	6.0	5.2
Public	8.4	2.4	2.7	6.6	0.9	2.1	-0.8	-1.4	-0.6	5.6
Investment										
Gross fixed	8.9	-15.9	-28.3	6.4	7.9	-11.8	-0.6	6.4	5.9	13.4
Private	6.7	-17.1	-22.1	7.9	12.2	-10.4	4.3	13.6	9.5	13.6
Public	12.3	-14.2	-36.0	4.1	0.9	-14.2	-9.8	-9.1	-3.6	12.8
Expenditure										
Private	6.6	-2.1	-8.1	3.9	4.8	-3.4	0.6	3.9	6.6	6.6
Public	10.2	-6.7	-16.0	5.7	0.9	-3.8	-3.7	-3.7	-1.5	7.6
Exports (free on board)	9.9	13.7	13.6	5.7	-4.5	3.2	9.8	3.0	3.1	5.2
Imports (cost, insurance, freight)	9.6	-37.1	-33.8	17.8	11.0	-12.4	4.5	38.8	20.7	22.9

a. Average annual growth rate.
Source: Secretaría de Programación y Presupuesto, various years; Banco de México, Informe anual, 1990.

Table 9-5. Balance of Payments in the Mexican Economy, 1977–90
(billions of U.S. dollars, unless otherwise noted)

Indicator	1977–82ᵃ	1982	1983	1984	1985	1986	1987	1988	1989	1990
Current account balance	−33.3	−4.9	5.3	4.2	1.2	−1.7	4.0	−2.4	−6.0	−6.3
Goods and no factorial services balance	−1.4	6.8	14.4	13.9	9.1	5.6	10.4	4.1	−0.3	−2.3
Interest payments	33.2	11.3	10.2	11.7	10.2	8.3	8.1	8.6	9.3	9.0
Payments net of interest	—	—	8.9	9.6	8.3	6.9	6.2	6.1	6.7	6.4
Capital account	50.2	8.6	−1.1	0.0	−1.8	1.8	−0.6	−1.4	3.0	9.7
Direct foreign investment	4.3	0.7	0.5	0.4	0.5	1.5	3.2	2.6	3.0	2.6
Errors and omissions	−18.0	−8.4	−0.9	−0.9	−1.9	0.4	2.7	−2.8	3.4	−0.1
International reserves (variation)										
Gross	—	−3.2	3.1	3.2	−2.3	1.0	6.9	−7.1	0.4	3.2
Net	−1.0	−4.7	3.3	3.4	−2.4	0.6	6.1	−6.7	0.3	3.4
Capital flight	18.8	6.5	2.7	1.6	0.7	−2.2	0.3	1.1	−2.9	—
External debt										
Total	317.2	92.4	93.8	96.7	96.6	101.0	107.5	100.4	95.1	98.2
Public	225.5	59.7	66.6	69.4	72.1	75.4	81.4	81.0	76.1	77.8
Ratio of external debt to GDP (percent)	—	49.0	62.6	54.2	52.4	76.3	73.6	59.1	48.5	41.9
Debt service ratio to exports (percent)	—	62.2	50.4	42.8	43.8	48.6	42.8	43.4	35.9	29.4

— Not available.
a. Accumulated flows.
Source: Lustig 1992, tables I.5, II.2, and II.4; Banco de México 1978; Banco de México, *Informe anual*, 1980–85; Banco de México, *Indicadores económicos*, October 1991, pp. IV-1–IV-2.

however, suggest that these deficits were driven primarily by the high inflation premium built into the interest costs of domestic public debt. Estimates that correct for the amortization component of these expenditures (the operational budget) show that deficits from 1984 to 1987 were well below the 1977–82 average (see table 9-6). The primary budget (all noninterest accounts) was in surplus between 1983 and 1987, while primary deficits averaged 4 percent from 1977 through 1982. The persistence of high inflation in the face of such deep fiscal efforts supports the view that inertial factors and exogenous disturbances were playing a decisive role (for the government's view on the subject, see Presidencia de la República 1987, pp. 27–32). Of course, the high speed with which the peso was devalued gave a strong impetus to inflation, especially during the second half of 1986. In this context, existing inflationary expectations were jolted by strong new pressures on the exchange rate during the third quarter of 1987 (Zuckerman Behar 1989). One important source of demand for dollars resulted from a FICORCA settlement on private sector external debt negotiated during the preceding year. Rather than extend the payout period, as the agreement specified, many external creditors offered deep discounts for the prepayment of hard currency debts, an offer that many Mexican debtors hastened to accept (Banco de México, *Indicadores económicos,* 1987, p. 25).

More important was the crash of the stock market on October 19. During the preceding eighteen months, the government had delayed correcting a drift toward negative real interest rates; this had encouraged a shift of funds into the market and a speculative boom. In October, with the fall in world stock markets, the situation reversed itself, and investors shifted from stocks to dollars. In the thirty days following the October crash, Mexican stock prices lost approximately 70 percent of their value, reflecting the increasing demand for hard currency (Presidencia de la República, Dirección General de Comunicación Social, 1988b, p. 188). Finally, as occurred toward the end of other presidential terms, the uncertainties associated with a year of political transition encouraged holders of liquid capital to hedge their bets. Both the stock market crash and a massive new round of capital flight occurred within days of the designation of Salinas as the next president.

On November 18, the central bank attempted to protect reserves by withdrawing from the free exchange market, and in just one day, the price of the dollar soared from Mex\$1,712 to as high as Mex\$2,200, an increase of 28 percent. Despite these shocks, the bank expected to contain the inflationary spillover; reserves remained very high, and the controlled exchange rate, which governed most producer import prices, was held constant. The sharp rise in the free exchange rate, however, increased the uncertainty regarding future devaluations (Presidencia de la República, Dirección General de Comunicación Social, 1988b, p. 199). As a consequence, consumer prices rose almost 15 percent in December,

Table 9-6. Net Change Public External Indebtedness, Net IMF Disbursements, and Interest Payments in Mexico, 1982–90
(millions of U.S. dollars)

Indicator	1982	1983	1984	1985	1986	1987	1988	1989	1990
Total external debt, net change	7,429	5,087	2,613	763	73	2,961	−825	−1,190	2,168
Disbursements	11,196	8,774	6,231	4,817	11,197	9,535	8,434	4,908	7,687
Amortization	3,767	3,687	3,618	4,054	11,124	6,574	9,259	6,098	5,519
Long-run debt, net change	8,337	4,622	2,461	708	249	3,726	−1,142	−1,065	1,685
Disbursements	11,196	6,832	4,814	3,572	10,184	8,569	7,165	3,608	5,539
Amortization	2,859	2,210	2,353	2,864	9,935	3,289	8,307	4,673	3,854
Commercial bank debt, net change	5,975	4,537	2,884	860	−399	4,410	−2,970	−1,986	110
Disbursements	7,770	5,209	3,075	1,287	253	4,782	1,176	44	430
Amortization	1,795	672	191	427	652	373	5,125	2,030	320
Bilateral debt, net change	486	281	55	318	676	1,442	733	346	743
Disbursements	853	781	619	1,005	1,802	2,666	1,770	1,749	2,243
Amortization	367	500	564	687	1,126	1,223	1,037	1,403	1,500
Supplier debt, net change	4	216	−119	1	−9	−31	−12	24	91
Disbursements	46	319	143	65	53	34	21	50	123
Amortization	42	103	262	64	62	65	33	26	32
IDB AND IBRD debt[a], net change	1,147	178	603	711	913	393	697	701	706
Disbursements	1,375	505	979	1,166	1,446	1,086	1,642	1,615	1,772
Amortization	228	327	376	455	533	694	945	914	1,066

(continued on next page)

Table 9-6 (continued)

Indicator	1982	1983	1984	1985	1986	1987	1988	1989	1990
Bonds, net change	725	−588	−473	−488	−519	−934	1,389	−149	34
Disbursements	1,151	17	0	49	0	1	2,556	150	971
Amortization	426	605	473	537	519	935	1,167	299	937
Short-run debt, net change	−908	465	152	55	−176	−764	316	−125	483
Disbursements	0	1,942	1,417	1,246	1,013	966	1,268	1,300	2,147
Amortization	908	1,477	1,265	1,191	1,189	1,730	952	1,425	1,664
Commodity Credit Corpora-tion, net change	145	1,254	−59	−370	−445	−23	217	159	−53
Disbursements	145	1,309	742	260	157	272	532	491	396
Amortization	0	55	801	630	602	295	315	332	449
IMF, net change	201	1,003	1,204	296	616	320	−69	303	731
Disbursements	201	1,003	1,204	296	741	600	350	943	1,608
Amortization	0	0	0	0	125	280	419	640	877
Interest payments	−12,203	−10,103	−11,716	−10,156	−8,342	−8,097	−8,891	−9,377	−9,064

a. Inter-American Development Bank and the International Bank for Reconstruction and Development.

Source: Lustig 1992, table II.V.

sending clear signals that the economy was entering a major crisis (see tables 9-7 and 9-8).

The Initial Response: The Actors and Negotiations

The explosion of prices, detonated just at the outset of a presidential transition year, sent shock waves throughout the Mexican system. Within government circles, ongoing debates about the merits of a stabilization pact acquired new urgency. Discussions with major business leaders had been initiated in July, but the basic blueprint of the program was hammered out during the last days of November and the first two weeks of December.

In the public sphere, the impetus for these negotiations appeared to come from new wage demands issued by the normally quiescent official labor movement. On November 23, union leaders called for a 46 percent adjustment to compensate for the decline in income caused by the November 18 devaluation and threatened a general strike if this adjustment was not put into effect by the middle of December (Presidencia de la República, Dirección General de Comunicación Social, 1988b, p. 191). On the surface, the tripartite agreements announced on December 15 responded to this demand. In reality, however, government, business, and labor brought very different resources and levels of political strength to the bargaining table.

Characteristically in the Mexican system, the executive elite provided the most important source of initiative. Especially important for the pact was the network of financial officials allied with Carlos Salinas in the Ministry of Budget and Planning, the Bank of Mexico, and the Ministry of Finance. The magnitude and scope of the inflation crisis took this group by surprise, and many of its immediate decisions were ad hoc and improvised. Most key policymakers, however, attached considerable importance to the inertial factors that underlay the Mexican inflation and were familiar with the risks and advantages of wage-price controls. When the crisis hit, therefore, the financial officials were well positioned to assume leadership in designing a relatively coherent project. At the same time, with Salinas designated as the next president, they could count on the collaboration of other segments of the bureaucracy as well.[3] Officials in SECOFI, though skeptical about the acceleration of trade reform, were entrusted with the task of negotiating the details of the price control system.

In its contacts with the private sector, the officials attached to Salinas had at least three big sticks for getting what they wanted. First, they represented the future administration, and their negotiating partners knew that for the next six years they would hold public power. Second, after the reconciliation with external creditors, they were viewed favorably by the international community, which implied a reasonable possibility of mustering the financial resources to implement their plans. Fi-

Table 9-7. *Prices and Wages in Mexico, by Quarter, 1987 and 1988*
(percentages unless otherwise noted)

Indicator	1987				1988			
	First	Second	Third	Fourth	First	Second	Third	Fourth
Nominal exchange rate (pesos per dollar)[a]								
Free	1,019	1,232	1,454	1,917	2,266	2,298	2,298	2,298
Controlled	1,016	1,229	1,451	1,771	2,230	2,257	2,257	2,257
Nominal interest rate[b]	28.3	26.8	26.1	32.0	23.9	11.4	8.3	8.3
Change in the nominal legal minimum wage[c]	23.0	20.1	23.1	34.7	32.0	0.0	0.0	0.0
Change in consumer prices[c]	23.5	25.3	24.7	34.2	31.5	7.2	3.2	4.3
Real exchange rate (1970 = 100)[a]	174.7	175.2	165.5	164.1	153.9	141.9	132.4	132.9
Real interest rate[b]	4.8	1.5	1.4	-2.2	-7.5	4.3	5.1	4.1
Change in the real legal minimum wage[c]	-0.4	-4.2	-1.3	0.4	0.4	-6.7	-3.1	-4.1

a. Simple arithmetic average of monthly data.
b. Annual rate of each month divided by twelve and accumulated during the period.
c. Accumulated increase over the previous quarter.
Note: Increases in the real legal minimum wage are increases in the real minimum wage index, defined as the nominal legal minimum wage index divided by the consumer price index. The real interest rate is defined as the nominal interest rate minus increases in consumer prices.
Source: Banco de México, *Indicadores económicos*, December 1988, October 1991; data from the Comisión Nacional de Salarios Mínimos.

Table 9-8. Prices and Wages in Mexico, by Month, 1987 and 1988
(percentages unless otherwise noted)

	1987			1988					
Indicator	*October*	*November*	*December*	*January*	*February*	*March*	*April*	*May*	*June*
Nominal exchange rate (pesos per dollar)									
Free	1,603	1,909	2,241	2,231	2,269	2,298	2,298	2,298	2,298
Controlled	1,599	1,692	2,023	2,202	2,231	2,257	2,257	2,257	2,257
Nominal interest rate[a]	8.2	9.6	11.3	13.0	12.8	6.7	4.5	3.7	2.8
Change in the nominal legal minimum wage[b]	25.1	0.0	7.7	28.1	0.0	3.0	0.0	0.0	0.0
Change in the stock market	-41.8	-43.2	-7.0	32.1	43.7	-13.1	-11.6	22.0	-0.8
Change in consumer prices[b]	8.3	7.9	14.8	15.5	8.3	5.1	3.1	1.9	2.0
Real exchange rate (1970 = 100)	160.1	161.0	171.2	162.9	151.2	147.4	145.1	142.5	138.2
Real interest rate[a]	-0.1	1.7	-3.5	-2.5	4.5	1.6	1.4	1.8	0.8
Change in the real legal minimum wage[b]	15.5	-7.3	6.2	10.9	-4.9	-4.9	-3.0	-1.9	-2.0

a. Annual rate divided by twelve.

b. Increase over the previous month.

Note: Data for monthly increases in the manufacturing wage are not available. The real interest rate is defined as the nominal interest rate minus the inflation rate. Increases in the real legal minimum wage are increases in the real minimum wage index, defined as the nominal legal minimum wage index divided by the consumer price index.

Source: Banco de México, *Indicadores económicos,* December 1988; data from the Comisión Nacional de Salarios Mínimos.

nally, they had the backing of de la Madrid. In Mexico's presidential system, this meant that they were the only group with any possibility of controlling the crisis.

On the business side, initial consultations were restricted to a very small number of major business leaders. The heads of all the main industrial and commercial associations were included in the negotiations. Especially important, however, were Augustín Legoretta, president of the Coordinating Council of Entrepreneurs, the financial elite's main peak association, and Vicente Bortoni, president of the National Confederation of Industrial Chambers (CONCAMIN), which was dominated by larger manufacturing firms.

Relations between these groups and the government were seriously strained during the 1970s and then again after the bank nationalization of 1982. Like their government counterparts, however, representatives of the business community were deeply alarmed by the growing threat of economic and political instability and thus had strong incentives to go along with the agreements proposed by the government. Their adhesion to the December pact in effect committed them to deploying their personal prestige and substantial economic weight to gain the adherence of their affiliates in follow-up negotiations and to collaborate on monitoring and enforcing subsequent price agreements.

Negotiations with representatives of the official labor movement were shaped by the corporatist links to the government and the official party. For many decades, cooperation with the government and the PRI had produced substantial material and political payoffs for both union leaders and their membership; for most union leaders, continued cooperation appeared to offer the best long-term hope of defending wage and employment levels and political privileges during the hard times of the 1980s. But unions were clearly the subordinate partners in the relationship with the government, and their bargaining power was weakened considerably by the prolonged recession and factional realignments that had occurred under de la Madrid (Collier 1992; Collier and Collier 1991). Thus, although union protest served as an important (though possibly staged) catalyst to the negotiations, labor had only limited room to maneuver in the ensuing tripartite bargaining.

Throughout 1988, union leaders criticized business elites and the pact itself, but they were generally constrained to accept the restrictive incomes policy established by the financial bureaucracy and the business sector. Wage agreements reached in December (an immediate 15 percent increase in wages, and another 20 percent increase on January 1) were well under the original demands, as were the revisions reached in March. Throughout the rest of 1988, unions accepted a freeze in nominal wages, in spite of a sharp deterioration in the level of real public sector and minimum wages. Acceptance of these conditions was partly compensated, however, in ways not explicitly laid out in the agreements. Employment levels were generally maintained in the public sector, formal job descriptions were upgraded, permitting some salary adjustments, and wages in the manufacturing sector were generally allowed to keep pace with changes in the price level (see appendix 9-1 for further discussion).

Design of the Program: Initial Assumptions and Conditions

As it was announced on December 15, 1987, the Economic Solidarity Pact envisioned a two-step process for bringing inflation under control (Presidencia de la República, Dirección General de Comunicación Social, 1988b; Zuckerman 1990). During the first two months, emphasis was to be placed on opening trade and realigning relative prices, with provisions made for raising substantially public sector prices and the controlled exchange rate. These steps were to be undertaken in conjunction with commitments by the government and unions to hold expenditures and wages to specified levels and a vaguer pledge by representatives of the business sector to restrain prices. The general understanding was that the first phase would be a period of persuasion and adjustment for firms in the private sector. Until the end of February, firms signing onto the pact would be able to raise their prices, but it was hoped that the increases would be restrained by import competition and the blandishments of business and governmental elites.

A second phase was to begin with a new agreement scheduled for completion by the end of February (Presidencia de la República, Dirección General de Comunicación Social, 1988a). At that point, enterprises that had entered the pact were expected to freeze their prices, and the exchange rate, now substantially adjusted, was to serve as the nominal anchor for the program. In the new agreement signed in February, nominal wages were raised 3 percent and then frozen for the duration of the agreement. This provision revised commitments made in December to grant successive monthly adjustments on the basis of anticipated increases in inflation. Finally, the February agreement also provided that the pact would be renegotiated at three-month intervals, rather than monthly as originally planned, and the general terms were in fact renewed on schedule until the end of the de la Madrid period.

The acceleration of the trade opening actually began prior to the pact, at the beginning of December, when the government removed licensing requirements for most key consumer products and virtually eliminated official reference prices. By the end of the year, only about 25 percent of industrial production—primarily oil, agriculture, and automobiles—was covered by quantitative restrictions (Ros 1991, p. 35). In most of these areas, the government did not consult the business community, although its actions formed a context for subsequent negotiations. Tariff reductions were explicitly incorporated as part of the pact. On December 15, the uniform 5 percent surcharge on imports was abolished, and existing tariffs were slashed in half. Tariff levels were reduced from seven to five, and the maximum tariff reduced from 40 to 20 percent ad valorum (Reyes Heroles 1989; Secretaría de Comercio y Fomento Industrial 1988a, p. 135).

As is often the case with this type of policy, initial expectations of success were extraordinarily low. Virtually no one, either the signatories or their opponents, believed that the initiative would work. Within the business sector, negative expectations were clearly reflected in capital flight and in the high real interest rates demanded for government bonds. Union leaders, in turn, publicly expressed doubts that their private sector counterparts would comply with the agreement. Meanwhile, on December 19, opposition parties of the left organized demonstrations against the pact in front of the National Palace, and Manuel Clouthier, presidential candidate for the National Action Party, publicly condemned the price controls and the accelerated trade opening (Presidencia de la República, Dirección General de Comunicación Social, 1988b, p. 199).

Opinion surveys taken during 1988 indicated comparable skepticism within the general public. Even in April, as inflation began to decline, only about 25 percent of a Mexico City sample had a good or very good opinion of the pact, and at the end of May, the population approving the pact still remained at less than 40 percent. More than 30 percent of the sample felt that prices would be higher in June, and almost 92 percent thought inflation would increase during the next presidential term (Centro de Estudios de Opinión Pública 1988).

Seen from the perspective of the almost euphoric atmosphere of the early 1990s, such pessimism is striking and raises an important question about how a program that depended so heavily on expectations could ultimately have been so successful. What went right? A significant part of the answer lies in favorable preconditions established during the previous presidential term. Three prior developments deserve particular emphasis.

First, depreciation of the peso and containment of demand, in combination with the inflow of new external financing, had created favorable conditions for using the exchange rate as an anchor during the initial twelve months of the pact. During the last quarter of 1987, reserves averaged more than $14 billion, a historic high, and they climbed still higher during the months following the November devaluation, reaching more than $16 billion in May 1988 (CEESP 1989, p. 30). The current account balance was similarly strong, with a surplus of about $4 billion (table 9-5).

The consensus within government about the importance of limiting public deficits was a second major factor, and as shown in the next section, a well-developed administrative machinery was in place to put this consensus into operation. Both publicly and in interviews, representatives of the leading business organizations identified quantified commitments to reduce expenditures as a key condition of their participation in the pact; and this feature of the Mexican program is what most distinguishes it from the far less successful heterodox experiments undertaken earlier in Argentina, Brazil, and Peru.

Finally, by the outset of the pact, the Mexican government had passed through the serious 1985–86 conflicts with external creditors and begun a longer-term process of normalizing relations with the international financial institutions and private creditor banks. The government did not turn the corner in this respect until the change of presidential administrations in both countries and the conclusion of the Brady Plan agreements of 1989–90. Nevertheless, the agreements of 1986 and 1987 helped lay the foundations for this broader process of reconciliation and thus for the longer-term credibility of the program as a whole.

The eventual success in bringing down inflation was thus the result of a rather large combination of factors, which operated simultaneously on several fronts: high reserves and a fixed exchange rate, external political and financial support, deep fiscal restraints, and, of course, price and wage controls themselves. The impact of these factors is discussed at greater length in the appendix to this chapter.

Implementation of the Pact: The Stabilization Program

This section examines the implementation of stabilization measures incorporated in the Economic Stabilization Pact; the next focuses on trade reform. In each policy area, three sets of questions are posed: What were the principal political and economic challenges encountered during 1988? What were the mechanisms and resources that induced or inhibited government and business compliance with commitments? What were the outcomes for the fulfillment of the original policy expectations or for the economy? The discussion of stabilization policy focuses first on macroeconomic management, then on the politics of *concertación*.

Fiscal and Interest Rate Policy

In the area of macroeconomic management, the government's intensified fiscal adjustment marked a departure from more typical electoral-cycle patterns in Mexico. Normally, incumbents increase expenditures at the end of the term, in order to strengthen support for the PRI candidate or to complete favored projects. de la Madrid, in contrast, generally met the commitments made in December 1987. Noninterest expenditures, previously projected to reach 22 percent of GDP, were in fact reduced to 20 percent (Banco de México, *Informe anual,* 1988, p. 51). Despite a sharp drop in oil revenues in June, moreover, the financial deficit in 1988 was reduced to 12 percent of GDP, from 16 percent the preceding year (table 9-1; see also tables 9-9 and 9-10). The primary surplus of 6 percent of GDP was the largest of the six-year administration.

What accounts for achievements so strikingly at variance with historical patterns? First, the lack of competition in the Mexican electoral

Table 9-9. *Public Finances in Mexico, by Quarter, 1987 and 1988*
(percentages unless otherwise noted)

Indicator	1987				1988			
	First	Second	Third	Fourth	First	Second	Third	Fourth
Total revenue	100.0	100.0	100.0	100.0	100.0	100.0	100.0	100.0
Oil revenue/total revenue	12.7	20.5	14.8	19.2	12.6	12.6	10.8	9.5
Tax revenue/total revenue	38.6	34.2	35.0	34.0	40.8	39.9	39.7	39.3
Income tax/tax revenue	39.9	37.3	35.1	36.5	42.3	39.1	43.9	39.1
Value added tax/tax revenue	28.7	29.8	31.6	30.3	28.6	30.4	29.4	30.2
Total expenditure	100.0	100.0	100.0	100.0	100.0	100.0	100.0	100.0
Budget expenditure/total expenditure	98.9	94.4	96.9	98.2	96.3	96.4	95.7	97.5
Programmable expenditure/budget expenditure	43.4	46.7	46.4	52.1	30.4	44.7	55.2	58.6
Nonprogrammable expenditure/budget expenditure	56.6	53.3	53.6	47.9	69.6	55.3	44.8	41.4
Total interest/total expenditure	47.2	42.5	56.1	42.1	54.2	46.9	36.1	34.1
Internal interest/total expenditure	36.3	32.5	34.5	34.0	43.6	38.7	25.6	26.7
External interest/total expenditure	10.9	10.0	11.6	8.0	10.6	8.3	10.5	7.3
Deficit (billions of pesos)								
Financial	4,287	5,823	6,128	14,763	11,361	11,787	11,845	13,742
Economic	3,841	5,294	5,531	14,395	9,925	10,141	10,050	12,365
Primary	−2,647	−2,383	−4,336	230	−10,274	−8,374	−4,040	−977

Source: Banco de México, *Indicadores económicos*, December 1988, October 1989.

Table 9-10. Public Finances in Mexico, by Month, 1987 and 1988
(percentages unless otherwise noted)

	1987			1988					
Indicator	October	November	December	January	February	March	April	May	June
Revenue									
Total	100.0	100.0	100.0	100.0	100.0	100.0	100.0	100.0	100.0
Oil revenue/total revenue	15.7	15.5	25.0	1.6	25.8	10.7	11.9	13.3	12.5
Tax revenue/total revenue	32.5	34.2	35.1	43.2	39.4	39.9	41.0	39.1	39.7
Expenditure									
Total	100.0	100.0	100.0	100.0	100.0	100.0	100.0	100.0	100.0
Budget expenditure/total expenditure	96.6	93.6	100.0	96.9	96.4	95.5	98.6	95.3	95.1
Programmable revenue/budget expenditure	46.9	49.5	57.1	34.9	41.0	24.8	35.3	59.2	50.5
Nonprogrammable expenditure/budget expenditure	53.1	50.5	42.9	65.1	59.0	75.2	64.7	40.8	49.5
Interest									
Total interest/total expenditure	45.1	41.7	39.2	50.8	49.0	62.7	55.2	42.7	42.0
Internal interest/total expenditure	36.3	32.9	32.4	38.6	39.5	52.5	48.0	35.1	31.9
External interest/total expenditure	8.8	8.8	6.8	12.2	9.5	10.2	7.2	7.5	10.1
Deficit (billions of pesos)									
Financial	4,228	3,504	7,031	3,353	4,773	3,055	5,069	3,579	3,140
Economic	3,911	3,208	7,275	3,309	4,384	2,232	4,485	2,904	2,752
Primary	−386	−1,005	1,621	−2,643	−1,929	−5,703	−3,286	−2,329	−2,760

Note: Data for monthly increases in manufacturing wages are not available.
Source: Banco de México, *Indicadores económicos*, December 1988.

system considerably reduced the political costs of fiscal discipline. Once designated as the PRI's presidential nominee, Salinas was assured of election and of a six-year tenure in office. He thus faced fewer short-term risks than do candidates in more competitive elections and was more certain of gaining potential long-term benefits.[4] For de la Madrid, conversely, the prohibition against a second presidential term lowered the political costs of backing potentially unpopular measures.

Also important from a comparative perspective was the domination of a highly centralized executive over the budgetary process. In 1988, as before, the PRI majority in Congress guaranteed passage of the annual budget proposal.[5] In view of high deficits run in earlier years, executive dominance per se obviously did not guarantee fiscal discipline. The weakness of the Congress in the Mexican political system did, however, eliminate a potential constraint on a president who, like de la Madrid, was committed to holding the line on expenditures.

Within the executive branch itself, the key mechanism for controlling expenditures was the Commission of Expenditures and Financing, composed of the heads of the major financial agencies: the Ministry of the Treasury, the Ministry of Budget and Planning, the Bank of Mexico, and the Comptroller General. Under de la Madrid, the commission met weekly to review fiscal expenditures, first at the level of undersecretaries, then at the level of the secretaries themselves. At the outset of the budget cycle, this very reduced component of the larger cabinet was charged with establishing macroeconomic targets. Under the supervision of the Ministry of Budget and Planning, the commission instructed agencies to plan budgets within these parameters and reviewed all major requests to change the projections.

Although the commission existed under earlier presidents, it acquired new importance after 1982 because the president was personally committed to fiscal austerity as were his appointees in the relevant ministries. Throughout the 1980s, therefore, but especially in 1988, the commission served as an instrument for planning the budget and as the main gatekeeper for monitoring expenditures. During 1988, the intense pressures to reduce expenditures rapidly impeded systematic efforts to reallocate funds to priority areas; cuts were made across the board. Nevertheless, with strong backing from the president and a strong internal consensus, the committee blocked virtually all requests for expenditures from even reaching debate in the cabinet.

As the election approached, finally, these incentives were substantially strengthened because the program had begun to achieve its antiinflationary objectives. Growing signs of success gave government officials a strong stake in avoiding spending decisions that might antagonize the business sector and jeopardize the price freeze.

For macroeconomic policymakers, the most intractable problem was not fiscal expenditure, but management of public debt—or, more broadly, credit and finance. In this area, the question of interest rates posed especially complex dilemmas. With expectations still very uncertain, it was essential to maintain high real interest rates and protect reserves; otherwise, capital flight would threaten the fixed exchange rate and unravel the entire stabilization program. Accordingly, the central bank allowed the decline in nominal interest rates to lag well behind the general drop in the rate of inflation (Banco de México, *Informe anual,* 1988, p. 32).

In both the short and medium run, there were substantial costs to this decision. Notwithstanding high real interest rates, the drop in nominal interest payments led initially to a wave of political protests among depositors in the nationalized banking system as well as to a flow of funds into informal credit markets. Over a longer period, of course, real rates actually remained very high, which placed serious strains on public finance and private credit markets.

Throughout 1988, with confidence in the program still very shaky, there were no good answers to this dilemma. On the fiscal side, the real costs of financing the public debt increased, and continuing pressure was exerted on the operational deficit. More generally, the competition for credit between the public and private sector constituted a serious obstacle to overall recovery for the next several years.

Concertación

To understand the politics of implementing the price concertación, it is essential to emphasize that, for the private sector, the pact of December 15 was little more than a framework in which the heads of the peak associations agreed to the program in principle and pledged over the next several months to seek the adherence of their affiliates. In fact, even this limited commitment on the part of top business representatives created considerable discontent among the tens of thousands of businesses that were not part of the negotiations, and in virtually all business organizations extraordinary sessions were held to explain the reasons behind the agreement. In the last two weeks of December 1987 and throughout January and February, an increasing number of firms were formally incorporated into the accord. By the end of February, more than 40,000 firms had become formal participants in the pact (*El Universal* 1988, pp. 19–21).

As part of the machinery for supervising this process, the signatories of the December 15 pact established a high-level tripartite committee (the Commission of Monitoring and Prices) that met on a weekly basis to assess progress and monitor compliance. During the initial phase of incorporation, however, the adjustment and freezing of specific prices were generally handled in intensive bilateral negotiations between specific firms or sectors and government representatives, usually led by officials of SECOFI.

In negotiating incorporation and monitoring compliance, the mode of business participation varied significantly with the size of firms and with sectors.[6] In conformance with explicit provisions in the December agreement, the first accords were generally negotiated with leading firms in industry and commerce. These firms pledged not only to restrain their own prices but also to use their purchasing power to ensure the moderation of prices among supplier firms in their sector. At times these agreements were signed by the individual firms themselves, such as Aluminio, General Foods, Kimberly Clark, and Xerox. In other instances, the signatories were chambers and associations controlled by the firms. Most important among the latter were ANTAD (National Association of Self-Service and Department Stores) and chambers representing cement, chemicals, and automotives. Whether individual firms or sectoral organizations signed the accord, relations with the government were generally marked by considerable consultation and cooperation.

Bargaining was far more difficult with chambers representing decentralized economic sectors, such as services, apparel, footwear, and agricultural products. Stabilizing prices in many of these areas was especially difficult because contracts frequently lagged behind overall inflation, then compensated by overshooting changes in the general level of prices. Perhaps as important, the dispersion of firms made it more difficult to arrive at and enforce agreements. In such cases, the government frequently resorted to substantial intimidation to induce cooperation, threatening further tariff reductions, economic sanctions, formal price controls, and labor unrest. The initial months of December through February were particularly acrimonious, involving bitter public criticisms by leading government officials and exhortations to the public to denounce unauthorized price increases to the Federal Consumer Protection Agency.[7]

Even after the formal process of incorporation was concluded, the absence of oligopolies in the service and small manufacturing sectors continued to make policing more difficult than in the more concentrated sectors. Nevertheless, although some cheating occurred during the freeze, the fluctuation of prices and tensions among participants decreased significantly.

Several factors account for this level of cooperation. First, of course, the government's very tight macroeconomic policies compressed domestic demand, while the fixing of public tariffs—for example, in energy and transportation—contained the relative price of key production inputs. Second, controls were always applied with some flexibility, and producers were offered at least some opportunity to renegotiate price levels as conditions changed.

Finally, the power of large-scale retailers was crucial in policing the pricing behavior of their suppliers. In this regard, the close collaboration between SECOFI and ANTAD played a pivotal role. ANTAD's chain of supermarkets and department stores controlled between 35 and 60 percent of the retail market and bought only at prices authorized by the Department of Commerce.

Stabilization Outcomes

Although it is difficult to assess the separate contributions of fiscal restraint and price controls, the program's overall impact on price stability was extremely impressive. During January, inflation continued above 15 percent, indicating that many firms had hedged their bets about the long-term effectiveness of the scheduled freeze. However, by the end of February, monthly rates had declined to 8 percent and continued to decline for the rest of the year. Annual inflation rates remained between 20 and 30 percent in 1989 and 1990. Growth rates were also low in 1988 (less than 2 percent), and the real minimum wage declined around 13 percent (table 9-7). Thus, even with the concerted agreements, the stabilization was far from painless. Nevertheless, both the slow growth and wage deterioration would perhaps have been worse if the government had relied on orthodox fiscal and monetary instruments alone.

Three key challenges faced in any freeze in wages and prices are the possibility of shortages, misalignment of relative prices, and exit from the system of controls. In each of these areas, de la Madrid's administration encountered problems, but they generally seemed less severe and more manageable than those encountered in stabilization experiences elsewhere.

Shortages occurred almost exclusively in nondurable goods, particularly food products such as sugar, cooking oil, and meat, and at one point, the government had to subsidize beef imports in order to alleviate shortages in Mexico City. On the whole, however, these problems were relatively minor compared with earlier experiences in Argentina, Brazil, and Peru. Mexico experienced few, if any, shortages of durable goods, and difficulties with the food supply were probably attributable as much to weather and crop conditions (there was a serious drought in 1988) as to price controls (Reyes Heroles 1989, p. 9).

Price misalignments posed a more serious problem during 1988, with the lag in public sector prices increasing substantially during the course of the year. In this area, political factors offered a clear incentive to delay adjustment. Facing an election during the first semester and a prolonged controversy over the honesty of the electoral process during the second, the government strongly preferred to defer public rate increases until after the new administration was inaugurated. At least in hindsight, however, this did not pose fatal difficulties for the stabilization program. In early 1989, the incoming Salinas government raised public rates and then began another round of negotiations that was reasonably successful in inducing upstream producers to absorb portions of the cost. By the time final products reached consumers, monthly price increases remained in the range of 2 to 3 percent.

Engineering an exit from the system of price controls, as might be expected, was the most problematic feature of the program. For obvious reasons, this issue was not seriously addressed in the last year of de la Madrid's administration and was still at least partially unresolved in 1992. There are substantial grounds for optimism, however. Beginning in 1989 and 1990, negotiations between the Salinas administration and business chambers quietly expanded discretion over pricing in a range of economic sectors. This occurred without a serious resurgence of inflation, and there were reasons to believe that it could continue to do so as long as the government maintained control over fiscal deficits and other key macroeconomic variables.

Implementation of the Pact: Trade Reform

Unlike the consensus that prevailed over stabilization policy, the trade component of the pact was the result of a fierce battle within the administration over proposals for accelerated liberalization coming from the central bank and other parts of the financial bureaucracy (Córdoba 1991). The final decisions, made by the president himself, consolidated the shifts in power already well under way within the Mexican government elite. On the one hand, the explicit link between accelerated liberalization and stabilization—a connection formalized by the terms of the pact—allowed the financial bureaucracy to consolidate its control over trade policy. At the same time, the additional reduction in quantitative restrictions and the virtual elimination of official reference pricing dealt still another blow to the capacity of SECOFI to influence policy at the administrative level.

This section examines two important issues related to implementation of the pact. The first was how to cope with the general reaction of business sectors to acceleration of the reform. The second was how to reconcile the use of a nominal exchange rate anchor with trade policy objectives. This was a more technical issue but one with profound political implications as well.

Reactions of the Business Sector

At the outset of the pact, the government faced a private sector that harbored deep reservations about a radical opening of the Mexican economy. The extent of these reservations, of course, varied by sector and by company size, but there were few enthusiastic supporters anywhere in the business community for the government's decision to accelerate trade reform.[8]

Moreover, key steps regarding quantitative restrictions and tariffs had been decided with virtually no consultation outside the government elite itself and then included in the pact without extensive discussion. Consequently, even large industrialists complained that the government had in effect unilaterally discarded a schedule of tariff reductions negotiated with the private sector only three years earlier.[9]

Under these circumstances, one of the more surprising aspects of the program is the relative absence of public protest in 1988. During the month of January, most of the major associations, including the Coordinating Council of Entrepreneurs, criticized the appreciation of the exchange rate, but only the main industrial organizations demanded more gradualist trade policies, and even these demands generally disappeared in the second quarter of 1988.

To some extent, the propensity of business groups to oppose trade reform had already been weakened by the reduction in quantitative restrictions instituted in 1985. In the years following that initiative, high tariffs and depreciations of the peso continued to provide high levels of effective protection. The policy changes made at the end of 1987 reduced these barriers, and imports began to grow very rapidly. Thus, 1988 was, arguably, the first year in which the private sector actually felt the threat of international competition. Why the passive response?

One major reason has already been mentioned: the weakening of SECOFI's discretionary authority reduced an important source of access for firms seeking special exemptions from general policy decisions. At least two other factors, however, also muted the response of business.

The first was that trade liberalization was packaged as a component of the pact and as an important condition of stabilization (see chapter 3 of this volume). In fact, the time lag required for domestic firms to adjust to international competition made it unlikely that liberalization would affect domestic prices in the short run. The political effect was important, however. On the one hand, throughout the operation of the pact, trade policy remained one of the key political instruments used by the government to pressure businesses into complying with price restraint (*El Universal* 1987, p. 1). At the same time, however, links to the pact tended to disarm potential critics within the business elites whose uneasiness about liberalization was outweighed by their anxieties about hyperinflation and by the urgency they attached to closing ranks with the government at a moment of considerable political uncertainty. For such groups, liberalization was the price to be paid for economic and political stabilization.

Within the framework of this implicit bargain, the organization of power within the private sector also played a significant role. The centrality assigned to the Coordinating Council of Entrepreneurs in negotiating the pact was critical in this sense, because it magnified the interests of large financial-industrial groups that were in a reasonably good position to absorb the costs of economic liberalization. The same pattern extended to the internal organization of most of the other major business chambers (Alcazar 1970; Camp 1970; Heredia 1992). CONCAMIN, the national industrial congress, was dominated by very large manufacturing companies in sectors such as automobiles, fibers, and steel that generally preferred to criticize the trade opening only in very moderate terms. This tended to mute the impact of its member organization, CONACINTRA (the National Chamber of Transforming Industries),

which typically represented smaller manufacturing companies more inclined toward protectionism.

Management of the Exchange Rate

With business opposition neutralized or muted, the most pressing
trade policy question remaining during 1988 was how to manage the
exchange rate. As a pivot of both stabilization and trade reform, exchange rate policy typically poses well-known short-term tradeoffs between controlling domestic prices and establishing competitiveness in
international markets. After leaning strongly toward exports during
1986 and 1987, Mexico's policies in 1988 reflected the new emphasis on
stabilization. In January and February, the big devaluation of the official
rate was followed by the institution of a crawling peg; beginning in
March, the rate was frozen entirely for the rest of the year. The consequences for reserves and the reactions of exporters were both reasonably
predictable.

In the first place, doubts about the long-run sustainability of the program meant that not even the pull of very high domestic interest rates
could prevent a surge in the demand for dollars. Pressures were especially
strong after the June drop in petroleum prices, and reserve levels dropped
precipitously. A fairly steep decline, however, had already been anticipated. With a huge cushion of hard currency, officials calculated correctly that this was an acceptable price to pay for breaking the inertial
spiral and that they could afford to wait out the year before making a
correction (Banco de México, *Informe anual,* 1988).

Also quite predictably, exporters complained that appreciation of the
peso would damage their competitiveness. During the initial phase of the
pact, the Coordinating Council of Entrepreneurs and most of the other
peak associations claimed that exchange rate policy would inhibit the
growth of exports. These complaints ceased after the second-round
agreements were concluded at the end of February, as government and
business leaders consolidated their alliance. But scattered complaints
from individual exporters continued throughout the year, and the wisdom of the freeze remained a point of concern among economic observers (*El Proceso,* June 20, 1988).

In the face of these dilemmas, the decision to sustain the nominal rate
requires comment. The economic basis for the decision was that the peso
had become substantially *undervalued* during 1986 and 1987, so that
fixing the nominal rate in effect allowed the real rate to appreciate to a
more or less "historic" level of about 1985. Assessment of this argument
depends, among other things, on judgments concerning the appropriateness of 1985 as a base year, methods of measuring the real exchange rate,
and estimates of changes in the exchange rate among Mexico's competitors for U.S. markets. By the early 1990s, real appreciation had become
a legitimate cause for concern. Throughout 1988, however, the advan-

tages for stabilization of maintaining the nominal rate seemed to out-weigh the risks. The inflation-corrected exchange rate remained well below the noncompetitive levels reached in the early 1980s, and exports other than oil continued to grow, although at a rate somewhat lower than in 1987 (Banco de México, *Informe anual,* 1988, p. 36). Besides, the real wage fell sharply in 1988 so that there was no loss of compet-itiveness. As long as reserves remained adequate, therefore, it seemed reasonable to allow the freeze to continue and confidence in the stabiliza-tion program to deepen.

Whatever its merits, this economic argument was clearly reinforced by political considerations. As was the case with other adjustments in offi-cial prices, corrections in the nominal exchange rate implied risks that the government was not anxious to run during a volatile and uncertain transition period. Again, the government did not return to a crawling peg until the advent of the Salinas administration.

Outcomes of Trade Policy

The outcome of the trade policies described above will depend heavily on business adjustments that unfold over a relatively long period of time, as well as on external market conditions and trade negotiations under way in the early 1990s. An examination of the 1988 current account data presented in tables 9-11 and 9-12 shows three facts: (a) there was a major surge in imports (up almost 40 percent from the preceding year); (b) total exports grew only slightly, by 0.3 percent; and (c) as a result, the current account balance declined markedly from a surplus of $4.0 billion in 1987 to a deficit of $2.4 billion in 1988. The implications of these figures are extremely ambiguous, however, and a longer time frame is needed to assess their significance for trade reform.

On the export side, the low overall growth rate masks a 16 percent rise in exports other than oil, which was offset by the decline in oil revenues (Banco de México, *Informe anual,* 1988, p. 36). Some of this expansion, however, came from sectors that continued to be covered by export promotion schemes. In the automobile industry—which remained largely unaffected by the 1987 reforms—exports constituted approximately 40 percent of total production (Ros 1991; Banco de México, *Informe anual,* 1988, p. 26). Conversely, traditional sectors such as textiles, food, and wood products were generally badly hit by the reduction in trade barriers.

On the import side, the key issue is the extent to which appreciation of the peso and reduction of tariff protection for producers' goods encour-aged firms to import capital equipment aimed at strengthening future export capabilities. A disaggregation of the import data provides some indication of developments along these lines. About 20 percent of all imports did go to capital goods, more than 70 percent to intermediate products, and only 8 percent to consumer goods (Banco de México,

Table 9-11. Real Growth of Aggregate Supply and Demand in Mexico, by Quarter, 1987 and 1988
(percentage growth over the previous quarter)

Indicator	1987				1988			
	First	Second	Third	Fourth	First	Second	Third	Fourth
Domestic supply	-2.0	1.2	0.2	7.0	-4.9	-0.6	-0.3	7.2
Imports	-11.2	13.6	12.4	3.0	3.6	17.1	12.4	6.3
Total supply	-2.5	1.9	0.9	6.7	-4.4	0.7	0.7	7.2
Exports	-0.5	0.4	-3.1	5.1	4.6	-4.0	-5.8	5.5
Domestic expenditure	-2.9	2.2	1.8	7.1	-6.1	1.6	2.0	7.5
Consumption								
Private	-3.7	2.6	1.7	4.3	-6.2	2.9	1.1	7.0
Public	-0.2	-0.8	-2.4	-0.5	0.7	1.4	-1.2	0.6
Gross fixed investment	-6.8	12.2	7.6	8.4	-15.0	3.9	7.6	8.1

Note: The real growth rates correspond to the growth rates of the respective real index (1980 = 100) for the component.
Source: Banco de México, Indicadores económicos, October 1991, p. II-2.

Table 9-12. Balance of Payments in Mexico, by Quarter, 1987 and 1988
(billions of dollars)

Indicator	1987				1988			
	First	Second	Third	Fourth	First	Second	Third	Fourth
Current account balance	1.44	1.43	0.47	0.64	0.70	-0.04	-1.40	-1.70
Goods and no factorial services balance	3.01	2.94	2.19	2.24	2.48	1.52	0.17	-0.06
Interest payments	1.85	1.98	2.11	2.14	2.20	2.11	2.08	2.25
Payments net of interest	1.50	1.52	1.61	1.56	1.64	1.45	1.41	1.63
Capital account	-0.49	3.53	-1.62	-1.99	2.18	-1.50	0.63	0.14
Direct foreign investment	0.43	0.77	0.61	1.44	0.64	0.64	0.33	0.98
Errors and omissions	1.06	-0.11	1.96	-0.20	1.91	0.24	-3.39	-1.60
International reserves (variation)								
Gross	2.17	4.84	0.80	-0.88	2.08	-1.64	-4.25	-3.32
Net	2.01	4.85	0.80	-1.59	2.23	-1.31	-4.16	-3.49

Source: Banco de México, Indicadores económicos, December 1988, February 1991.

Informe anual, 1988). Interestingly, firms within the hard-hit textile industry were among the most active importers of capital goods. By the early 1990s, however, it was still impossible to know for certain how much of this activity represented a speculative buildup of replacement goods and producers' supplies, stimulated by the relatively cheap dollar and new import opportunities.

Even without being able to draw clear conclusions about supply responses, it is possible to say with somewhat greater confidence that the reforms marked an important turning point in the credibility of the government's commitment to opening trade. Prior to 1988, businesspeople had reason to be skeptical about the speed and consistency with which the government would move toward its announced objective, since liberalization initiatives had already been reversed in the mid-1970s and early 1980s. The reforms of 1987–88 drastically reduced the ground for such skepticism. Both interviews and the public discourse of the business sector suggest strongly that the private sector was at last convinced that the trade opening would not be abandoned or delayed, even in response to a serious economic crisis.

Institutional and Structural Influences on Outcomes of the Pact

Notwithstanding the many challenges that still confronted Mexico at the end of 1988, the first year of the pact can be considered a clear success in the analysis of stabilization and structural adjustment. The reform package was remarkably coherent, especially given the crisis conditions in which it was conceived, and left the economy much better off than might have been expected a year earlier. To be sure, the agenda of issues left to be tackled by the new Salinas administration was daunting. It included the need to adjust relative prices, exit from the price control system, increase the level of wages, and of course, reignite economic growth. Nevertheless, the pact had laid the groundwork for a recovery, without creating unmanageable new problems. What explains this success?

The previous sections emphasized how the crisis itself provided the administration with incentives to experiment with policies, package trade and stabilization measures skillfully and creatively, and negotiate with key business groups. These processes occurred, however, within a highly centralized system of power that reduced the political costs of policy adjustments and enhanced the possibility of securing the cooperation of economic sectors affected by them. The remaining pages of this chapter look more closely at some of the key features of this system and its relations with the private sector and the United States.

State Capacity: Internal Coherence and External Linkages

The capacity of the Mexican state to undertake and implement reforms can be discussed in terms of mutually reinforcing internal and external aspects of institutional organization. Internal capacity is reflected in the skills, cohesion, and informational resources of the bureaucratic apparatus. High internal capacity implies relative autonomy of an organization's norms of recruitment, budget, and mission. External capacity refers to the institutional resources available for communicating with economic groups and inducing their cooperation in policy projects (Evans 1992). The Mexican government's success in framing and implementing the pact reflects high capabilities in both respects.

Although much of the Mexican state was characterized internally by high levels of patronage and corruption, the principal economic decision-making agencies generally sustained high standards of professionalism and economic training. The Bank of Mexico—an institutional power for decades—was especially impressive in this regard, but very high standards were also maintained within the finance and budget ministries and in parts of SECOFI.

Among other things, high levels of technocratic skills implied a substantial capacity to collect and analyze economic data and an ability to draw on ongoing policy research while framing options. In the case of the pact, which was improvised rapidly in the face of crisis, this reduced the risk of internally incoherent choices. Broad contingency plans had already been on the table for more than a year; top officials and their staffs had studied experiences in other countries and had deliberated about possible applications to Mexico.[10]

Finally, because of the extensive appointment powers of the president, the social and professional cohesion of the economic bureaucracy increased substantially in the 1980s. Most officials recruited into decision-making positions during this period came from a common social background, had attended elite schools in Mexico, and possessed advanced degrees—often in economics—from prestigious graduate programs in the United States. Although shared backgrounds and training did not preclude bitter bureaucratic and political rivalries, they did facilitate common perspectives on the importance of fiscal discipline and market-oriented reforms.

The external capabilities of the Mexican state were based principally on the deployment of corporatist and bureaucratic resources that had characterized the Mexican system since the late 1930s. Peasant organizations were almost exclusively dependent on the PRI and had virtually no political independence in the negotiations over agricultural policy. Although the views of official union leaders carried somewhat greater weight in policy negotiations, their control over their rank and file depended heavily on government sponsorship and patronage, which limited their leverage in conflicts with officials. Notwithstanding moments of criticism and dissent, unions were, as discussed, constrained to accept incomes policy decisions reached within the leadership of the financial bureaucracy.

Finally, although more subtle means of persuasion and collaboration were used to induce the cooperation of business groups, these means were backed up as well by formidable instruments of influence and social control. As with the case of labor, corporatist chambers were crucial channels of communication and monitoring, especially within the more dispersed economic sectors. To bolster these, the government frequently deployed other resources. Recalcitrant businesses faced implicit threats of labor unrest from official unions. The possibility of tax audits magnified the voice of the finance minister in negotiations. And the manipulation of tariff and trade regulations remained an important instrument for inducing cooperation.

The Partnership with the Private Sector

Business groups, of course, were partially shielded from the power of the Mexican state by the control that private firms exercised over investment resources and marketing decisions. As happened throughout the 1970s and early 1980s, this meant that Mexican business sectors could wield significant pressure on state authority when they perceived serious threats to their interests. It also implied that inducement and persuasion would necessarily be significant components of any bargains struck with public authority.

The pact was an important political turning point in this respect, because it capped a sustained effort begun under de la Madrid to end the long period of adversarial relations between the business sector and the state. Prior to 1988, tensions had already been reduced by the government's assistance in managing private debt through FICORCA and by a favorable settlement on the bank nationalization. Nevertheless, at the outset of the pact, business relations with the government continued to be characterized by considerable mistrust, and both sets of actors had relatively low expectations that the other would be able to keep its side of the agreement. Doubts began to dissipate, however, as it became clear that the government would meet its fiscal commitments and that the stabilization was in fact taking hold. And, of course, incentives for cooperation were strengthened considerably by Cuauhtémoc Cárdenas's surprisingly strong electoral showing in mid-1988.

By the beginning of the Salinas administration, the representatives of major business groups had ceased to campaign against the concentration of power within the political system or the potential abuses of discretionary presidential authority. Relations between government and business had begun to evoke comparisons with the "stabilizing development" period of the 1950s and 1960s.

As in the stabilizing development period, however, the establishment of a partnership between the state and business depended heavily on the extension of privileged, behind-the-scenes political access to the top elites of the business sector.[11] For the elites who participated most extensively in the agreements, the costs posed by trade liberalization and fiscal austerity were lower than those that would have been incurred by failure to reach agreement; but this was not necessarily the case for smaller, more vulnerable firms that were not directly included in the bargaining process. Because power was concentrated within the business sector, however, the cooperative bargains struck by the business elites tended to restrict the economic and political options of their less powerful counterparts.

The implications of this concentration of power were probably clearest in the process of breaking the inertial inflationary spiral that threatened Mexico in the late 1980s. In important respects, inertial inflation can be understood as a prisoner's dilemma in which incentives to cheat on individual price or wage decisions lead to suboptimal outcomes for the collectivity as a whole. In the Mexican case, these incentives were reduced substantially by the power of a highly centralized government and a powerful business elite to police their constituents and enforce their respective commitments.

At the same time, the business elite's close, privileged access to government had a more complex impact on the formulation and implementation of trade policy during the 1980s. During the 1950s and 1960s, cooperative relations with the private sector had been forged in the context of an import-substitution industrial development strategy that offered ample scope for discretionary inducements to individual business groups. In the case of the pact, in contrast, the behind-the-scenes bargains struck with top business leaders seemed less consistent with the principles of a neutral and transparent trade regime that the government envisioned for the 1990s. Such bargaining did, however, enable the government to avoid political isolation with respect to its accelerated program of liberalization. What remains unclear is whether the traditional forms of cooperation reestablished in 1987–88 can be sustained in a context free of rent seeking and special political privileges.

Finally, the concentration of public and private power associated with the initiation of the pact raises important questions about the eventual prospects of democratic reform. Over the long run, it is quite conceivable that prospects for such reforms can be enhanced by the processes of economic liberalization set into motion during the 1980s. A more stable, market-oriented economy can provide the basis for the continued expansion of a Mexican middle class and for more insistent demands for participation within the political system. A reduction in the economic resources flowing through the public sector can also be expected to reduce the scope of political patronage available to local bosses and to the groups that control the levers of power within Mexico's corporatist system. Nevertheless, the initiation of the liberal reforms depended substantially on the capacity of de la Madrid's government to wield these levers and to enlist the support of the business elites.

During the first years of the Salinas administration, a series of steps have been taken that appear to move toward a more competitive and open political system (Bizberg 1990b; Castillo Peraza 1992; Gómez and Bailey 1990; Woldenberg 1991). Electoral laws have been reformed to reduce the possibility of cheating, and greater scope has been provided for the National Action Party to exercise influence in the legislature and in state and local government. These steps, however, have not yet altered Mexico's basic power hierarchies. As of the early 1990s, reaching the goal of political pluralism still implied major transformations in the state institutions and in the political bargains that had thus far guided the economic transformation.

The Reconstruction of Relations with External Creditors

Throughout most of 1988, external creditors—the U.S. government, international financial institutions, and private banks—did not play a large, direct role in the episode examined here. There is no evidence, moreover, that the main actors in the pact anticipated that their agreements would lead to the specific opportunities for debt reduction and trade opening later offered by the Brady Plan and the North American Free Trade Agreement negotiations.

As suggested throughout this chapter, however, the reestablishment of positive political and economic relations with creditor groups was crucial to the success of the adjustment process both in the 1980s and over the longer run. Successful negotiations with creditors in 1986 and 1987 were essential to the successful outcome of the pact itself. That success, in turn, laid the groundwork for the much more extensive process of rapprochement that followed under Salinas and U.S. president George Bush—a prospect that may well have been anticipated in general terms by at least some of the actors in the policy episode described.

Accommodation with external actors affected both financing and the expectations of economic actors. Crucial financing steps were taken in 1986 and 1987 and were followed later, of course, by the Brady Plan agreements in 1990. In addition, the easing of tension with the Reagan administration probably reduced economic uncertainty in some measure. In November 1988, for example, a $3.5 billion credit extended by the United States government helped calm tensions associated with the transfer of presidential power, even though it was not actually used by Mexico.

Nevertheless, under de la Madrid, the accommodation reached with the United States and external creditors was far more tentative than the close working relationship reestablished with the domestic business elite.

Continuing tensions with creditors, in turn, jeopardized the credibility of the adjustment program—although precise effects are obviously difficult to gauge. In any event, despite the dramatic drop in inflation in 1988, doubts about the sustainability of the program persisted throughout de la Madrid's administration, placing at risk the gains made during that time.

In this respect, the more extensive rapprochement following the change of administrations in Mexico and the United States marked a pivotal change in the context of adjustment. With the ratification of the trade treaty, of course, these relationships will evolve. But the credibility of the steps initiated in the 1980s was vastly strengthened when the Brady Plan negotiations were concluded in 1990, coinciding directly with a reduction in interest rates and a reversal of the capital flight that had plagued de la Madrid's administration.

Appendix 9-1: The Economics of Disinflation

The pact successfully reduced inflation in the course of 1988 because the government firmly pursued a strategy that involved simultaneous actions on several fronts (Banco de México, *Informe anual,* 1988, pp. 17–23; Lustig 1991). Such actions included (a) fixing the exchange rate at the start of the pact's third month of operation, (b) fixing the prices of most public goods and services, as well as those of key consumer goods produced in the private sector such as bread and tortillas, (c) controlling most other private sector prices, (d) severely cutting programmable public expenditure and implementing a restrictive fiscal and monetary policy, and (f) reducing trade barriers suddenly and across the board. This appendix discusses the role of these measures, each of which was an important ingredient in the overall operation of the pact.

The decision to fix the exchange rate may have been the most important single step in the anti-inflationary package. The measure not only eliminated the strong pressures that the rapid rate of depreciation had imposed upon costs since mid-1986, but also signaled the government's firm commitment to price stabilization.[12]

The political timing of the decision was crucial to enhancing the credibility of the fixed exchange rate; failure to sustain the rate in the midst of a complex electoral process would have entailed prohibitive political costs. The most fundamental bases of credibility, however, were the high level of reserves and the sizable trade surplus in December 1987. The high level of reserves was partly the result of the inflow of external credit that accrued because of arrangements negotiated with foreign creditors in the summer of 1986. Also important in explaining the central bank's accumulation of reserves—as well as the large surplus in the trade balance that caused it—was the policy of rapid depreciation of the peso pursued by the government from mid-1986 up to the last months of 1987.[13]

The decision to fix key public and private sector prices was a second major ingredient of the pact. Particularly significant in this regard were the prices of energy, transport, and important popular consumption items such as sugar, flour, corn, and wheat. The existence of prior subsidy schemes proved helpful for fixing many of these prices.

Fixing these prices led in the medium run to higher public deficits and higher inflation, but in the short run it had a very positive influence on costs as well as the general level of prices. Furthermore, the increase in these prices during the initial months of the pact reduced the fiscal costs of maintaining prices fixed during the following months.

Also critical was the establishment of an extensive system for controlling the prices of goods and services produced by the private sector. Even though controlled prices for key products in the *canasta básica* had existed in the past, the control over virtually all private sector prices constituted the most novel and heterodox component of the pact.

Controls over other private sector prices tended to be, understandably, less effective and more flexible than controls over public sector prices and consumer items traditionally subject to price controls. For a number of reasons, however, the system introduced under the pact proved to be more effective than might have been expected: (1) business associations provided firm support in promoting and ensuring compliance from their affiliates, (2) the government managed price controls realistically and flexibly, and (3) imports were used as a threat against firms that failed to comply with concerted price levels.

No published studies fully assess the importance of this ingredient of the anti-inflationary package. Nevertheless, the contrast with the Argentine and Brazilian experiences suggests that both the absence of shortages as well as the absence of massive imports of consumer goods during implementation of the pact had a lot to do with the system of extensive and concerted price controls.

A third element in the government's all-out attack on inflation was wage policy. Evaluating the contribution of the evolution of wage levels to price stabilization is difficult, however, because the evidence is ambiguous. In the course of 1988, real minimum wages fell 13 percent (table 9-2). The fall in average real wages in manufacturing, on the other hand, was almost nil. How does one explain these two markedly different trends, and what was the effect of wage policy on price stabilization?

The differences in large part reflect priorities implicit in the stabilization policy. On the one hand, the government was firmly committed to fixing the minimum wage because doing so is important for shaping the expectations that economic agents have about price levels. The government paid less attention to controlling manufacturing wages, however, in part because most workers in manufacturing were unionized and received salaries that exceeded the minimum wage, while minimum-wage workers were typically unorganized and had less political influence. Also important in accounting for trends in manufacturing wages, however, were market conditions themselves. The resumption of industrial growth toward the end of 1988 increased the demand for labor and pushed manufacturing wages upward. Market pressures, along with union pressures, thus appear to have contributed significantly to the 5 percent increase in manufacturing wages from December 1987 to December 1988 (table 9-2).

The evidence suggests, then, that the contribution of wage policy to stabilization concerned the government's ability to obtain the support of unions for reducing real minimum wages and, thus, to avoid incurring the costs of more strikes. In return for such support, unions received the space they needed to protect the salaries of their rank and file through private contractual negotiations with individual firms and sectors.

Even where the salaries of unionized workers did drop sharply—as in the case of public sector employees—unions were inclined to remain inactive, and thus loyal to government, until after the contractual negotiations were complete.

Another critical ingredient of the pact was fiscal policy. As indicated by the central bank's annual report, the primary budget balance showed a surplus of 7.6 percent of GDP in 1988, which exceeded by 0.7 percent of GDP the primary budget surplus of 1987. This was the result of a 1.6 percent of GDP fall in programmable public expenditure, an increase of 0.9 percent in tax income, an increase of 0.8 percent in nontax income, as well as a drop in oil income that amounted to 2.3 percent of GDP.[14]

In the course of 1988 and in spite of a sharp reduction in external oil revenues, the public sector reduced its demand for nonfinancial goods and services and increased both its tax and its nontax revenues. Fiscal policy led to the contraction of demand in many markets and to an overall reduction of inflationary pressures throughout the economy. Such results show, then, that the government did, in fact, adopt a markedly restrictive stance in fiscal policy while implementing the pact.

The sharp rise in real interest rates, however, generated an equally significant increase in domestic financial public expenditures, which rose from −0.7 percent of GDP in 1987 to 7.0 percent in 1988. The cause of this increase was the need to compensate holders of domestic public debt for the risks that a sudden devaluation or the freezing of public debt would entail.

The increase in public debt that resulted from the rise in real interest rates obviously affected the balance of both the total as well as the operational budget. The balance of the operational budget moved from a surplus of 1.8 percent of GDP in 1987 to a deficit of 3.6 percent in 1988, which entailed an overall increase of more than 5 percent of GDP (table 9-1).

A superficial glance at the evidence suggests that the increase in the operational deficit entailed an expansionary fiscal policy during 1988;

such an increase was the result of the need to pay domestic savers so as to ensure their willingness to continue holding public debt. However, the effects of such expenditure were, in fact, restrictive rather than expansive. That is to say that, if the interest expenditure had not risen, total expenditure would probably have risen even more.

Failure to adjust interest rates upward would have led to the liquidation of domestic debt and, thus, to a simultaneous rise in the demand for foreign exchange, heightened expectations of devaluation, and a steep rise of demand in nonfinancial markets, all of which would have had strong inflationary effects. Although not sustainable in the long run, then, the increase in domestic financial public expenditure had an important short-run anti-inflationary effect.

Stabilization during the operation of the pact, in sum, was possible due to a firmly restrictive fiscal policy, especially with regard to the reduction of government expenditure in nonfinancial goods and services, and not only to price controls and a fixed exchange rate.[15]

Nevertheless, the magnitude of the 1988 increase in domestic financial public expenditure as well as of the associated levels of real interest rates was not sustainable over the long run. Due to various wealth effects, the expenditures of the groups receiving interest payments were bound to increase sooner or later. Very likely, in fact, government domestic financial expenditures in 1988 led in subsequent years to lower levels of disinflation, greater inertial tendencies, and higher levels of imports.

The acceleration of trade liberalization constituted another piece of the pact. In December 1987 most import licenses and official prices were eliminated and tariff levels were significantly reduced, reaching an average value of almost 6 percent.[16]

Since most of the 54 percent increase in merchandise imports, which amounted to almost $19 million in 1988, occurred among liberalized sectors, opening trade did spur the growth of imports. Although final consumer imports rose 150 percent, their total value amounted to only $1.921 million and thus constituted a very small fraction of total domestic consumption.

These figures indicate that trade liberalization contributed to disinflation by allowing part of the excess demand to flow abroad. Equally true, however, is the fact that such a measure did not directly affect either prices or competitiveness in the markets for most consumer goods. Rather than acting directly on consumer prices, trade liberalization helped to reduce them indirectly through its effects on intermediate imports and thus on production costs. However, such contractionary effects were probably mitigated by the strongly oligopolistic nature of the Mexican economy. In fact, what appears to have been most decisive about the relative importance of the trade component of the pact was the implicit—and often explicit—threat of higher imports of final consumer goods as a means to keep those prices in line.

In order to assess the significance of trade liberalization for price levels, more detailed studies of the various effects associated with opening trade are required. It is clear, however, that opening commerce did contain a potential resurgence of inflationary pressures.

A lot more could be said about the various measures that made up the pact as well as about the conditions that facilitated its implementation.[17] This analysis clearly shows that the success of the anti-inflationary strategy pursued by the Mexican government from December 1987 to December 1988 was the result of the complex, and often unexpected, combination of orthodox and heterodox components of the Economic Solidarity Pact.

Fiscal policy partially canceled itself out, because interest payments had to be increased and the public debt defended. It thus would have been insufficient in and of itself. Without a restrictive fiscal stance and rapid removal of trade barriers, though, the effectiveness of price and wage controls would have been severely reduced. Moreover, without the initial effectiveness of all those measures, the decision to fix the exchange rate would have proved unsustainable.

Finally, the agreement among government, business, labor, and foreign creditors in support of the pact was decisive. Without this agreement, few of the other measures discussed would have been sustainable. Unfortunately, as the evolution of the Mexican economy from 1983 to 1987 shows, no good recipe tells how to conclude agreements of this kind at the appropriate time.

Notes

1. Contrary to popular impression, the group most concerned about a moratorium was the Mexican financial establishment. From historic experience, this group feared that confrontation with creditors would be linked to populist policies directed against them and allied sectors of big business.

2. All dollar amounts are in U.S. dollars. A billion is 1,000 million.

3. Labor Minister Arsenio Farell, in particular, played a pivotal role in winning the cooperation of business leaders as well as of unions. Farell's influence in the negotiations with business leaders rested in part on his importance in dealing with potential labor conflicts and in part on his position as a respected senior member of the cabinet.

4. The timing of developments in the election campaign also played a role. The opposition candidacy of Cuauhtémoc Cárdenas was not perceived as a serious threat until May. By that time, inflation had declined significantly, and the stabilization program was viewed as a political asset.

5. PRI congressional losses in the 1988 elections provided the opposition National Action Party with some leverage in the legislature after 1989. But the bargaining power was restricted to constitutional issues—most notably electoral reform amendments—which required a two-thirds' majority.

6. This section is based primarily on interviews conducted with business leaders.

7. Negotiations with weak chambers tended to proceed more or less as follows. The heads of the chamber were called into the meetings chaired by the minister of trade, but where the ministers of finance, budget and planning, and labor were also present. One interviewee used the term "traumatic" to describe these meetings, and all of them said they were directly cajoled into signing the *Acuerdos de Concertación*. At first, each of the chambers thought it was being treated especially hard. Members soon realized, however,

that all were being subject to the same intimidation. The most frequently used tactics were the threat of labor unrest, the opening of trade, and the imposition of strict price controls. In subsequent meetings, where specific agreements were drawn up, pressure decreased somewhat.

8. According to two of the most outspoken advocates of rapid opening within the central bank (Gil Díaz and Zepeda Payeras 1991), the most intense opposition to trade liberalization came from the owners of large firms in the intermediate manufacturing sector (for example, cement, glass, paper, secondary petrochemicals, aluminum, and steel) as well as from firms covered by sectoral programs (for example, pharmaceuticals, automobile parts, electronics).

9. The original schedule for tariff reductions was formalized in the Program to Reduce Tariffs, 1983–88, launched in April 1986. The program established a two-and-a-half-year period for reducing the level of tariffs, at the end of which maximum tariffs would reach 30 percent ad valorem. Protection for inputs and intermediary goods would be reduced to 10 percent, and locally manufactured consumer products would retain high levels of tariff protection (Secretaría de Comercio y Fomento Industrial 1988b, pp. 133–34).

10. The fact that such contingencies had been debated in a relatively insulated bureaucratic setting was also important, because it diminished the possibility that leaks about a prospective freeze might trigger speculative behavior.

11. In May, Augustín Legoretta was reported to have boasted that the economy could be controlled by 300 businessmen: "a closed group that can talk directly with the president in a presidentialist system" (El Proceso, May 30, 1988). Although Legoretta later denied making these statements, reports of his talk created substantial controversy.

12. For some time, in general terms, prices in the Mexican economy have been virtually indexed to dollar prices (McLeod and Welch 1992).

13. One might ask whether it made sense in 1987 to establish an exchange rate that built reserves but induced inflation, only to have to stabilize and lose those reserves in 1988. Why create a problem that had to be solved later? Would it not have been better to implement the pact earlier? The delay may be attributable, in part, to the timing of the Mexican electoral cycle, but a simpler explanation would rest on the learning experience of Mexican decisionmakers. Only at the end of 1987 did they have the experience to create and implement an anti-inflationary program that included massive price and wage controls, as well as a fixed exchange rate (Córdoba 1991).

14. These figures differ from those in table 9-1, which refer to total primary expenditures, including budgetary and other expenditures. In any case, the adjustment to this last figure was greater. Figures in the text refer to information quoted in the yearly report of the Bank of Mexico about economic developments during 1988, and they are more or less consistent with figures reported in table 9-1. Subsequent revisions have not altered the sense of the assessments made in the text.

15. In 1981, in the face of obvious inflationary pressures, some authors proposed a fixed exchange rate as *the* effective anti-inflationary instrument while questioning the utility of controlling demand (Eatwell and Singh 1981). Ros (1992) questions the effectiveness of demand management policies in the late 1980s.

16. Some of these exceptions were licenses in the agricultural sector and in industrial sectors covered by so-called engineering programs (cars and many automotive inputs, computers, office equipment, chemicals, weapons, and so forth).

17. Among other questions, the following should be explored: (a) What were the efficacy and later consequences of the initial price realignment that occurred between January and March 1988? (b) Which entrepreneurial groups failed to maintain price discipline and moved capital abroad, and why? (c) How precisely did the labor market function? Was this exclusively the result of market mechanisms, or did it also involve negotiated agreements?

References

Aguilar Zinser, Adolfo. 1988. "La crisis de las relaciones con los Estados Unidos y el cambio político en México." In Rolando Cordera, Raúl Trejo, and Juan Enríque Vega, eds., *México: El reclamo democrático.* Mexico City: ILET / Siglo XXI.

Alcazar, Marco Antonio. 1970. *Las agrupaciones patronales en México*. Mexico City: El Colegio de México.

Arriola, Carlos. 1988. *Los empresarios y el estado, 1970–1982*. Mexico City: Universidad Nacional Autónoma de México/Miguel Angel Porrúa.

Banco de México. Various years, 1980–90. *Informe anual*. Mexico City.

_____. Various years, 1987–91. *Indicadores económicos*. Mexico City.

_____. 1978. *Estadísticas históricas de balanza de pagos, 1970–78*. Mexico City.

_____. 1992. *Criterios generales de política económica*. Mexico City.

Bazdresch, Carlos, and Santiago Levy. 1991. "Populism and Economic Policy in Mexico, 1970–1982." In Rudiger Dornbusch and Sebastian Edwards, eds., *The Macroeconomics of Populism in Latin America*. Chicago, Ill.: University of Chicago Press.

Bizberg, Ilan. 1990a. "La crisis del corporativismo mexicano." *Foro Internacional* 120 (April–June), pp. 695–735.

_____. 1990b. *Estado y sindicalismo en México*. Mexico City: El Colegio de México.

Buffie, Edward, and Allen Sangines Krause. 1989. "Mexico 1959–86: From Stabilizing Development to the Debt Crisis." In Jeffrey D. Sachs, ed., *Developing Country Debt and the World Economy*. Chicago, Ill.: University of Chicago Press.

Camp, Roderic A. 1970. *Entrepreneurs and Politics in Twentieth Century Mexico*. New York: Oxford University Press.

Carpizo, Jorge. 1978. *El presidencialismo mexicano*. Mexico City: Siglo XXI.

Carr, Barry, ed. 1986. *The Mexican Left, the Popular Movements, and the Politics of Austerity*. Monograph Series 18. La Jolla, Calif.: Center for U.S.-Mexican Studies, University of California, San Diego.

Castañeda, Jorge G., and Robert A. Pastor. 1989. *Límites en la amistad: México y Estados Unidos*. Mexico City: Joaquín Mortiz/Planeta.

Castillo Peraza, Carlos. 1992. "Las cifras de la crisis." *La Jornada*, April 6.

CEESP (Centro de Estudios Económicos del Sector Privado). 1989. *Marco económico 1989*. Mexico City.

Centro de Estudios de Opinión Pública. 1988. *Jornada nacional*. Mexico City.

Collier, Ruth Berins. 1992. *The Contradictory Alliance: State-Labor Relations and Regime Change in Mexico*. Berkeley: University of California, Berkeley, Institute for International Studies.

Collier, Ruth Berins, and David Collier. 1991. *Shaping the Political Arena*. Princeton, N.J.: Princeton University Press.

Córdoba, José. 1991. "Diez lecciones de la reforma económica en México." *Nexos* 158 (February), pp. 31–48.

Cornelius, Wayne A., Judith Gentleman, and Peter H. Smith, eds. 1989. *Mexico's Alternative Political Futures*. La Jolla, Calif. Center for U.S.-Mexican Studies, University of California, San Diego.

Cosío Villegas, Daniél. 1973. *El sistema político mexicano*. Mexico City: Joaquín Mortiz.

Eatwell, John, and Ajit Singh. 1981. "Está sobrecalentada la economía mexicana? Un análisis de los problemas de política económica de corto y mediano plazo." *Economía Mexicana* 3.

Evans, Peter. 1992. "The State as Problem and Solution: Predation, Embedded Autonomy, and Structural Change." In Stephan Haggard and Robert R. Kaufman, eds., *The Politics of Structural Adjustment*. Princeton, N.J.: Princeton University Press.

Gil Díaz, Francisco, and Manuel Zepeda Payeras. 1991. "Mexico's Recent Experience Regarding Commercial Openness." Unpublished ms. Mexico City. Processed.

Gómez, Leopoldo, and John Bailey. 1990. "La transición política y los dilemas del PRI." *Foro Internacional* 121 (July–September), pp. 57–87.

González Casanova, Pablo. 1977. *Democracy in Mexico*. New York: Oxford University Press.

Gurria Treviño, Angel. 1988. "La restructuración de la deuda: El caso de México." In Stephany Griffith-Jones, ed., *Deuda externa, renegociación y ajuste en América Latina*. Mexico City: Fondo de Cultura Económica.

Hansen, Roger D. 1971. *The Politics of Mexican Development*. Baltimore, Md.: Johns Hopkins University Press.

Heredia, Blanca. 1992. "Politics, Profits, and Size: The Political Transformation of Mexican Business." In Douglas Chalmers, Atilio Borón, and María do Carmo Campello de Souza, eds., *The Right and Democracy in Latin America*. New York: Praeger.

Hernández Rodríguez, Rogelio. 1988a. *Empresarios, banca y estado: El conflicto durante el gobierno de José López Portillo, 1976–1982*. Mexico City: FLACSO/Miguel Angel Porrúa.

————. 1988b. "Los hombres del presidente de la Madrid." *Foro Internacional* 28:1 (July–September), pp. 5–38.

Kaufman, Robert R. 1990. "Stabilization and Adjustment in Argentina, Brazil, and Mexico." In Joan M. Nelson, ed., *Economic Crisis and Policy Choice: The Politics of Adjustment in the Third World*. Princeton, N.J.: Princeton University Press.

Loaeza, Soledad. 1988. *Clases medias y política en México*. Mexico City: El Colegio de México.

López Portillo, José. 1988. *Mis tiempos*. Mexico City: Fernández Editores.

Lustig, Nora. 1991. "El pacto de solidaridad económica." In G. Rozenwurcel, ed., *Elecciones y política económica*. Buenos Aires: CEDES.

————. 1992. *Mexico: The Remaking of an Economy*. Washington, D.C.: Brookings Institution.

McLeod, Darril, and John Welch. 1992. "El libre comercio y el peso." *Economía Mexicana, Nueva Epoca* 1:1 (January–June), pp. 193–235.

Maxfield, Sylvia. 1990. *Governing Capital: International Finance and Mexican Politics*. Ithaca, N.Y.: Cornell University Press.

Maxfield, Sylvia, and Ricardo Anzaldúa, eds. 1987. *Government and Private Sector in Contemporary Mexico*. Monograph Series 20. La Jolla, Calif.: Center for U.S.-Mexican Studies, University of California, San Diego.

Middlebrook, Kevin J. 1989. "The Sounds of Silence: Organized Labor's Response to the Economic Crisis in Mexico." *Journal of Latin American Studies* 21:2, pp. 195–220.

Molinar Horcasitas, Juan. 1991. *El tiempo de la legitimidad: Elecciones, autoritarismo y democracia en México*. Mexico City: Cal y Arena.

Poder Ejecutivo Federal. 1983. *Plan Nacional de Desarrollo 1983*. Mexico City.

Presidencia de la República. 1987. *Criterios generales de política económica, 1987*. Mexico City.

Presidencia de la República, Dirección General de Comunicación Social. 1988a. "Pacto de solidaridad económica: Firma del acuerdo de concertación, 28 de febrero de 1988." In Presidencia de la República, Unidad de la Crónica Presidencial, *Las razones y las obras: Crónica del sexenio 1982–1988, sexto año*. Mexico City.

———. 1988b. "Pacto de solidaridad económica: Firma del pacto de solidaridad económica, 15 de diciembre de 1987." In Presidencia de la República, Unidad de la Crónica Presidencial. *Las razones y las obras: Crónica del sexenio 1982–1988, sexto año*. Mexico City.

El Proceso. 1988. May 30, June 20, July 11.

Reyes Heroles, Jesus G. G. 1989. "Mexico's Strategy for Price Stability and Economic Growth." Paper presented at the Overseas Development Council, Washington, D.C., March 21.

Reyna, José Luis, Francisco Zapata, and Marcelo Fleury. 1976. *Tres estudios sobre el movimiento obrero en México*. Mexico City: El Colegio de México.

Reyna, José Luis, and Richard Weinert, eds. 1977. *Authoritarianism in Mexico*. Philadelphia, Penn.: Institute for the Study of Human Issues.

Ros, Jaime. 1987. "Mexico: From the Oil Boom to the Debt Crisis. An Analysis of Policy Responses to External Shocks, 1978–1985." In Rosemary Thorp and Laurence Whitehead, eds., *The Latin American Debt Crisis*. London: Macmillan.

———. 1991. "Mexico's Trade and Industrialization Experience since 1960: A Reconsideration of Past Policies and Assessment of Current Reforms." Paper presented at the UNU/WIDER Conference on Trade and Industrialization Reconsidered, Paris, OECD Development Center, August 31–September 3.

———. 1992. "Macroeconomic Adjustment, Structural Reforms, and Growth in Mexico." University of Notre Dame, Notre Dame, Ind. Processed.

Secretaría de Comercio y Fomento Industrial. 1988a. *Balance sexenal del sector comercio y fomento industrial, 1982–1988*, vol. 1. Mexico City.

———. 1988b. "Programa de desgravación arancelaria, 1983–1988." *Balance sexenal del sector comercio y fomento industrial, 1982–1988*, vol. 1. Mexico City.

Secretaría de Gobernación and Dirección General de Comunicación Social de la Presidencia de la República, eds. 1986. *Cuadernos de renovación nacional*, vol. 7. Mexico City: Fondo de Cultura Económica.

Secretaría de Hacienda y Crédito Público. 1986. *Deuda externa*. Mexico City.

Secretaría de Hacienda y Crédito Público, Dirección General de Planeación Hacendaria. Various years, 1977–86. *Estadísticas de finanzas públicas*. Mexico City.

Secretaría de Programación y Presupuesto. Various years. *Sistema de cuentas nacionales, Resumen general y oferta y utilización de bienes y servicios.* Mexico City.

Shafer, Robert. 1973. *Mexican Business Organizations: History and Analysis.* Syracuse, N.Y.: Syracuse University Press.

Solís, Leopoldo. 1981. *Economic Policy Reform in Mexico: A Case Study for Developing Countries.* New York: Pergamon Press.

Tello, Carlos. 1979. *La política económica en México, 1970–1976.* Mexico City: Siglo XXI.

_____. 1984. *La nacionalización de la banca.* Mexico City: Siglo XXI.

Ten Kate, Adriaan. 1990. "La apertura comercial de México: Experiencias y lecciones." In Eduardo Gitli, ed., *Estudios sobre el sector externo mexicano.* Mexico City: Universidad Autónoma Metropolitana, Unidad Azcapotzalco.

Ten Kate, Adriaan, and Fernando de Mateo. 1989. "Apertura comercial y estructura de la protección en México: Estimaciones cuantitativas de los ochenta." *Comercio Exterior* 39:4, pp. 312–29.

Trejo Delarbre, Raúl. 1990. *Crónica del sindicalismo en México (1976–1988).* Mexico City: Siglo XXI.

El Universal. Various years, 1987–88. December 28, 1987; March 9, 1988.

Woldenberg, José. 1991. "Democracia y sistema electoral." In José Luis Barros Horcasitas, Javier Hurtado, and Germán Pérez Fernández del Castillo, eds., *Transición a la democracia y la reforma del estado en México.* Mexico City: Universidad Nacional Autónoma de México/FLACSO/Miguel Angel Porrúa.

Zuckerman Behar, Leo. 1989. "El proceso de toma de decisiones de la política económica en México: Del crack bursátil al pacto de solidaridad económica." Undergraduate thesis, El Colegio de México, Centro de Estudios Internacionales, Mexico City. Processed.

_____. 1990. "Inflation Stabilization in Mexico: The Economic Solidarity Pact: December 1987–December 1988." M.Sc. thesis in Public Policy in Latin America, University of Oxford, Oxford, Eng.

10

Thailand: Economic and Political Gradualism

RICHARD F. DONER AND ANEK LAOTHAMATAS

THAILAND MOVED FROM ECONOMIC DISTRESS TO STABILIZATION, growth, and structural change during the 1980s. Levels of inflation and external debt fell, gross domestic product and exports grew, and economic activity became increasingly diversified.[1] Systematic economic reforms undertaken in conjunction with borrowing from the World Bank and the International Monetary Fund (IMF) were key to this impressive performance. This chapter explores the political bases of economic reform in Thailand during the 1980s. After a brief examination of the 1973–79 period, the principal focus is the major stabilization and trade reforms undertaken during 1981–85. This period overlaps with the fifth five-year plan (1982–86) and with the tenure of General Prem Tinsulanond (1980–88), the leader whose government is most closely associated with the reform effort.

Two central puzzles are addressed. First, how did this country manage to initiate and sustain macroeconomic reform in a period of ostensible political instability? During 1980–88 Thailand experienced two coup attempts, three unplanned elections, and a government (in 1986) that seemed doomed by opposition to its austerity program. Second, why

The authors thank Peter Brimble, Chaturon Chaisaeng, Supote Chunanuntathum, Choomchun Poolsawat, Vichote Vanno, Skon Varanyuwatana, and Amnuai Viravan.

were Thailand's successes in macroeconomic stabilization not matched by achievements in trade liberalization during the reform period?[2]

The first argument has to do with the nature of the democratic transition and institutions in Thailand. Prem was successful at macroeconomic stabilization because of the restrained democracy of his regime and the insulation, cohesion, and expertise of his officials. Thailand's political regime under Prem was democratic in the sense that it resulted from free elections, allowed a free press, provided extensive opportunities for party competition, and was viewed as preferable to military authoritarianism by a broad range of political forces. These forces strengthened the government's ability to resist military opposition to devaluation and to restrictive fiscal and financial policies. But Thai democracy was clearly circumscribed by the threat of a military takeover. That threat was the principal reason why democratic elements supported Prem and his reform measures. Democratic or authoritarian forces alone would have derailed reform. Their interaction within a restrained democracy facilitated it.

The regime was insulated in its approach to macroeconomic policy by virtue of two factors: legal constraints on the fiscal policy process and the lack of clear positions on economic issues taken by political parties. What seems to have been a highly competitive and fragmented party system was, in fact, closer to a single dominant coalition that did not exert pressure during electoral cycles. Finally, the regime acted coherently in that macroeconomic policy was largely the domain of experienced technocrats operating in close proximity to the prime minister.

The second argument is that the principal interest groups either supported stabilization or were not strong enough to impede it. Although import substitution dominated Thailand after the postwar period, an entrenched import substitution coalition did not exist in large part because agricultural exports were so important and because export firms coexisted with import-competing firms often within the same group or bank. Business opposition to stabilization policies was thus blunted by cross pressures and by an increasingly strong export component within the manufacturing sector. Labor, for its part, did not constitute an effective opposition to the reforms because it had no links with either the parties or the military and few opportunities existed for labor absorption in the countryside and the Middle East. The strongest opponent of stabilization efforts—the military—did not constitute an effective obstacle because it was weakened by internal differences and lacked legitimacy as a defender of national interests and because military authoritarianism was widely feared.

The final argument concerns the composition and design of the reform program. Some of the factors that promoted stabilization also undermined trade and sectoral reform efforts. Political parties, whose support was necessary for Prem's stabilization policies, ran the economic ministries and generally obstructed trade and sectoral reforms. Technocrats were insulated from party representatives, and although this isolation allowed them to design flexible macroeconomic policies, it also meant that they showed little political acumen when adopting strategies to implement sectoral reform. A conflict arose between the political requirements of stabilization and those of structural reform in early stages of the democratic transition. The insulation and political support that were effective for stabilization may not have been useful for trade and sectoral reform.

The first section of this study outlines the conditions forming the background to the reform. The second reviews and evaluates Thailand's reform policies, examining whether such policies were implemented and the degree to which they were solidified by legal and institutional measures. The next four sections analyze explanations of Thailand's policy performance: the impact of Thailand's political transition on the reform efforts, the organization and interests of business and labor and the ways in which these groups influenced reforms, the ways in which the organization of the state influenced the reforms, and the impact of the program's design.

Background of the Reform

Thailand faced an impending crisis rather than an actual economic breakdown. Its economic institutions were intact and allowed for healthy and timely supply responses to stabilization measures. Nevertheless, Thai officials, encouraged by international financial institutions, viewed economic conditions with considerable alarm. By the early 1980s, Thailand faced some of the most difficult economic conditions in its history. The country's real gross domestic product (GDP) grew slower and inflation was higher than in past years (see table 10-1). The current account (trade balance) had moved into a persistent and substantial deficit, leading in turn to a growing external debt.

External shocks played an important role in these problems. Until 1983, rising world interest rates increased Thailand's financial burden and reduced the country's disposable income. Thailand's terms of trade, reflecting increased oil prices and, following the second oil shock, global recession and the commodity slump, deteriorated sharply between 1975 and 1984 (GATT 1991). But the impact of external shocks was mediated by expansionary economic policies undertaken by two types of regime: those of the 1973–76 democratic period and those of the 1976–80 authoritarian period leading up to Prem's tenure. Two somewhat counterintuitive lessons concerning the impact of regime type on economic policies emerge from an examination of these periods. First, the 1973–76 democratic opening clearly led to fiscal expansion but not to the profligate populism one might expect given the Latin American experience. Any

Table 10-1. Economic Indicators in Thailand, 1975–90
(percent)

Year	Growth in GDP	Rate of inflation	Debt service ratio[a]	Growth in exports
1975	5.6	5.3	15.1	25.6
1980	7.9	19.7	17.3	19.1
1981	6.3	12.7	17.4	23.1
1982	4.1	5.2	18.0	20.0
1983	7.3	3.8	22.9	−8.4
1984	7.1	0.9	24.8	19.7
1985	3.5	2.4	27.5	10.3
1986	4.9	1.9	24.8	24.8
1987	9.5	2.5	19.8	31.6
1988	13.2	3.8	14.9	36.2
1989	12.0	5.4	13.0	25.7
1990	10.0	—	10.9	14.9

— Not available.

a. Percentage of exports of goods and services.

Source: Data from the Bank of Thailand and the National Economic and Social Development Board; Robinson, Byeon, and Teja 1991, p. 47; Warr and Nijathaworn 1988, pp. 97–98; World Bank 1990, p. 2.

move toward populism (rural populism in the Thai case) was impeded by parties with little mass base or capacity to form stable, policy-based coalitions, by the political weight of urban interests, and by the influence of new business interests that balanced their own populist tendencies with a belief in the positive role of the private sector and foreign investment.

Second, however, the post-1976 authoritarian regimes did not facilitate stabilization. Thailand's rent-seeking did not result in the levels of inflation and declining growth rates normally associated with the idea of economic crisis. In the context of the second oil shock and traditional Thai concerns with healthy external balances, however, they did encourage levels of debt that economic policymakers viewed as quite alarming.

Economic Policies of the 1970s

The most important economic trend in the 1970s was the expansion of public investment, which resulted in public sector deficits averaging 6 percent of GDP from 1980/81 through 1985/86 (see table 10-2). Under the third plan (1972–76), the focus of this spending was rural development. Under the fourth (1977–81), overseen by the military, the share of public spending in agriculture, health, and education fell while that in defense, administration, energy, transport, and industry rose. Some sixteen state enterprises were established during the 1970s, most involving infrastructural activities (Ingavata 1989, table 1). Overall growth in public sector spending reflected three components of government policy in

Table 10-2. Balance of Payments and Fiscal Deficits in Thailand, 1975–90

Year	Current account of balance of payments as percentage of GDP	Consolidated public sector surplus (deficit) as percentage of GDP[a]
1975	−4.1	—
1980	−6.4	−6.9
1981	−7.4	−8.0
1982	−2.8	−6.0
1983	−7.3	−4.6
1984	−5.1	−6.0
1985	−4.1	−4.8
1986	0.7	−1.6
1987	−0.7	−1.2
1988	−2.8	4.3
1989	−3.6	4.8
1990	−8.6	—

— Not available.

a. Consolidated accounts of central government, local governments, and nonfinancial public enterprises; figures refer to fiscal years; for example, 1980 is 1980–81.

Source: Bank of Thailand; National Economic and Social Development Board; Robinson, Byeon, and Teja 1991, pp. 3, 15.

the mid- to late 1970s: (a) the decision to subsidize prices and public utility charges, (b) the desire to develop an alternative local source of energy through public investment (Warr and Nidhiprabha 1988, p. 66; Warr and Nijathaworn 1988, p. 34), and (c) the effort to maintain growth through public investment despite a deterioration in domestic savings.

The growth of public sector spending reflected an expansion of external borrowing, initially for the military and subsequently for state enterprises. Military borrowing, which was facilitated by a 1977 decree loosening Thailand's traditionally strict controls on overseas loans, accelerated in 1978 and 1979 but then slowed and was displaced by public enterprise loans.[3] Interest payments on public debt for military purposes rose from 14 percent in 1978 to 56 percent in 1981 (Warr and Nidhiprabha 1988, pp. 78, 80). External debt as a percentage of exports rose sharply in the late 1970s. Combined with the baht's[4] linkage to an artificially strong dollar, growth in domestic spending and external borrowing resulted in growing trade deficits and weak balance of payments.

There was no coherent macroeconomic policy response to this deterioration prior to 1979. The government instead stressed slight shifts in the exchange rate and protectionism. In early 1978, the Bank of Thailand announced that the baht would no longer be tied to the dollar, but rather to a basket of currencies in which the dollar would be a major component.[5] By the end of the year this was replaced by a system of daily fixing, which encouraged speculation against the baht and was abandoned as well. In response to the worsening trade deficits, the government announced an import ban and an extensive tariff increase in 1978 (Fish 1978, p. 78; Phongpaichit 1991, p. 12).

These policies, especially when exacerbated by the emergence of negative real interest rates in the late 1970s, contributed to a skewing of relative prices (Robinson, Byeon, and Teja 1991, p. 9). Domestic imbalances were compounded by subsidized energy prices that both affected Thailand's fiscal position and, by discouraging conservation, intensified the impact of higher foreign oil prices on the external account. Only in July 1979, in the face of a new round of price increases by the Organization of Petroleum Exporting Countries and a growing shortage of refined products throughout the country, did the government of General Kriangsak Chomanan announce significant increases in retail prices. These, in turn, generated a corrective inflation, broad political opposition, and Kriangsak's overthrow by the military in February 1980.

The Politics of Economic Policy under Democratic Regimes, 1973–76

These relatively expansionary policies constitute something of an anomaly in Thai economic history. The decade's growth in spending and external borrowing stands in marked contrast to Thailand's traditionally conservative monetary and fiscal policies (Brown 1988; Ingram 1955). This puzzle can only be explained by referring to political factors: the nature of Thailand's democratic transition, the preferences and organization of interest groups, and the characteristics of state agencies responsible for macroeconomic policy.

Thailand began a democratic transition in 1973 when a broad range of forces, led by students and intellectuals but also including the country's growing middle class, overthrew the long-standing military regime (Anderson 1977, pp. 15–16; Prizzia 1985). The expulsion of the military leaders was followed by three years of civilian governments. Although preceded by a 1968 constitution and a parliamentary interlude in 1969–71, the overthrow of the military in 1973 nevertheless marked an important break in Thai political history.[6] Most important, it allowed for mobilization of new social forces in the countryside, the emergence of new parties, and the empowering of the House of Representative's previously proscribed right to call a no-confidence vote. Under the 1974 constitution, some forty-odd newly legalized parties campaigned for positions in the lower house of a bicameral legislature. Democratic elections in 1975 and 1976 resulted in three governments, the last of which was overthrown by the military in October 1976.

These developments led to the growth in expenditures for rural areas and external borrowing noted earlier. Although none of the parties was rooted in the countryside, one of the leading parties, the Social Action Party, emphasized the need to develop a rural base by pledging to distribute resources to the countryside. This would be done through budgetary and investment mechanisms stipulated in the fourth plan and through price supports for agricultural commodities.

The 1973–76 period thus marked an important step in Thailand's democratic transition: Thai politics had clearly shifted away from the "bureaucratic polity" status in which the role of extrabureaucratic forces was minimal and decisions were limited to the patronage needs of bureaucrats and soldiers (Laothamatas 1992a). Thailand's political opening was fueled by an increasingly active middle class, intensified party competition, and Bangkok-based protests and press coverage. In an unprecedented development, protests spread to rural areas. Although this was not a classic case of inflationary spending generated by electoral cycles, it was a significant instance in which extrabureaucratic pressures led to growing state expenditures.[7]

The Social Action Party's approach to rural poverty never generated a lasting base of support for the party. First, the effort was weakened by opposition from other parties and by the fact that the politicians supporting it had no leverage over its implementation. The policy was taken over by the bureaucracy. Rather than strengthening political accountability, this enriched local administrators (Anderson 1977; Christensen 1991). Critical to this development were the parties' organizational weakness and relatively shallow social base: none of the parties commanded widespread allegiance or drew on mobilized popular sectors. Instead, it was the military and, especially, industrialists who emerged with significant influence in the newly active parties. The presence of an appointed Senate further moderated any strong redistributive tendencies.

Redistribution through price supports also ran up against an urban-rural conflict. As an integral part of its efforts to address rural poverty and develop electoral support in the countryside, the government of Kukrit Pramoj in 1976 deliberately raised the price of rice. Even more authoritarian regimes had failed to reconcile this dilemma: a similar increase in 1973 had resulted in riots and collapse of the military regime. The 1976 effort was met by a combination of labor and student strikes in Bangkok and an opposition move to bring down the government. The policy was withdrawn, although efforts to address rural poverty by modifying agricultural prices remained an integral part of Thai public policy in subsequent years (Bowring and Nations 1976; Christensen 1991, p. 43).

Third, a strain of economic policy new to Thailand emerged toward the end of the 1973–76 period. As enunciated by Boonchu Rojanastien, a founder of the Social Action Party, head of the Bangkok Bank and Thai Bankers Association, and finance minister in the 1975 Kukrit government, this approach used welfare-oriented capitalism to pacify the increasingly radicalized masses. The policy also involved active promotion of foreign investment and exports and strong support for cooperation between the public and private sectors, an approach later termed "Thailand Inc." Underlying it was a consensus on the need for private sector–led export promotion, even among persons who differed on macroeconomic questions. This was, in sum, a much milder and, in fiscal and financial terms, more responsible approach to reform than that seen in the populist regimes of Latin America.

Finally, the institutional cohesion of the government's economic and planning machinery suffered during the democratic period. This was in part simply the result of the national focus on alleviating rural and urban poverty, issues that technocrats simply had not addressed in the past. It was also a function of a tremendous growth in businessmen entering the parties, the House of Representatives, and the cabinets.[8] The fourth five-year plan's formulation was fragmented and delayed by changes in government, indecision on the very utility of a plan, resentment against Boonchu's perceived efforts to centralize planning within the Ministry of Finance, and the requirements of an increasingly democratic regime.

Politics of Economic Policy under Authoritarian Resurgence, 1976–80

The political factors that weakened macroeconomic discipline seem to have disappeared in 1976 following a bloody military coup that pitted university students against security forces and right-wing groups in Bangkok. The coup installed a new prime minister, General Thanin Kravixien, and initiated a period of authoritarian rule by military leaders. However, economic discipline was undermined by the military itself, as well as by other domestic and external pressures.

An immediate problem involved conflicts between Thanin's intense authoritarianism and anticommunism and the more moderate policy preferences of the Bangkok middle class and the local business community. Thanin's alienation of these forces led to his replacement in 1977 by a more flexible representative of the military: General Kriangsak (Christensen 1991, p. 59). Yet the country remained under martial law until 1978 when a new constitution was promulgated. The constitution was strongly promilitary and allocated little power to elected representatives. Having appointed the senators one month previously, Kriangsak was elected prime minister in 1979 despite the support of less than one-third of the members of the House of Representatives. His cabinet included numerous military officials.

With military support and a restrictive constitution, Kriangsak seemed well positioned to address the country's economic woes. In fact, his ability to do so was severely constrained, in part by the revenue needs of his major political support: the military. The withdrawal of U.S. troops from Southeast Asia in 1975 prompted a loss of U.S. financial support for, and panic within, the military (Christensen 1991, p. 60). Despite the negative consequences for Thailand's debt position, an alternative source of funding was found in foreign loans, which grew substantially in the 1976–79 period. The military's reliance on state-owned enterprises for extra revenues also constrained the government's capacity to limit state expenditures.

Parliamentary pressure for rural development also weakened constraints on spending and borrowing. Despite the authoritarian character of the constitution, the 1979 elections resulted in the emergence of opposition in the lower house to Kriangsak's hand-picked Senate. The opposition was led by the Social Action Party, whose strong electoral showing was based largely on rural support and reflected the continuing broad popularity of a plan for rural development initiated by the 1975 Social Action Party government under Kukrit.[9] This pressure, along with World Bank concern over increasing relative poverty (Fish 1979a, p. 40), resulted in Kriangsak's declaring 1979 to be the "Year of the Farmer." The plan involved agricultural and infrastructural initiatives and required that overseas borrowing originally stipulated for the fourth five-year plan be revised upward by 29 percent (Fish 1979a). As in the 1973–76 period, extrabureaucratic forces contributed to expansionary fiscal policies, although those forces now had a distinctly more electoral tone.

Kriangsak, then, relied largely on the military but could not ignore the parties. Even as he appointed numerous military officials to the cabinet, he resorted to a new institutional mechanism for co-opting party opposition: the expansion of cabinet positions. The 1978 constitution enlarged the cabinet from thirty to forty-four posts. These seats were typically located in the ministries of agriculture, commerce, and industry, which implemented sectoral economic policies and thus provided parties with rent-seeking opportunities.[10]

The entrance of politicians into the ministries constrained nonpolitical, technocratic participation in macroeconomic policy. The Ministry of Finance lost control over borrowing by the military and by state enterprises in 1977, and Kriangsak acted as his own finance minister for about nine months in 1979 and 1980. To these domestic constraints on Thai technocrats must be added an important and somewhat ironic external one: in the late 1970s, the World Bank encouraged borrowing by state enterprises to address Thailand's urban-rural imbalances. Because the proposed borrowing exceeded recommendations of the National Economic and Social Development Board (NESDB), the Bank began to view the board as a bureaucratic obstacle to be circumvented (author interviews; Fish 1979b).

Kriangsak's efforts to impose some economic restraints revealed the weakness of his coalitional support. His decision to pass on to Thai consumers the full impact of shifts in the price of oil led to broader inflation and political opposition. Labor demonstrations forced the government to reduce its initial price increases 10 to 18 percent (Fish 1979a, p. 40). Tight money policy, adopted to correct inflationary and trade imbalances, prompted protests from businesses forced to rely on the high-interest, unorganized money market (Rowley 1979, pp. 100–103). Finally, Kriangsak suffered from a series of finance company failures and from commercial bank resentment at government pressures for mandatory lending to the rural sector. All of these pressures helped solidify opposition by the elected members of Parliament who, despite access to cabinet positions, perceived themselves as having too little influence over policy (thus, for example, Kriangsak's industry minister threatened to resign over oil pricing and procurement; Rowley 1979, p. 100).

Kriangsak also lacked solid military backing. Opposition was developing between his main allies—the older, active generals—and a group of "Young Turks"—middle-level officers whose experience in rural areas during communist suppression operations imbued them with an avowed distaste for corruption among their elders and a belief in the need for greater democracy (McBeth 1979, p. 33). The thinness of this support became evident when, after a near no-confidence vote in the House of Representatives and Kriangsak's resignation, General Prem Tinsulanond formed a new government with military backing.

In sum, the military-dominated regimes of the late 1970s were ill-equipped to address the deficiencies of their democratic predecessors. The military itself, weakened by its own needs and contradictions as well as by the expanding role of parties and business, was unable to provide the political base necessary to address the second oil shock. This meant that Kriangsak was unable to buffer the conservative technocrats who had historically guided Thailand's macroeconomic fortunes.

Sense of Crisis

These political factors did not cripple the country's economy, but they did produce a perception that "major structural and financial adjustments were required . . . to prevent the problems from escalating into an external crisis" (Leeahtam 1991, p. 18). One source of concern involved relatively short-term problems with the capital account. Foreign investment was dropping drastically in response to the worsening situation on the Cambodian border, and higher offshore interest rates were attracting an outflow of short-term capital (Ho 1979, p. 94). The balance of payments was relatively healthy until 1977, when the bill for imported oil rose $120 million (Ho 1979, p. 96). External indebtedness, which was smaller than that of most developing countries during the 1971–75 period, jumped sharply in the latter part of the 1970s, more rapidly than all developing countries in the same period. The fact that the growth of debt in Thailand exceeded that in the Philippines was much in the mind of Thai technocrats. The debt profile was also of concern since many of the loans for defense and state enterprises had commercial terms (Leeahtam 1991, pp. 15–16).

The World Bank and the IMF viewed the economy with alarm and played an important role in sensitizing Thai officials to the dangers of an impending crisis. Indeed, the country's traditionally strong reputation among foreign financial institutions was weakening. The first and second structural adjustment loans received in 1982 and 1983, respectively, were roughly 90 percent of the rest of the foreign debts incurred by the government in those years (Tinnakorn and Patamasiriwat 1985). Reflecting the kingdom's low creditworthiness at the time, Governor Nukul found it unprecedentedly difficult for the Bank of Thailand to obtain foreign commercial loans in 1979–80 (author interviews).

These problems were viewed as especially serious given certain longer-term weaknesses in the Thai economy. The country's capital-intensive import substitution strategy had helped it become the developing world's fifth largest net importer of petroleum (Ho 1979, p. 96). Problems in the agricultural sector created doubts about Thailand's ability to pay for rising imports through the traditional means of agricultural exports.[11]

Policy Performance in the 1980s

This sense of crisis led to a wide range of policy initiatives. This section focuses on the degree to which such policies were actually implemented and institutionalized. The government was markedly more successful in macroeconomic stabilization than in trade and sectoral reforms. It cut public sector deficits, devalued the exchange rate, and maintained oil prices at reasonable levels. The tariff structure remained largely unchanged, however, and, with the exception of certain agricultural goods, industry-specific measures to promote exports and improve efficiency were not implemented. Those reforms that were implemented were only moderately solidified through legal and institutional changes. But this weak institutionalization did not undermine subsequent reforms because the country's existing macroeconomic policy structure was strong and initial reform policies produced beneficial results.

Early Efforts

Thailand's reform efforts began prior to the first structural adjustment loan and the submission of the first letter of development policy on February 4, 1982. The early context for stabilization was set by the fifth five-year plan, which covered the 1982–86 period but was drafted well before 1982. Indeed, some of the measures proposed by Thailand for the first structural adjustment loan drew on the fifth plan. Although the plan stipulated poverty alleviation as its primary objective, it actually emphasized sectoral adjustment, rationalization of the incentive structure to give the government greater flexibility in dealing with external shocks, and reduction of fiscal and financial imbalances through the mobilization of domestic resources. The one area in which the plan required revision involved delaying or rephasing certain large-scale development projects.

This general effort was preceded and accompanied by a number of more discrete but timely moves. The first occurred in 1979 when the newly installed governor of the Bank of Thailand, Nukul Prachuabmoh, convinced Parliament to raise the country's sixty-year-old limit of 15 percent on lending rates. The limit, imposed by the civil and commercial code to prevent usury, was leading to rapid outflows of capital that reportedly left Thailand with reserves to cover only two weeks of imports (Nations 1979b; author interviews). Other early actions included reduction of export taxes, an approximate 10 percent devaluation of the baht against the dollar in 1981, initial moves to raise petroleum prices and remove subsidies, reassertion of Ministry of Finance control over military loans, the imposition of a no-growth budget, and the establishment of several committees on industrial and fiscal policy (Sahasakul, Thongpakde, and Kraisoraphong 1989, pp. 20–21).

Fiscal Policy

Government policy during the first half of the 1980s attempted to correct public sector deficits by reducing expenditures (this summary draws on Robinson, Byeon, and Teja 1991. Budgetary limits of 19 to 20 percent of GDP were stipulated by ceilings on government wages, cuts in capital expenditure (eventually totaling around 1 percent of GDP), and a series of ceilings on public sector foreign borrowing. Additional revenue measures included several increases in prices charged by state enterprises such as telephones, railways, and waterworks in 1983 and 1984 (Leeahtam 1991, p. 31). Financial criteria for state enterprises were also set to reduce subsidies financed from the budget. State enterprise financing went from a deficit of 3 percent of GDP in 1980–81 to a surplus of 0.3 percent of GDP in 1985–86. Although these measures were important in setting "the tone for expenditure policy for the remainder of the decade" (Robinson, Byeon, and Teja 1991, pp. 14–15), they did not reduce fiscal deficits during the first half of the decade. Revenue shortfalls were a major problem, in part because of low elasticity of tax revenues, tax reductions on the export sector, and the general slowdown of economic activities. The 1985–86 period was, however, quite important for promoting "substantial structural adjustments in both expenditure and revenue" (Leeahtam 1991, p. 51). During these years, the government (a) adopted a series of discretionary fiscal packages (including higher oil taxes, customs tariffs, transfers of state enterprise profits, and zero-growth budgets) and (b) imposed new constraints on the external borrowing of state enterprises.

Fiscal problems were much less serious by the second half of the decade: public sector deficits disappeared by 1987 and moved into a surplus of almost 5 percent by 1989 (table 10-2). The government's tendency to inflate revenue in its budgetary assumptions was reversed in 1986–87; conservative revenue estimates have since constrained expenditures and have "imparted an institutional bias toward the generation of fiscal surpluses" (Robinson, Byeon, and Teja 1991, p. 14). Efforts to improve tax efficiency through a value added tax were not, however, successful.

Monetary Policy

In the early 1980s the government's principal goals were to mobilize savings, restrain credit, and align domestic interest rates with high over- seas rates to reduce the outflow of capital. These concerns were ad- dressed through a tight monetary regime: the 1979 measures to raise interest rate ceilings, the freeing of domestic rates, and the control of commercial bank access to Bank of Thailand funds. Direct credit con- trols were used only in 1984 in response to a sharp growth in credit and the trade deficit. Following a period of negative rates in 1978–80, real interest rates were positive for the rest of the decade (Robinson, Byeon, and Teja 1991, p. 9). After a decline in the growth of credit between 1984–86, interest rates were lowered to encourage the expansion of credit, and savings continued to be mobilized because interest rates were positive. Monetization of the economy increased rapidly throughout the rest of the decade, although this growth was probably due more to a shift of funds out of the informal sector than to the increase in private savings (Robinson, Byeon, and Teja 1991, p. 22).

This account of monetary policy management leaves out an important problem. With the exchange rate fixed, interest rates had to serve not domestic credit objectives but balance of payments concerns (Leeahtam 1991, p. 36): reserves would flow out unless domestic rates followed overseas rates. Although high interest rates had some effect, a shift in the exchange rate was clearly necessary.

Exchange Rate Policy

Until 1984, the baht was linked to the U.S. dollar. Pressure for deval- uation grew in 1981. First, the dollar rose after the second oil crisis and drove the baht up as well. The baht then continued to appreciate against the deutschmark, yen, and sterling, severely hurting Thailand's export income from the sale of certain agricultural commodities usually quoted in deutschmarks and sterling. This led to two devaluations in 1981, together amounting to roughly 10 percent. The first, in April, was only 1.07 percent and triggered panic buying of dollars by importers and bankers (Phongpaichit 1991, pp. 16–17).[12] This was followed by a sec- ond devaluation of 8.7 percent in July. However, the baht remained tied to the dollar, which continued to rise, bringing the baht up with it. The government initially refused to address the problem of overvaluation and opted to impose credits limits on commercial banks. Following the fail- ure of numerous small firms, the government finally devalued the baht 14.7 percent in 1984. The Bank of Thailand also formally abandoned the link to the U.S. dollar, basing the value of the baht on a basket of currencies. However, as the dollar was presumably the major component of this basket, the baht depreciated more than 20 percent between 1985 and the end of 1987 as the dollar moved down.

Energy Pricing Policy

Raising energy prices was politically risky, having led to the downfall of the Kriangsak government in 1979. The country was significantly more successful in pricing energy during the 1980s, although luck played no small part. Oil prices were raised significantly in 1981, and the Oil Fund was in surplus by 1982. When global oil prices dropped, the government reduced domestic prices but at a rate less than that of the price of imports. The difference was kept for the Oil Fund and used to cushion domestic prices through 1985, a form of what Waterbury (1989, p. 54) has termed "desubsidization by stealth" (Leeahtam 1991, p. 31). However, almost half of the Oil Fund, amounting to nearly 0.2 percent of GDP, was used up in this manner. If global prices had stayed at their 1985 level, the entire fund would have disappeared and the government would have had to increase retail prices. With the economy in a shaky state, such increases would have seriously threatened the government's survival (Leeahtam 1991, p. 60). In the event, global prices declined sharply in 1986, allowing further accumulation of Oil Fund reserves.

Privatization

As of 1989, some sixty-seven state-owned enterprises remained of the one hundred originally operating. Many had been liquidated or privatized in the 1960s after the perceived threat of Chinese economic domination disappeared (Ingavata 1989, p. 329). More recent privatization efforts were initiated in 1983, but real efforts did not begin until 1986. Progress was not impressive during the period under review, with only some thirteen cases of actual privatization (Vanno 1991, p. 245) and the more successful cases being those under direct control of the Ministry of Finance. The Electricity Generating Authority of Thailand was the most important firm moving toward privatization at the end of the decade. In several cases, more partial steps were taken to promote efficiency. Thus, the private sector was allowed to bid for particular jobs such as installing telephones for the Telephone Organization of Thailand. The state-owned Thai Airways International was merged in 1988 with the domestic carrier, Thai Airways, in hopes of reducing capital requirements and streamlining operations (Vanno 1991, p. 330).

Trade and Sectoral Reform

As suggested at the beginning of this study, Thailand's success in export growth is not reflected in trade liberalization. The average level of effective protection rose, and export-oriented producers were disadvantaged relative to import-competing sectors (the following discussion draws on Akrasanee, Dapice, and Flatters 1991; GATT 1991; Robinson, Byeon, and Teja 1991, pp. 27–29). The two principal obstacles to liberalization were (a) the importance of import taxes for government tax revenue—while export taxes declined from roughly 5 percent of total tax revenue to almost zero between 1980 and 1990, import taxes remained between 20 and 25 percent (GATT 1991, p. 48)—and (b) the complexity of the trade regime.

Some progress was made in reducing nontariff barriers such as the proportion of goods subject to import restrictions and the use of specific surcharges by the Board of Investments. And in 1982, as part of the fifth five-year plan, the maximum tariff rate on most products was cut to 60 percent. However, this was offset by the immediate imposition of surcharges and tariffs on raw materials and intermediate goods for revenue purposes. Between 1985 and 1989 the tariff structure remained broadly unchanged (exceptions included reductions in tariffs on electrical and electronic goods to reduce smuggling). According to one participant in the process, Thailand engaged in a number of superficial tariff reform measures to assuage the World Bank even as it imposed other measures, such as surcharges, that were not on the official tariff books. The Bank's (belated) recognition of this fact and its belief that Thailand was backsliding on liberalization contributed to Thailand's not drawing on a third structural adjustment loan (author interviews; the other factor was that the Thais themselves opted not to draw on it).

The tariff structure also became increasingly complex during this period. The government imposed more than twenty duty rates between 1981 and 1987, applied tariffs flexibly, changed rates on individual products, and implemented alternate tariffs for some 25 percent of items, especially in agriculture. These differential duties resulted in an increase in the average applied tariff during the 1980s from almost 10 percent in 1982 to 11 percent in 1990 (GATT 1991, p. 52). In addition, the scope of import licensing grew, affecting around 8 percent of all product categories in 1991, up from 6 percent in 1982 (GATT 1991, table IV.11, p. 73).

The government did initiate industry-specific measures to improve efficiency and promote exports. Proposals for industrial restructuring included reductions in local content, improved linkages among up-, mid-, and downstream parts of an industry, as well as improved policymaking processes and expanded technological capacity (Industrial Management Company 1983, 1985). With the exception of the electrical goods sector, these efforts largely failed, although there is evidence of overall low rates of protection for Thailand's major source of manufactured exports: textiles and apparel (Sahasakul, Thongpakde, and Kraisoraphong 1989, pp. 62–65). The government was fairly successful in its efforts to liberalize agricultural exports, especially rice. The premium on rice exports was reduced to zero in 1986 after being as high as B5,200 per ton in 1974;

export duties on rice were reduced from 5.0 to 1.5 percent in 1985 and then to zero in late 1985; and export quotas, abandoned but also reimposed in 1984, were discontinued in 1986.

Financial Reform

Despite not being a formal component of the structural reform program, changes in the financial system merit note. Thailand was hit by financial crises in 1979 and 1983. In both cases, manipulation, insider trading, and improper loans by finance and securities companies triggered large-scale losses, including, in 1978, the collapse of the Securities Exchange of Thailand. Also problematic was a proliferation of high-yield pyramid fund pools in the informal market. These crises prompted legislation that empowered the Bank of Thailand to expand its supervisory functions and to intervene directly in bank affairs when necessary (Doner and Unger 1992). The Bank of Thailand also mobilized support of the private financial sector for ailing financial institutions (Chaisut, Samkoset, and Ponpatarakul 1987).

Institutionalization

Thailand's reforms were solidified through legal and institutional changes in the areas of exchange rate and fiscal policy management. The 1984 shift to a more flexible system of exchange rates helped reduce economic disruptions, accustomed the public to daily movements in the rates, and encouraged businesses to adapt to changes. Perhaps most important, it "did not give ground for opportunists to score political advantage and thus made it more flexible as an instrument for economic management" (Leeahtam 1991, p. 72). The government also introduced a series of expenditure and tax reforms that were critical to enhancing the long-run flexibility of the fiscal system.[13]

These changes were accompanied by rationalization of the economic policy machinery. Macroeconomic policymaking was centralized in the hands of a small group of economic advisers. Authority for imposing petroleum taxes was shifted from the Parliament to the cabinet alone. The Ministry of Finance was empowered to centralize all borrowing needs of government agencies and state-owned enterprises and to establish a high-level State Enterprise Committee (Leeahtam 1991, pp. 53, 63, 76).

On the other hand, many changes were less than permanent. Agricultural export liberalization took the form of reducing to zero rather than abolishing premiums and export duties. Efforts to adopt a value added tax were unsuccessful. Limits were imposed on external debt, but these ceilings could be and were raised. Even legislation to raise the ceiling on interest rates avoided a frontal assault on the civil and commercial code (author interviews). And as developments in the Chartchai administration were to show, the more cohesive and centralized macroeconomic policy machinery did not result in the establishment of permanent structures.

In retrospect, this modest degree of institutionalization was not all that damaging to subsequent reforms. The positive outcomes of initial efforts bolstered support for sustaining and even expanding reform. In addition, Thailand's preexisting rules and institutions governing macroeconomic policy were relatively well suited to stabilization. Thailand had a relatively cohesive set of technocrats in the Ministry of Finance and Bank of Thailand, a relatively insulated budgetary process, parties without clear policy positions, and rules limiting government guarantees of private sector loans. These arrangements were weakened during the 1970s, but they were clearly not destroyed. As economic conditions (such as declining export revenues) threatened the stability of both state finances and significant private interests, the political space for these stabilization-supporting rules and institutions expanded.

Political Transition and Reform

The plethora of stabilization measures undertaken and implemented during the Prem administration indicates a government with relatively long time horizons and significant capacity. This seems puzzling in light of the considerable opposition generated by the reform and the resulting political instability. Parties opposed sectoral liberalization efforts, sectors of business and the military criticized the 1984 devaluation, the military was frustrated by general fiscal constraints, and sections of business suffered under the crackdown on informal financial markets (Hewison 1987, pp. 72–75). Coups were attempted in 1981 and 1985, and unplanned elections occurred in 1983, 1986, and 1988. How was reform possible under these circumstances?

Balance of Power and Regime Type

The achievements (as well as limitations) of the Thai reforms under Prem reflected Thailand's political transition to a restrained, semi-democratic system. This was essentially a Bonapartist balance of two major contending forces—the military and the parties—within a semi- or restrained democratic system. Central to this balance was Prem's position as an outsider acceptable to both forces. By playing these forces against each other, by using their fear of each other, and by capitalizing on the desire of each force to have him lead the regime, Prem was able to protect his proadjustment cabinet ministers and senior technocrats from the groups hurt by adjustment.

Prem's position as an independent balancer did not spring full blown upon his becoming prime minister in February 1980. More reliant on the military until 1983–84, Prem's ability to forge a more independent stance was in part a result of policies encouraged by the economic crisis and the response of a section of the military to those policies. Understanding this dynamic requires an examination of the constitutional arrangements, the principal political actors, and the impact (or lack) of electoral cycles.

Constitutional Arrangements

During the Prem period Thailand continued under a parliamentary system with a bicameral legislature. The provinces were divided into constituencies with parties or independent candidates standing as individuals. The evolution of parliamentary rules, however, reflects an important shift in the political balance away from the military. Prior to 1983, the power of the government-appointed Senate was equal to that of the elected House of Representatives. Active military officers and civilian bureaucrats could hold cabinet positions. These arrangements were provisional. According to the constitution, in 1983 the Senate would become an advisory body, active military and civilian officials could no longer serve in the cabinet, and candidates for the House of Representatives would stand as members of parties, not as individuals.

The military, however, initiated a constitutional amendment to preserve the old system. This effort was opposed by a broad coalition of parties, students, academics, and even dissidents within the armed forces. Following the Parliament's defeat of this amendment, Prem called a snap election to legitimate the expanded role of the parties and widen his political base beyond the military. He also established closer ties with functionally organized business and exhibited greater allegiance to the king, a point whose importance emerged during the devaluation crisis.

The parties' expanded role under Prem was reflected in their leverage over the trade liberalization process. Prem's strategy for co-opting the parties was to allow them access to those agencies yielding the greatest patronage opportunities: the ministries of commerce, agriculture, and industry. This required continuing the expansion of ministerial posts initiated under Kukrit in the 1970s (Christensen 1991, p. 58). This also allowed the parties to weaken industrial reform efforts.[14]

But party influence did not translate into power over macroeconomic stabilization. In essence, Prem's provision of patronage opportunities was part of a broad bargain in which parties were compensated or mollified for their lack of voice over major fiscal and monetary decisions. This powerlessness over macroeconomic policy was more the result of an institutionalized hard budget constraint than a short-term political compromise: constitutionally, neither the Senate nor the House of Representatives was permitted to initiate a money bill. Politicians during this period obtained rents at the point of deciding who got to do a particular project, not which project was actually approved (author interviews). The budget process was and continues to be centralized. The Parliament set

> ceilings on levels of taxation, but adjustments underneath that ceiling are the preserve of permanent officials. With little law-making author-

ity, MPS [members of Parliament] spend much of their three months in session shuffling around the annual budget to extract money for their districts, in addition to debating no-confidence motions against cabinet ministers (Christensen 1991, p. 62).

Prem further limited party impact on policy by retaining veto power to promote or transfer senior civil servants (a power ceded largely to elected cabinet ministers under the succeeding Chatichai government; Christensen 1991, p. 61).

The Parties

These constitutional constraints worked in part because the party system was relatively uncompetitive and parties feared the military. The first point goes against what seems to be a fragmented and competitive system of multiple parties. In fact, the system can be understood as a single dominant coalition composed of three major parties—the Social Action, Chart Thai, and the Democrat parties—none of which was able to establish clear hegemony. With minor exceptions, these have been largely clientelist organizations with little interest in or capacity for developing general policy positions (Christensen 1991, p. 3). This state of affairs is in part a function of the lack of systematic party linkages to broad sectors of business (as opposed to particular firms), labor, or the peasantry. The parties were generally fragmented on policy issues and deficient in policy-related information. With the partial exception of Social Action Party's rural emphasis, the parties were not sophisticated enough to formulate any economic vision or strategy. With a few exceptions, they were ill-equipped even to debate broad policy issues with the technocrats under Prem.

Party initiatives generally involved distributive issues rather than ideology or broad development policy.[15] The Chart Thai Party's decision to quit the government coalition in 1983 illustrated the numerous divisions among and within Thai parties. After Chart Thai emerged from the 1983 elections as the largest party, its leader attempted to lead an opposition coalition; it failed when the Social Action Party invited Prem to continue as prime minister. Meanwhile, the party that had been the most effective opposition force, Prachakorn Thai, was lured into the government coalition as Chart Thai was left out in the cold and cast as the irresponsible oppositionist.

Despite its weakness, the Chart Thai–led opposition did reflect a widespread deterioration of economic conditions and broad skepticism as to both the utility of austerity measures and Prem's competence. By 1986 the opposition was bolstered by an alliance between the head of the military and a dissident group of Social Action Party members. Finance Minister Sommai Hoonakul was a specific target of the opposition because of both his support for austerity measures and his unwillingness to allocate money for the Social Action Party's program to intervene in the price of rice. As further austerity measures became politically impossible, Prem decided that he could no longer govern and called a snap election (Leeahtam 1991, pp. 40–41).

This was the only election during this period that involved substantial debates on economic policy. The majority view seemed destined to doom the adjustment effort: "All political campaigners advocated a more expansionary financial stance" (Leeahtam 1991, p. 41). Former minister Boonchu even advocated a three-year moratorium on all government debt-servicing obligations—domestic as well as foreign—so that more of the budget could be used to move the economy. The election, however, returned Prem as prime minister. Sommai resigned as finance minister but was replaced by a close associate who maintained stringent financial measures.

There was, in sum, continuity in stabilization policy. What accounts for this result? One factor involves the cohesion and beliefs of macroeconomic policymakers. More important, however, was Prem's pivotal political position. Stated simply, the major parties needed Prem as head of government to sustain the shaky process of political reform. He had, first of all, allocated more cabinet positions to political parties than his predecessor, Kriangsak. Second, Prem had demonstrated a commitment to democratization through his opposition to the 1983 military proposals for a constitutional revision. And finally, he had demonstrated an ability to withstand coup attempts.

In sum, the ruling parties saw in Prem a military man who was willing to share power with them and who could advance the democratization process. Lacking an alternative champion for their most basic interests, they were, to a significant extent, beholden to Prem (Laothamatas 1992b). Underlying this reliance was the parties' fear of the alternative: a return to military control.[16]

The Military

Several general features characterize the military at the inception of the adjustment period. The end of regional hostilities and the defeat of Thailand's own rural insurgents placed the overall security function of the military into question. The military also lost much of its financial autonomy. Viet Nam's 1979 invasion of Cambodia and the initiation of the arms trade with China did permit the maintenance of sizable military budgets. But with the end of U.S. military aid and the ban on loans by the military, the armed services went from a position of rarely having "to explain anything to anybody with regard to their defense budget" to one of involvement in the domestic budgetary process (Phongpaichit 1991, pp. 5, 23).

At the same time, a section of the military exhibited strains of anticapitalism and antipathy to political parties. These tendencies reflected the military's own view of its function as the guardian of the national interest, its experience with poverty in rural areas, and its status as perhaps the only channel of political mobility for ethnic Thais who are not part of the nobility. But the military itself benefits from economic activities involving real estate, commerce, and finance. Profits from arms procurement are reportedly quite important. The range and increasingly personalized form of economic activities, combined with questions about its overall mission, increasingly fragmented the military.

This portrait is of a group threatened by and suspicious of but still attempting to benefit from Thailand's booming capitalist system. The sense of threat, as well as its efforts to maintain a corporate identity, help explain the military's initial support for Prem. After the problems of Thanin and Kriangsak, Prem was appreciated by many in the military not only as one of their own, but as someone principled, clean, and capable (see, for example, McBeth 1979). In 1981, Prem further consolidated his ties to the military by appointing as army chief General Arthit Kamglangek, who played a prominent role in suppressing the coup attempt earlier that year.

The relationship began to cool in 1983–84, however, as financial and political reforms threatened both corporate and particularistic interests of the military. On the financial front, military leaders were displeased with Finance Minister Sommai's opposition to their planned purchase of F-16s. They may also have been concerned with Prem's inability to protect them from unusually active questioning of their budgetary requests by members of Parliament in the House Budget Scrutiny Committee.[17] A further issue of contention was Sommai's decision to ban the booming chit fund pyramid schemes in which various sectors of the armed forces were reportedly involved. Politically, tensions increased with the military's unsuccessful efforts to maintain its role in Parliament through constitutional revision and to extend Arthit's term as military chief.

The event that most seriously weakened the military's role in the economic policy debate and reflected its inability to organize systematic opposition to stabilization was the November 1984 devaluation. Arthit and other senior generals were furious about the 15 percent adjustment because Prem made the decision swiftly and secretly, because the devaluation would significantly reduce their capacity for purchasing weapons overseas, and because Arthit was reportedly connected to business interests with large overseas loans and thus vulnerable to losses from the devaluation (this account draws on Laothamatas 1992b; Phongpaichit 1991, p. 20; author interviews).

Soon after the devaluation, Arthit launched a fiery televised attack on the government: he demanded a reversal of the devaluation, criticized the government's 1984 tight money policy, attacked the ban on chit funds, and called for a change in the cabinet, meaning the dismissal of Finance Minister Sommai. He seemed to be on solid political ground. In response to the devaluation, the Chart Thai Party called for a no-confidence vote. Members of the cabinet not involved in the decision attacked Sommai. The Association of Thai Industries complained that local industrialists with overseas loans would suffer huge losses. Labor threatened a general strike in support of Sommai's dismissal and demanded an increase in the minimum wage and price controls. Some labor leaders praised Arthit for sympathizing with the workers. Despite rumors of an impending coup, however, the devaluation was sustained without a change in cabinet. Members of the cabinet announced their support of the devaluation. Even senior members of the military criticized Arthit's intervention as inappropriate.

The ability to make the devaluation stick was largely a function of political factors.[18] First, Arthit's previous efforts to modify the constitution and extend his own term delegitimized his stance on the devaluation, which was seen as simply one more instance of self-aggrandizement. Second, links between the military and affected groups such as labor were weak at best. And finally, the king intervened with a show of support for Prem. Within the system of a single dominant coalition party described earlier, the military provided the only effective opposition to the reforms for dissenting politicians and businesses as well as labor, farmer, and student groups. Its links with these groups were, however, too weak to constitute an effective opposition.

Electoral Cycles

A final factor facilitating Thai stabilization was the weak electoral cycle. Three national elections took place in 1983, 1986, and 1988, each a snap election called by Prem to prevent the formation of alliances between extraparliamentary forces (military, labor), on the one hand, and opposition parties or dissenting elements within government parties, on the other. None was preceded by any significant fiscal expansion.[19]

The weakness of electoral pressures on economic policy seems odd in light of the fact that Thai parties are heavily pork-based. A partial explanation for the absence of an electoral cycle is found in Thailand's economic fortunes. Had the economy continued to deteriorate in 1987–88, an electoral dynamic might have emerged. Also important is the constitutional limit on parliamentary influence over government spending. The party system also contributed to a weak electoral cycle. Because none of the three major parties had clear economic positions, no clear alternative governing coalition emerged. Party pressure for policy-based elections was neither useful nor necessary. Also, because the parties were not well institutionalized, elections could not be expected to maximize the chance of incumbents being reelected, even with expansionary policies. The potential for a political-business cycle was also weakened by the fact that the prime minister had no party of his own; Prem's premiership was contingent not on a clear parliamentary majority of a particular party or parties but rather on complex, ad hoc negotiations between the parties and the military and among parties. Elections, in sum, posed little threat to stabilization, and even served to strengthen the hand of the technocrats.

Organization of Interests

Comparing the Thai reform experience with that of other countries highlights the absence of broad-based, participatory politics in Thailand. Demonstrations and protests occurred, and political parties decried the recessionary consequences of stabilization. But reform politics in Thailand were largely an elite affair handled by technocrats interacting sporadically with the military and parties. This raises two questions: (1) What explains this relative political passivity, especially on the part of business and labor? (2) How did this passivity influence outcomes of the reform efforts?

Business

Why, despite widespread bankruptcies and foreign exchange losses, did Thai business respond to tight money policies and a hefty devaluation so timidly? With regard to the devaluation, part of the answer has to do with the export-oriented structure of assets and activities of powerful private actors (unless otherwise noted, the following discussion of business preferences draws on Doner and Unger 1992). Agricultural exports have been a long-standing and large, albeit declining, portion of commercial bank portfolios. Commercial banks are tightly linked to the country's expanding, domestic-oriented industrial sector, but some of Thailand's most powerful firms had already begun to move toward exports. The peak association of manufacturers, the Association of Thai Industries, lodged only half-hearted protests against the devaluation because its members were not highly dependent on imports; their stance offset the complaints of firms more reliant on imported inputs (Siam Cement, the country's largest industrial group, complained, while Saha Union, a major textile group, and Charoen Pokphan, the largest agroindustrial group, generally welcomed the move; author interviews). The Thai Bankers Association was similarly passive in the face of the devaluation, although small banks disagreed publicly about the benefits of the devaluation (*Bangkok Post,* November 3, 1985, pp. 1, 2). The Bangkok Bank, the country's largest financial institution, simply reduced its foreign exchange exposure in anticipation of the devaluation.[20] In sum, cohesive opposition to the devaluation was precluded by economic cross pressures and the fact that major business interests had market-based options for adjusting to the new exchange rate.

Nor did business have strong links to the state. As noted, the military was generally suspicious of business, especially large firms. Relations between business and political parties were considerably closer, but parties did not represent collective business interests. Trade associations, whose numbers and access to policymakers increased during the Prem administration, had few links as associations to electoral politics. Patterns of support were further blurred by competing businesses supporting the same party even as different parties obtained support from the same firm (Christensen 1991).

In addition to crosscutting interests and lack of collective business representation, the potential for an alliance between disgruntled business interests and political forces was weakened by the access of business to the Prem government and by Prem's position as a symbol of the democratic transition. Technocrats under Prem expanded consultation with the peak associations through the establishment of joint public-private sector consultative committees (Laothamatas 1992a). These provided direct channels through which associations could articulate their concerns on issues such as credit limits, bureaucratic inefficiency, high taxation, and export incentives and helped defuse potential opposition to painful stabilization. They also drew the attention of policymakers to obstacles preventing greater economic efficiency. The government thus engineered a useful tradeoff by providing political access to business and satisfying demands in some areas in return for cooperation on inflation and the current account deficit.

Labor

Labor occasionally demonstrated against aspects of the reforms, such as increased bus fares and the devaluation, but, by and large, labor resistance did not impede the reforms. This was in part due to compensatory measures such as modest increases in the minimum wage and effective monitoring of price increases after the devaluation. It had more to do, however, with factor mobility, levels of organization, and links with organized political forces.

The impact of stabilization measures on labor was cushioned by the opportunity to find work and sustenance in the countryside or overseas. A more permanent urban labor force had developed in Thailand by the 1980s, but migrant workers were still present in manufacturing and services. Many moved back and forth between seasonal farm work in the country and urban wage work (Phongpaichit 1991). Migrant labor, especially in the Middle East, offered another cushion for labor.[21] Workers' remittances constituted the third largest foreign exchange earner in 1983 and 1984 (Leeahtam 1991, p. 21).

Thai workers were also not that significant in numbers or in organization. There were four peak associations, but only around 10 percent of Thai labor was in manufacturing and less than 2 percent of the country's work force was unionized; the majority of unions were found in the state enterprise sector (unless otherwise noted, the discussion of labor is drawn from Vanno 1991; author interviews). Labor has had no consistent links with political parties. It has shown no strong preference for any one party, not even for the Democratic Labor Party, which was established by labor. The parties, for their part, have shown no interest in labor except to recruit them to be campaign workers. Under these conditions, labor's resistance to the reforms depended on its willingness and ability to link up with the military. A brief examination of three issues—the minimum wage, devaluation, and privatization—suggests that such a strategy was only moderately feasible.

Organized labor presented a demand for a modest increase in the minimum wage (from B66 to B72) during the summer of 1984. The government Wage Committee initially refused any increase, but labor intensified its demand after the 1984 devaluation and obtained an increase of B4. Critical to this partial victory was a labor strategy designed to take advantage of the government's fear of military intervention. Labor leaders knew of the government's concern to prevent labor agitation and strikes that would justify a military coup.

The limits of this strategy were evident in the devaluation crisis, however. Following the November announcement, labor demanded an across-the-board wage increase equal to the devaluation, as well as price controls. These demands were followed by contacts between the peak labor associations, some of the parties, and the military. Demonstrations were planned but eventually abandoned. Labor was itself split, with a majority unwilling to engage in direct political action that would threaten the Prem government. As was the case with business, the specter of military rule lay in the background. Most labor leaders were "economic oriented" and careful to ensure that "their action would not be interpreted by the military as support for a coup" (Vanno 1991, p. 100).

The government's privatization efforts, beginning in 1983, could have been expected to generate unified, military-labor opposition. State enterprises were important sources of military wealth and influence as well as the major locus of organized labor. Labor opposition, in the form of protests and the emergence of ad hoc groups, did develop, but labor never established common cause with the military, and the public did not support state workers whose job security and benefits exceeded those of their private sector counterparts. As economic growth highlighted the need for greater efficiency in areas such as communications, public transport, and port facilities, various forms of privatization gained public backing.

Impact on Outcomes

High factor mobility, weak organization, and fragile links to political actors representing business and labor enhanced the state's ability to pursue reform, especially in the area of stabilization. However, some of these factors undermined other aspects of the effort.

The disadvantages of weakly organized private interests were most evident in trade reform and industry restructuring. The major obstacle to tariff liberalization, in addition to state fiscal requirements, was the difficulty of reconciling the needs of different groups of firms, especially upstream and downstream producers. The problem was especially acute in the automotive and textile industries. In automobiles, differences in local content, tariffs, and export requirements emerged between Japanese and western assemblers and local assemblers and parts firms (Doner 1991; Sahasakul, Thongpakde, and Kraisoraphong 1989, pp. 63–64; Thanamai 1985). In textiles and apparel, conflicts developed among spinners, weavers, and garment producers. Only in the electrical goods industry were tariff liberalization efforts implemented. This occurred because, due to the large number of electrical goods smuggled into Thailand, the industry was never that protected in the first place. Thus, "tariff reductions would lower an incentive to smuggle electrical goods from abroad, which then increased the sale of domestic firms" (Sahasakul, Thongpakde, and Kraisoraphong 1989, pp. 63–64). The lack of corporatist-like private sector organizations, as well as close ties between technocrats and those organizations, undermined the government's ability to reconcile the problems of collective action inherent in any trade reform.

Organization of the State

The Prem government's long time horizon on stabilization policy was strengthened by the continuity and cohesion of its macroeconomic policy officials. Most, but not all, of these individuals were nonpartisan (or nonparty) officials. The party system and Prem's position as a political balancer helped buffer them. It would, however, be wrong to assume that technocrats were highly insulated. They were, in fact, careful to avoid alienating career officials in the ministries as well as party members in the cabinet itself (the following discussion draws on author interviews; Leeahtam 1991; Samudavanija 1989).

No specific commission or agency was solely responsible for formulating and implementing structural adjustment. A commission charged with monitoring the reforms and headed by the NESDB secretary general, Snoh Unakul, did participate in the secretariats of relevant ministries, but Snoh did not consider the commission all that important. The critical locus of adjustment plans and decisions was the economic cabinet, sometimes called the Council of Economic Ministers. The council was headed by Prem, with Snoh as secretary.

This was, in effect, a supercabinet authorized to make economic decisions that were binding on the entire cabinet. The council was composed of the following: (a) economic ministers with party backgrounds such as Industry Minister Ob Vasuratana; (b) officials whose allegiance was largely to Prem, such as Finance Minister Sommai, ministers involved in the Bureau of the Budget and Board of Investment, officials of the Energy Policy Committee; (c) Prem's personal advisers, most of whom had academic backgrounds; and (d) career officials heading important technocratic agencies such as the governor of the Bank of Thailand and head of the NESDB; the latter was a former governor of the Bank of Thailand.

Advisers, bureaucrats, and nonparty politicians far outnumbered party-based cabinet members (Samudavanija 1989, p. 26). Fragmented among themselves and lacking the resources and political base to develop clear policy positions, the parties were at an intellectual disadvantage as well. Decisions were made by consensus, not vote, and the technocrats usually prevailed because they held better information and shared a common intellectual perspective. All were trained and believed in neoclassical economics, all were deeply suspicious of government micromanagement, and all were part of a Thai intellectual tradition emphasizing fiscal conservatism and realistic exchange rates as a source of national independence. Further, "Prem's men" consulted among themselves, drew on the knowledge of outside experts, and prepared common positions before council meetings.

But the council was not sealed off from career bureaucrats and party politicians. Nonparty members reportedly went to great lengths to persuade and, if necessary, compromise with party-based cabinet members heading the ministries of commerce, industry, and agriculture. Prem's political instincts avoided harsh policy measures, and compromise was further facilitated by the lack of an entrenched import-substitution industry in the private sector and the cabinet. Even Industry Minister Ob, one of the major opponents of the devaluation and of tight fiscal and monetary policies, was a strong advocate of export promotion.

Monetary Policy and Exchange Rates

This combination of political savvy and intellectual cohesion and continuity was probably best reflected in the areas of monetary policy and exchange rates. These, along with issues such as oil prices, were the responsibility of the Bank of Thailand, which is itself under the finance minister's jurisdiction. Fiscal policy is largely the responsibility of the Ministry of Finance, but from the Bank of Thailand's perspective, the high government deficit weakened the utility of fiscal policy and made its own role especially important during the early Prem period (author interviews).

Thai monetary authorities are distinguished by their relative cohesion and autonomy from political forces, especially the parties. These features were critical to the Bank of Thailand's ability to raise the ceiling on interest rates in 1979, to impose a credit ceiling on the banks in 1984, and to implement a devaluation in the same year. This independence was not absolute, however; neither does it imply isolation. The Bank of

Thailand's strength reflected not only its capacity to formulate policy independently but also the congruence of its preferences with those of the Thai private sector, especially the banks (Doner and Unger, 1992). The banks did not call for deflationary measures or devaluation; neither did they oppose them.

Budgetary Process

Although government deficits themselves constrained fiscal policy, spending limits were a central component of the stabilization process. Several institutional aspects of the budgetary process encouraged healthy fiscal performance: legislative weakness, absence of cyclical-related expenditure, and a gradual centralization of executive agencies during this period.

Thailand is distinguished by the general lack of legislative involvement in the budgetary process (the following description draws on Pillai and Sopchockchai 1986; author interviews). The central institutional fact is that the Parliament is legally prohibited from initiating spending bills. The budgetary process was essentially a trichotomous one limited to the executive:

- The planning agency, the NESDB, was responsible for establishing the overall size of the budget and broad sectoral allocations; the Ministry of Finance, especially the Fiscal Policy Office, was responsible for revenue projections and control; and the Bureau of the Budget, housed within the Office of the Prime Minister, was responsible for incorporating priorities and revenue projections into a draft after consulting with the other two bodies and considering requests from within the ministries. The draft was sent to the prime minister who approved and sent it to the cabinet for further amendments and approval. The cabinet rarely changed the draft. When political problems emerged, the finance minister's role became more prominent. Thus, the only nontechnocrat with input into the original draft was the finance minister, and under Prem this was the highly technocratic Sommai (and after 1986 his deputy).
- The Budget Bureau then sent the amended draft, with budget lists classified by ministries, to the ministries for approval or suggested changes. The ministers themselves had minimal input because budget requests from the bureaucracy came not from the ministerial level but from the departments headed by career directors general. The opportunity for party-based ministers to influence the budget was largely limited to the allocation of contracts for projects already approved.
- The Budget Bureau incorporated the suggested amendments from the ministries and submitted the new draft to the cabinet and prime minister. On approval, the draft became the fiscal budget bill and

only then, in early to mid-June, some five months after the process began, was the bill submitted to the Parliament with supporting documents. The documents contained only explanations of spending categories; they did not identify the problems to be addressed through spending or expected time frames. The House of Representatives was empowered only to cut the budget. Its deliberations were to be completed rapidly so that the budget could be in place by October 1. Debate within the full body of the House over whether to accept the bill was reportedly limited to one or two days.

If the legislature was not a source of inflationary pressure, its actual role remains unclear. One view is that legislative activity was largely limited to monitoring implementation, such as reviewing whether funds were in fact spent as planned (author interview). Even this function was constrained because most monitoring was the responsibility of an Audit Council within the prime minister's office. Others emphasize that the legislature exercised two budgetary functions through the House Budget Scrutiny Committee: it was the major locus of project-based lobbying and, representing business, the primary source of public restraint on military budgets (Phongpaichit 1991). Yet the Scrutiny Committee's scope of activity was limited by time and information, as well as by the tendency of government parties to defend the budget.

A second institutional feature of the budgetary process that enhanced fiscal restraints was "the virtual absence of cyclical-related expenditure in the budget" (Leeahtam 1991, p. 75). Unlike many other countries, the Thai budget contained no social security payments or unemployment entitlements; nor, due to the prohibition on government guarantees of private debt, was it encumbered with significant financial supports for private enterprises. Finally, the budget was "freed of subsidy on food and other consumer items . . . common in developing countries" (Leeahtam 1991, p. 76).[22]

Although the executive dominated the budgetary process, it did not do so all that efficiently at the beginning of the reform period. During the 1981–84 period, policy was poorly coordinated among the Ministry of Finance, NESDB, and the Budget Bureau; this fragmentation "was partly responsible for the unsuccessful fiscal adjustment during this period" (Leeahtam 1991, p. 35). Undermining efforts to reduce existing budgets was a sharp demarcation between the administration of revenue and expenditure. Spending cuts required approval from relevant ministers. Finally, there was no centralized supervision of state enterprise finance. The board of each state-owned enterprise controlled all operations except for certain sensitive tariffs that required cabinet approval. Each enterprise belonged to a ministry and became a vested interest for parties and military representatives. The representatives of core agencies on the boards tended to "become informally representatives of these enterprises in the core agencies instead" (Leeahtam 1991, p. 79). NESDB scrutinized individual enterprise investment plans outside the overall macroeconomic framework.

But the executive underwent a centralization under pressure of the "crisis imperative" of the 1980s (Phongpaichit 1991). Working groups were established to coordinate and monitor the implementation of fiscal policy. The Fiscal Policy Office was strengthened by new personnel and by technical assistance from the IMF. The Ministry of Finance was empowered to centralize all external borrowing, and Prem strengthened the previously porous Foreign Debt Policy Committee, both of which constrained the expansion of state enterprises. Harder budget constraints were imposed on state firms in the form of requirements to contribute 30 percent of profits as government revenue (to equal the corporate income tax rate on private, listed companies). The government also eliminated cross arrears among state enterprises to lessen liquidity shortages.[23]

Trade Policy

In practice, the most important institutional influence on trade policy was the Ministry of Finance, with other executive agencies playing subsidiary roles. Legally, any change of statutory tariffs required legislative changes. But the finance minister, on the recommendation of an executive tariff committee and with cabinet approval, was empowered to modify applied tariffs without legislative approval. The applied tariffs for numerous products thus differed from statutory levels (GATT 1991, p. 49). Import surcharges were levied by the Ministry of Commerce, with cabinet approval, and by the Board of Investments with a view to protecting promoted industries. Conversely, the board also had the power to grant tariff and tax concessions (on, for example, necessary machinery or raw materials) for industrial promotion.

That the Ministry of Finance played such an important role in tariffs is consistent with the fact that tariffs in Thailand function primarily to generate government revenue rather than to nurture particular industries (Corden 1967). Protected industries did emerge and were represented in the ministries of industry, agriculture, and commerce and, to some degree in the Board of Investments. These industries, as noted, were not that strong politically, and tariff decisions were generally a function of fiscal health rather than political influence. Thus, the mid-1980s' reversal of the early-1980s' trade liberalization resulted from government deficits rather than the political strength of the import-competing sector. Conversely, trade liberalization occurred in 1990–91 as a result of fiscal surpluses under the Chatichai government, a government certainly more penetrated by business and party influence than was the case under Prem. (The Board of Investments, commonly assumed to favor large, import-competing firms, showed surprising flexibility. This was attributed by some as proof that rents could be obtained by granting incentives for exporters as well as industries emphasizing the domestic market.)

There was, however, an important disadvantage in tariffs functioning as an instrument of fiscal policy more than of trade or industrial policy. It meant that the persons controlling the trade regime had few institutional links to and little real knowledge of particular industries. When the NESDB initiated efforts to liberalize and restructure particular industries in the 1980s, the agency found itself without the means necessary to reconcile the diverse interests in each industry. The high-level Restructuring Committee established to oversee industrial reform rarely met and had little impact. According to one observer close to the process, it was "something set up for the [World] Bank" in the first place and enjoyed little integration with public or private officials with experience in particular industries (author interviews).

Agricultural Liberalization

It is in this context that Thailand's success in agricultural liberalization merits explanation (this discussion is drawn from Pantasen and Chenvidyakarn 1988; Pintong 1986; Siamwalla and Na Ranong 1990; author interview). Liberalization in this context refers to ending the premiums, duties, and taxes on exports that had contributed so much to government revenues and constituted important opportunities for rent seeking by parties controlling the ministries of commerce and agriculture. Agricultural liberalization was largely focused on rice exports, although maize was freed up as well.[24] Nevertheless, rice was a significant case. It constituted the country's number one export item for decades, the major agricultural export item, the occupation of some 60 percent of the population, and an important source of rents for the parties.[25]

The changing structure of government revenues encouraged liberalization of the rice trade. The contribution of export taxes to total tax revenue had declined from a high of 13–14 percent in 1974 to less than 5 percent by 1982, thus making liberalization less fiscally burdensome (GATT 1991, p. 48). The government's increased sensitivity to rural constituencies was equally important. The premium levied on exporters resulted in their reducing the price paid to rice farmers; the premium was, in essence, a form of tax levied on farmers. Boosting agricultural prices, especially the price of rice, was widely seen as a way to address problems of rural poverty. Parties jumped on this bandwagon, although political intervention was largely confined to providing development funds to rural areas and making government purchases to raise the price of paddy. No systematic action on rice liberalization emerged during the 1970s.

In the early 1980s, declining prices generated broad public recognition that higher prices should be paid to rural cultivators. Not until the fifth plan, however, did liberalization emerge as a full-fledged program. The effort was backed up by the leverage of technocrats under Prem. One of Prem's advisers headed the Ministry of Agriculture in 1981–82 and helped liberalize the maize trade. The Ministry of Commerce, long a stronghold of the Social Action Party, was more intractable. Yet Finance

Minister Sommai was able to block a price support scheme of the Social Action Party in 1986. The liberals' strategy reflected Prem's political base and insistence on compromise. Although Prem's advisers pushed for reform every time world prices declined, they also abstained from demanding an absolute end to the rice premium. Believing that the legal abolition of the premium would be too costly in a political sense, they simply reduced the rate to zero.

Program Design

Thailand's economic resurgence occurred, first of all, because the government did not do the wrong thing in reaction to the impending economic crisis. The government often *abstained* from further actions as evidenced by its halting large infrastructural projects that could well have become white elephants. The relative absence of political opposition to the reforms that were implemented was due in no small part to the gradual and orthodox nature of the reforms, as well as to numerous compensatory measures.

These measures seem to have been not part of some well thought-out, overarching strategy, but rather a response to short-term pressures. The conditions facilitating Thailand's program design should be considered as well. The country was facing an impending crisis, not an actual economic breakdown. Its basic economic institutions were sufficiently strong to permit a healthy supply response. And finally, Thailand's state institutions were sufficiently cohesive and well informed to generate timely macroeconomic policy responses. Where such conditions do not obtain, especially where the magnitude of the crisis is significantly larger, the gradualism and compensatory measures characterizing Thai reforms will be less feasible economically and politically.

Pace

The Thai reforms were generally orthodox and gradual. Inflation was largely controlled through traditional monetary and fiscal instruments, including the avoidance of large capital projects. More discrete, interventionist measures were adopted but much more slowly. Zero-growth budgets and ceilings on external borrowing were only implemented in the mid-1980s. Energy prices were raised but, as noted earlier, more through failure to pass on savings to consumers than through direct increases. Tariff reforms were initiated as early as 1982 but then reversed in the mid-1980s. Privatization efforts began in earnest only in 1986 and even then were not implemented quickly. One partial exception to the orthodox picture involves wages. Although not indexed or formally controlled, wages were clearly limited. The average annual increase in the minimum wage during the Prem administration was 4 percent compared with a 23 percent annual average for the 1973–80 period (Vanno 1991, table 9, p. 263). Between 1982 and 1989 government employees received no substantive raises (Robinson, Byeon, and Teja 1991, p. 25).

The more significant departure from gradualism was the devaluation. On the one hand, Thailand's exchange rate policy was quite gradual, moving from a small devaluation in 1981 to an almost 15 percent change in 1984. From the Thai perspective, on the other hand, the latter move qualified as a type of "shock treatment" (Leeahtam 1991, pp. 33, 38): the size of the 1984 devaluation surprised the market, and unpegging the baht from the dollar led to a daily variation in the exchange rate unprecedented in Thailand, provoking opposition from the military, labor, and several sectors of business.

The absence of clear counterfactuals makes assessing the pace of Thai reform fairly post hoc. Some tentative conclusions are nonetheless possible. The gradual approach to macroeconomic stabilization was probably the only one feasible given the Thai political context. The approach clearly had its economic costs in that correcting fiscal deficits required a good five years. However, any attempt to impose rapid and comprehensive reforms (to couple trade liberalization with stabilization measures) would have been likely to generate greater fragmentation and hostility than credibility. The political uncertainty of 1984–86 merits special attention here. Although the 1984 devaluation generated export growth, this was still a period of economic slump, of military restiveness reflected in an unsuccessful 1985 coup attempt, of border hostilities, and of declining business confidence (this portrait is drawn from Leeahtam 1991, pp. 40–41). The cabinet rejected a deficit reduction package in early 1985 and the finance minister was a primary target for a no-confidence motion in the Parliament. An election was called in which all campaigners pushed for a more expansionary financial stance. Despite these pressures, economic adjustment continued for reasons that will be discussed, but anything more aggressive would have surely undermined the basis even for gradual measures.

The success of the 1984 devaluation suggests the utility of rapid, bold moves in areas where a number of conditions obtain. There were significant and immediate gains for a broad sector of business. Also, the devaluation was facilitated by the simplicity of its implementation. Unlike fiscal policy, shifts in the exchange rate did not require the cooperation of spending agencies (Leeahtam 1991, p. 38).

Compensation

The Thai reforms were supplemented by a range of compensatory measures. These measures did not involve large sums, nor, as noted, were they part of a coherent, anticipatory strategy. The need for large sums was obviated by the relatively small scale of the crisis itself. Any tendency toward broad compensation was dampened by the political strength of fiscally conservative technocrats. But many measures, such as temporary price controls, were at least symbolically effective in compensating losers. Others, such as export incentives, provided positive, nonzero–sum incentives and signals for firms to move in new directions.

One type of compensation involved transfers to sectors adversely affected by reform measures, especially devaluation. These measures included the abolition of import surcharges, imposition of temporary price controls on items such as cement, reduction of bank lending rates, a promise not to raise oil prices, a pledge of B3 billion to the military, modest increases in the minimum wage, and mandatory transfers of exchange profits from commercial banks to compensate those hurt by the devaluation.[26] Unlike the period following Kriangsak's raising of oil prices, government control of profiteering during this period was reportedly effective (*Nation*, November 7, 1984, pp. 1, 2).

A second type of compensation, most apparent after the mid-1986 election, involved modest, general spending to weaken political pressures for stimulation that would have generated even more serious inflation (Leeahtam 1991, p. 76). Third, despite spending changes in the fifth plan, the technocrats directing the adjustment effort did not neglect the plan's original concern with rural development. Rural funds were maintained, albeit not increased, and one participant in the process argued that Thai adjustment in fact exhibited a "human face."[27]

Fourth, designing and timing measures to even out or obviate short-term impacts were important. In the early 1980s the government implemented expenditure savings measures on an across-the-board basis so as to reduce resentment among officials in the various ministries (Leeahtam 1991, p. 28). Timing was especially important in the 1984 devaluation. Unlike the 1981 devaluations, the 1984 adjustment was undertaken when Parliament was in recess. Prem also did not consult the military. The government thus had more time to make its case clear to the public. Further, the move was timed to benefit farmers rather than middlemen.[28]

Fifth, the general combination of sequencing and positive incentives for trade reform operated as an indirect but highly effective form of compensation. The priority throughout the Prem government was stabilization rather than trade liberalization and sectoral restructuring. As noted, tariff reductions were reversed in the mid-1980s, and elaborate restructuring plans drawn up for the NESDB were not implemented. Exports were encouraged. In addition to the critical 1984 devaluation, the Prem government adopted a broad range of incentives, including an increase of central bank rediscounting facilities for exporters, the initiation of a long-term financing program, expanded Board of Investment incentives, and exemptions or reductions on export taxes for most items (GATT 1991).

These incentives were quite circumscribed and did not constitute any coherent package. Yet export promotion measures did have the virtue of not attacking import-competing interests. As such, they helped to attract foreign, export-oriented firms and to generate rapid export growth by local as well as foreign firms and by small and medium as well as larger firms.[29]

To some degree, this hands-off approach toward the trade regime was necessitated by the importance of import taxes and the country's pressing fiscal requirements. The strategy appears to have been deliberate.[30] Whatever the source, the approach was astute in the context of considerations about economic, political, and institutional capacity. Economically, it established a macroeconomic basis for industry-specific growth. It encouraged domestically oriented firms to move gradually into exports and thus reduce the pain of eventual tariff reductions. Politically, this expanded the coalition of forces supporting further reforms. Of greater short-term political importance, the approach was predicated on the correct assumption that a frontal assault on protection was not feasible for several reasons. Control of the trade regime tended to be industry- or sector-specific, and party and other particular interests had the greatest direct involvement on these levels. More specifically, two parties well known for rent-seeking behavior, the Chart Thai and Social Action parties, dominated the ministries of industry and commerce, respectively (Christensen 1991, pp. 78–82).

In terms of institutional capacity, macroeconomic policymakers had little knowledge about or contact with actors in particular industries. As their initial efforts to restructure autos and textiles show, more aggressive efforts would have alienated rather than mobilized business (Doner 1991; Thanamai 1985). Indeed, political constraints were illustrated even in the provision of positive incentives for exports: in 1988, "potential losers" blocked a Bank of Thailand attempt to raise its short-term rates for export financing to traditional, large exporters and lower them for smaller, new exporters (Leeahtam 1991, pp. 119–20).

Mounting a direct attack on protection would thus have undermined political support for macroeconomic stabilization efforts. As one academic involved in the reform noted, leaving the micro (sector-specific incentives) alone provided the political base to attack the macro problems (author interview). Put somewhat differently, the approach reflected the implicit bargain central to Thai politics: macroeconomic policymakers enjoyed relative independence in exchange for yielding influence over industries and sectors to parties and particular interests.

Conclusions

Thailand's reform achievements during the 1980s illustrate the benefits of a particular type of restrained or semidemocratic regime. The country's democratic transition, begun in 1973, resulted in a balance of forces between the military and a multitude of parties rather than a solid political coalition in a majority-dominated legislature. Prem's pivotal role as an honest broker within this balance provided space for economic technocrats to formulate and implement stabilization policies. The Thai party system also bolstered technocratic initiatives. Not only were the parties fragmented, but they also lacked clear policy positions and strong links with societal interests adversely affected by stabilization. Under these conditions, the opportunities for struggles among parties and for broad mobilization that could paralyze reform were thus limited. Thai economic reformers were, in sum, able to capitalize on the partial nature of the transition itself.

Stabilization efforts were also strengthened by institutional features of the state itself. Prem's technocrats constituted a cohesive group following a long Thai tradition of fiscal and monetary caution. These officials enjoyed significant autonomy in macroeconomic policy due to tight legal constraints on political influence in budgetary and monetary decisions. They were not isolated, however. Stabilization policies found at least partial favor with Thai business already beginning to expand exports, and business resistance to reform was weakened by expanded consultation with government officials through joint public-private sector consultative committees. These groups encouraged business leaders to take broad views on economic policies while allowing them to articulate particular concerns about the reforms. This in turn provided technocrats with information useful in designing appropriate reform policies. Thai reforms were gradual, with the important exception of the 1984 devaluation. The government also provided losers with modest but symbolically important compensation while adopting positive incentives for business to expand exports.

Thailand's particular transition and the state's institutional features also impeded efforts to extend reforms beyond stabilization. The parties, whose support was critical to stabilization, used their ministerial influence to weaken trade reform and industry restructuring. The technocrats lacked the willingness and capacity to offset party opposition. Their concern with fiscal surpluses was much stronger than their desire for trade reform. Their traditionally weak ties to particular industries also deprived them of the expertise and contacts necessary to engineer sectoral changes. Only in agriculture did politics facilitate reform: boosting agricultural prices (by ending the export premium) was a way of reducing rural poverty, an issue to which Thai governments had become increasingly sensitive during the transition process.

The Thai case thus suggests at least a short-term conflict between the political needs of stabilization and sectoral reform in the early stages of the democratic transition. Over the longer term, the high rates of growth ushered in by Prem's stabilization policies paved the way for subsequent trade reforms initiated under the democratically elected Chatichai government that followed Prem in 1988.

The longer-term consequences of the Prem government for Thailand's

transition to democracy and sustained economic growth are more problematic. Reliance on technocratic austerity in the 1980s did little to
strengthen the parties institutionally. Under Chatichai, politicians found
new sources of patronage both inside the ministries and in control of the
infrastructural projects necessitated by rapid economic growth (Christensen 1991, p. 62). This corruption helped legitimize the military overthrow of the Chatichai government in 1991. The military was forced to
govern the country indirectly through technocrats and respected business
figures, and the regime was replaced by a democratically elected civilian
government in 1992. The problem of poorly institutionalized parties
remains, however, as does fragmentation of the state officials charged
with sectoral policies. These weaknesses continue to plague Thai efforts
to address the human and physical infrastructure needs resulting from
the country's rapid economic growth (Santikarn Kaosa-ard 1992).

Notes

1. Between 1980 and 1990, agriculture's contribution to the gross national product
(GNP) declined from 23 to 13 percent, while that of manufacturing rose from 21 to 26
percent (Thailand Development Research Institute 1993, p. 5). Manufactured exports
expanded nearly 40 percent annually from 1986 to 1989, accounting for more than two-
thirds of total exports in 1989 compared with less than half before 1985 (Akrasanee,
Dapice, and Flatters 1991, p. 5).
2. An analysis of the 1982–87 period notes that despite public announcements indicating
a shift toward a more export-based strategy, "the actual incentives created by taxes and
import tariffs and export duties have been increasingly import-substitution-oriented"
(Akrasanee, Dapice, and Flatters 1991, p. 23). Important trade liberalization measures
were subsequently implemented under both the more democratic and subsequently authoritarian regimes following Prem: in 1988 Chatichai Choonavan became the country's first
elected prime minister since 1976; Chatichai was overthrown in February 1991 by a military coup that installed a technocrat-led government. Tariffs on capital goods were reduced
from 20 to 5 percent in October 1990. The government of Anand Panyarachun initiated
reductions of import taxes on raw materials, intermediate goods, and finished products and
drastic cuts in tariffs on computers and automobiles. See Guyot 1991, p. 72.
3. The military obtained fifteen loans amounting to $366 million in the twenty-four
months prior to June 1979 (Nations 1979b, p. 53). All dollar amounts are U.S. dollars.
4. Thailand's currency is the baht.
5. Less than 20 percent of Thailand's trade is with the United States, but much of its
trade is denominated in U.S. dollars.
6. This event itself was preceded by elections in 1969 in which the parliamentary majority was a party organized by the military. The Parliament was overthrown in 1971.
7. For one thing, elections did not occur until 1975. Further, the very proliferation of
parties in these governments led to highly fragmented coalitions wracked by numerous
policy differences. One of the more important ones, the speed of the U.S. withdrawal after
the defeat in Viet Nam, contributed to the demise of both coalition governments in 1975
and 1976. The weaknesses of the parties and the fragility of the coalition undermined any
significant budgetary role for the Parliament. As one observer notes, until the late 1970s the
Parliament generally "acted as a rubber stamp for the budget" (Phongpaichit 1991, p. 6).
8. Twenty-seven of the fifty-one members of the executive committees of the three leading
parties in 1974 were businesspeople. After the 1975 election, businesspeople constituted
the largest group in the House. The proportion of cabinet members with business backgrounds grew tremendously during the 1973–76 period: over half of the Kukrit-Boonchu–
led cabinet, formed in March 1975, were businessmen (Laothamatas 1992b).
9. This Tambon Fund allowed farmers to borrow money from banks without collateral.

The plan was never completely implemented. A further indicator of the popularity of rural development programs is that the other major party, Chart Thai, drew all forty-seven of its parliamentary seats from the provinces rather than Bangkok (Prizzia 1985, table 4, p. 97).

10. For example, in Kriangsak's 1979 government the number of seats reserved for the deputy agriculture minister was raised from one to four; see Christensen 1991, p. 57; Prizzia 1985, p. 99.

11. By the early 1980s, agricultural exports had stagnated, the crop area was no longer growing, and the agricultural sector seemed to be encountering a "land frontier" (Phongpaichit 1991, pp. 13–14).

12. The Japanese were reportedly speculating against the baht at this time; see anonymous 1983, p. xi.

13. These changes included the introduction of a program-based budgeting system, decentralization and computerization of tax administration, revision of excise tax codes, and review of customs duties (Leeahtam 1991, p. 30).

14. For example, Ob Vasuratana, party leader and industry minister, was in part responsible for halting the implementation of technical studies on trade liberalization and industry restructuring (Doner 1991; Sahasakul, Thongpakde, and Kraisoraphong 1989, p. 62).

15. Thus the Social Action Party's March 1981 departure from the government resulted not from political principle but from a conflict with the Chart Thai Party concerning a Saudi oil deal. The Social Action Party rejoined the government later that year.

16. This discussion has not addressed party attitudes toward privatization. Parties are often assumed to oppose privatization because of the rent-seeking opportunities provided by state enterprises. Leeahtam (1991, p. 90) notes the existence of some common interests between the privatization drive and parties. Presumably this refers to the opportunities available to party backers for controlling former state enterprises.

17. Phongpaichit (1991) argues that the parties, acting through the House Budget Scrutiny Committee, represented business opposition to the military's budgetary requests. Although a few members of Parliament opposed the military budget, business in the Prem government was at best an ally of the Ministry of Finance in checking excess purchases of military arms. The major battle was fought between the Ministry of Finance and the military. No parties took an official stance on reducing the defense budget.

18. Also important were the compensatory measures noted earlier and a fall in oil prices that reduced the inflationary impact of the adjustment and the relative weakness of import-substitution industries.

19. The 1983 election was a response to the military's proposals for a constitutional change. The 1986 election was the only one that involved significant debate over stabilization policy. That election was preceded not by expansionary fiscal policy but by the first zero-growth budget in fiscal 1986/87. Following the election, the finance minister approved some growth in capital expenditure to defuse political pressures, but the overall fiscal balance was maintained by cutting other expenditures and by delaying implementation of the program (Leeahtam 1991, pp. 56, 76). The 1988 election, held amidst phenomenal economic growth, resulted from rifts within the ruling Democrat Party over the allocation of ministerial positions. A prior (1987) relaxation was probably not gauged to boost the government's electoral chances since the next full-term election was scheduled for 1990. Only a brief relaxation in 1982 might be seen as anticipating the 1983 election.

20. An official of the bank discounted the need for any opposition to the devaluation: some of his clients were hurt, but others benefited (author interview).

21. The outflow of contract migrants from Thailand jumped from slightly more than 9,000 in 1979 to almost 21,000 in 1980, 25,000 in 1981, and then 108,000 in 1982 (Abella 1984, p. 492; Quibria 1986, p. 85).

22. A related point is that the temptation to bolster revenues by drawing on windfalls from the global decline in the price of oil was blocked by exclusion of the Oil Fund from the fiscal deficit. The Oil Fund was purposely kept in a separate, commercial bank account under the Comptroller General, not the Ministry of Finance, and state enterprises had no access to it (Leeahtam 1991, p. 78).

23. Government agencies reportedly attempted to circumvent spending limits by postponing utility payments to state firms that had no sanctions to enforce payment by the agencies (Leeahtam 1991, p. 90, fn. 133).

24. Liberalization did not extend to all agricultural products. The ministries of commerce and agriculture imposed bans on the export of kenaf and castor oil to ensure that

infant agribusiness industries (gunnysack factories and castor oil refineries) would have sufficient raw materials.

25. The rice premium allowed the Ministry of Commerce to engage in government-to-government rice trading without fear of suffering a loss. The Ministry of Agriculture benefited because, since 1974, the money collected by the Ministry of Commerce was turned directly to the Farmers Aid Fund. The fund was supervised by the Ministry of Agriculture, which had significant discretion in spending it. For example, they could use it to purchase paddy and raise prices in geographical areas they considered important. Perhaps the most egregiously political use of rice policy for political means occurred under the Social Action Party's agriculture minister, Kosol Krairerk (1983–86). Kosol reintroduced a policy suspended in 1974 under which only traders allocated quotas were empowered to export. After this policy proved unworkable in world markets, Kosol proposed a government purchase scheme to guarantee minimum paddy prices. The proposal was defeated by Finance Minister Sommai.

26. Leeahtam 1991, p. 35; Vanno 1991, p. 276; author interviews. A billion is 1,000 million.

27. Author interview. The sharp drop in farmers' incomes in 1985 and 1986 was somewhat offset by a decline in inflation. As a result of consistent state finances for improving cultivated land, occupational skills, and health services, the number of absolute poverty districts declined from 286 in 1982 to 197 within three years (Leeahtam 1991, pp. 131–32).

28. The 1981 adjustments occurred when exporters held large stocks of unsold agricultural products. Sommai explicitly announced that the 1984 shift "would help the farmers since their products were still in their possession" (Warr and Nidhiprabha 1988, pp. 48, 55).

29. The share of export-oriented firms in the total number of foreign investments promoted by the Board of Investments rose from roughly 10 percent in 1984 to three-quarters in 1988 (GATT 1991, p. 44, fn. 26). Since incentives included allowing full foreign ownership for export-oriented foreign projects, foreign shares of foreign investment projects have grown. This expansion has probably been most pronounced in areas such as consumer and industrial electronics, textiles, and automobiles. Yet between 1985 and 1988, local investment has dominated the expanding lower-technology industries such as jewelry, shoes, leather goods, furniture, artificial flowers, toys, steel tubes, and auto parts (Phongpaichit 1989, p. 345).

30. Author interviews; also note NESDB Chief Snoh's 1985 statement that the government's approach was to tackle easier problems first (Unakul 1985).

References

Abella, M. 1984. "Labor Migration from South and Southeast Asia: Some Policy Issues." *International Labor Review* 123:4 (August), pp. 491–506.

Akrasanee, Narongchai, David Dapice, and Frank Flatters. 1991. *Thailand's Export-Led Growth: Retrospect and Prospects.* Policy Study 3. Bangkok: Thailand Development Research Institute.

Anderson, Benedict. 1977. "Withdrawal Symptoms: Social and Cultural Aspects of the October 6 Coup." *Bulletin of Concerned Asian Scholars* 9 (July–September), pp. 13–30.

Anonymous. 1983. "Forceful but Cautious." *Euromoney* (October), pp. xi–xii.

Bangkok Post. 1985. November 3, pp. 1, 2.

Bowring, Philip, and Richard Nations. 1976. "Kukrit's Fight for the Farmers." *Far Eastern Economic Review,* January 30, pp. 34–36.

Brown, Ian. 1988. *The Elite and the Economy in Siam c. 1890–1920.* Singapore: Oxford University Press.

Chaisut, Narit, Warakorn Samkoset, and Chunruthai Ponpatarakul. 1987.

"Krongsang lae panha kong sataban karn-ngern nai rabob settakit tai [Structure and problems of financial institutions in the Thai economic system]." Paper presented at the Symposium on the Security of Financial Institutions, Thammasat University, Faculty of Political Science, Bangkok.

Christensen, Scott R. 1991. "The Politics of Democratization in Thailand: State and Society since 1932." Unpublished ms. Thailand Development Research Institute, Bangkok. Processed.

Corden, W. M. 1967. "The Exchange Rate System and the Taxation of Trade." In T. H. Silcock, ed., *Thailand: Social and Economic Studies in Development.* Singapore: Donald Moore.

Doner, Richard F. 1991. *Driving a Bargain: Automobile Industrialization and Japanese Firms in Southeast Asia.* Berkeley: University of California Press.

Doner, Richard F., and Daniel Unger. 1992. "The Politics of Finance in Thai Economic Development." In Stephan Haggard, Chung Lee, and Sylvia Maxfield, eds., *The Politics of Finance in Developing Countries.* Ithaca, N.Y.: Cornell University Press.

Fish, Peter. 1978. "Thailand's Phase Two Tightens the Squeeze." *Far Eastern Economic Review,* March 24, pp. 78–79.

———. 1979a. "Oiling the Wheels of Inflation." *Far Eastern Economic Review,* August 3, pp. 38–40.

———. 1979b. "Thailand Grasps the Nettle." *Far Eastern Economic Review,* January 5, pp. 40–44.

GATT. 1991. *Trade Policy Review Mechanism: Thailand.* Geneva: GATT Secretariat.

Guyot, Eric. 1991. "The Army Has Given Me a Fairly Free Hand: Interview with Prime Minister Anand." *Asian Finance,* September 15.

Hewison, Kevin. 1987. "National Interests and Economic Downturn: Thailand." In Richard Robison, Keven Hewison, and Richard Higgot, eds., *Southeast Asia in the 1980s: The Politics of Economic Crisis.* Boston, Mass.: Allen and Unwin.

Ho, Kwon Ping. 1979. "A Bitter Pill for Thailand." *Far Eastern Economic Review,* December 14, pp. 94–96.

Industrial Management Company. 1983. *Industrial Restructuring Study for the National Economic and Social Development Board: Summary.* Bangkok.

———. 1985. *Industrial Restructuring Study . . . : Technology Development and Promotion for the Engineering Industries.* Bangkok.

Ingavata, Poonsin. 1989. "Privatization in Thailand: Slow Progress amidst Much Opposition." ASEAN *Economic Bulletin* (March), pp. 319–35.

Ingram, James C. 1955. *Economic Change in Thailand since 1850.* Stanford, Calif.: Stanford University Press.

Laothamatas, Anek. 1992a. *Business Associations and the New Political Economy of Thailand.* Boulder, Colo.: Westview Press.

———. 1992b. "The Politics of Structural Adjustment in Thailand: A Political Explanation of Economic Success." In K. Jayasuriya and A. Macintyre, eds., *The Dynamics of Economic Policy Reform in Southeast Asia and the Southwest Pacific.* Singapore: Oxford University Press.

Leeahtam, Pisit. 1991. *From Crisis to Double-Digit Growth*. Bangkok: Dokya.

McBeth, John. 1979. "The Premier on Probation." *Far Eastern Economic Review*, August 17, pp. 32–33.

Nation. 1984. November 7.

Nations, Richard. 1979a. "Bangkok Loosens the Purse-Strings." *Far Eastern Economic Review*, November 30, pp. 68–70.

_____. 1979b. "Thailand's Tactical Retreat." *Far Eastern Economic Review*, July 6, pp. 52–53.

Pantasen, Apichai, and Montri Chenvidyakarn. 1988. *Karnmuang ruang kao [Rice politics]*. Bangkok: Social Science Association of Thailand.

Phongpaichit, Pasuk. 1989. "Thailand: Miss Universe 1988." In Ng Chee Yuen, ed., *Southeast Asian Affairs 1989: An Annual Review*. Singapore: Institute of Southeast Asian Studies.

_____. 1990. "Technocrats, Businessmen, and Generals: Democracy and Economic Policy-making in Thailand." Unpublished ms., Faculty of Economics, Chulalongkorn University, Bangkok. Processed.

_____. 1991. "The Politics of Economic Policy Reform in Thailand." Paper presented at the seminar on the politics of economic policy reform, Manila, October 15–16.

Pillai, Vel, and Orapin Sopchockchai. 1986. "Budgeting, Financing, and Planning in Thailand: Study of a Trichotomous Process." *Public Budgeting and Finance* (winter), pp. 34–42.

Pintong, Chermsak. 1986. "Karnmuang ruang kao." Paper presented at the Conference on the State Capital and Labor: Crisis without a Solution? Chulalongkorn University, Bangkok, February 8–9.

Prizzia, Ross. 1985. *Thailand in Transition: The Role of Opposition Forces*. Honolulu: University of Hawaii Press.

Quibria, M. 1986. "Migrant Workers and Remittances: Issues for Asian Developing Countries." *Asian Development Review* 4:1, pp. 78–99.

Robinson, David, Yangho Byeon, and Ranjit Teja. 1991. *Thailand: Adjusting to Success: Current Policy Issues*. Washington, D.C.: International Monetary Fund.

Rowley, Anthony. 1979. "Kriangsak's Other Battlefront." *Far Eastern Economic Review*, September 21, pp. 100–103.

Sahasakul, Chaipat, Nattapong Thongpakde, and Keokam Kraisoraphong. 1989. "Lessons from the World Bank's Experience of Structural Adjustment Loans (SALS): A Case Study of Thailand." Thailand Development Research Center, Bangkok.

Samudavanija, Chai-anan. 1989. *The Economic Cabinet [in Thai]*. Bangkok: Thailand Development Research Institute.

Santikarn Kaosa-ard, Mingsarn. 1992. "Manufacturing Growth: A Blessing for All?" *Thailand's Economic Structure: Towards Balancing Development?* Bangkok: Thailand Development Research Institute.

Siamwalla, Ammar, and Viroj Na Ranong. 1990. *Pramual kwanroo ruang kao [Compendium of knowledge about rice]*. Bangkok: Thailand Development Research Institute.

Thailand Development Research Institute. 1993. *Thailand Information Kit.* Bangkok.

Thanamai, Patcharee. 1985. "Patterns of Industrial Policymaking in Thailand: Japanese Multinationals and Domestic Actors in the Automobile and Electrical Appliances Industries." Ph.D. diss., University of Wisconsin, Madison.

Tinnakorn, Prani, and Direk Patamasiriwat. 1985. "Ni tang pratet kong pratet doi pattana lea koroni suksa ni tang pratet pak rattaban kong tai [Developing country foreign debt and the case of Thai government foreign debt]." *1985 Symposium on the Foreign Debt Crisis of the Thai Government,* pp. 1–38. Bangkok: Thammasat University, Faculty of Economics.

Unakul, Snoh. 1985. "Karn pattana karn song ork [Developing exports]." Speech to the commercial counselors of the Ministry of Commerce, printed in *Warasarn Settakij Lae Sangkhom [Journal of economy and society],* February 25, p. 65.

Vanno, Vichote. 1991. "The Role of Trade Unions in the Political Development of Thailand, 1958–86." Ph.D. diss., City University of New York.

Warr, Peter, and Bhanupongse Nidhiprabha. 1988. "Macroeconomic Policies, Crisis, and Growth in the Long Run: Thailand Country Study." Research Project 673-99, pt. 2. World Bank, Bangkok.

Warr, Peter, and Bandid Nijathaworn. 1988. "Macroeconomic Policies and Long-Term Growth." Research Project 673-99, pt. 1. World Bank, Washington, D.C.

Waterbury, John. 1989. "The Political Management of Economic Adjustment and Reform." In Joan Nelson, ed., *Fragile Coalitions: The Politics of Economic Adjustment.* New Brunswick, N.J.: Transaction Books.

World Bank. 1990. *Thailand Financial Sector Study,* vol. 2. Washington, D.C.

11

Nigeria: Economic and Political Reforms at Cross Purposes

JEFFREY HERBST AND ADEBAYO OLUKOSHI

IN FEW COUNTRIES OF THE WORLD HAS THE GAP BETWEEN ACTUAL AND POTENTIAL economic and political performance been wider than in Nigeria. Africa's most populous country, Nigeria has about 90 million people, an excellent agricultural base, and significant oil reserves, making it one of the largest producers of petroleum in the world. Despite these attributes, Nigeria's economy declined at a rate of 0.4 percent annually during the 1980s, and in 1990 its per capita income was roughly lower than that of India or Kenya, making it the seventeenth poorest country in the world (World Bank 1992b, p. 218). Indeed, in 1984, after ten years of an oil boom, the per capita income of the average Nigerian was no higher than it had been a decade before (Husain 1987, p. 1). Similarly, against the background of a vibrant civil society, a vociferous press, and multiple centers of power, Nigerians have shown a strong national commitment to democracy, and the country has been more innovative than most in Africa in its attempts to ameliorate the effects of cultural pluralism through constitutional engineering. Nevertheless, the democratic experiments of the first (1960–66) and second (1979–83) republics ended ignominiously in coups d'état. As a result,

The authors are grateful to Stephan Haggard, Ishrat Husain, Steven Webb, and their colleagues on this project for helpful comments.

Nigeria has been ruled by generals for all but ten of its thirty-one years of independence.

During the 1980s, new strategies were developed to meet the increasingly severe economic and political challenges facing Nigeria. After a long period of delay, the government of Ibrahim Babangida (1985 to the present) adopted a broad range of measures sanctioned by the International Monetary Fund (IMF) and the World Bank in order to stabilize and, eventually, adjust the economy in the hope that growth would again be possible. At almost the same time, a new program to foster a political transition to a democratic third republic was announced, making Nigeria the first African country to promote programs of political and economic reform simultaneously.

The central concern addressed in this chapter is why the regimes of Shehu Shagari (1979–83) and Muhammadu Buhari (1983–85) felt unable to adopt the promarket measures recommended by the multilateral agencies and why the Babangida administration was subsequently able to do what had been widely viewed as politically impossible in Nigeria. This chapter examines the dilemmas faced by a government compelled to introduce economic reforms that would inevitably be widely disliked while seeking to retain enough popular support so that its transition program to civilian rule can proceed. Also assessed is the extent to which the Babangida government has implemented its market reform program in the face of strong and persistent resistance from interest groups. Finally, it analyzes how successful the Babangida regime has been in changing the logic of Nigerian politics, especially the reliance on state controls, expenditure, and patronage to gain political support.

Since oil accounts for more than 90 percent of Nigeria's exports and provides most of the government's revenue, this chapter begins with the Shagari government's response to the collapse of the oil market in the early 1980s. This collapse triggered the Nigerian crisis, exposing in sharp relief the structural deficiencies of the economy and the hollow base on which the development process rested. It then evaluates the economic program of crisis management adopted by General Buhari's government and analyzes the economic and political reforms introduced by General Babangida's administration. It concludes by reviewing the Nigerian response to the small oil boom that occurred in 1990–91 and analyzing whether the reforms implemented in the latter half of the 1980s fundamentally altered the political basis for making economic policy.

Brief Review of Nigeria's Political Economy

Chief Awolowo noted in 1947 that one of the fundamental problems facing Nigeria was that it was, in many ways, little more than "a geographic expression" (Joseph 1987, p. 184). The postcolonial period witnessed far-reaching political, economic, and social programs aimed at accelerating the processes of nation-building within a federal system. Today, the country is much more than a geographic expression and has taken on many of the characteristics of a modern nation-state. Nevertheless, a constellation of ethnic, regional, religious, and class conflicts continues to pose tremendous problems and still has the potential (as demonstrated in the civil war of 1967–70) to threaten national unity. These conflicts have had a significant impact on the economic policymaking and reform process. Indeed, many of the economically inefficient public investment projects of the 1970s can be attributed directly to the myriad ethnic, regional, and religious competitions that are always a component of Nigerian politics.

Of the many cleavages in Nigerian society, one of the most important is the rivalry among ethnic groups and their conflicting claims on state resources, which sometimes lead to violence. The complex ethnic divisions of the country, coupled with religious polarization between Muslims (concentrated in the north and parts of the southwest) and Christians (in the middle belt, southeast, and parts of the southwest) mean that, from independence, Nigerian governments have had to engage in balancing acts aimed at allaying fears of ethnic domination and religious expansionism. The consequence is that resource allocation has always had a strong political bias. Nigerian governments have always had to mollify fears in southern Nigeria of Hausa/Fulani political domination while at the same time attempting to win the confidence of the peoples of the relatively less developed north through the deliberate allocation of industrial, infrastructural, and commercial assets. Indeed, the peoples of the south, especially in oil-producing areas, sometimes openly protest what they see as enrichment of the north via the state at the expense of the south. It is little wonder that the conflict over revenue allocation is unending. Indeed, the Babangida regime alone has introduced four revenue allocation schemes in its constant attempts to balance competing claims.

Since independence, the state has played a critical role in attempts by nationalist politicians to promote unity. Also, given the urgent need to develop economic and social infrastructure, the state has assumed a central and constantly increasing role in the economy. In line with the conventional wisdom of the 1960s and 1970s, the state has championed investment projects and attempted to mediate the competing claims on federal and local resources. As a result, the state is a principal focal point for developing and nurturing patron-client relations. Correspondingly, patron-client relations have had a particularly significant role from the outset in holding this multiethnic, multireligious country together.

Indeed, clientelism has characterized *all* postcolonial regimes, at least through 1992, whether military or civilian. At one level, establishing patron-client ties has been one way for successive governments to promote national unity. As Richard Sandbrook (1986, p. 330) has noted, clientelism is the classic response of government leaders to the problems posed by an unintegrated peasantry thrust together inside boundaries drawn by colonialists. Therefore, clientelism as it is practiced in Nigeria should not be seen merely as rent seeking by individuals raiding the coffers of the state. Rather, as Richard Joseph (1987, p. 67) has noted, the distribution of state offices "is legitimated by a set of political norms according to which the appropriation of such offices is not just an act of individual greed or ambition but concurrently the satisfaction of the short-term objectives of a subset of the population."

The tendency toward clientelism and patrimonialism was greatly aggravated by the oil windfall that Nigeria received in the early 1970s due to domestic increases in production and to increases in prices by the Organization of Petroleum Exporting Countries (OPEC). In 1970, oil exports equaled N510 million; a decade later they had increased to N14.2 billion.[1] Since almost all of the oil revenue was funneled through the state, government expenditures increased more than 3,000 percent during the same period (Federal Office of Statistics 1991, pp. 7–8). As a result, control of the state became exceptionally valuable, and the explosion of oil revenue fueled the creation of larger and more elaborate patron-client networks. Indeed, the oil boom greatly expanded the ranks of the indigenous trading, contracting, and manufacturing classes, many of whose members were utterly dependent on the state for their continued existence. With the constant flow of oil revenue, it seemed in the 1970s and early 1980s that government revenue could indefinitely finance the parasitic classes that had developed.

The great inflow of revenue caused by the oil boom also created other strong constituencies that would later have an interest in opposing structural adjustment. The public expenditures program of the state was greatly expanded so that utilities and social services were delivered relatively cheaply. For instance, primary education was made free and mandatory, creating an enormous market for school buildings and textbooks, all of which had to be allocated through the state. The strong exchange rate also enabled the importation of cheap food and consumer goods. Moreover, speculators, contractors, commission agents, importers of all commodities, local and foreign manufacturers, and the urban working class all benefited to varying degrees from the massive increase in state expenditures. Finally, the military was well rewarded, especially with imported equipment and other expensive perquisites.

The inability of Nigeria to develop a stable political system in the 1980s or earlier also encouraged informal systems of resource allocation. Nigeria only infrequently had a democracy, and when the military was in power even the generals usually stated that their rule was transitory. The expectation that at any given time the current government was transitory made the continual pledges to reduce corruption meaningless. Indeed, the rapid turnover of regime reinforced the tendency of civilian and military holders of public office to raid the state's coffers to buy support.

Figure 11-1. Real Effective Exchange Rate of the Naira, 1977–90

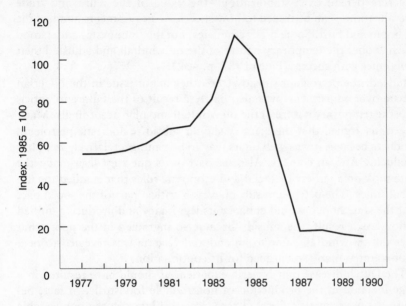

Source: IMF 1991.

Evolution of the Economy

Naturally, the oil boom also had a profound impact on the Nigerian economy. The analysis of Nigeria's structural economic problems is by now well developed using the basic Dutch disease model (Cassing, Wells, and Zamalloa 1987; Collier 1988; Struthers 1990). The extra foreign exchange provided by the oil boom increased the supply only of those goods that were internationally traded (tradables). Demand for all goods increased, however, so that the price of goods not traded internationally (nontradables) increased significantly. As a result, the exchange rate (which can be thought of as the price of nontradables relative to the price of tradables) appreciated. Between 1977 and 1984, the real exchange rate increased more than 100 percent (see figure 11-1).

Successive Nigerian governments treated the sudden increase in oil revenue as a permanent flow of income that could always be counted on even though it was clearly a temporary windfall. Indeed, as many African governments had done in the past, the Nigerian government overspent the massive windfall it received from the oil boom. Further, even after the global market for oil collapsed, Nigeria was reluctant to take steps that would allow the economy to adjust. The real exchange rate continued to appreciate long after the oil boom had ended in the early 1980s. Since the market could not regulate imports given the distorted exchange rate, the government had to resort to increasingly elaborate administrative mechanisms for allocating imports. Thus, two of the three issues in the Nigerian debate over stabilization—the value of the naira and trade liberalization—can be traced to how successive governments handled the oil boom and bust. Some other countries, notably Indonesia, understood much sooner the temporary nature of the oil windfall and adjusted their economies with success (Pinto 1987, p. 432).

Indeed, the petroleum subsidy (the other major issue in the Nigerian debate over adjustment) was also partly a result of the failure to antici-pate the temporary nature of the oil windfall and plan accordingly. Many Nigerians argued that the country should subsidize domestic petroleum products because it was well on its way to becoming a relatively rich, oil-producing African country. Also, as part of its quest for legitimacy, the state took on a variety of social and economic roles that entailed the use of subsidies. The petroleum subsidy was a critical part of the social pact that the state hoped would enhance its legitimacy and produce a unified nation. As a result, the subsidy became so ingrained in the polity that once the oil windfall came to an end and Nigeria was revealed to be a poor country, many still argued for its continuation.

The Dutch disease that Nigeria experienced should have resulted in a large increase in the production of nontradable foodstuffs. In fact, be-cause the government allocated resources and labor to the nontradable service sector (construction, retail), a significant amount of labor shifted out of agriculture and per capita production decreased markedly (Collier 1988). Although huge sums were invested in agricultural development programs, often with World Bank support, the artificially cheap price of imports made it impossible for some farmers to compete. Of course, agricultural tradables were hit hard by the real appreciation of the naira and the diversion of resources to other sectors. Agricultural exports as a percentage of total exports decreased from 73 percent in 1962 to 1 percent in 1981 (Okonkwo 1989, p. 377). Indeed, oil accounted for more than 93 percent of exports between 1973 and 1981 (Federal Office of Statistics 1991, p. 8).

Finally, due to the high exchange rate, the overwhelming majority of factories were concentrated in light processing activities; the intermediate and capital goods sectors were especially underdeveloped. Local value added was very low for practically all manufacturing subsectors. Thus, after the oil windfall was over, Nigeria was left with a much less diver-sified economy than it had in the 1960s.

Shagari and the Initial Crisis, 1979–83

The Shagari government, which faced Nigeria's first great economic crisis of the oil era, was the country's second experiment with democracy. The generals who led Nigeria between the end of the first republic in 1966 and initiation of the second republic in 1979 rejected another attempt at Westminster-type democracy and designed a political system based on the U.S. political system. The National Assembly was divided into two houses. The Senate was composed of five senators from each of the (then) nineteen states. The House of Representatives was made up of 450 members elected from the nineteen states on the basis of population. In addition, significant attempts at constitutional engineering were made to prevent the parties from duplicating the ethnically based organs that had driven the first republic into disarray and led, eventually, to the Nigerian civil war. The constitution demanded that each party be national in origin by requiring that it have a presence in a certain number of states and that it be open to all Nigerians. In addition, the 1979 constitution required that the winner of the election gain at least one-quarter of the vote in two-thirds of the states. Finally, the composition of ministers, civil servants, and the military had to reflect the diversity of the nation.

The federal system and the demand that parties represent more than one region originated in the determination of Nigerians to change the political dynamics so that ethnic and religious ties would become less salient. Many of these provisions, well intentioned though they were, aggravated the tendency toward clientelism that had always been inherent in Nigerian politics. Indeed, in many ways, the reforms, especially the creation of nineteen states from the original four regions, attempted to reduce the importance of ethnic ties by explicitly providing incentives for cross-ethnic patron-client relations.[2] Each state required a capital, the usual complement of elected officials, a full civil service, a university, and all of the improvements in infrastructure that have always been associated with graft in Nigeria. Indeed, state creation became a major avenue by which groups sought not only to broaden their patronage nets but, equally important, also to win greater access to the resources of the rentier federal state. At the very least, the federal system means that powerful constituencies demanding an increase in overall government spending are always present because most of the states' funds come from oil wealth.

Shehu Shagari, the candidate of the northern-dominated National Party of Nigeria, won only 34 percent of the vote in the 1979 elections. Although his electoral strength was overwhelmingly from the north, he managed to capture at least 25 percent of the vote in twelve states and convinced the legal authorities that he met the constitutional tests (Kirk-Greene and Rimmer 1981, p. 39). In the 1979 election, the Nigerian plurality system of voting produced the usual bias in favor of the winning party when votes were translated into seats: with 34 percent of the vote, the National Party of Nigeria won 37 percent of the seats in the House (see table 11-1).

The margin of victory was thin enough, however, to suggest that Shagari did not have an absolutely secure electoral base. In addition, the government would be vulnerable if the opposition parties managed to

Table 11-1. Results of Elections in Nigeria, 1979 and 1983

Party and candidate	Number of presidential votes		Percent of total vote		Number of seats in House		Percent of all seats	
	1979	1983	1979	1983	1979	1983	1979	1983
National Party of Nigeria (Shagari)	5,689,757	12,047,648	33.7	47.3	168	264	37.4	68.4
Unity Party of Nigeria (Awolowo)	4,916,641	7,885,434	29.2	30.1	111	33	24.7	8.5
Nigerian People's Party (Azikwe)	2,822,522	3,534,633	16.7	28.4	78	48	17.4	12.4
Great Nigerian People's Party (Waziri)	1,686,489	640,128	10.0	2.5	43	0	9.6	0.0
People's Reform Party Aminu	1,742,154	n.a.	10.3	n.a.	71	n.a.	15.8	n.a.
Yussuf	n.a.	1,037,481	n.a.	4.1	n.a.	41	n.a.	10.6
National Advance Party (Braithwaite)	n.a.	308,842	n.a.	1.2	n.a.	0	n.a.	0.0
Total	16,862,208	16,862,208	100.0	100.0	449	450a	100.0	100.0b

n.a. Not applicable.

a. Elections were not held in two states.

b. Percentages were calculated from the total number of seats contested.

Source: Nwolise 1988, pp. 53–63.

Figure 11-2. Oil Revenue in Nigeria, 1978–90

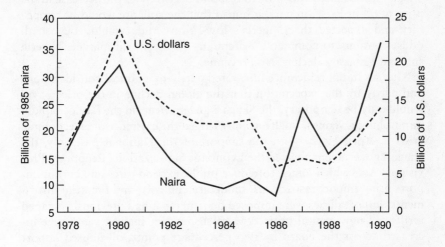

Source: Federal Office of Statistics 1991; IMF 1991; World Bank 1991b: Central Bank of Nigeria 1991.

form a coalition. Thus, the Shagari government had every incentive to develop an expenditure and resource allocation regime that would open new inroads for it in marginal areas where the opposition parties were most vulnerable. The carrot of state expenditure was also used to divide the ranks of the opposition to the advantage of the ruling National Party of Nigeria. The new regime also had resources available since, as figure 11-2 shows, the country was deluged with revenue as a result of the second oil boom that followed the fall of the shah of Iran. Indeed, the corruption trials that occurred after Shagari was overthrown suggest that government officials threw themselves into the task of elaborating Nigeria's patronage system with unprecedented enthusiasm.

The Shagari government should have faced a significant stabilization crisis almost immediately upon coming to power in October 1979, but the second oil boom allowed the government simply to increase spending without taking serious steps to bridge the widening gap between rich and poor or diversify the country's economic base. Indeed, the second oil boom seemed to confirm in the minds of many political officials that they could always count on oil to bail the country out of practically any difficult economic situation.

Therefore, when the oil market collapsed in the early 1980s, Nigerian officials were especially unprepared. Obviously, the decrease in oil prices from $38.97 per barrel in 1982 to $31.50 per barrel in 1983 hurt

Nigerian exports (Central Bank of Nigeria 1984, p. 26). Further, the Shagari government was slow to respond decisively to the decrease in the price of oil because, in part, it hoped that the collapse would be temporary and expected that Nigeria's low-sulfur crude would, against all odds, continue to command a premium on the world market. Nigeria suffered a massive decline in oil revenue.

After an initial reluctance motivated partly by political considerations and partly by the expectation that the global decline in the price of oil would only be temporary, the Shagari government, in the face of rapidly diminishing revenues, finally acknowledged the existence of an economic crisis in April 1982. With the support of the National Assembly, the Shagari government enacted the Economic Stabilization (Temporary Provisions) Act, which aimed to reduce public expenditures and curtail imports using import restrictions, monetary controls, and financial instruments. Import duties were imposed on items that had previously escaped tariffs, all new capital projects were suspended, interest rates were increased across the board by two percentage points, all unused import licenses were recalled, the public investment expenditure was cut 40 percent, and tariffs and gasoline prices were raised.

Records of the National Assembly's brief debate on the economic stabilization act prior to its adoption do not reveal any sharp divisions. Many of the legislators apparently shared the hope of the executive that the world market for oil would recover quickly to permit a resumption of business as usual. A few legislators were concerned that the sacrifices be equally borne across class, ethnic, and regional divisions. No doubt, the lack of debate was due in good part to the mildness of the proposed measures. This consensus was also shared by the executive. In particular, an influential group within the presidential policy advisory circles, led by Professor Edozien, economic adviser to the president, stressed that the government did not need to take any actions other than those listed in the act. This minimalist approach attracted skepticism from some government economists in the presidency and the central bank.

Although these measures had some effect, the government did not appear to take actions that accorded with its rhetoric. The gap between actual and projected expenditures, a recurring problem in Nigeria, actually increased significantly in 1982, although it declined substantially in 1983 (see figure 11-3). Reviewing the continued economic deterioration during 1982–83, the Central Bank of Nigeria wrote, "although laudable policies had been adopted to address these [economic] problems, implementation has been faulty and particularly disappointing" (Central Bank of Nigeria 1984, p. 12). The central bank noted, for instance, that, although the balance of payments improved in 1983, this advance was only a "technical expression" because Nigeria was not paying its short-term trade debt. The economy went further into depression in 1983.

Table 11-2. Economic Growth in Nigeria, 1979–89

Year	Real change in GDP	Inflation (consumer price index)
1979	5.3	9
1980	−8.4	10
1981	−0.3	21
1982	−5.4	8
1983	−5.1	23
1984	9.4	40
1985	3.1	5
1986	−0.5	5
1987	9.9	10
1988	5.3	38
1989	5.2	41

Note: These statistics can only be partially reconciled with data provided by the Central Bank of Nigeria.

Source: World Bank data base for Nigeria; Central Bank of Nigeria, various years, 1991; IMF, various years.

Industrial production declined 12 percent, manufacturing output dropped 20 percent, and agriculture slumped 9 percent (Central Bank of Nigeria 1984, p. 12). As table 11-2 notes, the economy declined sharply during this period.

There were strong expectations in the government and the National Assembly that the provisions of the 1982 act would help stabilize the Nigerian economy, particularly if the decline in the world price of oil proved to be short-lived. Therefore, the government was initially extremely reluctant to invite the IMF and World Bank to participate in its crisis management program at a time when extensive news reports focused on bread riots in Egypt and Sudan. Even as the world market for oil continued to deteriorate and the government's fiscal crisis deepened, the Shagari government approached private international financiers for a loan of $2 billion to help clear the country's trade arrears rather than negotiate with the IMF and the World Bank.[3] The government also drew on its reserves, which decreased from $2.1 billion in 1982 to $441 million in 1983 (IMF 1990, p. 491).

In late 1982, when it was clear that Nigeria no longer had credibility on the international financial markets, the Shagari government exercised its right to withdraw its gold tranche from the IMF (Olukoshi 1990). These funds only offered short-term relief. Indeed, by October 1982, the economy was burdened by three months of arrears in its short-term debt. The arrears prompted foreign banks to begin to curtail the confirmation of letters of credit from Lagos, a development that put further pressure on the economy and the government. The massive increase in Nigeria's debt during the early 1980s was driven mainly by a significant jump in trade arrears (see figure 11-4).

Figure 11-3. Nigerian Fiscal Management: Budgeted and Actual Recurrent Expenditures, 1981–90

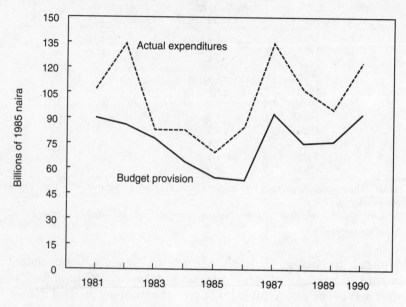

Source: Central Bank of Nigeria; various years; Federal Republic of Nigeria various years; Federal Office of Statistics 1988.

In early 1983, faced with growing pressure from western financiers and in the context of rapidly diminishing economic fortunes, the government invited the IMF to send a team to Nigeria to examine the nature and dimensions of the country's economic problems and to suggest solutions. At the same time, in April 1983, the government submitted an application to the IMF for an Extended Fund Facility loan of approximately $2.5 billion. Another application was sent to the World Bank for a structural adjustment loan of between $300 million and $500 million. Also, several teams of financial advisers were appointed by the government to negotiate with thirty western banks on the financing of nearly $2 billion in trade arrears (Olukoshi 1990). At the same time, a National Economic Council Expert Committee was established to review critically the state of the nation in light of the worsening economic crisis.

In responding to the Nigerian government's application for an Extended Fund Facility loan, the IMF insisted that the Shagari administration should carry its economic recovery program well beyond what was contained in the 1982 act by adopting a more comprehensive structural adjustment program. According to the IMF, devaluation of the naira had to be the centerpiece of any acceptable adjustment program. Further, the government had to reduce its capital expenditures drastically between

Figure 11-4. Evolution of Nigerian Debt, 1980–90

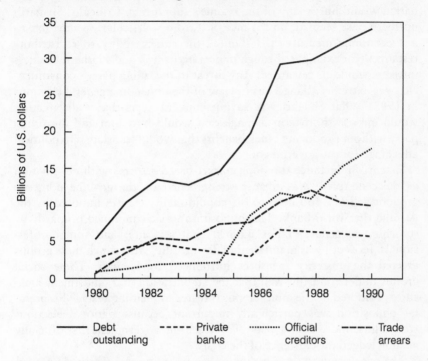

Source: World Bank 1990c, 1991a.

1983 and 1986. The IMF suggested that all projects requiring N300 million or more for their completion should be shelved, while viable parastatals should be privatized. It also suggested deregulating prices and interest rates, promoting nonoil exports, and liberalizing trade.

While accepting the IMF's recommendations for reducing capital expenditure and rationalizing some public enterprises, the Shagari regime was extremely reluctant to accept the other policy recommendations. The demand that the naira be devalued caused particular resentment. According to Shagari, "Devaluation is irrelevant in the Nigerian situation" (Olukoshi 1990, p. 90). Shagari's refusal to devalue was based on the contention that, since Nigeria's only export was priced in dollars on the world market, a devaluation would have no effect. This argument was, of course, misleading. Overvaluation of the naira had, after all, led to the dominance of oil in the export sector.

The argument forwarded by Shagari does, however, begin to make more sense given the tenets of Nigerian politics sketched earlier. The ruling National Party of Nigeria depended for its cohesion on an elaborate network of patron-client relations, much of it centering on import licensing. The adoption of market-based reforms would disrupt many of

these relationships, and the dramatic shifts in income generated by devaluation would hurt many of the regime's supporters. Critically, Shagari's
northern base seemed, on the face of it, to be particularly vulnerable to
any economic measures that limited the state's ability to redistribute
resources (for example, through import licensing), and southern business
interests would be rewarded. Any threat to the ruling party's constituencies was extremely dangerous in view of the impending general elections
in 1983. What Shagari was saying implicitly was that a devaluation
would impose short-term damage that would hurt him and the ruling
party without producing quick benefits that would translate into political
advantage for the government.

Shagari's reluctance to adopt market-based reforms with devaluation
as the centerpiece was further strengthened by the genuine domestic
groundswell of opposition to the conditionality clauses imposed by the
IMF and the World Bank. This opposition was championed primarily by
students, academics, labor unions, civil servants, and some professionals. Its depth was manifested by the hostility with which these groups
greeted the austerity measures introduced by Shagari. These social
groups understood full well that the stabilization and adjustment measures promoted by the multilaterals threatened their interests. This popular opposition was particularly important because national elections
were a little more than a year away when the government first officially
acknowledged the existence of the crisis.

The opposition to the devaluation could use several extremely powerful arguments so that their protests appeared to be driven by the national
interest rather than by special interests. The imposition of World Bank
and IMF conditionality struck a nationalist nerve in Nigeria, which made
the debate over economic reform extremely emotional. Changes in the
exchange rate were not seen merely as normal economic policymaking
but also as a highly important political issue that, among other things,
implied how important the country was to the rest of the world.[4] There
was also genuine hope that the world oil market crisis would, like the
1977–78 downturn, be short-lived and followed by a dramatic increase
in prices to the benefit of Nigeria. Thus, Shagari found that opposition to
the multilaterals was extremely powerful despite his own colossal mis-
management of the economy.

In the face of this powerful opposition, the only constituency that was
explicitly advocating structural adjustment was the central bank. In November 1983, the central bank submitted a memorandum to the government calling for a wide range of reforms. The bank's diagnosis of
Nigeria's problems included "excessive budget deficits, considerable
waste in government fiscal operations, . . . the crowding out of the
private sector by the Government, and industrialisation strategy based
on the importation of inputs, [and] a faulty agriculture policy." It called
for a "radical departure" from current practices including moving away

from import substitution, privatizing certain parastatals, and decreasing government intervention in the economy (Central Bank of Nigeria 1984, p. 12). Although its recommendations effectively demanded a change in foreign currency policy, even the central bank could not bring itself to call explicitly for a devaluation.

The unwillingness to accept a devaluation led to a stalemate in negotiations with the multilaterals. As a result, commercial lenders refused to roll over Nigeria's short-term debt. Official creditors, led by the U.S. Export-Import Bank and the British Import Credit Guarantee Department, also refused to lend more to the country, making any new support for Nigeria contingent upon an agreement with the IMF. Nigeria received practically no new capital inflows from official creditors during 1982–83.

Shagari's party won the August 1983 election and massively increased its presence in the National Assembly (table 11-1). However, the 1983 elections were widely perceived to be fraudulent since the Shagari regime could not serve credibly as both referee and player in the balloting. The ruling party, insistent on staying in power, used blatant physical force, and the opposition replied in kind. Despite his victory, Shagari had no mandate to do anything other than simply continue to try to hold his constituencies together. The country continued its downward economic spiral for the rest of 1983, and, finally, on December 31, 1983, the military intervened to end the second republic.

The Buhari Regime, 1983–85

In the context of the rapidly deteriorating economic situation and the political turmoil that followed the 1983 elections, a military government led by General Muhammadu Buhari was sworn in on January 1, 1984. In its bid to grapple with the deepening economic crisis, the new regime adopted a blueprint that combined the provisions of the 1982 stabilization act with the key recommendations submitted to the Shagari regime by the Council of Economic Advisers and with elements that the new regime considered to be the "positive" elements of the IMF recommendations to its predecessors. Cost recovery measures in health and education were introduced, a wage freeze (that included public sector employees) was imposed, and 250,000 public sector employees were laid off (Callaghy 1990, p. 305).

The Buhari regime represented a major change from the Shagari regime because it made some real attempts to achieve stabilization. The new military leaders seemed to have recognized that they faced unsustainable fiscal and balance of payments deficits that would undermine the country if not addressed. Indeed, the Buhari regime significantly curtailed at least some government expenditures. As table 11-3 indicates, government spending and the deficit declined in 1984 and 1985. Especially after the prolific and irresponsible spending under Shagari, the

Table 11-3. Government Expenditures and Deficits in Nigeria, 1980–90
(as a percentage of GDP)

Year	Expenditures	Revenue	Deficit
1980	21.6	18.5	3.1
1981	25.4	13.7	11.7
1982	20.4	13.0	7.4
1983	21.2	11.7	9.6
1984	14.6	10.5	4.2
1985	13.6	11.2	2.5
1986	17.4	14.7	2.7
1987	27.4	17.5	10.0
1988	23.6	12.7	10.9
1989	22.9	17.1	5.8
1990	23.2	20.3	2.9

Note: Statistics from the Central Bank of Nigeria and the World Bank for 1988–90 cannot be reconciled. This table presents data from World Bank 1992b for the contested years.

Source: World Bank 1990a, 1990b, 1990c, 1992a, p. 405; Central Bank of Nigeria, various years, 1991, p. 2.

Buhari measures were a significant development. Moreover, Buhari also limited overspending. Indeed, the Buhari regime was the first Nigerian government since the late 1960s (that is, an entire generation before) to implement real cuts in government spending and change the trajectory of overall expenditures.

This economic compression was implemented, as might be expected given how dependent so many had become on state expenditure, in a framework that brooked no political opposition at home. The regime required 5,000 prominent political figures from the previous government to appear before tribunals for interrogation and jailed many of the disgraced politicians on corruption charges (Mwalimu 1991, p. 547). In addition, a rash of decrees was passed to forestall any manifestation of political opposition. For instance, the regime placed unprecedented restrictions on Nigeria's vibrant press and passed laws that allowed it to jail reporters who printed material "calculated to bring the Federal Military Government . . . to ridicule or disrepute" (*West Africa,* April 7, 1984, p. 968). It also used preventive detention of opponents on grounds of security (decree no. 2) and banned all demonstrations, processions, and unauthorized meetings. In the face of growing popular pressure to set a timetable for the return to civilian rule, the regime forbade public discussions of Nigeria's political future. These restrictions prompted almost immediate clashes with the politically active elements of Nigeria's civil society. Students contested the regime's cost recovery measures in the education and social sectors, which resulted in proscription of the National Association of Nigerian Students. Doctors called a strike protesting the funding of the public health system, which led to a ban of the

Nigerian Medical Association and the National Association of Resident Doctors, the arrest and detention of the strike leaders, and the temporary imposition of emergency martial rule on teaching hospitals. These measures were extraordinary given the vibrancy of Nigeria's polity (under both military and civilian regimes) and its history of a free press.

While implementing some politically difficult fiscal measures, the regime also rejected fundamental structural and institutional changes that would allow Nigeria to adjust to the changing oil market. Indeed, the Buhari regime's stringent measures can be read as the reaction of a government that knew it must tighten its belt for a short period of time but genuinely believed that administrative controls worked and that, perhaps, the oil market would eventually save the country. Thus, the regime refused to devalue the naira, in part because it believed that it could administratively allocate foreign goods until the import constraint was loosened. Accordingly, all imports were placed under licensing in 1984, and Nigeria's borders were closed. A cascading system of advance deposits for imports was introduced, and the currency was changed to deter smugglers (Struthers 1990, p. 316).

Further, the Buhari regime held many of the Shagari regime's preconceptions concerning devaluation. Once again, devaluation was rejected as inappropriate for Nigeria. Also, the highly nationalistic military officials thought of devaluation as demeaning, especially in the context of IMF conditionality. As one government publication noted, "The IMF aroused the indignation of all self-respecting and patriotic Nigerians when it started insisting . . . that the government must carry out its dictates" (Ministry of Information and Culture 1988, p. 19).

Like its predecessors, the Buhari regime was unwilling to adopt many of the other proposals put forth by the IMF and the World Bank. For instance, although it was prepared to reduce grants to parastatals and public enterprises, the government rejected the idea of fundamentally changing the pattern of ownership.[5] Similarly, although it agreed to abolish the approved user scheme and to promulgate a new customs tariff decree in 1984 incorporating some of the IMF demands, it refused to liberalize and, instead, adopted strong trade restrictions. Finally, the Buhari government argued that removing the petroleum subsidy would complicate its economic problems and opted instead to campaign against smuggling.

Inevitably, some of the economic and political measures adopted by Buhari threatened the patrimonial system of politics that had developed, particularly during the second republic. Buhari and some of his close associates seemed to have a strong moral aversion to the way politics had evolved in Nigeria. The Buhari regime did, in fact, attempt to challenge existing patronage networks. A campaign against indiscipline was launched, rent-seeking activities such as the hoarding and smuggling of essential commodities were attacked, and some offenders were jailed.

Also, some contractors, importers, and oil brokers were arrested as part of the effort to undermine the patron-client networks of the disgraced civilian politicians. The failure to reform basic economic structures and practices meant that these measures, however stringent they appeared, would only be somewhat effective. Indeed, the regime's decision to enhance the regulation of imports created vast new rent-seeking opportunities for determined smugglers and individuals or groups with privileged access to foreign exchange who were not seriously deterred by a slight increase in enforcement. Similarly, petroleum products continued to be smuggled out of Nigeria because gas and other refined products were so much more expensive in the surrounding countries.

During 1984, unable to sort out their differences, a stalemate emerged in the negotiations between the Buhari regime and the IMF. Of course, this stalemate also affected Nigeria's negotiations with insured trade creditors that were organized under the auspices of the Paris Club. Members of the Paris Club refused to accept the regime's terms for refinancing the country's trade arrears, insisting that an agreement be reached first with the IMF before any serious discussions could occur. When the Buhari regime rejected this cross-conditionality, Nigeria's lines of credit were cut. The World Bank also withheld consideration of the regime's application for an adjustment loan as well as applications for water supply and health projects.

In a bid to avoid cross-conditionality and to restart financial flows, the Buhari regime approached the Saudi government for a $1 billion loan as an alternative to IMF financing. When this loan was not forthcoming, the regime tried to win western financial confidence on its own by massively increasing debt repayments and further draining its reserves.[6] The regime began to pay off loans at such a high rate that the debt service ratio increased significantly, and net transfers turned negative (see table 11-4). While welcoming this commitment, the Paris and London clubs nevertheless insisted on a "comprehensive economic adjustment program" as a precondition for fresh flows of capital to Nigeria (Olukoshi 1990).

The worsening problems of the economy and the authoritarian practices of the government reinforced popular opposition to the regime and provided a basis for Buhari's overthrow in a palace coup led by General Ibrahim Babangida on August 27, 1985. The coup should not have been surprising because, in many ways, the Buhari regime had tried to stabilize by the most difficult means possible. Its economic policies, especially the cut in expenditures, layoffs, increased fees, and wage freezes, provoked considerable anger and opposition. Its authoritarian political outlook and practices, including its refusal to discuss a timetable for the return to civilian rule, only aggravated its political problems. Its refusal to adopt promarket reforms such as devaluation meant that it was unable to receive substantial inflows of new funds from the multilaterals or diversify the economy away from oil. Also, its attempt to buy goodwill

Table 11-4. Debt Repayment in Nigeria, 1980–90

Year	Total debt service over exports of goods and services	Net transfers (millions of U.S. dollars)
1980	4.2	−1,357
1982	16.2	1,738
1983	23.8	805
1984	33.8	−1,535
1985	33.3	−2,348
1986	32.7	−497
1987	13.4	252
1988	29.4	−973
1989	23.2	1,504
1990	20.3	−1,653

Source: World Bank 1990c, 1991b.

from western banks simply increased the economic drought when the Paris Club held to the IMF conditions. As a result, the regime was thrown into a spiral of having to adopt ever-harsher measures without being able to demonstrate any real economic gains or greater acceptance of Nigeria by the international financial system. Buhari's strategy was not sustainable.

The Babangida Regime, 1985–91

By 1985, opinion within governmental policy circles was becoming increasingly polarized as to the appropriateness of the policies adopted for crisis management. As the Babangida regime took power, there was no clear support for an alternative adjustment strategy, particularly one as controversial as those put forward by the multilaterals. However, the new government was aware, from the outset, that if the economy was not to suffer from continued lack of access to international credit, it would have to seek accommodation with the IMF and the World Bank by adopting an adjustment program that the multilaterals were prepared to support. To differentiate himself from his immediate predecessor, General Babangida assumed office in August 1985 on a platform that promised, among other things, to relax the political restrictions and repressive measures imposed by the Buhari regime and to respect human rights and freedom of the press.

Indeed, Babangida had to move with great urgency because the collapse of the global oil market forced the price of crude to as low as $10 per barrel in 1985 and threatened to deal the Nigerian economy a mortal blow. Table 11-5 indicates the extent to which the economy was starved for foreign exchange, since reserves had not been replenished (IMF 1990, p. 491), by portraying exports as a percentage of gross domestic product

Table 11-5. Exports as a Percentage of GDP in Nigeria, 1979–89

Year	Exports as a percentage of GDP
1979	25.5
1980	28.1
1981	22.6
1982	18.5
1983	13.9
1984	15.0
1985	16.7
1986	12.9
1987	27.6
1988	22.0
1989	30.9

Source: World Bank data base.

(GDP). Certainly, the marked declines in the price of oil probably dispelled any illusions that the country could simply buy time until the oil market improved. The collapse in hard currency earnings also meant that the entire postcolonial basis of politics, including important aspects of the patron-client networks, were put under great stress and could not be sustained in their existing forms much longer.

Setting the Stage for the Reform Program, 1985–86

In a bid to gauge the mood of Nigerians, the new government invited the citizenry to debate publicly the question of whether the country should agree to an IMF loan and the attendant conditionalities. This debate formed part of the regime's strategy to build confidence, which also entailed releasing many political prisoners, abrogating decree no. 2, publicly disgracing the National Security Organisation, and embracing the principle of dialogue and consultation with Nigerians. These measures captured the popular imagination, especially after the authoritarian Buhari administration, and greatly enhanced the legitimacy and approval rating of the Babangida administration in the early days after the coup. Even the noted Nigerian author Wole Soyinka, hardly an enthusiast for military rule, said that "the government is not deaf" (*West Africa,* January 12, 1987, p. 48). The new regime hoped that it would be able to use its honeymoon with Nigerians and, in particular, the press to win acceptance of structural adjustment.

To coordinate the national debate, the government established a committee of officials from the central bank, the civil service, and the universities. The committee was mandated to receive written and oral testimonies and report its findings back to the government. While the debate proceeded, the government began discreet discussions with the World Bank on an adjustment package. Given the deep suspicion with which some Nigerians inside and outside the government viewed the IMF, it was much easier for the regime to seek reentry to international financial markets through a deal with the World Bank than with the IMF. Also, Ishrat Husain, the World Bank's representative in Lagos at the time, proved to be widely popular in business circles and among senior economic bureaucrats and was particularly adept at negotiating with the regime.

The regime also declared a fifteen-month national economic emergency beginning October 1, 1985, that included wage and salary cuts of between 2 and 20 percent for public and private sector employees. In addition to enabling the government to cope with its worsening fiscal crisis as oil prices declined, the declaration of the emergency sent a signal to Nigerians that the economic situation was bad and that, finally, structural measures would have to be taken. The wage freeze also told multilaterals that the new regime was serious about structural adjustment, irrespective of the outcome of the national debate.

The labor movement bitterly resented the salary cut, which was effectively a 22 to 42 percent decline in real wages. The Nigerian Labour Congress publicly condemned the wage and salary cuts and called for protest strikes. It felt that the government had acted unilaterally and was subjecting workers to further hardship when corporate profits could have been taxed further. These protests symbolized the deep suspicion beginning to emerge across the country concerning Babangida's intentions and marked the beginning of the end of the honeymoon. It was only after the government promised to refund monies deducted from the wages of workers that the Nigerian Labour Congress relented.

As the national debate on the IMF continued, it became clear that the overwhelming majority of Nigerians were opposed to the IMF and its conditionalities. This opposition cut across class, ethnic, regional, and religious lines. Mechanics, industrial workers, petty traders, manufacturers, the leading chambers of commerce, academics, traditional rulers, doctors, lawyers, accountants, and even members of the elite Eighty-second Airborne Battalion publicly expressed opposition to any role for the IMF. This groundswell of unanimity was unprecedented in Nigerian politics. When the Babangida regime's first finance minister angrily dismissed the voices of opposition as ignorant and irrelevant, popular hostility forced the president to move him to the far less sensitive Ministry of National Planning.

The groups who stood to benefit from structural adjustment failed to press their views as forcefully as the opposition for several reasons. First, many Nigerians opposed the loan because they believed that the money would simply be siphoned directly into the patronage nets, as had happened with so much of the country's oil money over the years. Second, many manufacturers, in particular, benefited from the tariff structure and were ill-prepared to compete with goods produced on the international market. Indeed, the bottlenecks in the Nigerian economy, espe-

cially concerning the flow of information, were so great that many potential beneficiaries of structural adjustment could not explicitly identify
themselves as winners before the program was adopted. For instance,
given the overvaluation of the currency and all the problems in the systems of credit and infrastructure, only the most visionary manufacturers
could believe that they might be able to reorient their production to
become a successful net earner of foreign exchange.

Finally, the nationalistic urge to reject reforms imposed from the
outside—usually ignored in most economic models as a touching
irrelevancy—did affect the preferences of a significant number of people
used to thinking of their country as Africa's leader and an emerging
superpower. As the debate continued, it became impolitic to voice any
support for economic reform, and the few voices supporting the IMF loan
were drowned out in the press.

In late 1985, flooded with submissions critical of the IMF and its policies, the committee established by the government to coordinate the
national debate recommended that Nigeria should reject the IMF loan.
The failure of the president to state whether his government had accepted
or rejected the recommendations several weeks after the report was submitted led to fresh apprehensions about the regime's real intentions.
Clearly, the regime had not decided how to handle the popular verdict
against the IMF since it was itself generally in favor of the loan and
adjustment. Amid growing public suspicions of its motives, the regime
announced that it had uncovered a plot to overthrow Babangida with
violence and accused the plotters of scheming to collect the IMF loan.
This unproven and dubious accusation sparked sympathy demonstrations in support of the government.

A few days after announcing discovery of the plot, the president went
on national television to say that his government had decided to accept
the popular wishes of Nigerians and would reject the IMF loan. He also
noted, however, that he interpreted the consensus to mean that reforms
should proceed as long as the loan was not taken:

> It is clear that the IMF issue is basically one of whether this country
> should face the challenge of our economic recovery through a struc-
> tural adjustment based entirely on the efforts of our citizens or through
> a combination of efforts and help by way of a loan from the IMF
> (quoted in Foreign Broadcast Information Service 1985, p. T3).

Rejection of the IMF gave Babangida particular credibility when he
claimed that the structural adjustment program had been designed by
Nigerians rather than imposed from the outside (see the interview in *West
Africa*, September 28, 1987, p. 897). Indeed, the decisiveness with which
Babangida acted and his ability to cloak his actions in nationalist sentiment temporarily disarmed his opponents, who had thought, and had
been led to believe, that opposition to the IMF and opposition to economic reform were synonymous.

The call for a national debate and the subsequent announcement of a reform program, despite the consensus to the contrary, are sometimes seen as a case of "clever politics," which enabled the regime to implement reforms that had previously been considered untouchable (Callaghy 1990, p. 303). Babangida did seem to revel in being called the Maradona of Nigerian politics. Indeed, there may have been no other way to initiate the reform program. Conducting a national debate that reached a conclusion and then using clever tactics to slip the initial program through had real costs, however, which became apparent as the reform program progressed. In particular, the regime probably forfeited the opportunity to develop an explicitly proreform constituency centered on a critique of fundamental Nigerian economic institutions and practices. Instead, Babangida's actions symbolized that reform would progress primarily by disarming the opposition through further subterfuge and through separate deals with individual constituencies so that no group would feel too badly hurt. In many ways, Babangida's style was not that different from the style of previous regimes, although the logic of the government's adjustment program implied that it was trying to change the fundamental rules of resource allocation in Nigeria. Indeed, therein lies both the strength of the Babangida approach and its potentially devastating weakness.

Implementing the Reforms, 1986–88

In January 1986, armed with its interpretation of the outcome of the national debate, the Babangida government, in the budget address, announced what it hoped would be the basis for introducing an IMF/World Bank–sanctioned adjustment program and insisted it would be homegrown. Babangida addressed the three critical issues that the World Bank and IMF demanded be included in any reform program, although not in the manner that the multilaterals had hoped. First, he declared that the government would "continue its policy of realistic adjustment of the external value of the naira" (Federal Republic of Nigeria 1986, p. 7). The value of the currency did not change, however; instead, a 30 percent levy was placed on all imports.

Trade liberalization, the second issue that had been isolated as critical, was not addressed in a way that the multilaterals found persuasive. Although Babangida admitted that the import-licensing system led to corruption and inefficiency, he only promised to make the system work better. The Nigerian National Supply Company, which the Buhari government had refused to abolish, was disbanded, and a package of incentives for exporters was announced.

The budget did reduce the petroleum subsidy—the third critical issue—80 percent. It also committed the government to a number of other fiscal measures to limit Nigeria's chronic overspending and budget deficits. In particular, the government promised to pay unparalleled attention to implementing its expenditure control program. Babangida

declared that "we cannot afford to allow the machinery of policy implementation to jog along at its leisurely pace during the next twelve
months. Government is therefore determined to pursue at all levels of
administration, a strategy of close monitoring of all policies and pro-
grammes enunciated in this budget" (Federal Republic of Nigeria 1986,
p. 4).

Finally, the Babangida regime committed itself to privatization and
commercialization of public enterprises. As a first step, nonstatutory
transfers to all economic and quasi-economic parastatals were reduced
50 percent. It also promised to divest holdings in agriculture, electronics,
and all nonstrategic industries. Overall, Babangida was pleased to note
that he had, for the first time in recent memory, balanced the budget.

The 1986 budget did not, however, satisfy the multilaterals or
Nigeria's creditors. The Paris Club and, soon after, the London Club
declared that no debt would be rescheduled until Nigeria signed a
standby agreement with the IMF, which presumably would include devaluation. In response, Nigeria floated the idea of a two-tier exchange rate
system that would, in effect, partially devalue the currency. The World
Bank was apparently willing to support such a program, although it
could not, by itself, endorse the two-tier scheme, in part because of
pressure from the IMF and the U.S. treasury.

Finally, on August 27, 1986, the regime formally announced the adoption of a comprehensive structural adjustment program in cooperation
with the World Bank and with IMF clearance. The Nigerian structural
adjustment program had as its centerpiece devaluation of the naira
through a two-tier system. The First-Tier Foreign Exchange Market was
used temporarily to handle debt servicing and official transfers to international organizations at the prevailing nominal exchange rate of the
naira. All other transactions were to be handled through the Second-Tier
Foreign Exchange Market, where the naira was determined on the basis
of bids submitted by banks for the foreign exchange that the central bank
supplied to the market. The strategy was to ensure that through the
gradual convergence of the administratively determined first-tier exchange rate and the market-determined second-tier rate, the naira would
be drastically devalued. At the same time, the government would phase
out import licenses over the next eighteen to twenty-four months.

Although the IMF has traditionally opposed multiple exchange rates
because they are so cumbersome, it signed a letter of intent with Nigeria
in September 1986. Ishrat Husain and some of the key Nigerian players
apparently convinced the IMF that the two-tier system was the best way
forward and that the government would move rapidly to unify the rates.
The standby agreement allowed Nigeria to draw approximately SDR650
million. However, the government announced that it would not actually
take any money from the IMF, thus deferring to the majority view expressed during the national debate and assuaging some of the popular

fears about the diversion of new loans. Even though Nigeria did not take the IMF's money, the IMF had the same monitoring and reporting responsibilities that it would in any standby agreement. In October 1986, the World Bank agreed to extend a $450 million loan for Nigeria and, critically, the London Club agreed that rescheduling would be contingent on progress being made on the conditionalities included in the World Bank's loan. In November 1986, the London Club agreed to reschedule $3.8 billion and extend new loans. In December 1986, the Paris Club also agreed to reschedule $6.5 billion in official debts.

Rationale for the Structural Adjustment Program

Why did the Babangida regime introduce structural adjustment reforms, especially devaluation, that successive Nigerian governments had resisted for so long? First, the declining price for oil on the world market, which reduced Nigeria's oil revenue from $11.9 billion in 1985 to $5.5 billion in 1986 (UNCTAD 1989, p. 357), and the concomitant exacerbation of the fiscal crisis put a great deal of pressure on the government to act before it faced a totally unmanageable situation. Indeed, the collapse of government revenue threatened the entire governmental structure and had the potential for further complicating an already dismal economic situation, with all the adverse political repercussions that would follow. Devaluation would at least boost the government's revenue in nairas even if the country's dollar earnings from oil exports continued to decline.

Indeed, since the Nigerian state is overwhelmingly a net seller of hard currency, devaluation caused a "naira boom" that was, in many ways, similar to the earlier petroleum bonanzas. The devaluations that have occurred since 1986 have generated an enormous increase in oil revenue. Clearly, the great challenge posed by the reform program was for the government to see its way through the "naira illusion" and finally get control of government spending. In particular, there was the danger that the naira boom would simply reinvigorate the clientelist networks that had been put under so much strain by the fiscal crisis of the state.

Second, the regime adopted the reform program because it knew that it could only reenter the international credit market if it reached some kind of settlement with the IMF and the World Bank. Once again, cooperation with the multilaterals posed enormous challenges. To be seen as cooperating too closely with the multilaterals would be politically difficult, especially since the regime based much of its own legitimacy on designing and implementing an indigenous plan. Although the government received significant inflows of capital immediately after announcing the reform package and avoided publicly humiliating itself before the IMF, relations with the multilaterals were particularly difficult because of the regime's approach to reform.

Third, there was a growing realization within official policy circles, particularly among the key advisers whom Babangida brought into government, that the interventionist framework used by both the Shagari and Buhari regimes had been exhausted and that the time had come, with a new government in place, to promote an alternative development strategy. Some of the officials who pushed for market-based reforms also hoped that they would help not only to change the basis for economic activities in the country but also to undermine ethnic and regional political advantages. This was especially true in the north, which had accumulated much power through years of privileged access to the state's vast resources.

Institutional Arrangements to Promote Reform

To implement the economic recovery program, the president relied on a core group of officials from the key economic ministries and the presidency. Particularly prominent were the ministers and director-generals of the ministries of finance and of budget and planning, the governor of the central bank, the secretary to the federal military government, and their advisers. Besides this core group, the president also established the Presidential Advisory Committee, independent of all ministerial control and located in the presidency. Headed by a prominent economist, the advisory committee became a key part of the process of formulating economic policy, producing a budget, and providing a platform for internal debates on policies and ways to manage their repercussions.

Political Transition Program

In addition to winning the confidence of Nigerians by declaring its commitment to human rights, the government sought to win acceptance of the structural adjustment program by declaring its intent to return Nigeria to civilian rule. Almost side by side with the introduction of the structural adjustment package, the regime spelled out an elaborate political transition program based partly on the report of the Political Bureau established in 1986 to coordinate a national debate on the country's political future.

The initial purpose of the commitment to a civilian transition was both to stabilize support for the government by giving Nigerians something to look forward to and to distinguish Babangida from his predecessors. As the government attempted to implement its adjustment program, however, it amended the political transition program in order to sustain the economic reforms. Indeed, the military had always been committed to guiding any future transition to civilian rule. Retired General Danjuma—a critical official in the Murtala-Obansanjo regime—argued,

> Soldiers have no business going into government unless we are going to play politics, and playing politics means you must ensure that there is going to be an orderly step-by-step transition from the military to the civilian regime. No government which is worth its name can be indifferent to its successor (*West Africa,* January 30, 1984, p. 197).

Thus, the military government wanted to turn power over not only to civilians but also to politicians who would follow the economic policies developed by the Babangida regime. For instance, the Political Bureau recommended that Nigeria adopt a socialist socioeconomic system in which the state held the "commanding heights of the economy" (Political Bureau 1987, p. 50). The government rejected this approach but agreed to create a two-party presidential system. Thus, from the very beginning of its transition program, the government was faced with the contradictory goals of democratizing the country and of implementing a program of radical economic reform. As a result, the transition was guided less by ideas and institutions than by political expediency.

Implementation of the Reform Program

A significant difference has always existed between the formulation of policy initiatives and their implementation and sustainability in Nigeria. As an authoritarian regime, the Babangida government rarely allowed debate before adopting a specific policy procedure and often did not even announce that a particular measure was about to be implemented. Thus, interest groups in society can only bring their political influence to bear once a policy is adopted, and the regime is then faced with the problem of implementing an unpopular policy. As a result, a consistent pattern of relatively easy adoption of even controversial reform policies followed by considerable difficulty and backsliding in implementation characterized the Babangida regime since 1985. Indeed, it is no coincidence that those reforms that the government found easiest to sustain—especially devaluation and the abolition of agricultural marketing boards—required little implementation beyond a government decree.

The Babangida government also faced a particularly severe implementation problem because it depended on the military for its continued existence. Unfortunately, next to nothing is known about the dynamics of Babangida's relations with the rest of the military. It is obvious, however, that to continue to rule, Babangida needed the support of officers who had the capability, and certainly the precedent, to overthrow him. A military government differs from an elected civilian regime in that it cannot replace its fundamental constituency. For instance, a reforming civilian regime could conceivably move from a political base that consists of import-substituting businesses and the urban population to a constituency that revolves around exporters and the peasantry. Indeed, economic reforms in Africa are predicated on such a political transformation. The Babangida regime could not afford to lose the support of the military, irrespective of whatever other groups supported it.

This is a particularly important point because the military was an obvious loser from structural adjustment. The Nigerian military is overwhelmingly a net importer and was therefore hurt by devaluation. It also had privileged access to some goods (notably food and housing) at subsidized prices. Finally, it benefited from bribes associated with many of the illegal activities that grew up around Nigeria's economic distortions. For instance, soldiers at the border were undoubtedly paid off by smugglers shipping Nigeria's artificially inexpensive petroleum to neighboring countries.

Thus, Babangida was in the extremely difficult position of having to retain at least the nominal support of an organization whose interests would be hurt by the very reforms he proposed. Accordingly, his strategy was to announce the reforms and then respond by extending patronage (which aggravated fiscal problems) or by backtracking on reforms when he sensed increasing anxiety among officers and their soldiers. It is hardly surprising that implementation has been such a significant problem in Nigeria.

The Second-Tier Foreign Exchange Market opened in September 1986 with the naira equivalent to $0.217, a depreciation of approximately 66 percent. On October 10, 1986, the method of auction was changed, and the amount of foreign currency available was increased from $75 million to $80 million. As a result, the naira underwent a 44.5 percent appreciation from N1 = $0.198 to N1 = US$0.294. The second-tier exchange rate remained stable for the rest of 1986 and for the first half of 1987 (see figure 11-5).

On July 2, 1987, the first and second tiers of the exchange rate were merged to form the Foreign Exchange Market, but a dual rate remained. An auction rate was determined fortnightly by the central bank using funds from oil revenue and the World Bank. This rate was available to the government, banks, official foreign exchange dealers, and some importers. An interbank rate determined by market forces and drawing upon all other sources of foreign exchange fixed the value of the naira for all other purchasers of foreign exchange (International Currency Analysis 1991, p. 146). The exchange rate of the naira did not change noticeably on the Foreign Exchange Market in the second half of 1987, and the gap between the auction rate and the parallel market rate actually widened.

Initially, there was little obvious opposition to the government's exchange rate policy, and the regime appeared to have successfully exorcised the antidevaluation sentiment. Many were surprised that the Babangida government had finally taken action and were disarmed by the nationalist cloak with which the regime initially draped its policies. Also, so many goods were already being allocated through the parallel market that, in many ways, the depreciation simply legalized the prices consumers were already paying. Finally, abolishing the 30 percent import levy, which occurred when the Second-Tier Foreign Exchange Market was adopted, further ameliorated the effects of the change in the value of the naira.

The relative ease with which the naira was initially devalued through

Figure 11-5. Value of the Naira, 1986–89

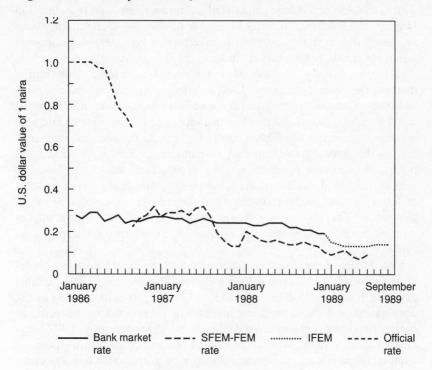

Source: International Currency Analysis 1991; World Bank 1991a.

the second-tier market was matched by the effortless manner in which the notorious import-licensing system, around which so much of the preadjustment rent seeking revolved, was abolished. The government's task in this matter was made easier by the fact that import licensing as a means of allocating foreign exchange had become almost completely discredited as a result of the blatant abuses perpetrated by politicians in the second republic and the notorious loopholes associated with the rationing system for foreign exchange adopted by the Buhari regime. Many members of the Manufacturers Association of Nigeria, who were at the receiving end of the corrupt import-licensing deals of the second republic and whose situation was not improved by the rationing formula adopted by the Buhari regime, welcomed the abolition of import licensing.

The rent seekers who had benefited from the import-licensing program also did not significantly oppose the reforms. First, due to the drop in oil revenue in 1986, many of the licenses they held were essentially worthless. As a result, many of the old arguments against devaluation became moot. Second, it would have been illegitimate for them to object to a reform that was eliminating a system so many saw as dysfunctional. Third, as some of the best capitalized and most flexible entrepreneurs in Nigeria, the holders of licenses were able to shift to other activities with far less problem than, say, the manufacturer who assembled imported goods for the domestic market. Indeed, the Babangida regime, for whatever reason, always allowed other distortions to emerge while implementing the reform program. This, in effect, provided alternative business opportunities for rent seekers who, due to the economic reforms, faced a sudden windfall loss. For instance, the quantitative restrictions on imports and the significant gap that emerged between the exchange rate of the central bank and that of commercial banks provided new, potentially lucrative opportunities for groups that would nominally be hurt by reform. The distortions subsequently introduced were undoubtedly less harmful to the economy than the tremendous overvaluation of the naira. The government's tolerance of other rent-seeking opportunities certainly mitigated the opposition to reforming the exchange rate.

The Babangida regime also had some success in its efforts to implement fiscal reform. As table 11-3 indicates, Nigeria made considerable progress in closing its deficit in 1985 and 1986, primarily because of the devaluation and the subsequent increase in oil revenue as measured in nairas. In addition, the marked decline in net debt service in 1987 (documented in table 11-4), which came about because of the inflow of capital from multilaterals and debt rescheduling agreements, also had a positive impact on government financing. Nevertheless, recurrent expenditures continued to outpace budgeted recurrent expenditures by a substantial margin in 1986 and, especially, in 1987.[7] Indeed, the central bank warned that the government deficit for 1987 was more than twice what the government had projected at the beginning of the year (Central Bank of Nigeria 1988, p. 10). Of course, the continued inability to control recurrent expenditures was particularly worrisome because the improvements due to the naira boom and debt servicing were only temporary.

Development of the Opposition

Although the regime was able to implement parts of the reform package, especially the price changes announced as part of the initial program in 1986, opposition quickly mobilized around several central issues. The first reform to attract significant opposition was the trade liberalization component of the structural adjustment program. The introduction of an interim tariff structure in September 1986, at about the time the Second-Tier Foreign Exchange Market was inaugurated, triggered a rash of protests from members of the Manufacturers Association of Nigeria who described it as a traders' tariff designed to stifle local production.

Manufacturers soon developed a rather long list of grievances against the government. For the Manufacturers Association of Nigeria, opposition centered on the cost implications of the drastic devaluation of the naira for their import-dependent factories. Manufacturers also faced a difficult internal market due to a collapse of consumer purchasing power, which left them with significant unsold stocks. Relations with the government were further aggravated when, one year after the structural adjustment program was announced, the central bank issued circular no. 21 abolishing all forms of controls on interest rates. The bank also raised its minimum rediscount rate from 11 to 15 percent. As a result, interest rates shot up to about 18 percent in the second half of 1987 and hovered around 20 percent for much of 1988.

The Nigerian Labour Congress's principal concern in opposing the adjustment policies was to restore workers' purchasing power and defend existing subsidies on social services and the pricing of petroleum. Its campaign against devaluation dovetailed with that of the Manufacturers Association of Nigeria, and the two organizations had occasions to express themselves jointly in support of restoring consumer purchasing power and ending what they saw as undervaluation of the naira. On several occasions, particularly over the privatization program and the petroleum subsidy questions, the Nigerian Labour Congress spearheaded the opposition against the government's policies. Correspondingly, student and professional groups such as the National Association of Nigerian Students resisted significant aspects of the reform program, notably reduction of the petroleum subsidy, cuts in the financing of social services and education, and privatization of public enterprises. Indeed, practically no year has passed since 1986 without incidents in which students clash violently with the government and universities are closed.

The opposition to the structural adjustment program soon began to have a real impact on implementation. The rapid slide of the naira after the foreign exchange auction was introduced caused the petroleum subsidy to reappear because the world price of oil in naira terms skyrocketed while the government continued to sell petroleum products at pre-auction prices. In December 1987, the government, acting through the Nigerian National Petroleum Corporation, launched an active campaign in newspapers and through posters to prepare Nigerians for further price increases. The proposed actions were vigorously opposed by the Nigerian Labour Congress, which countered the government's arguments with its own newspaper advertisements and posters. Faced with the popularity of the opposition's campaign and the support it enjoyed among the majority of Nigerians, the government was forced to back down and suspend the planned increase in prices.

Also, because of opposition among students, professionals, and workers and because of the need to maintain Nigeria's delicate ethnic, regional, and religious balances, the government moved very carefully on the question of privatization. Northern elites, in particular, feared that southern entrepreneurs would benefit disproportionately from privatization, given their management expertise and access to capital. Therefore, only two years after formal introduction of the structural adjustment program and under explicit pressure from the IMF and the World Bank, the government established a technical committee to prepare for privatization.

The composition of the technical committee reflected Nigeria's ethnic and regional diversity. The members were also given a mandate to ensure that shares of the firms to be privatized were available to all groups. For instance, shares in companies to be privatized were advertised in all states through banks, local government councils, and state ministries. Priority was given to local governments, trade unions, educational establishments, cooperatives, and professional associations. Workers in enterprises whose shares were to be sold were allocated a percentage of the offering. In exceptional cases, the committee was empowered to make an allocation directly to investment houses owned by state governments until the citizens of the state(s) concerned could afford to participate. As much as possible, the privatization exercise was undertaken on the stock exchange in order to ensure transparency. The committee was also mandated to target small investors as opposed to institutional or big investors. Thus, the committee made an extremely credible effort to address northern concerns that their region would lose out disproportionately if a significant privatization program was implemented.

As a result, the government was more successful in implementing the privatization program than many other aspects of the economic reform program and generally exceeded expectations in this area. Privatization emphasized disposing parts of the federal government's share of commercial banks, insurance companies, and multinational oil subsidiaries. Seventeen enterprises, mostly agroindustrial, were privatized in 1986. As of December 1990, fifty-five state companies had been sold and 400,000 new shareholders created (World Bank 1991a, p. 403). A considerable effort was also made to commercialize enterprises that continued to be operated by the state (World Bank 1990b, p. 396). The government also abolished all commodity marketing boards and sold their assets to private groups.

Responding to the Opposition, 1988–90

In December 1987, a significant turning point in the adjustment program occurred. When mass protests against adjustment culminated in a call by former head of state General Obansanjo for "adjustment with a human face," the Babangida government felt compelled to introduce a reflationary budget. The new program incorporated several adjustment relief measures and programs such as meal subsidies for civil servants, a mass transit scheme, the National Directorate of Employment Scheme, and the Open Apprenticeship Program. Overall spending was projected to increase 37 percent. The regime adopted a strategy of selectively accommodating the opposition's demands, including the erection of its own patron-client network. In other words, the Babangida regime responded to opposition in the traditional official Nigerian manner despite the obvious contradictions this implied for the logic of its economic program.

Indeed, the regime, starting in 1987, began to change key personnel in its economic decisionmaking team in order to develop a more accommodating response to the burgeoning protests against reform. For instance, the regime added persons who were not economists (including specialists in sociology, political science, history, and international relations) to the Presidential Advisory Council in response to increasing pressure to introduce structural adjustment relief measures. These specialists played a prominent role in designing the reflationary budget.

The reflation had an immediate impact on government expenditures. Actual expenditures during 1988 were even higher than the government had projected. At the same time, the leveling off of the currency devaluation in 1987 meant that the government was no longer receiving an increasing number of naira for each barrel of oil produced. Not surprisingly, the government's deficit increased to a very high 11 percent of GDP in 1988.

The 1989 budget was more conservative than the reflationary budget of 1988, and the rate at which spending rose slowed dramatically. Nevertheless, that budget was again increased at mid-year in response to riots protesting the structural adjustment program. Among the concessions made was the creation of the soft loan, nonprofit Peoples Bank targeted at the urban poor; the unfreezing of wages; the lifting of the ban on recruitment into the civil service; and the introduction of a new minimum wage. The increase in the budget was possible because the currency had once again begun to depreciate, and the government was again receiving what it must have viewed as a windfall of naira. The 1988 and 1989 budgets seemed to set a precedent whereby fiscal expenditures would be increased significantly if the government was confronted with serious protests against the reform program. Apparently, the government could not ignore the protests while it was relying on a nascent proreform constituency.

Also, starting in 1989, the regime had to fund a large number of new, costly programs. The regime's electoral transition program, the construction of the new capital city of Abuja, the intervention in the Liberian war, and the national census all exerted unceasing pressure on the budget. As might be expected toward the end of any government in Nigeria, the regime's clients were increasingly driven to feed at the trough of public expenditures while they were still well placed. Indeed, the creation of nine new states, and their corresponding capitals, civil services, and related infrastructure, can be interpreted in part as an effort to buy off the regime's supporters. At the same time, the Babangida regime alien-

Table 11-6. Rate of Growth of the Money Supply in Nigeria, 1984–90
(percent)

Year	Rate of growth
1984	11.6
1985	9.0
1986	2.0
1987	22.4
1988	32.9
1989	10.7
1990	35.4

Source: World Bank data base.

ated the powerful politicians who had dominated the politics of the first and second republics by banning them for varying lengths of time from participating actively in the third republic. In order to keep some of these politicians quiet and possibly even obtain their support for the adjustment program, the regime extended generous lines of patronage to them. Ironically, the bribes provided politicians with the resources they then used to intervene in the political transition process and ultimately compelled the regime in December 1991 to lift the ban it had imposed.

Monetary policy was also very loose in 1988. As table 11-6 indicates, the money supply increased 33 percent, well above the target. In August, however, the central bank tried to dampen the overheated economy by restricting the growth of loans issued by commercial and merchant banks to no more than 7 percent per quarter. This was the first of a series of increasingly severe monetary actions that the Nigerian government used to try to reign in a system that tended toward fiscal disequilibrium.

Indeed, in April 1989, in response to the problems of controlling fiscal expenditures and the emerging gap between the official exchange rate and the parallel market rate, the central bank announced several anti-inflation measures, including a sharp monetary squeeze and credit restrictions. All levels of government and parastatals were forced to transfer their deposits from commercial banks to the central bank, resulting in a tremendous contraction in bank liquidity (World Bank 1990a, p. 10). As a result, growth in the money supply was dramatically reduced. In fact, the central bank actually overperformed on its monetary targets (World Bank 1990b, p. 397). Again, the regime had at least partially compensated for its profligate fiscal ways with sudden, sharp decreases in the economy's money supply.

It was politically difficult for the regime to use monetary policy to compensate for an expansionary fiscal policy because nominal interest rates were a lightning rod for opposition to the regime. Indeed, by 1990, partially in response to restrictive monetary measures, nominal interest rates had increased to 28 percent. Once again, the spirited protests of the Manufacturers Association of Nigeria and other business groups forced the government to intervene and, in 1991, through the budget announced in January, to peg the rate at 21 percent. Thus, monetary policy—which the regime used to compensate for its inability to hold expenditures in check—alienated a group that should have been one of the reform program's principal supporters. The difficulties of implementing the reform program through too great a reliance on old-style political practices had become clear.

The high deficits were partially due to the high debt service ratio (debt service has averaged approximately 24 percent of exports since 1987). Government finance before debt repayment has been in surplus most years since 1985. Had this debt been used primarily to enhance the country's capital stock, the government's need to resort to further deficit spending could be viewed in a more positive light. As noted, however, the social pressures for increased public expenditure and the imperatives of patron-client networks substantially determined the path of government spending. Under the Babangida regime, perhaps more than with any of its predecessors, unbudgeted expenditure, extrabudgetary accounts (especially for the armed forces and the myriad security agencies established since 1986), and secret accounts became as significant, and perhaps more significant, than regular budgetary expenditure. Of course, these high levels of expenditures were themselves reflected in greater debt service in future years.

Some observers (Ishrat Husain, personal communication, 1992) place greater weight on debt service as a reason for high government expenditures. Although debt service is an important factor in Nigeria's continuing fiscal problems, the Nigerian government, in the face of intense domestic suspicion of the IMF, felt it politically expedient not to draw down on the standby facilities made available to it by the IMF. Thus, in order for its adjustment program to get off the ground, the government declined several billion dollars that might have eased some of its immediate fiscal exigencies. In addition, a considerable portion of the overspending can be tied to interest group pressure. If the causal factor for Nigeria's debt problems had been primarily due to debt service (a predictable expense), Nigeria would presumably not have constantly breached its fiscal expenditure guidelines.

EVOLUTION OF THE EXCHANGE RATE. These fiscal and monetary policies had a direct impact on the exchange rate. Throughout 1988, the gap between the Foreign Exchange Market auction rate and the parallel market rate widened. In January, the auction rate was 25 percent greater than the parallel market rate; by May, the differential had increased to 50 percent, and by December the auction rate was nearly twice the rate of the parallel market. Between the fourth quarter of 1987 and the fourth quarter of 1988, the World Bank estimates that the currency appreciated almost 26 percent in real terms.[8] The monetary measures introduced in 1989 went a considerable way to reducing this gap.

In early 1989, the government replaced the auction with the Interbank Foreign Exchange Market whereby the central bank determines the exchange rate daily. The Interbank Foreign Exchange Market stemmed the naira's appreciation and led to a further depreciation of the currency. Since funding still fell short of demand, however, a gap remained between official rates and the parallel market. Therefore, in September 1989, the authorities allowed *bureaux de change* to trade foreign currency freely. The bureaus opened with rates 40 percent lower than the official rate, approximately N1 = $0.09 (Smith 1990, p. 8). Overall, Nigeria managed to sustain the devaluation begun in 1986.

TRADE LIBERALIZATION. Progress was also made on trade liberalization. In 1988, the government introduced a new tariff structure that set specific rates for a seven-year period and eliminated a wide range of exemptions (World Bank 1990b, p. 396). The World Bank estimates that the level of protection under the new scheme is lower than the pre-1984 level but higher than the interim tariff adopted in 1986 (World Bank 1990a, p. 22).

The Babangida regime also tried to satisfy the manufacturers who were deeply concerned about the impact of trade liberalization on their import-substitution industries. The government attempted to meet their demands by incorporating tariff increases for several imports and greater protection for the productive sector in the revised tariff structures. These efforts did not satisfy many of the manufacturers, who continued their protests and sent delegations to the president. As a result, the government established a tariff review board to hear their cases and offered redress that went some way to assuaging their concerns. Not surprisingly, the tariff review board served as a "lightning rod" for the complaints that various members of the organized private sector (including the Manufacturers Association of Nigeria and the Nigerian Association of Chambers of Commerce, Industry, Mines, and Agriculture) leveled toward aspects of the structural adjustment program (Robertson 1992, pp. 191–92). As a result of the pressure directed toward it, the review mechanism has changed tariffs every year since 1988. Simple average tariffs in agriculture increased from 39 percent in 1989 to 40 percent in 1991, while those in industry increased from 35 to 36 percent during the same period. The tariff rates for some product categories (primary cells and batteries, fluorescents, jewelry, starches) increased from between 10 and 100 percent to between 25 and 300 percent. Nigeria has bound only one tariff rate (stockfish) under rules of the General Agreement on Tariffs and Trade. It has therefore failed to eliminate uncertainty in the tariff structure (GATT 1991, pp. 3, 9, 64–65).

Also, in the 1989 budget, imports of fifteen items, including livestock, vegetables, and some fabrics, were banned outright. Wheat imports were also banned. These bans created new opportunities for smuggling. Indeed, some of the rent-seeking opportunities lost due to the devaluations were made up for in the illegal importation of wheat and other contra-band widely available in Nigeria. The export of unprocessed cocoa was initially banned until pressure from cocoa farmers and exporters forced the government to rescind this decision. Although the structural adjust-ment program technically reduced the number of goods banned from seventy-three to fifteen, the actual coverage remained substantially the same because of the significance of the still outlawed imports in the economy (Robertson 1992, p. 187).

PETROLEUM SUBSIDY. In April 1988, the government was also forced to revisit the question of the petroleum subsidy because the IMF threat-ened that, if no progress was made on the matter, a new standby loan would not be approved to replace the one that had expired at the end of 1987. The World Bank withheld disbursement of the $500 million struc-tural adjustment loan for the same reasons. With this pressure, the gov-ernment decided, after suspending the Nigerian Labour Congress in Feb-ruary 1988, to increase the price of petroleum products 3 percent. The response from the public, led by university students and workers, was immediate, violent, and, in many respects, unexpected by the govern-ment. All over the country, protest meetings and demonstrations were held, forcing the government to back down.

It was not until January 1989, through that year's budget, that the government was able to effect an increase in petroleum prices using a two-tier pricing structure that froze the amount paid by commercial vehicle operations at their prebudget level and increased the price paid by private motorists 43 percent. The two-tier structure was later abolished: prices were unified at N0.6 per liter, which private motorists paid, and a voucher system was introduced to provide a discount to commercial drivers. Prices were not increased between 1989 and 1992.

ABSENCE OF A COALITION OF SUPPORTERS. By the middle of 1988, when the formal structural adjustment program ended, the reform effort was clearly running into significant problems. Indeed, despite the limited success on the petroleum question, the IMF did not immediately renew the standby agreement in 1988. Of course, since Nigeria had not drawn down its loan, the IMF's unfavorable review may have had less impact on the regime than would have been the case in other countries. Eventually, in February 1989 and October 1990, after the government had made progress on critical issues, standby agreements with the IMF were signed. The Babangida regime continued its practice of not drawing on the loans. The regime also negotiated further debt reschedulings with the Paris Club (March 1989) and the London Club (April 1989). Under the latter agreement, the entire stock of medium- and long-term debt was rescheduled over a twenty-year period with three years' grace (World Bank 1990b, p. 399).

Other than the multilaterals and the creditors, relatively few groups emerged to support the economic reforms and serve as the political base for further reforms. Part of the reason for the lack of support was the government's tactics. In phasing the structural adjustment program, it is not at all clear that the regime was guided by calculations of who would win or lose from specific policy measures. Rather, the approach was simply to introduce the policy measures. Also, in contrast to the students and workers, supporters of the reform program were not well organized and could not cloak their arguments in popular terms that would appeal to the general population.

Finally, the economic growth that Nigeria experienced in recent years has not been great enough to win over a significant portion of the population. In 1987, as table 11-2 indicates, GDP increased almost 10 percent. In 1988 and 1989, the economy began to respond to the new incentives plus the infusion of capital, and real GDP grew 5 percent annually (Central Bank of Nigeria 1991, p. 3). These growth statistics must be kept in perspective. Measuring growth since the advent of the reform package is somewhat misleading because, as noted, the reform package was introduced when the oil market was near the bottom of a trough. Much of the growth simply represents the recovery of oil revenue due to higher prices. More important for most Nigerians, who recognize the cyclical nature of the oil market, was the fact that at the end of 1989 the overall economy was 5 percent smaller (in real terms) than in 1980 but, in the meantime, the population had increased 30 percent (World Bank 1990a, p. 401).[9]

Several groups were, in fact, winners at the beginning of the program: manufacturers and farmers who produce for the export market (Husain 1987, p. 20). Manufacturers, who were potential beneficiaries if they could reorient their production, were active participants in the coalition opposing aspects of the reform program, particularly devaluation, interest rate deregulation, and trade liberalization. Indeed, the generalized opposition of manufacturers, as represented by the Manufacturers Association of Nigeria, continued despite the increase in capacity use among some of them (especially in the sectors allied with agriculture) and despite the regime's efforts to promote nontraditional exports.[10] In addition to devaluation of the naira and the removal of export controls, the regime implemented tax holidays, export credit guarantees, and insurance; enabled exporters to retain all the foreign currency they earn from their transactions; and designated duty-free ports and zones.

The response to these incentives was sluggish. Given how oil dominates the economy, even if nontraditional exports started to grow impressively, a considerable amount of time would pass before they had an impact on the economy. Indeed, at the end of 1989, oil still accounted for 91 percent of all exports, although this was down from 94 percent in 1986 (World Bank 1990b, p. 402). Thus, manufacturers only slowly supported the reform program because it took them a long time to reorient their production strategies and even longer to become a significant political presence, given oil's dominance of the economy. Perhaps not surprisingly, in 1987, the World Bank projected that nonoil exports would reach $1 billion by the early 1990s. In 1991, they only reached $425 million, well below the 1987–88 average of $575 million (Hawkins 1992, p. iii).

Similarly, Nigeria's peasant farming community, expected to emerge as winners from the adjustment process, had a mixed experience as inflation, the increased cost of farm imports caused by the withdrawal of subsidies and devaluation, and the activities of intermediaries ate deeply into rural incomes.[11] Cocoa farmers in Ondo State, for instance, appeared to enjoy a boom between 1987 and 1989, with producer prices at one point exceeding prices prevailing on the world market. By the end of 1989, however, they suffered a severe reversal when prices decreased from N25,000 to N3,500 per ton. The speculative buying of cocoa was the result of attempts by entrepreneurs to repatriate earnings that had been lodged with the central bank for transfer abroad before adjustment was introduced but that were released after the Second-Tier Foreign Exchange Market was inaugurated. Once speculators had repatriated their earnings, cocoa prices collapsed, much to the anger of farmers. In addition, cocoa farmers were badly hurt by the collapse of the world market for their produce. Between 1986 and 1989, the volume of cocoa produced in Nigeria increased 35 percent, although dollar earnings from cocoa were actually 5 percent lower in 1989 than they had been three years earlier (World Bank 1990b, p. 402). Of course, it is not the fault of the adjustment program that international cocoa prices went against Nigeria precisely when the country was trying to increase production. The collapse of the international market did, however, mitigate at least some of the positive effects of the adjustment program for farmers.

Most of the cocoa farmers of Ondo State who, at the height of the speculative buying that characterized the 1987–90 period, praised the government for its agricultural policies vehemently criticized it after the price collapse in the fourth quarter of 1989. The price collapse threw some cocoa farmers into debt since they had borrowed money, mostly from the informal sector, to purchase inputs and buy consumer goods. Their expectations were that high prices would be sustained over a long period of time. The adverse market developments at the end of 1989 forced many into financial crisis, compelling them to stage angry demonstrations against the government's hands-off policy. The Ondo State government finally agreed to meet their representatives and negotiate terms on which the authorities might intervene to protect farmers' interests and provide them with financial relief. The state government also agreed to provide subsidies for inputs. A leading member of the Ondo State Farmers Congress, when interviewed, stated that for him and for other farmers "the middlemen were cheating us, and the government did not come to the rescue. Even when we sent out an sos, they [the government] did not answer until we marched to them." It is hardly surprising that cocoa farmers were not enthusiastic supporters of the adjustment program, even though many welcomed the abolition of the Cocoa Marketing Board, which siphons off their profits.

The experience of the cotton farmers of northern Nigeria—another potential set of winners—was slightly different but no less disheartening. The abolition of the Cotton Marketing Board was perhaps welcomed by farmers who had many grievances against the board, including low prices, delays in the supply of inputs, and the difficulty of doing business with it. The crucial role played by the board's ginnery in assisting farmers to process their crop was, however, ignored when the decision to abolish it was taken. As a result, for at least one buying season after the board's abolition, farmers were stuck with unginned cotton. It took the intervention of the government in cotton-producing states like Kano for a new management system to be worked out.

Cotton farmers also complained about the increased cost of farm inputs, particularly fertilizer and seeds. Their complaints were substantiated by a Central Bank of Nigeria survey noting "phenomenal increases in the prices of essential farm inputs such as fertilizers, pesticides, tractors, tools, and implements" (Central Bank of Nigeria 1991, p. 68). Farmers were also unhappy with the Kano State Agricultural Supply Company, a parastatal run by the Kano State government and charged with bulk-purchasing and supplying inputs to farmers in the area. They blamed the parastatal for the periodic shortage of inputs. The arrangements for marketing their output were also an issue of great concern. As one farmer noted,

> Before, the Cotton Board bought all of our cotton. Now, we wait for the buyers, and they don't come quickly. So we send to them to beg them to buy. And they tell us the price they can pay. We can either take it or leave it.

As with cocoa farmers, cotton farmers also incurred some debt, mostly from small moneylenders. Unlike cocoa, cotton production increased 42 percent between 1988 and 1990.[12]

Even with a growing agricultural sector, farmers did not provide the Babangida regime with an important political constituency. As an authoritarian regime, the Babangida government did not benefit from the sheer demographic weight of the peasants it sought to aid. Farmers had been marginalized for so long that they would have been difficult to engage as an immediate constituency even if the Babangida government had shown an interest in cultivating political support from rural areas. As General Babangida himself noted in his 1992 New Year's speech, "The absence of truly grass-roots commodity-based farmers' associations has also for long hindered small-scale farmers from participating in the policy process. Existing associations were not real apex organizations, making it difficult for government to verify competing claims of clientele" (quoted in Foreign Broadcast Information Service 1992, p. 35). Finally, the highly structured political transition program may actually have prevented the emergence of even an informal political movement based on farmers because the regime only sanctioned the creation of two parties.

Beyond the increased cost of inputs that accompanied the devaluation, the deteriorating conditions in the Nigerian countryside increased the level of apathy and hostility to the government. Many rural schools and health centers were in a state of advanced decay, lacking all basic facilities and suffering from gross underfunding. In many states, schools and health centers—the only symbols of government presence and concern—were allowed to close. In others, particularly in eastern Nigeria, only community efforts kept schools and rural clinics open. Rural water and electricity supply schemes begun in the 1970s at the height of the oil boom were discontinued in many states, and the failure to maintain or service existing facilities led to their collapse. Life in rural Nigeria, as A. R. Mustapha (1992) has noted, is still characterized by worsening cases of disease, acute poverty, malnutrition, and declining household purchasing power.

Creation of the Directorate of Food, Roads, and Rural Infrastructure (DFRRI) in 1988 did little to alter the dismal fate of rural Nigeria. The program suffered from the inefficiencies and corrupt practices that characterize many government policies in Nigeria. In Anambra State, for instance, a presidential monitoring team reported that it was "told by DFRRI officials in Enugu that 360 communities had been supplied with potable water at a cost of N5,322 million [N5.322 billion]. However, after a ten-day tour of the area, the team found that 64 of the communities listed as beneficiaries did not exist and 153 had no functioning water scheme" (*West Africa,* July 17, 1989, p. 1187). Retired Commodore Larry Kainyan, chair of DFRRI, was forced by overwhelming evidence of fraud in his organization to state that "there are those who believe that the measure of their success is the amount of public funds they spend irrespective of what it was spent on, why, and the results achieved" (quoted in Mustapha 1992, pp. 122–23). Not surprisingly, many rural smallholders became increasingly dependent on remittances from relatives living in the urban areas (Zakari 1990).

One group that profited from adjustment includes bankers, especially merchant bankers, easily Nigeria's nouveau riche class, boasting very high naira earnings, enjoying access to foreign exchange, and living a high-flying lifestyle. In 1986, Nigeria had 41 licensed banks; by 1991, the number had tripled to 120 (Callaghy 1992, p. 17). Bankers were (until March 1992) permitted to make easy money because of the significant gap between the naira price of dollars that they bought from the central bank and the price at which they were allowed to sell dollars on the open market. Some of these banks were apparently established by interests previously associated with the import-licensing system, which, after the system was abolished, shifted their resources to the interbank and bureaus of change markets.

While profiting from deregulation, merchant bankers were not an active constituency in support of adjustment, partly because of the apparent love-hate relationship between them and the government. This relationship arose from the government's attempt to deflect political blame for the wild, downward fluctuation of the naira onto "irresponsible" bankers. As public criticism of the increasing "undervaluation" of the naira mounted, the government was often compelled to take actions against bankers. In the third quarter of 1991, within the space of one month, bank executives were summoned to three separate meetings with the finance minister, the vice president, and finally the president. At these meetings, they were requested to cut down on their lifestyle and salaries and to take steps to ensure the appreciation of the naira. This hardly made bankers enthusiastic supporters of the adjustment process.

IMPLEMENTING THE REFORM PROGRAM WITHOUT SUPPORT. The Babangida regime's response to the lack of domestic political support was multifaceted. Caught between sustained domestic opposition to adjustment and pressure from international financial institutions, the state sought to accommodate local demands and establish its own clients. Groups opposed to or critical of the government (for example, the Bar Association, the Nigerian Labour Congress, and the Nigerian Union of Journalists) received millions of nairas in personal gifts from the president or his wife. So, too, did numerous individuals and members of the armed forces.

While providing these carrots, the regime also resorted to repression. Some of the most vociferous critics of the government's policies were arrested. Journalists, university lecturers, students, and trade unionists were targeted for intimidation by the state security services. The National Association of Nigerian Students was banned shortly after the regime came to power. In 1988, the Academic Staff Union of Universities was proscribed, and the Nigerian Labour Congress was dissolved as part of the regime's attempt to encourage the emergence of a more manageable labor leadership. Not surprisingly, an attempt in August 1990 to convene a national conference initially under the sponsorship of two nominally disparate groups—the so-called progressives, consisting of radical lawyers, academics, students, and doctors, and the so-called technocrats, made up predominantly of retired senior civil servants from the Gowon days—was called off after a show of force by the government. Increasingly, the human rights cloak worn by the regime at its inception in 1985 became ill-fitting. Indeed, the Lawyers Committee for Human Rights wrote, "the Nigerian Police Force are responsible for numerous and widespread violations of human rights. Increasingly under the military government of Ibrahim Babangida, police officers have been implicated in arbitrary arrests, beatings, torture, extra-judicial killings. The Nigerian military government continues to tolerate these widespread abuses of human rights" (Lawyers Committee for Human Rights 1992, p. 33).

The regime also experimented with a number of government reforms as part of its bid to institutionalize structural adjustment. Perhaps the most important institutional change introduced was the removal in 1989 of the central bank from the jurisdiction of the Federal Ministry of Finance and its placement in the Office of the President. Under the new arrangement, the governor of the central bank reported directly to the president. Interviews with central bank personnel in August 1991 suggest, however, that the institution gained only limited real autonomy. Officials of the Central Bank of Nigeria were skeptical of the reforms and doubted that they would mean much under civilian rule. Certainly, the central bank acted, sometimes dramatically, to control the money supply as part of its fight against inflation. Yet, it was powerless to forestall government overspending other than to write periodic confidential reports warning of the adverse effects of fiscal expansion.

Finally, the Babangida regime attempted to institutionalize the economic reforms through the political transition itself. Indeed, as opposition to structural adjustment gathered strength, the Babangida administration increasingly manipulated its transition program to civilian rule as one means to sustain its reforms after returning to the barracks. Although the regime moved swiftly to release most of the disgraced second republic politicians whom Buhari had detained or jailed, the government proceeded to ban most of them, and other "old breed" politicians who participated in the first and second republics, from holding office either for life or until after 1996. A transition to civilian rule decree was promulgated, making "attempts by an individual or groups to distract us or put obstacles in the path of a planned and effectively supervised return to civic order" an offense that would be viewed as sabotage and treated as such (*West Africa,* September 7, 1987, p. 1731). The decree was partly directed at banned politicians but was also applied to other opponents.

The Political Bureau had recommended that the country adopt a two-party system within the framework of a socialist ideology. This recommendation brought out in sharp relief the potential conflicts that could arise between the adjustment program and the attempt to promote political reform. Not surprisingly, the government rejected most of the recommendations of the bureau, retaining only those planks that would permit the political transition program to be monitored with a view to guiding the process to a desired outcome. A rash of decrees was therefore promulgated granting extensive, unprecedented powers to the National Electoral Commission to accept or reject candidates for elective offices.

In April 1989, the government announced that it had accepted a two-party system as a basis for the return to civilian rule and the creation of the third republic in 1992.[13]

The government lifted the ban on politics in May 1989 by inviting Nigerians to form parties that would compete for recognition from the Armed Forces Ruling Council. In response, more than fifty political associations were launched, including one sponsored by the Nigerian Labour Congress. Parties were required to fulfill very stiff conditions, including supplying the addresses of their members on a ward-by-ward basis and stating clearly their attitude toward the structural adjustment program. By July 1989, thirteen associations had approached the National Electoral Commission for recognition as one of the two parties that would compete for political power.

The government refused to recognize any of them because—it claimed—they had discernible religious or ethnic allegiances and because many were under the influence of banned politicians. In October 1989, in an extraordinary move, the government created two parties: the National Republican Convention and the Social Democratic Party. According to the president, the National Republican Convention was supposed to be "a little to the right" and the Social Democratic Party "a little to the left." The government also wrote the constitutions and manifestos of the two parties. The platforms committed both parties to promoting the goals and objectives of the structural adjustment program even before they had members or officers. The government then provided them with officers and appointed senior civil servants to recruit workers and arrange their inaugural congress. All Nigerians were invited to join the party of their choice except political and religious radicals and extremists. A decree was passed legalizing the operations of the two parties; all other political associations were banned and forbidden to meet, canvas, or attempt to field candidates. The power of elected officials of the National Republican Convention and Social Democratic Party to amend the manifestos bequeathed them was also severely constrained.

An Evaluation of Progress, 1986–90

By the end of 1989, the government had made considerable progress in key areas. Perhaps most important, the naira had been devalued 84 percent in real terms between 1985 and 1990 (IMF, various years, 1991, p. 398). There had been some reform in trade liberalization and considerable progress made on privatization and the promotion of agriculture. Overall, significant changes had occurred in the incentives producers faced and considerable encouragement given to the nonoil export sector.

The inability of the government to control fiscal expenditures remained, however, and reflected the political reality: opposition to key aspects of the adjustment program continued, and only a very weak coalition offered outright support for the economic reforms. As a result, the government undertook several bouts of overspending only to be followed by severe monetary policies that attempted to mop up some of the economy's liquidity and relieve some of the pressure on the naira. The tough monetary policies exacted a high political cost because they alienated the manufacturers who had the potential to support reform.

The continuing dominance of oil and the concomitant centrality of the state suggest that for all the changes brought about by liberalizing the market (and they are substantial), the basic framework of politics in Nigeria, especially the complex dynamic of ethnic, class, and religious cleavages mediated by patron-client networks, remain essentially unchanged. Although some social groups adopted the rhetoric of the market, they did so primarily for the purpose of gaining or justifying access to the rentier state. The Nigerian political system was perhaps more resilient than the Babangida regime itself realized. Certainly, to push through its own policies, it had to develop its own patron-client network. Therefore, the fundamental question for the Babangida regime was whether the old dynamics of the political system would, over time, threaten the very important reforms that had been adopted.

Coping with the Oil Windfall, 1990–91

The small oil boom of 1990–91 provided an excellent test of the sustainability of key aspects of the economic reform program. Indeed, given that the weak link in Nigeria's structural adjustment program was fiscal policy, the oil windfall associated with the Iraqi invasion of Kuwait in August 1990 presented an ideal opportunity to test the degree to which the Babangida government was able to institutionalize controls on spending and answer the other questions posed at the beginning of this chapter. Certainly, the sudden, rapid rise in oil prices after August 1990 had a profound effect on Nigerian finances. The World Bank estimates that total oil export revenue in 1990 was $14 billion, a 49 percent increase over the level for 1989 (World Bank 1991a, p. 404).

The government said, from the start of the Persian Gulf crisis, that it was going to treat the increase in revenue as a temporary exogenous shock that would not have a long-term effect on the level of government spending. Indeed, General Babangida, in his 1991 budget address, went out of his way to stress that his administration had learned the lessons of the 1973 and 1979 oil windfalls and was committed to handling the huge increase in revenue in a responsible manner. Babangida (1991, pp. 5–6) said that "most of the extra earnings [from the oil windfall] were in fact sterilised in building up the nation's foreign exchange reserves." If the money had been treated in such a manner, it would have been nothing short of a revolution in Nigerian finances, given the fiscal irresponsibility of previous regimes over the past twenty years.

Despite these intentions, the Babangida regime experienced powerful pressure to increase spending after the Iraqi invasion of Kuwait. First, opposition to the structural adjustment program was still strong, and a visible proreform coalition had not developed. Indeed, the manufacturers' association announced in April 1990 that first-quarter capacity use had actually decreased below its 1989 level. The regime therefore felt the need to increase expenditures in order to buy popular acquiescence. Second, also in April 1990, an amateurish coup attempt by junior officers came surprisingly close to succeeding. Although their grievances centered around ethnic and religious issues (they sought to expel the states in northern Nigeria from the federation), Babangida attempted to buy more support from the military. As a result, a large expenditure program for rehabilitating police and military barracks was initiated; spending on security, including a proposed but controversial national guard, was increased; new weapons were procured; and special grants to improve the welfare of officers were approved. In February 1992, $50 million was allocated to purchase 3,000 Peugeots for the private use of captains and majors in the Nigerian army. Similar presidential gifts were promised to the officers of the navy and the air force. Third, the states made a strong appeal for their share of the oil revenue. Finally, more money may have been needed to grease the wheels of the political transition program.

In fact, the government ratcheted up spending almost as soon as the spot oil market responded to the Iraqi invasion by dramatically increasing the price of crude. Especially worrisome was that the deficit spending appeared to be financed in good part by the domestic banking system, leading to the possibility that local investment would be crowded out. Net banking system claims on the government in 1990 increased 15 percent, compared with a decrease of 34 percent in 1989. Not surprisingly, monetary policy could not act as a counterweight to fiscal expenditures given the enormous sums that Nigeria was suddenly taking in. The narrow measure of the money supply increased 45 percent in 1990, compared with 22 percent in 1989. The target for 1990 had been 13 percent (Central Bank of Nigeria 1991, p. 1).

The overall evidence suggests that, at least for the second half of 1990, the government did not sterilize the money received from the windfall. Rather, it increased expenditure massively by funding the intervention in Liberia and the purchase of new military equipment (estimated at a cost of $250 million to $500 million), failing to curb spending on the Ajaokuta steel plant (at an initial price of $1.4 billion and a final price estimated at $4 billion), continuing the commitment to a dubious $2.4 billion aluminum smelter, and sponsoring the 1990 Organization of African Unity summit ($150 million; Keeling 1991, p. 4). Indeed, the central bank complained that the high level of deficit spending in the second half of the year caused "considerable pressure" on the naira (Central Bank of Nigeria 1991, p. 1). William Keeling, the *Financial Times* correspondent in Lagos, also reported that, by June 1991, Nigeria had spent at least half of the oil windfall (Keeling 1991, p. 4). A World Bank report completed in early 1991 also noted that there was

> a breakdown in fiscal and monetary discipline in 1990 . . . not only characterised by additional spending and monetary expansion but also by a major surge in expenditures bypassing budgetary mechanisms for expenditure authorisation and control (quoted in Holman 1992, p. 14).

The report noted that "significant domestic currency spending appears to have occurred without any apparent budgetary authorisations." In particular, inconsistencies in the Federal Stabilisation Account, if they are equivalent to actual expenditures, "imply spending outside normal accounting and budgetary mechanisms which exceed total budgetary nondebt service spending of the Federal government in 1990" (quoted in Holman 1992, p. 14).

The Babangida government's handling of the Persian Gulf windfall may very well have been better than the Nigerian response to the 1973 or 1979 OPEC shocks. That comparison sets, however, a very low standard for judgment. Although not all the figures are in, the government apparently did not successfully match its rhetoric by managing the exogenous shock in what could be considered a fiscally responsible manner. Certainly, the experience in 1990–91 did not offer much reassurance that the recovery program would stop being exceptionally vulnerable to loose fiscal policies that threaten the entire macroeconomic framework of the reforms instituted to date.

Conclusions

The Babangida government implemented significant reforms between 1986 and 1992. The reforms of the exchange rate, privatization, and elimination of marketing boards in particular promised to eliminate some of the most glaring inefficiencies in the Nigerian economy and provided significant incentives to expand the nonoil sector. Nevertheless, there is very little evidence, despite strenuous attempts by the government, that politics in Nigeria was transformed in any significant manner. Buhari, not Babangida, represented the most significant attack on clientelism, and his reforms failed due to internal contradictions in his program and due to lack of support by creditors. Indeed, Babangida's *diktat* that the artificially created political parties could not even discuss the economic reform program during the election campaign suggests that the government itself did not believe that it had successfully challenged the postcolonial syndrome in Nigeria.

The inability to change the nature of Nigerian politics was repeatedly demonstrated by the government's failure to keep spending under control. Critically, when pressure to limit expenditures temporarily abated

during the Persian Gulf conflict, government spending increased danger-
ously. The government did not institutionalize controls on spending or
credit. Nor did it create a strongly independent central bank. As a result,
the pattern of Nigerian politics—with its seemingly insatiable desire for
side payments, bribes, and patronage—continued to threaten the reform
program's goals, irrespective of the government in power. Although rent-
seeking activities probably became less important economically (primarily because of reforms in management of the exchange rate), they remain
vital to the political system. Babangida was not able to develop an alternative means to mobilize popular political support.

Notes

1. Nigeria's currency is the naira. A billion is 1,000 million.
2. The Nigerian federation now has thirty states following the latest state creation
exercise carried out in August 1991.
3. All dollar amounts are in U.S. dollars.
4. Even in 1991, after five years of structural adjustment, many Nigerians, even in the
commercial banking sector, refused to believe that the value of the naira was the outcome of
monetary and fiscal policy and continued to insist that there was a "just price" for their
currency.
5. Anecdotal evidence suggests that subventions to public enterprises did decrease. The
data are too poor, however, to make a conclusive judgment.
6. Reserves were valued at $425 million in 1983 but decreased to −$498 million in 1984
(IMF 1990, p. 491).
7. The improvement in net debt service appeared as part of the government's capital
account rather than its recurrent expenditures.
8. World Bank 1990b, p. 8; the IMF estimates exchange rate appreciation at only 10
percent (IMF, various years, 1991, p. 398).
9. This assumes a 3 percent annual growth in population. The actual rate of Nigerian
population growth is unknown.
10. The actual growth in manufacturing is unclear because World Bank and Central
Bank of Nigeria statistics cannot be easily reconciled. Manufacturing appears to have
grown approximately 6 percent a year.
11. This section is based on fieldwork done by Olukoshi in 1991 to test actual support
for structural adjustment in the countryside.
12. Central Bank of Nigeria 1991, p. 69. The magnitude of increase in production
should be viewed as only a rough estimate given Paul Mosley's work on errors in Nigerian
agricultural statistics; see Mosley 1992, p. 227.
13. When he took office, Babangida promised a return to civilian rule by October 1990.
The slippage reflects the severe problems that the government had in guaranteeing that its
successor would sustain the economic reform program as well as the logistical difficulties
associated with any significant political program in Nigeria.

References

Babangida, Ibrahim. 1991. *1991 Budget Speech*. Lagos: Federal Republic of
Nigeria.

Callaghy, Thomas M. 1990. "Lost between State and Market: The Politics of
Economic Adjustment in Ghana, Zambia, and Nigeria." In Joan M. Nelson,
ed., *Economic Crisis and Policy Choice*. Princeton, N.J.: Princeton University
Press.

_____. 1992. "Democracy and the Political Economy of Restraint and Reform
in Nigeria." Philadelphia. Processed.

Cassing, James H., Jerome C. Wells, and Edgar L. Zamalloa. 1987. "On Resource Booms and Busts: Some Aspects of Dutch Disease in Six Developing Economies." *Eastern Economic Journal* 13:4.

Central Bank of Nigeria. Various years. *Annual Report and Statement of Accounts.* Lagos.

Collier, Paul. 1988. "Oil Shocks and Food Insecurity in Nigeria." *International Labour Review* 127, pp. 761–82.

Federal Office of Statistics. 1988. *Economic and Social Statistics Bulletin.* Lagos.

_____. 1991. *Nigeria's Principal Economic and Financial Indicators, 1970–1990.* Lagos.

Federal Republic of Nigeria. Various years. *Budget.* Lagos.

Foreign Broadcast Information Service. 1985. *Foreign Broadcast Information Service: Middle East and Africa.* December 13.

_____. 1992. *Foreign Broadcast Information Service: Africa.* January 7.

GATT (General Agreement on Tariffs and Trade). 1991. *Trade Policy Review: Nigeria,* vol. 1. Geneva.

Hawkins, Tony. 1992. "An Urgent Need for Debt Relief." *Financial Times,* March 16, p. iii.

Holman, John. 1992. "'Inconsistencies' in State Funds." *Financial Times,* March 16.

Husain, Ishrat. 1987. *Perspectives on the Nigerian Economy.* Lagos: Nigerian Institute of International Affairs.

International Currency Analysis. 1991. *World Currency Yearbook 1989.* London.

IMF (International Monetary Fund). 1990. *Balance of Payments Yearbook.* Washington, D.C.

_____. Various years. *International Financial Statistics Yearbook.* Washington, D.C.

Joseph, Richard A. 1987. *Democracy and Prebandalism in Nigeria.* Cambridge, Eng.: Cambridge University Press.

Keeling, William. 1991. "Nigeria May Prove World Bank's Acid Test." *Financial Times* 27, p. 5.

Kirk-Greene, Anthony, and Douglass Rimmer. 1981. *Nigeria since 1970.* London: Hodder and Stoughton.

Lawyers Committee for Human Rights. 1992. *The Nigerian Police Force: A Culture of Impunity.* New York.

Ministry of Information and Culture. 1988. *20 Questions and Answers on SAP.* Lagos.

Mosley, Paul. 1992. "Policy-Making without Facts: A Note on the Assessment of Structural Adjustment Policies in Nigeria, 1985–1990." *African Affairs* 91 (April), pp. 227–40.

Mustapha, A. R. 1992. "Structural Adjustment and Agrarian Change in Nigeria." In Adebayo Olukoshi, ed., *The Politics of Structural Adjustment in Nigeria.* London: James Currey.

Mwalimu, Charles. 1991. "Police and Human Rights Practices in Nigeria." *Emory International Law Journal* 5, pp. 515–69.

Nwolise, O. B. C. 1988. "Political Parties and the Electoral Process." In Victor Ayeni and Kayode Soremekun, eds., *Nigeria's Second Republic*. Lagos: Daily Times Publications.

Olukoshi, Adebayo. 1990. *Nigerian External Debt Crisis: Its Management*. Lagos: Malthouse.

Okonkwo, I. C. 1989. "The Erosion of Agricultural Exports in an Oil Economy: The Case of Nigeria." *Journal of Agricultural Economics* 40:3.

Pinto, Brian. 1987. "Nigeria during and after the Oil Boom: A Policy Comparison with Indonesia." *World Bank Economic Review* 1:3, pp. 419–45.

Political Bureau. 1987. *Report of the Political Bureau*. Lagos: Government Printer.

Robertson, James W. 1992. "The Process of Trade Reform in Nigeria and the Pursuit of Structural Adjustment." In Chris Milner and A. J. Rayner, eds., *Policy Adjustment in Africa*. London: Macmillan.

Sandbrook, Richard. 1986. "The State and Economic Stagnation in Tropical Africa." *World Development* 14, pp. 319–32.

Smith, Patrick. 1990. "Nigeria: Adjustment's New Phase." *Africa Recovery* 4 (April–June), pp. 5–12.

Struthers, John J. 1990. "Nigerian Oil and Exchange Rates: Indicators of 'Dutch Disease.'" *Development and Change* 21, pp. 309–42.

UNCTAD (United Nations Conference on Trade and Development.) Various years. *Commodity Yearbook*. New York.

West Africa. Various years, 1984–87.

World Bank. 1990a. "Nigeria: Medium Term Prospects." Western Africa Department. Washington, D.C.

————. 1990b. *Trends in Developing Economies 1990*. Washington, D.C.

————. 1990c. *World Debt Tables, 1990–1991*, vol. 2. Washington, D.C.

————. 1991a. *Trends in Developing Economies 1991*. Washington, D.C.

————. 1991b. *World Debt Tables, 1991–1992*, vol. 2. Washington, D.C.

————. 1992a. *Trends in Developing Economies*. Washington, D.C.

————. 1992b. *World Development Report 1992*. Washington, D.C.

Zakari, K. 1990. "Resource Flows between Rural and Urban Nigeria in a Period of SAP." Processed.

Contributors

Alberto Alesina is professor of economics and government at Harvard University. He holds a doctorate in economics from Harvard, and has published extensively in academic journals. He most recent book is *Partisan Politics, Divided Government, and the Economy*, with Howard Rosenthal (Cambridge University Press, 1994).

Genero Arriagada Herrera has served on the Christian Democratic Party's Political Council in Chile since 1975 and is now a prominent member of the Frei government. He was one of the primary leaders of the democratic opposition in the late 1980s. He is the author of books and articles on such topics as the Chilean aristocracy and civil-military relations, including *Pinochet: The Politics of Power* (Unwin Hyman, 1988).

Carlos Bazdresch is general director of the Center for the Research and Teaching of Economics and director of *El Trimestra Económico*, a Mexican journal. He has written several articles and reviews on the economic history of Mexico. Recently he edited *Mexico, auge, crisis y ajuste* (Fondo de Cultura Económica, 1993).

Nancy Bermeo teaches politics at Princeton University. She writes on the causes and consequences of changes in regime in Southern Europe. Her publications include a book on Portugal's democratization and an edited book, *Liberalization and Democratization: Change in the Soviet Union and Eastern Europe* (Johns Hopkins University Press, 1992).

Richard F. Doner is associate professor of political science at Emory University. His current research addresses problems of collective action in economic development and the political challenges of flexible production in developing countries. He is the author of *Driving a Bargain: Automobile Industrialization and Japanese Firms in Southeast Asia* (University of California Press, 1991).

José García-Durán is professor of economics at Barcelona University. He studied at the London School of Economics and has published work on industrial organization and applied macroeconomics. His most recent book is *Macroeconomía española: hechos e ideas*, with Antonio Argandoña (McGraw Hill, 1993).

Carol Graham is a visiting fellow in the office of the vice president for human resources at the World Bank, and adjunct professor of government at Georgetown University. She has published articles in several journals on the political economy of compensation during reform. Her most recent book is *Safety Nets, Politics, and the Poor: Transitions to Market Economies* (Brookings Institution, 1994).

Stephan Haggard is professor of international relations and Pacific studies, University of California, San Diego. He has written on the political economy of the East Asian and Latin American newly industrializing economies, the debt crisis, and the politics of finance in developing countries. His most recent book is *The Political Economy of Democratic Transitions*, with Robert Kaufman (Princeton University Press, forthcoming).

Jeffrey Herbst is associate professor of politics and international affairs at Princeton University. He has written on the politics of economic and political reform in Africa. His most recent book is *The Politics of Reform in Ghana, 1982–1991* (University of California Press, 1993).

Blanca Heredia is associate professor of international studies, Instituto Tecnológico de México. She has written on business and politics in Mexico and on the politics of economic reform. Her most recent essay is "Making Economic Reform Politically Viable: The Mexican Experience," in *Latin American Political Economy in the Age of Neoliberal Reform: Theoretical and Comparative Perspectives for the 1990s*, edited by William C. Smith, Carlos H. Acuña, and Eduardo A. Gamarra (Transaction, forthcoming).

Simon Johnson is assistant professor of economics at the Fuqua School of Business, Duke University, and director of the Fuqua Center for Manager Development in Saint Petersburg. His research deals primarily with postcommunist countries, particularly Poland, Russia, and Ukraine. His most recent book is *Managing Business Enterprises after Communism*, with Gary W. Loveman and David T. Kotchen (Harvard Business School Press, 1994).

Samba Ka is a historian and political scientist. He has taught at the University of Dakar and at the Foreign Service Institute in Washington. He is presently a program officer at the African Capacity Building Foundation in Harare, Zimbabwe. He has published articles in many reviews and journals.

Robert R. Kaufman is professor of political science at Rutgers University. He has written extensively on the politics of economic reform, with a particular focus on Latin America. His recent works include *The Politics of Economic Adjustment*, co-edited with Stephan Haggard (Princeton University Press, 1992), and *The Political Economy of Democratic Transitions*, co-authored with Stephan Haggard (Princeton University Press, forthcoming).

Marzena Kowalska is deputy editor-in-chief of *Życie Gospodarcie*, the Polish economic weekly. She is a graduate of the Warsaw School of Economics in finance and Warsaw University in journalism. She has published widely on fiscal and monetary policy, economic policy, and institutions in transition.

Anek Laothamatas is professor in the Faculty of Political Science at Thammasat University in Bangkok. His current research concerns democratization in Thailand and Southeast Asia. He is the author of *Business Associations and the New Political Economy of Thailand: From Bureaucratic Polity to Liberal Corporatism* (Westview, 1992).

Adebayo Olukoshi is a senior fellow at the Nigerian Institute of International Affairs, where he edits the monthly *Nigerian Forum*. His doctoral thesis at the University of Leeds was on the role of multinational corporations in the industrialization of northern Nigeria. He has been researching the Nigerian adjustment program since 1987, and has published extensively in journals.

Ziya Öniş is associate professor of economics and international affairs at Boğaziçi University in Istanbul. His research and publications concern various aspects of the political economy of development. His most recent book is *Economic Crises and Long-Term Growth in Turkey*, with James Riedel (World Bank, 1993).

Dani Rodrik is professor of economics and international affairs at Columbia University. He has published widely in the areas of international trade, economic development, and political economy. He is a research associate of the National Bureau of Economic Research, a research fellow of the Centre for Economic Policy Research, and a senior fellow of the Institute for Policy Reform.

Nicolas van de Walle is associate professor of political science at Michigan State University. His research and publications focus on both democratization and the politics of reform in Sub-Saharan Africa. He is the author of *Of Time and Power: Leadership Duration in the Modern World*, with Henry Bienen (Stanford University Press, 1991).

Steven B. Webb is a senior economist at the World Bank, where he sees the political economy of adjustment firsthand. He has done research on policymaking in Germany and in countries now undergoing adjustment, and on central bank autonomy. His most recent book is *Adjustment Lending Revisited: Policies to Restore Growth*, edited with Vittorio Corbo and Stanley Fischer (World Bank, 1992).

Index

African Independence Party (Senegal), 311
AID (U.S. Agency for International Development), 291
Akbulut, Yildirim, 134
Alesina, Alberto, 11, 43–46, 48–52, 56
Alessandri, Jorge, 272
Allende, Salvador, 244–45, 272
All-Poland Alliance of Trade Unions, 190, 218, 238 n22
Ames, Barry, 12, 46
Anand Panyarachun, 447 n2
ANAP. *See* Motherland Party (ANAP, Turkey)
Argentina, 12, 13, 82
Association of Thai Industries, 432, 433
Aylwin, Patricio, 261, 267
Aylwin, Patricio, government of. *See* Concertación de los Partidos por la Democracia (Chile)

Babangida, Ibrahim, regime of (Nigeria): bureaucratic reform in, 15; concurrent political and economic reform in, 7; core group of officials in, 478; coup attempt against, 498; declaration of national economic emergency by, 473; establishment of tariff review board by, 488; exchange rate policy of, 475, 476–77, 480, 487–88; fiscal policy of, 475, 482, 496–97, 499–500; import bans under, 488; monetary policy of, 486–87, 497; political parties under, 11, 496; political repression by, 494; Political Transition Program of, 478–79; privatization under, 476, 483–84; public debate over IMF loan encouraged by, 472–75; reflationary budget of 1988 of, 484–85; relations with military of, 479–80; structural adjustment program of, 476–78; trade reform under, 18, 465, 469, 475, 482, 488–89; weakness of proreform coalition in, 494
Baker Plan, 369
Balcerowicz, Leszek, 193, 195, 199, 231
Balcerowicz Plan (Poland): absence of coherent alternative to, 233; compared with Beksiak plan, 193–94; compensa-

507